The Hardball Times Baseball Annual 2010

Featuring contributions by THT's staff writers:

Richard Barbieri • Brian Borawski • Evan Brunell
Craig Brown • Craig Calcaterra • Matthew Carruth
Mike Fast • David Gassko • Jonathan Halket
Brandon Isleib • Chris Jaffe • Max Marchi
Jeff Sackmann • Dave Studenmund • Steve Treder
Tuck • John Walsh • Geoff Young

With additional contributions by guest writers:

Bill James • Craig Wright • John Dewan
Tom Tango • Ben Badler • Sean Smith
Sky Andrecheck • Dave Allen • Corey Dawkins
Jack Marshall • Greg Rybarczyk • Warren Corbett

Produced by Dave Studenmund

Edited by Joe Distelheim, Bryan Tsao, Ben Jacobs, Jeremiah Oshan and Carolina Bolado

The Hardball Times Baseball Annual 2010

New articles daily at www.hardballtimes.com

Edited by Joe Distelheim, Bryan Tsao, Jeremiah Oshan, Carolina Bolado, and Ben Jacobs
Stats developed by Dave Studenmund and Bryan Donovan
Cover design by Tom Wright
Typesetting by Dave Studenmund

Published by: ACTA Sports
5559 W. Howard Street
Skokie, IL 60077
1-800-397-2282
info@actasports.com
www.actasports.com

ISBN: 978-0-87946-408-0
ISSN: 1940-4484
Printed in the United States of America by Worldcolor Press.
Year: 16 15 14 13 12 11 10 09
Printing: 10 9 8 7 6 5 4 3 2 1

What's Inside

Welcome to Our Book 5

The 2009 Season

The American League East View.............. 9
by Evan Brunell
The American League Central View 13
by Craig Brown
The American League West View............ 17
by Matthew Carruth
The National League East View 21
by Jonathan Halket
The National League Central View 25
by Jeff Sackmann
The National League West View 29
by Steve Treder

Commentary

Ten Things I Learned This Year 34
by Dave Studenmund
The Year in Frivolity 40
by Craig Calcaterra
Trivia Time.. 50
by Brandon Isleib
The Annotated 2009 in History 53
by Richard Barbieri
All the World's a Ballpark 57
by Max Marchi
The Latin America Scandals................... 63
by Ben Badler
The Baseball Biz in 2009 67
by Brian Borawski
Serious Aches and Pains 71
by Corey Dawkins
Strong Seasons Leading Index............... 76
by Bill James
The Content of their Character............... 86
by Jack Marshall
The Rebuilding Team Fan's Survival Guide 94
by Geoff Young

History

Pete and Honus 100
by Craig R. Wright
The Best Series? Get the Hook............. 104
by Chris Jaffe
The Year the Players Were Set Free...... 111
by Craig Brown
Reaping What You Sow 119
by Steve Treder
Paul Richards in a Box 126
by Warren Corbett

Analysis

Championship Leverage Index 132
by Sky Andrecheck
Hit Tracker 2009 138
by Greg Rybarczyk
And the MVP Goes To.......................... 147
by David Gassko
What the Heck is PITCHf/x? 153
by Mike Fast
Where Was That Pitch? 159
by Dave Allen
Miles Per Starter................................ 167
by Tom M. Tango
Relievers Yesterday And Today............. 176
by Sean Smith
A New Approach to MLE's.................... 183
by Jeff Sackmann
Better Than We Thought...................... 188
by John Walsh
Oh Lucky Men! 194
by Dave Studenmund

Statistics

It's the Hardball Times Statistics.......... 203
The Tiger and the Mariner................... 207
by John Dewan
American League Team Stats 212
National League Team Stats 217

What's Inside (cont.)

Arizona Diamondbacks 222
Atlanta Braves.................................. 226
Baltimore Orioles 230
Boston Red Sox 234
Chicago Cubs 238
Chicago White Sox 242
Cincinnati Reds................................. 246
Cleveland Indians............................... 251
Colorado Rockies 256
Detroit Tigers.................................... 260
Florida Marlins.................................. 264
Houston Astros................................. 268
Kansas City Royals............................ 272
Los Angeles Angels of Anaheim........... 276
Los Angeles Dodgers.......................... 280
Milwaukee Brewers 284
Minnesota Twins 288
New York Mets.................................. 292
New York Yankees............................. 297
Oakland Athletics.............................. 301
Philadelphia Phillies 305
Pittsburgh Pirates 309
San Diego Padres.............................. 313
San Francisco Giants 318
Seattle Mariners 322
St. Louis Cardinals 326
Tampa Bay Rays 330
Texas Rangers................................... 334
Toronto Blue Jays.............................. 338
Washington Nationals 342
Appendix: Win Stats.......................... 347
The Hardball Times Glossary 356
Trivia Answers.................................. 360
The Virtual Who's Who....................... 363

Welcome to Our Book

The baseball annual is a time-honored tradition that dates back to Henry Chadwick's first *Beadle Dime Base-Ball Player* in 1861. The Sporting News' *Official Baseball Guides*, for instance, are a vital part of any historcial baseball book collection. Bill James revolutionized the baseball annual in the early 1980s with his Abstracts and there has been a surge of basell annuals ever since, such as Ron Shandler's *Baseball Forecaster, Baseball Prospectus* and James' *Gold Mine.*

This is the sixth *Hardball Times Annual*, and we'll proudly take a place next to any of them. This year's book follows the same format as our previous Annuals. Half of it is full of articles and commentary and the other half is taken by statistics and graphs. Baseball is like that — wordy and nerdy — and the Annual pays homage to both sides of its schizoid fans.

The first section, covering the 2009 season division by division, is a good example. Each article begins with a division race graph and some key comparative stats, and then a THT "staff" writer highlights key events of the year. The next section is called "Commentary" and it consists of articles that touch on any number of subjects (all related to the 2009 season in some way) by THT writers and special guests.

Those writers include Bill James himself, Ben Badler of *Baseball America* and THT's own Craig Calcaterra. Some of these essays report the year's news in a straightforward manner, others are humorous, and some are, well, nerdy. Something for everybody.

We've got five articles in our History section, including a guest piece from famed sabermetrician Craig Wright. THT's Chris Jaffe, who's about to have a book about baseball managers published, contributes too.

And then, for those who like or just like hearing about baseball stats, there is our Analytic section. Noted baseball analysts like John Dewan, Tom Tango and Sean Smith have contributed and you'll find interesting articles about the latest technologies, such as Hit Tracker and PITCHf/x.

There are also a couple of special features sprinkled throughout these sections. Brandon Isleib has contributed some fantastic trivia challenges — Brandon has a mind for these sorts of things — and Tuck has contributed seven "toons," satirical drawings that touch on the more controversial aspects of major league baseball.

That's half the book. The other half is all baseball stats. It has its own introduction so I won't get into any details here, other than to say that our stats are totally awesome.

In order to get this book published as quickly as possible, we decided to send it to the printer before the postseason even finished. As I write these words, the very last part of the book to be written, the World Series hasn't even started. The good news is that those of you who purchase the *Hardball Times Annual 2010* will be able to download an article that covers the postseason in our own unique way. That article will be available by the time you hold this book in your hands.

We have several other downloads, including a couple of spreadsheets with some truly cutting-edge stats and a PDF file of all of my weekly Batted Ball Reports, which were only available on a subscription basis during the year. That's like getting another 100-plus pages of baseball coverage. The instructions for downloading these files are in the Statistics introduction.

It takes a lot to publish a book and I'm always amazed that we manage to pull it off each year. ACTA Sports is our publishing partner and Greg Pierce, John Dewan and Charles Fiore are terrific to work with. The stats are supplied by Baseball Info Solutions and we've received tremendous assistance from Damon Lichtenwalner and Steve Moyer for six years now.

One of the reasons the Hardball Times is such a well-respected baseball Website is that we have a crack staff of editors who just love to pounce on the mistakes of clueless writers like me. Bryan Tsao, Joe Distelheim, Carolina Bolado, Ben Jacobs and Jeremiah Oshan also set aside time to edit all of the articles in the Annual while maintaining their sitely duties. I am truly humbled.

The Hardball Times is a Website and a book, but really we are a bunch of people who like baseball and like to write about it. All of the writers and editors at THT have that common bond — a passion for baseball — but they are also excellent people and it's a pleasure to know them.

Alas, John Brattain, who had written for THT for several years and was a beloved member of our little "family," passed away unexpectedly this summer. John left behind a wife and two teenage daughters, not to mention a rapt audience that always enjoyed what he had to say (and how he said it). John is deeply missed by us and by many, many baseball fans. We dedicate the Annual to John's memory.

I cannot do justice to John's spirit, but I know that he would want me to end with our traditional sign-off.

Happy Baseball,

Dave Studenmund

The 2009 Season

The American League East View

by Evan Brunell

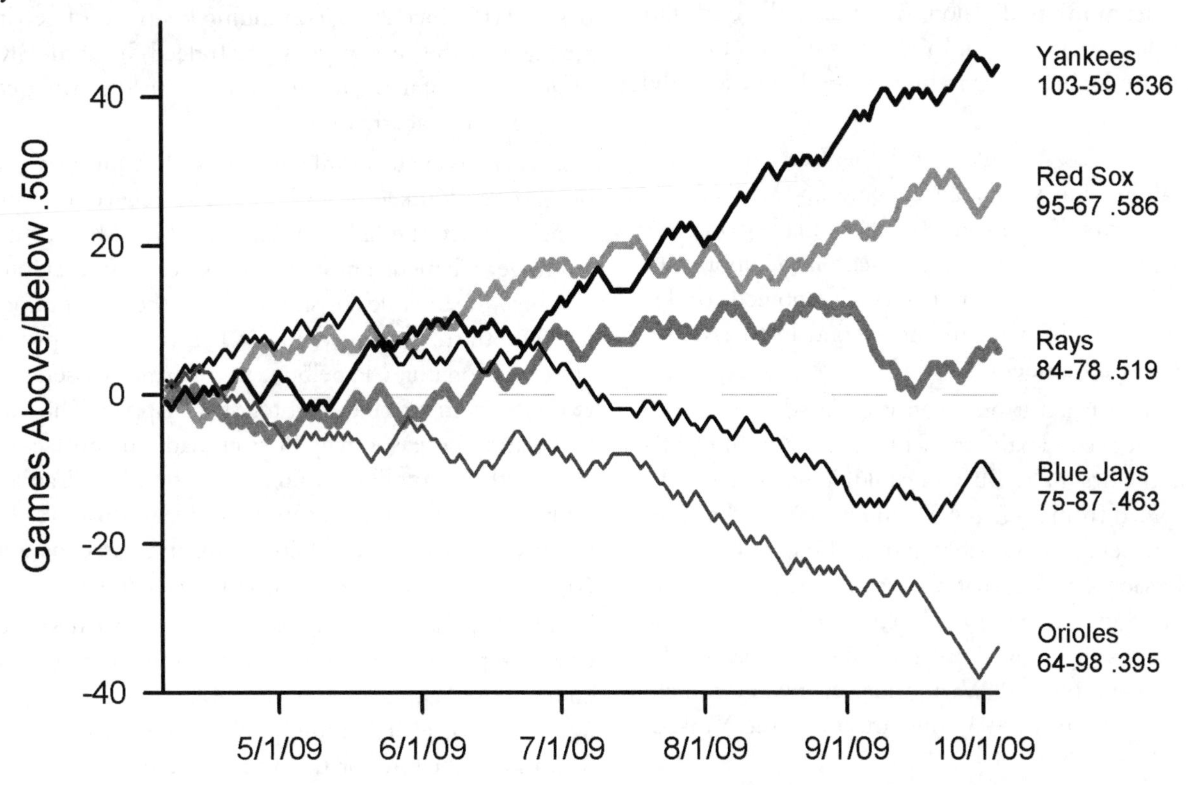

Play Against Other Divisions			
Division	**W**	**L**	**Win%**
AL Central	110	76	.591
AL West	79	95	.454
NL East	49	35	.583
NL Central	2	1	.667
NL West	1	2	.333
TOT	**241**	**209**	**.536**

Head to Head Records						
Team	**BAL**	**BOS**	**NYA**	**TB**	**TOR**	**TOT**
BAL		2	5	8	9	24
BOS	16		9	9	11	45
NYA	13	9		11	12	45
TB	10	9	7		14	40
TOR	9	7	6	4		26

To find wins, read across; losses are read from the top.

Top Players		
Player	**Team**	**WAR**
Zobrist, Ben	TB	8.5
Jeter, Derek	NYA	7.4
Halladay, Roy	TOR	7.3
Longoria, Evan	TB	7.3
Lester, Jon	BOS	6.2
Sabathia, CC	NYA	6.0
Youkilis, Kevin	BOS	5.5
Crawford, Carl	TB	5.4
Beckett, Josh	BOS	5.3
Teixeira, Mark	NYA	5.2
Pedroia, Dustin	BOS	5.2
Bartlett, Jason	TB	4.8
Drew, J.D.	BOS	4.6
Rodriguez, Alex	NYA	4.6
Scutaro, Marco	TOR	4.4
Cano, Robinson	NYA	4.3
Hill, Aaron	TOR	4.3
Shields, James	TB	4.1
Posada, Jorge	NYA	4.0
Lind, Adam	TOR	3.7

WAR stands for Wins Above Replacement and is defined in the Glossary.

Pitching ruled 2009 in the American League East division. Indeed, the final standings were a reflection, top-to-bottom, of the state of the pitching staffs in the league. One might think that patently obvious, that the best team in the division would have the best staff and it would trickle down. In fact, it is not common for pitching to dictate the standings as strikingly as it did in 2009.

The New York Yankees led the East in pitching ERA, addressing what had become an Achilles heel in recent years. The Bronx Bombers made a massive outlay of $243.5 million in the offseason to import C.C. Sabathia and A.J. Burnett. The two combined for 437 innings, fourth in baseball and second in the AL for any two-starter tandem.

Sabathia turned it on when it counted, with a 2.74 ERA in the second half after a pedestrian (for him) 3.84 ERA in the first half. Burnett couldn't match that—his ERA spiked from 3.77 to 4.33, and he garnered a reputation for being inconsistent and clashing with catcher Jorge Posada. Indeed, that clash caused the Yankees to assign backup catcher Jose Molina to Burnett in the playoffs, costing New York an important bat in the games Burnett pitched. Warts aside, the two new pitchers sent the team to 103 wins, the most the Yankees have had since 2002.

Finishing second was New York's hated rival 206 miles north, Boston, with 95 wins on the backs of Josh Beckett and Jon Lester. This tandem gave Sabathia and Burnett a run for their money for the best American League top two, ranking fourth in the AL with 415.2 innings and being crucial to Boston nabbing the wild card. The starting rotation, headed by Beckett and Lester, had Daisuke Matsuzaka, Tim Wakefield and Brad Penny to kick off the season. Down on the farm, Clay Buchholz and Michael Bowden were biding their time while John Smoltz waited for his shot and Justin Masterson practiced his craft in the bullpen. An embarrassment of riches, right? Think again.

Three months later, the rotation was a disaster which contributed to the Sox sinking quickly out of first place into a distant second. Penny pitched barely decently enough to hang onto his job until the Sox released him Aug. 27. Smoltz's Hall of Fame career was stained by his Boston tenure, Matsuzaka had a lost season after a late return and Wakefield made only four starts in the second half after leading the majors with 11 wins on July 21. It got so bad at one point the Sox had to bring Paul Byrd out of retirement. While the pitching situation improved noticeably by the time the playoffs came around, the struggles were enough to drop the Sox eight back to end the season.

Things never got bad for New York even once you got past the first two starters. Andy Pettitte posted his best WHIP since 2005, continuing his trend of getting stronger as the season goes on. Indeed, his 3.31 ERA after the All-Star break ranked ninth in the American League, with Sabathia fourth.

The emergence of Phil Hughes as a late-inning weapon gave the Yankees their best starter-reliever one-two punches since the halcyon days of 2001's Mike Mussina/Roger Clemens and Mariano Rivera/Mike Stanton combos. Meanwhile, Boston boasted the best bullpen, top to bottom, in the division. When you have a proven closer in Jonathan Papelbon, two former closers and two closers-in-waiting, that tends to happen. The bullpen was a big reason why Boston made the postseason even with its rotation in flux all season. The Yankees bullpen may not have been as good as Boston's, but when your offense scores 915 runs and has consistent Nos. 1 through 4 starters, it doesn't have to be.

Joba Chamberlain impressed as the fourth starter, despite repeated calls for his shift to the bullpen. After an ill-advised application of the "Joba Rules" in August (a day off for every inning pitched), his season began to unravel. Luckily for the Yanks, the division was all but sewed up so Joba got a chance to work through the rules. While he ended the season on a down note and was shifted to the bullpen for the playoffs, it was the foundation for future success, and he did pitch well in the first half, when the Yankees really needed it to stay close after a slow beginning.

The word "foundation" is how Baltimore approached its 98-loss, cellar-dwelling season—a season that could be considered the team's most promising in years.

The Orioles certainly didn't start the season that way, choosing to dump starts off on Cubs castoff Rich Hill and baseball castoff Adam Eaton. It's okay, though ... they weren't looking to contend and needed warm bodies. The two quickly left the rotation once the club was ready to bring up its two top pitching prospects. Chris Tillman, acquired along with Adam Jones in the Erik Bedard trade of 2008, made his big-league debut as did Brian Matusz, drafted just a year ago. The two topped the prospect charts to enter the year, suggesting that a good new one-two tandem in the East may be on the rise.

Tillman's debut may not look like it was successful: A 5.40 ERA and 1.55 WHIP can do that. However, Tillman is just 21. He projects to be a staff ace down the line, but he'll have to start working his fastball lower in the zone, especially if he has only two other pitches to play off his fastball. He likes to leave his fastball up, making him a flyball pitcher. Matusz pitched slightly better, checking in at a 4.63 ERA and 1.48 WHIP.

Like Baltimore, the Tampa Bay Rays saw a glimpse of the future in David Price and prospect Wade Davis. Also like Baltimore's, Tampa Bay's future looks good.

Take Price, for example. He channeled Ervin Santana circa 2006-'07, struggling massively on the road. As the season wound on, however, Price grew more comfortable on the mound, holding three playoff quality offenses (Detroit, Boston, New York) in check during one three-start stretch in early September.

While the Rays somewhat surprisingly pulled the plug on Scott Kazmir, sending him to the Angels and getting out of his contract, Tampa didn't get the short end of the stick. The Rays acquired three minor league players from the Angels in return. One, Sean Rodriguez, could be the starting second baseman in 2010 and crank 20 home runs. The team also recalled right-hander Davis from Triple-A, where he posted a 3.70 ERA in 158.2 innings along with 140 whiffs. He still needs to firm up his command, but the consensus is that Davis could emerge as an ace. He turned some heads in the bigs, posting a cumulative 3.72 ERA along with an excellent 36/13 K/BB ratio in 36.1 innings.

Unfortunately for the reigning American League champions, the Rays had to look ahead to next year because of inconsistent performances from their top starters, who couldn't compete with the names New York and Boston were rolling out. Tampa saw the emergence of Matt Garza and Jeff Niemann to boost its pitching staff, but Andy Sonnastine and Kazmir combined to derail it. When your eventual third-best starter (Niemann) barely ekes out a job out of spring training as a rotation placeholder for Price, you know the season isn't going as planned.

So the season didn't go as the Rays hoped, but Price, Niemann and Davis joining James Shields and Garza in the rotation will keep them in contention for years to come. In the bullpen, the Rays lost Troy Percival to injury and a second retirement, necessitating J.P. Howell stepping into the closer's role. He quickly established himself as a closer to watch.

Other new pitching names that emerged in the AL East were in Baltimore: Brad Bergesen, David Hernandez and Japanese import Koji Uehara. For a team looking to emerge out of the doldrums, they are names to watch. Uehara, 34, made 12 starts and showed an understanding of how to pitch, walking a skimpy 1.6 batters per nine innings. In the American League East, that's tough to do. Uehara will continue to serve as an above-average pitcher, something in short supply for Baltimore recently. Hernandez has a long way to go to become a solid mid-rotation starter, but will get every chance to do so. Bergesen, like Uehara, skimps on the walks but may not strike out enough to last once baseball gets the book on him.

With Jake Arrieta in the minors waiting for his shot, the Orioles are suddenly flush in young, capable starters. There was nothing special about the O's bullpen, especially when Baltimore traded George Sherrill, but that did open the closer's job for Jim Johnson. He, like Baltimore's young starters, had growing pains.

The other team in the East—the fourth-place Toronto Blue Jays—saw its general manager, J.P. Ricciardi, fired at season's end. The club couldn't handle the heat in the East; the offense suffered and the rotation was in flux all year because of injuries. So was the bullpen. Remember when B.J. Ryan received a ton of money to close for Toronto? Well, one Tommy John surgery and 87-mph fastball later, the Jays got two closer-caliber years out of a five-year, $47 million contract.

If the pitching had been able to stay glued together, it's possible Toronto could have battled the Rays for third place. Still, the Jays were able to fashion themselves an impressive stable of youngsters for 2010, a common theme among non-playoff teams in the East.

Shaun Marcum, Dustin McGowan, Jesse Litsch and Casey Janssen all missed chunks of time in 2008 and 2009. To compensate, Ricky Romero and Marc Rzepczynski both turned in fine rookie years while the touted 22-year-old Brett Cecil also made his career debut. Former independent league hurler Scott Richmond became the latest success story from the indies.

Perhaps Toronto's biggest story line of the season was the Jays' highly publicized Roy Halladay affair. Ricciardi adopted a hard line in deadline trade talks, so Halladay played out the rest of the season for a below-.500 team. For a team desperate to clear payroll, it's unfathomable that the Jays couldn't turn Halladay into integral pieces for a shot in 2012-13. After all, Halladay reportedly plans to test free agency when eligible after 2010.

You could consider 2009 a year of transition for pitching staffs. Take New York. The Yankees had to work two brand new starters (Sabathia and Burnett) into the team while handing Chamberlain the keys to a spot for the entire year. They had to move Hughes to a bullpen spot and now will have to move him back to the rotation, which will give them a one-through-five combo to fear entering 2010.

For Boston, the transition lasted the entire year. Pitchers were shuttled in and out behind Beckett and Lester until the right mix was found. You could argue it still hasn't been. Down in Bird Land, it has. The Orioles are committed to their young pitchers and will spend 2010 trying to get them acclimated to the majors. The Jays are in a similar position, with green pitchers looking to carve out a niche for themselves. Tampa was forced to re-evaluate its thinking once Price struggled, Sonnastine was demoted and Kazmir was traded.

Unsurprisingly, the various levels of transition manifested themselves in the standings. The good transitioning (bringing established talent in) belonged to New York. Boston and Tampa Bay had to contend with injuries and attrition, but the overall level of Boston's talent won out. Toronto and Baltimore had the bad type of transitioning—at least, the bad kind when it comes to competing—by helping pitchers make the jump to the majors.

Now that 2009 is over, all five teams are better off in 2010 for it. Every team's rotation is largely settled entering opening day and will not be an issue to specifically address in the offseason, barring a major trade.

For years, the East has been fixated on offense. The Red Sox offense broke records in 2003-04 while the Yankees became known as an all-offense, zero-pitching team during the decade. The Rays attempted to bring back old times with Greg Vaughn and Fred McGriff. The Blue Jays had an up-and-coming offense before it fell apart and Baltimore had an underrated offensive group for several years.

Now, the teams are realizing the importance of pitching. Now, you're seeing the teams listen to former Orioles manager Earl Weaver, who once said: "Nobody likes to hear it, because it's dull, but the reason you win or lose is darn near always the same—pitching."

The American League Central View

by Craig Brown

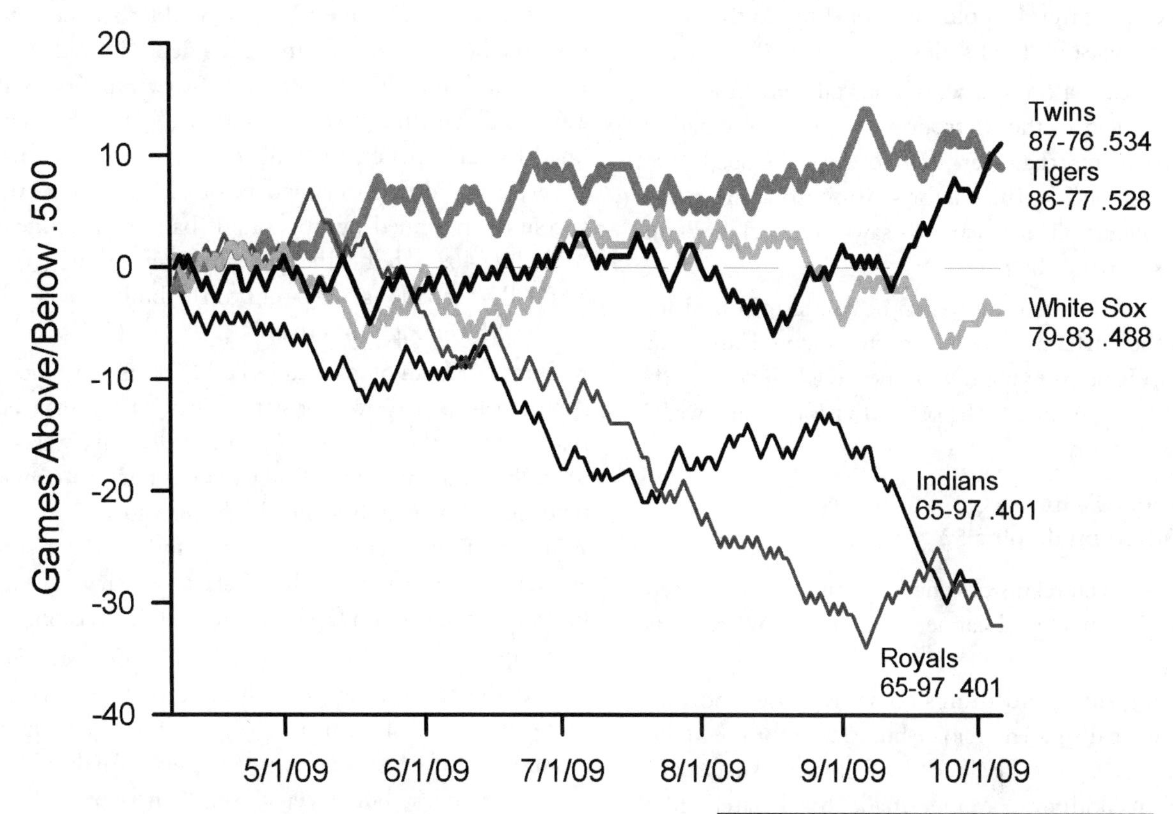

Play Against Other Divisions			
Division	**W**	**L**	**Win%**
AL East	76	110	.409
AL West	78	96	.448
NL Central	43	38	.531
NL West	4	5	.444
TOT	**201**	**249**	**.447**

Head to Head Records						
Team	**CHA**	**CLE**	**DET**	**KC**	**MIN**	**TOT**
CHA		10	9	9	6	34
CLE	8		4	10	8	30
DET	9	14		9	7	39
KC	9	8	9		6	32
MIN	12	10	12	12		46

To find wins, read across; losses are read from the top.

Top Players		
Player	**Team**	**WAR**
Greinke, Zack	KC	9.4
Verlander, Justin	DET	8.2
Mauer, Joe	MIN	8.2
Cabrera, Miguel	DET	5.5
Choo, Shin-Soo	CLE	5.1
Floyd, Gavin	CHA	4.5
Lee, Cliff	CLE	4.2
Span, Denard	MIN	3.9
Jackson, Edwin	DET	3.5
Baker, Scott	MIN	3.5
Buehrle, Mark	CHA	3.4
DeJesus, David	KC	3.3
Granderson, Curtis	DET	3.2
Morneau, Justin	MIN	3.2
Polanco, Placido	DET	3.2
Cabrera, Asdrubal	CLE	3.1
Kubel, Jason	MIN	3.0
Blackburn, Nick	MIN	3.0
Danks, John	CHA	2.9
Bannister, Brian	KC	2.8

WAR stands for Wins Above Replacement and is defined in the Glossary.

For the second consecutive season, it took 163 games to decide the winner of the AL Central. Thanks to a three-game sweep of the hapless Royals, the Twins stood at 86-76 at the regular season's end. The Tigers matched that after dropping two of three to the White Sox in the season's final series.

That meant a one-game, winner-take-all showdown would be held in the Metrodome. It was only natural that two teams that were so close would need extra innings to decide the victor—Minnesota. It was a fitting conclusion to a year that saw no one club distinguish itself from the pack.

The story of the Central can be found in run differential, the difference between runs scored and runs allowed. It helps explain why the division went to the wire and why, unlike in the other divisions, there wasn't a runaway winner.

Minnesota Twins
Run Differential: plus 52

Of the seven teams that had a positive run differential in the American League, only one came from the Central.

Proving that good things come to those who wait, the Twins really had no choice but to wait for Joe Mauer to return from the disabled list following surgery on one of his kidneys. Mauer made his belated 2009 debut on May 2 and homered on the first pitch he saw. From that moment, the Minnesota catcher turned on the power like never before. Mauer's previous career high for home runs was 13, a mark he needed just 39 games and 143 at-bats to match this past summer. He finished with a line of .365/.444/.587, league-high numbers across the board, and a career-high 28 home runs.

Under manager Ron Gardenhire, the Twins have developed a reputation for playing "small ball," but this year's version could swing some mighty bats. Overall, the Twins posted a team batting average of .274, which was the third best in the league, and slugged .492, which was seventh best. Their 172 home runs wasn't a huge total, but it was 61 more than the team hit the previous year and it was the most since the Twins banged 191 over the fence in 2004.

Mauer was joined in the power department by Michael Cuddyer, who hit a career-high 32 home runs with a .520 slugging percentage, and Jason Kubel, with a career-high 28 home runs and .539 slugging percentage. Justin Morneau kicked in 30 before ending the year early with a stress fracture in his lower back.

It was a good thing the Twins hitters were on fire because the starting rotation, thought to be a strength entering the season, struggled almost from the get-go. Scheduled opening day starter Scott Baker opened the year on the DL due to right shoulder stiffness and was roughed up when he made his debut in mid-April. He found life difficult over the first two months with a 6.32 ERA in his first nine starts. With Baker sidelined for the opener, the ball went to Francisco Liriano, who proceeded to spend most of the year getting absolutely pounded by opposition bats to the tune of .279/.361/.469. He hit the DL with arm fatigue (and a 5.80 ERA) in August and went to the bullpen when he was healthy enough to return.

Starters Kevin Slowey and Glen Perkins were inconsistent before they were lost to injury. That left Nick Blackburn as the staff ace. With just 98 strikeouts and 41 walks in 205 innings, Blackburn is a pitch-to-contact type pitcher who relies on his defense to make plays. While the Twins' defense wasn't outstanding, it was solid enough to let him win 16 of his 33 starts, which was fitting for the best pitcher on the best team in this division.

While the pitching struggled, the offense often carried the team, scoring at the rate of five runs per game, the fourth-best in the league. The Twins hung around for most of the summer, never further than five games back, but never closer than two. Following a 3-1 loss to Cleveland on Sept. 6, Minnesota fell seven behind Detroit, its largest deficit of the year. A finishing kick that saw their offense hit .295/.364/.460 and win 19 of their final 27 games was just enough to propel the Twins past the Tigers and to the summit of the Central.

Detroit Tigers
Run Differential: minus 2

Detroit received a breakout season from Justin Verlander on the mound and another MVP-caliber year from first baseman Miguel Cabrera, but the rest of the roster was a study in mediocrity.

Verlander led the league with 240 innings pitched and topped the strikeout charts with 269. At times, he was dominant—he made seven starts in which he struck out 10 or more batters and he struck out at least eight in 20 of his 34 starts. He owned a 6.75 ERA through April, but he quickly turned his fortunes around. His best outing of the season came on May 8 in Cleveland, when he tossed a two-hit shutout against the Indians while striking out 11 and walking two. From there, he was outstanding, finishing with a 3.45 ERA.

Behind Verlander, Edwin Jackson also was terrific through the first two months of the season. Following his start June 6 against the Angels (a four-hitter), his ERA stood at 2.16. Rookie Rick Porcello (3.96 ERA in 31 starts) gave the Tigers a strong third starter.

While the Tigers were getting quality starts from their top three in the rotation, the Detroit offense was scuffling. Overall, the team hit .260 and scored just 4.56 runs per game. Both marks ranked 11th in the league, but in the AL Central, they were good enough for third-best. Cabrera once again paced the Tigers with the stick, hitting .324/.396/.547 and leading the team with 34 homers and 104 RBIs. Unfortunately, his accomplishments were overshadowed by a late-season altercation with his wife that resulted in a 911 call, two days before the scheduled end of the regular season.

The rest of the offense showed warts all season, especially at the top. Leadoff man Curtis Granderson's .249 batting average and .327 on-base percentage were the worst full-season rates of his career. No. 2 hitter Placido Polanco hit .285 with a .331 OBP, both roughly 15 points below his career marks. And in the middle of the order Magglio Ordonez hit just nine home runs and slugged .428, his lowest rate since his rookie year in 1998.

Despite the season-long struggles for most of the offense, the pitching was able to keep the Tigers in contention. Behind five strong innings from the rookie Porcello, they moved into first place in the AL Central on May 10. It was a perch they would keep for the next four and a half months.

With 16 wins, September was one of the Tigers' better months. However, a closing slide of just four wins in their final 11 games brought, for the second consecutive year, a playoff to decide the champion of the Central. When Detroit lost a three-game lead with four to play, the Tigers assured their spot in the pantheon of great late-season collapses.

Chicago White Sox
Run Differential: minus 8

As you might expect based on their run differential, the South Siders hovered around the .500 mark all summer. The high point of the White Sox season came on July 23. Not only did Mark Buehrle toss his perfect game against the Tampa Bay Rays that afternoon, but the victory pushed the Sox to a season-high five games over .500 and gave them a share of first place in the Central with the Tigers.

The next evening, undoubtedly not lacking for optimism, the White Sox traveled to Detroit for a double-header to kick off a four-game series. In the first game, Verlander shut down the Sox, allowing just one run on six hits. In the nightcap, reliever Matt Thornton walked in the go-ahead run in the bottom of the eighth, which was the difference in a 5-4 Tigers win. As if a double-header sweep at the hands of the Tigers wasn't bad enough, the Sox were delivered another crushing blow the next evening. With Chicago protecting a one-run lead in the ninth inning, Granderson doubled off Sox closer Bobby Jenks, driving in the game-tying run. In the 10th, D.J. Carrasco gave up three consecutive singles and the ballgame was over. In the span of 48 hours the White Sox had gone from the high of the Buehrle perfect game, which vaulted them into a first-place tie in their division, to the low of falling three games back.

Chicago won the next night to salvage something from the series in Motown, but didn't sniff first place for the rest of the season. It's rare that a division is decided over four games in July, but the Detroit series neatly encapsulated the White Sox summer. They were good enough to hang around in the Central, but they weren't good enough to stay on the summit.

The issue for the Sox seemed to be extended cold streaks from several of their key players. When Buehrle got the final out of his perfect game, his ERA stood at 3.28 and the Sox had won 15 of his 20 starts. In his six starts following that, he allowed 26 earned runs in 37 innings (a 6.21 ERA) and the Sox won just once. Fellow starter John Danks hit a similar rough patch in May when, over eight starts, he saw his ERA balloon to 5.10.

Offensively, the problems lasted much longer. After hitting a home run on July 18 against the Orioles, right fielder Jermaine Dye was hitting a robust .302/.377/.574 with 21 home runs. From there, he went into a tailspin and didn't bottom out for two months. In 49 games from mid-July to Sept. 18, Dye hit .160/.255/.238 with just four home runs. It didn't help that fellow slugger Paul Konerko found himself in a similar, albeit shorter, slump at roughly the same time. He was hitting .302/.353/.521 with 18 home runs through July 20, but over the next month he hit just .161/.295/.299 with only four home runs.

The Sox were just good enough to stay in the hunt for most of the season, but they couldn't sustain success long enough to remain relevant.

Cleveland Indians
Run Differential: minus 92

For the second consecutive season, a slow start submarined the Indians' hope of contention.

The Indians opened the year with five consecutive losses and dropped 12 of their first 18. Wins were so scarce that Cleveland didn't have a three-game winning streak until the week of Memorial Day. It didn't help that leadoff man Grady Sizemore endured a stretch beginning on April 21 in which he hit just .184/.236/.289 in 26 games.

However, because it was the Central, a bad start didn't doom the Indians' chances immediately. On May 28, Cleveland was seven games under .500, yet only 6.5 games out of first. Then, a June swoon cast the Indians into a double-digit deficit from which they never were able to dig out.

Entrenched in last place, the Tribe moved Cliff Lee to Philadelphia, stripping the team of the only bright spot of the starting rotation. While Lee wasn't matching his Cy Young campaign from the previous year, with a 3.14 ERA and 107 strikeouts in 152 innings, he was clearly the best of a sparse rotation. Lee was followed out of Cleveland by Carl Pavano (5.37 ERA in 125.2 innings) leaving a rotation in which Jeremy Sowers, at 26, was the elder statesman. It wasn't an ideal situation.

Meanwhile, closer Kerry Wood was proving why it's hardly ever a good idea to pay big money to a ninth-inning pitcher. He was just 20 of 26 (77 percent) in save situations and posted a gaudy 4.25 ERA in 55 innings.

The Indians waved the white flag with vigor in September, when they won just seven of their final 25 games. In that stretch they were outscored 183-120, which accounted for more than half of their negative run differential. Whether the late-season slide cost manager Eric Wedge his job is up for debate (some think his fate was sealed as early as April), but what cannot be debated is that, for the second consecutive season, the Indians failed to live up to some lofty expectations.

Kansas City Royals
Run Differential: minus 156

The Royals owned the worst run differential in the Central because of a disastrous rotation, a slipshod bullpen and an offense that ranked last across the board in the American League.

The lone bright spot on the mound was Zack Greinke. He was brilliant over the first two months of the season, allowing more than two runs in a start only once and winning eight of 11 starts with a sterling 1.10 ERA. Greinke didn't allow a home run until his 12th start of the season, a streak that reached 83 innings. He finished the season with an AL-best 2.16 ERA and 1.07 WHIP.

Young first baseman Billy Butler became a doubles machine—he hit 51 on the year—and was clearly the Royals' best hitter, posting a final line of .301/.362/.492 with 21 home runs to go along with all those doubles.

However, beyond the Greinke/Butler nucleus, there wasn't much to get excited about.

The trades that brought Coco Crisp and Mike Jacobs to Kansas City came at the expense of the bullpen. The pen, which had been fairly solid in 2008, wasn't good at all in 2009 with a 5.02 ERA, worst in the league. Perhaps that was why manager Trey Hillman rode his starters to the breaking point. After Gil Meche threw 132 pitches in a shutout against Arizona on June 16, he was rocked in his next two starts, going just 8.1 innings and allowing 13 runs on 14 hits. The Royals became alarmed when Meche reported a "dead arm" and decided to monitor his health before his next start. After throwing a successful bullpen session and being declared fit to make his start, Meche threw 121 pitches in a loss to the Twins. Two starts later, Meche was on the DL. He returned in August but was largely ineffective. In his final six starts, before shutting down for the year at the end of the month, Meche posted an 8.01 ERA with 19 strikeouts and 17 walks in 30 innings of work.

Starter Brian Bannister hit a similar barrier at the end of his season. After throwing more than 100 pitches in five consecutive starts at the end of July, Bannister was shelled in his next six starts. He had a 9.29 ERA in those 31 innings before the Royals shelved him for the year in early September with what the team said was shoulder fatigue.

The Royals were going to go as far as their pitching would take them. Despite the brilliance of Greinke, the rest of the staff crumbled, leaving the Royals battling for fourth place, a position all too familiar.

The American League West View

by Matthew Carruth

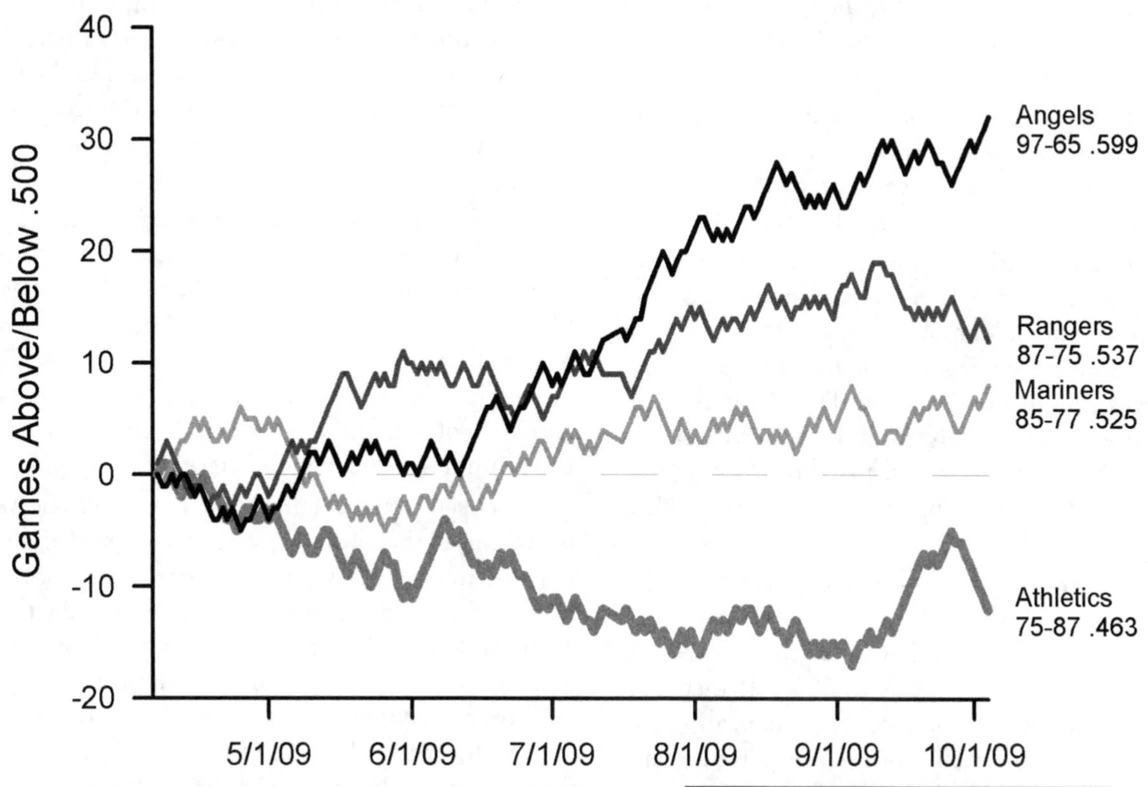

Play Against Other Divisions			
Division	**W**	**L**	**Win%**
AL East	95	79	.546
AL Central	96	78	.552
NL Central	5	1	.833
NL West	34	32	.515
TOT	**230**	**190**	**.548**

Head to Head Records					
Team	**LAA**	**OAK**	**SEA**	**TEX**	**TOT**
LAA		12	10	8	30
OAK	7		5	11	23
SEA	9	14		8	31
TEX	11	8	11		30

To find wins, read across; losses are read from the top.

Top Players		
Player	**Team**	**WAR**
Hernandez, Felix	SEA	6.9
Figgins, Chone	LAA	5.9
Gutierrez, Franklin	SEA	5.8
Suzuki, Ichiro	SEA	5.1
Kinsler, Ian	TEX	4.6
Morales, Kendry	LAA	4.3
Lackey, John	LAA	3.9
Weaver, Jered	LAA	3.9
Young, Michael	TEX	3.9
Sweeney, Ryan	OAK	3.9
Aybar, Erick	LAA	3.8
Anderson, Brett	OAK	3.8
Hunter, Torii	LAA	3.8
Davis, Rajai	OAK	3.7
Cruz, Nelson	TEX	3.6
Rivera, Juan	LAA	3.5
Feldman, Scott	TEX	3.3
Napoli, Mike	LAA	3.2
Andrus, Elvis	TEX	3.0
Braden, Dallas	OAK	2.9

WAR stands for Wins Above Replacement and is defined in the Glossary.

The American League West had an anticlimactic season in 2008, and with another divisional crown for the Angels, 2009 loomed as the same. By spring training, projections almost uniformly foretold a mediocre division. No team seemed dominant, or even worthy of competing with the big three in the AL East.

Underneath that, however, was a season filled with turbulence and change, perhaps not in the results, but in the process. Each franchise in the division had shifted team-building strategies over the past winter.

Perhaps none of the teams underwent as much change as the Seattle Mariners. A new front office came in and immediately revamped the organization from top to bottom. Many organizational fixtures, both beliefs and the people who upheld those beliefs, found themselves relocated or dismissed. The Mariners transformed from one of the organizations least receptive to advanced analysis to a team that employed a full division devoted to it, bringing in respected analyst Tom Tango to consult.

The Mariners came off a 61-win season in 2008 with little salary room, due to the many bad contracts still on the books from the Bill Bavasi era, so they seemed to have little room to compete in 2009. Rather than simply wait out the bad contracts, though, new general manager Jack Zduriencik focused on defense and went to work acquiring as many undervalued assets as possible.

To accomplish that, Zduriencik moved closer J.J. Putz, prospect Luis Valbeuna and a couple of spare parts to bring back elite defensive outfielders Endy Chavez and Franklin Gutierrez, along with numerous role players. With those players, holdovers Ichiro Suzuki and Adrian Beltre, and a midseason jettison of Yuniesky Betancourt, the Mariners became one of the best defensive teams in baseball this past season.

Surprising many, the Mariners grabbed the division lead at the beginning of the season. Ken Griffey Jr., returning after a decade away from the city where he made his name, homered on opening day against Francisco Liriano. Even with Ichiro on the shelf with an ulcer problem to begin the season, the Mariners raced out to a 7-2 mark and would finish April at 13-9. The season peaked for them, however, just a few days later.

On May 4, the 14-10 Mariners, playing the 9-12 Athletics, found themselves trailing 4-3 in the bottom of the ninth inning facing Russ Springer, who had given up Jose Lopez's game-winning hit two nights earlier. A Kenji Johjima home run tied the game and sent it to extra innings. In the top of the 13th, the Athletics plated three runs on a Landon Powell double and Orlando Cabrera's single to make it 7-4, surely enough for a victory. Except a single, fly out, single, walk, walk, ground out and single netted the Mariners three runs to equalize. In the bottom of the 15th, a single, error and intentional walk set the stage again for Lopez, who delivered another game-ending single. The Mariners had come from behind when their win expectancy for the game hit lows of 11 percent and 4 percent.

People like to trumpet statement games and if there was an example of such a game, that was it. The surprising Mariners, now 25 games into the season, held a 15-10 record and, according to Baseball Prospectus' PECOTA playoff odds, a roughly 40 percent chance of making the playoffs. They had come from behind twice in their last three games and just had won a series with two walk-off victories. They should have had all the momentum if such a thing mattered much.

It seems that actual talent mattered more. The Mariners dropped their next six games, fell to third place and that was that. Seattle would only for one day escape up to second place in the division and never really threatened the lead. Still, for a team coming off 101 losses and, in the eyes of the pundits, no dramatic offseason makeover, spending 27 days in first place and more days above .500 than below has to be considered a rousing success, one built almost entirely on a league-leading defense.

Seattle was not alone in trumpeting defense. The Rangers, perhaps figuring that they had some surplus offense, moved Michael Young off shortstop to third base to make room for the slick-fielding Elvis Andrus. Andrus seemed destined to be a liability at the plate and the move seemed to ruffle Young's feathers, but things settled down and the new defensive alignment stayed. Andrus even ended up surprising with some respectable hitting, while Young had a good season with the bat and seemed to adjust to playing third.

Texas was the team that took over the AL West lead from the Mariners when they faltered from their hot start. After a 10-11 mark in April, the Rangers surged ahead with a 20-9 record in May, giving them a 5.5-game lead in the division after May 30. At that point, PECOTA, regressing the Rangers' performance against their run differential and projections (which were dismal coming into the season), still had the Rangers with nearly a 50 percent chance of making the playoffs. CoolStandings.com, which relies more on run differential, had the Rangers' chances as high as 81 percent on that date in May.

Those odds would tail off sharply with an 11-15 June, which saw the Rangers surrender their divisional lead. A 17-8 July kept them on the cusp of wild card contention as reinforcements for the pitching staff, including Darren O'Day and Neftali Feliz, arrived. However, postseason play was not in the cards this season for Texas. The Rangers finished the year much as they began it, a touch below average, going 29-32 over the final two months.

Still, an 87-75 record was a nice eight-game improvement over 2008 and was the first time since 2004 that the Rangers finished above .500. Andrus' play at short, plus the heavier usage of Nelson Cruz in the outfield and some major strides by Ian Kinsler, helped revitalize Texas' defense in what was, along with Seattle's, a marked departure from the past ways of thinking and performance. The defense certainly deserves a lion's share of the credit for the Rangers 227-run drop in runs allowed during 2009 compared to 2008. Unfortunately for Texas, the offense also dipped, by 117 runs, but that still gave them a 110-run improvement in run differential, a massive amount for just one season.

Moving in the opposite direction were the Oakland Athletics. Accustomed to bargain shopping, Oakland's front office encountered new-found competition for defensive assets and turned instead to a group of players most hurt by the collapsing free agent market: veterans.

But before that, general manager Billy Beane had made a surprising splash by trading for Matt Holliday from the Rockies, without surrendering much irreplaceable talent. Then, however, Beane brought in long-ago stars Nomar Garciaparra and Jason Giambi; the hope seemed to be that those two, along with Holliday, would revitalize Oakland's anemic offense. They would have had to for the Athletics to compete, since that offense was joined by a nearly completely untested starting rotation, part of which was fresh up from Double-A.

It was that move to aging hitters that marked the difference for Oakland from the previous year's team. While the A's continued to get younger on the pitching front with their extraordinarily young starting rotation, their average hitter's age jumped almost two full years from 27.2 in 2008 to 29.1 in 2009. That number would have been even larger had the Athletics not fallen out of the race so fast and turned to younger position players.

Those veteran signings also had another impact, one that played to Oakland's quick demise in the 2009 season and will test your sense of pattern recognition: yes, that means defense. Oakland went from a top-notch defensive team in 2008 to one of the league's worst in 2009. In fact, the A's lost in the vicinity of 70 runs. Oakland's two-of-three series win in Anaheim to begin the year marked the only time the A's were above .500, and by the time they reached a 13-22 record, their poor play had nearly extinguished their hopes for the playoffs. They were in last place, already nine games out of the lead.

Pitching ended up being the only strength for Oakland, a bit of a surprise considering the players involved. The youngsters in the rotation performed up to task for the most part, ending the season at roughly an average level of performance as a unit. The bullpen however, with newcomer Andrew Bailey leading, or rather finishing, the way, was a tremendously talented group and one of baseball's best.

They were not good enough, however, to make up for a disappointing season by the offense. Holliday initially struggled mightily with his move to the American League and eventually was shipped to St. Louis. Giambi never recovered his Oakland stroke and ended up in Colorado after being released. That the A's scored more than 100 more runs than in 2008 was far more of a testament to how putrid the offense was in 2008 than it was a good mark for the 2009 team; Oakland still managed only 759 runs, nearly one a game fewer than the division champion Angels.

The Mariners and Rangers both got younger and more defensively focused. The Athletics did the opposite, at least on the positional player side. So what of the Angels? Well, their change was not so much a planned strategy than one that was forced on them. Even before the sudden loss of Nick Adenhart in a fatal car accident, the Angels' rotation was in trouble. John Lackey, Kelvim Escobar and Ervin Santana were all still on the shelf with injuries to begin the season. The Angels' pitching, long the bedrock of their divisional successes, was in shambles.

It was not just the rotation, though. The Angels had also relied on a dependable bullpen in years past. This season, with Francisco Rodriguez departed for Citi Field in New York, there were more questions at the end the game than you would want for a team with so many new questions at the start. In fact, the Angels would use 25 different pitchers in 2009, the most for the franchise since the 2000 team matched that number, which was last exceeded by the 1996 team.

As the start of the season approached, prospects looked dimmer for Anaheim than they had in recent memory. Normally, the Angels had been a team built on speed and pitching depth, but in 2009 the offense stepped up in a huge way, giving the pitching staff room to breathe. The 883 runs the Angels scored marked a franchise record.

Anaheim's injuries were not limited to the pitching staff. Vladimir Guerrero played in just 100 games because of chest and knee injuries and he was hampered enough to post the first sub-.800 OPS since his nine-game debut season in 1996. The Angels had to turn to others for run production and found it, getting solid years out of a variety of players, from Kendry Morales to Chone Figgins to Bobby Abreu.

On a team level, however, the Angels were right around league average in home runs, strikeouts, walks, extra base hits and ball in play rates. How, then, did they manage to score enough runs to finish second in the league?

In short, because of two somewhat related numbers: the Angels' batting average on balls in play and their batting average with runners in scoring position. The Angels as a team posted a .322 BABIP compared to a league average of .299. They also hit .297 with runners in scoring position compared to the league's .269. Those are two metrics that are going to point a lot to luck. Some might point out that the Angels typically rely on team speed and thus should be expected to have higher than league-average numbers in those categories. While that's probably true, such a large deviation isn't attributable to speed alone.

The Angels stood just 25-25 on June 3, but from there would win 38 of their next 53 games, ending play on Aug. 2 with a 63-40 record and a four-game lead in the division. With so few games left to play, and the Angels a clearly superior team to the Rangers or Mariners, the division race was mostly over at that point. Both PECOTA and CoolStandings pegged the Angels as about 82 percent favorites to take the division. They would reach 90 percent about 10 days later and never slide back, finishing with 97 wins and another postseason date with the Red Sox

The past AL West season may not have seen a dramatic race to the playoffs, but it did feature a lot of change and 29 more total wins from the four teams combined. Expect even more player turnover this winter: Each team has some big holes to patch.

The National League East View

by Jonathan Halket

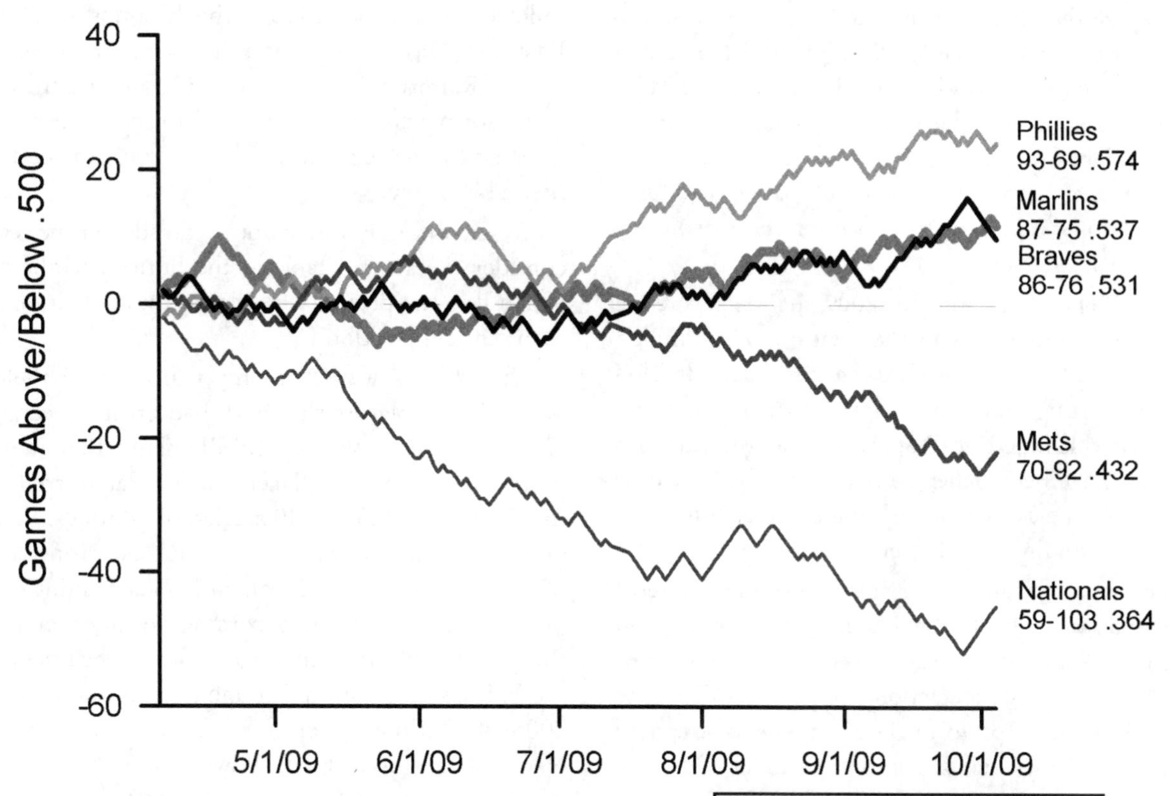

Play Against Other Divisions			
Division	**W**	**L**	**Win%**
AL East	35	49	.417
NL Central	99	101	.495
NL West	80	85	.485
TOT	**214**	**235**	**.477**

Head to Head Records						
Team	**ATL**	**FLA**	**NYN**	**PHI**	**WAS**	**TOT**
ATL		8	13	10	10	41
FLA	10		11	9	12	42
NYN	5	7		6	10	28
PHI	8	9	12		15	44
WAS	8	6	8	3		25

To find wins, read across; losses are read from the top.

Top Players		
Player	**Team**	**WAR**
Utley, Chase	PHI	7.7
Ramirez, Hanley	FLA	7.3
Zimmerman, Ryan	WAS	7.1
Vazquez, Javier	ATL	6.6
Johnson, Josh	FLA	5.5
Howard, Ryan	PHI	4.9
Werth, Jayson	PHI	4.7
McCann, Brian	ATL	4.4
Nolasco, Ricky	FLA	4.2
Ibanez, Raul	PHI	4.1
Jurrjens, Jair	ATL	3.9
Escobar, Yunel	ATL	3.9
Hamels, Cole	PHI	3.8
Victorino, Shane	PHI	3.4
Wright, David	NYN	3.3
Morgan, Nyjer	WAS	3.0
Beltran, Carlos	NYN	2.9
Prado, Martin	ATL	2.9
Uggla, Dan	FLA	2.9
Jones, Chipper	ATL	2.8

WAR stands for Wins Above Replacement and is defined in the Glossary.

If 2007 was tragedy and 2008 farce, then 2009 was a disappointment. This season featured no Phillies comeback; their fans could safely buy playoff tickets by the All-Star break. There was no September Mets crash, since they had already skidded down the standings months earlier. Hanley Ramirez and the rest of the Marlins could not look forward to sinking the Mets' playoff hopes in the final series of the season for the third straight year. Chipper Jones couldn't savor his Shea Stadium September home runs anymore. Only in the nation's capital were hopes for the season low enough to avoid a letdown.

In the THT predictions for 2009, the Mets were the consensus favorites to win the division. The Phillies, as defending champions and back-to-back division winners starting the season with virtually the same team that celebrated at Tropicana Field the previous fall, must have been galled to once again be picked by many pundits as bridesmaids. Some projections even had the Braves finishing better.

Of course, the injuries to key Mets players are the most apparent reasons why there will be no pennant flag to add to their new stadium this year. Nevertheless, the NL East in 2009 mostly met expectations, despite the Mets. The Phillies' star players performed well enough to be carried into first place by their supporting cast. The Marlins' pitching remained inconsistent and Hanley Ramirez's supporting cast was not strong enough to carry out a Tampa Bay Rays-like insurgency. The Braves' starting pitching was as good as advertised, but their lineup was mediocre and unable to handle the decline of Chipper Jones. The Mets' bit players were not all that good once thrust into the spotlight. The Nationals did indeed get stronger offensively with the addition of Adam Dunn, but their pitching remained dreary.

Though a team's outfield is not destiny, it is instructive to use each team's outfield circa this past April to see how much better placed Philadelphia was to win this season. For, apart from perhaps the Nationals, the infielders were expected to be the dynamos for each NL East team. For the most part they were: Brian McCann, Hanley Ramirez, Chase Utley and Ryan Howard would all perform well. The outfields for each team had new faces and lingering uncertainty, as you can see in the first table below.

To see how that uncertainty evolved over the season, consider the second table at the bottom of the page, which lists the players who played the most innings at each outfield position.

The Phillies were the only team able to field an outfield with players that both had great expectations and the good fortune to fulfill them. Ibanez was a more than suitable replacement for Pat Burrell. His first half of .309/.367/.649 carried the Phillies. Victorino's 2009 season, while not quite as strong as his 2008, was still solid. Meanwhile Werth built on his breakout 2008 season, becoming yet another power threat in the Phillies' lineup. And it was the lineup that the Phillies relied upon through the All-Star break. In 2008, the Phillies' pitching staff was fifth-best in the National League in runs allowed. For the first three months of the 2009 season, the staff was the fifth-worst. Fortunately, during the same time, their lineup was the second-best in runs scored, one run behind the Rockies.

The Phillies' top three starters from 2008 struggled in the first half of 2009. On July 1, Cole Hamels had a 4.98 ERA and a 5-5 record. Still that was better than Brett Myers, who sped out to a 4.66 ERA by May before going to the DL for the next four months with a hip

Projected Regular NL East Outfields

	Phillies	Marlins	Braves	Mets	Nationals
Right Fielder	Jayson Werth	Cody Ross	Jeff Francoeur	Ryan Church	Adam Dunn
Center Fielder	Shane Victorino	Cameron Maybin	Jordan Schafer	Carlos Beltran	Lastings Milledge
Left Fielder	Raul Ibanez	Jeremy Hermida	Garret Anderson	Daniel Murphy	Austin Kearns

Most Innings in NL East Outfields

	Phillies	Marlins	Braves	Mets	Nationals
Right Fielder	Jayson Werth	Jeremy Hermida	Jeff Francoeur	Jeff Francoeur	Elijah Dukes
Center Fielder	Shane Victorino	Cody Ross	Nate McLouth	Carlos Beltran	Willie Harris
Left Fielder	Raul Ibanez	Chris Coghlan	Garret Anderson	Gary Sheffield	Josh Willingham

injury. Jamie Moyer lost his age-defying form from the previous year and began July with 6.05 ERA.

The starting staff would get better in the second half. By the end of May, J.A. Happ was starting. Though not touted as their best pitching prospect (that honor would belong to the now less-coveted Carlos Carrasco), his 2.82 ERA quickly found a place in the rotation. In July, the team came to terms with Pedro Martinez and traded for Cy Young winner Cliff Lee (giving up, among others, Carrasco). Lee would give up no more than one earned run in each of his first four starts for them while Martinez had a 5-0 record in his first seven starts.

The Phillies' bullpen, which led the NL in ERA in 2008, was an open wound in 2009. Brad Lidge, who did not blow a save in 2008, blew 11 in 2009, also posting an 0-8 record and a 7.21 ERA. Ryan Madson performed admirably as their set-up man, but seemed to wilt when handed the closer's role, first when Lidge was on the DL and later when manager Charlie Manuel lost patience with him.

The Marlins' outfield was mostly a tale of talent unfulfilled in 2009. Maybin failed to produce to start the season and was sent down. Ross showed some power, but his inability to take a walk meant that his OPS was still below .800. Hermida was the Marlins' big hope for a breakout player but never materialized. Coghlan was a pleasant surprise but not to the degree that he could carry a team.

The same tale could mostly be told about the Marlins' starting pitching as well. Only Josh Johnson routinely pitched well. Anibal Sanchez and Ricky Nolasco were pictures of inconsistency. Both Sanchez and Nolasco were very hittable through late spring; the latter was sent down to the minors and the former to the DL.

There was nothing unsatisfying about Hanley Ramirez, however. If there was any doubt about which NL East team had the league's best shortstop, this season should put that to rest. Ramirez's .342/.410/.543 season was overshadowed by Albert Pujols's, but if Pujols is the consensus MVP then Ramirez should be the consensus runner-up.

Meanwhile, the goal for the Braves' outfield for 2009 must simply have been to not be as bad as in 2008. Francoeur did manage to put up an .836 OPS, only he did it for the Mets. During his time on the Braves, he had only a .642 OPS. Schafer, like Maybin, was an immediate disappointment and was optioned back to the minors in June. To make up for Schafer's letdown, the Braves traded for Nate McLouth in June from the Pirates, who had themselves been let down by his inability to build on his 2008 performance. Once on the Braves, McLouth continued to stagnate. Anderson mostly lived up to expections of low power and declining batting average.

It is a shame that the Braves could not muster a bit more from their offense, since their pitching was great. They had the best starting pitching in the majors, despite getting a 4.67 ERA from free-agent pickup Derek Lowe. Their other free-agent starter, Javier Vazquez, lived up to expectations, striking out 238 with at least five in every start. Tommy Hanson lived up to his hype, striking out 116 in only 127.2 innings pitched. Jair Jurrjens didn't disappoint either, posting a 2.60 ERA.

The Braves' rotation made manager Bobby Cox's penultimate season in the dugout reminiscent of the team's decade dominance in the '90s. What this year's team was lacking was a young Chipper Jones. The injury problems that had started to eat into his playing time over the past couple of seasons finally seemed to eat into his on-field performance this season, as he posted a .264/.388/.430 line, well down from 1.000-plus OPS marks of yesteryear.

The Braves did manage to reacquire Adam LaRoche, filling what had become an offensive black hole for the team at first base. He promptly showed his pleasure at being back in Atlanta by hitting 12 home runs and batting .355 in his first 47 games with the team. Perhaps the Braves would have made the postseason if they had managed to acquire him directly from the Pirates rather than later via the Red Sox.

For the Mets, the problem was attrition, not delayed acquisitions. Before the injuries started piling up, the season seemed to be fairing rather well.

On May 10, Carlos Delgado's final game before leaving with a hip injury, the Mets were one game up on the Phillies for the division lead. Ten days later, when Jose Reyes left for the year with calf problems, the Mets were just one game behind the Phillies. Even on June 21, right before the Mets sent Carlos Beltran to the DL for almost three months, they were only two games behind the Phillies (but only one game over .500). Other, mostly later, injuries to starting players John Maine, Oliver Perez, Johan Santana and David Wright were just icing on the cake.

Most Mets fans would have penciled in their team for a trip to the World Series on April 1 if they had heard that Luis Castillo, their white elephant last season, was going to hit .302 in 2009 while Livan Hernandez, their emergency fifth starter, would have a 4.04 ERA through his first 15 starts. That these comebacks of sorts were wasted in a year of injuries must have disappointed fans. Every team needs a bit of luck to win and instead the Mets received heaping doses of misfortune.

However, what galled the fans more was how poorly the rest of the team played once their brightest stars were removed from the foreground. Probably Castillo's game-losing drop of an infield fly against the Yankees was most memorable. But for fans of the now slap-hitting team with a huge home field, the numerous base running mistakes by Pagan and Murphy (among others) must have been more exasperating. The team led the league in "outs on base" (a statistic that counts outs made by base runners, not including force outs, caught steal-ings or pickoffs). The Mets were worst in the majors in fielding, as measured by their Ultimate Zone Rating (a metric that combines measures of fielding range, arms, double plays and errors)—a disastrous result given the dimensions of their new field. The pitching staff was second-worst in the majors in walks allowed.

Since trading away Xavier Nady in 2006, the Mets' apparent strategy for their corner outfield spots (traditionally cheap sources of offense) has been:

- Fail to develop and lose faith in (with or without cause) players with growth potential, like Lastings Milledge, Carlos Gomez and Ryan Church.
- Acquire well-past-prime stars with significant injury risks, like Moises Alou and Gary Sheffield.
- Convert infielders to fill gaps when necessary.

To start the year, the corner outfield was mostly a make-do bunch. The Mets quickly added Gary Sheffield and then mostly hoped that Church, Murphy and Fernando Tatis could fill the gaps when Sheffield needed time off or when the Mets needed more than one corner outfielder on the field at a time. Murphy could not figure out the outfield while Tatis soon showed that his resurgent 2008 was mostly a fluke. Mets manager Jerry Manuel and Church did not talk to each other. Later, the Mets did acquire Francoeur (for Church), who turned out to provide at least some offensive ballast and defensive capability.

Perhaps, without any (or at least many) of the key injuries, the Mets could have survived such weak corner outfielders. However, the injury to Delgado exposed the outfield. Corner outfielders are often emergency first basemen (see Adam Dunn). The Mets were no different, with Tatis and, mainly, Murphy moving to first once Delgado went down. But corner outfielders, along with corner infielders, are usually a team's power hitters. Without Delgado and with David Wright going through a season-long home run drought, the Mets' biggest power threat was the oft-sidelined, 40-year-old Sheffield. Until September, he held the Mets lead for home runs, with 10. Their leader at the end of the season was Murphy with 12 and the Mets finished last in the majors in home runs with 95—the next-worst team was San Francisco with 122. The power outage was not just a park effect, as the Mets were just league average in doubles and had more home runs at home than away.

The Nationals experimented with their outfield line-up the entire season. Dunn had one of his best seasons, complementing his usual power (38 home runs) with a respectable batting average (.267). Josh Willingham finally grew into his expectations with a .260/.367/.496 season. Dukes and Milledge failed their tests, but midseason acquisition Nyjer Morgan blossomed before breaking his left hand in August.

But while Ryan Zimmerman, with 33 home runs and more than 100 runs and RBIs, claimed the title of best third baseman in the division from Chipper Jones and David Wright, the pitching staff was the worst in the league by nearly any metric. Nationals pitchers had the most walks, the fewest strikeouts, and the most runs allowed (almost 10 percent more than second-worst Brewers and 15 percent more than third-worst Pirates). Starters and relievers were equally bad. No wonder Stephen Strasburg was the most talked-about Nationals pitcher without pitching a single major-league pitch.

While the Nationals are probably more than a year away from endowing their fans with postseason hopes, an embryo of a competitive team seems to be emerging. Zimmerman and Dunn should anchor a competent if not spectacular offense. Strasburg could lead a decent staff with John Lannan and, in 2011, Jordan Zimmermann. If the team could find one or two decent bullpen arms, it might find its way out of last place next year.

The National League Central View

by Jeff Sackmann

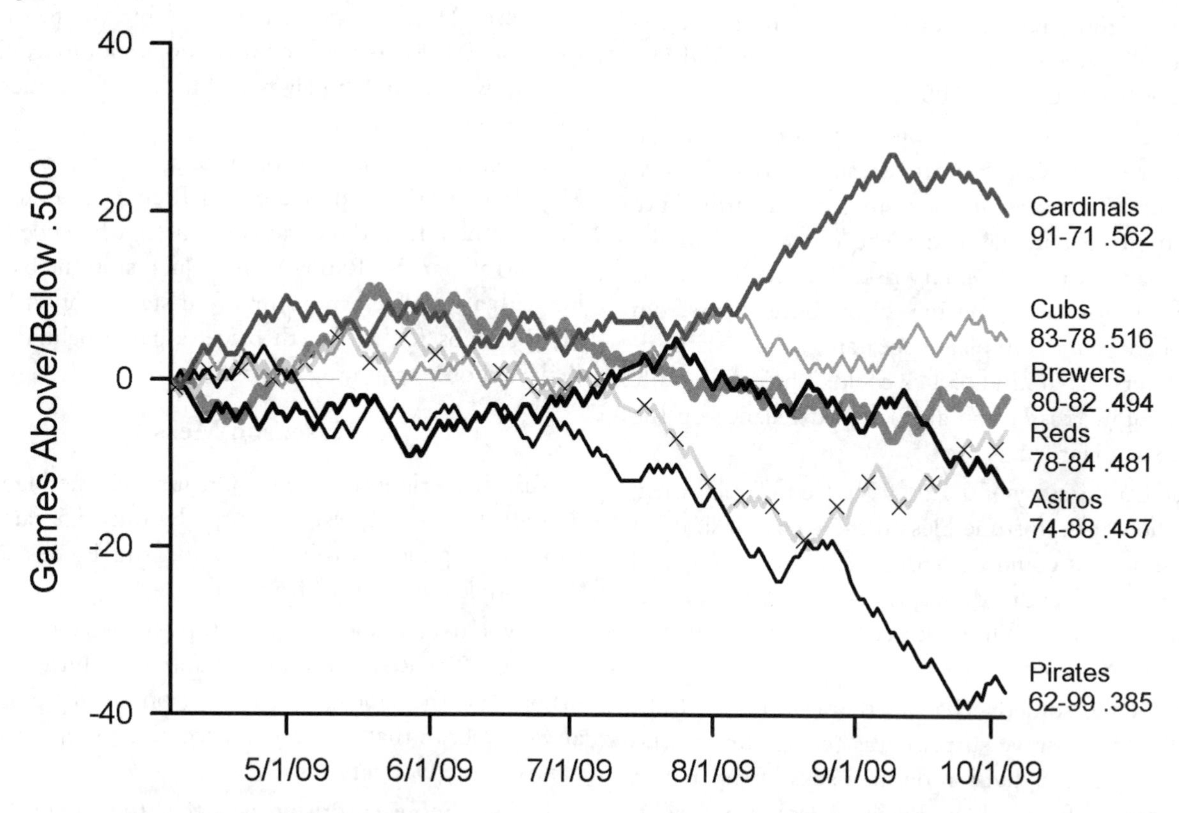

Play Against Other Divisions

Division	W	L	Win%
AL East	1	2	.333
AL Central	38	43	.469
AL West	1	5	.167
NL East	101	99	.505
NL West	91	116	.440
TOT	**232**	**265**	**.467**

Head to Head Records

Team	CHN	CIN	HOU	MIL	PIT	STL
CHN		10	11	10	10	6
CIN	5		12	8	13	8
HOU	6	4		5	10	6
MIL	7	7	10		9	9
PIT	4	5	5	5		5
STL	10	8	9	9	10	

To find wins, read across; losses are read from the top.

Top Players

Player	Team	WAR
Pujols, Albert	STL	8.4
Fielder, Prince	MIL	6.7
Wainwright, Adam	STL	5.7
Carpenter, Chris	STL	5.6
Lee, Derrek	CHN	5.3
Pineiro, Joel	STL	4.8
Braun, Ryan	MIL	4.7
Votto, Joey	CIN	4.4
Cameron, Mike	MIL	4.3
Bourn, Michael	HOU	4.2
Rodriguez, Wandy	HOU	4.0
Lilly, Ted	CHN	3.7
Dempster, Ryan	CHN	3.6
Zambrano, Carlos	CHN	3.6
Molina, Yadier	STL	3.4
McCutchen, Andrew	PIT	3.4
Pence, Hunter	HOU	3.4
Phillips, Brandon	CIN	3.2
Maholm, Paul	PIT	3.2
Ryan, Brendan	STL	3.2

WAR stands for Wins Above Replacement and is defined in the Glossary.

Back in March, few baseball fans would've been surprised if you told them the NL Central would be a one-horse race, featuring a 91-game winner and a bunch of also-rans.

Most of those fans, however, wouldn't have believed that the 91-game winner came from St. Louis and that the Cubs barely cracked .500.

The Chicago club that entered the season was an impressive one. Coming off of back-to-back division titles and 97 victories in 2008, they could hardly have been more heavily favored. The only chink in the Chicagoans' armor was injury risk. The 2008 club was reasonably fortunate, getting 29 or more starts from four pitchers and 550 plate appearances from six position players. That kind of luck couldn't hold, especially with an aging roster and an increased reliance on the fragile Rich Harden.

Much of the story of the 2009 NL Central race, then, is just how little fortune blessed the Cubs. Just about everything that could go wrong went wrong. General Manager Jim Hendry didn't deserve a disaster of this magnitude, but as we'll see, his club's decline wasn't just fate striking a blow.

Of course, someone had to outperform the Cubs as well. The positive surprise was the Cardinals, who ran away with the division on the backs of superlative performances from Albert Pujols, Adam Wainwright, and Chris Carpenter. St. Louis wasn't immune to bad luck—for example, Troy Glaus was limited to 29 at-bats—but depth and aggressive management kept the team strong into September.

Setting The Tone

The Cardinals didn't waste any time proving they could contend. On May 1, they notched their 17th victory in 24 contests, good enough to lead the second-place Brewers by four games. The St. Louis bats were hot from the get-go: Pujols posted a typically spectacular 1.132 OPS in April, supported by Chris Duncan (.938) and Yadier Molina (.902). The pitching was nearly as strong, as the staff limited opponents to a little more than four runs per game.

But it wouldn't remain that easy. In mid-May, the Brewers swept a three-game set from the Cards in St. Louis, taking a three-game lead in the division. The Crew held a share of first place as late as July 4, but in retrospect, that series sweep in May was the beginning of the end: It coincided with the loss of Rickie Weeks, whose .857 OPS suggested he was finally ready to step forward as an important cog in the Milwaukee offense.

The Brewers would suffer a number of such blows, notably injuries to Weeks and Dave Bush along with performances from J.J. Hardy, Bill Hall and Manny Parra that fell far below expectations. Craig Counsell and Casey McGehee performed well, but the fact that they got 750 at-bats between them does a lot to explain why Milwaukee didn't play many meaningful games in August and September.

The Cubs were headed south for similar reasons. In May, both Carlos Zambrano and Rich Harden spent time on the DL, as did Aramis Ramirez, who ended up missing 50 games. Randy Wells helped stop the bleeding with a 1.80 ERA in his first four starts, but on May 31, the Cubs fell to fourth place, a game behind the Reds and only a game above .500.

A Midseason Mess

Yes, that's right: the Reds. On June 11, the biggest division in baseball was separated by only 5.5 games. Cincinnati pulled within 1.5, while the Pirates and Astros duked it out for fifth place.

It would take some time before this mess sorted itself out. The Reds hung around until early July; a 22-1 drubbing at the hands of the Phillies on July 6 presaged an 8-19 month that included consecutive sweeps at the hands of the Dodgers and Cubs.

Perhaps more surprising was that the Pirates and Astros were still within striking distance. Houston got as close as a single game out of first on July 22, due as much to the mediocrity of the division as to their own success. A breakthrough season from Wandy Rodriguez (14-12, 3.02 ERA) gave the Astros another arm to complement Roy Oswalt. Ultimately, however, the rest of the rotation was too much of a shambles: Guys like Mike Hampton, Brian Moehler, and Russ Ortiz couldn't keep their team in the race.

The Pirates never threatened for the division lead, though they did come within four games of the top spot in June. They were three games below .500 at that peak; more impressively, they had scored more runs than they had allowed. Pittsburgh management never overestimated their chances for success, trading away Nate McLouth, Adam LaRoche, and Jack Wilson, among others. That cleared the way for exciting youngsters such as Andrew McCutchen, but it ensured the Bucs would be a non-factor in the division race.

Once the Brewers, Reds, and Astros felt the effects of injuries and dreadful pitching from fourth and fifth starters, the Cardinals and Cubs settled in for a premature race to the finish. In late July, Chicago reeled off five in a row, taking a slim lead.

But the northsiders couldn't sustain the pace. The Cardinals took advantage of an easy August schedule to seal the deal, going 11-3 from July 31 to August 16. In that stretch, they went from a half-game back to five games up. No other team came within five games for the remainder of the season.

How To Plug Holes And Win Divisions

It's easy to look at the NL Central in retrospect and see a simple explanation for its outcome. The Cardinals got an unexpectedly spectacular season from Chris Carpenter and better-than-promised performances from Adam Wainwright and Ryan Franklin, enough to get them from last year's 86 wins to this year's 91.

At the same time, the Cubs lost an all-star slugger in Aramis Ramirez, saw a mediocre season from Geovany Soto and suffered a dreadful one from Alfonso Soriano. A similar narrative can be constructed for the Brewers, who had to do without Rickie Weeks and got less than expected from Hardy, Bush, Parra, and Braden Looper—any of which may have been injury-related.

That narrative greatly underestimates what the Cardinals accomplished. Consider what Tony LaRussa had to contend with. Last year, Troy Glaus, Ryan Ludwick, and Rick Ankiel combined for 89 home runs. This year: 33. Ankiel and Ludwick each lost 175 points of OPS. No one replaced that production until Matt Holliday arrived mid-season. On the other side of the ball, Todd Wellemeyer's 3.17 2008 ERA morphed into a 5.89 mark in 2009. Kyle Lohse went from 3.78 to 4.74.

Consider, as well, the strokes of good fortune that benefitted the Cubs and Brewers. Both had a Rookie of the Year candidate come out of nowhere: Randy Wells was arguably as valuable as any Cubs starter, and Casey McGehee batted .300 and plugged a gaping hole at third. The Brewers struck gold with cheap midseason acquisition Felipe Lopez, while the Cubs got a huge bounce-back season from Derrek Lee.

What, then, was the difference? Certainly luck plays a role in who gets hurt and who performs to expectations, but it's much more appealing to point to good and bad decisions that influenced the outcome of the season.

Senior Moments

The oldest regular position player on the 2009 Cards was Ryan Ludwick, at age 30. (34-year-old Mark DeRosa arrived in midseason.) Chris Carpenter was the only starting pitcher over 30.

Contrast that to the Cubs. Every regular except for Geovany Soto was 29 or older. Derrek Lee and Alfonso Soriano—as important as any cogs in the offense—were both 33. The rotation was on the young side, and as it turned out, that was the strength of Chicago's season.

The Brewers were a mixed bag. The offense was built around two 25-year-olds (Prince Fielder and Ryan Braun), but depended on Mike Cameron (36) and even Craig Counsell (38). The rotation was split between youngsters such as Yovani Gallardo and Manny Parra and veterans like Jeff Suppan and Braden Looper.

What does all is this mean? There are hardly any eye-popping differences in the makeups of these three teams.

What jumps out at me is the difference between upside risk and downside risk. If your team is going to give a starting job to a player projected to hit .270 with 15 home runs and 75 RBIs, you'd probably rather that guy is a 26-year-old with a chance of turning into a star than a 35-year-old with a chance of pulling his hamstring for the third time. Upside risk isn't limited to young players and downside risk doesn't only apply to veterans, but that guideline is a good place to start.

Cardinals: Lots Of Upside

In a perfect world, then, your team will collect upside risk and limit downside risk. The Cardinals outfield is a great example. While Rick Ankiel and Ryan Ludwick both posted excellent seasons in 2008, no one really expected Ludwick to manage another .966 OPS.

Instead of trading one, the Cards brought back both, along with platoon candidate Chris Duncan and top prospect Colby Rasmus. That outfield wasn't projected to be the strength of the 2009 club, but even if something went wrong (as it did, when Duncan stopped hitting and Ankiel followed suit), it wouldn't be a disaster. Downside risk limited. While the potential upside didn't pan out, Rasmus' stellar first half showed just how high it could have been.

Of course, a big part of the 2009 Cards outfield production came from midseason acquisition Matt Holliday. Picking him up wasn't cheap. That's another form of collecting upside risk: Keeping a few million payroll dollars in reserve leaves the option of picking up an impact player. The Brewers applied a similar strategy and got a similar boost from CC Sabathia in 2008.

The Cardinals' starting rotation is also worth looking at. While Lohse and Wellemeyer exceeded expectations in 2008, no one expected them to replicate those performances. But, between the two of them and Joel

Pineiro (all 30-year-olds), it was reasonable to plan on getting one or two average-or-better seasons.

Of course, there was no planning for the greatness that was Chris Carpenter's season. No one knew what exactly he would contribute upon return, only that at his best, he's a Cy Young contender. There it is again: Lots of upside risk. St. Louis had the arms to make it through the season without Carpenter, and they may well have won the division even if he didn't pitch a single game. But the opportunity to win the lottery was there.

Brewers: Not This Year

Milwaukee constructed a similar sort of team. Yovani Gallardo, returning from injury, was their Carpenter, while Parra, Bush, and Looper can be compared to Pineiro, Wellemeyer, and Lohse. The offense was built around a couple of big bats; if anything, the Brewers had reason to expect more from this part of their club.

The Brewers were built to make a run at 85-88 wins, but there was more downside risk than anyone could have foreseen. Hardy, a young player coming off of seasons with OPS marks of .786 and .821, fell all the way to .659. Corey Hart, another promising youngster, didn't recover his 2007 form and posted another below-average season. In a way, these disappointments were worse than Weeks' injury, because it was so much harder to spot and correct the problem.

A similar story applied to the pitching staff. Looper and Jeff Suppan are veterans with consistent track records; their downside couldn't be that low, could it? Looper coughed up a club-record 39 home runs, while Suppan posted a 6.24 ERA in the second half. Parra was even worse, following up a breakthrough season with a fully deserved 6.36 ERA.

The Brewers had the depth to plug the hole at shortstop and deal with Bill Hall's decline at third base, but struggled all year to find starting pitching. These things happen when at least three of your starters underperform your worst-case scenario for them.

Cubs: All Downside

As I've noted, the Cubs entered 2009 with a great team on paper. Bringing back an improved version of a roster that won 97 games is great for ticket sales, but it usually means you have nowhere to go but down.

Just about everyone on the 2008 Cubs had a good or great year. Geovany Soto posted an .863 OPS as a rookie; Ryan Theriot got on base at a .387 clip; Soriano, Ramirez, and Mike Fontenot (!) topped .875 in OPS. Ryan Dempster's ERA was below 3.00, Ted Lilly struck out nearly a batter per inning and Carlos Marmol dominated in a setup role. Even important newcomers Milton Bradley (replacing a spectacular performance from Jim Edmonds) and Kevin Gregg (replacing Kerry Wood) posted career years in 2008.

It was a near certainty that some of those performances wouldn't repeat. At the same time, there were not very many important roster spots where someone (like Soto in '08) could step forward and make up for other losses. Only Randy Wells and Jeff Baker filled that role; perhaps Jake Fox could have done so given more playing time.

With a little more luck, the Cubs could've ended closer to 90 than 80 wins. But in retrospect, those slam-dunk pre-season projections appear misguided.

Upside In 2010?

The team with massive upside risk in 2010, of course, is the Pirates. McCutchen and Garrett Jones have already arrived; Pedro Alvarez is one of a handful that could make a similar impact in 2010. It won't be enough to launch the Bucs into contention, but it may mean we have to take them seriously the following year.

The picture is less rosy for the Reds and Astros. Cincinnati has already gotten solid seasons from several young players, and Edinson Volquez is out for 2010. The Astros have gaps in their rotation and unless they unearth two or three more Bud Norrises from within, that may not be a solvable problem.

The disappointment of the Cubs' season presents an opportunity for 2010. While the Cardinals can't count on repeat performances from Wainwright, Carpenter, or Franklin, Chicago can expect more from Soto and Ramirez, and management knows the club can be improved at closer and second base.

The same advantage is available to the Brewers. While many of 2009's starting pitchers will be back for another go-round, it's almost impossible that they will be as bad; if they are, the team won't be patient enough to give them as many innings. Similarly, J.J. Hardy will probably be traded, giving Alcides Escobar a chance to shine, and Rickie Weeks will be an early favorite for comeback player of the year.

But you can't predict who will make those big comebacks, which Rule 5 picks will make good, or which veteran will collapse in his early 30s. In a tight division, any of those things could mean the difference between a trip to the playoffs and a lost season.

The National League West View

by Steve Treder

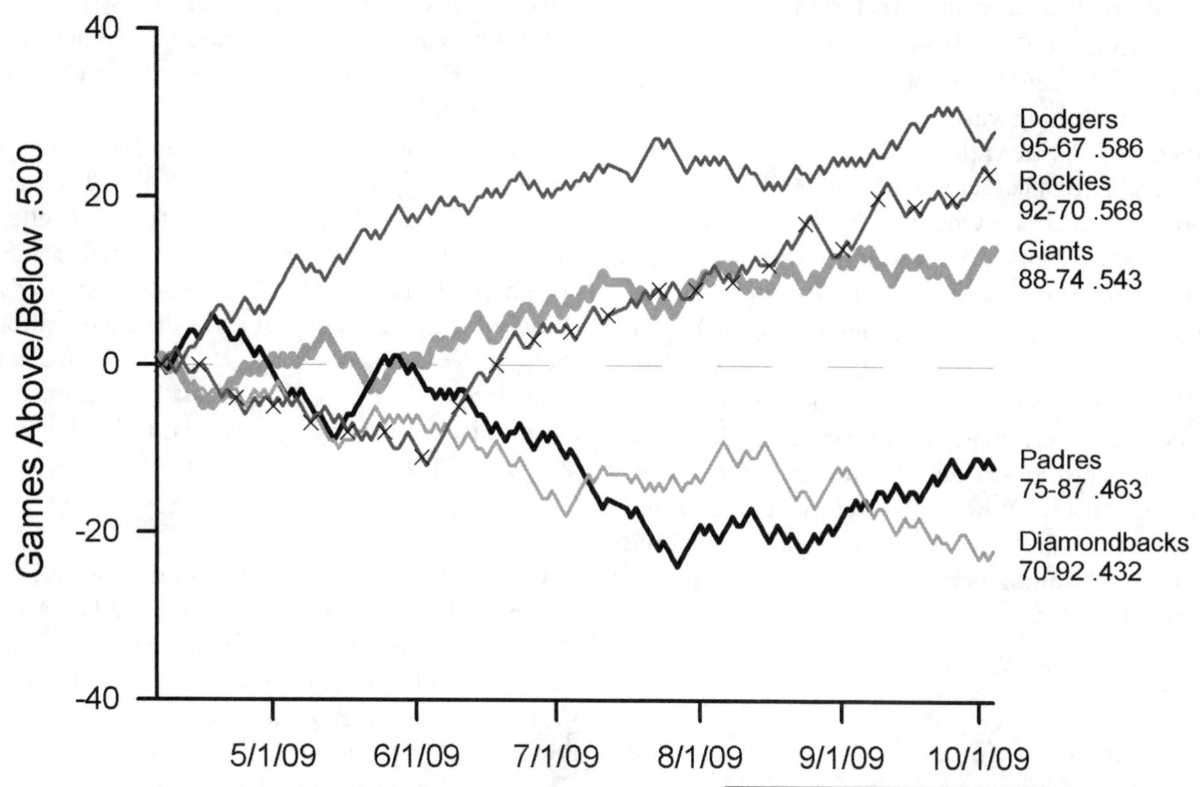

Play Against Other Divisions			
Division	**W**	**L**	**Win%**
AL East	2	1	.667
AL Central	5	4	.556
AL West	32	34	.485
NL East	85	80	.515
NL Central	116	91	.560
TOT	**240**	**210**	**.533**

Head to Head Records						
Team	**ARI**	**COL**	**LAN**	**SD**	**SF**	**TOT**
ARI		7	7	11	5	30
COL	11		4	10	8	33
LAN	11	14		10	11	46
SD	7	8	8		10	33
SF	13	10	7	8		38

To find wins, read across; losses are read from the top.

Top Players		
Player	**Team**	**WAR**
Lincecum, Tim	SF	8.2
Gonzalez, Adrian	SD	6.4
Haren, Dan	ARI	6.1
Jimenez, Ubaldo	COL	5.7
Tulowitzki, Troy	COL	5.5
Sandoval, Pablo	SF	5.1
Kemp, Matt	LAN	5.1
Upton, Justin	ARI	4.4
Blake, Casey	LAN	4.3
Kershaw, Clayton	LAN	4.2
Reynolds, Mark	ARI	3.9
Marquis, Jason	COL	3.8
Hammel, Jason	COL	3.8
de la Rosa, Jorge	COL	3.7
Helton, Todd	COL	3.6
Cain, Matt	SF	3.6
Montero, Miguel	ARI	3.3
Furcal, Rafael	LAN	3.3
Scherzer, Max	ARI	3.2
Billingsley, Chad	LAN	3.1

WAR stands for Wins Above Replacement and is defined in the Glossary.

Among the most tired of sports clichés is the old standby, "That's why they play the games." Like most clichés, this one keeps getting dusted off by drive-time sports talk hosts and ex-jock color commentators for a reason: It rests on an eternal truth.

That truth is this: Prediction is a most worthy enterprise—indeed, how would we get through a day without anticipating what will likely happen next?—but predicted results aren't the same thing as actual results, and actual results have a way of confounding our best efforts at prediction. One need look no further than the National League West for ample evidence of the perils of prediction based on past performance.

In this space last year we presented a table listing the collective performance of the NL West against other-division opponents (including interleague) over the past decade. There is just no better metric of divisional strength than this; you can't get any more direct than "wins and losses." Why don't we update that information, only this time let's look at it graphically. Here's the year-by-year winning percentage of this division over the past 10 seasons:

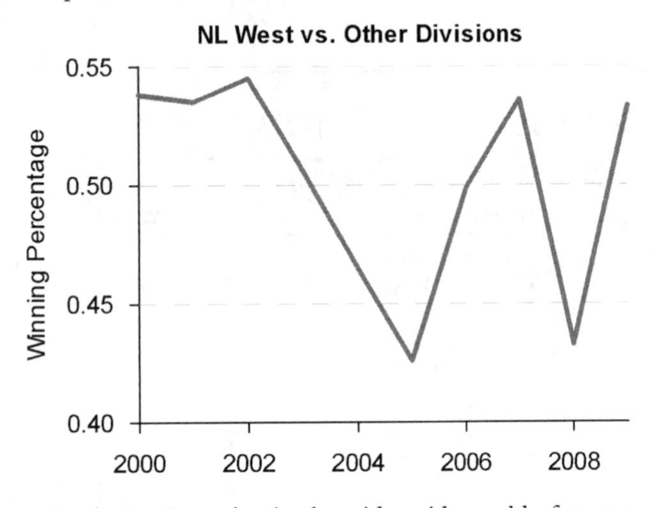

I ask you: Just what in the wide, wide world of sports is going on here? Is there any rhyme or reason to this whatsoever? Have you ever seen a more wildly careening roller coaster?

And most relevant to our "that's why they play the games" lesson: A year ago, did you predict that the NL West in 2009 would suddenly vault from the status of worst division in baseball to best in the National League?

Neither did I. Well, we're forced to admit, that's why they play the games.

But, never being one to allow fair and reasonable warning—such as the persistent futility of prediction we've just illustrated—to inhibit foolish action, I'll say right now that the strength the NL West demonstrated in 2009 is real, and will probably be sustained in 2010 and over the next few years. Indeed, my assessment is that the 2008 plunge in NL West performance was a fluke, a perfect storm of simultaneous disasters (which we chronicled in this space), and that another pratfall along those lines is unlikely to be encountered soon by this division.

The basis for such a prediction (well, other than, you know, stubborn foolishness) is simply this: The success exhibited by the 2009 NL West was largely manifested in young players. In fact, while the aggregate farm system production of the franchises in this division consistently ranked as the worst in the majors through the past decade, that era is now distinctly over. The farm systems feeding the NL West have dramatically improved, and are poised to render this division highly competitive for the foreseeable future.

Let's Start At The Top

One illustration of the strength of the 2009 NL West was the fact that both of its top teams, the Los Angeles Dodgers and Colorado Rockies, qualified for the post-season. A look at their rosters reveals something more they had in common: The primary force propelling both ball clubs was a core of exceptional young talent. To be sure, both also enjoyed the contributions of veterans, but it was whiz kids doing the heavy lifting.

In Los Angeles, most of the media attention was absorbed by the adventures of 37-year-old left fielder Manny Ramirez: his sizzling early-season hitting, his subsequent 50-game PED suspension, and his comparatively lackluster performance over the second half. But while this should hardly be considered surprising—the colorful Manny always makes for great copy—the focus on the veteran superstar was disproportionate to his role in the Dodgers' 95-win success. Quite unlike 2008, Ramirez in 2009 wasn't the best ballplayer clad in Dodger blue. That distinction was earned by their extraordinary 24-year-old center fielder Matt Kemp, in just his second full year in the majors—unless, that is, one might decide that 27-year-old right fielder Andre Ethier was even better.

Kemp and Ethier combined for 67 doubles, 57 home runs, and 207 RBIs, and for good measure Kemp piled on 34 steals in 42 attempts. The pair emerged as one of the best young outfield combos in any lineup in many years. They were joined in manager Joe Torre's regular starting eight by two more youngsters from the Dodgers system: 26-year-old catcher Russell Martin and 25-year-old first baseman James Loney. We must acknowledge that both Martin and Loney endured, by their standards, disappointing years with the bat in 2009, but both are still generally considered among the more impressive young performers at their positions.

Yet the key to the Dodgers' winning formula wasn't their hitting, it was the exceptional depth and quality of their pitching—the staff ran away with the league lead in ERA. Here again, much of the best work was contributed by youngsters. Southpaw Clayton Kershaw, in his first full major league season at the tender age of 21, placed in the league's top five in ERA and strikeouts per inning, and led the league in fewest hits per inning. Fellow starter Chad Billingsley, 24 years old, had a rocky second half but still topped the LA staff in wins, and was right behind Kershaw in strikeouts.

No bullpen in the league was better than that of the Dodgers, and it was anchored by three burly young right handers: 26-year-old setup men Ramon Troncoso and Ronald Belisario, and the massively strong flame-throwing closer, 25-year-old Jonathan Broxton.

For the Rockies, longtime star first baseman Todd Helton, at the age of 35, bounced back from an injury-wracked 2008 to deliver a splendid performance. But aside from Helton, no other front-line contributor on the Rockies' roster, in any role, was over the age of 30. Colorado's best player (indeed, emerging as one of the premier players in the game) was their tremendous all-around shortstop, Troy Tulowitzki—all of 24 years old, in just his third full year in the big leagues. Colorado's best pitcher (indeed, emerging as one of the better young starters in the game) was their hard-throwing right hander, Ubaldo Jimenez—all of 25, in just his second full year.

The Rockies' top-flight closer, Huston Street, was also 25. Twenty-four-year-old third baseman Ian Stewart, in his first full major league season, muscled his way into the lineup with 25 homers in 425 at-bats. Outfielders Seth Smith and Carlos Gonzalez, 26 and 23 respectively, also gained prominent roles over the course of the season by wielding loud bats, while 23-year-old rookie Dexter Fowler manned Colorado's extra-spacious center field most of the year, holding his own at the plate and providing superb defensive range along with 27 stolen bases. The Rockies' primary catcher, one of the better-hitting backstops around, was 26-year-old Chris Ianetta.

All of these youngsters are recent graduates of the Colorado farm system, with the exceptions of Street and Gonzalez, both of whom were acquired in a November 2008 trade for another Rockies farm product, star outfielder Matt Holliday. While it's never a happy decision for a franchise to cash in a centerpiece asset for prospects, rather than risk losing him to impending free agency, in this case Rockies' GM Dan O'Dowd appears to have played it shrewdly. After tumbling to 88 losses in 2008 following the Rockies' surprise pennant of '07, this year's Colorado team robustly bounced right back. With this foundation of first-rate young talent in place, we should expect the Rockies to contend in 2010 and beyond.

Looking forward, the Dodgers may have a few holes to patch. Manny's late-season drop-off is cause for concern, and it might be that he and/or a few of their other veteran regulars (particularly 35-year-old third baseman Casey Blake) will soon be in need of replacement. But just as in Colorado, it was the outstanding young talent that paved their way past 90 wins in 2009, and it's the outstanding young talent that promises continued success.

The Freak, The Panda And Other Giants

When last seen in the company of contenders, the San Francisco Giants were heavily dependent upon the sensational slugging of ultra-veteran Barry Bonds, and supported him with a lineup full of fellow graybeards. That was, alas, a long time ago: in 2004, which was, in fact, the last time the Giants presented a ball club losing fewer than 85 games.

The last time, that is, until 2009, when after four dreary seasons, San Francisco sprang back into contention. And this year's Giants bore precious little resemblance to the Bonds-era power-centric geriatrics: The '09 team frequently struggled to score runs, but reliably prevented them with a dominating pitching staff, and their key contributors in both halves of the inning were callow youths.

The most prominent leader of the San Francisco resurgence was, of course, Tim Lincecum, the 5-foot-11, 160-pound "Freak" with the gymnastic motion and the array of untouchable stuff. Smooth-cheeked and long-haired, he appears even younger than he is, but at age 25 Lincecum was still quite young in 2009, in just (though difficult to believe) his second full season in the big leagues, exceeding 260 strikeouts for the second time.

Yet brilliant as Lincecum was in 2009, he'd been nearly as brilliant in 2008, and those Giants were still buried in 90-loss depths. Their '09 breakout was a function of Lincecum being joined in stardom by two teammates, both even younger than he: switch-hitting 22-year-old third baseman Pablo Sandoval and 24-year-old right-handed starter Matt Cain. Sandoval, dubbed "The Kung Fu Panda" for his combination of roly-poly size and jovial personality, came out of nowhere to suddenly stand tall amid the premier young hitters in the game, while the strong-as-a-bull Cain stepped forward as the fully-formed ace he'd long been predicted to become.

Yet another youngster made news in San Francisco in 2009. In a July start, 26-year-old left-hander Jonathan Sanchez threw a no-hitter that was a lone infield error removed from being a perfect game. Overall Sanchez was inconsistent, surrendering too many walks and posting a so-so 4.24 ERA, but he placed fourth in the league in strikeouts per inning, and may be on the verge of stardom himself.

To be sure, the '09 Giants were still making use of long-in-the-tooth veterans in central roles, and they must add significant ingredients to rise to the next level. But for the first time in many, many years this franchise is presenting young talent as its core strength. Moreover, two of the Giants' September call-ups in 2009, 22-year-old catcher Buster Posey and 19-year-old starting pitcher Madison Bumgarner (how's that for a couple of colorful names?), have compiled glittering minor league stats and are widely considered among the elite prospects in the game.

Even At The Bottom, Things Are Looking Up

Everything didn't turn out peachy in the NL West in 2009. Though it was the best division in the league, it still included two losing teams, and one of those entries—the last-place Arizona Diamondbacks—was widely expected to do much better. For the Diamondbacks, the 2009 season can't be considered anything other than a letdown.

Yet even in disappointment there was reason for optimism. Neither the D-backs nor their fellow strugglers, the fourth-place San Diego Padres, wasted much energy on short-term fixes in 2009; instead, both ball clubs invested significant playing time in young talent. This is, of course, the time-honored preferred method of rebuilding, and if history is any guide, either or both of these teams will find their nurturing efforts rewarded with blossoming ballplayers in 2010 or shortly thereafter.

Unlike the Diamondbacks, San Diego wasn't expected to be competitive in 2009; the Padres went into the season ready to give the kids room to grow. The San Diego youth movement was accelerated when two of their veteran standouts soon encountered problems: 38-year-old right fielder Brian Giles gave up the ghost with a miserable, injury-plagued performance and played his final game in mid-June, and 28-year-old ace starter Jake Peavy, the league's Cy Young Award winner as recently as 2007, was mostly hurt as well, and was dealt for prospects at the July 31 trade deadline.

Thus fully unburdened by expectation, the Padres fully focused on development. Twenty-two-year-old Everth Cabrera, a Rule 5 draft pick (from the Rockies' rich system), was given most of the innings at shortstop. Chase Headley and Nick Hundley, each 25 and each in his first full season, emerged as regulars at left field and catcher, respectively, while 26-year-olds Tony Gwynn Jr. and Will Venable also saw significant action in the outfield. A 6-foot-6, 285-pound 22-year-old rookie outfielder-first baseman named Kyle Blanks clouted 10 homers in 148 at-bats before going down with a foot injury. The starting rotation was almost entirely given over to prospects and projects.

Unsurprisingly, San Diego spent much of the season taking heavy lumps. The Padres reached their low point in late July, at 38-62. But from there (interestingly, almost exactly the point of the Peavy trade) the Padres were quite good, going 37-25 the rest of the way, giving cause to expect competitiveness in 2010. And, by the way, San Diego's one-and-only star in 2009, 40-home run-slugging first baseman Adrian Gonzalez, was just 27 years old.

Meanwhile, the silver linings within Arizona's 92-loss gloominess were many and genuine. Right fielder Justin Upton, at only 21 years of age, burst out as an all-around star. Third baseman Mark Reynolds ignited 44 bombs (and, remarkably, swiped 24 bags) at the age of 25, and another 25-year-old, catcher Miguel Montero, blossomed into stardom as well. Twenty-six-year-old Stephen Drew remained one of the better-hitting shortstops in the league, while 24-year-old right-hander Max Scherzer emerged as one of the league's more impressive young starters.

The Diamondbacks' season didn't offer the optimistic trajectory of San Diego's—Arizona, after a slow start, played winning ball in July and August before falling apart again in September—but Arizona's young offensive core is better than San Diego's. And, by the way, the D-backs' one-and-only pitching star in 2009, Cy Young candidate Danny Haren, was just 28 years old.

Commentary

Ten Things I Learned This Year

by Dave Studenmund

Time goes on, baseball is played and wonders never cease. Okay, maybe not wonders—even I don't take baseball that seriously—but curiosities, insights and new things jump out of the sports page nearly every day of a baseball season. When there are 15 games, 135 innings and 600 plays every day, something new and unexpected is bound to happen.

The 2009 term was no different. We think we know this game, those of us who watch it and ponder it obsessively. But we don't, and that is what keeps bringing us back, and keeps supplying fodder for these Annual articles of mine.

For the third year in a row, there was a thrilling one-game playoff to determine the postseason's final contestants. Two new ballparks opened, Derek Jeter became the all-time Yankees hit leader, Manny Ramirez was suspended for 50 games and Joe Mauer had a season so superb he may never replicate it.

That's a good place to start.

Joe Mauer Had A Really, Really Good Year.

A lot of players had big years. Albert Pujols, obviously. Zack Greinke, too. But it was the Twins' Mauer who most captured my imagination. Consider...

- 23 percent of Mauer's batted balls were line drives. That figure didn't lead the majors, but it was in the top 20. The major league leader, Jason Bartlett, was at 26 percent and the major league average was 19 percent.
- He hit only **one** infield fly, one percent of all his flies. Didn't quite lead the majors, but was very close to the guy who did, Ryan Howard (also at 1 percent). The major league average was 11 percent.
- 21 percent of his outfield flies were home runs, another top 20 figure. The major league average was 11 percent.
- He struck out in only 10 percent of his plate appearances, yet another top 20 figure. The major league average was 18 percent.
- He walked in 13 percent of his plate appearances, above the major league average of 10 percent and not quite in the top 20.
- He hit .279 on his ground balls. The major league average was around .250. Not a top-20 figure, but not exactly chopped liver, either.

This is a remarkable batting profile, with no below-average traits. Most of this year's great batters had at least one flaw.

- You can't really say Pujols has hitting flaws, but his line drive rate was 16 percent and his infield fly rate was 12 percent. Not Maueresque.
- Ryan Braun is an outstanding hitter, but he had a 17 percent infield fly rate last year.
- Prince Fielder had a superb year but he isn't a line drive hitter.
- Miguel Cabrera is a solid all-around hitter, with strong batted ball fundamentals, but he didn't match Mauer in a single one of the batted-ball categories I just mentioned.
- Chase Utley? Mauer Lite.

When you go down the list of great major league hitters, the only one who might match Mauer in all-around awesomeness is Hanley Ramirez. But ground-ball batting average is the only batted ball category in which Ramirez bested Mauer. That's it.

One other thing: Mauer is a catcher. We all know what the tools of ignorance do to the knees and the bat—they wear them down. The standard for batting greatness for catchers is much lower than that for any other position, which makes Mauer's year even more remarkable.

I spent the season researching and writing about batted-ball hitting and pitching. In fact, one of the benefits of purchasing the *2010 THT Annual* is that you can download all of my weekly Batted Ball Reports in one master PDF file. Read through them, if you'd like, because there were a number of new things I learned and shared during my research.

But perhaps the most significant thing I learned was the awesomeness of Mr. Mauer of Minnesota.

They Still Hit Ground Balls In Cleveland

Park effects were the big topic early in the year, thanks to a simultaneous home run deluge and drought in New York.

In the new Yankee Stadium, 15.7 percent of the Yankees' and their opponents' outfield flies were home runs. On the road, that figure was 11.8 percent. The difference (3.8 percentage points) was by far the largest in the majors; the second-highest difference was 2.2 percentage points in Cincinnati.

There's a trade off in this sort of thing. Shorter fences, or funky wind currents or whatever, make for home run havens. But they also make it easier to catch in-play fly balls for outs. In Yankee Stadium, outfield flies that weren't home runs were caught for outs 85 percent of the time. On the road, they were caught for outs 80 percent of the time. That difference was also the largest in the majors (once again by a wide margin; second largest spread was Washington's three percentage points).

The net effect was that teams created .021 more runs per fly ball in Yankee Stadium than on the road. That's something, but not compared to some other ballparks such as Fenway (.061 more runs per fly) or Cincinnati's Great American Ballpark (.029 more runs per fly).

Overall, the Yankees and their opponents scored .10 more runs per game at home than on the road. A hitter's park, but not overwhelmingly so.

Meanwhile, across town in the new Citi Field in Queens, something more bizarre was happening. The Mets' offense seemed to disappear into the heights of the Jackie Robinson rotunda as they (and their opponents) scored .32 fewer runs per game at Citi than on the road.

Actually, the Mets' offense disappeared everywhere. The new field didn't help, but its overall impact might surprise you.

As your favorite obsessive-compulsive TV detective might say, here's the thing: Despite Citi's well-publicized impact on home runs, the Mets and their opponents actually scored 0.15 *more* runs per fly ball at home than on the road. Citi Field's impact on fly balls was almost as positive as the new Yankee Stadium's!

Later in these same pages, Greg Rybarczyk, of the fantastic Hit Tracker Website takes a closer look (actually, a *very* close look) at both new New York ballparks. He finds that Citi did indeed rob Mets batters (and their opponents) of many home runs. But most of those unhomers fell in for extra-base hits and other Citi flies fell for hits too. The net result on all of the Mets' outfield flies was about the same.

I know these are totally counterintuitive results, perhaps unlikely to be repeated next year. We shall see. And they still hit more ground balls in Cleveland (45 percent) than on the road (42 percent)—a phenomenon we first noted about four years ago. I still have no idea why.

Relievers Are Fickle

Relievers are inconstant bedfellows, aren't they? Seriously.

Let me put this in Biblical terms: Relievers are not patient; they are not kind. Relievers are jealous, they put on airs, they are snobbish. They are rude, self-seeking, prone to anger; they brood over injuries.

Relievers fail.

Okay, perhaps I'm being a bit dramatic (not to mention sacrilegious), but have you considered Brad Lidge?

- On May 23, Lidge entered the bottom of the ninth with the Phillies leading 4-2 against the Yankees. He gave up three runs, including a two-run homer to A-Rod.
- On June 5, he inherited a 3-2 lead in the bottom of the ninth, loaded the bases and then gave up a game-winning double to Andre Ethier.
- Aug. 15, with a 3-2 lead over the Braves, he gave up two runs in the bottom of the ninth again. The key play was his own error handling a bunt.

I could go on, but you get the picture. At the Hardball Times and Fangraphs we like to use something called WPA to judge relievers. WPA, which stands for Win Probability Added, is defined in the glossary at the back of the book. It tracks the impact of each play on the team's probability of winning and assigns the difference in probability to the players involved in each play.

As games progress, probabilities increase, which makes late-inning plays big events. And that's where relievers come in. For instance, when Lidge entered that May 23 game against the Yankees, the Phillies had a 89.5 percent probability of winning. Since Lidge gave up the game, his WPA for that game was -.895. In WPA terms, he lost the game all by himself.

Thirty-three times in 2009 a "closer" pitched the ninth inning for his team and gave up a lead such that he received a WPA score of -.80 or worse. Five of those times it was Lidge. No other closer did it more than three times.

Overall, Lidge posted a WPA of -4.54, the worst mark of any player in the majors last year. That figure is in stark contrast to 2008, when he seemed to lead the Phillies to their World Series title with his magical closer arm, posting the second-highest WPA in the majors: 5.37.

The bottom line is that Lidge's fall from the grace of 2008 to the hell of 2009 was record-breaking. No other pitcher in the history of Fangraphs' WPA records (from 1974 to now) has ever lost so much WPA from one season to the next. Starting pitchers and position players who play the entire season just aren't likely to post pronounced differences like that. Only relievers are given the "opportunity" to reach such highs and lows.

Sometimes relievers just don't justify our faith in them.

Maybe There Is Such A Thing As A Clutch Hitter

One of the best things about WPA is that it has birthed a second stat—a descriptive stat, really—called Leverage Index. The stat measures the importance of a situation by examining its potential impact on the outcome of the game. Leverage Index is set so that an average situation equals 1.0, but late-inning situations of close games can reach an LI of eight or nine—10, even. Last year, there were 20 plays with an LI of 10 or more.

Leverage Index is a natural way to measure clutch hitting (and pitching). You may be familiar with the concept of clutch play—its existence, predictability and usefulness have been debated in sabermetric circles since before Bill James was a security guard in a bean factory.

I like to use LI as a tool for judging clutch play and clutch impact. My measure of choice is performance in situations with an LI greater than 3.0. About 3.5 percent of all situations had an LI of 3.0 or more last year, which makes it the right combination of rare and important.

Last year, we anointed the Dodgers' Andre Ethier the best clutch hitter in the majors based on his performance in high-LI situations. We've run the numbers again this year and the winner is ... Andre Ethier.

This year, the Dodgers right fielder came to bat 41 times with an LI of 3.0 or more. That was the second-highest figure in the majors; only Aaron Hill came to bat more often in high-leverage situations (43 times). It seems that no matter what list you put together, there will always be a Blue Jay there to surprise you.

Anyway, in those 41 appearances, Ethier…

- Homered three times
- Doubled twice
- Singled four times
- Walked or was hit by a pitch 13 times
- Made an out 18 times.
- Reached base on a dropped third strike once

Ethier made an out less than half of the time he batted in high-leverage situations. Other batters had better batting averages in 3.0-plus LI plate appearances (Raul Ibanez batted an impressive .500 in 12 high-leverage plate appearances, with three home runs), but Ethier gets credit for performing better in more clutch situations than anyone.

That's two years in a row for Ethier, Clutch King. Think he can make it three in a row? I'll bet a lot of sabermetricians out there are chomping at the bit to take that bet.

I Love Playoff Games

We've not only witnessed three consecutive years with playoff games, we've witnessed three consecutive years of exciting playoff games. I have a simple method of judging a game's excitement: I tally up the total changes in win probability that occurred during the game. The more swings in win probability between the two teams, the more exciting the game.

Running the figures, this year's final game between the Twins and Tigers was right up there. In fact, on a "real-time" basis, it was not only the most important regular season game, it was the third-most exciting. Only two other games had more swings in win expectation between the two teams.

Oddly, the most exciting game of the year was also played between the Twins and Tigers, back on May 13. That game was a crazy 14-10 slugfest in Minnesota, won by a two-out Joe Crede grand slam in the 13th.

In case you've forgotten how much fun we had, I've included a graph of the swings in win probability, as well as the Leverage Index (that gray bar at the bottom with the scale on the right) of each play from the fabulous 2009 playoff game.

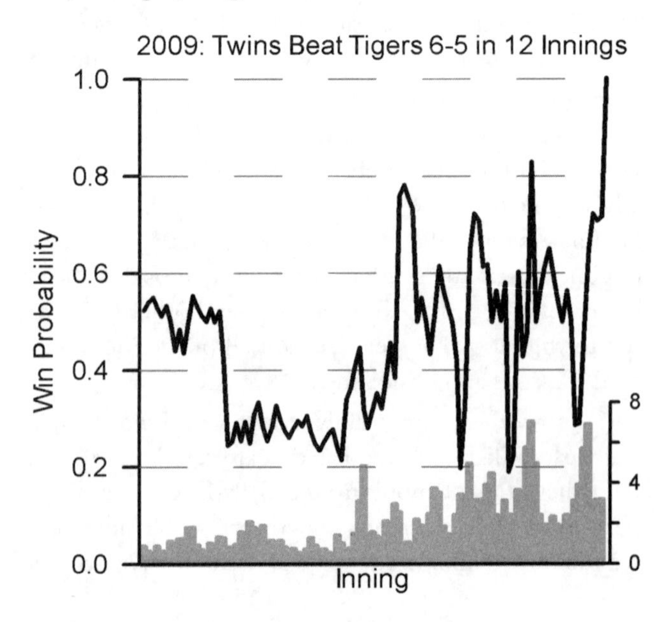

Of course, the 2008 playoff game between the Twins and the White Sox wasn't exactly humdrum either. Although 1-0 contests don't have many swings in probability, they're just as memorable. You can literally see Jim Thome's seventh-inning home run leap up the line.

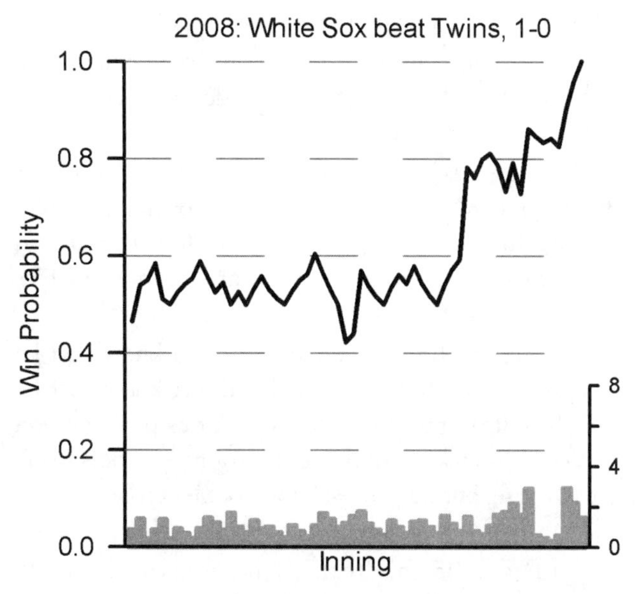

And let's not forget 2007's whopper between the Padres and Rockies. That game had the wildest swing of all, from feast to famine, in the 13th (or famine to feast, depending on your perspective).

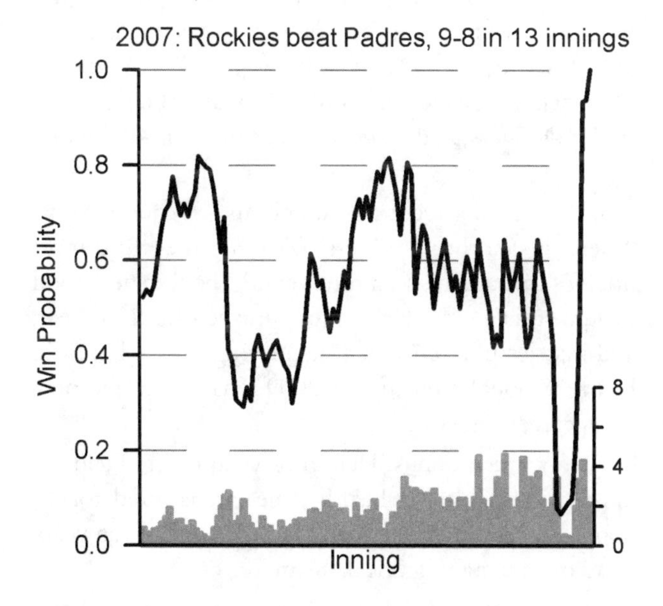

Even with that wild 13th inning swing, 2007's playoff game doesn't equal 2009's in win probability swings. In 2009, importance and excitement merged at the end in a way very few games do.

What Leverages Championships

Last winter, Sky Andrecheck, a writer for Baseball Analysts, and I developed and published a similar idea. I called mine the Drama Index and he called his Championship Leverage Index, but they amounted to the same thing. We both took the notion of Leverage Index (the "real-time" importance of a play during a game) and applied it to the season (in other words, the "real time" importance of a game during the season).

We both found that playoff games, like the ones above, had about 20 times as much "leverage" as the average game. Things that occurred during those games were magnified 20 times in terms of their "real time" importance.

We then applied each game's Leverage Index to its WPA outcomes for each player and tabulated the "ultimate MVP stat," which calculated how much each player contributed to his team's chances of making the postseason based on the criticality of each situation all year long.

It was a great idea carried to its logical extreme, and it did what all good ideas do in the extreme: It started to fall apart.

I'm not going to go into all the hoary details. You can read them on the web or, even better, you can read them in Sky's article entitled "Championship Leverage Index" in this very Annual. He explains much better than I could.

And, like WPA, there are some very salvageable ideas that came out of our exercise. In particular, Sky's Championship Leverage Index is a great measure of how important each game was and how dramatic each team's season was. We've included it in each of our team graphs in the statistics section.

What WAR Is Good For

If you're like me, you're probably tired of newfangled baseball stats. It seems like everyone has a new version of how runs are created or how pitchers rely on their fielders—or not—or how players contribute to wins. I'm not sure I need to see any more stats. There are plenty of numbers on my plate, thank you.

But I'll make an exception for WAR. Wins Above Replacement is kind of a generic name, but it's a singularly good stat. The basic methodology was developed by Tom Tango and friends at the Book Blog the past couple of years, and a couple of sites have implemented their version of it.

Fangraphs posted WAR totals for 2009, and they have also graciously donated their WAR totals to us, and you. Sean Smith has also developed WAR figures for every player in baseball history, and his WARs are particularly useful for the "Retrosheet era."

In this very Annual you hold in your hands, there are two articles that make fantastic use of WAR: Sean's review of the evolution of relief pitching and John Walsh's analysis of the players of the past 40 years we most "under-appreciated." Plus, you can download a spreadsheet that contains many of the cutting-edge "win stats" available today: WPA, WAR and Bill James' Win Shares.

There are other "win stats" out there, such as Baseball Prospectus' WARP and Pete Palmer's Total Player Rating. John Dewan is developing a new system called Total Runs.

But the sabermetric blogosphere, including most of us at THT, are converging around WAR as the win stat of choice, with a nod to WPA, which really measures something different. (In fact, Sean's article about relief pitching is a great example of how WAR and WPA can be combined for a fuller story).

So stay tuned to WAR and watch it grow.

The Doubles Record Is Going To Fall

Bill James had this to say during the year: "I wanted to go on record … the career record for doubles will be broken within 20 years." I wasn't sure about Bill's proclamation at first, but now I'm convinced.

Bill's rule of thumb for this sort of thing is pretty straightforward. If a career record represents 15 to 18 years of league-leading performance, the record is vulnerable. If it represents less than 15 years of league-leading performance, it will almost surely be broken.

According to Bill, his rule has held true for many career marks, such as home runs, stolen bases and strikeouts. And now, it seems, doubles are due. I won't go into the details—you can read them in a couple of articles in Bill James Online which, unfortunately, requires a paid subscription—but his logic is certainly interesting and, as usual, insightful.

The record for most doubles in a career is held by Tris Speaker, who finished his spectacular play in 1928 with 792 doubles. Over the past 10 years, the average league leader has hit around 51 doubles a year, or 15.5 years of Speaker's total. That is right on the line of doom.

But who, among today's players, is likely to break the record? The closest batter among today's players is Manny Ramirez (531 doubles through the age of 37). He hit 36 doubles last year, 24 in two-thirds of a year this year—36 a season seems like a reasonable rate for Manny. He'll have to produce at that level for more than seven more years to break Speaker's record at the age of 44. Doable, but a huge stretch.

Other than Ramirez, other close candidates seem unlikely. Ivan Rodriguez has 547 doubles, Griffey Jr. has 522, Garret Anderson has 516.

But there is someone else on track to crack the career doubles record. He holds the record for most doubles through his first three years. Also his fourth, fifth and sixth years. And he just set the record for most doubles through his ninth year.

I'm talking about Albert Pujols. You know that he is a great hitter, but you probably didn't know that he had this bit of intrigue going. Most of us pay attention to records such as most home runs or hits. Pujols won't break those, but he may take the doubles crown.

Still, that is a long way away. Pujols hit 44 doubles last year and 45 this year. If he keeps swatting 45 doubles a year, he'll tie Speaker's mark at the age of 38, in nine years. If he drops to 40 a year, it will take him 10 more seasons to make it. A lot can happen in 10 years.

To underscore the point, the man with the second-most doubles through the first nine years of his career was another famous Cardinal, Ducky Medwick. Medwick was beaned in his 10th year, after being traded to the Dodgers, and he never hit as many as 40 doubles again.

Still, this is a record to watch and, to quote Yoda, "there is another." Guess who hit the third-most doubles through his first nine years? The Rockies' Todd Helton, that's who. Helton just finished his 13th year, and injuries have curtailed his playing time a bit. Still, he hit 38 doubles during his 2009 renaissance and now has a career total of 509.

As an added bonus, Helton plays in Coors Field—a haven for doubles. If healthy, the guy is good for 40 doubles a year, maybe more. That puts him seven years away from matching Speaker's mark.

I'm thinking Bill James is a little off base here. The career record for doubles may be broken in 10 years.

Sometimes I Make Mistakes

This is the fifth "Ten Things" column I've written for the THT Annual. When I write it, I like to stretch for things that I think are interesting but relatively unknown. I thought I had a good one last year when I found that the major leagues had gotten younger in 2008 by over a year — a record for a one-year age change in the majors. I led off the column with it and even got a little press out of it.

Well, I was wrong. Turns out that one obscure cell in one of my spreadsheets (not so obscure now!) had a bad year reference and all players were calculated to be one year younger than they actually were. Really, that's a terrible mistake and I should have caught it. No excuses.

I'd like to make it up to you by reproducing a graph that shows the average "Win Shares Age" of all major leaguers throughout major league history. As you can see below, the major leagues have been getting younger (a trend that continued this year) but not as much as I thought. The average Win Shares hasn't even declined a full year since it reached its peak back in 2004.

Win Shares age, by the way, is simply the weighting of each player's age by the number of Win Shares (another win stat!) he contributed to his team. It reflects playing time and production, probably the best way to measure each year's relative age.

I don't mean to end on a downer, but not everything we learn is pleasant. Speaking of which, I managed to stay away from the "S" word this year, although there is still plenty to say about the subject. In fact, you'll find more said in the Annual.

As we send this book to press, the World Series has not yet concluded and I've learned it's hard to write a column like this when you don't know the season's ultimate winner. In fact, I've left the 10th item for you (fill in the blank: "The World Champions are BLANK!") because you know something that I don't yet know.

Which means that I'm luckier than you. I still get to watch baseball.

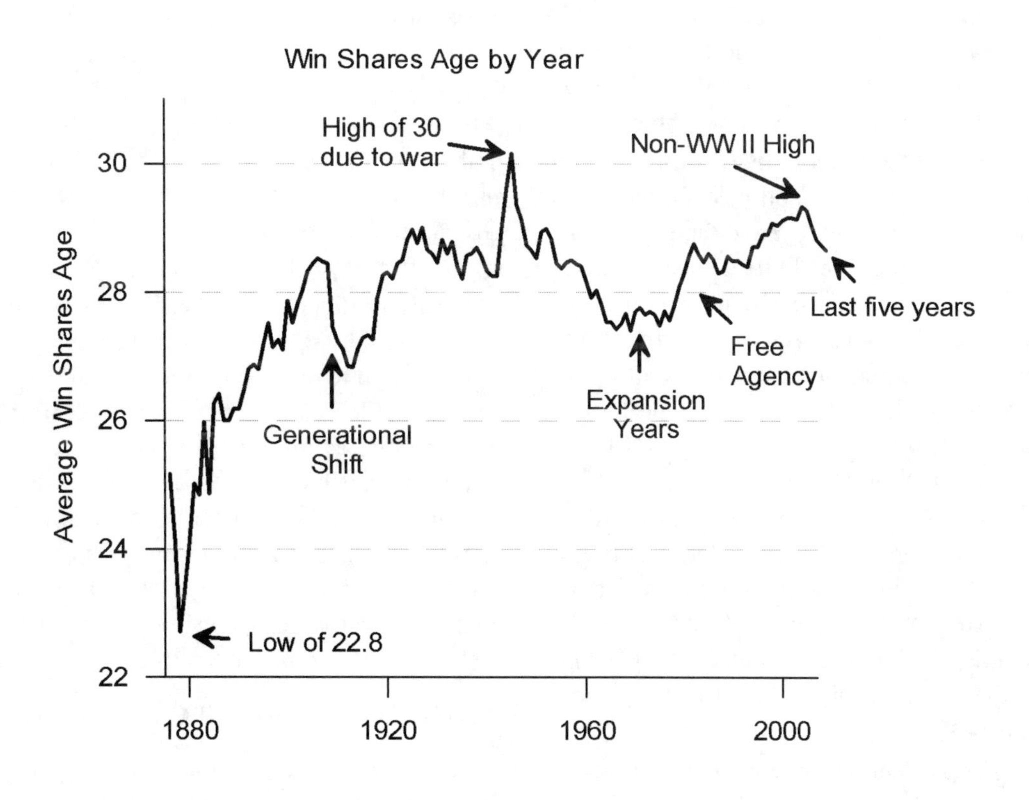

The Year in Frivolity

by Craig Calcaterra

This book is chock full of information about the 2009 baseball season. If you read even a portion of it and don't know who won, who lost and why this past year, there's no helping you.

But you can be forgiven if you forgot the year's ephemeral, trivial, embarrassing and pathetic events. That stuff doesn't stick in a fan's mind like who won the MVP. That's why I'm here. So, without further ado, I give you an overview of all things funny, sad, stupid and ignominious about the 2009 baseball season!

February: A-Rod's Winter of Discontent

Red Sox owner John Henry is engaged to girlfriend Linda Pizzuti. In doing so, Henry overruled the advice of Bill James and other Red Sox advisers who counseled him to go after someone younger than 30 who can be locked up in a long-term deal on the cheap.

Bud Selig receives a $3 million raise, and will earn $17.5 million for the 2009 season. Critics complain that he is overpaid, citing his lackluster defense and poor batting eye. Supporters note that, at the very least, this shows that major league owners are no longer making the mistake of overpaying for past performance, because nothing in Selig's past justifies a fraction of this salary.

The next day, Selig announces that, contrary to all of the chatter during the rainy and cold Phillies-Rays World Series, baseball will never move the Fall Classic to a neutral, warm weather site. During the same press conference, Selig likewise rejects the idea of an alcohol ban in all ballparks, returning shorts to the White Sox uniforms and re-segregating baseball. Contrary to this trend of shooting down patently stupid ideas, Selig insists that the All-Star Game will still determine home field advantage in the World Series.

Citi Financial Group, recipient of federal bailout dollars and wary of negative publicity, suggests that it would like to get out of the naming rights deal for the Mets' new ballpark. Within months, Citi is joined by tens of thousands of season-ticket holders who likewise would like nothing to do with anything that happens in the Mets ballpark.

Alex Rodriguez is identified as having tested positive for steroids in 2003. As predicted by the multiple hand-wringing articles published in the wake of the news, the Yankees' 2009 season is rendered a misery-filled slog of failure, ill-will and depression, and Rodriguez becomes a millstone around the neck of the team's hopes.

In the space of 24 hours, the Dodgers sign Jeff Weaver and Jose Lima to contracts while Manny Ramirez remains unsigned. There's no joke here. I'm just amazed this happened and wanted to share it with you all.

Darryl Strawberry comes out with an autobiography, the bulk of which explains how alcoholism and hard drug use derailed the competitiveness of a fabulous Mets team and a number of fabulous young Mets talents. Most commentators respond with the verbal equivalent of a wistful smile and a strong suggestion that these tales of booze, coke and speed are colorful. They then resume writing about how players who used steroids in order to enhance their competitiveness are history's greatest monsters.

Byung-Hyun Kim is unable to join his South Korean teammates for practice at the World Baseball Classic because he lost his passport. Police suspect that he lost it somewhere in 2003, around the same time he lost his control, velocity and effectiveness.

Entering spring training, Braves fans are atwitter over a trade involving John Smoltz, the prospect of a shaky Tom Glavine taking the hill a handful of times and the possibility that an aging, but still famous, Ken Griffey may patrol left field. Wait, I'm sorry, that item was a repeat from 1987.

Royals outfielder Jose Guillen makes news when he bypasses the team's medical staff and yanks out his own ingrown toenail. Observers recall that a few years before, Guillen's girlfriend was robbed after taking his Washington Nationals-issued paycheck to one of those storefront check-cashing places. While it's tempting to make fun of Guillen for all of this, in light of his prescience regarding the eventual breakdown of the banking system, experts believe that his avoidance of doctors conclusively establishes that our nation's health care system is doomed as well.

March: World Baseball Classic Rivets Dozens

Jim Bowden resigns as the Nationals general manager. Given the state of the team's roster, Bowden's own erratic and polarizing behavior, and the fact that he embroiled the team in a wide-ranging bribery and corruption scandal in the Dominican Republic, the fact that this was a resignation rather than a termination ranks as the biggest surprise of the spring.

Milwaukee right-hander Braden Looper pulls an oblique muscle sneezing. If you win 20 in the show, you can pull an oblique sneezing and the press will think you're colorful. Until you win 20 in the show, it means you're, well, hell, I have no idea what it means.

Whispers start to filter through spring training camps that baseball is thinking about contracting two teams, probably the A's and Marlins. Contraction, of course, would require the owners of those teams to be bought out to the tune of hundreds of millions of dollars. The reason they would arguably need to be contracted: No one can raise hundreds of millions of dollars to build them new stadiums. Scientists remain baffled how the owners of baseball teams became billionaires.

Strawberry, doing publicity for his autobiography, is asked whether he would do steroids if he were still in the game: "Hell yeah I would have used them. Are you kidding me ... if that was going on in the '80s, that probably would have been in my system too." Given that steroids were actually "going on" while he was still playing, one can only assume that he was too boozed and coked up to find a steroid dealer. In other news, taking steroids is still thought of as the worst thing that a ballplayer has ever, ever done to himself.

On March 4, free agent Manny Ramirez agrees on a two-year, $45 million deal to stay with the Dodgers. The deal won't become final until he takes a physical a few days later. No one is worried, however, because all involved are certain that there is no danger that doctors will find anything amiss inside of Manny's body.

Bernie Williams gives his annual "I'm not retired yet and I would still like to play in the major leagues" quotes. He vows to continue to do so until he becomes eligible to draw Social Security, at which point he'll play it closer to the vest so his benefits won't be cut for having outside employment.

Observers wonder if newest Yankees star CC Sabathia's performance will suffer as a result of his being required to shave off the beard he sported during his 2007 Cy Young Award season in Cleveland and his 2008 second-half surge in Milwaukee. Many laugh, but Yankees experts agree that if it weren't for the fact that Don Mattingly had to shave his sideburns, they wouldn't have missed the World Series every year between 1982 and 1995.

A new Manny Ramirez biography called *Becoming Manny* is published, the bulk of which consists of a profile by a clinical psychologist. Publishing industry insiders remain quietly skeptical as to how it took 250 pages and a clinical psychologist to get to "Manny being Manny."

Aaron Rowand reveals that Willie Mays has been giving him pointers in center field during spring training. Later that month it's revealed that Superman is going around telling people that "You just have to sort of will yourself up and you'll be jumping tall buildings in a single bound in no time" and the ghost of Miles Davis is going around telling junior high school trumpet players to "Just blow, baby."

Pudge Rodriguez signs with the Astros, all but assuring he will surpass Carlton Fisk for the record for most games caught. Fisk successfully lobbied to have Ed Wade's, Humberto Quintero's and J.R. Towles's names added to the record book, because without their particular brand of excellence, Rodriguez would almost certainly not have a shot at the record.

The Mets announce that Livan Hernandez will be their fifth starter. Despite this and the curious roster construction it suggests, people still buy the story that their woes in 2009 were the result of subsequent injuries. And people say that Omar Minaya is bad at PR.

Curt Schilling announces his retirement. Reporters everywhere are thankful that Schilling has finally been relieved from practicing the taciturn discretion required of a working major league ballplayer and can finally open up and tell them how he really feels about things.

The wife of Pirates minor leaguer Jose Tabata is arrested for stealing an infant from a Florida hospital. The arrest was made quickly because given that she was 43 years old and Tabata was 20 years old at the time of the incident, police already had her under investigation for cradle-robbing.

On the eve of Opening Day, there is real concern that the Mets may not completely sell out their new ballpark. A meeting is held to try to figure out why this is. No one connects it with the Livan Hernandez announcement.

April: Here Come the Royals!

Aubrey Huff goes on record admitting that he really didn't work out at all in the offseason, citing his excellent 2008, which was preceded by an offseason of no physical activity due to surgery. The results of the Bob Horner, David Wells and Dimitri Young workout: A .241/.310/.384 season and a trade away from Baltimore. Repeat: The Orioles didn't think he was worth keeping around. Early reports for the 2009-2010 offseason reflect that 100 percent of players are in compliance with team conditioning goals, and vegetable intake is approaching record highs.

The Royals get a lot of hype as "this year's version of the Rays." This despite the presence of Sidney Ponson and Horacio Ramirez in the starting rotation. Last year's Rays wait the season out, and then sue everyone for slander.

The Reds break camp with a rotation consisting of Edinson Volquez, Johnny Cueto, Aaron Harang, Bronson Arroyo and Micah Owings. Many writers observe that the first letters of their last names can be arranged to spell "HAVOC." The definition of "havoc" is "Widespread destruction; devastation; disorder or chaos." While the Reds pitching staff ended up not being too terrible in 2009, unfortunately, that definition only really applied to Volquez's elbow.

Catholics in Detroit and Milwaukee are faced with a dilemma due to the fact that their teams scheduled day game home openers on Good Friday. In Detroit, many Catholics urge a boycott of the game. Milwaukee's Archbishop approaches things differently, saying that it's okay to go to the game, but it is not OK to eat brats or sausages at the game. Sadly, this does not ease the souls and spirits of the flock, as they are left to determine which is greater sin: eating meat on Good Friday or not eating brats at Miller Park.

Opening Day! The Braves beat the Phillies behind a sold performance by Derek Lowe. Even better: Jeff Francoeur tees off for a home run on the first pitch he sees! Such a performance, most agree, no doubt presages a startling return to late-2005 form for the kid they call "The Natural!"

The Yankees release a list of all of the "official sponsors" of their new stadium. At the time I wrote a blog post mocking it by inserting a phony, ridiculous sponsorship into a list of six of the actual sponsorships and challenging readers to guess which one was bogus. It read as follows: (1) Official Automobile Classified Company: Autotrader.com; (2) Official Supermarket Retailer: Stop & Shop; (3) Official Rail Fare: Amtrak; (4) Official Non-Dairy Creamer: Nestlé Coffee-Mate; (5) Official Deli Meat: Boar's Head; (6) Official Pudding: Kozy Shack; (7) Official Non-Kosher Hot Dog & French Fry: Nathan's. As I sit here today, just over six months later, I can't for the life of me recall which of those was supposed to be the fake, silly one.

Curtis Granderson, who had spent the previous couple of years blogging over at ESPN.com, moves his in-season blog to Yahoo! One can only assume that he got sick of Rob Neyer stealing his lunch from the office fridge and Buster Olney reminding him to put his cover sheets on his TPS reports.

Randy Johnson, now in a Giants uniform, begins his quest to win his 300th game. Writers chronicling his chase note that the Big Unit may be the last man to 300. This makes him the first last man to 300 since Glavine, who in turn was the first last man to 300 since Greg Maddux. Maddux, in turn, took the last man to 300 title from Roger Clemens. Prior to Clemens, there were so many men to 300 that no one ever considered the concept. Why no, no one learned a lesson from all of that. Why do you ask?

Mets starter Oliver Perez gives up eight runs in four innings in his season debut. That's funny, I seem to recall reading in the offseason that he was the best left-handed pitcher since Koufax. Boy, I hope the guy who opined thusly—a fellow named Boras—wasn't pulling our legs on that one.

In a sign that Twitter has jumped the shark, Fox broadcaster Joe Buck opens an account and starts tweeting. Among his first tweets: "Cold in the booth in STL. Tim (McCarver) and I are bundled up. And snuggling." This is the 12,567th instance of Buck breaking the single most important rule of baseball announcing: If you can't imagine Vin Scully saying it, you shouldn't say it.

Elijah Dukes is fined $500 for being a few minutes late to the Nationals' April 18 game. He receives a tremendous amount of sympathy when it is revealed that the reason he is late is that he was out in the community signing autographs for little leaguers in suburban Virginia. Our Elijah Dukes moral compass is restored to its normal telemetry, however, when it is learned that he was charging the little leaguers $500 for his appearance. He then exceeds even all Elijah Dukian expectations when it is revealed that the little league for which he was signing actually took up a fundraising effort to pay off Dukes' fine, and Dukes accepted the money. As Annie Savoy said, the world is made for people who aren't cursed with self-awareness.

In the glow of the Mark Teixeira signing, *Newsday's* Wallace Matthews pens a nastygram to Jason Giambi, noting that the Yankees won no championships between 2002 and 2008, and that what "every one of those teams had in common was the presence of Giambi." Matthews curiously forgets to mention two other things those teams had in common: the presence of Derek Jeter at short and the presence of Wallace Matthews in the press box.

Major League Baseball Advanced Media announces that it is launching an online tabloid to run on MLB.com, the purpose of which is to contrast MLB.com's news reporting with some real unvarnished, in-your-face opinion. And don't think that just because Major League Baseball is paying the writers' salaries that it means the writers will be declawed. For example, the first article out of chute—"Commissioner Selig: Merely great, or the greatest ever?" really got tongues wagging!

The Yankees, after a month of constant criticism for setting the prices too high in their new stadium—and a month of embarrassment as a result of many, many empty premium seats because of it—actually announce that they are considering raising the prices of said premium seats 4 percent in 2010. Lackeys to Hal Steinbrenner and Randy Levine fall all over themselves to congratulate the bosses for their staunch refusal to play silly public-relations games. And silly supply-and-demand games. And silly acknowledgement-of-reality games.

A man named Dennis Mascari makes the news for selling something called "Eternal Skyboxes," which are basically a premium area, designed to resemble Wrigley Field, for the interment of ashes of deceased Cubs fans in an Illinois cemetery. Plots aren't cheap, either: $1,295 a pop, not including the cremation. Mascari quickly sells more premium real estate in his new park than the Yankees did in theirs. Patrons say that it's simply a better value to spend your time dead in Mascari's place than alive in Steinbrenner's.

May: Manny Gets Bannied

A tell-all book comes out with salacious allegations involving (1) performing-enhancing drugs; (2) the tipping of pitches to opposing players in blowouts; and (3) phony rape charges against young men. The charges were trumped up beyond anything even a shred of evidence could support, yet smeared the name of the innocent and lit a fire under a bogus prosecution which will no doubt dog the wrongly accused for decades. Afterwards, the accuser did not even stop to apologize once the campaign was shown to be built on a foundation of sand and lies. Despite the fact that (1) and (2) involved the book's subject and (3) described the acts of the book's author, the former was expected to explain himself against the accusations of the latter.

President Obama's short list to fill Justice David Souter's soon-to-be vacant seat on the Supreme Court includes Judge Sonia Sotomayor of the U.S. Court of Appeals for the Second Circuit. Judge Sotomayor's record includes membership in anarchist political parties, staunch opposition to the Bill of Rights and a virulent pro-crime agenda. She is also the judge who, on March 30, 1995, issued the preliminary injunction against Major League Baseball preventing the owners from unilaterally implementing a new Collective Bargaining Agreement and using replacement players, effectively ending the 1994 baseball strike, thereby clearing the way for the Atlanta Braves to win the 1995 World Series. Accordingly, she has my full support.

The Mets, claiming that they don't want the players "exposed to the 'bad vibes' from the tabloids after back-to-back September collapses" remove the *Post*, the *Daily News* and *Newsday* from the team's clubhouse. At least that's the Mets' story. A competing interpretation is that the Mets only have four guys over the age of 35 on the team, one of whom is Gary Sheffield, who doesn't seem like a big reader, and another is Ken Takahashi, who doesn't seem like a big English reader. The rest of the team was rather amused by it all, wondering aloud what a "newspaper" was.

Francoeur is asked why he doesn't try to raise his on-base percentage. His response: "If on-base percentage is so important, then why don't they put it up on the scoreboard?" Within hours of his statement, numerous Braves bloggers find multiple examples of the Turner Field scoreboard clearly showing on-base percentage. They then recall that, as recently as a year prior, there were strong rumors that the Royals were considering trading Zack Greinke to the Braves for Francoeur and spare parts. After considering the memory, numerous Braves bloggers commit suicide.

Manny Ramirez is suspended for 50 games following a positive test for banned substances. As a result of his suspension, Ramirez is unavailable to the Dodgers until early July. Ramirez's defense—"Hey dudes, you didn't have me until July 31 last year, so we'll be nearly a month ahead of the game when I come back this year!"—somehow falls on deaf ears.

Following numerous games in which multiple premium seats went unused, hundreds of premium Yankees tickets begin turning up on StubHub. Speculation mounts that the team itself, unable to sell them on a retail basis, is posting them with the secondary market broker. A team official denies this, claiming that demand for Legends Suites tickets is as strong as ever. The official adds that "there are no American infidels in Baghdad," and that the "faltering forces of infidels cannot just enter a country of 26 million people and lay besiege to them!"

The Diamondbacks fire manager Bob Melvin and hire A.J. Hinch. Some question whether a man with no managerial experience is the best person for a major league manager's job. Many more question whether a man named "A.J." is the best person for any job.

In the wake of the Manny Ramirez business, some baseball owners say they would love to have the option of voiding the contracts of players caught using drugs. Their arguments might have gained more traction if they hadn't claimed about 125 other reasons why they would like void player contracts when it suits them.

Bobby Jenks is fined $750 for throwing a pitch behind Ian Kinsler. Most observers agree that the fine had less to do with the pitch itself than the fact that Jenks admitted after the game that, yeah, he was trying to send a message. This is remarkably similar to the time when Jenks had that M15 agent strapped to his automated death machine and, just before flipping the switch that would bring eventual, presumed death to his enemy, told him all about his plans to fire missiles at the San Andreas Fault, sinking half of California into the ocean and rendering his vast Central Valley land holdings into valuable oceanfront property.

The Florida Marlins, thankful that public officials of Miami and Dade County authorized the use of tax dollars for the construction of their new ballpark, announce that the plans for the new stadium will be cost-conscious, sensitive to the sacrifice of taxpayers in difficult economic times and will contain only the essentials to the enjoyment of baseball. The plans themselves contain a gigantic, luxurious pool. Just kidding: They made no promises that the plans would be cost-conscious or sensitive to taxpayers whatsoever.

Cal Ripken makes a personal appearance at a banquet for the Jewish Federation of Palm Beach County, but refuses to eat with the people who paid $100 a ticket plus a $250 minimum individual gift for the federation and paid for his first-class round trip airfare and for his room at the Four Seasons Resort. Indeed, he met only with those who were invited to a VIP room, and then he disappeared for the rest of the evening. In other words, his appearance was much like his final years on the Orioles: He showed up, collected his check, and then didn't do a whole lot of anything.

The sale of the Chicago Cubs drags on and on. In May, details of the intricate financing of it all are revealed. The upshot: It's big and complicated and involves three banks and seemingly unsupportable debt. In light of the 2008-09 financial collapse, it's sort of like turn-back-the-clock night.

The Indians' season in a nutshell: On May 17, Rays manager Joe Maddon screws up the lineup card by listing two third basemen and no DH, thereby causing the pitcher to have to bat. Even worse, the pitcher, Andy Sonnanstine has to bat third. Despite this, he goes 1-for-3 with a double and an RBI, leading the Rays to a 7-5 win.

The Yankees enter into an agreement allowing Notre Dame to play a handful of football games in Yankee Stadium. Fans are thrilled about finally having one-stop shopping for all of their insufferable self-important sports team needs.

June: There Go the Royals!

The Houston Astros announce they will be buyers at the trade deadline. Which makes total sense given that they're the oldest team in baseball, expensive and noncompetitive.

Tony La Russa sues Twitter. Which is strange, because you'd think that a guy who thinks he's a genius and who invented hyper-specialized bullpen usage would be in league with a product for self-absorbed people with short attention spans.

The Braves shock their players and their fans by releasing team legend and future Hall of Famer Tom Glavine without giving him a shot in a big league game. The release sets off a cycle of negativity in Braves nation, as some fans think the team owed Glavine at least one or two starts to see if he really had lost it, while others believe there's no place for nostalgia and that fresh blood is needed. For a team with such a stable operation over the previous 20 years, the controversy is disorienting. Thankfully, Francoeur restores a sense of normalcy to the team by striking out with the bases loaded in the sixth inning of a close game. In trying times, we all crave the familiar.

Sixteen-year-old prospect Bryce Harper is profiled in *Sports Illustrated.* Despite his age, his parents want to get him into the 2010 baseball draft. Oh, and he's being advised by Scott Boras. The odds against this turning into a circus are only outweighed by the odds against Harper going through five stints of rehab before he's arbitration eligible.

Because being allowed to be painted green and getting dressed up like Yankee Stadium by Billy Crystal, becoming the site for a "Bud Bowl," becoming overgrown with weeds, and finally, being slowly dismembered by wrecking balls over the course of months wasn't a bad enough end for Tiger Stadium, whoever is in charge of the place decides the last appearance by anyone in the old ballpark should be Val Kilmer filming some straight-to-video movie as opposed to, you know, a ballplayer giving the place a proper goodbye.

Randy Johnson wins his 300th game. Experts agree that we can finally close the book on the Mark Langston trade and declare Seattle the winner.

The Braves start to shop Francoeur. The first big rumor is that he's going to Boston in exchange for Brad Penny. The Braves already have Derek Lowe, Javier Vazquez, Jair Jurrjens, Kenshin Kawakami, Kris Medlen and Tommy Hanson pitching decently in the rotation. Experts in such matters normally counsel against bringing in a seventh starter, but since such a deal would involve getting rid of Francoeur, the experts believe Atlanta could put Penny in right field and still experience a net upgrade.

The Diamondbacks and Padres play an 18-inning game. Despite getting twice the usual amount of baseball for their money, fans demand a refund on the grounds that it meant they had to watch more of the Diamondbacks and Padres.

On June 9, the Tigers beat the White Sox 5-4, with the Sox putting forth a spectacularly poor effort in the loss. After the game, Ozzie Guillen says "If this was the 1980s, (none) of these guys would be in the big leagues right now, because if you hit .210-.230 and you can't execute, I don't think you should be out here." Given his career lines, Ozzie apparently demands nothing short of an empty .260 and a failure to execute.

MLB Network debuts its first reality series, entitled "The Pen," which chronicles the exploits of the Philadelphia Phillies' bullpen. Given that life in the bullpen mostly consists of sitting around in warm-up jackets while watching other people play, there are concerns that the series will lack drama. And suddenly Brad Lidge's surprising cardiac arrest-inducing 2009 season is cast into a whole new light.

Just a month after making all of the headlines, Selena Roberts's tell-all book about Alex Rodriguez vanishes from best-seller lists after having sold just 16,000 copies. The same article that breaks the story about Roberts's sales reveals that James Frey's *A Million Little Pieces* is currently outselling Roberts' book. That means that Roberts isn't even heading the lists in the lucrative Unsubstantiated Baloney genre.

The Royals announce they will be holding an open free-agent tryout in Eau Claire, Wisc. at the end of the month. Any man older than 12 and younger than 50 with even a modicum of lateral movement and something less than a 100 percent fear of a pitched baseball is encouraged to attend. Those criteria eliminate Tony Pena, Jr. or Mike Aviles from the running, but then again, that was kind of the point.

In what turns out to be his last action of the year—and maybe of his baseball career—Dontrelle Willis gives up eight walks in 3.2 innings to a Pittsburgh Pirates team that ain't exactly known for plate discipline. Penguins forward Bill Guerin threw out the first pitch at the game and even he had better command than Dontrelle did. Tigers officials believe it was worth giving Willis seven starts to mess around, however. I mean, it's not like one game is going to sink this team's chances this year, right?

Because they haven't yet squeezed every last red cent from their fan base, the Yankees auction off everything that is and isn't nailed down in old Yankee Stadium, including 1'x1' pieces of live sod ($120) and "Final Season Crystals with Genuine Dirt from the original Yankee Stadium" ($80). Don't worry, though: It all comes with certificates of authenticity. I mean really, what would be worse than finding out someone is trying to sell you fake dirt from the Bronx. You want the real McCoy, champ!

Tom Hicks's Rangers, still saddled with debt and nearly insolvent, lays off front-office staff. Some people wonder whether this is a sign that, contrary to popular belief, sports teams are not recession-proof. Most realize, however, this proves nothing more than the fact that sports are not spendthrift owner-proof.

Sammy Sosa is revealed to have tested positive for steroids in 2003. This is not exactly shocking news. But, unlike all that has come before on the subject of Sosa and PEDs, it is actually news as opposed to gossip, thereby giving the anti-Sammy Sosa dogpile some sort of official imprimatur. Meanwhile, Sosa's attorneys all ask for an apology regarding that whole testify-before-Congress in Spanish thing. Listen to your lawyers, kids, they'll keep you out of trouble.

The Padres beat the A's 4-1 on Father's Day. The fathers of Brian Giles, Edgar and Adrian Gonzalez, Luke Gregorson, Kevin Kouzmanoff, Cla Meredith, Edward Mujica, Joe Thatcher, Tony Gwynn and Kevin Correia threw out the first pitch to their respective sons before the game in honor of Father's Day. Then, in the true spirit of baseball fathers everywhere, they all got drunk and paced behind the backstop while angrily yelling at the coach to put their boys in.

MLBPA executive director Don Fehr announces that he is stepping down after 24 years at the helm. By every measure short of PR, Fehr did an excellent job for the players he represented. Casual fans, however, ignored everything he did except for the stuff that fomented the bad PR, and for that stuff he was excoriated. Against that backdrop, it's no surprise that the list of people who want his job is a short one.

It is revealed that Sidney Ponson tested positive for a stimulant during the World Baseball Classic. The drug was Phentermine, which is generally used as an appetite suppressant. Observers believe that someone obviously spiked his urine sample, because there's no way Sidney Ponson has ever been on an appetite suppressant in his life.

July: The Midsummer Contrivance

Former major leaguer Jim Leyritz is arrested on charges of domestic battery against his ex-wife, just two months before his trial on a DUI manslaughter charge was set to begin. The same ex-wife who moved back in to help with expenses and the kids when he was in desperate straits following the fatal accident. It has already been established that Leyrtiz is an idiot, but the court will accept cumulative evidence on this point.

The All-Star rosters are released. There aren't a ton of outrages until you get to the NL backups, which seem to reflect a conspiracy! Fact: Charlie Manuel manages the NL team this year. Fact: He has constructed an All-Star roster with too many first basemen and nary a legitimate center fielder to be found. Fact: The league that loses the All-Star Game costs its World Series representative home-field advantage. Fact: The Phillies stand a decent enough chance to go back to the World Series this year. Fact: The Phillies have been a much better road team than home team this year. Theory: Charlie Manuel is deliberately tanking the All-Star Game in the hopes that the Phillies lose home-field "advantage." Charlie Maunel: crazy like a fox.

Nomar Garciaparra makes his first trip back to Fenway Park since the 2004 trade. The event reminds the reader that Nomar turned down a four-year, $60 million contract in the spring of 2004. Nomar reminds the reader not to remind him of that painful, painful memory.

A giant controversy is set off after Jeter is called out attempting to steal third base even though he isn't tagged. The reason according to the ump: "He didn't have to tag you; the ball beat you." The controversy could have been avoided if he said Jeter was out on account of the idiot tax, assessed for trying to steal third base with nobody out in the first inning.

On July 10, the Nationals beat the Astros 11-10. Because it was a continuation of a rain-suspended game from earlier in the season, Joel Hanrahan gets the win in this game despite no longer playing for the Nats and Nyjer Morgan scores the winning run even though he was playing for the Pirates when the game started. Even stranger: Both men were succeeded by vice-presidents named Johnson who were southern Democrats and former senators, Hanrahan had a secretary named Morgan, and Morgan had a secretary named Hanrahan!

The Royals acquire Yuniesky Betancourt from the Mariners in exchange for a couple of decent young arms. On the same day, the Mets acquire Francoeur from the Braves for Ryan Church. What's left of the Mets and Royals fan bases go on 24-hour suicide watch.

Manny Acta is fired after leading the Nationals to a .299 winning percentage at the break. But maybe the most telling thing about this move is that it immediately leads to heat on the Mets' Jerry Manuel, with the thinking being that "Hey, Acta's available." Mets baseball: It's fantastic!

During his annual All-Star Game press conference, Commissioner Selig is asked to comment on reports that the union may be considering lodging a collusion complaint arising out of the treatment of free agents following the 2008 season. Selig said "They're entitled to their opinion ... This is one sport where I can't even fathom that anybody could think that." When the reporters noted that Selig himself was one of the architects of baseball's three previous collusion cases, the commissioner did that old Ronald Reagan trick of pretending he couldn't hear the questions above the noise of the helicopter. There was no helicopter, however.

The All-Star Game goes off without much of a hitch. Good baseball. Quick pace. Not a lot of time for in-between inning and in-between at-bat and pitching-change nonsense. The only people who are not happy about this run the Fox network, which sells most of its advertising space based on promises of nonsense.

CNN's Larry King reveals that his friend, Mets owner Fred Wilpon, lost way more money to fraudster Bernie Madoff than he originally let on. And speaking of King: Say what you want about your other vegetables, but in my book, nothing beats asparagus ... What ever happened to variety shows? Flip Wilson, now there was an entertainer ... Got a pair of black brogues yesterday, and I feel like a million bucks ... Caller, do you have a question for Dane Cook about the hostage crisis? ...

As the Royals' season spins out of control, manager Trey Hillman is given a vote of confidence by GM Dayton Moore. Which is kind of like being thrown a leaky life preserver by the guy in the water next to you after the ship hits the iceberg.

On July 22, Manny Ramirez hits a pinch-hit grand slam in the sixth inning to break a 2-2 tie and power the Dodgers past the Reds. The crowd goes bonkers! Wow! Oh, wait, I forgot: We're not supposed to be enjoying this. Bad Manny. Bad, bad, bad. You have ruined baseball.

Following A-Rod and Sosa, David Ortiz is revealed to have tested positive for PEDs in 2003. And with this news, the steroid story takes a more tragic turn. I mean, it's one thing when robots like Bonds and McGwire are juicing, but when they start naming the cuddliest of ballplayers, the end is truly nigh.

August: When Prince Fielder Attacks!

On Aug. 4, the Dodgers beat the Brewers 17-4. After the game, in a scene out of 1980s WWF, Prince Fielder runs through the underground tunnels to go put a hurt on Guillermo Mota in retaliation for a ninth-inning plunking. Fortunately for Mota, Fielder is stopped at the Dodgers' clubhouse door. No word on whether he had a folding chair with him. All in all it was kind of a bush league move on Fielder's part, I mean, everyone knows that if you're going to go after a guy, you don't do it in the clubhouse. You become friends with him and then you ambush him in a heel-turn during the next taping of Piper's Pit.

On the same August day, the Red Sox designate Smoltz for assignment, the A's release Giambi, and those of us who aren't all that much younger than Smoltz and Giambi suddenly feel very, very old.

Following news that he has been placed on waivers by the Mets, Gary Sheffield goes on a public relations tear, and in the space of two days states that he plans to hang around to get 3,000 hits and that if someone gives him a full-time job in 2010 he'd hit 35 home runs. Sources with Major League Baseball say that the dramatically stepped-up drug testing to which Sheffield is subjected beginning the next day is totally coincidental.

Actress Kate Hudson, who has been dating Alex Rodriguez for months, tells friends that she'd like to have a baby with the $250 million man. Minds reel trying to picture a family gathering involving Hudson, Goldie Hawn, Kurt Russell, ex-husband/father of first child/Black Crowes singer Chris Robinson, Rodriguez and assorted children milling about. A-Rod could probably talk to former Met and Brave Matt Franco, though, seeing as though he's Russell's nephew.

Kevin Youkilis shows just how tough he is by charging the mound to go after Rick Porcello after getting hit in the back by a pitch. And how tough is he? Hard to say, because the people who measure such things drop their instruments in laughter after Youkilis throws his hat at Porcello like a purse and then is thrown to the ground by the much younger, much smaller and presumably much weaker Tigers pitcher.

Reds starter Bronson Arroyo gives an interview to *USA Today* in which he admits to taking all manner of supplements that aren't approved by Major League Baseball. Arroyo is lauded for his honesty by some. Everyone else, however, reminds him that baseball is a part of corporate America, and that corporate America is not a big fan of honesty.

A fan in Wrigley Field throws a full cup of beer on the head of Phillies outfielder Shane Victorino. After intense public pressure for his dastardly deed, the culprit turns himself in. At the press conference, Mayor Richard Daley says "the acts of this young man were utterly deplorable. To see someone waste a precious, delicious beer like that on national television made me ashamed to call myself a Chicagoan."

In an interview, Hank Aaron says Barry Bonds is the real home run champ and that asterisks in the record book are a dumb idea. His statements cause people to stop ranting and raving about Bonds and steroids and immediately form committees to advocate for Bonds's induction in the Hall of Fame.

Carlos Delgado suffers a setback in his rehabilitation. It is described by Mets officials in *The New York Times* as "a good thing" in that it allows Daniel Murphy to play more first base. Because there's nothing better than Daniel Murphy playing more first base.

The Yankees sign first-round pick Slade Heathcott for $2.2 million. The guy is not terribly notable as prospects go, but the news is picked up far and wide as people register their surprise that "Slade Heathcott" is a ballplayer's name and not the name of, say, a rakish dandy with ulterior motives attempting to woo a wealthy widow in late Victorian England.

Five months after a lot of talk about how the Rangers were gonna trade all of their catching depth for some pitching, Texas trades for Pudge Rodriguez. Nothing personal, Texas. We all make a lot of plans that don't pan out.

Stephen Strasburg signs with the Nationals for $15.1 million. Many people declare this a victory for the Nats inasmuch as it's far, far below the $50 million number that had been floated for months. Boras sits back and smiles, wondering how it is possible that he's been in this business with these same people for so many years, yet none of them have yet caught on to his baloney.

Royals GM Dayton Moore is given a four-year contract extension. Experts ask themselves if they, in their own profession, made a mistake equivalent to trading for Yuniesky Betancourt, would expect to be fired, or given five years of lucrative job security? They further ask themselves how Royals owner David Glass is able to run the most successful corporation on the planet in Wal-Mart, yet is still capable of making a judgment like "Dayton Moore has the organization pointed in the right direction"?

September: Dead Wedge Walking

Alex Rodriguez, trying to rehabilitate his reputation following last spring's steroids revelations, is reported to be doing anti-drug lectures in public schools. His pitch: "Hey kids, taking illegal drugs may have brought me fame, a quarter billion dollars and Kate Hudson in my bed every night, but they could do really bad things to you, so just say no."

While the Braves are still in the race, commentators note that 2010 may be their real year to contend. The reason: With the return of Tim Hudson and the emergence of Tommy Hanson, Atlanta will have six effective starting pitchers under contract, a development characterized as a "nice problem to have." Frank Wren is a problem solver, however, and he vows to do what he does best and turn those six good pitchers into three good pitchers, two retreads and a couple of past-their-prime corner outfielders by the time camp breaks next April.

Former Mets and Phillies outfielder Lenny Dykstra finds himself in bankruptcy court. At a hearing, Dykstra testifies about the business plan for one of his properties, saying the Louis Vuitton company has promised to commit $10 million for a stake in the relaunch of Dykstra's *Players Club* magazine. *The Players Club,* Dykstra informs the court, completely oblivious to the irony of the situation, is a publication meant to help professional athletes manage their finances.

Tom Glavine, months after being released from the Braves and receiving no interest from any other team, announces he is not planning on pitching in 2010. In other news, agents for Charlie Leibrandt and Phil Niekro, the estate of Warren Spahn, and a historian writing a biography of Lefty Tyler have all indicated that their guys are going to sit 2010 out as well. Zane Smith's people could not be reached as of press time.

A story appears about the San Francisco Giants' "going green" initiative, which has them adopting the use of all manner of Earth-friendly products at AT&T Park. One example given in the article is the use of all-natural, "nonhormone disrupting" cleansers. Environmentalists agree that it was a good thing the Giants were using the non-natural, hormone-disrupting cleansers before, because if their hormones weren't at least partially disrupted in the early part of the decade, Bonds probably would have exploded and flooded the park with testosterone.

Angels outfielder Torii Hunter was named the recipient of the 2009 Branch Rickey Award. The Rickey award is given out each season to honor those players who do the most to set the single-game record for stolen bases allowed, to crush the independent minor leagues, to deal sharply with players renegotiating their contracts and business partners attempting to buy them out, and to those players who do their best to integrate baseball.

In a classy move, the MLB Network announces that it is going to name three production studios after Ernie Harwell, Mel Allen and Vin Scully. Plans to name appropriate rooms after announcers Joe Morgan, Tim McCarver and Rick Sutcliffe are put on hold when it is discovered that modern broadcasting facilities no longer have abattoirs, outhouses or vomitoriums.

Pedro Martinez pitches the Phillies past the Mets 1-0 in the backend of a Sept. 14 doubleheader. Adding insult to the Mets' season of injuries, Tom Glavine comes out of retirement the following day and throws a three-hitter against New York, getting run support from Mo Vaughn, who hits for the cycle, while Vince Coleman coaches third base and Bobby Bonilla coaches first.

Aaron Crow, who was drafted by the Nationals in the 2008 draft but held out (1) for more money; and (2) to get away from a train wreck of an organization signs for (1) less money than the Nats offered him; with (2) the Kansas City Royals. This was not exactly how Crow and his agent drew it up on the conference-room white board last year.

The Cardinals, seemingly forever one game away from clinching the Central Division, are reported to be travelling with 25 cases of champagne on their current road trip, anticipating the clinch. Conservative estimates put that at four to five bottles per player. And people are wondering why they came out sluggish in the Division Series against the Dodgers.

A late season Pirates-Reds day game leads to the lowest attendance in the history of PNC Park. Team officials blame the World Economic Summit taking place in Pittsburgh and all of its attendant road closures and security measures. In so doing, they ignore a much simpler solution for the poor turnout, that being the fact that it was a late season Pirates-Reds day game.

A few days later Pirates manager John Russell lifts Zach Duke one out away from a complete game. Russell's explanation: That he wanted to give Duke a standing ovation as he left the mound. Given that there is no law preventing fans from applauding following a complete game, the explanation seems less than plausible. A better explanation is revealed when it is discovered that Russell is in a fantasy league in which complete games are a countable stat and the guy he's battling for first place owns Duke.

Eric Wedge is fired with a week to go. He's asked to remain in place as some sort of zombie manager for the last seven games, however, because back in July Indians team owner Larry Dolan assured Wedge and the public that Wedge would have a job through the end of the season and it would not look good for management to have been wrong.

There's Only One October, and This Year it Lasts into November!

The Blue Jays announce their second round of front-office layoffs, ruining the lives of two dozen workers. On the bright side, the layoffs pay for nearly one-twelfth of Vernon Wells' raise for 2010.

Tony La Russa and Dave Duncan accuse the Reds' Bronson Arroyo of somehow arranging for properly pre-rubbed game balls to be replaced with slick, unrubbed balls, thereby putting Cardinals starter John Smoltz at a disadvantage. They accuse Arroyo of using pine tar to compensate. La Russa even goes so far as to hoard collected game balls as "evidence" and cornering reporters in his office, explaining the whole conspiracy whether anyone wants to hear it or not. "Ahh, but the game balls! That's ... that's where I had them," La Russa said. "They laughed at me and made jokes but I proved beyond the shadow of a doubt and with ... geometric logic ... that a duplicate key to the clubhouse ball locker *did* exist, and I'd have produced that key if they hadn't of pulled the Caine out of action ..."

Giants general manager Brian Sabean, who has wasted millions on declining veteran talent, is given a contract extension, and Padres general manager Kevin Towers, who has put together surprisingly good teams on a shoestring budget is fired, thereby proving the universe is an arbitrary, godless expanse of unfathomable injustice.

Despite a surprisingly good pitching staff in Cincinnati and the seeming resurrection of Homer Bailey as a legitimate prospect, Reds pitching coach Dick Pole is fired. Yep, he really got the shaft on that deal. Totally boned if you ask me.

The Tigers drop two of their last three games over the final weekend of the season to fall into a first place tie for the AL Central with the Twins following the completion of 162 games. There are always a million things one can point to over the course of a season that could have meant the difference between a single win and a loss. In the Tigers' case 999,998 of them have to do with the trade that brought Willis and Miguel Cabrera over from the Marlins two years prior.

The playoffs are played, and a World Series champion is crowned, but nothing remarkable, exciting, silly, frivolous, sad, pathetic or notorious occurs in the process. Damndest thing, really.

Trivia Time

by Brandon Isleib

If there's one thing subdivided into two parts we know in the golden sunny land of THT, it's that our readers know stuff, and that we want to help them know more stuff. You may have noticed that we wrote a book this year to help you know more stuff, and that we do it every year. This time, we're going whole hog and admitting that there's some stuff we'll help you know that isn't particularly useful in any way, shape or form—trivia.

According to dictionary.com, trivia is not only "matters or things that are very unimportant, inconsequential, or nonessential"; it's also the plural of trivium, which was the "grammar, logic, and rhetoric" part of medieval curriculum—matters that to precision-craving minds are far from trivial. I won't inundate you with more trivia trivia—if you want that, pick up Ken Jennings' book *Brainiac*—but from this alone we can see that the word trivia can denote things both important and unimportant. Which sense you mean is based simply on how you're using it.

And we're using our trivia to help you, the stuff-knower, slake your thirst for knowable things. In short, we're using the unimportant trivia to assuage the important brain, which is grammatically correct, logically sound, and rhetorically florid. Just so you don't feel like we picked random things to throw at your brain, there are differently themed challenges here.

First Trivia Challenge: Dodecatrivia

In the first, we have a dozen crafty queries, all on the number 12. Some of the connections to 12 are listed. Some aren't, and if they aren't, you can bet your bottom shilling the answer hinges on you figuring out the connection.

Although some of you may find 12 questions on a theme of 12 to be gross, without further ado, here are the questions.

1. The Nationals on April 24 and the Red Sox on April 26 earned what distinctions this year?
2. George Foster's 52 home run season in 1977 carries with it at least three significant connections to the number 12. Because that's kind of a vague question, full credit if you come up with any of them.
3. Ray Durham's 192 home runs are the record for what?
4. One of the most famous in-game 12s of all time was beaten by a pitcher with a different 12. Without the loss he received in that game, however, he would not have become the first pitcher in history (and still just one of four) to win exactly 12, lose exactly 12, and intentionally walk exactly 12 in a single season. Who's the guy, and what are the unidentified 12s?
5. Speaking of wins and losses … a handful of teams have had three pitchers with a 12-x record. Another handful of teams have had three pitchers with an x-12 record; no team has had more than three of either set. Our mystery team had three pitchers with 12-12 records, tying for the team lead in wins and losses. What's the team and who are the pitchers?
6. His career All-Star appearances are equal to the amount of singles plus walks he earned in those games is equal to his uniform number is equal to the millions of dollars asked for in a lawsuit against him. As you might have guessed, the number in question is 12. Who's the dozened denizen?
7. It was considered a big deal on April 5, 2000 when it happened for the first time in history. On May 7, 2009, when it happened for the second time, it generated little if any fanfare. What is it?
8. Jim O'Toole pitched a 10-inning shutout in his 12th-to-last major league game, on May 13, 1967. Jim Deshaies, in a 12-win season (which were his first 12 major league wins at that), struck out the first eight batters of the game on Sept. 23, 1986, setting a major league record. But despite the 12s that surround their performances, the Jims' performances are linked by a different 12. What's the 12?
9. On July 11, 1944, Whitey Kurowski drove in his Cardinals teammate Walker Cooper with a double in the seventh inning. It was the last hit of the game, making it the last time the event in question will ever happen, barring the absurdly improbable. It had only happened once before. What is it?

10. This list of 12 (okay, 15, but it's a tie for 12th) is the all-time leaderboard for something. What is it?

Mike Piazza	49
Barry Bonds	38
Larry Walker	27
Cliff Floyd	25
Moises Alou	23
Chipper Jones	23
Pat Burrell	21
Ken Griffey	21
Craig Biggio	20
Glenallen Hill	19
Dmitri Young	19
Kevin Millar	18
Olmedo Saenz	18
Mark Sweeney	18
Gary Sheffield	18

11. Here's a team made up of 12 players. What do they have in common?

C: Scott Hastings
1B: Bill Kenworthy (I had to put somebody there)
2B: Billy Herman
SS: Henry Baldwin
3B: Pat Patterson
LF: George Rooks
CF: Steve Behel
RF: Jimmy Sheckard
SP: Slim Harriss
P: Jim Baskette
P: Kid Camp
P: Billy Buckner

Don't miss the last Docecatrivia question on the next page...

12. The 12 most frequent last names in the United States as of 1990 are listed in alphabetical order. The active streaks in which the majors have fielded at least one player with that last name are listed in reverse order of length. Match the names to the active streak. I've listed their longest historical streak after the semicolon unless the active one is longest, in which case there's something else to identify them.

Anderson	Inactive ; 1920-48
Brown	2009- ; 1954-79
Davis	2009- ; 1911-2007
Johnson	1971- ; their only Hall of Famer is a manager
Jones	1962- ; two of them combined for 995 career steals and 113 in the same single season
Miller	1957- ; missed only two years before 1900
Moore	1951- ; 1884-1946
Smith	1950- ; 1948-49 are the only two years since 1882 without one
Taylor	1950- ; didn't field a player until 1899, the latest for these dozen names
Thomas	1945- ; 23 first-round draft picks and a World Series-winning manager have yielded no Hall of Famers
Williams	1939- ; three players of this last name that also shared first names: an American Leaguer in 1912; a National Leaguer in 1913-14; and a Federal Leaguer in 1915, all as their entire careers
Wilson	1907- ; that's clue enough to get this one

That's it for our first Trivia Challenge. Look for two more Challenges further in the Annual. The solutions to these questions and all Challenges are in the back of the book, starting on page 360.

The Annotated 2009 in History

by Richard Barbieri

Each week at The Hardball Times I look back on an event from the past week in history in the Annotated Week in Baseball History. For the Annual, however, I need to look only at the past year in baseball to find events of historical interest. While some of these events were major news, others might have slipped below the radar. But all were important in a historical context, so read on.

November 2008: Cliff Lee Wins Cy Young Award

If we were writing this headline for November 2007, it would be C.C. Sabathia winning the same award. The link between these two, of course, is that both won their awards pitching with the Cleveland Indians and neither is pitching for Cleveland any longer. That is just another sign of the decline of the Indians since their appearance in the 2007 ALCS. Leading 3-1, the Indians lost three straight games to the Red Sox, being crushed a collective 30-5 in the three.

Riding high going into the 2008 season, the Indians slumped to .500—despite Lee's 22-3 record—and lost almost 100 games in 2009. Meanwhile, as of this writing, Sabathia and Lee were pitching and winning in the postseason while Victor Martinez was batting third in the Red Sox lineup. Excluding teams built exclusively for one year like the 1997 Marlins, it is hard to recall a recent team that so badly imploded after being so close to a World Series.

In the bottom of the first inning of Game Five of the 2007 ALCS, already down a run, the Indians had a first-and-third situation with nobody out. Travis Hafner hit into a double play; the tying run scored. Though Cleveland could not have known it at the time, that would represent its high point, the equivalent to the Confederates reaching the Union lines at Gettysburg. Whether the Indians can rally again remains to be seen.

December 2008: Yankees sign C.C. Sabathia

As is probably well-known by now, landing Sabathia was part of Yankees GM Brian Cashman's master plan. Rather than trading for the equally excellent Johan Santana, Cashman held on to young players like Phil Hughes and Melky Cabrera and opted to wait for Sabathia to hit the free agent market.

The strategy looked rough in 2008 as the Yankees missed the playoffs and virtually all the players Cashman was unwilling to trade underperformed expectations. But it has turned around to make the GM look brilliant

Of course, Cashman's plans were predicated upon some serious dollars being spent. Sabathia cost the Yankees $161 million for seven years (assuming he stays through the life of the deal; there is an opt-out after the third year). That is the largest contract ever given to a pitcher, going along with the deal they gave Alex Rodriguez after the 2007 season—the largest for a position player. With big money also going to Mark Teixeira and Derek Jeter, if Sabathia plays out his contract the Yankees will have paid for the four largest deals in baseball history. Cashman deserves credit for having a plan and sticking to it, but both he and Yankees fans should be grateful for the money they have to spend.

January 2009: MLB Network Launched

I adore the MLB Network. In the midst of a long, cold winter—when, like Rogers Hornsby, I stare out the window and wait for spring—I will watch just about any baseball game, even old ones I've seen a bunch of times. Maybe especially old ones I've seen a bunch of times.

Besides satisfying addicts like me, MLB Network reflects two elements that dominate modern sports. One is the sheer amount of money involved. The contracts handed out by the Yankees last offseason received much press, but they're small potatoes compared to the network. While the economic collapse may mitigate projections somewhat, when the network was founded analysts believed that by 2015 revenue would exceed $200 million a year. At those rates, it would have a total value of more than a billion dollars.

Moreover, the MLB Network reveals just how ubiquitous coverage of sport has become. Between the MLB Network, national games on FOX, ESPN and TBS, and further coverage like "Baseball Tonight," there is easily 200 hours of baseball coverage many weeks of a year. That is a dramatic turnaround from 20 years ago, when NBC cancelled its longstanding "Game of the Week" coverage.

February 2009: Oliver Perez Signs with Mets

Now we come to my third year of discussing the All-Bust starting rotation. The rotation is currently composed of Barry Zito, Jamie Navarro, Mike Hampton and Carl Pavano. It is probably a little early for Oliver Perez to join that group, but if he has two more years like his 2009 there definitely will be a spot for him.

After missing out on the rest of the free agent crop, including A.J. Burnett and Derek Lowe, the Mets brought Perez back on a three-year deal averaging $12 million a year. And what did they get for their money in 2009? A 3-4 record and a 6.82 ERA in just 66 injury-plagued innings. Meanwhile, while worth nothing close to the $18.5 million the Giants were paying, Zito at least had his best season as a Giant.

Zito probably would need a miraculous return to his Oakland form to have any chance of removing himself from this list, so pending Perez's performance the next two years, the rotation remains unchanged.

March 2009: Aaron Boone Undergoes Open Heart Surgery

I'm a Yankees fan, so I will always have a soft spot in my heart for Aaron Boone. Boone was dreadful up to—and after—his famous pennant-winning home run in the 2003 ALCS, but such was the import of the home run that most Yankees fans I know look back on him fondly.

No matter one's rooting allegiance, Boone's surgery (which included replacing his aortic valve) was one of those events—like Jon Lester's cancer, for example—that prompts a number of clichés. It "puts everything in perspective" and "reminds us that it is just a game," which are all true. And part of the reason we fall into cliché is because there are so few words to describe something so serious.

Luckily, Boone's story has a happy ending. He made his season debut Sept. 2. Playing in 10 games, he reached base just once in 14 plate appearances, on a hit by pitch no less. It is rare that a player appearing in 10 games with a .000/.071/.000 line can be said to have had one of the best years in baseball, but for Boone it is definitely the case.

April 2009: Yankee Stadium Opens

It has been a long time since anyone could truly write that sentence, since the 1976 opening day of the renovated park really only counts for half. The new Yankee Stadium is, not unlike the team that plays there, incredibly controversial.

Some cite its billion dollar-plus price tag (the most expensive baseball stadium in North America), the "moat" separating frequently half-empty Legend Suites behind home plate and other features as reasons it's a park simply for the elite, those who cannot be bothered to sit through a whole game. Some admire the Yankees' willingness to spare no expense in building the park and cite the features that are an upgrade on the old park.

Whatever one's view, it is interesting to note that Yankee Stadium—along with its cross-town cousin CitiField—is leading the last wave of new ballparks. Since 1992, when Baltimore's Camden Yards opened, 19 teams have moved into new parks, while the Royals and Angels extensively remodeled their homes.

The Twins will get a new stadium next spring, and the Marlins shortly thereafter. With those parks complete, every team except the A's and Rays is likely to play in its current park for at least the next decade. Barring unexpected news, 2013 and 2014 will represent the first back-to-back seasons without a new park opening since 1983-84.

May 2009: Tom Glavine Wins Minor League Game

Glavine won 305 games in his major league career, ranking 21st all-time. He won 20 or more games five times, including a 62-25 stretch from 1991 through 1993. He won two Cy Young Awards, was World Series MVP and appeared in 10 All-Star games.

Not only was Glavine performing well, he was also a model of health, throwing more than 200 innings 14 times. Excluding those seasons shortened by strike, Glavine pitched 200 or more innings for 11 straight years.

It is no surprise, therefore, that he was not spending a lot of time in the minor leagues. After his permanent call-up to the Braves in 1987, Glavine would not throw another pitch in the minors until 2008, for an injury rehab stint during which he went 0-1.

In 2009, while pitching in relief for the Triple-A Gwinnett Braves, Glavine recorded the win—his first at a level less than major league since 1987, a gap of more than 20 years. That might not be the longest stretch between wins in the minor leagues—records for that kind of thing are sketchy—but it is certainly up there.

No doubt to Glavine's dismay, while he would win another game in the minors (for the Single-A Rome Braves) the Braves released him rather than return him to the major league team. So for now, Glavine's last victories came for Gwinnet and Rome. That is probably not how he imagined going out, but one doesn't always get to choose.

June 2009: Aaron Cook Breaks Rockies Win Record

I suppose I could have used this for any month after June, because Cook kept resetting the record with each game he won. He finished the season with 63 career wins with the Rockies, five ahead of Jason Jennings. That's not an especially impressive win total to lead a franchise.

The Rockies' 1993 expansion counterpart Florida Marlins can top it, with Dontrelle Willis's 68 wins. (In fairness, Cook is likely to pass that next season, and the current Marlin with the most wins is Ricky Nolasco at 40.) The Diamondbacks came into the league after Colorado but have two players ahead of Cook, Randy Johnson (118) and Brandon Webb (87) and only Cook's record-setting win pushed him ahead of Curt Schilling's Arizona total.

(Needless to say, none of these are even close to the kind of totals possessed by the leaders of long-standing franchises that existed in the days of four, or fewer, men in the rotation. Christy Mathewson won 372 for the Giants, Warren Spahn 356 for the Braves and so on.)

But as with so many things, Cook and the Rockies are at least ahead of the Rays. Their franchise leader is now-departed Scott Kazmir, who won 55 times during his time in Tampa Bay. James Shields needs 13 wins next season to pass Kazmir and allow me to write this same little essay again.

Roy Oswalt needs just eight wins to take over the Astros' record from Joe Niekro. That figures to be the only change in the leader boards, though. The next closest is Roy Halladay, 27 behind David Stieb in Toronto. Halladay seems unlikely to stay with Toronto past this season, but if he does, he figures to take the top spot there.

July 2009: President Obama Throws Out First Pitch

This first pitch came at the All-Star game and Obama—apparently more of a basketball man—spent time practicing so that he would not bounce the pitch. He did not, thanks in no small part to a nice catch by Albert Pujols. Pujols, I learned while researching this bit, was wearing a specially made glove for the occasion. I wonder if the Secret Service had to approve that.

Obama is the latest in a long line of Presidents and other dignitaries to throw out a first pitch, although the first President since Gerald Ford in 1976 to throw out the first pitch at an All-Star game. The custom was started by William Howard Taft; it's odd that a man most famous for his enormous girth is forever associated with commencing an athletic competition.

Traditionally, Presidents would attend the Opening Day game in Washington. Since Taft began the practice—in the early days the President threw the pitch from his seat, which would have saved Obama considerable trouble—every President has thrown out a first ball at either an Opening Day or a World Series. During the 1920s and '30s, the President attended almost every Opening Day. Though World War II forced Franklin Roosevelt (and later Harry Truman) to miss many games, it was Dwight Eisenhower's choice to pass on Opening Day to play golf that earned a President much grief. Ike caught a lucky break: The game was rained out, so he was able to attend the make-up. Sufficiently chastised, he did not miss an opener for the rest of his presidency.

George H.W. and George W. Bush are of course the only father-and-son pair to have thrown a presidential first pitch, but Eisenhower's son David filled in for father-in-law Richard Nixon before the Senators' 1970 opener.

Given the nature of the President's current schedule, it seems unlikely we will ever return to the days of a President appearing at the game in D.C. every year. But at least we can have moments like the All-Star Game to remind us how important baseball is in the American consciousness.

August 2009: Derek Jeter Sets Shortstop Hit Record

This was a good year for Derek Jeter breaking hit records; see below. The record here is hits recorded while playing shortstop—the Yankees captain passed Luis Aparcio.

Depending on how you shift the goalposts around, the record can come and go from Jeter.

For example, if we take all hits by players who saw at least 50 percent of their time at short, Jeter drops to No. 5 all-time. At two-thirds, he moves up to No. 4. For now, Jeter is second behind Luke Appling among those who saw 90 percent of their games at short, but barring a lightning strike he will move ahead next season: He needs just three hits.

Meanwhile, the hit-leader list of players who have never played anywhere but shortstop is rather different. The current leader is the Rockies' Troy Tulowitzki, who has 460 in his brief career. Elvis Andrus ranks No. 3, based solely on his performance for the Rangers this season. Since it seems likely that both Tulowitzki and Andrus will someday find themselves elsewhere than short, the long-term leader figures to be John Gochnauer, who hit .187 during 1901-03 while manning only short.

So Derek Jeter might be No. 1 when it comes to hits accumulated at short, but if you want the purest possible record in the future, it would seem Gochnauer is your man.

September 2009: Derek Jeter Breaks Yankees Hit Record

Jeter tied this record at a game I attended, which was pretty fun to see. If you lived outside the New York area, you probably saw this story repeated quite a bit. If you live in the New York area—as I do—this story was occasionally in the news in the same sense that the Atlantic Ocean is occasionally wet.

Notwithstanding the 200-hit year of Robinson Cano, Jeter figures to hold the Yankees hit record for the foreseeable future. Jeter joined Todd Helton (Colorado), Carl Crawford (Tampa Bay) and Ivan Rodriguez (Texas) as franchise hit leaders who played for their team this season. Luis Castillo (Florida) and Garrett Anderson (Angels) are the other active players who lead teams.

Jeter is still shy of 3,000 hits, but if he is able to reach it without leaving the Yankees, he will become the 11th player with 3,000 hits for a single team, joining some good company like Hank Aaron, George Brett and Stan Musial.

Crawford's rebound season brought his hit total to 1,296, which also dropped Castillo and the Marlins to the lowest total for a franchise hit leader.

For next season, the wild card is Ivan Rodriguez. If he were to re-sign with the Rangers, even as a part-time player, it would be difficult for Michael Young—currently 85 hits behind—to pass him in 2009. If Pudge does not return to Arlington, Young almost certainly will grab the title. Meanwhile, Vernon Wells needs to match his career hit total next season to pass Tony Fernandez in Toronto, but appears more likely for 2011.

October 2009: Brad Lidge Makes Final Regular Season Appearance

As you probably heard, this was not a good season for Brad Lidge. Owner of zero blown saves and a 1.10 ERA in save situations in 2008, Lidge blew 11 this season and had a 7.78 ERA with the game on the line. That went along with a less-than-sterling performance in non-save situations to give Lidge a 7.21 ERA for the season.

But despite his troubles and his bloated numbers, Lidge recorded 31 saves this season. That made him one of 16 pitchers with 30 or more this year, and is one of 368 player seasons of 30 or more saves since 1901. (In fact, they're all since 1965, when Ted Abernathy had the first 30-save season, for the Cubs.)

And how does Lidge's 2009 rank among those 368 player seasons? Pretty badly. Lidge's 7.21 ERA is the highest ever for a pitcher with 30 or more saves, relieving former Rockies closer/current problem gambler Shawn Chacon from that dubious honor. For good measure, Lidge also has the worst ERA+, coming in at 59, the only season below 60.

Lidge had the fourth-highest HR/9 at 1.69, behind Todd Worell's 1997, in which he saved 35 but give up 12 homers in less than 60 innings. Lidge is also 11th for worst BB/9, coming in at 5.22, which is at least well behind Chacon's 7.39 from 2004. Finally, Lidge has the second worst WHIP of 30-save seasons, again behind Chacon's 2004.

Terrible as Lidge's season was (and it was) it is worth remembering that the fourth highest ERA in a 30-save season belongs to ... Brad Lidge, in 2006. So if he could bounce back from those depths to reach the heights of 2008, we can only imagine what heights Lidge might reach in the future.

All the World's a Ballpark

by Max Marchi

When you are planning the perfect coup, you must be careful about timing. Even though the theater of action didn't include Europe, living there looked like a fortunate occurrence. Hence, the plan was easily contrived.

Wake up at four in the morning to catch the first of two games from the Far East. China, which lost 4-0 to defending champions Japan the previous day, was playing Taiwan, who lost to the Koreans 9-0 just 18 hours before. The losing team would be out of the second World Baseball Classic before most of the nations had even played.

After the game, there'd be a good three hours to have breakfast and get ready for the next contest from the Tokyo Dome: the latest installment of Japan vs. Korea, with the winning team clinching a berth for round two and the loser going to a win-or-die game against the surviving team from the first game.

Then, from around 2pm till 5pm, do whatever else I had to do, lunch included, because there wouldn't be another break all day or night, with the Dominican Republic facing European champions the Netherlands in Puerto Rico at 5pm, followed by the United States playing Canada in the Rogers Centre in Toronto, followed by Panama playing Puerto Rico, with Italy and Venezuela in Toronto as the nightcap, starting at two in the morning.

And that was just day two of the 2009 World Baseball Classic, with Mexico, South Africa, Australia and Cuba scheduled to debut the following day in the thin air of Mexico City.

The Tournament

The WBC was back, but not exactly the same. At the end of the inaugural edition back in 2006, it was apparent that some tweaking was needed to improve the tournament. It adopted a double elimination format to increase competitive fairness. Pitch count limits were slightly increased to 70 in round one, 85 in round two and 100 in semi-finals and final, and the tournament adopted Olympics-style extra innings, with the batting team starting with runners on base beginning in the 13th inning. Venues for the Classic included San Diego (the site of the finals in 2006) and Miami, with the 2009 semifinals and final held at Dodger Stadium.

The Players

However, going into the tournament it seemed like one big player after another was pulling out: no Joe Nathan, no Albert Pujols, no Manny Ramirez. Then it looked like Johan Santana might miss even opening day, let alone the WBC.

Then Alex Rodriguez made headlines when he chose to play for the Dominican Republic after suiting up for the Stars-and-Stripes in 2006. He then made even more headlines when he admitted using steroids during his years in Texas. Finally, just as he was ready to start his path to redemption in the WBC, he was back in the news when he suffered a hip injury that forced him to miss the tournament and the first few weeks of the regular season.

Nonetheless many great players were ready to represent their nations: Derek Jeter captained the USA; Ichiro and Daisuke Matsuzaka were back for Japan; Justin Morneau proudly wore Canadian red; not to mention guys like David Ortiz (Dominican Republic), Shin-Soo Choo (Korea), Joakim Soria (Mexico), Carlos Lee (Panama), Yadier Molina (Puerto Rico) and Magglio Ordonez (Venezuela).

There were also players using the tournament as a major league tryout. Age and a poor economy had left Ivan Rodriguez and Pedro Martinez without contracts. A couple of home runs early in the tournament convinced the Astros to shell out for Pudge. Martinez had a couple of strong outings, but made both outings against the offensively challenged Dutch. Concerns about the quality of his opponents, uncertainty about his health, and high salary demands left him looking for an employer until midsummer. Sidney Ponson traded Dutch orange for Kansas City blue at the end of the event. Even Bernie Williams made himself available for the competition, probably because he still wasn't sure about his recording career.

Speaking of new careers, word also leaked during the tournament that Ichiro and Akinori Iwamura were doing some pitching in Japan's training facility, just in case the pitch limit rules left their team without viable options on the mound. The Mariners immediately imposed a halt to the blossoming of a new hurler.

The Teams and the Games

The Netherlands were the darlings of the 2009 WBC. In 2006, they had but one bright spot, as Shairon Martis pitched a no-hitter against Panama. Before the 2009 tournament, they were expected to fight it out with Panama for third place in Pool D, since they were matched with Puerto Rico and the Dominican Republic.

The Orange were not a team that could pile up big offensive numbers, but they didn't need much hitting to pull off the biggest upset of the tournament against the Dominican Republic. In that game, they scored three runs in the top of the first without a single ball leaving the infield other than a harmless fly out. By the end of the game, the European side had totaled just three hits, but managed to hold on behind four innings from Sidney Ponson and a solid bullpen performance.

Three days later, David again had to face Goliath—fresh off sending Panama home scoreless—with a spot in the second round on the line. The rematch looked a lot like the first act. The Dutch barely scraped a couple of hits together over nine innings, but their pitchers held the powerful lumber of Ortiz, Hanley Ramirez and company quiet, with an encore of the the last game's impressive relief effort put on by Robbie Cordemans, Alexander Smit, Dennis Neuman, Leon Boyd and Diegomar Maxwell (who was not used in the first game). So, after nine innings, two matching lines of goose eggs stood on the scoreboard. In the top of the 11th, the Dominican Republic scored on a two-out throwing error by shortstop Gene Kingsale, seemingly ending the game. However, the Dutch offense awoke in the bottom frame, managing a couple of hits off Carlos Marmol to tie the game before completing the second upset on a pair of defensive errors and banjo hitting themselves into the second round.

Australia provided the surprising result in Pool B, rolling over host Mexico 17-7 in their first meeting. However, the surprises in Pool B stopped there, as the Aussies lost to 2006 runners up Cuba 5-4, with the go-ahead runs coming on a two-run homer in the eighth by Yosbany Peraza. Mexico had no trouble winning 14-3 against South Africa who, along with Panama, are the the only teams winless after two editions of the WBC. Mexico later paid Australia back with a 16-1 pounding.

The Cubans, who have built their international dominance on the long ball, also thrived in the thin air of Mexico City: they exploded with seven homers in their opening game against South Africa, winning 8-1. Then, after hitting only one (crucial) dinger to defeat the Aussies, added three more when they faced and defeated Mexico 16-4 to win the pool.

However, things were different for the Cubans in the second round, as they played in the pitchers heaven that is Petco Park. They managed just one win, 7-4 against Mexico, and didn't hit a single home run in the round. Instead, they were shut out twice by defending champions Japan, marking the first time Team Cuba has missed the finals of an international tournament in 58 years.

In Pool A, China's growth as a baseball country was the big under the radar story. They had come a long way since starting their national team program in 2005. During the 2008 Olympics, China defeated arch-nemesis Taiwan in a 12 inning affair, then duplicated the feat at the WBC, winning its first ever World Baseball Classic game 4-1. Their star of the tournament was Kansas City-born Ray Chang, who fell one triple short of the cycle against Taiwan. On the other side of the Taiwan Strait, Taiwan needs to reverse the decline of a team that is used to winning its share of games against top international competition, never finishing lower than fourth in the World Cup between 1982 and 1988 and earning the silver medal in the 1992 Olympics.

The Strategy

Leo Durocher used to say, "You don't save a pitcher for tomorrow. Tomorrow it may rain".

Well, back in March the Rogers Centre's roof was very well closed, so Canadian manager Ernie Whitt chose not to use Scott Richmond, his best available pitcher, in a win-or-die game against underdog Italy, in order to have him ready the following day to face the powerful Venezuelan lineup. Unfortunately, Richmond never had the chance to toe the rubber, because Team Italy pulled an upset of their own, winning 6-2 and sending the Maple Leafs home.

In the first of five matchups, Japan beat Korea 14-1 on WBC day two, but the Koreans promptly gained the right for a rematch—and to play in round two—beating China 14-0. The second bout, on March 9, was for seeding purposes only, but did contain a controversial managerial choice. After Korea scored one run early, Ichiro singled with one out in the bottom of the eighth. Manager Tatsunori Hara elected to bunt him to second, where he was stranded when Norichika Aoki grounded to pitcher Lim Chang-yong, leaving many people scratching their heads. It wasn't just saber-types who were unpleased by the strategy; Ichiro himself stated he was puzzled by the choice during the post game press conference. Even former Cuban dictator Fidel Castro took exception with Hara in his column "Reflections from Comrade Fidel."

Japan and Korea continued their rivalry, trading punches in the second round at Petco Park (after beating Cuba 6-0 and Mexico 8-2, respectively). On March 17, Korea won 4-1; two days later the Japanese team, after sending Cuba home, got revenge by winning 6-2, evening up their WBC records against each other.

They would cross bats for a fifth time in the championship game at Dodger Stadium. Bong, who has held Japan to six hits and one run in two Korea wins, started for Korea. He was opposed by Hisashi Iwakuma, who conceded just two hits in the 1-0 affair at Tokyo Dome and held the Cubans scoreless for six innings on March 18.

A slumping Ichiro opened the final game with a single and Hara bunted him to second, but Japan wouldn't manufacture any runs in the inning. In the third frame he even asked his cleanup hitter, Kenji Johjima, to lay one down with two men on and nobody out to stay out of the double play. Johjima ultimately grounded out on a fielder's choice, but Japan scored once. With his team still leading by one, the formerly slumping Ichiro opened the ninth inning with a double. Hiroyuki Nakajima, two-for-three on the night, is instructed to sacrifice, but also fails to execute. Japan can't increase its lead and Korea ties the game in the bottom of the ninth, despite tallying five hits to Japan's 12.

In the top of the 10th, Seiichi Uchikawa singled and Atsunori Inaba—surprise—bunted. Uchikawa came around to score on a two-out hit by the now rolling Ichiro, and Japan ended up winning 5-3. Hara had surely been a nightmare for all the statheads that March—a nightmare who ended up going all the way and winning the tournament.

The Fans

The 2009 WBC also attracted more interest than the inaugural version. Nearly 55,000 people watched the heartbreaking 10 inning final between two teams from the other side of the Pacific Ocean at Dodger Stadium . A grand total of more than 800,000 moved the turnstiles in five different countries for an average of more than 20,000 per game and an increase of nearly 9 percent from 2006. Every game in L.A. drew over 40,000, with Korea rolling over an error prone Venezuelan team in front of 43,378 on March 21 in the first semifinal, while Japan put a halt to the U.S. run before 43,630 fans the following day in the other semi.

A hot Puerto Rican team drew well in Miami, bringing 30,000-plus fans inside Dolphins Stadium in a mercy-rule victory over the United States on March 14 and 25,000 more two days later, when they lost 2-0 against Venezuela. Such crowds are hardly seen in South Florida during the summer. In Tokyo, attendance was over 40,000 when the home team was playing, and the Rogers Centre opened with 42,000 fans in attendance as the United States battled Canada in a 6-5 win.

On the negative side, crowds were sparse when the hosts weren't on the field: both Japan vs. Korea games averaged barely 15,000 fans at Petco Park and another couple of games there did not even reach 10,000. Twenty-thousand showed up at Foro Sol Stadium when Mexico battled against Australia and Cuba, but not many more than 10,000 were in attendance for the other games; Puerto Ricans packed Hiram Bithorn Stadium to watch the local team, but left it half empty when the Netherlands upset the Dominican Republic; Rogers Centre was deserted after the opening game.

Television ratings also experienced an improvement over the previous edition. ESPN's coverage of the event increased, along with its coverage on its Spanish language companion ESPN Deportes and Rogers Sportsnet was successful broadcasting the games in Canada while Team Canada was still alive. In Japan, everybody in the country seemed to tune into J-Sports to watch the WBC, as ratings ranged between 30 and 45 percent while the Japanese were playing.

The Injuries

If you see Adam Dunn standing near the first base bag wearing a glove, it's natural to suspect that something is not right. If in the same tournament you look toward left field and see Braves catcher Brian McCann patrolling the outfield, you know something is not right. Finally, if you learn that Cubs pitcher Ted Lilly was asked whether he felt like taking a turn in the outfield, something is definitely wrong.

Team USA went deeper into the tournament than it had three years before, but the run came at a high price. Manager Davey Johnson had his hands full dealing with injuries, putting players out of position, telephoning GMs and managers to apologize for improper use of their personnel and telling the world he was contemplating the idea of forfeiting a game in the event of further injuries.

Over the course of a few days, he lost Dustin Pedroia (abdominal strain), Chipper Jones (oblique strain), Matt Lindstrom (rotator cuff strain) and Ryan Braun (intercostal strain). The latter was the injury that forced Johnson to send McCann into the outfield during a win-or-go-home game against the Netherlands. After winning that game 9-3, the United States were again in a must-win situation against Puerto Rico, which they dealt with in the most dramatic way, thanks to a walk-off two-run single by David Wright to seal it 5-4. But they didn't escape unscathed, with Kevin Youkilis leaving the game limping and returning to the Red Sox training camp to nurse a sprained left ankle.

Team USA wasn't the only squad sending players back after injuries: Robinson Cano and Damaso Marte were returned to the Yankees from the Dominican team. The same was true outside of MLB as well, with Shuichi Murata returned in crutches to the Yokohama Bay Stars after delighting fans with thundering homers and diving stops at third for Team Japan.

PITCHf/x, International Edition

The WBC even gave us statheads a jump start on the 2009 season, as Sportvision's PITCHf/x tracking system was active in all the MLB parks hosting the event, allowing analysts to get their first looks at some top international talent. Iwakuma, Fujikawa (Japan) and Bong (Korea) are all approaching 30 years old, and are probably not on the radar for MLB clubs anymore, but getting a look at the likes of Yu Darvish (22 years old, right-handed, from Japan) and Hyun-jin Ryu (21 years old, left-handed, from Korea) was a stathead's dream.

What are dreams made of?

Ryu's change-up (at least the one he showed during the Classic) travels at 81.6 mph, while moving 7.9 inches horizontally and 8.0 vertically. If you are not a PITCHf/x disciple, you may wonder whether these NASA-like numbers mean the pitch is any good. Quick answer: they're Johan Santana-like. That's right, the Korean youngster's change-up is comparable to that of one of the most effective around. Check for yourself in the table below (though be aware that we are talking about a small sample of offerings).

His fastball is also quite similar to Johan's–same speed, a little less movement on the horizontal plane (or "tail" using scouting lingo) and a little more on the vertical plane (a bird dog would say that Ryu's heater "rides" more than Santana's).

Darvish's stuff is even more exciting, because it's literally off the charts. His fastball is consistently clocked at around 95 mph and has a lot of movement too, comparable to what you would usually see in lefthanded pitchers, but with way more velocity. Add a cutter–take Jon Lester's cutter, add a couple of miles and some more bite for good measure–and a swiping 83 mph slider that generates an insane quantity of swing and misses.

And he can throw all of the aforementioned pitches–plus a 73 mph curveball he didn't use many times during the tournament–for strikes.

Needless to say, MLB clubs have been following his performances for a long time, and offers will be sky high should he make himself available. However, he has made clear he's not interested in leaving his home country for a while.

For completely different reasons, Cuban pitchers are also forbidden fruit for American teams. Studying them brought to life the different approaches between veterans like Lazo and Vera (a great variety of pitches with fluctuating release points—maybe that's what we would have seen had PITCHf/x been installed in ballparks in Luis Tiant's heyday), and young flamethrowers like Garcia and Chapman (sporting fastballs in the mid- to high-90s). Chapman's performance became a lot more intriguing the following summer, when news broke that the 21-year-old had defected and planned on playing in the bigs.

Ryu and Santana Through the Eyes of PITCHf/x

Pitch type	Measure	Ryu	Santana
Change-up	Speed	81.6	81.4
	Horiz. Movement	7.9	7.8
	Vert. Movement	8.0	7.8
Fastball	Speed	90.8	90.5
	Horiz. Movement	5.3	6.1
	Vert. Movement	12.0	10.9

Odds and Ends

If you are one of those who don't like the World Baseball Classic, please stop reading now. (Why have you gone this far, for that matter?) I envy you. You won't have the unpleasant experience of feeling the crescendo of play-off baseball, only to abruptly find yourself back in spring training mode, where teams do not pay attention to the score, and regulars are hitting the showers before the seventh inning stretch. You won't get confused seeing Jeter play for the Yankees.

And, most importantly, you won't have to stay up 24 straight hours watching baseball.

OK, for those of you still reading, the good news is that the WBC is going to stick around for a while, especially now that baseball is out of the Olympics. It will be in March again, since the cons of every other option seem to outweigh their pros. However, there were several other options advocated.

Some have suggested a WBC week at midseason every four years, replacing the All-Star Break, similar to what NHL has done for the past three Winter Olympics. But the owners are probably not willing to sacrifice gate receipts when the weather is good and the schools are closed. Having many unselected players idle for a week is another point against a July WBC, but it seems to me a minor one, as hockey players have gladly taken the chance for a midseason rest in the past.

Another option is playing in November, but that would limit the the number of playing venues available due to weather issues. Hockey could also suggest another possibility: Holding the WBC during the playoffs in October would mirror hockey's practice of holding the World Cup during the Stanley Cup playoffs. Players from the eliminated teams are in top shape and their teams won't need their services for a few months. While this might be an ideal solution in terms of easing club concerns about availability and quality of competition, it has the obvious drawback of pitting the WBC against the playoffs.

All in all, March seems a good time to hold the World Baseball Classic: the football season is in the books, the NBA and NHL are one month away from their playoffs and even soccer is hardly at its apex in any of the soccer-crazy countries. The only competing event is March Madness, a great draw in the States, but hardly a factor in the rest of the baseball world.

Thus, barring someone coming up with a revolutionary idea, we'll probably see you again in March 2013.

The Results

Round 1, Pool A - Tokyo Dome, Tokyo, Japan

Date	Match-Up
Thu., Mar. 5	Japan 4, China 0
Fri., Mar. 6	Korea 9, Chinese Taipei 0
Fri., Mar. 6	China 4, Chinese Taipei 1
Sat., Mar. 7	Japan 14, Korea 2
Sun., Mar. 8	Korea 14, China 0
Mon., Mar. 9	Korea 1, Japan 0

Round 1, Pool B - Foro Do Sol, Mexico City, Mexico

Date	Match-Up
Sun., Mar. 8	Cuba 8, South Africa 1
Sun., Mar. 8	Australia 17, Mexico 7
Mon., Mar. 9	Mexico 14, South Africa 3
Tue., Mar. 10	Cuba 5, Australia 4
Wed., Mar. 11	Mexico 16, Australia 1
Thu., Mar. 12	Cuba 16, Mexico 4

Round 1, Pool C - Rogers Centre, Toronto, Canada

Date	Match-Up
Sat., Mar. 7	United States 6, Canada 5
Sat., Mar. 7	Venezuela 7, Italy 0
Sun., Mar. 8	United States 15, Venezuela 6
Mon., Mar. 9	Italy 6, Canada 2
Tue., Mar. 10	Venezuela 10, Italy 1
Wed., Mar. 11	Venezuela 5, United States 3

Round 1, Pool D - Hiram Bithorn Stadium, San Juan, Puerto Rico

Date	Match-Up
Sat., Mar. 7	Netherlands 3, Dominican Republic 2
Sat., Mar. 7	Puerto Rico 7, Panama 0
Sun., Mar. 8	Dominican Republic 9, Panama 0
Mon., Mar. 9	Puerto Rico 3, Netherlands 1
Tue., Mar. 10	Netherlands 2, Dominican Republic 1
Wed., Mar. 11	Puerto Rico 5, Netherlands 0

The Results (cont.)

Round 2, Pool 1 - Petco Park, San Diego, United States

Date	Match-Up
Sun., Mar. 15	Japan 6, Cuba 0
Sun., Mar. 15	Korea 8, Mexico 2
Mon., Mar. 16	Cuba 7, Mexico 4
Tue., Mar. 17	Korea 4, Japan 1
Wed., Mar. 18	Japan 5, Cuba 0
Thu., Mar. 19	Japan 6, Korea 2

Round 2, Pool 2 - Dolphins Stadium, Miami, United States

Date	Match-Up
Sat., Mar. 14	Venezuela 3, Netherlands 1
Sat., Mar. 14	Puerto Rico 11, United States 1
Sun., Mar. 15	United States 9, Netherlands 3
Mon., Mar. 16	Venezuela 2, Puerto Rico 0
Tue., Mar. 17	United States 6, Puerto Rico 5
Wed., Mar. 18	Venezuela 10, United States 6

Semifinals and Finals, Dodger Stadium, Los Angeles, United States

Date	Match-Up
Sat., Mar. 21	Korea 10, Venezuela 2
Sun., Mar. 22	Japan 9, United States 4
Mon., Mar. 23	Japan 5, Korea 3

The Latin America Scandals

by Ben Badler

Even by the standards of the expect-the-unexpected world of Latin American scouting, 2009 was arguably one of the most bizarre years in the region in recent memory.

A Giants prospect, 19-year-old first baseman Angel Villalona, who signed for $2.1 million in 2006, was arrested in the Dominican Republic and charged with murder in the fatal shooting of a 25-year-old man in a La Romana bar. Dominican shortstop Alvaro Aristy, who signed with the Padres in 2008 for $1 million at age 16, played in the Dominican Summer League before being suspended 50 games upon failing a steroid test.

Sixteen-year-old Domincan outfielder Wagner Mateo agreed to terms with the Cardinals on July 2 for $3.1 million, the biggest bonus ever for a Latin American position player. Nearly three months later, the Cardinals voided Mateo's contract, citing a failed physical related to his vision. Soon after that, the Twins swooped in and signed 16-year-old Dominican shortstop Miguel Sano for $3.15 million after a long saga surrounding Major League Baseball's investigation into his age and identity.

Another major 2009 Dominican signing, 16-year-old shortstop Damian Arredondo, agreed to terms with the Yankees for a high six-figure bonus on July 2. But the deal fell apart when it turned out the player wasn't 16, wasn't named Damian Arredondo and tested positive for steroids.

The market for Cuban talent expanded when hard-throwing left-hander Aroldis Chapman defected in July, while 19-year-old shortstop Jose Iglesias signed with the Red Sox for $8.25 million as part of a major league contract during the summer. Right-hander Michael Ynoa, who signed an international record $4.25 million bonus with Oakland in July 2008 at age 16, didn't throw a pitch in 2009 due to an elbow injury.

Meanwhile, several teams fired scouts and high-ranking team officials amid federal investigations into bonus skimming, a process in which team employees pocket a percentage of a player's signing bonus, often but not always in conjunction with a player's trainer.

Latin American trainers, also referred to as buscones, find and begin to train players when they are as young as 12 or 13 years old. Trainers will often provide equipment, a field, food and sometimes housing, all in exchange for a substantial cut (often 25 to 40 percent) of a player's signing bonus. If a player has the potential to command a substantial bonus, his trainer might enlist the services of an experienced agent to negotiate it. Many of the wealthier and more powerful trainers also at times purchase the rights to a star player from a less powerful trainer, who stands to make an instant profit and won't have to worry about not receiving any compensation if his player leaves him in the future. These trainers, who are largely unregulated, wield a considerable amount of power when it comes to Latin American signings.

Yet for major league teams and prospect analysts, one of the biggest issues in Latin American baseball is rampant age fraud, which became an explosive issue in 2009 in the wake of the Esmailyn Gonzalez scandal with the Nationals.

July 2, which marks the beginning of the international signing period, is like Christmas in the world of Latin American scouting. When a player from Latin America turns 16, he becomes eligible to sign with a major league team on the following July 2. If a player turns 16 during the international signing period, which lasts through the end of August, then he becomes eligible to sign on his 16th birthday. Once a player becomes eligible, he can sign at any point thereafter.

Gonzalez, a shortstop from the Dominican Republic, signed with the Nationals for $1.4 million on July 2, 2006. That amount of money immediately raised suspicions, although that's not uncommon for any high-dollar signing in the world of scouting 15- and 16-year-old kids in Latin America. While most organizations refrain from commenting on signing bonus amounts, the Nationals trumpeted the $1.4 million bonus in an official press release.

Gonzalez spent the 2007 and 2008 seasons in the Rookie-level Gulf Coast League, where he hit .307/.412/.415 in 84 games. Meanwhile, the FBI was investigating Gonzalez's background, a process that culminated just before the 2009 season. The investigation revealed that Gonzalez's real name was Carlos Alvarez Daniel Lugo and he was not 19 but 23 years old. Not only was Alvarez's prospect status diminished, but it's questionable whether he even will be allowed back into the country, as he spent the 2009 season playing in the Dominican Summer League. The Nationals shortly thereafter parted ways with general manager Jim Bowden and special assistant Jose Rijo.

The Gonzalez scandal changed the way MLB operated in Latin America. At the request of the U.S. Consulate, MLB reevaluated the cases of several recent Latin American players who had cleared their investigations and signed with teams in the past year. Whereas in the past the U.S. Consulate was primarily concerned with verifying a player's identity before issuing him a visa, it began scrutinizing age more closely. (The government's need to know the identity of people entering the country is obvious, but knowing someone's age is also important with regards to a person's rights as an adult or as a minor.)

"That's when it became more difficult to get in because everyone's scrutinizing age," one international scouting director said. "What changed in the months after Esmailyn is the U.S. government got embarrassed. They come across as an entity that's allowing someone to come in who isn't who he says he is. That's embarrassing for national security to have it be on ESPN ... After that happened, players visiting the consulate who had entered the country in recent years were having their investigations reevaluated."

The Indians found out that Dominican shortstop Jose Ozoria, whom they signed for $575,000 in 2008, was not 17; he's a 20-year-old named Wally Bryan. Padres third baseman Jefri Pena, who signed in 2008 for $325,000 in August 2008, turned out to be using a false identity and is four years older. Both players received their bonuses after coming up clean in MLB's initial investigations.

Cuban center fielder Felix Perez, who had presented himself as a 19-year-old and reportedly agreed to a $3 million bonus with the Yankees, became the first Cuban player in recent memory to be suspended for misrepresenting his age—it turned out he was 24. With MLB's more vigorous and time-consuming investigations, several of the top prospects for 2009 remained unsigned months after July 2, though the skyrocketing bonuses from 2008 combined with an economic recession also played a role.

It's easy, perhaps even fashionable, to blame the corruption on Major League Baseball. Yet while there are things that MLB could do to improve the situation—instituting in May 2008 a one-year suspension for players caught misrepresenting their ages or identities was a long overdue move—those closely involved in Latin American scouting say the problem goes beyond what MLB can control.

Identifying papers in the Dominican Republic are not warehoused the way they are in the United States. Birth certificates aren't notarized the way they are in the United States and are often subject to forgery. Sometimes the changes to birth certificates or school records are made with something as basic as Wite-Out, but the cover-ups can be more elaborate. Some of it is nearly untraceable; one agent recalled a player who signed using the birth certificate of a younger brother who died at birth as "a buscone's dream."

"These buscones will move a mountain if they can to get kids signed for big money," another agent said. "It's important to be informed and have a good legal team, and do things the right way. MLB has been doing a better job, but the issue is really in the country. It's not really an issue where MLB can go in and structure how these birth certificates are administered."

MLB has tried to move quickly within the last year to improve its investigations in Latin America. When a team agrees to terms with a player for a contract, that player must first pass MLB's investigation. Teams will also request that MLB investigate some of the more prominent players in advance of July 2. Lou Melendez, MLB's vice president of international baseball operations, told *Sports Illustrated* in March that two investigators were fired this year, one for "sloppy" work, the other for the "mishandling of funds." Three other investigators were fired in the spring of 2008, at least one of them for accepting bribes.

MLB's New York-based department of investigations, which was created in January 2008 at the recommendation of the Mitchell Report, took over the investigations of ages and identities after the Gonzalez scandal. The department hired eight new investigators—including six native Spanish speakers with backgrounds in law enforcement and narcotics enforcement, with two of its most recent hires working full-time in the Dominican Republic—as well as two analysts and a support staff.

The investigators are given lie detector tests and have their cases reviewed by people with backgrounds in investigations. In the past, the people reviewing the investigations didn't necessarily have that background, which led to poor quality control and made it easier for investigators to have two sources of income: one from their employer and one from whomever wanted to bribe them in exchange for a clean investigation.

"They've tried to improve the investigation process as a whole," said a National League international scouting director. "MLB spent a lot of time hiring new investigators, changing the protocol, which needs to be done from the clubs' standpoint because we have to have some faith because we rely on what they tell us. If they clear the investigation, we're assuming the identity and age is correct."

The investigators have tools at their disposal, but each one has its limitations. Investigators can conduct a DNA test on a player, but all that does is verify if the people the player claims are his parents are his real parents; it does nothing to verify age. Growth plate testing and bone grafts that some teams perform on players provide an estimated age range on a player, but the tests' margins for error are large enough to prevent the pinpoint accuracy necessary for this purpose.

Just as important for investigators is the field work. After getting a player's birth certificate from the government, an investigator will go to the hospital the player was born in and get a hospital certificate. School records are scrutinized to look for any inconsistencies in the records. Investigators also go into the player's neighborhood to interview family, friends, neighbors, teachers and anyone else who might be able to verify or dispel a player's true identity.

While the fraud gets more media attention now than it did in the past, players misrepresenting their ages is nothing new. Miguel Tejada, Vladimir Guerrero, Rafael Furcal, Tony Pena and Edinson Volquez are just a handful of the prominent players who use different birth dates now than when they signed. The difference today is that top international amateur free agents have become exponentially more expensive to sign. It creates more risk for teams and provides more incentive for players and trainers to fudge their ages.

"It's been a problem for years," one long-time scout said. "It's not a new thing. The hardest part is, if a guy can throw 95 and he's 15 years old, this is a phenom. This is a guy from another planet. But even if he's older, you still want to sign him because you can see the talent. The problem is, are you going to give him $3 million? There are kids who did it right, they have the right age, but they're throwing 89-91, and maybe when they're 20 they might be 94-95. But that kid might get passed up and have to settle for less money."

Others suggest that, while players lying about their ages has been going on for years, it has become more commonplace recently and the tactics used to deceive teams have become more difficult to trace if parents can obtain false documents for their children at a very young age.

"They've been telling people to do this for the last 15 years," said one Latin American agent, "and now is pretty much when all the papers are going to be older. Fifteen years later is when we're actually seeing the backlash. The kids getting caught these days are the parents who just didn't know about it when their sons were born, and they're trying to fudge it and it's past the fact."

One international scouting director relayed a story about how one prominent Dominican minor league prospect showed up to a tryout camp his team held claiming to be 16. Two years later, the same player showed up and again claimed to be 16. The scout said he wasn't fooled, but the player signed a seven-figure bonus with another organization.

The industry itself could better allocate its resources if teams worked cooperatively to report which players aren't who they claim to be (or to report any other misappropriate conduct), but having a competitor spend $1 million of its budget on a player lying about his age is an advantage for the team that has done its homework.

"You go to the school, hospital, other records and the kid's neighborhood," said a National League international scouting director. "You do all that, the only way you're going to be deceived is if the guy does an incredible job deceiving. The record-keeping in Venezuela is more modernized, more records—it's harder to commit fraud. But people find a way to do it, because where there's money there's a way."

While the problem of players misrepresenting their ages seems to be more widespread in the Dominican Republic, it's still an issue in Venezuela. The record-keeping in Venezuela is more advanced than it is in the Dominican Republic, but the political climate in Venezuela makes it more difficult for MLB to conduct a thorough investigation.

"The Venezuelan government isn't as open as it is in the Dominican Republic," said one agent. "The U.S. and MLB comes into the D.R. and they can knock over tables and look at everything. If Venezuela says a kid is 16 or 17, MLB can't do as much."

Commissioner Bud Selig has talked about MLB's push for some type of worldwide draft, though the purpose of the draft would be to curtail skyrocketing bonuses rather than reducing age manipulation.

Whether or not an international draft of any magnitude is logistically possible, the increased signing bonuses have magnified the age fraud in Latin America and increased the frustration of international scouts. Not only are potentially millions of dollars at stake, but the time and resources it takes to properly evaluate a player within the disorganized environment of Latin American scouting creates a significant opportunity cost that goes down the drain if a player isn't who he claims to be. It also means that international scouts have to be part scout, part Sherlock Holmes.

"It just makes everyone's job tougher," said an American League international scouting director. "Unfortunately, we live in an age where part of your job is not only evaluating players but the extent you can evaluate their age. You go to the neighborhood, go to the school—you almost have to play investigator as a scout because your reputation is on the line.

"If I ask one of my scouts if he did a background check and he tells me no, I just tell him you're not doing your job. You don't want to count on MLB completely. Part of your job should be getting to know the kid. Nobody should know the kid better than the scout who is supposed to be evaluating."

The stakes aren't quite as high for those of us who try to project players at either the amateur or professional level when we don't have millions of dollars at stake. From the evidence we have based on players we know misrepresented themselves when they signed and the shortcomings of MLB's investigations process, we cannot place a 100 percent confidence in a Latin American player's age when attempting to project his future talent level.

For established major league players, an age difference of one or two years might not make a huge impact on his year-to-year projections. But two years can be critical for minor league prospects. A 21-year-old mashing in the high Single-A Florida State League is usually a promising prospect. A 23-year-old doing the same is much less notable.

But as Esmailyn Gonzalez and others have proven, players can get away with shaving more than just a couple of years off their ages. Pablo Ozuna, Baseball America's No. 8 prospect entering the 1999 season, went from future star to fringe big leaguer overnight when it was revealed that he was four years older than he presented himself to be when he signed. There are certainly many more players we will never know about who misrepresented their ages to sign and never reached the big leagues.

While MLB has improved its processes, it's a problem that teams and analysts will have to deal with for the foreseeable future.

"There's always going to be a deal here and there, unfortunately," said an international scouting director. "It's going to continue to happen no matter what you're going to do because people never think they're going to get caught. But people are getting fed up with it."

The Baseball Biz in 2009

by Brian Borawski

In many ways, the 2008 season marked the end of an impressive run for baseball. It was the first time in five years that the majors didn't set an attendance record and the postseason was played with the backdrop of one of the biggest stock market crashes in our history. Many felt 2009 was going to be a unique year. From September on, at least outside of baseball, the news was mostly bad; as I write this, the unemployment rate is just under 10 percent with the expectation of more job losses.

The economic downturn has had a significant effect on the baseball landscape, one that still is being played out, and will probably have an impact on the sport for years to come. Still, not all of the news was bad. New York opened two new stadiums, attendance took a big dip that could have been a lot worse and minor league baseball held its own. The elephant in the room, though, is how long this downturn is going to last and what its lasting effects will be on the sport.

Attendance: Back To 2004

It's funny how you can spin just about anything. MLB had its worst attendance since 2004, a year it drew 73,022,969. But 2009's attendance of 73,418,479 was also the fifth highest of all time, so while there was a big downturn, the league just went back to where it was when the recent upturn started.

For the first time since 2002, the New York Yankees did not lead the majors in attendance. This year's crown went to the Los Angeles Dodgers, who sold 3,761,669 tickets. That's the second most in Dodgers history, less then 100,000 short of their 2007 record. Last year's World Series champions, the Philadelphia Phillies, set a team record with 3,600,693, third overall in baseball.

In the American League, the Yankees' 3,719,358 tickets sold fell well short of 2008's AL record 4,298,543. The past year's figure also broke a streak of four straight seasons over four million, but it's the seventh straight year the Yankees have led the American League in attendance. The Yankees' division rival, the Boston Red Sox, managed to squeeze more fans into Fenway Park and set a franchise record with 3,062,699. The Los Angeles Angels of Anaheim, who have finished second in American League attendance to the Yankees the past six seasons, also topped the three million mark for the sixth straight time.

Only the Phillies and Red Sox set team attendance records; seven teams did in 2008. Nine teams sold more then three million tickets compared to 10 the year before. Nineteen teams topped the two million mark, down from 23 in 2008 and 24 in 2007.

For the first time since 2005, the Florida Marlins weren't at the bottom of the attendance list and it's the first time since 2004 that a team from Florida didn't claim the dubious distinction. In 2009, it was the Oakland Athletics that finished last with 1,408,783 tickets sold. A tough economy combined with a bad baseball team doesn't do a franchise any good at the gate. The Marlins did finish 29th despite being in the playoff race most of the year, but their 1,464,109 tickets sold was an 8.8 percent increase. It'll be interesting to see what the Marlins do to entice fans into Dolphin Stadium in anticipation of their new ballpark that's set to open in 2012.

For the first time since 2001, when Barry Bonds and the San Francisco Giants led the way, a National League team led baseball in road attendance. The Chicago Cubs led with an average of 34,931, just ahead of the Yankees' 34,475. Last year's winner, the Red Sox, finished third with 33,869 per game. The Cubs benefited from strong attendance in the NL Central. The St. Louis Cardinals and Milwaukee Brewers were both in the top 10 in attendance, with the Houston Astros at number 13. The Red Sox' road dip was attributable to the Yankees' big home attendance decrease. There was a lot of weakness even when it came to popular teams drawing in road ballparks.

The big question is where things go from here. The stock market is up from its lows but it isn't likely to reach any records anytime soon. We're in the middle of what many are calling a jobless recovery, but there are still several risks. Unemployment may be even higher by the beginning of next season. This means a lot of people who were on the fence but bought in 2009 might be looking to give up their season tickets in 2010.

There's also the chance that the 2006 through 2008 period, when attendance topped 76 million each year and peaked just under 80 million in 2008, was an anomaly. We might look back five or 10 years from now and call it an attendance bubble that popped along with the credit and real estate bubbles. My prediction is that things keep going down. There's even a chance we could see attendance drop to below 70 million for the first time since 2003. The patterns probably will be regional, though. The Red Sox, Yankees, Cubs and Dodgers should continue to sell well, but teams like the Detroit Tigers and Milwaukee Brewers, coming off near-record highs and disappointing seasons, are likely to see further slides.

One final concern is with revenue. While attendance was down, it was still good historically, but I'm curious to see what teams did to get fans into the parks. If tickets across the board were discounted significantly just to get to 2004's level, then baseball could be headed for some problems, because teams will be paying most of their players at 2007-2008 levels for some years to come. That could hurt the bottom line. We should start seeing the effect of this during the offseason: If some marquee free agents are looking at significantly lower salaries than you'd expect, you will know the teams are hurting.

The State Of Minor League Baseball

Minor League Baseball's downturn was less severe. With the minors being a more affordable, fan-friendly option for baseball fans, this shouldn't surprise, but there still wasn't enough support to help the minors to a sixth straight attendance record. Overall attendance came in at 41,644,518 over 10,269 games, an average attendance of 4,055. This compares to an overall attendance of 43.2 million fans in 2008, but because of all the games lost to weather in 2009, average attendance dropped just 2.9 percent, or 119 fans per game.

Two Triple-A teams opened new ballparks in 2009, with the Columbus Clippers playing their first game in Huntington Park and the Gwinnett Braves opening Gwinnett Stadium. The new park helped elevate the Clippers to the top of the minor league attendance list with an overall attendance of 666,797. Gwinnett didn't have as successful an opening: Its average attendance was well short of capacity, with an average draw of 5,965. While this is in part due to the tough economy in the Atlanta area, the fact that Gwinnett is actually competing with the Atlanta Braves because of their proximity can't help either.

The Florida State League showed the biggest improvement in year over year attendance with a 12.2 percent increase from 2008, and the Midwest League set an attendance record for the third consecutive year. Leading the Midwest League was the Dayton Dragons, who have sold out every game in their 10-year history. Their 704 consecutive sellouts are the second most by a professional team; they trail only the NBA's Portland Trailblazers, who sold out 814 consecutive games.

My prediction is that, as in 2009, we see a slight downturn in 2010. However, I don't think the downturn will be as bad as in MLB. Families strapped for cash view a minor league game as a nice weekend activity, while taking a family to a major league game is viewed by many as an extravagance. As with the majors, though, attendance will vary by region, and venues will matter more than in years past.

Stadium Games

Two new ballparks opened in the city of New York in 2009, both with high expectations and both with extra financing from public bonds to get the stadiums ready for Opening Day. The 21st century edition of Yankee Stadium opened on April 16, and it didn't take long to determine that this was going to be a hitters' park. It also didn't take long for the Yankees to realize that they might have made some pricing mistakes, with the Legends Suite section running as high as $2,625 a seat. The Yankees cut their prices once it became embarrassing to have those seats empty when they were on national television.

The Mets opened Citi Field, and while the ballpark was nice enough, the team fell flat. With the bullpen a concern in their prior two end-of-season collapses, the Mets got relievers Francisco Rodriguez and J.J. Putz, but Rodriguez was nowhere near as effective as he was the year before and Putz, along with many of the team's other big names, landed on the disabled list. The result was a 70-92 finish, and the poor season showed at the attendance booths. A year after becoming one of just four teams ever to top four million in attendance, the Mets had less than a 93 percent capacity with an attendance just over three million in their brand new ballpark.

The only new major league park set to open for the foreseeable future is Target Field, which will be the new home of the Minnesota Twins starting in 2010. It'll be interesting to see how the state of Minnesota handles an open air stadium, especially in April, but early reviews on the ballpark have it as one of the nicest in baseball.

The Florida Marlins had to push back the projected opening of their new ballpark from 2011 to 2012 after legal and bureaucratic problems caused several delays, but ground finally was broken on July 18, 2009.

While the Marlins got their stadium deal pushed through, the Athletics gave up on their Fremont, Calif., stadium in late February. Without a backup plan, the Athletics began trying to line up potential suitors, with San Jose topping the list. In June, the Athletics asked San Jose to hold off on a public referendum until next year so they can sort out their situation with the league. San Jose is in the San Francisco Giants' territory and it looks like the A's are playing it safe rather then trying to cut a deal with their cross-bay rivals after the fact.

In the midst of news about new or prospective construction, the city of Detroit lost its historic ballpark. After the Old Tiger Stadium Conservancy failed to convince Detroit officials to keep a portion of the stadium for amateur games, the old home of the Detroit Tigers was torn down. Had the group succeeded, it would have been the first time a former big league ballpark was at least partially preserved. Unfortunately, the shortsightedness of the city didn't allow that to happen.

Baseball Teams for Sale

There was plenty of activity in the MLB transactions department in 2009. You had some actual team sales and quite a few rumors, most of which centered on someone's financial hardships.

Things kicked off before 2008 even ended as Tribune Company, the owner of the Cubs and Wrigley Field, filed for bankruptcy. In a process that has been dragging out like the Montreal Expos' sale, Sam Zell has been trying to sell the Cubs ever since acquiring the Tribune Company in 2007. Zell needed a ton of debt to make the purchase and one of the assets he determined to sell to pay off some of that debt was the Cubs. To make things even more complicated, he also owned a piece of the Chicago White Sox. A year and change later, the company sat in Chapter 11 bankruptcy and was more or less looking for ways to raise big chunks of cash. Whether this helped expedite things isn't clear, because here we are almost a year later, and while a purchaser and a price have been accepted, the sale still hadn't closed at season's end.

The question was whether to sell the Cubs and Wrigley Field together or separately. Twice, the Cubs were in talks to sell the ballpark to the Illinois Sports Facility Authority, but a deal was never consummated. This left Tribune with the option of selling the Cubs and Wrigley as a package, and in January Tom Ricketts, whose family founded TD Ameritrade, came forward as the head of the group that would buy the team.

Major League Baseball has approved the $845 million sale, but as of mid-October one more bankruptcy court OK is still needed before it could become final. Even then we may hear more. Tribune Company is using some aggressive tax planning to defer a large tax hit on the sale. This shouldn't hold up the sale, but it wouldn't surprise me if the Internal Revenue Service takes a good long look at the deal.

Near the first of the year, Kevin McClatchy divested himself of the last of his share in the Pittsburgh Pirates. After several losing seasons, McClatchy stepped down as the managing partner and has since just served on the board. This transaction finalized his relationship with the Pirates.

Around the same time, the San Diego Padres were sold. After months of speculation surrounding his divorce, John Moores agreed to sell the Padres to Jeff Moorad, the former agent and chief executive officer of the Arizona Diamondbacks. Moores plans to sell his 90 percent stake in the team over the next five years, but Moorad has effectively taken control. The team's former chief executive, Sandy Alderson, departed and Moorad took over that function as well.

With the financial turmoil came several rumors. Tom Hicks, the owner of the Texas Rangers, became late on his debt payments on March 31. Like Tribune (but without the bankruptcy) he needs to do some liquidation, so he's testing the waters by putting the team up for sale. Hicks has valued the team at $600 million, but the final number, in this buyers' market, probably will come in well south of that. Six prospective buyers have shown an interest and while names haven't been announced, Nolan Ryan's has popped up, as has Fort Worth auto dealer David McDavid's. Still, Hicks doesn't appear motivated to do a quick sale, so odds are nothing will get done until next season at the earliest.

In December 2008, Bernie Madoff's $65 billion Ponzi scheme was uncovered. One loser was Mets owner Fred Wilpon. It hasn't been revealed exactly how much Wilpon lost, but rumors began to fly when Erin Arvedlund's book on the Madoff scandal was being publicized. She said that it wasn't a matter of if but when Wilpon would sell the team and that his losses were estimated at $700 million. Wilpon said the number is a lot lower and that he has no interest in selling the Mets.

Heading into 2010, there's a lot of uncertainty in the economy. Assuming Wilpon isn't blowing smoke, the only pending sale on the horizon concerns the Rangers. Still, it wouldn't surprise me if another owner or two reveals that his market losses are forcing him to sell his the team.

War in the Desert

For the past few years, we've seen team after team move spring training from Florida to Arizona. In 2010, the Cincinnati Reds will become the latest team to make the move. They'll share a two-team facility in Goodyear with the Cleveland Indians. That will mean that the Cactus League will have as many teams as the Grapefruit League in 2010.

There's also an intrastate change coming. In June, both the Colorado Rockies and Arizona Diamondbacks announced that they were going to leave their spring training home in Tucson. A month later they chose a new site, the Salt River Indian Reservation in Arizona. The problem is, they plan on playing in their new facility in 2011, but both have leases with the city of Tucson that extend beyond that. Odds are it'll either go to court or the teams will have to buy off the city, as the Chicago White Sox did when they paid Pima County $5 million so they could begin playing in their new facility.

This obviously is making cities skittish. At this writing, the city of Mesa was in negotiations with the Chicago Cubs to make sure that team stood pat.

Summing Things Up

The economy is still running near empty and it looks like it's going to be the consumer who's the last to recover. This can't be good for baseball, so I'd expect an even more tepid free agent season and another drop at the gate. I don't think we'll drop below 70 million in attendance, but a mark close to 71 million might be realistic. Also, keep an eye on what teams have to do to get those fans in the seats. If there are more fire sales of tickets, that can only mean even tougher times ahead because that will hit the teams' bottom line.

One final thing to keep in mind is that the latest—and friendliest ever—collective bargaining agreement between players and management is set to expire after the 2011 season. That seems like a long way away, but the poor economic backdrop might be a way for the owners to get some of the concessions they've been wanting, so you'll probably begin to see some jockeying as early as this offseason. I have a feeling we'll be hearing from Bud Selig and others about how bad things are right now and how bad they're going to get. But it's hard to sort through the noise because of all the mystery surrounding a given team's financial situation.

Serious Aches and Pains

by Corey Dawkins

The human body can endure a tremendous amount of pain and damage and still perform at a high level. During my time at a major Division I football and baseball program, I quickly realized that a player is 100 percent healthy only when he takes the preseason physical. I also realized that relatively few injuries ever show up in the media reports.

Sports medicine has advanced dramatically in the last 25-30 years. Surgeries that once were considered career-ending are becoming close to routine. We will never be able to get to the point of predicting or avoiding every injury or recovery, but we are reaching a point where we can somewhat predict certain injuries in professional sports. The game would be very different if there were no Tommy John survivors and scoring would not be nearly as high without players getting stronger through strength and conditioning exercises. Whether you're involved in the actual game or you're a fantasy competitor, it is critical to gain a greater understanding of injuries.

The evolution of sports medicine and injury-tracking has led me to believe that there is a common group of signs and symptoms for injuries to the lower back, elbow and shoulder. One crucial piece to gaining an advantage is recognizing these signs and symptoms early.

Good baseball general managers recognize this and try to be proactive in their approach to injuries, especially with pitchers. Bad general managers are those who, among their other failures, don't focus on the risk/reward of potential injuries. Professionals put in countless hours rummaging through all sorts of information to try to get a competitive edge. Players, managers and general managers go through an immense amount of film, tables of statistics, scouting reports and injury information.

Injury information is just like any other piece of information: It helps someone make a more informed decision and helps reduce the risk associated with the decision. As people understand why repeated elbow inflammation and tendinitis can be indicative of the need for future Tommy John surgery or why pitchers with repeated biceps tendinitis are likely to require surgery on their labrum eventually, they can begin to make proactive decisions regarding their personnel. Making proactive decisions is key to running any team in professional or fantasy baseball: It allows you to find hidden value, but even more importantly, it prevents overpaying for someone who will not produce daily.

It has been extremely difficult to find consistent and helpful information about injuries in one centralized location. No one has the time or the patience to search through hundreds of player pages to find all the information about injuries. Here, I've gathered that information for you. As of this writing, in my database, I have all major league disabled list transactions dating back to 2001, day-to-day injuries for 2009, major offseason injuries to major league players and high level prospects and most of the DL transactions for the minor leagues in 2009. By the start of 2010, I will have all minor league DL transactions dating back to 2001. When I reference numbers from here on out, it is from my database unless otherwise noted.

Lower Back Injuries

The first type of injury to be wary of is multiple instances of lower back problems. In my data set I have 252 instances (164 players) in which a lower back injury of some sort caused a player to miss time. Even though there are not many clear diagnoses of bulging or herniated discs, several different injuries usually occur before such determinations. Each lower back surgical case was preceded by 3.28 other bouts of lower back pain/injury, compared to the 0.28 for athletes who didn't require surgery.

Imagine the spine and discs as the foundation of a house. The first problems with a bad foundation typically aren't cracks in the foundation walls but small issues throughout the house. There may be cracks in the walls somewhere in the house (muscle strains) or the doors and windows may jam when opened (inflammation and spasms). It's not until a couple of these things happen that it's recommended to look at the foundation. By that time, the problem is usually significant enough that some sort of repair is required to the foundation or its supporting structures. Inflammation, spasms and strains can occur because the discs are the basic stabilizing structure for everything else to work. Sports medicine professionals believe that if the core is weak or compromised, there is a much greater chance of injury to anything connected to it. Strains and spasms occur because of the body's innate instinct to protect the spine from excess motion. If the discs don't provide that stability, it has to come from somewhere.

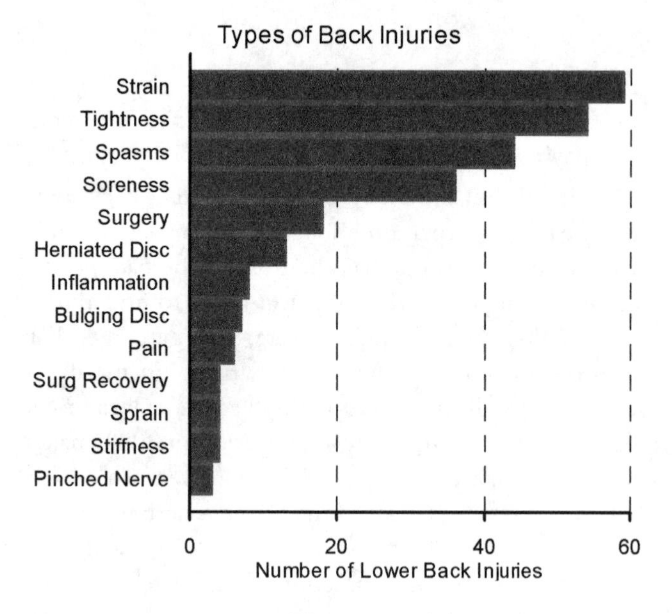

Playing baseball requires a lot of torsion, shearing and compression forces, so having a strong lower back and core is essential to the overall health of the athlete. If a player's lower back is dysfunctional, it can lead to problems in other areas of the body such as the shoulder and elbow. The crux of the problem with lower back injuries isn't that they often require surgery, it's that they tend to silently sap production. Repeated injuries without specific mechanisms usually indicate an underlying chronic pathology. In the case of repeated lower back injuries, the first thing I worry about is that something may be wrong with the discs that could end up requiring surgery.

Herniated and bulging discs also become part of the process known as degenerative disc disease. That basically occurs as everyone ages, but it also is accelerated during activities associated with baseball such as repeated jumping and twisting movements. As the condition worsens, the tougher outer part of the disc can have small tears, allowing the more fluid inside part of the disc to bulge out or, worse, become herniated and break into fragments. Once the injury reaches these last stages, usually the only way for baseball players to truly have relief is to undergo surgery

A classic example is Mark Kotsay's DL history, which is listed below.

Kotsay has quite an extensive injury history with his lower back. There was a time when he was quite useful to the Oakland A's and in AL-only fantasy leagues. In 2004 and 2005 he was a decent third outfielder with some pop, hitting 15 home runs in each of those seasons. Fantasy managers should have known to drop or trade him when the repeated cases of inflammation, spasms, strains or tightness/stiffness in his lower back came to light. They would have avoided his horrible 2006 season, when he hit only seven home runs and drove in barely 50 despite having more than 500 at-bats, not to mention the 2007 season in which he underwent surgery in spring training and finished with fewer than 230 at-bats.

Mark Kotsay's Injury History

Date On	Date Off	Position	Body Part	Injury	Severity Description	Surgery Date
04/23/2003	04/26/2003	OF	Low Back	Spasms		
5/19/2003	06/05/2003	OF	Low Back	Strain		
08/18/2003	08/19/2003	OF	Low Back	Spasms		
06/04/2005	06/07/2005	OF	Low Back	Spasms		
07/25/2005	07/31/2005	OF	Low Back	Spasms		
08/08/2005	08/11/2005	OF	Low Back	Spasms		
08/29/2005	09/06/2005	OF	Low Back	Spasms		
06/15/2006	06/20/2006	OF	Low Back	Spasms		
08/07/2006	08/14/2006	OF	Low Back	Spasms		
09/03/2006	09/04/2006	OF	Low Back	Tightness		
09/07/2006	09/15/2006	OF	Low Back	Spasms		
03/23/2007	06/01/2007	OF	Low Back	Surgery	Herniated Disc	03/10/2007
08/05/2007	08/10/2007	OF	Low Back	Spasms		
08/15/2007	10/01/2007	OF	Low Back	Soreness		
05/26/2008	07/01/2008	OF	Low Back	Soreness		
01/29/2009	03/27/2009	OF	Low Back	Surgery	Microdiscectomy	01/29/2009
3/27/2009	06/02/2009	OF	Low Back	Recovery from Surgery	Microdiscectomy	01/29/2009

The Elbow and Tommy John Surgery

Spinal disc injuries are not the only ones that are somewhat predictable. Tommy John surgeries have claimed seasons or parts of multiple seasons of 118 players (47 starting pitchers, 54 relievers, 17 position players). How many times have you heard about a pitcher (usually) complaining about forearm cramping, tightness or inflammation, then coming back to pitch? Then, either later that season or the following season, after it's originally been reported that the pitcher will be shut down for a few weeks to reduce inflammation, he ends up on the surgeon's table. His career gets a new lease on life after undergoing Tommy John surgery and he is out for 12 to18 months. To explain why this occurs, let's look at some anatomy around the elbow.

The ulnar collateral ligament (UCL) is composed of three bands of tissue that lie on the medial (inside) aspect of the elbow. It connects the two largest bones in the upper extremity, the humerus to the ulna, which prevents what's called a valgus force. ("Valgus" means turning outward, or twisting.) To imagine this force, with the palm facing forward, keep your elbow and upper arm stationary and then have someone move your forearm toward your thumb.

Directly over the UCL is a large muscle mass known as the flexor/pronator mass. Those muscles contract to pronate the hand/forearm (turning the hand over from seeing your palm to seeing the back of your hand) and also flexes the wrist. This muscle mass is extremely important in providing dynamic stability to the medial elbow in addition to the static stability provided by the UCL. This stability is most tested in the late cocking stage and the acceleration phases of pitching, when a valgus force is placed on the medial elbow and it gaps open.

The relationship of the ligament to the flexor/pronator mass is so important that I want to go into a little further detail to explain why we see the progression from tendinitis to Tommy John surgery. Everything is related:

1. If we assume the ligament is normal, the flexor/pronator mass does not have to work as hard to stabilize the medial elbow, allowing it to focus its energy on other aspects of pitching.
2. If the ligament is loose, the flexor mass must absorb valgus forces that it was not designed for, which leads to microscopic breakdowns resulting in inflammation and tendinitis in the flexor/pronator mass.
3. If we assume the flexor mass to be compromised, the UCL will be damaged further as the muscle fatigues earlier and a greater amount of stress must be absorbed through the ligament, leading to microscopic failure of the ligament, and eventually its complete disruption.
4. Compounding the situation, the ligament almost always tears from the inside out, involving the deepest layer of the ligament first and then progressing to the outer layers as the injury worsens. Therefore, it is difficult to diagnose the early stages of ligament damage on normal MRIs.

An example of this is Anthony Reyes, who had Tommy John surgery after repeated bouts of elbow inflammation last year. Once one of the Cardinals' top prospects, he was the first player from the team's 2003 draft class to make it to the majors. That was in 2005, before injuries and ineffectiveness caused the Cardinals to trade him to Cleveland. In 2006, arm fatigue cost him nine days. In 2007 he had shoulder soreness and missed the final couple of weeks of the season.

The next year, the problems in his elbow showed up: He twice was limited by elbow inflammation, costing him 19 days in one stretch, 23 in another. Then, unfortunately, it all caught up with him. He underwent Tommy John surgery and ulnar nerve transposition surgery on June 12, 2009. This is why it is important to monitor players with a history of injuries in the kinetic chain: It provides an important early warning that something is off and, if taken care of properly, surgery may be able to be avoided.

Shoulder Injuries

Injuries to the shoulder are almost a last frontier for sports medicine in baseball. Velocity is often the first thing to be affected by shoulder problems, with control being the first sign of an elbow issue. While it's not an everyday thing, I have 130 players since 2001 in the database with multiple instances of shoulder inflammation, tendinitis, strain, impingement, fatigue, weakness and soreness—more than 800 total shoulder injuries.

The shoulder is a complex joint with secondary attachments from the hips to the skull and elbow to the spine. It has the most mobility of any single joint in the body, but unfortunately that comes with a price of stability. Because of its inherent skeletal instability, it greatly relies on the dynamic stability provided by the musculature. The rotator cuff, long head of the biceps, pectoralis major, deltoids and latissimus dorsi muscles are all major stabilizers of the shoulders, so when one of these is injured in any way, the stability of the shoulder joint also is affected. Much like lower backs, everything needs to be working perfectly to function properly.

The rotator cuff is generally well known for its role in the shoulder's health, but the biceps is less well understood. The long head of the biceps is important because it is attached directly into the labrum and often is involved in a specific type of labral tear known as the SLAP tear. SLAP tears come in all shapes and sizes and some do not even include the biceps tendon, but no matter what, it is a debilitating injury. When the biceps becomes fatigues or injured, the biomechanics of that attachment site changes and at the very least microscopic failure of the labrum begins.

One of the best examples I came across for this is Jason Schmidt. He was extremely effective in 2003 and 2004, striking out more than 200 batters in 2003 and more than 250 in 2004. His disabled list history is laid out in the table at the bottom of the page.

So we saw three instances of shoulder injury before he required surgery in 2007. We had episodes in successive years in 2004 and 2005 but then nothing in 2006 until the eventual downturn in 2007. Using my guidelines, we may have missed out on a relatively useful 2006 season, but as soon as he went on the DL again in 2007 with another shoulder injury, a fantasy player should have either traded him immediately or dropped him and picked up someone useful.

Looking Forward

What's in the past is in the past, but most people (particularly fantasy baseball players) want to know what is going to happen next year and beyond. Who do I see having an increased risk in the coming seasons by using these methods?

A.J. Burnett isn't my No. 1 player to avoid for next year, but he is questionable because of what I see about his elbow and other areas. He already has had one Tommy John surgery, in early 2003, but he has continued to have problems with the kinetic chain, specifically his elbow and shoulder. I see several warning signs. First, he's suffered two more bouts of vague symptoms (soreness and inflammation) inside his elbow in 2006 and then two more injuries in the kinetic chain in his shoulder in 2007. Four injuries within the kinetic chain in such a short period of time worries me. Second, his BB/9 has me concerned:

Season	Team	BB/9
1999	Marlins	5.44
2000	Marlins	4.79
2001	Marlins	4.31
2002	Marlins	3.96
2003	Marlins	7.04
2004	Marlins	2.85
2005	Marlins	3.40
2006	Blue Jays	2.59
2007	Blue Jays	3.59
2008	Blue Jays	3.50
2009	Yankees	4.28

Clearly, he already had control issues when he came into the big leagues, but appeared to be improving until the 2003 season. That season he underwent Tommy John surgery, which helped to correct some of his control issues. For a couple of years, his was in good health, but in 2006 and 2007 he had the elbow and shoulder injuries which caused his control to worsen. It has only gotten worse for the last three or four years, including the 2009 season, spiking by around .75 BB/9 in one year. Worsening control to go along with his injury history have me concerned that he will end up on the DL for an extended period next year.

One player I was considering reviewing in my section about back injuries, Joe Crede, announced plans for surgery at the end of the season. Another is Tim Wakefield, whose usefulness in fantasy baseball is

Jason Schmidt's Injury History

Date On	Date Off	Position	Body Part	Injury	Severity Description	Surgery Date
03/26/2004	04/14/2004	SP	Shoulder	Tendinitis	Rotator Cuff	
05/08/2005	05/24/2005	SP	Shoulder	Strain		
04/17/2007	06/05/2007	SP	Shoulder	Bursitis		
06/18/2007	09/30/2007	SP	Shoulder	Surgery	Labrum, Biceps Tendon, Bursa	06/20/2007
03/21/2008	09/28/2008	SP	Shoulder	Recovery from Surgery	Labrum, Biceps Tendon, Bursa	06/20/2007
09/10/2008	09/10/2008	SP	Shoulder	Surgery	Scar Tissue, AC joint arthritis	09/10/2008
03/30/2009	07/20/2009	SP	Shoulder	Recovery from Surgery	Scar Tissue, AC joint arthritis	09/10/2008
08/07/2009		SP	Shoulder	Soreness	from surgery	09/10/2008

extremely suspect because of his age (43) and the unpredictable nature of the knuckleball. A better example is Chris Snyder, whom I would avoid even though he was predicted to have a breakout year in 2009 and catching talent is always at a premium.

Catchers have a tremendous amount of wear and tear on their knees and their lower backs. Squatting at least 150 times per game 150 times per year, not including the rigors of travel, spring training and hitting four or five times a game, breaks a player down rather quickly. Few catchers catch every day anymore, and those who do tend to wear down as the season progress. Snyder was placed on the DL twice in 2009 (June 19-July 28 and Aug. 26 to the end of the year) with issues related to a bulging disc in his low back. After being diagnosed with a lower back strain the first time, he underwent further testing after the second incident and was diagnosed with the bulging disc; he was contemplating surgery as the season wound down. Even if he doesn't undergo surgery, I would avoid him because generally these conditions do not heal themselves.

I also recommend avoiding Roy Oswalt. For all his grit and guile, he has been breaking down a lot lately, with injuries being mentioned 14 times since the beginning of 2008. He has suffered hip strains, numbness in his hand and fingers, and multiple bouts of lower back soreness and inflammation. Since 2005, he has suffered at least six instances of lower back injury. I am concerned that in July 2008, he was officially diagnosed with a mild herniated disc (L5) which has worsened to the point that it has given him problems four more times. The herniated disc is pressing on the nerves coming out of his spine and causing numbness and tingling down his left leg.

After receiving a second opinion in the fall of 2009, he is determined to focus on strengthening his core in hopes he can avoid surgery. The fact that he needed to get a second opinion on his back, coupled with his history, is more than enough for me to recommend avoiding him.

For the shoulder, the biggest fantasy impact would be Max Scherzer. During his senior season in college, he battled shoulder tendinitis multiple times, including within the biceps tendon. That's my main concern. The Diamondbacks were so concerned with his shoulder after they drafted him in 2006 that they had Dr. Lewis Yocum evaluate him to determine whether he required surgery. He did not pitch until late 2007 due to a contract dispute, then had problems ranging from shoulder inflammation in 2008 that shut him down for 30 days due to fatigue in the 2008-2009 offseason before being placed on the disabled list at the start of 2009 with shoulder tightness.

If the same body area being injured five times in four years doesn't scare you enough, looking at the PITCHf/x data will give you additional pause. Velocity is the first thing to go with shoulder injuries, so that's what I'm looking at in PITCHf/x. His velocity, while not atrocious, is similar to where it was when he first went on the DL with shoulder inflammation in 2008. Before going on the DL in 2008, he averaged around 93-94 mph on his fastball, which is what he averaged in 2009. When he came back from the minor league DL in 2008, he was at 95 mph or greater in five of his six starts. For the 2010 season, I would look hard at the combination of his velocity loss, his previous injuries and concerns in his shoulder before drafting him.

Summary

Injuries, for the most part, are unpredictable. But a select few follow a certain path which, if recognized early, can become the competitive advantage that everyone searches for. I know that recognizing injuries early on and following them during their progression provided me with a greater respect for those in the game who deal with roster construction and gave me a greater respect for the game itself. Ultimately, I hope that everyone who reads this has the same feeling—and maybe even gets a fantasy championship or two out of it.

Strong Seasons Leading Index

by Bill James

Kevin Kouzmanoff finished the 2009 season with 18 homers, 88 RBI, a .255 average and a .722 OPS. What are the odds that he will do better than that in 2010? What are the odds that Joey Votto will hit better than the .322 that he hit in 2009, or that Chipper Jones will have a better year than his career-worst 2009 campaign, or that Scott Podsednik will continue to thrive?

This is the kind of question about which we have information all over the map. We know that Chipper Jones is getting up in years. We know that Joey Votto had a .373 in-play batting average in 2009, and we know that he is unlikely to repeat that. We know that Scott Podsednik, who hit .304 in 2009, is not historically a .300 hitter. These things are indicators of the likelihood of a better season.

The goal of this article is to round up as many of these indicators as we can into a single number, thus producing a list of the players who are most likely—and most unlikely—to sustain or improve on their 2009 seasons. I'll explain how I developed the method as I go along.

The first thing I should say is that this method was developed to work with players who had 400 or more plate appearances in their most recent season, and I can demonstrate that it does "work"—it does have predictive value—with players who have 400 or more plate appearances. Whether it would work with players with fewer than 400 plate appearances, I don't know. I wouldn't make any assumptions.

Also, I should warn you at the outset that we are going to get values at the end of the article which average well below 50 percent. This is because if you take most of the players who are regulars in any season, a majority will not have as good a season the next year. Some percentage of players in any group get injured, lose their jobs to a red-hot rookie, stop working hard enough, or just discover that they can't pull the trigger on a fastball. It happens; let's say it's 30 percent. Of the remaining 70 percent percent half will play better, and half will play worse. Since our system looks for players who play as much *and* play as well, the norms tend to be in the 35-40 percent range, rather than 50 percent. If you want players who will *probably* have better seasons, you need to study a different group of players.

Okay, we'll start with age, as age is the most obvious indicator of likely movement. These are the 2009 ages of the players mentioned above, and let's throw a couple more into the mix, just to liven it up:

Kevin Kouzmanoff	27
Joey Votto	25
Chipper Jones	37
Scott Podsednik	33
Jorge Posada	37
Dioner Navarro	25

Age is working for Votto and Navarro, against Jones and Posada. We have a 38-point system, of which nine points are based on age. The formula is:

Int[(39-age)/2]

But not less than zero, not more than nine. If a player is 26 or 27 years old, he gets six points. If he's 36 or 37, he gets one point. The values for these six players are:

Kevin Kouzmanoff	6
Joey Votto	7
Chipper Jones	1
Scott Podsednik	3
Jorge Posada	1
Dioner Navarro	7

So Votto and Navarro are ahead in our race to see who is most likely to have a better year in 2010, and Chipper is in last place. However, we also know that Chipper Jones in 2009 had an OPS of .825, whereas his career mark is more than 100 points higher than that. We also know that players tend to move back toward their historic norms. A player who has an OPS which is 100 points below his historic norm is likely, based on that fact, to have a better season next year.

That's Section B of our system; Section A is age. Section B is OPS compared to career OPS. Section B, Step 1: Subtract the player's OPS in his most recent season from his career OPS. Step 2, credit points as per the chart below:

.225 or higher	10
.175 to .224	9
.125 to .174	8
.075 to .124	7
.025 to .074	6
-.024 to +.024	5
-.025 to -.074	4
-.075 to -.124	3
-.125 to -.174	2
-.175 to -.224	1
-.225 or less	0

There will be a Step 3. Chipper's 2009 OPS was 129 points lower than his career OPS at the end of the 2009 season; that's eight points on the chart above.

Except that it isn't, because the points a player may be credited with in Section B are also constrained by his age. A player whose OPS is 100 points below his career norm at age 26—Grady Sizemore—may be presumed likely to bounce back. A player whose OPS is 100 points below his career norm at age 37 may have reached the end of his career. Yes, we accounted for age separately, but my point is: having an OPS 100 points below your career norm at age 40 is not the same as doing so at age 25.

So Step 3 is, figure the points awarded in Section A (age), add one, and double them. This is the maximum number of points a player may be awarded in Section B of the process. For Chipper, who had one point in Section A, this makes four. Therefore, Chipper gets only four points in Section B, not eight.

Podsednik had a .764 OPS in 2009 vs. a career total of .721; that's -.043, which is four points in this section. Votto had a .981 OPS vs. a career total of .924; that's -.057, which is four points. Kouzmanoff had a .722 OPS against a career norm of .743; that's +.021, which is five points. Navarro had a .583 OPS against a career norm of .676;, that's +.093, which is seven points, and Posada had an .885 OPS against a career norm of .859, which is -026, which is four points:

	Sect A	Sect B
Kevin Kouzmanoff	6	5
Joey Votto	7	4
Chipper Jones	1	4
Scott Podsednik	3	4
Dioner Navarro	7	7
Jorge Posada	1	4

So the scores now are Navarro 14, Votto 11, Kouzmanoff 11, Podsednik seven, Chipper Jones five, Posada five.

The next thing we look at is the Adjusted Ball in Play Average, figured as follows:

Hits

Minus 1.3 times home runs

Plus at-bats/30

Divided by at-bats, minus home runs, minus strikeouts

The highest Adjusted Ball in Play Average ever with 400 or more at-bats, was by Jesse Burkett in 1895, .461. The highest since 1900 was by George Sisler in 1922, .452. Jose Hernandez in 2002 had an Adjusted Ball in Play Average of .439.

The adjustment is made because players who hit home runs tend to hit the ball harder than players who don't hit home runs (duh). Because they hit the ball harder, they have higher in-play averages.

We're trying to reason that a player with a high in-play average is likely to decline next season because he is unlikely to sustain his high in-play average; this is generally known. However, he is *more* likely to sustain his high in-play average if he is a power hitter—other things being equal—than if he is a singles hitter. We're adjusting for that by giving the power hitters a little extra credit. The 1/30th at-bats is just a counter-adjustment to make the numbers look a little more normal; I took extra hits out, I put them back in. It doesn't exactly balance; so sue me.

Anyway, we compare the Adjusted Ball in Play Average to the chart below, and award points in Section C as follows:

Less than .260	6 points
.260 to .285	5 points
.286 to .311	4 points
.312 to .337	3 points
.338 to .363	2 points
.364 to .389	1 point
.390 or higher	So solly; no points for you

The historic norm is .325, so the average player gets three points. In 2009 the Adjusted Ball in Play Averages for these players were:

Kevin Kouzmanoff	.319
Joey Votto	.397
Chipper Jones	.320
Scott Podsednik	.377
Jorge Posada	.358
Dioner Navarro	.265

So Navarro gets five points here, Kouzmanoff gets three points here, Chipper gets three, Posada gets two, Podsednik gets one, Votto nothing. Which makes our tallies:

	Sect A	Sect B	Sect C	Total
Kevin Kouzmanoff	6	5	3	14
Joey Votto	7	4	0	11
Chipper Jones	1	4	3	8
Scott Podsednik	3	4	1	8
Jorge Posada	1	4	2	7
Dioner Navarro	7	7	5	19

We can pause for a moment and ask the question, "How do you know that you have the right weight on one factor, as opposed to the others?" The answer, of course, is that I don't know that I have them *exactly* right. However, I went through an orderly and quasi-scientific process to attempt to get the weights right, one versus another. The process was this. I started with a 20-point system, of which five points were based on age, two points were based on the Adjusted Ball In Play Average, and some points were based on things that are no longer part of the system. Using those initial assumptions, I figured a "20 point indicator score" for every player in major league history who had 400 or more plate appearances in a season. Some people had to be thrown out of the study for one reason or another, of course—probably for making out on the school bus—and I wound up with a field of a little more than 16,000 players who could be studied.

I then asked, about each player, "Did he in fact perform at least as well, in the next season, as he had in the base season?" Every player was a "1" or a "0"; 1 if he played at least as well the next season, and 0 if he did not. I'll explain later what the standards were for "played at least as well."

I then figured, for every level of "20 point indicator score," the percentage of players who had had seasons at least as good the next season. Let's say that for players at the level "8," 38 percent had seasons at least as good the next season, whereas for players at the level "12," 54 percent had seasons at least as good the next season.

I then tagged each player to his group norm. Suppose that a player had a 20-point indicator score of "8," but *did* go on to have a good season the next year. That would be a "contribution mark" of +.62—1.00, representing the fact that he *did* have a good season the next year, minus 0.38, representing the expectation that he would. If he was at level 8 and did not have a good season the next year, that would be -0.38. If he was at level 12 and did have a good season the next year, that would be +0.46; if he did not, that would be -0.54.

I then sorted the data by the indicator—in other words, sorted all players in order of age, in order of their Adjusted Ball in Play Average, etc. In this way, it became apparent whether a factor was over-valued or under-valued within the study. Let's say that the ball in play average was under-valued, which it initially was. When I sorted the data by ball in play average, then, the players at the top of the data would under-achieve relative to expectations. That is to say, they would have an aggregate "contribution mark" that was strongly negative, since I was not giving enough weight to the fact that their in play average in the base season was high. In this way, I was able to determine whether a factor had too little or too much weight relative to the other factors being considered.

I then adjusted the weights, worked my way up to a 24 point indicator score, and repeated the process of evaluating whether categories were over-weighted or under-weighted. I then adjusted the weights again, wound up with a 27 point indicator score, and repeated the process. I repeated the process until I was bored silly with the whole thing and couldn't stand to look at it anymore, at which point I decided I was done and would write it up and send it to Dave Studenmund.

Okay, when I was doing this, I kept coming up with the conclusion "we're under-weighting the OPS vs. career OPS factor." It was apparent that a player having a poor year relative to his career norms was the strongest indicator of a player who would likely do better the next season. I started with something like four points dedicated to that, expanded it and expanded it until it got up to 10, at which point it was still testing as under-valued.

It was under-valued, but I was no longer comfortable expanding it in the same format. I decided to test *essentially* the same thing, but in a different way. For Section D, I compared the player's runs scored and RBI to his runs scored and RBI in the previous season. Kouzmanoff, for example, had 71 runs scored in 2008, 84 RBI—a total of 155. In 2009 this total dropped to 138, down 17. I created a system which gave the player more points when this number was low than when it was high—in essence, arguing that when his runs scored and RBI totals go down one year, they are likely to go up the next year. The same thing we were measuring in Section B, but measured in a different way. For our test group, the data for 2009:

Kevin Kouzmanoff	-17
Chipper Jones	-6
Joey Votto	13
Scott Podsednik	86
Jorge Posada	96
Dioner Navarro	-27

And the points were awarded as follows:

-75 or less	6 points
-45 to -74	5 points
-15 to -44	4 points
+14 to -14	3 points
+15 to +44	2 points
+45 to +74	1 point
+75 or more	Get outta heah.

But this time, with no controls for age. Not everybody agrees, but this is my philosophy: The real world is complex and non-linear. Therefore, non-linear approximations resemble the real world much more than "true linear measurements," and therefore imbalanced non-linear approximations are more likely to be useful for prediction than are true measurements. By measuring essentially the same thing in different ways and with different standards, we create a complex non-linear tool, which is more likely to be useful to us than a strict mathematical model.

Anyway, Podsednik and Posada get no points here, Navarro gets four, while the other players get three each. This makes our totals as follows:

	Sect A	Sect B	Sect C	Sect D	Total
Kevin Kouzmanoff	6	5	3	3	17
Joey Votto	7	4	0	3	14
Chipper Jones	1	4	3	3	11
Scott Podsednik	3	4	1	0	8
Jorge Posada	1	4	2	0	7
Dioner Navarro	7	7	5	4	23

Okay, our next measurement, Section E, probably won't make any intuitive sense if I start by explaining the formula, so let me start by explaining the concept. Let's take Ferris Fain in 1950. I know you are all curious about Ferris Fain. He was a short, tough, left-handed hitting first baseman, nicknamed "Burrhead" because he wore a very short haircut and had little wiry hairs poking out all over his scalp. His father had been a professional boxer, and Fain also did some professional boxing early in his life, early in his pro career. Years and years later, when he was near 70, he was arrested and faced some pretty good prison time for cultivating and selling marijuana. He wound up with four months of house arrest. He was an outspoken man and a bit of a bigot with complete contempt for pot smokers, but you know, money is money. It's a market.

So anyway, in 1950 Burrhead hit .282 and with just 10 homers in 151 games, but he had 133 walks and 26 strikeouts; how's that for a strikeout/walk ratio? In other words, his strikeout/walk ratio was vastly better than his overall production.

On the other end of the scale we have ... well, Corey Patterson in 2004, or Cory Snyder in 1986, or Jeff Francoeur in 2006. These guys hit pretty well, but their strikeout/walk ratios were awful. In 2004, Patterson hit .266 with 33 doubles and 24 homers, but his strikeout/walk ratio was 168 to 45. In 1986, Snyder hit .272 with 24 homers in 103 games, but his strikeout/walk ratio was 123 to 16, and in 2006, Francoeur hit .260 with 29 homers and 103 RBIs, but with a strikeout/walk ratio of 132 to 23.

What we're essentially saying here is "I know you had a good year, Jeff (or Corey), but that strikeout/walk ratio is a problem. I really wonder whether you're going to be able to sustain your production with that kind of a strikeout/walk ratio. But as for you, Burrhead ... you're looking good. Your strikeout/walk ratio (five walks for each strikeout) suggests you may have better years ahead."

And, in fact, they did. Snyder fell off to a .236 average in 1987, and his career unraveled from there. You guys know what has happened to Francoeur, and Patterson fell off in 2005 from .266 to .215. Fain, on the other hand, hit .344 the next season, winning the American League batting championship.

Okay, so we have a formula, which is:

1.500 minus
OPS divided by 1.500
Times (walks plus 10)
Divided by (strikeouts plus 10)

I often add in 10 walks and 10 strikeouts so that a strikeout/walk ratio of 10-2 doesn't work out the same as a strikeout/walk ratio of 100-20. Anyway, this formula produces a number greater than 1.00 for a player like Ferris Fain, and a very low number for a player named Cory or Corey. These are the numbers for our test players in 2009:

Kevin Kouzmanoff	.325
Joey Votto	.584
Chipper Jones	1.070
Scott Podsednik	.578
Jorge Posada	.475
Dioner Navarro	.510

This is a four-point test, and our standards are

Over 1.350	4 points
1.000 to 1.349	3 points
.750 to .99999	2 points
.500 to .749999	1 point
Under .5000	No cigar

So Chipper gets three points here, Votto, Navarro and Podsednik get one, and Kouzmanoff and Posada get nothing. This makes our new totals:

	Total
Kevin Kouzmanoff	17
Joey Votto	15
Chipper Jones	14
Scott Podsednik	9
Jorge Posada	7
Dioner Navarro	24

Our next section, Section F, is a one-point test centering on speed. The formula is:

3 times triples
Plus stolen bases
Plus 1/10 at bats
Minus caught stealing
Minus GIDP
All that divided by plate appearances

The 1/10 at-bats is added into the system to prevent the numbers from being negative for guys who ground into double plays; I just didn't want to mess with the negative numbers. The highest figure of the modern era (that is, the era in which caught stealing and GIDP are available) was by Dave Collins in 1984. Collins hit 15 triples, stole 60 bases and did not ground into a double play in 128 games, 441 at-bats, giving him a "score" in this system of .275. The lowest score was by Paul Konerko in 2003—no triples, no stolen bases and 28 GIDP in 444 at-bats, giving him a score of .033.

All that matters is whether you're over .100 or under. If you're over .100, you get the point, if you're under, you don't. It's just a little thing ... speed guys age better than other players, meaning they are more likely to pop up with a good year later in their careers. This is just a small point to acknowledge that and nudge the system in that direction. In our test group we have scores of:

	Score
Kevin Kouzmanoff	.056
Joey Votto	.083
Chipper Jones	.073
Scott Podsednik	.137
Jorge Posada	.060
Dioner Navarro	.065

So Podsednik gets a point, making the new totals:

	Total
Kevin Kouzmanoff	17
Joey Votto	17
Chipper Jones	14
Scott Podsednik	10
Jorge Posada	7
Dioner Navarro	24

Our final two points, Section G, are just a little "central tendency" indicator. Over time, everybody gravitates toward the center. Suppose that you take a group of hitters whose OPS in Season 1 is .950, and a group at .550. In Season 2 the OPS of the top group will drop down to .910 or .920 or something, while the OPS of the bottom group will edge up to .570 or something. Everybody gravitates to the middle.

To adjust for this, we give one point to a player whose OPS in the base season is under .900, and two points to a player whose OPS is under .750. These were the OPS (OPSes? OPI?) of our test players:

	OPS
Kevin Kouzmanoff	.722
Joey Votto	.981
Chipper Jones	.818
Scott Podsednik	.764
Jorge Posada	.885
Dioner Navarro	.583

So Navarro and Kouzmanoff get two points here, Votto gets no point, and the other players get one each. That makes the final totals:

	Total
Kevin Kouzmanoff	19
Joey Votto	15
Chipper Jones	15
Scott Podsednik	11
Jorge Posada	8
Dioner Navarro	26

Navarro was not only the highest-scoring player among these six, but the highest-scoring player in the major leagues. Posada was not only the lowest-scoring player in these six, but the lowest-scoring player in the majors. It is very likely that Dioner Navarro will have a 2010 season at least as good he did in 2009. It is massively unlikely that Jorge Posada will.

What does that mean, "a season as good" as the previous season. What's the standard?

The standard is an OPS within .020 of the base season with at least 80 percent of the plate appearances as in the base season. Let us take Steve Buechele in 1986: 513 plate appearances, .712 OPS. To be considered to have had substantially as good a season in 1987, he has to have at least 411 plate appearances with an OPS at least .692. He actually had 400 plate appearances in 1987 with a .690 OPS, so he fails both tests: His OPS dropped by 22 points, and he had only 78 percent of his at-bats. On the other hand, Mark McLemore in 2002 just cleared both tests. His OPS dropped 16 points and his plate appearances dropped off by 16 percent—but he's clear.

As a practical matter, the great majority of players who qualify as having had at least as good a season have actually had seasons at least slightly better. There is a window there for performance to go down and be regarded as level, but it's a pretty narrow window, whereas the space *above* the bar—as in pole vaulting—is unlimited. It's just awkward to insist that players have a *better* year, because it leads to distinctions that seem silly. If a player's OPS drops one point but his RBIs increase by 30, he would score as a "no" because his OPS went down. That doesn't happen with these standards.

I will demonstrate in just a minute that our process does in fact predict the likelihood of a better season. The highest score ever was by Lou Bierbauer in 1891. Bierbauer:

A) Was just 25 years old, giving him a score of seven out of nine possible in Section A,

B) Had an OPS 136 points below his career OPS through the end of that season (.514 vs. .650), giving him a score of eight out of a possible 10 in Section B,

C) Had an Adjusted Ball in Play Average of .247, giving him six points out of a possible six in Section C,

D) Had only 106 combined runs scored and RBIs after having had 227 the previous season, giving him six points out of a possible six in Section D,

E) Had a very good strikeout to walk ratio relative to his abysmal OPS (28 walks, 19 strikeouts, .514 OPS), giving him four points out of a possible four in Section E,

F) Had a reasonably good speed score, giving him one point out of a possible one in Section F (annoying detail will follow),

G) Had an OPS below .750, giving him two points out of a possible two in Section G.

Altogether, that's 34 points out of a possible 38—the highest score ever. No one else is over 32.

The annoying detail that I enticed you with earlier is this. Players in the game's early history have no official record of caught stealing or GIDP, which interferes with the operation of our speed indicator. Those players, who have no GIDP and no caught stealing because none were recorded, have to have a speed figure of .150, rather than .100, to qualify for the one point. Bierbauer is just over the line, at .151.

Also, on a related point, in Section E we gave the player zero to four points based on a comparison of his productivity versus his strikeout to walk ratio. We have no strikeout data for some early players, so we can't do that. What we did is, we just gave all of those guys two points out of those four—treating them all as average since the data are unknown.

Anyway, Bierbauer did, in fact, have a better year in 1892 than he had in 1891, as our system expects that he would. On the other end, Eric Davis in 1998:

A) Was 36 years old, giving him a score of one out of nine possible in Section A,

B) Had an OPS 118 points above his career OPS through the end of that season (.970 vs. .852), giving him a score of three out of a possible 10 in Section B,

C) Had an Adjusted Ball in Play Average of .401, giving him zero points out of a possible six in Section C,

D) Had 170 combined runs scored and RBIs after having had 54 the previous season, giving him zero points out of a possible six in Section D,

E) Had an very high OPS with a strikeout to walk ratio of 108 to 44, giving him no points out of a possible four in Section E,

F) Had a "speed indicators" score of .071 (seven stolen bases and one triple), missing the point that is given for players who run well, and

G) Had an OPS over .900, giving him no points out of a possible two in Section G.

Altogether, that's four points out of a possible 38—the lowest score ever. Actually, there are three players who score at "four," all of whom did in fact have weaker seasons the next year; in fact, there are 13 players in history who score at four, five or six, and all 13 did in fact have poorer seasons in the follow-up season than in the base season.

There are 25 players who score at "seven" on this test, and 24 of those had weaker seasons the next year. The one exception was Andres Galarraga in 1997. He scored at "seven," but was able to have as good a season in 1998 as he had had in 1997. This chart summarizes the number of players historically at each level, and the number and percentage of those who were able to sustain performance at the same level (or do better) in the following season:

Score	No. of players	No. as good	Percentage
4	3	0	0%
5	4	0	0%
6	6	0	0%
7	25	1	4%
8	22	4	18%
9	65	7	11%
10	105	15	14%
11	198	32	16%
12	277	46	17%
13	446	98	22%
14	645	140	22%
15	841	226	27%
16	1104	314	28%
17	1364	423	31%
18	1543	531	34%
19	1684	645	38%
20	1695	668	39%
21	1621	651	40%
22	1390	669	48%
23	1049	489	47%
24	849	425	50%
25	524	297	57%
26	333	173	52%
27	174	105	60%
28	86	58	67%
29	38	23	61%
30	17	16	94%
31	3	1	33%
32	3	3	100%
33	--	---	---
34	1	1	100%

Obviously, the number of players having as good or better years increases alongside the indicators predicting that this would happen. We can smooth out the curves a little by grouping the cells. The data given for "30" in the chart below is the sum of all players between 29 and 31; the data for "17" is the sum of all players between 16 and 18:

Score	Entries	Held Performance	Pct.
5	13	0	0%
6	35	1	3%
7	53	5	9%
8	112	12	11%
9	192	26	14%
10	368	54	15%
11	580	93	16%
12	921	176	19%
13	1368	284	21%
14	1932	464	24%
15	2590	680	26%
16	3309	963	29%
17	4011	1268	32%
18	4591	1599	35%
19	4922	1844	37%
20	5000	1964	39%
21	4706	1988	42%
22	4060	1809	45%
23	3288	1583	48%
24	2422	1211	50%
25	1706	895	52%
26	1031	575	56%
27	593	336	57%
28	298	186	62%
29	141	97	69%
30	58	40	69%
31	23	20	87%

We are now in position to estimate, given any score, the likelihood that a player will perform at the same or a better level in the following season.

The only one of these players who is *likely* to have as good a season in 2010 as he had in 2009 is Dioner Navarro. Navarro's at 56 percent. The most likely of the others, Kouzmanoff, is at 37 percent. Votto is at 32 percent, Chipper Jones at 29 percent, while Scott Podsednik has only a 16 percent chance of having a 2010 season as strong as his 2009 season, and Jorge Posada only an 11 percent chance.

These are the "Strong Season indicators" for all major league players with 400 or more plate appearances in 2009:

Player	Total
Dioner Navarro	26
Chris Young	25
J.J. Hardy	25
Russell Martin	24
Grady Sizemore	24
Dustin Pedroia	23
James Loney	23
Ian Kinsler	23
B.J. Upton	23
Nate McLouth	23
Yuniesky Betancourt	23
Pat Burrell	23
Willy Taveras	23
Casey Kotchman	23
Curtis Granderson	22
Alex Rios	22
Alexei Ramirez	22
Aubrey Huff	22
Stephen Drew	22
Jeremy Hermida	22
Mike Jacobs	22
Elijah Dukes	22
Rick Ankiel	22
Ryan Garko	22
Jimmy Rollins	21
Jhonny Peralta	21
David Wright	21
Adrian Beltre	21
Gerald Laird	21
Corey Hart	21
Mike Fontenot	21
Chris Davis	21
Nick Markakis	20
Vernon Wells	20
Dan Uggla	20
David Ortiz	20
Justin Morneau	20
Kevin Kouzmanoff	20
Brian McCann	20

Player	Total
Yadier Molina	20
Elvis Andrus	20
Alfonso Soriano	20
Edgar Renteria	20
Hank Blalock	20
Ben Francisco	20
Nick Punto	20
Ty Wigginton	20
Brandon Moss	20
Delmon Young	20
Cesar Izturis	20
Jacoby Ellsbury	19
Adrian Gonzalez	19
Ryan Theriot	19
Placido Polanco	19
Jose Lopez	19
Hunter Pence	19
Jorge Cantu	19
Jeff Francoeur	19
Kurt Suzuki	19
Lance Berkman	19
Daniel Murphy	19
Ryan Ludwick	19
Jason Kendall	19
Milton Bradley	19
Rod Barajas	19
Brendan Harris	19
Anderson Hernandez	19
Shane Victorino	18
Andre Ethier	18
David DeJesus	18
Chase Headley	18
Nick Swisher	18
Yunel Escobar	18
Randy Winn	18
Jermaine Dye	18
Carlos Pena	18
Melky Cabrera	18
Kaz Matsui	18
Colby Rasmus	18
Emilio Bonifacio	18
Luke Scott	18
David Murphy	18
Andrew McCutchen	18
Ian Stewart	18
Tony Gwynn	18
Everth Cabrera	18

Player	Total
Gordon Beckham	18
Chris Getz	18
Jose Bautista	18
Jack Wilson	18
Albert Pujols	17
Chase Utley	17
Rafael Furcal	17
Denard Span	17
Billy Butler	17
Evan Longoria	17
Matt Kemp	17
Carlos Lee	17
Mark Reynolds	17
Brandon Phillips	17
Jack Cust	17
Andy LaRoche	17
Skip Schumaker	17
Mark Teahen	17
Erick Aybar	17
Cristian Guzman	17
Aaron Rowand	17
Alex Rodriguez	17
Adam Jones	17
Magglio Ordonez	17
Martin Prado	17
Lyle Overbay	17
Melvin Mora	17
Gerardo Parra	17
Scott Hairston	17
Jerry Hairston	17
Mark Ellis	17
Howie Kendrick	17
Ryan Braun	16
Mark Teixeira	16
Ryan Howard	16
Miguel Cabrera	16
Carl Crawford	16
Adam Dunn	16
Bobby Abreu	16
Alberto Callaspo	16
Adam LaRoche	16
Paul Konerko	16
Cody Ross	16
Clint Barmes	16
Asdrubal Cabrera	16
Luis Castillo	16
David Eckstein	16

Player	Total
A.J. Pierzynski	16
Ryan Sweeney	16
Bengie Molina	16
Dexter Fowler	16
Josh Willingham	16
Freddy Sanchez	16
Willie Bloomquist	16
Ken Griffey Jr.	16
Maicer Izturis	16
Mike Napoli	16
Brendan Ryan	16
Jason Varitek	16
Nolan Reimold	16
Vladimir Guerrero	16
Aaron Hill	15
Prince Fielder	15
Brian Roberts	15
Orlando Cabrera	15
Ryan Zimmerman	15
Shin-Soo Choo	15
Marco Scutaro	15
Robinson Cano	15
Matt Holliday	15
Hanley Ramirez	15
Jason Bay	15
Brandon Inge	15
Pablo Sandoval	15
Orlando Hudson	15
Pedro Feliz	15
Kosuke Fukudome	15
Chipper Jones	15
Justin Upton	15
Mark DeRosa	15
Juan Rivera	15
Chris Coghlan	15
Joey Votto	15
Hideki Matsui	15
Nelson Cruz	15
Torii Hunter	15
Mike Lowell	15
Miguel Montero	15
Manny Ramirez	15
Alex Gonzalez	15
Geoff Blum	15
Juan Pierre	15
John Baker	15
Michael Bourn	14

Player	Total
Jayson Werth	14
Victor Martinez	14
Troy Tulowitzki	14
Johnny Damon	14
Jason Kubel	14
Nick Johnson	14
J.D. Drew	14
Garret Anderson	14
Chone Figgins	13
Derek Jeter	13
Felipe Lopez	13
Miguel Tejada	13
Franklin Gutierrez	13
Joe Mauer	13

Player	Total
Marlon Byrd	13
Michael Young	13
Brad Hawpe	13
Adam Kennedy	13
Scott Rolen	13
Nyjer Morgan	13
Juan Uribe	13
Miguel Olivo	13
Adam Lind	12
Michael Cuddyer	12
Todd Helton	12
Mike Cameron	12
Ben Zobrist	12
Kevin Youkilis	12

Player	Total
Raul Ibanez	12
Casey Blake	12
Ivan Rodriguez	12
Jim Thome	12
Rajai Davis	12
Ichiro Suzuki	11
Kendry Morales	11
Derrek Lee	11
Scott Podsednik	11
Jason Bartlett	11
Russell Branyan	11
Craig Counsell	9
Matt Diaz	9
Jorge Posada	8

The Content of their Character

by Jack Marshall

Wanted: Baseball Heroes

Many baseball historians, commentators and analysts steadfastly believe that determining the greatness of any baseball player is and should be a simple process. All one needs are the abundant statistical tools the emerging discipline of sabermetrics has provided. With them, we can make accurate assessments of relative player quality and talent across the seasons and decades, avoiding the illusions that inflated and deflated reputations in the ignorant past. Then, assessing a player's greatness would be as simple as measuring the player's Fantasy avatar, or his Strat-O-Matic card.

But there is a catch. Baseball still holds fast to the archaic belief that great athletes should also be cultural heroes, whose exploits parents and grandfathers can use to inspire America's youth. Be brave, my son, like Lou Gehrig, saying good-bye to the fans, knowing his death was near. Sacrifice yourself for your comrades, daughter, like Kirk Gibson, hitting a pinch-hit game-winning home run in the World Series, though he could barely walk to the plate. Be kind to the weak and unfortunate, my children, like Teddy Ballgame working for the Jimmy Fund, or like the Babe, hitting a homer for that sick little boy in the hospital.

The National Baseball Hall of Fame, which has been the arbiter of what constitutes baseball greatness since it opened its doors in 1939, embraces this romantic ideal of "greatness," and it is hardly surprising. It was part of the Hall of Fame movement in America that began in 1901 with the establishment of the Hall of Fame for Great Americans on the Bronx campus of New York's City College. The turn-of-the-century concept of fame was far removed from today's Paris Hilton version, for fame was not mere celebrity, but *deserved* celebrity. "Fame" meant "renown": accomplished, acclaimed and admirable. When the Cooperstown shrine called itself a "Hall of Fame," this was the definition of fame it accepted, and if there was any doubt, its admission criteria erased it:

Voting shall be based upon the player's record, playing ability, integrity, sportsmanship, character, and contributions to the team(s) on which the player played.

This standard asserts that it isn't enough to be outstanding at the game of baseball as measured by mere statistics. A player must also be *good* ... sufficiently admirable to stand as a symbol of the game's aspirations and values. The Hall of Fame requires a hero, in other words, or more accurately, in Merriman-Webster's words: *"a man admired for his achievements* (wins, saves, hits, homers, runs batted it, championships and the rest) *and noble qualities* (integrity, sportsmanship, and character)."

How inconvenient. As time has passed and the media have become more intrusive, the lives of public figures have become impossible to mythologize. The concept of "hero" is under increasing post-modern attack. There are no heroes, say the cynics. Everyone is flawed. And since everyone is flawed, nobody has a right to pass on another's virtue or human worth. When it comes to baseball, this attitude calls for us to ignore character entirely, to stop looking for baseball heroes and simply enshrine the players with the best VORP in their respective eras.

Someday, the National Hall of Fame may adopt that philosophy, and I, for one, will be sorry. America still needs heroes, and heroes have never had to be flawless, only sufficiently virtuous to make their flaws irrelevant. We don't need a Hall of Fame to distinguish the players with the best lifetime statistics, if that's all the sport cares about. Why use a place of honor to enshrine *statistics*? But if we are going to honor human beings, it makes perfect sense to require that they be honorable human beings ... players baseball can be proud of, not just because of what they did on the field, but how they did it, and how they lived their lives. There is no reason why baseball can't, or shouldn't, maintain a Hall of Fame for players who meet a standard of heroism—men *"admired for their achievements and noble qualities."*

You are welcome to disagree; however, disagreement is irrelevant right now, because integrity, sportsmanship and character are included in the Hall of Fame's criteria for greatness. But unlike achievements on the field, there are no statistics to measure these qualities, so applying them to the rest of a player's career is a problem.

Consider:

- *In the middle of a key game, a bat flying out of a hitter's hands seriously injures a child in the crowd. The home team's star slugger leaps into the stands, scoops up the child, and carries him into the dugout for immediate medical attention. Most agree that the player's quick actions saved the child's life. The slugger is a borderline Hall of Fame candidate upon his retirement. How much, if at all, should his dramatic rescue of the stricken child enhance his qualifications as a baseball immortal?*

- *Years after his retirement, one of baseball's greatest relief pitchers falls on hard times and bad health. Reeling from clinical depression over the death of his son, and abusing medication, he robs a jewelry store. Should this kind of sad post-career incident disqualify a player for Cooperstown?*
- *One of baseball's greatest pitchers, in a sudden fit of fear and anger, attacks an opposing player with a baseball bat during a game. To what extent should this incident weaken his credentials for admission to the Hall of Fame?*
- *A player recognized for his work ethic, willingness to play hurt and exemplary skills on the field amasses accomplishments that qualify him for serious Hall of Fame consideration. He is also widely regarded as a racist, and once lied to his team, the press and the public about the origins of a serious injury. To what extent, if any, should the latter factors influence the judgment of Hall of Fame voters?*

For many years, it seemed as if the character requirements for Hall of Fame admission were *passé.* Some players whose on- and off-the-field conduct might have revived the issue, such as Albert Belle, Juan Gonzalez and Jose Canseco, saw their careers flame out before Hall consideration was feasible. Some who experienced genuine scandals in their careers, like Wade Boggs, had such overwhelming credentials that character never became an issue. The one player, Pete Rose, whose consideration would trigger a full scale-debate on the subject, remains ineligible for election.

And then came steroids.

Mark McGwire, whose more than 500 home runs make him an easy Hall of Fame admittee by past standards, has been rejected by voters for presumed (though yet to be proved) conduct impugning his integrity, sportsmanship and character. Many members of the Baseball Writers' Association of America say that they will similarly reject Barry Bonds, Sammy Sosa and Roger Clemens, though all have somewhat different settings for their alleged misconduct. Predictably, defenders, cynics and contrarians have seized on the opportunity to ask about the current Hall of Fame "heroes." Wasn't Ty Cobb a racist? Wasn't Grover Cleveland Alexander a drunk? Juan Marichal tried to kill John Roseboro, didn't he? What about them?

Good questions. It is fine to look for heroes, but if the recipe for baseball greatness is going to contain character, integrity and sportsmanship, we had better decide what they are, how we are going to measure them, and how much we need to have. They need to be to be defined and weighed. Now that there are heated debates over the integrity, sportsmanship and character of individual players, it is apparent that there is no consensus about what is relevant and what isn't, and the assumption appears to be that trying to move the argument beyond seat-of-the-pants opinion is futile. Maybe it isn't, however. Integrity, sportsmanship and character are concepts that have meaning, and determining their meaning within the world of major league baseball should be possible, if not especially easy.

Integrity, Sportsmanship And Character

When Manny Ramirez was suspended for testing positive for banned substances this past season, several commentators, including *Boston Globe* sportswriter Dan Shaughnessy, the Yankees' Johnny Damon and Manny himself, employed what I regard as the worst of all rationalizations for misconduct, the "It's not the worst thing in the world" argument. This vile shrug of a defense seeks to minimize every wrongful act by comparing it to a worse one. Their version was the "it's not like he killed someone" variation. It caused me to wonder about the hierarchy of perceived bad conduct in baseball. Using banned substances is far, far less of an offense than murder in the real world, of course, but it would seem that baseball necessarily regards the two acts as less disparate in negative value. Could it even be possible that in the world of baseball, steroid use, or other misconduct, is as bad as murder, or even worse?

Determining this must begin with identifying the factors that determine how particular conduct relates to a player's integrity, sportsmanship and character. Let's begin by defining what we mean by each of them.

First, let's understand "integrity," since it is mentioned first in the Hall's criteria. It is a complicated concept in philosophy, but the Hall of Fame can fairly be assumed to mean the term as it would most logically relate to playing baseball. Integrity implies the kind of consistency of character that encourages and supports trust. The quality includes honesty and responsibility, the determination to live by ethical principles and the courage to hold to them under duress.

"Sportsmanship," sandwiched between integrity and character, is a specialized virtue that relates to games and competition. It includes fair play, professionalism, respect for the game, its participants and fans, and "playing the game the right way." Sportsmanship also includes grace and humility in victory, accountability and graciousness in defeat.

Because breaches of sportsmanship would almost always be violations of integrity (cheating, for example), it appears that the criteria's integrity/sportsmanship dichotomy is intended to represent non-baseball and baseball conduct. This is logical, and it is also helpful. The inclusion of both integrity and sportsmanship tells us that it isn't only baseball-related conduct that matters when a player seeks hero status.

"Character" encompasses integrity and sportsmanship, but a lot more. Among the other most commonly cited markers of good character are...

trustworthiness; honesty in communication; candor; truth-telling; reliability; sincerity; honesty in conduct; humility; loyalty; respect; civility; courtesy; decency; dignity; courage; tolerance; responsibility; diligence; pursuit of excellence; competence; accountability; perseverance; self-restraint; prudence; fairness; openness; impartiality; proportionality; consistency; equity; caring; charity; benevolence; consideration; empathy; generosity; humility; and citizenship.

These virtues are broad enough to encompass both baseball and non-baseball conduct: off- the-field conduct that goes beyond integrity, and baseball-related conduct that may not involve sportsmanship.

Weighing Conduct

Measuring integrity, sportsmanship and character requires observed, documented, proven or reasonably certain conduct. It also requires weighting the significance of the conduct according to when it occurs. This creates a problem. In judging the character of a human being, distinctions between personal and professional conduct are generally illusory. An untrustworthy butcher is likely to be untrustworthy outside of the butcher shop as well; if he isn't, it is because some other factors are inhibiting him. Honest people don't lie, cheat and steal, ever, or anywhere.

But the National Baseball Hall of Fame honors baseball players who are deemed honorable because of their baseball-related achievements, and it is reasonable to conclude that baseball-related conduct should also weigh most heavily in the calculation of their character. It is a similar problem to the dilemma of whether war veterans should be buried in Arlington National Cemetery if they committed serious crimes after their discharge. The American Legion had opposed restrictions, arguing that if a soldier served his country honorably in war, his subsequent failings as a citizen shouldn't diminish the honor. Then Timothy McVeigh, a decorated Gulf War veteran, blew up a government building in Oklahoma City, and it didn't seem so clear any more.

The temporal factors in weighing player conduct:

When: Did the conduct occur before, during, or after the player's career? If during his career, did it also occur during the baseball season? What were the cultural norms in the game and in society when the conduct occurred?

Pre-career: In most cases, what a player did before he became a major league player is not held against him, though good conduct in this period may still raise the assessment of his character somewhat. It is as if the player's life begins when he puts on a big league uniform. Indeed, a pre-baseball life of serious misconduct can even burnish a player's reputation for character, because it casts baseball as the symbol of his redemption. Former Detroit outfielder Ron LeFlore, for example, never reached the career accomplishments that would qualify him for the Hall of Fame, but it is inconceivable that his pre-baseball conviction for armed robbery would have been used to disqualify him. As for especially virtuous pre-career conduct, it may become part of the case for integrity and character, subject to being superseded by subsequent events.

Post-career: After a player's career is over, his notable conduct, good or bad, will be linked to his baseball career, and to the institution of baseball. Perceived bad conduct can embarrass the player's team and the sport. Thus the embarrassing revelations about Steve Garvey's sexual indiscretions affect how posterity will regard his integrity and character. Orlando Cepeda's post-career arrest, conviction and imprisonment for drug possession impeded his candidacy for the Hall of Fame for many years. Players who remain in the game as coaches or managers, serve as teachers and role models for young players, perform special service to the game or its players (like Don Newcombe or Mark Belanger), or those, like U.S. Sen. Jim Bunning, who have significant achievements in a different field, add to their reputation for character because they are "credits to the sport."

During career: Clearly, conduct that occurs during a player's career is the most relevant to assessing his character as it relates to baseball, and will have the most impact on his reputation. Bad conduct may have direct negative consequences on the team's performance and is likely to create more serious damage to public perception of the sport and its personnel than any pre- or post-career conduct. The revelation in 1989 of Boggs' extramarital affair with Margo Adams helped to throw the 1988 division-winning Red Sox' season into disarray, and is still more remembered than Garvey's indiscretions. A player's exemplary conduct also will have more impact and perceived significance when it occurs during his career, when the public attention will be most intense.

There is also significant difference in perceived relevance to a player's character according to the timing of the conduct within a player's career. Offseason conduct usually will have less impact on assessments of a player's character than conduct during the season, unless the conduct is extreme. Conduct actually occurring during a game, such as Rick Monday's famous outfield rescue of the American flag from a would-be flag-burner, or Ty Cobb's infamous attack on a handicapped heckler in the stands (the spectator was missing hands), may become a prominent part of the player's public image for all time.

Note that two factors are intertwined here: conduct that indicates character (or lack of it), and the publicity such conduct receives. The fact that conduct occurs at a time in a season, or in a period of a player's life, when a player attracts media attention truly changes the character and the seriousness of the conduct. A player who has a DUI arrest after he retires drove a vehicle while intoxicated, which is bad, but a player who commits the same offense while active as a player during the season has also brought embarrassment on his team, his city and his sport. A DUI arrest before an athlete becomes a professional baseball player may never become generally known at all; even though it is the same conduct, it is less serious because there were no baseball duties breached.

The "When" impact hierarchy, therefore, is

1. During major league career (during a game)
2. During career (during the season)
3. During career (off-season)
4. Post-career conduct
5. Pre-career virtuous conduct
6. Pre-career negative conduct

There is large gap between the perceived importance of mid-career conduct and post-career conduct, and an even larger gap between post-career and pre-career conduct, with one special exception. In the rare case where a player overcomes unusual adversity to become a successful baseball player, pre-career conduct can become extremely relevant to character evaluation. This would apply to the inspiring stories of handicapped players like Jim Abbott, William "Dummy" Hoy, Pete Gray or Jim Eisenreich.

There is one additional aspect of timing that can be critical to an overall assessment of a player's conduct and how it reflects on his character, and that is cultural context. It is only fair to judge Babe Ruth's hedonistic lifestyle in the context of America in the 1920s and 1930s, for example. Confirmed steroid-users who broke the rules after the Mitchell Report should be regarded even more severely than those who used PEDs when they were epidemic in baseball and ignored by the game's leadership. Applying cultural context is so subjective and difficult that one is tempted to forego the effort. To do so would be unjust, however. Time gives all of us, including baseball players, opportunities to learn from history and experience. It is wrong to be excessively harsh in our judgment of those who didn't know they were wrong, when it may have taken us decades to learn what was right.

What: What was the conduct? Was it good or bad in absolute terms, in the context of baseball only, or some combination of the two?

In society, the worst crimes involve murder, because murder threatens to destroy society by throwing civilization into chaos and violence. In baseball, the worst conduct is conduct that threatens the game, rather than society. What threatens the game? As with all competitions, the greatest threat to baseball is a public perception that the game is a fraud—rigged, deceptive, and unworthy of trust and belief. Since 1919, as even the most casual baseball fan knows, gambling on baseball games has been pronounced an unforgivable sin, following close behind intentionally hurting one's own team on the field and accepting bribes to do so.

Another type of conduct that threatens baseball itself is player violence directed at umpires, because such behavior undermines the authority of official arbiters that the game cannot function without. (In Philip Roth's wonderful *The Great American Novel*, a star pitcher receives a lifetime ban for intentionally injuring an umpire with a well-placed fastball. I think that's right.) These and other on-field transgressions reflect on a player's sportsmanship as well as his character and integrity. Somewhere in the same group are extensive steroid and other PED use, conduct that may involve a crime (as with bribery and assault) and conduct involving on-field activity (a steroid-using player might be harmless to the game if he never played), that affects the integrity of the game.

But what about murder? We can assume that a player who intentionally killed a player, fan, teammate or umpire during a game would attain instant and lifetime infamy, placing that act at least on par with the game-threatening conduct mentioned above. Murder committed by a player or former player in his non-baseball activities, however, might be considered less serious (though very serious still), implicating his character but not his sportsmanship or integrity. I am not sure of this; I am sure that murder, as well as other serious crimes, would so thoroughly disqualify any ballplayer for heroic status that whether it is more or less damning in baseball terms is hardly worth debating.

The hierarchy of misconduct begins with a set of acts that should always disqualify any player for "greatness" regardless of how impressive his career achievements might be. Cowardly though it might be, I'll list them in alphabetical order, and call them "Disqualifying Conduct":

- Armed robbery
- Child pornography
- First-degree murder
- Fixing or throwing a baseball game
- Gambling on baseball
- Intentionally inflicting serious injury on a player, umpire or fan
- Kidnapping
- Large scale felonies, such as mass frauds, drug trafficking, counterfeiting
- Rape
- Treason

Each of these would require only one incident to disqualify a player for hero status; even the current fashion of dismissing all celebrity misconduct with the mantra, "Anyone can make a mistake!" won't sufficiently cleanse the reputation of the baseball player who throws a game, or commits rape. Does any other conduct qualify for this "no tolerance list?

There are some strong candidates, each with their own confounding aspects:

Animal abuse: Could a baseball-playing equivalent of Michael Vick be admitted to the Hall of Fame? Clearly, many Americans could never admire any individual shown to engage in cruelty to animals. Others would put the conduct in the next category down, bad conduct that may be mitigated or forgiven after appropriate contrition and reform. Although I would not be shocked at the discovery that one or more current Hall members engaged in dog fighting or cock fighting, current American cultural values make it hard for me to imagine a Michael Vick being accepted into the Hall of Fame. I don't think animal abuse quite makes it into the automatic disqualifier list, but it is very, very, close.

Demonstrable bigotry or racism: America's long history of racial conflict and its painful process, still ongoing, of striving to become a color-blind society make racism intolerable today. A vocal and avowed racist, or a player who committed blatant acts of racism (either mid-career, before or after) would be a difficult, if not impossible American hero in the 21st century. Still, designating an opinion, attitude or belief a definitive character flaw may be unfair. Attitudes toward race often are implanted by upbringing and culture: in some ways, an individual who recognizes that a personal bias is wrong and works to overcome it is more impressive that someone comfortably raised to be without prejudice of any kind. (I once had a roommate in law school who was an admitted racist, but who treated everyone respectfully and whom several African-Americans regarded as a good friend. He also raised and gave donations to the United Negro College Fund! When I noted that his actions seemed at odds with his biases as I had heard him express them, he answered, "I'm trying!")

Racism also raises the cultural evolution problem. It is a reasonable guess that the majority of baseball greats in the first half of the last century, and even a number of the later players, held racist beliefs, but unlike today, they were typical of white America generally. Does this mean that a particularly odious character trait can be "grandfathered" into the definition of acceptable character for a baseball hero today?

No. Let's use the American presidents as a comparison. Some of our most admired and successful presidents, including George Washington and Thomas Jefferson, were slave-holders in a culture that accepted the practice. It would be absurd and unfair to judge their character by the same standards we would use to judge an individual today who was found to be keeping slaves in his basement. Even Abraham Lincoln held many racist views that would disqualify him for public office today. We cannot reasonably require or expect heroic figures of the past to meet standards of conduct that evolved after their lifetimes, nor is it possible to devise timeless, universal standards of good character that can be applied to all individuals from all eras. The racism of Ty Cobb must be regarded differently than present day racism.

Racism, I think, requires a complex standard. The label of "racist" should not be applied to a player's character based on words alone. As we have seen in today's political rhetoric, some are far too willing to see racism where none may exist. Unambiguously racist conduct by a present-day player, however, at any time in his life, would probably disqualify him for the Hall of Fame's definition of "greatness." A 400-game winner who became a Grand Wizard in the KKK could not be enshrined, despite a career without blemish. As for older baseball greats, their racism ought to be treated as different in kind.

Racism and bigotry, then, also belongs in the gray zone beneath the automatic disqualifying conduct.

Spousal abuse: Like animal cruelty and racism, this conduct today is culturally taboo, and also like them, this was not always the case. Both the law and society acknowledge that domestic violence is unique, and that one incident may not make someone an abuser. My assessment would be that unlike animal abuse, a one-time incident of spousal abuse would weigh against a player's character but not decisively. A habitual wife-beater, however, should be disqualified for baseball greatness on the basis of character.

PED use: I am not so foolish as to aspire to settling this convoluted issue here. It is different than the other character-related conduct because it also implicates the legitimacy of the other side of the ledger, career statistics. Not to duck the issue, but that aspect of PED use, whether a PED-using player's on-field accomplishments can be taken at face value or should be discounted or even ignored, is not the topic of this inquiry.

The character, integrity and sportsmanship implications of PED use are serious enough. As most steroid and HGH use required violating laws (or inducing others to break laws), it shows a lack of integrity. It is cheating: surreptitiously using performance-enhancing substances others players assumed were unavailable to them because of legal restrictions was unfair conduct even before baseball specifically prohibited them. Cheating is the antithesis of sportsmanship.

Perusing the list of character values, secretly using illegal or banned substances to gain an unfair competitive advantage over both competitors and teammates violates trustworthiness, honesty in communication, candor, truth-telling, reliability, sincerity, honesty in conduct, loyalty, respect, responsibility, accountability, self-restraint, prudence, fairness, openness, equity, caring, consideration, empathy and possibly citizenship. That's bad, but the details matter. Was the PED use one time only, or for a major part of the player's career? Did the player respond to peer or competitive pressures? Was he persuaded to use by others? Did he honestly believe that "everybody was doing it," and that the game's leadership tacitly approved it? Was he trying to win games, or achieve money and fame? Did his use encourage others to do likewise? Did he lie about his PED use to the media and the public? Did he falsely present himself as opposed to PED use?

PED use certainly counts against a player's character, integrity and sportsmanship, but there are too many variables at work to declare the conduct unforgivable.

Chronic criminal conduct: I would add this to the disqualifier list. A baseball hero can't be accurately described as a criminal. Once a player has accumulated a rap sheet that continues during or after his playing career, he has flunked the character and integrity test.

What is the proper weight of *admirable* conduct? This is different from measuring bad conduct, because being an admirable person does not make an individual a more talented baseball player. I advocate "The Anti-Dibble Rule," named in honor of former gonzo-pitcher turned gonzo-radio pundit Rob Dibble, who last year went into an extended rant on his XM radio show when Ron Santo failed to be voted into the Hall of Fame by the Veterans Committee. "I mean, it's a joke!," Dibble raged. "With everything this guy has put up with, with all his courage, losing his legs and everything, plus his record, and they don't think he's qualified?"

The Anti-Dibble Rule holds that while admirable conduct off the baseball field may be used as a measure of a player's character and integrity, it can only enhance the measure of a player's greatness to the extent that it counter-balances misconduct or negative conduct. It cannot push a borderline great player into a higher category. Thus the impressive charity work of Ted Williams for the Jimmy Fund and his Korean War heroism can only help offset incidents showing poor character and bad sportsmanship in his career, such as spitting at the stands and refusing to tip his cap. Williams's admirable qualities and life achievements would give him legitimate hero status even if he had been a .260 lifetime hitter, but they wouldn't make him a great ballplayer.

The "What" of good and bad conduct reflecting on a player's character must also, in individual cases, be tempered by the "how" and "why." Former star closer Jeff Reardon's robbery attempt, described earlier, seemed to be completely out of character, prompted by grief and emotional illness. That conduct probably should have no bearing on our assessment of his character at all. Apparently Juan Marichal's attack on catcher John Roseboro has been accepted as the result of a form of temporary insanity, because the incident did not significantly impede his acceptance into the Hall of Fame. If he had killed Roseboro, presumably it would have hurt his candidacy more, although in character terms, there is little difference between trying to kill someone and succeeding. (The legal penalties for attempted murder are virtually the same as for murder itself.)

When I began this project, I intended to suggest a rough scoring system that would give numerical weights to various kinds of conduct. After some lively exchanges with wiser commenters on the *Hardball Times* website and Craig Calcaterra's blog, I decided that this was a foolish plan, and doomed to failure. Instead, I settled for the more moderate ambition of opening the subject for further analysis, and proposing some objective parameters for what has been, up to this point, a purely subjective topic.

To that end, here are some proposed guidelines for measuring player character, followed by a suggested hierarchy of non-disqualifying misconduct and character-supporting admirable conduct, and the application of these to some individual players:

Guidelines:

- In the case of the very greatest players, only misconduct that directly harmed the game of baseball or threatened to do so should disqualify the player for the Hall.
- Conduct showing bad sportsmanship should be considered more damaging to the measurement of a player's "greatness" than conduct implicating integrity or character generally.
- Personality should not be included in the assessment of character, except in extreme cases where it arguably affects team performance positively or negatively.
- Pre-career conduct is almost always irrelevant, unless it serves to explain, confirm or mitigate subsequent conduct.
- Good conduct, even unusual conduct that occurs during a game, should never elevate a player whose playing career is not Hall of Fame-worthy to Hall status. It can appropriately be used to counterbalance negative conduct that might otherwise show inadequate integrity, sportsmanship and character. It could reasonably be used to tip the scales in a very close call.
- Admissions, apologies and expressed regret for misconduct do not, by themselves, erase the significance of misconduct for purposes of assessing character, but may be used, as with other good conduct, as counter-balancing factors. When apologies are accompanied by genuine contrition and affirmative acts seeking to make amends, they should mitigate, but not erase, serious misconduct. They cannot remedy disqualifying conduct.
- Rumors, suspicion and supposition should not be the basis of judging any player's character. Reasonable conclusions based on obvious inferences from observed behavior, however, can be fair legitimate foundations for judgment.

Conduct rankings:

Bad conduct, indicating lack of integrity, bad sportsmanship or poor character (listed worst to best, not including "disqualifying conduct")

1. Attacks on fans or umpires.
2. Flagrant and extensive use of PEDs
3. On-field impairment affecting performance
4. Criminal conduct during the season
5. Criminal conduct during the player's career.
6. On-the-field cheating, unrelated to drugs (corking bats; tipping pitches to the opposition)
7. Chronic dishonest, uncivilized or other embarrassing personal conduct during a player's career.
8. Unprofessional conduct during a game (including lack of hustle, "flipping the bird" to fans or insubordination)
9. Post-career criminal conduct falling short of "disqualifying conduct"
10. Post-career conduct involving dishonest, anti-social or offensive acts
11. Habitual, unapologetic expression of extreme or offensive views (racist, homophobic, misogynistic, anti-American, etc.)
12. Betrayal of the confidences of teammates in printed material and interviews

Good conduct, indicating integrity, sportsmanship or good character, in descending order:

1. Team leadership
2. Unusual hustle, "playing the game right"
3. Special acts of courage, heroism or integrity during a game
4. Charity and community service
5. Special acts of courage, heroism or integrity during a season
6. Special acts of courage, heroism or integrity during the offseason
7. Post-career charity and community service

8. Distinguished post-baseball career
9. Outstanding military service
10. Distinguished career achievements after playing career
11. Post-career military or public service
12. Special individual acts of heroism, generosity, charity or other exemplary conduct, post-career.

Some Individual Cases:

Jim Rice: who saved the injured child during a game in 1979, was a borderline Hall of Famer elected last year. This incident, which was remarkable, apparently had no role in pushing him over the hump, but it is part of his legacy, and could have justifiably provided the final straw for those who felt he was barely short of Hall status.

Juan Marichal: whose pose in the famous photo of his 1965 attack on Dodger catcher John Roseboro is chilling, was apparently regarded as so outstanding a player and so well-liked an individual, not to mention a national hero in the Dominican Republic, that his criminal assault was not held against him by Hall of Fame voters. One reason seems to be the amazingly mild response his attempted on-field murder (for that is what it was) got from Major League Baseball. (He was suspended for only nine games and fined about $7,500.) Marichal and Roseboro reconciled and became friends, and the pitcher was genuinely remorseful.

I think an on-field attack like this is such a major sportsmanship breach that it should preclude Hall of Fame membership.

Jackie Robinson: Robinson's on-the-field courage and life sacrifices in his efforts to desegregate baseball make him a special case. He made the Hall of Fame on his merits as a player, but even if his statistical achievements had fallen short, he would be an exception to the principle that exemplary conduct cannot elevate a player to the status of greatness who doesn't have the numbers.

Gaylord Perry: Perry was an engaging and colorful pitcher who didn't need the spitball to win games until he was well past his prime. Nonetheless, his career-long use of the banned pitch was cheating, and I think the Hall of Fame would have been wise to leave him out.

Cap Anson: Anson's documented racism went far beyond attitude to aggressive conduct. Despite his status as an innovator and a major figure in baseball's early years, his pivotal role in segregating the game is impossible for me to reconcile with icon status.

Jeff Kent: Kent, whom many believe to hold racist views and who had an embarrassing incident of lying outright to the media about the source of an injury, is apparently an example of a seriously flawed human being who nonetheless was thoroughly professional as a ballplayer and who "played the game right." Those positive qualities, combined with his impressive career record, should outbalance his significant character negatives.

Manny Ramirez: My opinion is that Manny Ramirez epitomizes the otherwise great player whose lack of integrity and sportsmanship disqualifies him for baseball hero status. His unapologetic use of PEDs, testing positive after the game's tolerance of steroid use had changed, combined with his many incidents of atrocious sportsmanship culminating in his extorting Boston to trade him during the 2008 season by intentionally underperforming on the field, signal that he fails the Hall of Fame character test. He is very popular with many fans, however, and I have no illusions that my harsh assessment has any chance of prevailing.

Final Thoughts On The Hall Of Fame And Character

This exercise caused me to re-evaluate my perspective on the Hall of Fame, and to propose that others change theirs as well. Cooperstown is a Hall of Fame and Museum, after all, and there is no reason why the hall and the museum shouldn't have different standards. The museum should include and celebrate the exploits of Shoeless Joe, Pete Rose, Mark McGwire, Barry Bonds and Roger Clemens. That doesn't mean that the Hall of Fame has to honor those players, or that there is any void if they do not. If the hall decides, as so many believe it should, to enshrine players solely on the basis of their statistical worth, so be it. I'm not sure that I agree with the message that would send.

We should admire people for more than mere accomplishments, and the Hall of Fame's assertion that integrity, sportsmanship and character are equally important is valuable, inspiring and true. Perhaps the Hall should consider removing the plaques of those whose character, upon reflection, did not measure up to the values and standards of the game and society. Say good-bye to Cap, Juan, Gaylord ... maybe even Ty.

I could accept that. I think it would be better than giving up on our ideals, and baseball's.

The author wants to acknowledge the many suggestions he received from Prof. William Dechtel and other visitors to The Hardball Times.

The Rebuilding Team Fan's Survival Guide

by Geoff Young

It's the All-Star break and, as was the case for 30 percent of MLB teams in 2009, your team is already out of the playoff picture. Which of the following best describes your reaction?

A. If Mike Jacobs turns into Albert Pujols, Jose Guillen turns into Ryan Braun and everyone else in the division turns into zombies, we might have a chance.

B. These guys couldn't hit water if they fell out of a boat. Eh, baseball is lame anyway.

C. This isn't our year. I'm tired of all the losses; I wish there were another way to follow this team without worrying so much about outcomes.

You'll need a different kind of help for the first two, but if you chose (C), you're in luck. We can do something about that.

Introducing Modified Box Scores

In July 2009, at my Padres blog, Ducksnorts, I introduced Modified Box Scores as a way to track the season's remaining games with an eye toward the future. The idea was to stop fixating on wins and losses, and focus instead on the following questions:

1. Is the manager sticking the right players in the lineup?
2. Are those players producing?

The method I devised to evaluate these is simple yet effective. Perhaps more importantly, it helped make the second half of the season fun (or at least bearable). Here's how it works:

First, identify key unestablished players that might contribute to the team in the future.

Second, assign each targeted player points on a game-by-game basis as follows:

For Hitters:

1. Award one point if he gets at least four plate appearances. This is the playing time (PT) component. It rewards the manager for making the right decision in determining whom to play. It also rewards the team for producing enough offense to ensure that even guys at the bottom of the order get their requisite trips to the plate.
2. Award one point if he reaches base two or more times. This is the on-base (OB) component.
3. Award 1 point if he records four or more total bases. This is the slugging (SL) component.

For Pitchers:

1. Award one point if he works at least five innings. This is the endurance (End) component. Yes, it penalizes relievers, but very few unestablished relievers can be counted on to be a part of the rebuilding process for any team.
2. Award one point if his pitches per innings pitched is fewer than 15. This is the efficiency (Eff) component and helps measure the pitcher's command.
3. Award 1 point if his strikeouts are equal to or greater than his innings pitched. This is the power (Pwr) component.

The accounting method for hitters is straightforward enough. Reaching base and driving the ball lead to run scoring, which in turn helpsw lead to wins.

The pitching side is a little trickier. I like efficiency in a pitcher because it tends to correlate with working deep into games. I like strikeouts because a pitcher's ability to put the ball past hitters has been shown to increase his chances for long-term success.

Strikeouts often lead to elevated pitch counts, i.e., inefficiency. That said, a pitcher that racks up strikeouts while keeping his pitch count down (e.g., Greg Maddux, Roy Halladay, Chris Carpenter) is a mighty useful guy to have on your team. Hence, it is in these areas that I look for excellence from young pitchers.

Modified Box Scores In Action

We'll use the Padres for most of our examples because that is the team with which I am most familiar. Our first step is to identify the players to track.

This is a subjective exercise that depends on your opinion of an individual's ability to help the team going forward. For the 2009 Padres, I chose six position players (Kyle Blanks, Everth Cabrera, Chase Headley, Nick Hundley, Drew Macias and Will Venable) and one pitcher (Mat Latos).

From there it's simply a matter of perusing box scores and making a few quick calculations. Let's walk through the Padres' 4-2 victory over Atlanta at Petco Park on Aug. 3. We begin with the traditional box score, presented at the top of the next page.

Padres Boxscore, August 3, 2009

Hitters	AB	R	H	2B	3B	HR	RBI	BB	SO
Tony Gwynn Jr.	4	0	0	0	0	0	0	0	1
David Eckstein	3	1	1	0	1	0	0	1	1
Will Venable	4	1	3	0	0	0	1	0	0
Kevin Kouzmanoff	4	0	1	1	0	0	1	0	0
Chase Headley	4	0	1	0	0	0	0	0	1
Kyle Blanks	4	1	1	0	0	1	1	0	0
Eliezer Alfonzo	4	0	1	0	0	0	0	0	1
Everth Cabrera	3	1	1	0	0	0	0	0	0
Mat Latos	2	0	0	0	0	0	0	0	1
Oscar Salazar	1	0	1	0	0	0	1	0	0

Pitcher	IP	H	R	ER	BB	SO	HR	Pit
Mat Latos	7	6	2	2	2	3	1	94

Starting with the hitters, we'll eliminate everyone not on our list of tracked players, which leaves this:

Batter	AB	R	H	2B	3B	HR	RBI	BB	SO
Will Venable	4	1	3	0	0	0	1	0	0
Chase Headley	4	0	1	0	0	0	0	0	1
Kyle Blanks	4	1	1	0	0	1	1	0	0
Everth Cabrera	3	1	1	0	0	0	0	0	0

We next evaluate each player based on the criteria established in the introductory section. Venable gets one point for recording four plate appearances and another for reaching base at least twice. Headley gets one for plate appearances. So does Blanks, who also gets one point for recording four or more total bases (thanks to his home run).

Note that although Cabrera started, he gets no points because he failed to meet the plate appearances requirement. No, this is not his fault, but it hardly seems appropriate to reward manager Bud Black for batting one of his best young players so far down in the lineup. Also, had the Padres generated more offense on this night, Cabrera probably would have met the requirement, so this also penalizes the team for not doing a better collective job on offense.

(You may notice an additional factor in this instance. The Padres played at home, and because they led after 8½ innings, Cabrera didn't get a chance to bat a fourth time. I haven't figured out a satisfying resolution to this problem, so for now we'll just say, "Them's the breaks.")

On the pitching side, Latos gets one point for working at least five innings and one more for throwing fewer than 15 pitches per inning (94 pitches divided by 7 innings = 13.43 pitches per inning). In tabular form, we have this:

Batter	PT	OB	SL	Tot
Will Venable	1	1	0	2
Chase Headley	1	0	0	1
Kyle Blanks	1	0	1	2
Everth Cabrera	0	0	0	0
Totals	**3**	**1**	**1**	**5**

Pitcher	End	Eff	Pwr	Tot
Mat Latos	1	1	0	2

The only possible values for any given component are zero and one. The maximum "score" for any player in a game is three. It seems strange at first, but after a while, you'll find yourself saying things to yourself like, "Blanks is 1-for-3 with a homer; if he reaches base here, that's a 3-point game." Assuming, of course, you're in the habit of talking to yourself.

The Bigger Picture

Now that we've seen how Modified Box Scores work on a micro level, let's step back and look at the bigger picture. We know how to peruse an actual box score and modify it to serve our nefarious purposes; now what?

Well, we can do a few things. Two that immediately come to mind are to sum individual results and to look at trends over time.

On the summing side, if we know that a player went 1-for-4 yesterday and 1-for-3 today, we also know that he has gone 2-for-7 over the past two days. Keep adding, and eventually we arrive at a player's season line, which is knowledge worth having. We can learn something from the 1-for-4 or the 2-for-7, but we can learn much more from, say, .279/.361/.510 over 700 plate appearances.

On the trending side, if a player's successive monthly batting averages are .113, .203, .247, .275, .292 and .371, we can see that his numbers have improved over time. The caveat here is that because these comprise a subset of a larger collection of data, what appears to be a trend may be mere noise—small samples and all that. Still, this gives us another way to look at the available information, and it can be insightful, or at least interesting.

Again using the 2009 Padres as an example, here are a couple of methods I devised for tracking our chosen players over time. The first examines individual players, while the second focuses on the team.

Individual Totals

	8/17-8/23					Since All-Star Break				
	PT	OB	SL	Tot	A%	PT	OB	SL	Tot	A%
Blanks	2	3	3	8	.750	23	15	9	47	.511
Hundley	1	1	2	4	1.000	3	1	2	6	.500
Venable	3	3	2	8	.625	23	14	8	45	.489
Cabrera	4	4	1	9	.556	33	19	5	57	.421
Headley	6	2	0	8	.250	32	18	2	52	.385
Macias	0	0	0	0	-	2	0	0	2	.000
Totals	**17**	**12**	**8**	**37**	**.541**	**116**	**67**	**26**	**209**	**.445**

	Eff	Pwr	Tot	End	Eff	Pwr	Tot
Latos	0	0	0	4	2	2	8

This is just a random week, but it shows us how our players did during that time period and also gives a running total of their season to date (well, since the All-Star break, which is when we gave up our hope of winning and sought other methods for measuring success). For the hitters, I've added a column, A%, which is (OB + SL) / PT and which indicates the percentage of points that are earned on the basis of making positive contributions versus just showing up and collecting four plate appearances. (And yes, it is possible to accumulate "achievement" points without getting credit for "being there"—as happened, e.g., when Headley blasted a pinch hit homer against Colorado on July 18.)

Back to trending, we get something like this for the hitters:

Weekly Totals

	Week									Since ASB		
	G	PT	OB	SL	End	Eff	Pwr	Tot	T/G	G	Tot	T/G
7/16-7/19	4	12	3	1	0	1	0	17	4.25	4	17	4.25
7/20-7/26	7	21	8	4	1	0	0	34	4.86	11	51	4.64
7/27-8/2	7	22	13	7	1	1	0	44	6.29	18	95	5.28
8/3-8/9	7	24	12	5	2	1	1	45	6.43	25	140	5.60
8/10-8/16	6	20	18	1	0	0	0	39	6.50	31	179	5.77
8/17-8/23	7	17	12	8	0	0	0	37	5.29	38	216	5.69
8/24-8/30	6	22	13	3	1	1	0	40	6.67	44	256	5.82
8/31-9/6	6	17	9	2	0	0	1	29	4.83	50	285	5.70
9/7-9/13	6	23	12	5	0	0	0	40	6.67	56	325	5.80
9/14-9/20	6	21	9	3	0	0	0	33	5.50	62	358	5.77
9/21-9/27	7	26	12	4	0	0	0	42	6.00	69	400	5.80
9/28-10/4	5	16	8	1	0	0	0	25	5.00	74	425	5.74

Focusing on that rightmost column, which gives a running average of points per game, we can see that the Padres improved over the first few weeks and then flatlined. Were we so inclined, we could break things down further, noting how much of this improvement was due to Black playing the right guys (or at least the guys we think he ought to play), how much to increased on-base ability (that Aug. 10-Aug. 16 week sure looks nice) and how much to increased power. In other words, not only can we see *that* changes have occurred, we can also see *where* changes have occurred.

If we wanted to get real crazy, we could combine the previous two techniques and examine trends of individual players. For example, at the top of the next page is a week-by-week accounting of Cabrera's performance as measured by Modified Box Scores.

As with any other accounting method, the weekly individual totals comprise too small a sample to tell us much worth knowing. String together several weeks, however, and we begin to see patterns emerge and stories unfold. In Cabrera's case, that story is primarily one of consistency (which we might not expect from a player who spent the previous season in the Single-A South Atlantic League) and secondarily one of a young player that wore down toward the end (which should surprise us less given that he played every inning of every game at shortstop for the Padres in the season's second half).

Everth Cabrera

	Week							Since All-Star Break						
	G	PT	OB	SL	Tot	A%	T/G	G	PT	OB	SL	Tot	A%	T/G
7/16-7/19	4	4	0	0	4	.000	1.00	4	4	0	0	4	.000	1.00
7/20-7/26	7	7	4	1	12	.417	1.71	11	11	4	1	16	.313	1.45
7/27-8/2	7	7	4	2	13	.462	1.86	18	18	8	3	29	.379	1.61
8/3-8/9	7	5	2	1	8	.375	1.14	25	23	10	4	37	.378	1.48
8/10-8/16	6	6	5	0	11	.455	1.83	31	29	15	4	48	.396	1.55
8/17-8/23	7	4	4	1	9	.556	1.29	38	33	19	5	57	.404	1.50
8/24-8/30	6	6	4	0	10	.400	1.67	44	40	22	5	67	.403	1.52
8/31-9/6	6	6	4	1	11	.455	1.83	50	46	26	6	78	.410	1.56
9/7-9/13	6	6	2	0	8	.250	1.33	56	52	28	6	86	.395	1.54
9/14-9/20	6	6	3	1	10	.400	1.67	62	58	31	7	96	.395	1.55
9/21-9/27	7	7	1	0	8	.125	1.14	69	65	32	7	104	.375	1.51
9/28-10/4	5	4	2	0	6	.333	1.20	74	69	34	7	110	.373	1.49

Reality Check

Compiling numbers based on some contrived system is fun, but it's useful only inasmuch as it reflects reality in a meaningful way. With that in mind, let's evaluate the final Modified Box Scores totals for the players we tracked against their traditional numbers:

	Modified Box Scores				Actual			
	PT	OB	SL	Tot	PA	BA	OBP	SLG
Blanks	23	15	10	48	122	.288	.393	.635
Hundley	22	13	7	42	126	.241	.278	.440
Venable	52	27	15	94	257	.262	.325	.459
Headley	66	37	5	108	297	.293	.377	.421
Cabrera	69	34	7	110	330	.254	.343	.367
Macias	9	3	0	12	67	.172	.284	.207

As we would expect, the players that earned the most slugging points (relative to total points) by our accounting method also had the highest slugging percentages. Similar relationships exist between the PT component and plate appearances, and also between the OB component and on-base percentage. In other words, the numbers accrued through Modified Box Scores serve as a reasonably accurate shorthand for actual performance, which means that our method is useful as well as fun.

How about the pitchers? I've added the names of a few more young arms (Wade LeBlanc, Clayton Richard and Tim Stauffer) to the chart below so we have something to look at besides Latos' line:

	Modified Box Scores				Actual			
	End	Eff	Pwr	Tot	G	IP	ERA	K/9
Latos	5	3	3	11	10	50.2	4.62	6.93
LeBlanc	7	2	2	11	7	42	2.57	6.00
Richard*	9	2	2	13	12	64	4.08	6.75
Stauffer	10	3	4	17	13	66	3.68	6.27

**Padres numbers only.*

It's tougher to draw meaningful conclusions on the pitching side because there's not as much data (these guys pitch every five days) and there isn't necessarily a direct correlation between, say, the Pwr component and strikeouts per nine innings. This could be studied further to see if our method for evaluating pitchers needs additional refinements—one potential issue came to light when I added Stauffer: In his July 25 start at Washington, he struck out one batter in one inning; technically he gets his Pwr point for meeting our established criteria, but that doesn't seem right to me.

For grins, and so this article isn't exclusively about the Padres, let's see how another team's young pitchers fared according to our method. Baltimore's Brian Matusz played college ball at my alma mater, so we'll go with the Orioles. Jason Berken, David Hernandez, Matusz and Chris Tillman are young and they provide us with data points, which makes them suitable for demonstration purposes:

	Modified Box Scores				Actual			
	End	Eff	Pwr	Tot	G	IP	ERA	SO/9
Berken	11	4	3	18	15	73.2	6.96	4.89
Hernandez	8	0	4	12	14	69.1	6.10	6.62
Matusz	7	2	4	13	8	44.2	4.63	7.66
Tillman	10	1	3	14	12	65	5.40	5.40

I'm seeing a couple of problems, both related to Berken's performance. First, why are his Modified Box Scores numbers better than Hernandez's when the latter's real-world numbers are better? Berken's gains are in the End and Eff categories, so it is possible that the thresholds for those need to be tweaked—does a five inning outing deserve merit? What about six?

Here's another problem that didn't become evident until I looked at another team (I noticed this issue prior to Berken's final two starts, which is why his numbers below look a little different):

	Modified Box Scores				Actual			
	End	Eff	Pwr	Tot	G	IP	ERA	SO/9
Berken	10	3	3	16	13	65	6.78	4.98
Stauffer	10	3	4	17	13	66	3.68	6.27

Based on their Modified Box Scores numbers, we might expect a closer match in terms of traditional stats between Berken and Stauffer (incidentally, Berken-Stauffer would be a great name for a shoe), but Berken's ERA is more than three runs higher. Granted, Stauffer pitched half his games at the cavernous Petco Park and nothing in our method directly measures the number of runs allowed, but still ... this suggests that there is room for improvement (maybe walks, e.g., could be used to track efficiency).

That said, the tool is useful in that it gives us a general idea of how players are doing on a game-by-game basis. It also succeeds in helping those of us who might otherwise have trouble watching our favorite team get beat like a mule every night focus on something else within the game. The method may not be perfect, but it is fun ... like baseball is supposed to be.

Next Steps And Final Thoughts

Now that we have this tool at our disposal, where do we go from here? Well, you could tweak the parameters if you were so inclined. Maybe add a stolen base component if you're tracking a player (like Cabrera) who possesses good speed. The system lends itself to customization, so the only limit is your imagination.

Whatever you decide to do with this tool, I hope it serves you well as your team struggles through a rebuilding season. And I hope that at year's end, you won't need it anymore and you can pass it along to someone else who does. Perhaps you have a friend in Pittsburgh ...

The original article that spawned this work can be found at http://ducksnorts.com/blog/2009/07/smooth-jazz-and-other-questionable-ideas.html

History

Pete and Honus

by Craig R. Wright

When discussing Grover "Pete" Alexander, it is hard to go more than a few sentences without saying something about his shutouts. His most famous record is his 16 shutouts in a single season. Less well known but even more astounding is his record of 28 shutouts over a span of two seasons. Both are the major league records at the modern pitching distance, and his 28 shutouts in consecutive seasons are actually more than any other pitcher has managed in *three* consecutive seasons.[1]

Most Shutouts, Season
16 – Pete Alexander 1916
13 – Jack Coombs 1912
13 - Bob Gibson 1968

Most Shutouts, Consecutive Seasons
28 – Pete Alexander 1915-16
20 – Walter Johnson 1913-14
19 – Coombs, Mathewson, Walsh

The 1916 season is Alexander's most famous season. Besides the record-setting 16 shutouts, he had his career high in wins (33), which remains the single-season record for the National League after the introduction of the cork-centered ball in 1910. However, as great as his accomplishments were in 1916, he was even better the season before in nearly every other category, including-ERA, a better winning percentage, a nearly 50% better strikeout rate, a far superior hit rate, and half as many homers (see the table below).

Bill James's Win Shares methodology rates Alexander's 1915 pitching performance as the best in National League history under the modern rules (beginning with the modern foul strike rule, which was introduced in the NL in 1901). And only the amazing Walter Johnson of the American League ever had a better season since the introduction of the cork-centered ball in 1910.

When the 1915 season began, the single-season record for shutouts was 16 and belonged to the little-known George Bradley,[2] but that was in 1876 and under playing rules so foreign as to have little relevance to records set just a decade later. The single-season record for shutouts at the modern pitching distance was 13 by Colby Jack Coombs in 1910, and the National League record of 11 was set by Christy Mathewson in 1908.

In the 1915 season, Alexander actually got to pitch head-to-head for the first time against shutout king Colby Jack Coombs, who had just moved over from the to the Boston Braves from the Philadelphia Athletics. On June 26, in their only match-up of the season, the future shutout king appropriately bested Coombs with a shutout. It was Pete's best game of the year and arguably the best of his whole career. He took a perfect game into the eighth inning, when Hall of Famer Zach Wheat singled for the only base runner of the game.

That year Alexander also got to pitch three times against the National League shutout king, Christy Mathewson. Pete won all three games, and in their third match-up, he scattered seven hits to blank the Giants 2-0 for his 10th shutout of the year. A few days later, Mathewson watched from the bench as Alexander white-washed his Giants to tie his league record.

Alexander had five starts left in the season to break the National League record and possibly get Coombs's major league record as well. He did not come close to a shutout in his next two starts, but then nearly pulled it off on Sept. 19, when he held the Cardinals to four hits without an earned run—but the Cardinals managed to push across a couple of runs on defensive errors. His very next start was a similar miss: He five-hit the Cubs, did not allow an earned run, but again his defense let him down as a single unearned run crossed the plate.

					Per 9 Innings			
Alexander	ERA	W-L	W%	IP	H	K	BR	HR
1915	1.22	31-10	.756	376.3	6.1	5.8	7.8	3
1916	1.55	33-12	.733	389.0	7.5	3.9	8.9	6

To give Pete his best shot at setting the league record in his final start, he was given five days of rest for only the second time that year. On Sept. 29, against the Boston Braves, he pitched brilliantly, allowing a single hit, one walk, and no runs. Besides breaking Mathewson's record, that win also clinched a tie for the pennant, and it also set yet another record for Pete Alexander that still stands today—it was Pete's fourth one-hitter of the season. That tied an ancient record for most complete games of one hit or less in a season, and Alexander remains the only pitcher to do it at the modern pitching distance.

The Phillies won the pennant outright a couple of days later, and that ended any notion that the club would try to sneak in one more start for Alexander to try to tie the major league mark for shutouts. He took a final tune-up relief appearance of one inning before taking on the Boston Red Sox in the World Series. He came close to throwing his trademark shutout in the opening game of the Series. He was four outs away when Boston pushed across its lone run, and Pete won 3-1 for the Phillies' lone victory in that Series. In Alexander's only other start, he lost 2-1 on a walk-off hit by Duffy Lewis with two outs in the ninth.

It was an amazing season, but it could have been far more memorable with a few more breaks. 1915 was the best strikeout season of Alexander's career, but when he let the opposition put the ball in play, he suffered mightily from a lack of defensive support. An incredible 41 percent of the runs that scored with Alexander on the mound in 1915 were unearned, easily the most of his 20-year career. Compared to his record-setting 1916 season, he allowed a dozen more unearned runs in 1915, and they proved to be especially costly.

In going 31-10 in the 1915 season, Alexander suffered four defeats that were due to an unearned run, including back-to-back games where he lost on a walk-off error, one in the ninth inning and one in the 10th. And the unusual number of unearned runs also denied Pete a surprising number of shutouts. No fewer than *five* times Alexander threw a complete game without allowing a single earned run but missed getting the shutout due to an unearned run. He pitched very well in all five games, never allowing more than five hits and in one of the games he threw his season high of 12 strikeouts.

Looking at the peripheral numbers in those starts, Alexander pitched as well or better than he had in most games in which he recorded a shutout. He averaged fewer hits and more strikeouts in those five potential shutouts that were lost by the defense than he had averaged in the record 28 shutouts that did go into the books in 1915-16. It is not that far-fetched to say that with a few breaks Alexander could have finished the 1915 season with a record of 34-7 and *17* shutouts. (Under the assumption that with better defense, he would have gone 3-1 in the four games he lost on unearned runs.)

As bad as Alexander's luck was with his defensive support in 1915, it clearly did not carry over to 1916. Rather than 41 percent of his runs being unearned, that mark fell dramatically to 26 percent. While 26 percent still sounds like a lot by today's standards, it was very normal in that era. Indeed, it was right around the league average (24 percent). Rather than losing four games on unearned runs, Pete lost only one such game in 1916. And rather than costing Alexander shutouts, it appears his defense played over its head in preserving his shutouts. Most notable was a game on May 26, when with two outs in the sixth inning, Casey Stengel of the Brooklyn Dodgers was headed home with a run that would have tied the game 1-1 and ruined the shutout. The Phillies' right fielder, Cactus Gavvy Cravath, threw a perfect strike to the plate to nail Stengel and preserve the shutout, which Alexander completed, giving him six shutouts in his first 11 starts of the year.

That pondering of "what might have been" the year before in 1915 lends itself to an obvious question. *How many shutouts did Alexander lose to unearned runs in his record-setting 1916 season?* The answer is … none.

Now let that sink in for a moment.

The record for most complete games without allowing an earned run—does *not* belong to Alexander's season with the 16 shutouts but rather to his amazing 1915 season with its 17 "technical shutouts," which are complete games in which the pitcher never allowed an earned run.

And looking at the auxiliary numbers to his perfect ERA in the two sets of games, it seems clear that Alexander actually pitched *better* in his 17 "technical shutouts" in 1915 than he did in his 16 actual shutouts in 1916. Per inning, he struck out more batters, and he allowed fewer base runners and fewer hits.

		Per 9 Innings		
Technical Shutouts	**G**	**H**	**BR**	**K**
1915	17	4.0	5.6	5.7
1916	16	5.3	6.1	4.0

The Honus Wagner Effect

In researching Alexander's nearest misses at shutouts in 1915-16, seven games stood out, and it was startling to see how one player was at the center of stopping three of these "almost" shutouts. It was the ever amazing Honus Wagner, and adding to the charm of the story, for these particular seasons we are talking about a very *ancient* Wagner.

In 1915, the oldest pitcher in the league was Otto Hess, who at age 36 would appear in only four games and throw 14 innings. The position players aged only slightly more gracefully. The offense in those days was tremendously geared toward speed, and of the baseball skills, speed is the most vulnerable to age. In those days almost all position players were done as regulars by age 35. Honus Wagner was the most extreme exception.

In 1915, at age 41, Wagner played every one of his team's games and led the league in plate appearances. Technically, he was the second-oldest player in the league. His manager, Hall of Famer Fred Clarke, was 42, and although he had essentially retired as a player after his 1911 season at age 38, Clarke continued to sneak himself in for a brief appearance here and there. In 1915 he played a single game with two plate appearances. After Clarke and Wagner, the next-oldest players in the league were Miller Huggins and Tommy Leach, who both were 37 and would sit out at least 50 games.

On May 11, 1915, in the first game that Alexander lost a shutout while only allowing an unearned run, Alexander was pitching against Pittsburgh and it was the old warrior Honus Wagner, who reached base on an error, stole a base, and came around to score.

Wagner's most famous blow to deny Alexander a shutout is the time he hit a home run for the lone run by the Pirates' offense. That blast became a minor legend,with the facts getting a bit hazy over time. Some said it happened in 1915, others said 1916, and the most common version claimed that it was the only hit that Alexander allowed that day, thus also denying Pete what would have been the only no-hitter of his career.

The game behind the legend took place on July 9, 1915. Alexander did take a no-hitter into the eighth inning, when he got the first batter and then lost it on Wagner's over-the-fence home run at Baker Bowl. However, it did not end up the lone hit, as Pittsburgh collected a second hit after Wagner's blow.

In today's game, where home runs are about six times more common, such a hit would hardly be the stuff of legend, but in the context of that era, Wagner's blow was truly an electrifying event. The average pitcher allowed a homer every 54 innings, and a great one like Pete Alexander rarely ever allowed a homer—it was rarer still for him to allow a home run when throwing in top form. The *New York Times* heralded it as the first homer Alexander had allowed the whole season, but that was inaccurate. It was the second of three homers that Pete allowed that year, or about one for every 125 innings. Wagner's blow was a breakthrough for Pittsburgh fans, as their Pirates were a below-average offensive team in 1915, and they always seemed to catch Alexander on one of his best days. In Pete's first five appearances against Pittsburgh in 1915, covering 41 innings, the *only* earned run he allowed was Wagner's home run. Because it did not happen in 1916, it didn't keep Alexander from extending his record to a 17th shutout, but it did keep Pete from tying Coombs's major league shutout record in 1915.

In passing, allow me to comment on the unusual longevity of Wagner's power-hitting skills. Just 20 days after homering to break up Alexander's no-hitter and shutout, Wagner would become the oldest player to hit a grand slam, a record that would stand 70 years until broken by Tony Perez in 1985. Wagner ended up with six homers in 1915, becoming the first player to hit six homers in a season past the age of 40. Surprisingly that record lasted nearly 40 years into the Live Ball era. It remained unmatched until Hank Sauer passed him in 1958. Sauer, of course, did it in a very different era. Hank's 12 homers in 1958 ranked 35th in the league. Wagner's six homers in 1915 were the eighth-most in the NL.

Unfortunately for Pete Alexander, Honus did not follow through with his plans to retire after the 1915 season, and he continued to be a thorn in the side of the league's best pitcher. The closest that Alexander came to throwing a 17th shutout in 1916 came on June 12 in a game against the Pirates at the Baker Bowl. It was another brilliant game for Alexander, who threw a four-hitter without walking a batter, holding a 2-0 lead going into the ninth. That inning, the Pirates got a runner to third base with two outs and Honus Wagner stepped up to the plate. Wagner was now officially the oldest player in the league, and the oldest to play as a regular since Cap Anson back in 1896.

Yet the 42-year-old Wagner remained a dangerous hitter and came into the game hitting .305. Indeed, if it had been a one-run game, Alexander might have pitched around him, but with the two-run lead it made sense to take on the old warrior. Honus smoked a liner up the middle that hit Pete hard in the shin and bounced far enough away to score the runner.

That blow possibly cost Alexander more than just that one shutout. Pete did not miss a game, but that line shot off his leg may have had a lingering effect. He had a bit of a rough patch for the next six starts, including an extremely rare three-game losing streak. Beginning with the lost shutout on Wagner's shot off his shin, Pete went seven starts without blanking the opposition. It was his longest streak without a shutout that whole season.

Alexander's shutout records are truly amazing, but who knows how much better than they would have been if not for his nemesis Honus Wagner.

Footnotes

[1] Walter Johnson and Christy Mathewson each managed 27 shutouts in their best three-season run.

[2] An interesting coincidence is that the only two major league pitchers to throw 16 shutouts in a season were given both their first and middle names in honor of a U.S. president. Many know that Pete Alexander's given name is Grover Cleveland Alexander. Less well known is that George Bradley's middle name is Washington.

Second Trivia Challenge: Time Machine: Emit Enihcam

Who says that record books have to go forward? For this batch of trivia questions, the first season in baseball was 2008 (though games and seasons are still played forward) and history marches toward 1876. All career and single-season minima from above are applicable here: batting title and ERA title for single-season records, and 3,000 PA/1,000 IP for pitchers.

1. After the Red Sox took an early lead on world championships with their two in the 2000s, the Yankees became the first team to win three. Who was the second?
2. In just their fourth year of existence, they became the first National League expansion team to win a pennant.
3. This team stunned fans by becoming the first team to go from last place to the playoffs in consecutive years. Amazingly, it happened again the next two seasons with different teams.
4. Only one manager won a World Series in his rookie year. Who was he?
5. Although National League fans in 1994 and in 1930 found the feats amazing, they asterisked the would-be record holders since they didn't accomplish the feat over 162 games. To them, this beloved Canadian would always be the true record holder for his 1999 performance in this category.
6. Inheriting the mantle in 1999 from Brad Ausmus as the prototypical weak-hitting catcher, his record for lowest career OPS+ at the position was permanently surpassed only twice, once in 1940 and once in 1901.
7. With teams carrying fewer and fewer starters and 20-win seasons becoming more commonplace, it's hard to remember when 200 career wins was hard to come by. The first two pitchers to reach the then-venerated milestone, one right-handed, one left-handed, did so within 40 days of each other. Who were those initial legends?
8. On May 30, 1993, this person became the all-time home run leader with his 554th home run. On June 30, 1993, a different player became the second to hit 554. Name not only the two players but the previous record-holder.
9. On Aug. 5, 1991 against the Brewers, this 11-year veteran broke a record he had been working toward since his fourth season. Name the player and record.
10. It was the top of the eighth on April 17, 1988 with Don Mattingly at the plate and the Yankees down 5-1 against the Brewers (always in the right place at the right time). What record was set in this plate appearance?

The solutions to these questions and all Trivia Challenges are in the back of the book, starting on page 360.

The Best Series? Get the Hook

by Chris Jaffe

Everybody says that the Cincinnati-Boston World Series of 1975 was the best in history. I don't. I'll always maintain that the best Series I was ever in was the 1972 Series against Oakland.
–Sparky Anderson

When people talk of the greatest World Series of all time, the usual suspects come up: 1975 was the best for the Baby Boomers. In more recent times, the 1991 and 2001 Octobers are highly regarded. Some old-timers might recall the 1947 Series, and students of the game's history can point to 1912 and 1924.

It's quite possible that none of those was the greatest World Series of them all. Instead, the title might belong to an October overlooked by the game's collective memory, the 1972 Fall Classic. This Series, which featured the Cincinnati Reds and Oakland A's, was the most tightly played in history. Not only were a record six contests decided by one run, but there were only two innings in which either team led by more than two runs. In most games, the contest was in doubt until the final out.

Despite all that, the 1972 World Series lacks its rightful place in baseball folklore. People don't write best-selling books about it, ESPN misses it whenever it glosses over sports history, and Ken Burns's lengthy documentary on the national pastime never mentions it and features only two random pitches from this Series in a brief segment on the 1972-74 A's.

To understand why such a Series has been overlooked, you need to look at what made it so memorable and how that contrasts with what causes the general public to revere a particular World Series.

The 1972 World Series

Heading into the Series, the players on the Big Red Machine were openly confident. After defeating the Pirates in the fifth and deciding contest of the National League Championship Series, several Reds popped off that they already had proven they were baseball's best team. Bobby Tolan flatly declared, "As far as I'm concerned, the World Series is already over. The two best teams have played." Pete Rose announced that the NLCS "represented the world's championship."

Odds makers agreed, making Cincinnati the favorite. After all, the NL was widely regarded as the better league, having claimed victory in six of the nine previous World Series and 14 of the last 16 All-Star Games. The Reds also posted a better regular season record, and, since 1953, only once had an AL squad with a worse regular-season mark than its NL rival claimed the grand prize. Finally, the Reds had played in the 1970 World Series, giving them recent experience on the game's grandest stage.

The A's couldn't compete with that. It was the franchise's first pennant since 1931, when Connie Mack managed the club in Philadelphia. Prior to 1972, the A's possessed the longest World Series drought of any pre-expansion franchise. (By claiming the 1972 pennant, they pushed that unwanted designation to the Cubs.)

Most importantly, the A's were without their best player, Reggie Jackson. In the finale of the ALCS, Jackson injured his leg, and would be on crutches the rest of October. Jackson's roster slot went to pinch runner Allen Lewis, a rather steep decline in talent.

Oakland also appeared far more fractious that the Reds. Under the ownership of the continually obnoxious and predictably unpredictable Charles Finley, the A's seemed more interested in fighting each other than the opposition. In fact, moments after claiming the AL crown, Oakland pitchers Vida Blue and Blue Moon Odom engaged in a clubhouse fistfight. Champions were not supposed to behave like that.

For that matter, champions weren't supposed to look like Oakland. In a literal way, the 1972 Oakland A's looked nothing like any recent World Series competitor. Finley thought traditional baseball uniforms looked too staid and drab, and wanted to liven up the game's appearance by having his players wear gold and green colors. The Reds wore more sedate white home and gray road jerseys.

Just as baseball began to get used to Finley's brave new visual world, the A's launched another stylistic revolution upon the game in mid-1972: facial hair. In June 1972, Finley hosted "Mustache Day" at Oakland's ballpark in an effort to appeal to the changing times. He even offered his players bonuses if they grew whiskers for the game. This clashed with baseball tradition, in which many teams—including the Reds—mandated that players be clean-shaven. Many Oakland players kept their new look after the game ended, earning them the nickname "the Mustache Gang."

In the pre-cable days, the only chance people outside of Oakland had to see the A's was on NBC's Game of the Week or when they traveled on the road. For many viewers, the 1972 postseason marked the television debut of mustachioed baseball, and the visual difference between the two squads served as the most obvious contrast. It was longhairs from near Berkeley, Calif., taking on the conservative, well-scrubbed gentlemen from the heartland.

In many ways these images had little to do with the personalities of the players on the two clubs. After all, the supposedly rebel A's adopted their new look at their owner's urging. Still, the squads certainly possessed different cultures. It wasn't the Reds who got into fistfights in the clubhouse—it was those rebels from Oakland who did.

Game One

The A's won the Series opener in Cincinnati 3-2, thanks to an unexpected hero, Gene Tenace. He became the first player in baseball history to homer in each of his first two World Series at-bats, driving in all of Oakland's runs in the process. One of the more obscure members of Oakland's starting lineup, Tenace was a bench player for most of 1972, not claiming the starting job until the last six weeks of the season. Though Tenace developed into a dangerous power hitter over his career, after the game he told reporters he'd never hit two long balls in a professional game. The Reds fought hard, but couldn't convert on several opportunities to score late in the game, allowing the upstarts from the AL to eke out the win.

After the game, Reds manager Sparky Anderson told reporters their scouting reports indicated Tenace was a mediocre fastball hitter and that he twice went deep because pitcher Gary Nolan, by his own admission, threw two terrible pitches. Anderson believed they lost because of their inability to score when the opportunities presented themselves. Unfortunately for Cincinnati, the scouring reports were wrong—Tenace was a fastball hitter. The Reds' failure to adjust away from this faulty information would allow Tenace to torment them throughout the Series.

Game Two

The A's continued to surprise Cincinnati in the second game: They quickly took a lead, two runs to none, which they preserved into the final inning. In the bottom of the ninth, however, the entire day's effort nearly fell away from Oakland.

With a runner on first and no one out, Reds third baseman Dennis Menke launched a mammoth shot to left that many thought was destined for the grandstands. Instead, left fielder Joe Rudi made a circus catch for the ages to rob Menke of extra bases.

As he stared into Cincinnati's afternoon sun, Rudi caught the ball backhanded while diving into the wall. Battling nature and the building made it less a catch than a successfully run obstacle course. All who saw Rudi's grab considered it one of the greatest catches in October history, alongside Al Gionfriddo's grab of Joe DiMaggio's fly ball in 1947, Willie Mays' famous catch-and-throw in 1954, Sandy Amoros' game-saving play in 1955, and the desperation lunge Dwight Evans would make three years later in 1975 (also against the Reds).

In some ways, Rudi's catch might be the most important. Based on how the inning played out, if he hadn't made the catch, the Reds would've scored at least two runs that inning and possibly won the game. If the A's lose that game, Cincinnati takes the Series. Mays' team swept the Series, and the clubs of Gionfriddo and Evans lost their October contests. Amoros was the only other one whose famous catch not only was a great play, but potentially saved the day for a team that won in seven games.

As great as Rudi's moment was, Oakland manager Dick Williams maintained in his autobiography that it wasn't even the best defensive play of the inning. Cincinnati's next batter, Cesar Geronimo, hit a scorching grounder down the first base line that looked like a sure double. Instead, Mike Hegan, who had entered the game as a defensive replacement at first base, somehow snared the ball to retire Geronimo.

This pair of defensive gems proved especially important when Hal McRae, pinch-hitting for Cincinnati, singled in Tony Perez (who had advanced on Geronimo's shot) to make it 2-1. Had it not been for Oakland's spectacular defense, McRae would've singled home the go-ahead run for a 3-2 comeback victory. If the A's made only one of that pair of gems, the score would've been tied. Instead, Oakland retired the last batter to preserve the win.

Cincinnati was in an unenviable position. No team had won a Series after dropping the first two games at home. Anderson said he wasn't panicking, but he was getting close to it as the Series moved to Oakland.

Game Three

After a rainstorm pushed this contest back by a day, Game Three made history with its very first pitch: It was only the second night game in World Series history. Ever the iconoclast, Finley successfully lobbied for Oakland to host games that would appear on prime time TV.

To start during the East Coast's best viewing hours, the game was played in the West Coast's twilight, a fact that gave Cincinnati an opportunity. Hitters on both clubs had trouble battling the setting sun for the first half of the game, leaving it a scoreless stalemate for six innings.

In the seventh, Cincinnati claimed a lead on a routine single that became an unexpectedly dramatic play midway through. With one out and Perez on second base, Geronimo's hit appeared to allow Perez an easy road home. Instead, after rounding third Perez slipped and fell on the still-wet base paths. Luckily for him, the key Oakland defenders didn't notice Perez's pratfall because they were more concerned with preventing Geronimo from advancing to second. Perez scurried home before Oakland realized what happened.

Cincinnati sought to expand its 1-0 margin in the eighth inning, when one of the most famous moments of the Series occurred. The Reds placed runners on first and third with one out and 1972 National League MVP Johnny Bench at the plate. When the trailing runner stole second, a light bulb went off in manager Dick Williams' head. With a 3-2 count on Bench, Williams stormed to the mound to speak with pitcher Rollie Fingers and catcher Tenace. He motioned to the superstar slugger at the plate and the empty base at first, clearly indicating he wanted Bench intentionally walked.

Williams retreated to the dugout, and Tenace went to his position and motioned for an intentional pass. When Fingers threw, Tenace leapt behind the plate and caught a slider for strike three. All over America, people turned to those sitting next to them and burst out laughing. Williams had thought up a trick play, and the joke was on Bench.

Williams referred to the stunt as "my 15 minutes of fame." His managing eventually earned him a place in Cooperstown, and the hoodwinking of Bench became the signature move for the skipper known for his tactical smarts. Afterward, Bench maintained that he had not been caught off-guard, but that Fingers threw a pitch that was simply unhittable.

Regardless, the game remained 1-0, which was how it ended. Through three games, the home team had yet to win a single contest.

Game Four

For the second consecutive day, Oakland hosted a twilight night game, and again hitters had trouble making solid contact until the sun was safely past the horizon. Through seven innings, the only scoring came from Tenace's bat: In the fifth inning he turned another Cincinnati fastball into his third Series homer. Oakland led 1-0.

In the eighth inning, however, Williams—last night's hero strategist—quickly became a whipping boy for many Oakland fans. Even though Ken Holtzman was pitching a shutout, Williams pulled him with two out and a runner on second.

To comprehend this unorthodox move, you must understand Williams' mentality. By nature, he was a control freak, and the closely contested World Series games of 1972 magnified this characteristic. Simply put, the last thing Williams wanted was for Oakland to lose because he didn't do enough. The fact that Williams was widely renowned as one of the sharpest minds in the game furthered this desire to leave his mark whenever he could. If Williams thought Holtzman was losing his stuff, then Williams was going to make the move—second-guessers be damned.

One other factor may have pushed Williams into such an active managing strategy. Five years earlier, as a rookie manager with the Boston Red Sox, he piloted the team to an unexpected pennant. The Sox lost the Series in seven games, and this was Williams' first opportunity at October redemption. The combination of a controlling nature and a hunger for an unattained world championship in the midst of an incredibly close World Series ensured that Williams would be as active a manager as there had been in the Fall Classic.

When Holtzman saw Williams leave the dugout in the eighth, he might not have realized he was done for the night. Part of Williams' active managing strategy was to talk to his pitchers whenever he could before key moments. On at least one occasion he brought notes with him to the mound. Williams took advantage of the rulebook to do this.

In 1972, the rules stated that during the postseason, and unlike the regular season, the manager could visit the mound more than once an inning without removing the pitcher. By his own count, Williams made 42 trips to the mound this World Series. When Major

League Baseball changed the rule, Williams joked that the alteration should be named for him.

Whatever Williams' strengths, pulling Holtzman immediately backfired: Cincinnati promptly scored a pair of runs for a 2-1 lead. That remained the score entering the bottom of the ninth, when some key decisions Williams made before the Series paid substantial dividends for Oakland.

Most rosters in this era featured 15 position players and 10 pitchers. While teams normally constructed a similar bench for the postseason, Williams thought 10 pitchers were unnecessary in a short series. Instead, he loaded Oakland's roster with 17 position players and eight pitchers. This perfectly fit Williams' nature, as it gave him more opportunities to intervene. When Game Four's ninth inning began, a full complement of backups remained for his use.

With one out in the ninth, Williams dove into his bench. First, he called on pinch-hitter Gonzalo Marquez, who bopped a bouncer up the middle for an infield single. Williams wanted someone with a bit more speed to represent the tying run, so Oakland's pinch-runner, Allan Lewis—"the Panamanian Express"—went to first.

Williams refrained from calling on another pinch-hitter with World Series hero Tenace up next, and the catcher rewarded that decision with a single that sent Lewis to second base. With the number eight hitter due up, Williams called on veteran platoon specialist Don Mincher to pinch-hit against Cincinnati's relief ace, Clay Carroll. Mincher singled to center, sending Lewis home with the tying run and Tenace to third.

Williams went to his bench once again. Reserve outfielder Angel Mangual pinch-hit in the ninth slot, while Odom, a fleet-footed pitcher, replaced Mincher at first in hopes a double play wouldn't end the inning. The second pinch-runner proved to be unnecessary as Mangual rapped out Oakland's fourth consecutive single.

In the space of 10 minutes, Williams used three pinch-hitters and two pinch-runners to score two runs in the bottom of the ninth and claim victory, 3-2. The seventh inning's goat was again a genius.

Though extreme, Williams' hyper-involvement that inning typified the way he handled the Series as a whole. By the time the Series finished, Williams had called on nine defensive replacements, eight pinch-runners, and 13 pinch-hitters in 11 different at-bats. (Twice, Williams called on a pinch-hitter for a platoon advantage only to see Anderson bring in a new pitcher. On those occasions, Williams inserted a pinch-hitter for his pinch-hitter.) Much like his decision to sucker Bench in Game Three, these maneuvers kept working for him. For example, Oakland's pinch-hitters posted a .545 batting average. Marquez alone connected for three pinch-hit singles. If anyone rivaled Tenace's prominence in the Series, it was his manager.

In the Cincinnati dugout, Anderson considered himself the goat. An advance scout told the Reds that Marquez hit grounders up the middle, but Anderson declined to play shortstop Davey Concepcion closer to second, because Concepcion—who knew Mangual—told the manager the scout was wrong. When the ball bounced up the middle, a sure out became a rally-igniting hit. Years later, Anderson maintained that he blew the game and Series by ignoring the scouting report.

The Mustache Gang could clinch the world title with just one more victory.

Game Five

Down three games to one, it was do-or-die time for the Big Red Machine. Early on it looked like die, as Tenace continued to mock the scouting reports by blasting his fourth home run of the Series to give Oakland an early lead.

Cincinnati gradually clawed its way on top by scoring one run at a time. The most remarkable score came in the fifth inning when speedy Joe Morgan scrambled all the way home from first on a routine single to left by Tolan. Morgan, a very fast player, was attempting to steal before Tolan made contact, but this base-running feat primarily came from Morgan's rare combination of intelligence and aggressiveness on the field.

However, few things came easily in this Series, and trailing 5-4 the A's launched a rally in the bottom of the ninth. With one out and a runner on first, Williams went back to his extensive bench, installing Odom as a pinch runner for the second straight game and asking veteran catcher Dave Duncan to pinch-hit. Duncan cleanly singled to left, sending Odom to third. With still only one out and the top of the order coming up, the A's looked poised either to send the game into extra innings or win the Series outright this inning.

Shortstop Bert Campaneris hit a pop-up into Oakland's cavernous foul territory along the first base line. As Morgan raced to it from second, Odom got ready to take off for the plate, as Oakland's scouting report claimed Morgan had a mediocre arm. Right after Morgan caught it and Odom took off for the plate, the second baseman slipped on the foul territory's grass.

Let's pause here for a moment. The sight of Morgan's tumble must have been an electric one for the Oakland fans. Just the night before, the fans saw their team come back in the bottom of the ninth to win, and it looked like it was going to happen again. It seemed clear that Odom should be able to dash home with the game-tying run. Even if Oakland didn't win it that inning, the A's were in an excellent position go win the game and Series that night. The Series wouldn't go back to Ohio—the Oakland fans could see their team win it right before them. Morgan's slip seemed like the Fates intervening to give Oakland the world title.

That badly underestimated the tenacious Morgan. He immediately lifted himself up and fired a perfect strike to home plate, where Bench tagged Odom out for a game-ending double play. The stunned crowd in Oakland went from ecstasy to silence in a manner of seconds. Now the Reds claimed the Series' fifth consecutive one-run game, and sent the teams back to Cincinnati to finish it.

Game Six

Finally, after 45 innings of continual tension, the 1972 World Series produced a laugher: The Reds handily won 8-1 to force a seventh and deciding game. It was a little closer than the score indicated—the Reds didn't break the game open until a five-run seventh inning—but it was an unremarkable contest.

The only real drama occurred before the game when police received an anonymous tip that a Reds fan threatened to kill Tenace if he played again. Authorities found the fan outside Riverfront Stadium, and he indeed possessed a loaded revolver, for which he was promptly arrested. Tenace resolved to continue playing despite the unneeded drama. The injured Reggie Jackson quipped, "If you gotta go, Gene, at least it's on national television."

Game Seven

After a week of hard-fought games, it all came down to this. Oakland took a quick lead in the top of the first on an RBI single from, of course, Tenace. By the Series conclusion, he accrued nine RBIs for a team that scored only 16 runs. Tenace is the only person to drive in more than half a team's runs in a seven-game Series, and also the only player on a Series victor to achieve that. He also slugged more extra-base hits than all his teammates combined, five to four.

Oakland's starting pitcher, Odom, prevented Cincinnati from any scoring threats in the early innings, but that did not win him a vote of confidence from his manager. Not only was Williams the same man who pulled Holtzman in Game Four, but the high stakes inherent in a Game Seven made Williams acutely interested in leaving nothing beyond his reach. Williams later reminisced that he came to the park that day convinced he needed to work harder than ever for Oakland to win. In fact, by day's end he would've made 16 trips to the mound to confer with his pitchers.

As a result, when Odom began struggling with his control, Williams yanked him in the fifth inning even though he'd allowed only two hits. In fact, pulling Odom ensured that the A's staff, despite holding Cincinnati to two or fewer runs in five games, would amass zero complete games. For the era, that was astonishing.

Behind Tenace's bat and Williams' pitchers, Oakland led Cincinnati 3-1 entering the bottom of the eighth. With just six outs left in the season, the Big Red Machine launched a final rally. After a leadoff single by Rose chased Catfish Hunter from the game, Morgan greeted Holtzman, pitching in relief, with a double.

Years later, Morgan maintained that Cincinnati's undoing in the 1972 Series came at that moment. Morgan thought the blast was a triple that could've driven Rose in, but the third base coach wanted Rose to hold up at third. Morgan wrote in his autobiography, "What bothers me to this day is that I *know* the A's were not worrying about Pete Rose—he wasn't the tying run. *I* was. So Pete should have been able to score easily." The speedy Morgan had to stop at second.

Rose scored on a one-out sacrifice fly shortly afterward to make the game 3-2, but the third out came before Morgan could score. If Morgan's assessment of the inning was correct, and he was considered a very smart player, Rose could've scored on his hit, leaving Morgan himself to score the game-tying run from third on the sacrifice fly. What've, could've, might've—it all means didn't. The A's still led and the Reds had only three outs left.

The ninth was itself rather uneventful. With two outs reliever Fingers hit a batter, making this the fifth game of the Series in which the tying or winning run was on base at its conclusion. However, the next batter poked an easy fly to Rudi in left. Oakland could exhale.

Written off as the weaker team from the weaker league and playing without its best player, the Mustache Gang had done it. Even though Cincinnati scored more runs in the Series, the Oakland A's were champions of the world, thanks to four one-run victories.

1972 and Memory

So why has this World Series been largely ignored by the collective memory of baseball fandom? One possibility is that it was simply overshadowed by the 1975 Series. Putting two great events so closely together sometimes diminishes the memory of one. For instance, the 1950 NL pennant race was one of the best ever, but Bobby Thomson's Shot Heart 'Round the World in 1951 pushed it out of baseball's consciousness.

But the problem of remembering 1972 is deeper than that. It relates to what makes a World Series especially memorable. To live on in the popular memory, a Series needs a hook—something a little extra special to set it apart. To put it another way, it's easier to recall great moments than an entire extended series.

The most fondly remembered Series have a great game serving to represent them. Fisk's homer allows the 1975 Series to live in the game's folklore. The 1991 Series contained the 10-inning 1-0 Game Seven. Senators-Giants in 1924 had its 12-inning finale. The Subway Series of 1947 had the Bill Bevens game. Sometimes a Series might have more than one hook (1991 also has Kirby Puckett's walk-off homer, and 2001 had back-to-back game-ending blasts), but at least one all-time classic moment.

The 1972 classic, while a great Series throughout, lacked that one special game. If one made up a list of the 50 greatest games in World Series history, it's possible none would come from 1972. You might have four or five games from that Series in the top 100, but none in its upper reaches. In fact, about 10 years ago baseball historian Joseph Dittmar wrote a book called The 100 Greatest Games of the Twentieth Century, which featured 35 World Series contests, but none from 1972. Though 1972 had the most impressive depth of great games, no one remembers a World Series based on its fifth-best contest.

A disproportionately large number of baseball's best-remembered games ended when the home team scored the winning run in the bottom of the final inning. That was the case with the Fisk game in 1975, Kirk Gibson's 1988 homer, the 1993 Joe Carter blast, and the Game Sevens of the 1912, 1924, 1960, 1991, 1997 and 2001 World Series. Not all of the best-remembered games end that way, but it clearly helps keep a game in the public memory, and thus serve as a hook for an entire World Series. The 1972 Series featured a record-tying five games won on the road. One of the two home wins was the Game Six laugher. Game Four featured 1972's sole walk-off win.

This leads to the next problem for the 1972 World Series: It peaked at the wrong time, with its most impressive highlights occurring in Games Four and Five. Looking at all baseball history, it's Games Six and Seven that are best remembered. In Dittmar's book (not a perfect source, but an effective one for charting how games are remembered), 18 of its 35 World Series contests came from Games Six and Seven, but it lists only six contests from either Game Four of Five.

Also, sometimes people remember a World Series for providing a signature moment to a classic career. That was the case with Mays' 1954 catch, Bob Gibson's 17-strikeout demolition of the Tigers in 1968, and Jackson's three straight homers in 1977. These three aren't considered classic Series, but they are better remembered than 1972.

The big stars in 1972 were Tenace and Rudi, hardly immortals. Though Fingers pitched brilliantly, posting a 1.74 ERA in 10.1 innings in six games (the most games by any pitcher in a quarter-century), there was no signature moment. Besides, Fingers pitched even better in the following World Series: a 0.66 ERA in 13.2 innings.

The Series provided an encapsulating moment for one Hall of Famer, though: manager Williams, when he fooled Bench in Game Three. If Williams is the 1972 World Series' best hook, it is no wonder it left so little hold on the popular imagination. Even the best-remembered manager of all-time, Casey Stengel, is more renowned for his speech patterns than for any specific maneuver he made in a single game.

In fact, the fame of the Big Red Machine and Mustache Gang paradoxically limited the memory of the 1972 Series because the signature moments for both squads occurred in other Octobers. People remember great teams for their victories, so sensibly the Reds are more remembered for their victory in the legendary 1975 World Series and a sweep of the Yankees in 1976.

By the same logic, it seems that people should remember the A's for 1972, but that wasn't the case. Like World Series, teams are remembered for their hooks, and Oakland's best were Reggie Jackson, winning three straight championships and internal quarrels centering on Charles Finley.

Jackson missed the 1972 Series, but played in the other two, winning the 1973 Series' MVP Award. Furthermore, it was the 1974 Series that locked up the three-peat. In 1972, no one knew it was the first of three straight championships. It merely looked like an upset. Had the 1972 Series claimed a third straight title for Oakland, it would be much better known.

Also, though Oakland never had a peaceful clubhouse, its internal discord peaked in the 1973 Fall Classic when Finley tried (and failed) to use a fraudulent medical report to keep second baseman Mike Andrews from playing after he cost the team a game with shoddy defense. The mood became so ugly that Williams announced in mid-Series he wouldn't return the next year. That 1973 team was Oakland at its most clearly combustible.

Frankly, it's possible that the Series lacks a proper place in popular consciousness because, for many, the wrong team won. Oakland was the gang of longhairs who got into fistfights overseen by the obnoxious owner. That's not what baseball is supposed to be. By the time Oakland won proper respect by winning three straight Series, 1972 was already disappearing in the rear view mirror.

Actually, there was one moment in this World Series that got a segment in Ken Burns' documentary. Strangely, though, it had nothing to do with the games themselves. Just before Game Two, baseball held a special ceremony for a man who revolutionized the game a quarter-century previously: Jackie Robinson.

In ill health and nearly blind from diabetes, Robinson threw out the first pitch, and gave a brief speech in which he declared "I am extremely proud and pleased to be here this afternoon. But I must admit I'm going to be tremendously more pleased and more proud when I look at that third base coaching line one day and see a black face managing in baseball." The 1972 Series not only survived more as social history than brilliant baseball, but the former helped cast the latter in the shadows.

As great as the 1972 World Series was, seemingly every surrounding factor worked to minimize its reputation in the game's memory. The best World Series of all time may very well have been the 1972 edition, but best isn't a synonym for most memorable.

The Year the Players Were Set Free

by Craig Brown

In many ways, 1976 was a watershed year for America. You had the Bicentennial, the unveiling of the space shuttle and a presidential election in which an incumbent was defeated for the first time in more than four decades.

As crazy and exciting as 1976 was, it was just as crazy and exciting in the game of baseball. The end of the Oakland A's dynasty, the return of the New York Yankees to the World Series after an 11-year absence and the second championship in a row for the Big Red Machine highlighted the action on the field. But all that was overshadowed by what was happening off the field.

A new era was dawning in baseball. With the reserve clause dead, some players were playing the 1976 season without contracts, with an eye to the future when they would be free to negotiate and sign with the team of their choosing. Under the old system, they were bound to their clubs—and often the contracts they offered. The system in which the clubs ruled the players would be replaced by one in which the owners and players stood on equal footing. The players who didn't sign contracts were pioneers, risking short-term security for long term wealth.

It was baseball's first free agent class.

The Foundation

The seeds of free agency were planted in 1969, when outfielder Curt Flood challenged baseball's reserve clause following his trade from the St. Louis Cardinals to the Philadelphia Phillies. Flood refused to report to Philadelphia and asked that Commissioner Bowie Kuhn declare him a free agent with the ability to negotiate with any or all clubs. Kuhn refused. Flood sat on the sidelines for all of the 1970 season and eventually brought his case before the Supreme Court. Although the court ruled against Flood, his actions struck a chord with the players. They had to play for the teams that owned their rights, and their contracts were dictated by the clubs. There were holdouts from time to time, but nothing like what Flood did to protest the reserve clause. Although he was unsuccessful in his battle with baseball's power structure, he paved the way for free agency.

Baseball's first free agent didn't come until after the 1974 season. That October, with the Oakland A's in the World Series against the Los Angeles Dodgers, A's star pitcher Jim "Catfish" Hunter revealed that owner Charlie Finley had failed to pay $50,000 of the $100,000 that was called for by his contract. The $50,000 payment Finley didn't honor was to be made in a lump sum to an insurance company as a tax shelter for Hunter. When a three-man arbitration panel ruled 2-1 that the notoriously parsimonious Finley in effect didn't hold up his end of the agreement, Hunter was declared a free agent, available to all 24 teams. As the first (and only) free agent that winter, and as the reigning Cy Young Award winner (he led the league with 25 wins and a 2.49 ERA), Hunter was expecting a bidding war for his services. "I want the best contract I can get from all 24 clubs," Hunter told reporters.

He got his bidding war, with every club in baseball except the San Francisco Giants making bids, including Finley's A's. Twelve of the 23 teams visited Hunter at his home in Ahoskie, N.C. Interest was fierce as Hunter whittled the field to eight teams just after Christmas.

As negotiations continued, Hunter pared the field further and on Dec. 30 it was believed the teams still in contention were the Atlanta Braves, Cleveland Indians, Kansas City Royals, New York Yankees and San Diego Padres. A source reported that Hunter and his attorneys were seeking a five-year contract totaling $1 million, plus an additional $1 million signing bonus, a 10-year retirement plan totaling $500,000 and a $1 million life insurance policy as a tax shelter to be paid over 10 years. He also asked for $200,000 to cover attorney fees and $25,000 insurance policies for both of his children. That brought his total reported price tag to $3.75 million.

It was an enormous sum, but didn't scare the Yankees, who ultimately agreed to Hunter's asking price.

The contract rocked the sport. Not only was Hunter the highest-paid ballplayer of all time, it was believed to be one of the top sports contracts ever negotiated. To the Yankees he was worth every penny the follwing year, leading the league with 328 innings pitched and tying for the league lead with 23 wins. He finished second in Cy Young Award voting to Baltimore's Jim Palmer.

The challenge that ultimately changed baseball came from Andy Messersmith and Dave McNally. Under the reserve clause, each year's contract gave the club an exclusive option to employ the player for that and the following year. Pitchers Messersmith and McNally, though, played the 1975 season without signing their contracts, then sued in an effort to become free agents following the next season, their "option year." (McNally was involved as a formality. He was injured for most of 1975 and appeared in only 12 games for the Expos before retiring in June. The players association was afraid Messersmith would sign a contract with the Dodgers at some point during the '75 season, so used the retired McNally as a backup.)

Arbitrator Peter Seitz's bombshell came in December 1975. He ruled that clubs could renew a player's contract for only one year, effectively eliminating the reserve clause. Two appeals courts subsequently upheld his ruling, setting the stage for Messersmith to become a free agent.

While baseball teams had been enthusiastic in their pursuit of Hunter in the previous year, this time circumstances were different. This was a challenge to the reserve clause—the very rule that kept players tied to their teams and kept salaries depressed. Baseball executives didn't like that one bit. "This is the worst thing that has happened in my 37 years of baseball," Pirates general manager Joe Brown told the Pittsburgh Post-Gazette. Brewers owner Bud Selig told a reporter he was "deeply distressed by the whole situation."

Even some players didn't grasp how the dismantling of the reserve clause would impact the game. "I don't think any of the players are jumping up and down," Baltimore's Brooks Robinson told a reporter from the Associated Press, voicing an opinion common among players that winter. Robinson was happy in Baltimore and planned to stay. He felt many of his peers would similarly eschew free agency to stay with their current teams.

When Messersmith officially entered the market, both the player and his agent were surprised when response was lukewarm. Although Messersmith had won 19 games for Los Angeles with an ERA of 2.29 and finished fifth in Cy Young voting, only seven teams were known to have made offers for the right hander,and all the offers paled in comparison to what Hunter got. Offers ranged from $750,000 for four years from the White Sox to $500,000 for three years from the Mets. At one point in early April, the Yankees thought they had a four-year, $1 million agreement in place, only to see it crumble when they wouldn't guarantee Messersmith his salary, as they had for Hunter.

With negotiations between Messersmith and the interested teams falling apart at seemingly every turn, the Padres were incensed when he broke off talks over a reported split of as little as $5,000. The 1976 season opened with Messersmith still a free agent, still shopping for a team. Eventually, Ted Turner and the Braves stepped forward with a package totaling $1.4 million for five years.

While the Hunter and Messersmith cases had different particulars, the players noticed one similarity: the money. As Ted Simmons put it, "Curt Flood stood up for us; Jim Hunter showed us what was out there; Andy Messersmith showed us the way."

Indeed. The game was about to change in a big way.

The Circus of '76

The Messersmith ruling paved the way to free agency for players who didn't sign a contract for the '76 season. Because this was uncharted territory, there were plenty of misgivings on both sides. Ownership feared that more than 200 free agents would flood the market. Players feared injury leading to lost money.

The Seitz ruling, in effect, gave every player who didn't sign a contract for the 1976 season the right to offer his services to any team for the following year. With the applecart of stability overturned and spooked by the specter of free agency, the owners locked out the players in March of '76. Perhaps the owners couldn't prevent the tide of free agency, but they weren't going down without a fight to impose some sort of restrictions.

Again, the root of the problem was the reserve clause. The owners offered free agency following eight years of a player's service with a club. The players wanted to become free agents after six years of service. Another issue was a "draft" to disperse the free agent pool. The owners wanted to limit the number of teams with which a player could negotiate to eight. The players wanted to be available to all 24. The owners were also trying to set up a method of compensation for a team that lost a player as a free agent. The players were against this, fearing it would depress the market for their services.

Spring training finally opened after a delay of 17 days. When the players reported, at least 150, or 25 percent of all big leaguers, had yet to sign a contract for the 1976 season including stars such as Tom Seaver, Rod Carew and Bert Blyleven. According to a report in *Sports Illustrated*, at the same point in the previous spring, only 10 players were unsigned.

It was predicted that even with the high number of unsigned players, most would eventually sign contracts. That is, in fact, what happened: Players signed '76 contracts throughout the season. Late holdouts included Carlton Fisk, Rick Burleson and Fred Lynn of the Red Sox. All three waited to sign their 1976 contracts until early August. The last player to sign was utilityman Steve Braun, just hours before the end of the regular season.

Charlie Finley would have none of this. With nine of his best players unsigned in the spring, he began a purge of his dynasty. At the beginning of April, he sent 1973 MVP Reggie Jackson, who had hit a league-leading 36 home runs in 1975, and starter Ken Holtzman, who had won 18 games with a 3.14 ERA, to the Baltimore Orioles for Don Baylor, Paul Mitchell and Mike Torrez. Jackson and Holtzman were two of the nine A's who hadn't signed a contract.

Jackson asked Baltimore for a multi-year contract, reportedly for $3 million. The Orioles countered with a one-year deal for $200,000. Jackson, worried that injury could short-circuit his pending free agency, threatened to sit out the entire season. After four weeks on the sidelines, he agreed to report to the Orioles, although he still didn't sign a contract. Jackson debuted for the Orioles on May 2 (in a Holtzman start) and hit his first home run for Baltimore (a grand slam) 10 days later. He finished the season hitting .277 with 27 home runs and his slugging percentage of .502 led the majors.

Having orchestrated the first trade to get value from a pending free agent, Finley continued to deal—and innovate. He tried mightily to trade Joe Rudi, Vida Blue and Rollie Fingers, but couldn't find a partner who offered what Finley deemed to be "fair value." Thwarted in his trade attempts, Finley decided to hold a fire sale. Hours before the June 15 trade deadline, the he announced the outright sale of Blue to the Yankees for $1.5 million. He followed that by announcing he was selling Rudi and Fingers to the Red Sox for $1 million each. Three players, $3.5 million.

While Finley thought he was being proactive in getting compensation for his potential free agents, Commissioner Kuhn had other ideas. He vetoed the sale of the players, invoking the seldom-used power to act "in the best interests of baseball" and returned the three to Oakland. Finley strongly disagreed with the ruling, referring to the commissioner as "the village idiot" and threatening to sue. The executive director of the players association, Marvin Miller, charged that Kuhn had "single-handedly plunged baseball into the biggest mess it has ever seen."

At the heart of Kuhn's decision was a fear that the large-market teams would dominate the game as it entered the free agent era. The fact that the small-market A's were attempting to sell three of their top players to the large market Yankees and Red Sox was not lost on the commissioner. Although there had been such sales in the past, they had been gradual, as with Connie Mack's A's of the 1930s, and had since fallen out of favor as the game enjoyed a modicum of economic stability.

Finley held his three players out of action for almost two weeks while he prepared his lawsuit. The A's players weren't happy that some of their best teammates were sidelined by the owner and threatened to strike if they were not allowed to play. Finley countered by threatening to suspend his whole team and call up 25 minor leaguers to play out the season. The crisis was averted at the 11th hour when Finley agreed to reinstate the three players.

The Super Agent

In 1976, Jerry Kapstein was a New England attorney who represented the cream of the baseball crop. He stumbled into the game almost by accident. Kapstein received his agent's license when he represented his brother Dan, who was trying to catch on with the New England Patriots as a tight end. Dan didn't make it in the NFL, but soon the brothers became a team and began to represent baseball players.

Initially, Kapstein was just another player agent, making his bones arguing arbitration cases against Finley. Indeed, it was in the arbitration court where Kapstein began to place his fingerprints on the game. After Kapstein and Finley spent 10 hours over two days arguing the arbitration case for Ken Holtzman, MLB imposed a time limit on arguments. Kapstein was also one of the first in the game to use advanced statistics and comparable salaries to try to make sense of baseball's pay structure before an arbitration panel. Of course, the innovations wouldn't have meant anything, but for the bottom line … Kapstein often won.

Players noticed his arbitration successes and flocked to him.

His success made other agents jealous. Jerry Crasnick, in *License to Deal*, said Angels pitcher Ed Figueroa's agent, Tony Attanasio, charged him a $150 commission to renegotiate his contract in '75. It was a good contract for Figueroa and the pitcher seemed pleased, yet he switched to Kapstein the following year.

When Attanasio talked to Figueroa and asked why, he was told that because Kapstein was charging a higher commission, he must be doing a better job.

Kapstein also ran afoul of Miller, the director of the players association. Kapstein orchestrated the holdouts of Lynn, Fisk and Burleson from the Red Sox and all three missed most of spring training in 1976. The contracts Kapstein negotiated for the three players were for five years and granted the Red Sox a right of first refusal at the end of the deal, allowing them to match any competing offer when the players became free agents. This infuriated Miller, who believed such a clause would ultimately hurt potential free agents by limiting their movement.

For all that, Kapstein defied the stereotype of the flashy agent. He always wore the same corduroy jacket and famously drove a 1973 Pontiac Grand Prix. He was difficult to reach by phone: He was famous for never taking calls, only returning them. He didn't even have a proper office. Instead, he traveled to his clients.

While Kapstein may have been odd, you couldn't argue with his success. At the advent of the 1976 season, Kapstein represented roughly 60 players, including All-Stars Steve Garvey, George Brett, Fisk and Goose Gossage. Ten of his clients ultimately failed to sign contracts for 1976 and became free agents at the end of the year.

Jerry Kapstein was about to make 10 players very wealthy.

The Draft

The first free agent re-entry draft was held at the Plaza Hotel in New York City on Nov. 4, 1976. The rules were straightforward. The order of selection alternated between leagues based on reverse order of finish from '76. On a coin flip, the National League won the first pick. That gave the Montreal Expos, who had finished last in the NL East with a 55-107 record, the first selection. They were followed by the White Sox, and so on, all the way to the Cincinnati Reds and the New York Yankees, who had finished with the best records in their respective leagues.

But the Reds declined to participate in the draft.

Coming off a four-game sweep of the Yankees in the World Series and back-to-back titles, the Big Red Machine wasn't concerned or frightened by the specter of free agency. All the Reds' superstars—Pete Rose, Joe Morgan, Johnny Bench and Tony Perez—signed contracts for 1976 and were bound to the team for the 1977 season. The only player from the World Series roster who would be eligible for the draft was starting pitcher Don Gullett, who was widely considered the best pitcher available.

Plus, Reds president Bob Howsam understood the bidding war that was about to commence and how it would affect player salaries. He didn't want to risk alienating his big four by giving a large contract to a lesser player, just to get him to play for the Reds. "In fairness to the players who have won the world championship for us two years in a row, we do not feel it would be right for the Cincinnati club to get into the bidding contests that must come from this draft," he told the AP.

While the Reds were the only team that didn't participate in the draft, others chose players but never intended to sign any. Calvin Griffith's Twins selected seven players, but didn't to make a single offer. The same was true for the Chicago Cubs, who picked four players in the draft.

Once the draft was under way, each team could make one selection per round and teams could negotiate contracts only with those players they selected. The teams could select as many (or as few) of the available players as they liked. However, the maximum times a player could be selected was 12. After that, his name was removed from the board, and he was effectively locked in to negotiating with those 12 teams, plus his old club.

This wrinkle injected a touch of strategy in the draft. Do teams draft to fill their needs early, or do they go for the best player available, knowing that by the time the draft comes back to them, that player may be off the board? Or do teams gauge the potential demands of the players and draft according to how "signable" they deem a player? The rule also caused some teams at the bottom of the draft to sweat. Would Reggie Jackson, widely acknowledged as the best player in the draft, still be available when the 20th pick rolled around?

With more questions than answers, the 23 participating teams assembled in the hotel ballroom and began the draft (see table).

Despite a consensus that Jackson and Gullett were the top position player and pitcher respectively, there was a notable variety present in the first round. The most popular player was Joe Rudi, formerly of Finley's

First Round Selections

Team	Selection
Montreal	Reggie Jackson
Chicago White Sox	Joe Rudi
Atlanta	Gary Matthews
Milwaukee	Sal Bando
St. Louis	Bill Campbell
Detroit	Bobby Grich
San Diego	Joe Rudi
California	Joe Rudi
San Francisco	Rollie Fingers
Texas	Don Baylor
Chicago Cubs	Gene Tenace
Cleveland	Wayne Garland
Houston	Gary Matthews
Boston	Bill Campbell
New York Mets	Gary Matthews
Minnesota	Sal Bando
Pittsburgh	Joe Rudi
Oakland	Bobby Grich
Los Angeles	Don Gullett
Baltimore	Joe Rudi
Philadelphia	Joe Rudi
Kansas City	Gene Tenace
Cincinnati	Refused
New York Yankees	Bobby Grich

A's, who was selected by six teams in the first round. Rudi, who broke in as a 20-year-old for the Kansas City A's in 1967, wasn't necessarily a star, but he had built a reputation as a solid player. He was a three-time All-Star and finished second in the AL MVP vote twice—in 1972 when he led the AL in hits, and in 1974 when he led the AL in total bases. At that point in his career, Rudi was a .275/.320/.434 hitter. He nearly matched his career line when he hit .270/.323/.424 for Oakland in 1976.

In contrast, Jackson was selected by just one team in the first round: The Montreal Expos tabbed him with the first overall pick. Gullett also was chosen by a single team—the Dodgers—in the first round.

As the draft progressed, the first player selected by 12 teams and removed from the board wasn't Jackson, Gullett or even Rudi. It was catcher Gene Tenace, who hit .249/.373/.458 with 22 home runs and 66 RBIs in 1976. He was the first-round choice of two clubs and was selected by the full complement by the middle of the third round. Tenace, who had earned $41,000 the previous year and was the hero of the 1972 World Series for Oakland, was considered a "signability" pick. On the other hand, Jackson, who reportedly was seeking a $3 million payday, lasted until the 14th round.

In a bit of a twist, Finley's A's selected 16 of the 24 players eligible, including many of their former stars. The Chicago White Sox were the most active team in the draft, naming 18 players. It's interesting that Jackson lasted until the 14th round, because at that point in the draft, only the A's and the White Sox were still selecting players. Even though Finley actively participated and talked about re-signing most of his stars, he knew the writing was on the wall. "It's horse manure," he told a reporter. "It's like having someone come into your house and snatching up your children. It's unfair."

Kapstein represented 10 of the free agents. Of his players, Tenace, Baylor, Rudi, Fingers, Dave Cash, Bobby Grich, Gullett, Wayne Garland and Doyle Alexander all were picked by the maximum 12 teams. Only Bert Campaneris still had eligibility remaining at the end of the draft: He was selected by 11 teams. Of the players not represented by Kapstein, only Jackson and Sal Bando were picked by 12 teams.

Signings

With the draft sorted, the negotiations were set to get under way. Under the rules, all teams were allowed a maximum of two free agent signings, a mechanism to ensure that the teams with the deepest pockets couldn't monopolize the free agents. The lone exception was for those clubs who were to lose more than two players. Those teams would be allowed to match the players they lost with the same number of signings.

As with everything else in this painful process, there was controversy. Yankees owner George Steinbrenner wasn't happy that the Angels, who lost minor leaguers Paul Dade, Billy Smith and Tim Nordbrook in the draft, would be allowed to sign three major league players as replacements. Steinbrenner charged that the Angels acted in bad faith when they traded to get Nordbrook late in the year from the Orioles, knowing he was playing out his option in the minor leagues and they would lose him to free agency.

Then there was Braves owner Ted Turner's courtship of outfielder Gary Matthews. Before the draft, word leaked that Turner and the Braves had made a contract offer to Matthews in September of 1976, while he was still playing for the San Francisco Giants. The commissioner's office ruled that Atlanta was guilty of tampering, and in the first week of October fined the

Braves $10,000 for the offense and stripped them of their first-round choice in the next amateur draft. The matter was thought to have been settled, but then a Braves staffer threw a party for Matthews in late October before the draft. Then Giants owner Bob Lurie revealed that Turner bragged to him at a cocktail party that the Braves would beat any offer the Giants made for Matthews.

Although the party in Atlanta and Turner's braggadocio didn't violate any rule per se, Kuhn couldn't just look the other way. Again, the game was in uncharted territory with respect to free agents and Kuhn feared a Wild West mentality among owners. Ultimately, the Braves' overzelaous pursuit of Matthews earned Turner a suspension from Kuhn for the entire 1977 season. Turner accepted his ban with a humility that came naturally: "Abraham Lincoln, Jesus Christ, John F. Kennedy—if the world can get along without them, the Braves can do without me for a year."

The Signings Came Fast and Furious

The first free agent to sign was relief ace Bill Campbell, who went with the Boston Red Sox for four years and $1 million. Campbell had won 17 games and saved 20 more coming out of the bullpen for the Minnesota Twins in '75. Newspapers said Campbell was gambling with $8,000 by becoming a free agent. The Twins initially offered him a 1976 contract for $22,000. Campbell, however, was seeking $30,000. After a stalemate in negotiations, Campbell decided not to sign a contract. Shortly thereafter, the Twins acquiesced and agreed to the $30,000—if he signed his contract and surrendered his right to become a free agent.

By then, though, it was too late. Campbell decided he was going to take $8,000 less, play out his option and test free agency. It was considered a risky tactic, since his 1975 season (four wins, five saves, a 3.79 ERA) wasn't a good one. If he had had a repeat performance in '76, he could have cost himself some money. However, based on his performance in '76, that wouldn't be the case. He turned $8,000 into a cool million.

Tenace and Baylor were the first of the A's to relocate, with Tenace landing in San Diego and Baylor in Anaheim with the Angels. Tenace, who earned $51,000 in 1975, signed a pact totaling nearly $1.6 million for six years. Baylor's deal with the Angels equaled that. The next day, California nabbed another high-profile player, announcing Rudi's signing to a five-year deal valued at $2.1 million. A few days later, to no one's surprise, Matthews landed with Atlanta for five years and almost $2 million.

Presumed to be the best starting pitcher available, Gullett was the next to go when he signed a six-year contract with the New York Yankees, valued at an estimated $2 million. While the Reds claimed they wouldn't be participants in the free agent process, the loss of Gullett stung. Manager Sparky Anderson lamented his lack of loyalty and said he would never mention the pitcher by name again. Although it was expected that Gullett would command the top dollar among pitchers, the next day Wayne Garland signed with Cleveland for a whopping 10 years and almost $2.2 million. The same day, Sal Bando also moved to the AL East when he signed a five-year, $1.5 million deal with Milwaukee. Bando, who was drafted by 12 clubs, said two other teams offered more money, but went with the Brewers because he liked the organization.

Reg-gie

When the gates of free agency opened, the American League champion New York Yankees had two priorities: First, they wanted to sign a starting pitcher, which they accomplished by signing Gullett. Second, they wanted a shortstop. Fred Stanley played short for New York in 1976 and hit .238/.329/.273 in 110 games. Said Steinbrenner after the season: "We're not going to win a a championship with Fred Stanley at shortstop."

At the top of the list for the Yankees was Orioles second baseman Bobby Grich. Since the Yankees had 22-year-old Willie Randolph at second, they thought Grich, who hit .266/.373/.417 with 13 home runs in 1976, could slide to the other side of the bag and replace Stanley. Grich was such a priority for the Yankees that he was their first selection in the draft.

As negotiations progressed, it soon became obvious that Grich, a native of Long Beach, wanted to return to the West Coast. With the Angels offering a five-year package valued at over $1.5 million, on Nov. 24 Grich made the move to California.

Meanwhile, Jackson was being courted by the San Diego Padres, Montreal Expos and, with Grich no longer an option, the Yankees. Both the Padres and Expos, two teams perennially on the bottom of the standings, saw Jackson as an opportunity to immediately reverse their fortunes. The Padres offered a package in excess of $3 million. The Expos presented what they termed "a king's ransom" totaling nearly $4 million.

Although the Expos' money was difficult to turn down, Jackson went with the team that was in the best position to win: the Yankees. The contract he signed called for $400,000 a year for five years with a $900,000 signing bonus. Jackson didn't hit his goal of a $3 million contract, but with a total package of $2.9 million, he came awfully close. His new contract doubled his 1976 salary with the Orioles.

With the signing, Jackson was the first player in free agency that offseason to move to a team with a better 1976 record than his former club.

By the time baseball's spending spree had come to a close, *The New York Times* reported that Kapstein had earned between $750,000 and $1 million in commission for representing his 10 players.

Aftermath

With any new system, there will be a few willing to dive into the deep end. The Yankees, Angels and Padres were those teams, spending a total of $13 million on seven players. They also handed out the top six overall contracts, with the Angels the big spenders that winter, awarding three contracts totaling $5.2 million. In a lesson owners would need to be reminded of over and over, the Padres, like the Angels, struggled despite their new signings. Only the Yankees improved, winning 100 games and the AL East in 1977, up from 97 wins in 1976.

The Yankees found free agency a mixed bag. The money they gave Jackson was rewarded when he hit 32 home runs and drove in 110 during the regular season and added five more bombs in leading the Yankees to the World Series title. In his five years in New York, Jackson hit .281/.371/.526 and averaged 28 home runs a year. Four of his teams played in the postseason, with two of them winning the title.

On the other hand, the Bombers got next to nothing out of Gullett. Although still hampered by an ankle injury he suffered in the '76 World Series, Gullet did well for the Yankees in 1977, winning 14 of his 22 starts with an ERA of 3.58, but made only 30 starts over the life of his five-year deal. He threw his final pitch in the major leagues before he turning 28.

After spending big in free agency—and being the only team to sign more than two players—California had huge expectations for the 1977 season. The fans did, too: The Angels sold a club-record 6,000 season tickets. However injuries and a shallow starting rotation condemned the Angels to a 74-88 record and a fifth-place finish in the AL West, two games worse than their 1976 record.

Grich moved to shortstop for the Angels, but spent most of the '77 season in the trainer's room or on the disabled list with back issues. He appeared in only 52 games and was out for the year by mid-June for Gene Autry's Angels. The back was troubling him from the beginning of the season and he hit only .243/.369/.392, the worst season of his career to that point. The irony was, Grich injured his back trying to carry an air conditioning unit into a new apartment in Long Beach. He eventually underwent surgery on a herniated disc and didn't regain his strength until 1979.

His best year of his five-year deal was the last, in the strike-shortened campaign of 1981 when he tied for the AL lead with 22 home runs and led the league with a .543 slugging percentage, the best rate of his 17-year career. By tying for the league lead in home runs, he became the first second baseman to lead the league since Nap Lajoie in 1901.

Like his new teammate, Rudi found himself on the sidelines for most of the 1977 season. After being hit in the hand by a pitch in June, he initially was expected to be out of action for around three weeks. It was a blow to the Angels; Rudi, hitting .264/.333/.496, was enjoying one of the better seasons of his career. However, the injury failed to heal properly and Rudi underwent surgery in early September. He was never the same after the injury and he finished his career back in Oakland in 1982.

Baylor, the third new Angel, successfully avoided the trainer's room, but he was unable to contribute the production his new employers desired. Baylor admitted the expectations that came with his contract were a burden and partially blamed that for a slow start that saw him hit just .237/.328/.394 with 14 home runs over the first four months of the season. He eventually steadied himself and over his final 59 games, Baylor slugged 11 home runs and hit .275/.346/.498. By then, it was too late for the Angels.

Likewise, the going was rough for the Padres. Despite signing relief ace Rollie Fingers to a five-year, $1.6 million contract, and Tenace, his battery-mate from Oakland, Ray Kroc's team won only 69 games in 1977, four fewer than the previous year. The Padres' performance was no fault of the free agents: Fingers led the NL with 35 saves and Tenace hit .233/.415/.410 with a NL-best 125 walks. The Padres lacked quality starting pitching.

When the dust settled, 15 teams had signed players to contracts totaling over $24.5 million. A new day had dawned. Free agency would forever reshape the game.

The New Millionaires

Name	Contract	Bonus	Total
Reggie Jackson	5 years/$2,000,000	$900,000	$2,900,000
Wayne Garland	10/$2,185,000		$2,185,000
Joe Rudi	5/$1,000,000	$1,000,000	$2,000,000
Don Gullett	6/$900,000	$1,000,000	$1,900,000
Rollie Fingers	5/$1,000,000	$660,000	$1,660,000
Don Baylor	6/$1,020,000	$580,000	$1,600,000
Gene Tenace	5/$930,000	$660,000	$1,590,000
Dave Cash	5/$1,000,000	$560,000	$1,560,000
Bobby Grich	5/$950,000	$600,000	$1,550,000
Sal Bando	5/$1,250,000	$156,000	$1,406,000
Bill Campbell	5/$800,000	$500,000	$1,300,000
Bert Campaneris	5/$950,000	$60,000	$1,010,000

Reaping What You Sow

by Steve Treder

Readers of the *Hardball Times* site may recall a series of 14 articles we presented, beginning in August 2006 and concluding in October 2007, entitled "The Value Production Standings." The methodology is summarized in the note at the conclusion of this article, but the gist of it was this: we compared every team in the major leagues in every season from 1946 through 2007, on the basis of the total major league Win Shares delivered by the players produced by its farm system.

This "value production" was credited to the franchise whose system had produced a given player, regardless of whether the player was still playing for that team. Thus the "standings" were not a representation of how well or poorly any team might have done at retaining its home-grown talent, nor of leveraging it in the trade market; instead they were simply a measure of how well or poorly each team did at producing home-grown talent in the first place. It's not surprising that this manner of value production is positively correlated with actual team success, particularly in the long run, but the correlation is far from perfect: the analysis revealed quite a few franchises that have significantly over-performed or under-performed relative to their raw farm system harvest.

Attendees at this past July's Society for American Baseball Research (SABR) 39th annual convention in Washington, D.C., may recall that I presented a summarized version of the Value Production Standings research, updated through the 2008 season, and now depicted in graphical form. Among the slides I presented at SABR39 was something similar to this:

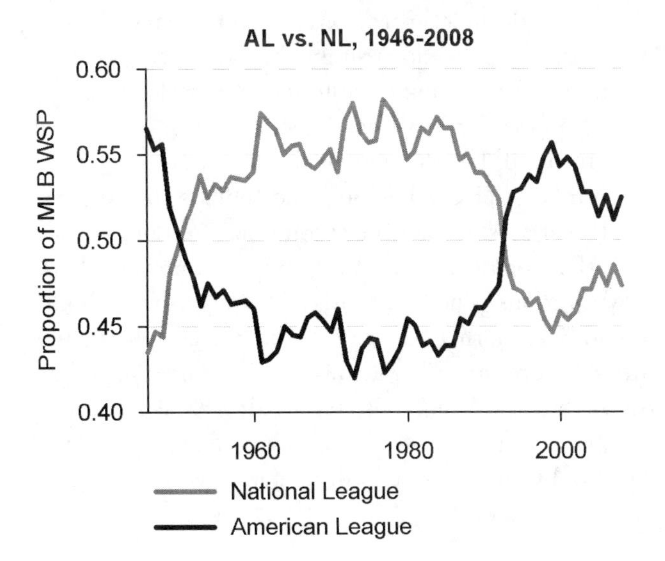

This graph aggregates the totals of team Value Production into their respective leagues and compares the two leagues in terms of the proportion of Major League Win Share production (WSP) credited to each. (The methodology prorates to adjust for differences in league size when necessary.)

If both leagues were to be exactly equal in WSP, then both would be right at the .500 point. But as we can see, very rarely in the more than 60 seasons over this period have the two leagues been exactly equal in WSP, or even close to it. Instead what we see is a pattern of one league or the other fairly dominating in WSP: initially the American League, which was quickly overtaken by the National, which sustained it for a very long time, finally to be surpassed again by the AL over the past decade-and-a-half.

Why is this? What are the factors that might have caused it? And what insight might this phenomenon provide on the issue of differences between the leagues in actual quality of play?

Digging Deeper: The Impact Of Expansion

To explore this, we first need to satisfy ourselves that the results we're seeing aren't an illusion or a distortion. As mentioned above, we've already addressed the issue of the periodic differentials in league size, so that isn't a concern.

But something directly related to differentials in league size might be: expansion. The data above includes the WSP of every team in every season, including expansion teams. And alas, because they haven't yet had a chance to get their farm systems into competitively productive status, expansion teams for their first several seasons routinely lag far beyond every established franchise in WSP. This is a concern for us, because the minimal WSP rates from young expansion franchises have the impact of significantly inhibiting league-wide average WSP, and since the two leagues have usually not expanded at exactly the same time or to exactly the same degree, the imbalanced impact of expansions are affecting the league data we see in the graph above.

The impact doesn't last forever; expansion teams eventually build up enough farm system production to become competitive with established teams. How long does this take? The data demonstrates that it takes about a decade; typically by the time an expansion franchise is around 10 years old, it's no longer automatically bringing up the rear of the league in terms of WSP.

So, let's reformulate the data we presented in the graph above, this time removing from consideration every expansion team for its first nine years, and instead introducing it to its league at the age of 10. Here's what we get:

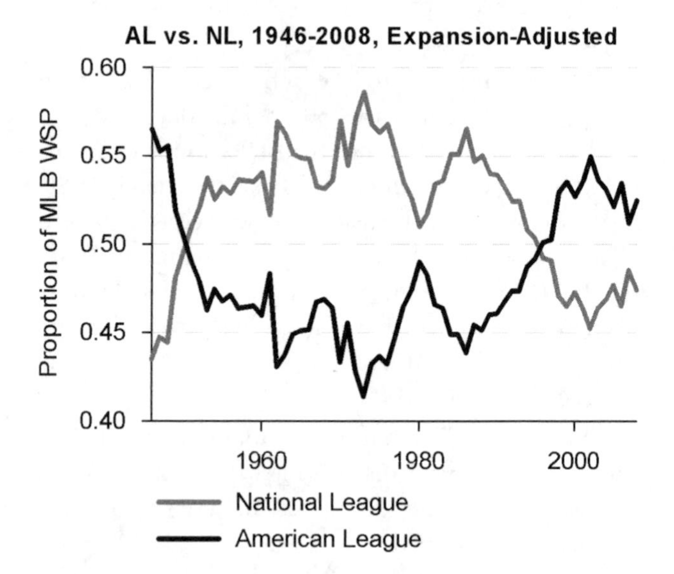

Well, then. This picture is different than the one we saw earlier. The AL briefly closes in on the NL in the late 1970s/early 1980s before falling back, and the "crossover" point of NL-to-AL superiority moves from 1993-94 to 1995-96.

But those are differences in detail. The prevailing pattern doesn't change at all: the NL remains dominant from the early 1950s until the early 1990s, and the AL remains the modern-era top dog. So our adjustment for expansion, while necessary, isn't sufficient to alter our initial impression. We can confidently conclude that we're seeing is real.

So, what of it, then?

Breaking It Down

Let's look more closely at this six-decades-plus saga by focusing on its constituent segments. We'll start with the period from the end of World War II to the dawn of the 1960s. No adjustment for expansion is necessary here, because of course there was no expansion in these years.

The pattern is stark: the AL started out with an enormous advantage in farm system production, but lost it with stunning suddenness. By the early-to-mid-

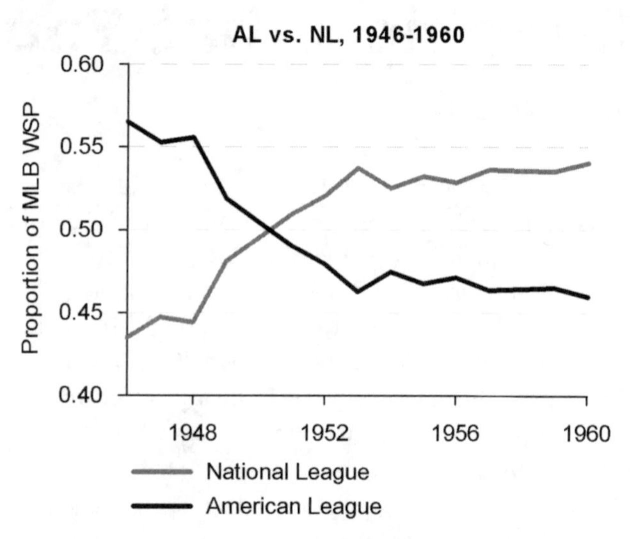

1950s, the NL had assumed a distinctly superior position, which it held steadily for the rest of the decade.

What happened in the late 1940s/early 1950s that can explain this dramatic turn of events? Well, racial integration is what happened. And racial integration was undertaken at anything but an even rate between the leagues: following Jackie Robinson's debut, nearly all of the franchises most eagerly engaged in signing and developing players of color were in the National League. So it is that the NL gets credit here not only for Jackie's Win Shares, but also those of Roy Campanella, Don Newcombe, Willie Mays, Ernie Banks, Hank Aaron, Roberto Clemente, Frank Robinson, Orlando Cepeda and so on, while the AL counters only with the likes of Larry Doby, Minnie Miñoso, and Vic Power—very good ballplayers, to be sure, but nothing close to the equal of their NL counterparts, either in quality or quantity.

But while that's a major explanation, it isn't all of it. As they built their farm systems in those years, National League organizations simply became more adept at signing and developing white talent as well. In 1946, the St. Louis Cardinals had by far the most productive system of all, but the best of the rest were in the AL: the Yankees, Tigers, Red Sox, and Indians all had more WSP that season than the second-best producer in the NL, the Dodgers. But in the years to come, several NL organizations joined the Cards and Dodgers with robust broad-based farms, particularly the Braves, Giants, and Reds, and meanwhile much of the AL failed to follow suit. Into the late 1950s, fully half of the American League's franchises—the Athletics, Senators, White Sox, and Orioles—were still operating with only rudimentary systems.

It's impossible to know exactly the impact of this newfound National League farm production dominance on overall league quality, but it had to be significant. Particularly in an environment without free agency, franchises with less productive farm systems were greatly inhibited in their capacity to construct competitive rosters; there's only so far you can get by "winning" trades. And thus a league with lesser farm production necessarily faces an uphill quality-of-play struggle compared to a rival league with greater production.

There was of course no regular-season interleague play in those days, so indicators of comparative league quality are difficult to come by. But what we have tells us this: the AL won every All-Star Game from 1946 through 1949, but from 1950 through 1960 the NL went on a 9-4 run. And after the Yankees completed their stupendous string of five straight World Series championships in 1953, the NL representative then took five of the next seven titles.

And there's an additional way to estimate league strength. Sean Smith's fascinating research (see the link at the end of this article) has identified all players who made significant appearances in both leagues and compared their relative success. He estimates that over the decade of the 1950s, the average AL team would have compiled a winning percentage of just .451 in the NL.

Add this WSP data into the mix, and it seems very clear that by the mid-to-late-1950s, the National League was presenting a superior caliber of competition.

Then came the 1960s.

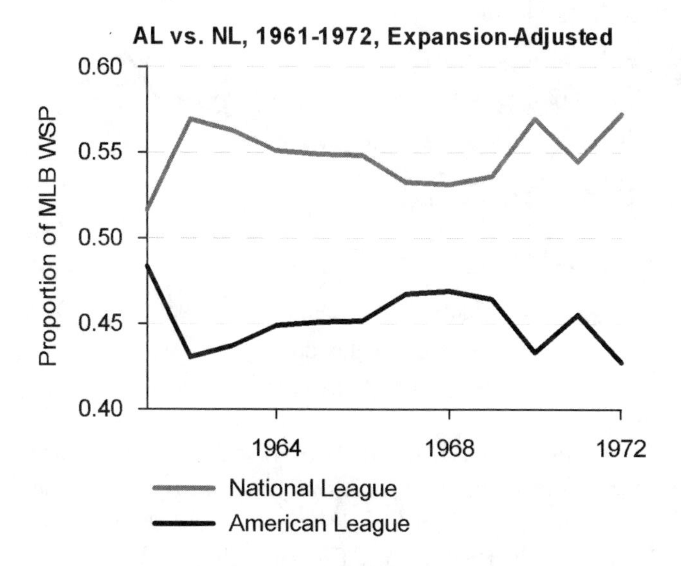

While we've adjusted this view for expansion, an effect of it still remains visible in one season above: 1961. In that year the original eight AL franchises had their WSP stimulated by largely stocking the rosters of the two new teams, via the league-specific expansion draft. But in 1962 the NL followed suit, negating the effect.

In any case, what we see is more than a decade of abject National League dominance in WSP. Building upon the foundation of advantage they'd gained by taking the lead in racial integration, NL farm systems consistently pumped out a greater volume and quality of talent than their AL counterparts all through this era.

In terms of attendance, there was just no comparison between the leagues: the NL easily outdrew the AL every season from 1961 through 1972, by an *average* rate of a whopping 29 percent. This is anything but an incidental issue with regard to farm production, as attendance directly links to revenue, and revenue directly links to the ability to spend, and farm systems are a very expensive enterprise, not a profit-generating venture. Not only does the operation of a farm system require compensation paid to players (both in signing bonuses and salaries), it also requires the investment in scouts, minor league managers, coaches, trainers, travel, and so on. The most productive farm systems tend to be the biggest farm systems, and the biggest farm systems are the most expensive.

Through this period, it was widely perceived that the NL was presenting a superior quality of play. Though World Series outcomes were a 6-6 draw between the leagues in these years, the NL went 11-2 in All-Star Games. In 1972, Roger Angell wrote in *The New Yorker*, "Among the ... hovering anxieties is the deepening disparity in quality ... between the two major leagues ... I believe that fans would respond with pleasure and alacrity to a ... solution to the American League's problems—better ball teams."

Sean's player-movement data estimates that for the 1960s, exactly as in the '50s, a team performing at a .500 rate in the AL would struggle to .451 in the NL.

But as the 1970s unfolded, the AL finally began to turn the tide.

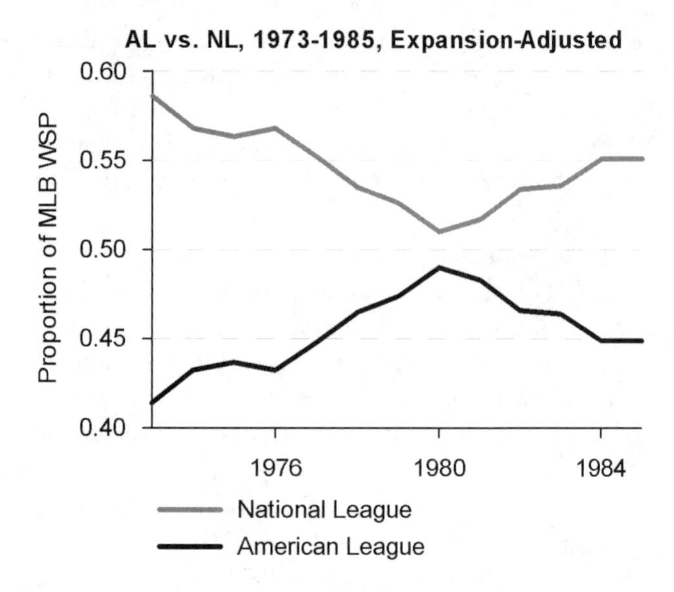

The NL's superiority in WSP reached its peak in 1973, but from that point the AL slowly but steadily began to restore equilibrium. By 1980 farm system production was nearly equal, only to subsequently see NL franchises reassert their dominance.

But it's worth noting that what we might be seeing here is a repetition of the expansion effect we saw above in the 1961 season. In 1977 the American League expanded from 12 to 14 teams, and this time the National didn't follow suit, with no NL expansion teams during the period. Thus even though we've excluded the newborn franchises from this analysis for their first 10 years, the existing AL franchises that were largely stocking the Mariners and Blue Jays' rosters via the expansion draft derive the WSP benefit here. Perhaps the 1977-80 drive toward equality is little more than that, and by 1981 its effect began to dissipate.

Because aside from the expansion factor, it isn't obvious what it was the AL did to regain WSP competitiveness in the '70s. National League franchises continued to enjoy a significant financial advantage, as the NL still led the AL in per-game attendance in every one of these years. Still, it is the case that the AL's adoption of the designated hitter rule beginning in 1973 had some effect on stimulating interest in its product and closing the attendance gap, as the NL's attendance-superiority margins weren't as staggering as they'd been in the '60s and early '70s, and by the mid-1980s the difference had become quite small.

Perhaps it was simply a vagary of chance that sooner or later the leagues' talent-development fortunes would move in the direction of convergence. There is, of course, no natural law that compels leagues or their farm systems to be equal in quality, but at the same time, since each club is independently operated and competing feely to acquire and develop talent, it isn't a given that any congregation of franchises will necessarily maintain its historical status vis-à-vis another congregation.

In any case, the 1970s saw the rise of several newly-robust farm systems in the AL, including those of the Athletics, Rangers, and Brewers, and meanwhile a couple of the NL's powerhouse systems of the '60s—the Giants and Reds—went into steep decline. The NL retook the initiative in the early '80s, but the gap wasn't as great as before.

Free agency came onto the scene in the late '70s, having some effect of de-linking farm production and roster strength, and the quality-of-play picture here is muddled. A couple of our limited indicators of league quality are essentially unchanged from the previous period: World Series championships effectively continued to be a draw, with the AL taking seven to the NL's six, while the NL sustained utter dominance in the All-Star Game, winning 12 of 13. Yet Sean's players-changing-leagues data interestingly gives a slight edge to the AL over both the 1970s (.512) and the '80s (.506).

But as the 1980s advanced into the 1990s, at long last unequivocal change arrived.

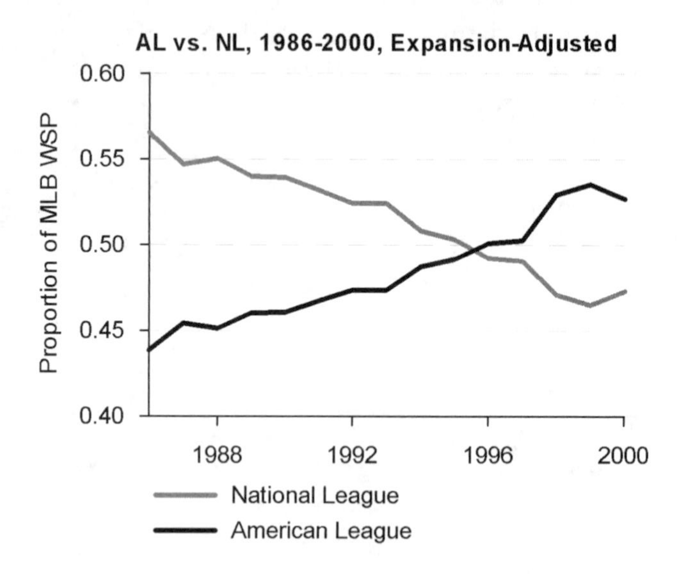

In 1987 the AL began an implacable climb toward WSP competitiveness, and this time didn't fall back at the point of reaching equality. Instead the AL met and surpassed its rival, for the first time since the 1940s.

The charge was led by the AL's two expansion franchises from 1977, the Blue Jays and Mariners, both of whom by the early 1990s were presenting first-rate farm systems. And it was also a function of the Yankees, whose once-tremendous system in the 1950s and '60s had endured a long period of mediocrity, finally re-emerging in the 1990s as one of the best in the game. Meanwhile the NL's two most productive systems of the early 1980s, the Dodgers and Phillies, both encountered rapid decline.

Again, no simple cause of this historic shift presents itself. Very likely it was a combination of multiple factors. Let's examine what they might have been.

Explaining The "Crossover"

Chief among the elements undermining the National League's decades-long WSP dominance would seem to be the lessening of reliance upon stadium attendance as the key revenue source for teams, as broadcasting contracts and merchandising of MLB-licensed products became far more lucrative than in the past. For example, in 1988 Commissioner Peter Ueberroth negotiated a 10-figure national TV deal with CBS that dwarfed anything that had come before. These shared MLB-wide revenue streams rendered the NL's attendance advantage less impactful in the funding of scouting and farm operations.

Moreover, in this period the two leagues finally became essentially equally popular anyway, as measured by per-game attendance. The NL led in 10 of these 15 seasons, but the margins were generally small; overall the NL outdrew the AL by just 1 percent.

But the changing dynamics of attendance and revenue only go so far as to explain the loss of the National League's superiority. To understand why the AL not only closed the gap, but went ahead and fully reversed positions, requires us to consider additional issues.

For instance, what about expansion? Let's remember that the NL expanded by two teams in 1993, and the AL didn't respond until 1998, and did so only by adding one franchise—an expansion that was matched by the NL's adding another of its own that year anyway. So even though we've kept all the expansion clubs themselves out of the WSP database until their 10th seasons, might the 1993 NL expansion in particular be a factor influencing the league-vs.-league WSP picture?

In short: no. Because the expansion draft in the fall of 1992 was the first in which all teams in *both* leagues made players available to the new teams. So the AL organizations as well as their NL counterparts stocked the rosters of the Rockies and Marlins, negating any league-specific expansion effect as we saw in 1961, and probably saw again in the late 1970s.

However, there is one expansion-related factor that is explanatory: the shift of the Milwaukee Brewers from the AL to the NL in 1998. Over the 1980s, the Brewers had presented one of the more productive farm systems in the majors, helping to fuel the AL's rise against NL WSP superiority. But by the time of their 1998 league transfer, the Brewers' production had stalled, and once in the NL it would decline. Thus the AL "bought low and sold high" on Milwaukee, leaving the NL holding the WSP bag.

Still, by 1998 the Brewers were just one of 30 organizations. To truly explain the fundamental transformation of league-to-league posture that transpired over this period requires the simultaneous improvement of multiple farm system operations in the AL, and a corresponding deterioration of multiple NL organizations. And this appears to be what took place.

The leading example of burgeoning AL systems was that of Toronto, who under general manager Pat Gillick, and then Gord Ash, built and sustained a scouting and development operation that was second to none. This was the period in which international amateur signings, particularly in Latin America, exploded in volume and quality as never before, and the organizations with the best Latin American operations were poised to win. This certainly describes the Blue Jays, but other AL teams such as the Yankees, Rangers, and Indians were also encountering great success in the international realm. The Red Sox, meanwhile, didn't do as well in that market, but made up for it by discovering and developing a bonanza of stateside talent: in this general period the Boston organization produced Roger Clemens, Jeff Bagwell, Curt Schilling, Nomar Garciaparra, Mo Vaughn, Brady Anderson and Ellis Burks.

A few NL systems kept pace; in particular the Expos effectively leveraged the Latin American talent pool. But most didn't. The Dodgers, for example, had reached a zenith of spectacular production in the early 1980s, but as Walter O'Malley's legacy faded into history the organizational excellence faded as well. In Philadelphia, Bill Giles purchased the franchise from the Carpenter family in 1981, and then attempted to run things as an old-school owner/general manager through much of the 1980s, and coincidentally or not, the long-robust production of the Philadelphia system thoroughly withered. Whether it was just coincidence, or whether it was complacency borne of decades of success, by and large in this period it was American League organizations displaying the ambition, innovation, and intolerance of mediocrity that had long been the National League hallmark.

Our old-fashioned indirect indicators of league quality suggest the AL finally gained the upper hand: in World Series play the American Leaguers enjoyed a 9-5 advantage, while in the All-Star Games the AL reversed the NL's longstanding rout, beating up on the National Leaguers 11-4. Furthermore, Sean's player-movement analysis gives a strong .537 advantage to the AL over the decade of the 1990s.

Yet in this period we finally were provided with a direct indicator of comparative quality, as regular-season interleague play debuted in 1997; if the results of interleague play aren't evidence of league quality, nothing is. And in these first four seasons of interleague games, it was the NL coming out slightly ahead, at 477-463 (.507)—not a resounding conclusion, but one indicating that in the late 1990s the leagues were of roughly equal strength.

Which brings us to the current era.

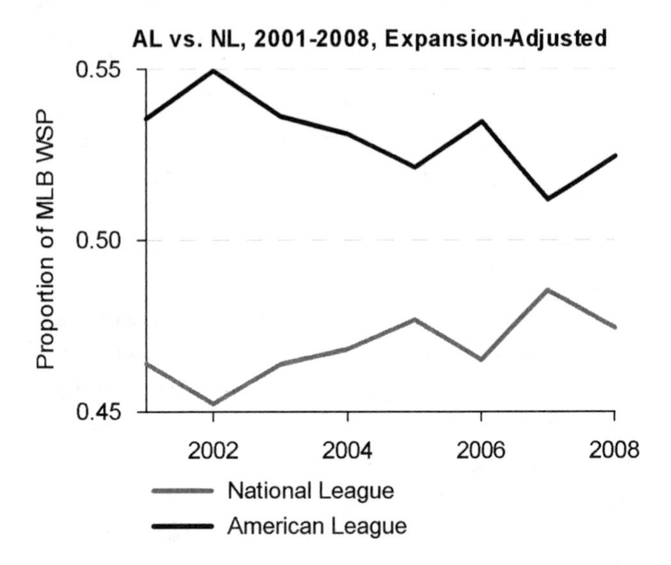

The AL has sustained the WSP advantage it achieved in the 1990s. The gap slightly narrowed over the 2000s (it will be interesting to see what 2009 yields; it was eclipsed here by our printing deadline). The AL's superiority doesn't approach that shown by the NL in previous periods, but it's been genuine. The AL's advantage hasn't been a function of monopolizing the best systems, since those of the NL's Astros and Expos/Nationals have been as productive through these years as the AL's best. But the AL has avoided having the least-productive systems, while the NL's Reds, Brewers, and Padres have competed for that lowly status.

As for quality of play, in the past few years it's been widely perceived that the AL has achieved distinct superiority. This hasn't been indicated by World Series results (always the weakest measure of league quality), as the league champs fought to a 4-4 draw from 2001-2008, but in All-Star play the AL has dominated to the tune of 7-0-1 (and now 8-0-1 if we include 2009). And the pattern in interleague play, the most direct and revealing indicator of league quality, has been striking: from 2001 through 2004 the NL maintained the same modest .507 advantage it had held from 1997 to 2000, but over 2005-2008 the NL's interleague performance collapsed to a dismal .429 (and was scarcely better in 2009, at .452).

The players-switching-leagues analysis echoes this, with an estimation of a .543 AL advantage in the 2000s, its strongest yet achieved. Yet, interestingly, the NL has re-established its traditional attendance advantage, leading the AL in per-game attendance in every year of this decade, though by an average rate of 7 percent, not nearly as dramatic as in previous eras.

Conclusion

Production of superior talent via the farm system isn't the same thing as presenting a superior team on the major league field. Through trades, and especially through free agency, it's possible for a team to construct a winning roster despite an inferior flow of talent from the minors.

But while it's possible, it isn't likely, especially in the long run. Even in the free agency era, strong farm production provides an inherent advantage for a ball club. And this principle equally applies to leagues (which are, of course, nothing more than collections of ball clubs); while a league-wide superiority in the production of talent doesn't guarantee a league-wide superiority in the quality of play, the two appear to have been rather strongly correlated over the decades since farm systems became ubiquitous.

As stated earlier, there's no underlying principle that requires the leagues to be even approximately equal in strength, regarding both farm system production and quality of play. Competitive pressure drives the inferior league to match its superior, but just as strongly, competitive pressure motivates the superior league to maintain its superiority. History demonstrates that fundamental shifts in the relative strength of the farm system production and the quality of play between the American and National Leagues have occurred—around 1950, tilting in the NL's direction, and in the 1990s, tilting back the other way—but these shifts have been rare, indicating a power of inertia that acts to hold the *status quo*. Thus, sooner or later the National League may regain the status of superiority in league-wide talent production it long enjoyed, but to do so would be a significant accomplishment.

Notes on WSP methodology:

First, we identify every player in the major leagues each season with at least five career Win Shares who was a product of the farm system. For each farm system-produced player, we identify which major league organization was responsible for originally signing and developing that player (or perhaps not originally signing him, but clearly being the organization most responsible for developing him). Finally, we credit every season's production of major league Win Shares by that player to that organization, regardless of whether he actually played that season for that organization.

Sometimes it's impossible to assign a player to one organization. Lots of players were signed by one team but then acquired by another organization while still young minor leaguers. For such players, we assign half-credit to each of the two organizations (and in a few cases, we assign one-third credit to each of three organizations). Examples of such players are Hank Sauer, Dick Bosman, and Jeff Nelson.

A few players never played in the minor leagues but were signed by major league teams while still very young, not fully-developed talents. We credit them to their signing team regardless, judging that they were "developed" by that organization, albeit at the major league level. Examples of such players are Eddie Yost, Sandy Koufax, and Dave Winfield.

A larger minority of players weren't the products of any major league team's farm system, having been purchased or signed as fully-developed free agents from independent teams, such as the Negro Leagues, the Mexican League or other non-aligned minor leagues, or the Japanese Leagues. The Win Shares of such players aren't counted in this analysis. Examples of such players are Ferris Fain, Luke Easter, and Ichiro Suzuki.

Sources

Roger Angell, "Starting to Belong," in *Five Seasons: A Baseball Companion*, New York: Simon and Schuster, 1977, pp. 27-28.

Sean Smith's estimation of historical league strength based on the performances of players changing leagues can be found at lanaheimangelfan.blogspot.com/2008_09_01_archive.html

Paul Richards in a Box

by Warren Corbett

Paul Richards was a lanky, pencil-necked Texan who never won a pennant in his dozen years in a big-league dugout, but he was recognized as one of the game's most brilliant and innovative minds when he managed the White Sox and Orioles in the 1950s and 1960s. Richards was the first sabermetrician in the dugout, although he probably never heard that word and certainly would not have liked the description. He once wrote that "well-kept statistics [can be] a method of disproving some old baseball assumptions." But he kept his ideas secret even from his closest associates. The full extent of his statistical innovations was unknown until now.

In his *Guide to Baseball Managers*, Bill James introduced the "manager in a box" as a shorthand way of describing a manager's style. James' framework helped guide my research for my biography of Richards. Here is Paul Richards in a box.

Year of birth: 1908. Richards started playing professionally in 1926, just as the batting explosion ignited by Babe Ruth and clean baseballs reached its height.

Years managed: Minors, 1938-1942; 1947-1950. Majors, 1951-1961; 1976. He got his first managing job before his 30th birthday; he said he decided to become a manager "when I found out I wasn't going to hit .300 in the major leagues. Of course, I found that out pretty early."

Record as a major league manager: 923-901, .506. Richards took on building projects with the White Sox and Orioles, two franchises that had been down so long they couldn't see the way up. He transformed both clubs into consistent winners. He took on another building project as general manager of the Houston expansion team.

Managers for whom he played: Wilbert Robinson, Max Carey, Donie Bush (in the minors), Bill Terry, Connie Mack, Steve O'Neill. He described Terry in terms that many others used to describe Richards: defense-oriented, distant from his players. He credited Bush as his most important mentor, but said the best lesson he learned from other managers was "what *not* to do."

Richards learned one of those lessons when he was the catcher and unofficial pitching coach for the wartime Tigers. Manager Steve O'Neill worked his top pitchers into the ground. With Detroit fighting for the 1944 pennant, Dizzy Trout and Hal Newhouser started 17 of 28 September games, including several on two days' rest. Trout started the season's crucial last game after just one day off. The Tigers lost the game and the pennant. In the seventh game of the 1945 World Series, O'Neill started Newhouser on two days' rest—and got away with it when the Cubs' starter, Hank Borowy, failed on one day's rest. This helped shape Richards' approach to handling pitchers. He said many times, "A tired pitcher is a badly handicapped pitcher" and he refused to send a man to the mound on short rest.

Others by whom he was influenced: As a young catcher with the Giants, Richards caught Carl Hubbell during Hubbell's dominant 1933 season, and they became friends. Hubbell said his screwball was such a devastating pitch because it was a change of pace. A change-up was Richards' first prescription for every pitcher.

Although he was a high-school dropout, Richards read widely in history. He studied military figures, including the Nazi Desert Fox, Erwin Rommel, for insights into leadership. The leader he most admired was Abraham Lincoln—remarkable for the grandson of a Confederate veteran who named one of his dogs Rebel.

Which managers did he influence? Earl Weaver worked for Richards as a minor league manager. When Weaver took over the Orioles in 1968, he used the detailed statistical breakdowns that Richards had pioneered. Tony La Russa began managing under Richards in the White Sox farm system. He said, "Paul's influence was a career maker for me." Dick Williams called Richards "my mentor," although he cited Bobby Bragan as his most important teacher. Sixteen of Richards' players became big-league managers, including Joe Torre, who despised him.

Characteristics as a player: After starting his career as an infielder (and occasional ambidextrous pitcher), Richards became a slugging minor league catcher. He never hit in the majors, but he won respect for his ability to handle pitchers and for his strong throwing arm. World War II extended his playing career because a knee injury disqualified him from military service. He made his reputation when he got credit for developing the wild, hotheaded young lefty Hal Newhouser into a two-time MVP.

What He Brought to a Ball Club

Was he an intense manager or more of an easy-to-get-along-with type? "Intense" is the word many players used to describe him. Infielder Fred Marsh: "There was a look fathers used to give their kids, where you just backed off when you saw it. Richards had that."

"No manager ever tries to win the love of his players," Richards said. "All he needs is their respect ... If you can't get them to respect you, you're in trouble." He earned respect because of his mastery of game situations; his players knew he would give them every chance to win.

Was he more of an emotional leader or a decision maker? A decision maker. He deliberately avoided emotional involvement with players, although he frequently exploded at umpires. Tony La Russa told his Boswell, Buzz Bissinger, that Richards taught him, "It's your ass. It's your team. It's your responsibility. There's a strategy for every situation. So start making some decisions."

Was he more of an optimist or more of a problem solver? A problem solver, with teams and with individual players. The best example: when his catchers couldn't hold Hoyt Wilhelm's knuckleball, he invented a giant mitt so they could at least knock it down. He tried to fix players' weaknesses—especially pitchers. He acquired players that he thought could fill his teams' needs, but if his first solution didn't work out he did not hesitate to dump that guy and try somebody else.

How He Used His Personnel

Did he favor a set lineup or a rotation system? He kept his best players in the lineup every day, but even when he had strong teams he was always moving players in and out to try to shore up the weak spots.

Did he like to platoon? He platooned extensively. Richards started tracking his players' platoon splits when he was managing in the minors in the 1940s, taping newspaper box scores into a notebook and calculating stats at the end of every week. With the 1959 Orioles he platooned at five positions. The next year his first-base pairing of Jim Gentile and Walt Dropo combined for 25 homers and 119 RBIs.

Did he try to solve his problems with proven players or with youngsters who still may have had something to learn? Youth. He told neophyte executive Tom Grieve, "Don't be afraid to go with your young players if you believe in them. Don't be afraid to make a mistake."

Many managers would give a rookie a small number of at-bats and send him down if he didn't produce right away. When Richards believed in a young player, he put him in the lineup and let him learn on the job, even if it took several years. See Brooks Robinson, Joe Morgan, Rusty Staub.

How many players did he make regulars who had not been regulars before, and who were they? Dozens. The list starts with Minnie Minoso, Brooks Robinson, Ron Hansen, Jim Gentile and the "Kiddie Korps" of young Orioles pitchers. As general manager in Houston he promoted Morgan, Staub and Jimmy Wynn, among many others. As general manager in Atlanta, Ralph Garr, Felix Millan, Darrell Evans, Earl Williams and Dusty Baker. In 1960 his Baltimore infield consisted of the 23-year-old "veteran" Robinson and three rookies. Five of his six top starting pitchers were 22 or younger. That team finished second, the highest of Richards' major league career.

He also gave regular jobs to longtime minor leaguers such as second baseman Billy Gardner, pitchers Saul Rogovin and Bob Keegan, and Negro League veterans Bob Boyd and Connie Johnson. Since he had spent most of his playing career in the minors, Richards recognized that some players could produce if they were given a chance.

Did he prefer to go with good offensive players or did he like the glove men? Glove men. Richards described himself as a defense-first manager, and his teams' defensive efficiency rates were usually exceptional. He said, "The most important thing to me is to get the other fellow out. Almost every game is decided by the loser giving it away rather than the winner winning it. A good defense, inclusive of pitching, is the most vital part of a successful team." He repeated this like a mantra: "Most games are lost rather than won."

Did he like an offense based on power, speed or high averages? He liked batters who could put the ball in play and run. One of his favorites was Nellie Fox, who struck out about twice a month and hit a home run every two months. Neither the White Sox's nor Orioles' ballpark was homer-friendly, but Richards realized that singles hitters could not beat the home-run offense that dominated the 1950s, so he was continually searching for power bats.

Did he use the entire roster or did he keep people sitting on the bench? He was a scorekeeper's nightmare, shuffling players in and out. He used the whole roster and then traded for some more. Richards carried nine or 10 pitchers, so he had more bench players than present-day managers. His liberal use of platooning, pinch hitters and defensive replacements meant that few players were rusting away on the bench. He had no doghouse; if he decided a man wouldn't do, he got rid of him

Did he build his bench around young players who could step into the breach if need be, or around veteran role players who had their own functions within a game? Veterans. He generally didn't keep young players on the bench, except for the bonus babies who were required to be there.

Game Managing and Use of Tactics

Did he go for the big-inning offense or did he like to use the one-run tactics? His teams and their spacious home parks were not suited to big-inning tactics, and that fit with his own preferences.

Did he pinch-hit much, and if so, when? He used pinch-hitters frequently, most often to get the platoon advantage. In 1961 switch-hitter Dave Philley pinch-hit 72 times for the Orioles. Like Casey Stengel, Richards would pinch-hit early in the game if he saw a chance for a big inning. He once used six pinch hitters in four innings.

Was there anything unusual about his lineup selection? How he juggled it. He often used more different lineups than Stengel. Of course, Stengel was juggling because he had so many good players; Richards did so because he had so few.

Did he use the sac bunt often? More often than any other manager of the 1950s, according to research by Steve Treder. Richards later changed his mind and said the sacrifice was a waste of an out.

Did he like to use the running game? His "Go-Go" White Sox led the league in stolen bases every year, but his Orioles were near the bottom. This reflects his adjustment to the power game of the '50s, when runners attempted to steal so seldom that it was a surprise play. However, he favored speedy players and may have paid more attention to teaching base-running than any other manager.

Did he hit and run very often? He hated the hit-and-run. In his instructional book, *Modern Baseball Strategy*, he listed six things that could go wrong on the play and, just for good measure, added that there was always the possibility that a runner might make it from first to third without a hit-and-run. He preferred the run-and-hit, where the runner takes off on a straight steal and the batter is not required to swing.

In what circumstances would he issue an intentional walk? Rarely. In his book he put this in italics: "*the intentional pass is a dangerous gamble*." Intentional bases on balls were first counted in 1955. All of his Orioles teams were at or near the bottom of the league in that category. In 1960, when he had the American League's best pitching staff, he ordered only 19 intentional walks. Stengel, whose Yankee staff was almost as good, issued 33.

Were there any unique or idiosyncratic tactics that he particularly favored? Richards was an experimenter—the knuckleball catcher's huge mitt is the most prominent of many examples. He defied "the book," baseball's conventional wisdom. He told La Russa, "Trust your gut, don't cover your butt."

At least four times Richards shifted his pitcher to a fielding position, brought in a reliever to gain the platoon advantage, then put the original pitcher back on the mound. When his pitcher ran to back up home plate in case of a throw, he instructed the pitcher and catcher to swap gloves, figuring the catcher could snare the ball easier with the pitcher's glove than with his pillow-like mitt. He ordered a runner at first base to let a ground ball hit him, spoiling a double play.

How did he change the game? He was the first manager to monitor pitch counts, 30 years before it became a widespread practice. He was the first manager to track on-base percentage, at least 40 years before it was recognized as a more important metric than batting average and before the statistic even had a name; he called it "B.A. with bases on balls." He calculated his hitters' and pitchers' platoon splits.

In Baltimore he wrote an instructional manual for minor league managers and coaches to ensure that players were taught the same techniques at every level. The manual was later expanded into a larger bible called "The Oriole Way," which guided the team's player development for decades. Building on the foundation laid by Richards and farm director Jim McLaughlin, the Orioles won more games than any other team from the mid-1960s to the 1980s.

Richards was responsible for three rule changes: a pitcher is now allowed to move to another position and back to the mound only once during an inning; the size of catchers' mitts is restricted; and an umpire may call a double play if a base runner deliberately allows a ground ball to hit him.

Handling the Pitching Staff

Did he like power pitchers or did he prefer to go with the people who put the ball in play? Above all he wanted pitchers who threw strikes. "Einstein couldn't be a smart pitcher unless he could throw strike one," he said. Most of his teams were among the stingiest in allowing walks. Several of his better staffs were near the top in strikeouts as well.

But he loved power arms. In 1960 he promoted left-handed flamethrower Steve Barber from Class D to the majors. Barber contributed 10 victories with a 3.22 ERA while leading the league in walks and wild pitches.

Did he stay with his starters or go to the bullpen quickly? He believed every pitcher had to be treated differently. His teams were usually among the leaders in complete games, but also used starters like Skinny Brown and Sandy Consuegra, who seldom finished games. He put several young pitchers on strict pitch counts and did not allow them to complete their starts.

Did he use a four-man rotation? Never. He believed pitchers needed at least four days of rest between starts at a time when the conventional wisdom called for three. Few of his pitchers started as many as 30 games in a season. That is one reason he never managed a 20-game winner.

Did he use the entire staff, or did he try to get five or six people to do most of the work? Except for those that he decided wouldn't do, he used everybody.

Was there anything unique about his handling of his pitchers? Nearly everything. He mandated four days' rest for starters and paid attention to pitch counts. He tried to teach all pitchers his favorite version of the change-up, the slip pitch, and he preached the value of an effective change-up. When he went after a veteran pitcher, he preferred to recycle those who had pitched for him before and presumably had bought into his program. (He did the same with position players.) Oddly, in both Chicago and Baltimore he kept the pitching coach he inherited from the previous regime. Ray Berres (White Sox) and Harry Brecheen (Orioles) were well respected, but they likely had little influence given Richards' pride in his own knowledge of pitching.

What was his strongest point as a manager? As the Orioles' scout Jim Russo put it, "teaching, teaching, teaching, 24 hours a day." Richards made his players practice the game's fundamentals and then practice them some more, "not just eight or 10 times, but 50 or 100 times," one player said. The teaching continued throughout the season; workouts on off-days were standard operating procedure. His hallmark was his ability to turn failed pitchers into winners. Dizzy Trout, Hal Newhouser, Billy Pierce and Phil Niekro were his most prominent turnarounds.

He told Donald Honig a manager's most essential trait was restraint: "Restraint under duress is absolutely necessary." He rarely showed up players publicly or ripped them in the newspapers.

Where did he stand on the most important moral issue of his lifetime? When Richards persuaded White Sox general manager Frank Lane to trade for the black Cuban Minnie Minoso in 1951, Chicago was only the third American League team to integrate. Richards also promoted Negro League veterans Bob Boyd and Connie Johnson to the Sox and later brought them to Baltimore.

In 1954 the Preserve Segregation Committee of Birmingham, Alabama, petitioned Richards to leave his black players out of the lineup when they came to that city for an exhibition game. Richards replied, "I am very sorry, but that question of racial segregation was settled more than 2,000 years ago on Mount Calvary ... Christ Jesus died for us all."

While Boyd and Johnson thanked him for giving them a chance, both believed he didn't like black players. When Richards was running the Houston club in the early 1960s, the spring training dormitories for minor leaguers were segregated.

Richards considered himself a Southerner and every one of his closest associates in baseball was a white Southerner. One of the leading black sportswriters, the Baltimore *Afro-American's* Sam Lacy, perceptively wrote: "Richards wouldn't be human ... if he didn't nurture prejudices ... There are some folk I don't like, and far be it from me to argue that I am free from prejudices ... but I am convinced that Richards nor Stengel nor Lopez nor Dressen permits his dislike of a player to interfere with what he considers to be the most advantageous handling of the team." (Ellipses in the original.)

If there was no professional baseball, what would he probably have done with his life? He would have started as a schoolteacher like his father and ended up as superintendent of schools or in some higher public office. His subordinates would have been terrified of him. Many teachers would have decided they would be happier selling insurance.

This article is adapted from Warren Corbett's The Wizard of Waxahachie: Paul Richards and the End of Baseball as We Knew It (Dallas: Southern Methodist University Press, 2009).

Third Trivia Challenge: Time Machine: The Advanced Class

For this one, we're going back in time quite a ways, but … what we're after is a bit different. Baseball from its inception has been a game that harbors dataheads, with an impressive array of numbers even before advanced metrics or a bevy of rate stats. But not all of those numbers were well-known in their day. Roger Connor now is known as Babe Ruth's prologue, but he wasn't then. In the same way, there are several fairly basic stats of the present day, and we now know who led them over the years, but their accomplishments were ignored.

For these 10 questions, name the player and their statistic where applicable. For each of these stats, all leagues traditionally considered major are major, and the record books start at 1876. For a rate stat, each batter qualified for the batting title and each pitcher qualified for the ERA title. Career stats require a minimum 3,000 plate appearances.

1. When Babe Ruth hit 54 home runs in 1920, he knocked this man out of a longstanding tie for 10th. Had it not been for the 1884 White Stockings and their oddity of a park, this man's 19 home runs would have shattered the previous record by five. But his production evaporated afterward, and by 1891 he was no longer in the majors.
2. One of the few times a career record is overtaken by someone associated with the same team, this Braves Hall of Famer had his record surpassed by Hank Aaron in 1972. He remained in the top 10 until 1993, when Dave Winfield passed him.
3. At a rate of 25.6 percent, this catcher went into the 20th century with the NL record in his stat. Mind you, from our current records, I have to specify NL record, and the stat can't be kept from 1897-1900, which might provide a clue. Three other hints: Babe Ruth was over 25.6 percent, but Joe DiMaggio wasn't; the average for all 19th century players who fit the career minimum is 14.8 percent; the NL's figure for 2008 was 29.5 percent.
4. The career leaders for this stat at the end of each season:

   Paul Hines 1884

   Ned Williamson 1885

   Harry Stovey 1886

   Dan Brouthers 1887-95

   Bill Joyce 1896-97

   Dan Brouthers 1898-1901

   Nap Lajoie 1902

   Buck Freeman 1903-04

   Dan Brouthers 1905-16

   Gavy Cravath 1916-21

   Babe Ruth 1922-2009

   Lifetime, Brouthers is one spot behind Bill Skowron and one ahead of Nick Johnson. Brouthers was knocked out of the top 10 in 1929, Cravath in 1931.
5. These players lead their position for a single-season offensive record. What is it?

   C: Mike Piazza

   1B: Mark McGwire

   2B: Fred Dunlap

   SS: Honus Wagner

   3B: Mike Schmidt

   LF: Barry Bonds

   CF: Mickey Mantle

   RF: Babe Ruth
6. This man played in only one season (1884) and didn't even lead his league in the category, but he remained in the single-season top 10 for this stat until 1956, when Herb Score and Sam Jones passed him. We don't know what hand he threw with, but he was a good pitcher at least for this one season.
7. When records were first available for this statistic in 1884, Will White set the record. Since then, only two men have broken his record: Gus Weyhing and Joe McGinnity. Since World War II, only Kerry Wood and Tom Murphy have come within half of the record.
8. Although primarily a third baseman, by 1885 he was the active leader, tied with Old Hoss Radbourn, in a pitching category, having led the majors in it in 1882.
9. Due perhaps to his home park, this Hall of Fame pitcher entered the 20th century as the all-time leader with 161. Although he wasn't passed until 1930, he was out of the top 10 a decade later.
10. Until Pedro Martinez, this right hander was the only pitcher whose career started in the modern era to have ended a season with a mark in this statistic above 4.00. Since Pedro, only Curt Schilling and Ben Sheets have ended a season this way. On top of that, he's the only player from my undergraduate alma mater to have made the majors, but not even Baseball Reference realizes his junior years were spent there.

The solutions to these questions and all Trivia Challenges are in the back of the book, starting on page 360.

Analysis

Championship Leverage Index

by Sky Andrecheck

There are a lot of ups and downs over the course of a baseball season and as the season progresses the games begin to take on either added or diminished importance. If your team is lucky enough to be in a pennant race, you may find your team's games becoming more meaningful each day as the race heats up. Similarly, those same late-season contests become nearly meaningless for a team that has fallen out of contention.

The Twins' Sept. 20 game against the Tigers had a playoff atmosphere and was much more important to the two teams' championship hopes than the average MLB regular season game. On the other end of the spectrum, the Astros' Sept. 20 game was meaningless to Houston's championship hopes. As a fan it's easy to sense the importance of a game in the context of a team's season. What I present here is a way to quantify the relative meaning of each game of the season, in what I call the Championship Leverage Index.

Some of you are probably already familiar with the concept of Leverage Index (LI) within the context of a single game. The concept was pioneered by Tom Tango, and puts a value on the importance of each moment in the game. For instance, leading off the bottom of the ninth in a tie game is a highly important situation. As a result, the at-bat has a Leverage Index of 2.3, meaning that the situation has 2.3 times the potential impact on winning as the average game situation.

Likewise, when leading off the bottom of the ninth down by five runs, an at-bat has an LI of 0.26, meaning that the at-bat is only 26 percent as important as the average major league at-bat. Since the game is already nearly a lost cause, the at-bat has lost a lot of its meaning and the low leverage index reflects this fact.

Championship Leverage Index, created independently by myself and Dave Studenmund, takes the same idea and applies it in the context of an entire season. Like its in-game cousin, Champ LI quantifies each team's games in terms of the impact they are likely to have on winning a championship. Late-season games for playoff teams will have a high Champ LI, while September games for teams out of the race will have a very low Champ LI, reflecting the fact that their result will do little to alter their team's playoff chances. Meanwhile, opening day games will have a Champ LI around 1.0.

The Nuts And Bolts Of Championship Leverage Index

Champ LI can be calculated in a few simple steps. First, the probability of each team making the playoffs is calculated based on the current standings and games remaining. In the second step, the probability is recalculated assuming the team wins its next game (and deals its opponent a loss). The increase in the team's probability of making the playoffs if they win is the game's potential impact. For instance, on June 20, the Red Sox had a 65.2 percent chance of making the playoffs. However, a win against Atlanta would increase their probability to 68.4 percent. This potential increase of 3.2 percent represents the foundation of Championship Leverage Index.

After we calculate this impact, the only thing left to do is to divide it by the average impact of a major league game. What is the average impact of a game on a team's playoff chances? Not coincidentally, the impact of an average game is equal to the impact of the first game of the season. Because nobody knows what the rest of the season will hold, the opening day game is, by definition, the average regular season game—depending on what happens later in the season, sometimes other games will be much less meaningful than opening day, and sometimes much more. The impact of the average opening day game happens to be approximately 2.4 percent, meaning that the average game of the season will increase or decrease a team's probability to make the playoffs by 2.4 percent.

So if we divide each game's impact by 2.4 percent, we get an index that is equal to 1.0 for an average game, greater than 1.0 for important games, and less than 1.0 for unimportant games.

The probabilities that go into the calculation are determined using a simulation, and the simulation makes a few assumptions. The biggest one is that all teams have a 50 percent chance to win each game. This places each team on equal footing and does not make any assumptions about the teams a priori. While of course each team's probability to win a game really does vary, determining the exact probability is difficult and would be open to bias. As an added convenience of this assumption, there is no need to calculate the impact of a loss since the absolute value of the change in probability will be identical to that of a win.

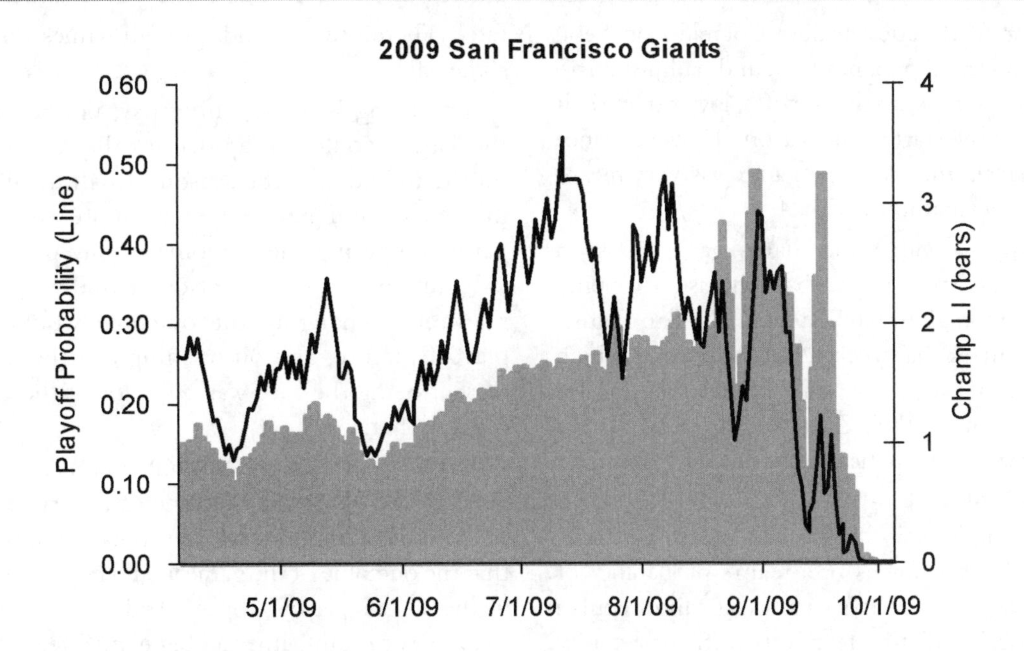

Champ LI In Action

Perhaps the easiest way get a grasp of Champ LI is by using an example. There are graphs of every team's Champ LI in the statistics section of this book, but let's go over the above graph of the San Francisco Giants' season in detail here. Each vertical bar on the graph shows the Champ LI of the game on a particular date of the season. The Champ LI of each game can be seen by looking at the right axis. Superimposed on the chart, and represented by the solid line, is the team's probability of making the playoffs (with the axis on the left).

Like everybody else, the Giants started off the season with a Champ LI of about 1.0. Since they were not playing a division rival, the first game on April 7 took on ever-so-slightly less importance, giving their first game a Champ LI of 0.97 and a pregame probability of making the playoffs of 26 percent. The Giants won that game, and of course, their probability of making the playoffs went up as well.

Since the win increased the chance that they would be fighting for the playoffs come September, they also increased their Championship Leverage Index to 1.02 for their April 8 game. The Giants slumped through April, and hence, their games lost some meaning and decreased to a low point of 0.68 when they fell to 3-8 before their game on April 19. Early in the season, each team's Champ LI tends to increase and decrease with their chances to make the playoffs. Good teams see their games gain meaning, while poor teams see their games quickly diminishing in value.

By May 8 the Giants had bounced back and were 14-13, in second place and 5.5 games behind the Dodgers. Their Champ LI the previous day was 1.01—almost exactly an average game. However, on the next day the Giants visited LA for a three-game series. You can see the three small spikes on the graph showing the added importance of the Dodgers games. On May 8, their Champ LI spiked to 1.23, indicating that the game meant about 20 percent more because it was against the first place Dodgers—a team which they were likely to be vying with at the end of the season for a playoff spot.

The added importance of games against division rivals is shown clearly by Champ LI, and you can see the spikes in the Champ LI on the graph. Late-season games against division rivals can have an even larger impact if the two teams are fighting for a playoff spot. Consider the Giants' mid-August series against the Rockies. On Aug. 20, their game against the Reds had a Champ LI of 1.99, but despite having lost that game, the Champ LI of the next day's game against Colorado skyrocketed to 2.54. In a strictly two-team race, games between the competing teams can take on up to double the importance of other games. This is an important fact to note, especially for managers who are considering juggling their pitching rotations to pitch their aces against their division rivals.

While the team's Champ LI is generally high when the probability of making the playoffs is high, late-season games can have a great deal of meaning even when the team's playoff chances are low. By the third game of their final series against Colorado on Sept. 16, the Giants were 2.5 games back and had just an 18 percent chance of making the playoffs, lower than their chances were at the start of the season. However, since there was so little time left, the game was very meaningful and had a Champ LI of 3.24.

After losing that game, the Giants' games took on progressively less meaning with each loss, dropping from 1.99 on Sept. 19 to 0.64 on Sept. 21. San Franciscans probably mark that weekend as the point at which they lost interest in the race and started focusing on the 49ers. Eventually, their Champ LI dropped to zero when they were mathematically eliminated from postseason contention.

While Championship Leverage Index generally follows the ups and downs of a team's probability of making the playoffs, a team's Champ LI can of course drop dramatically if the team's playoff probability becomes *too* high. Case in point, the New York Yankees' Champ LI rose steadily throughout the first half of the season, rising to a peak of 1.79 for their July 3 game against the Blue Jays when they led the wild card by two games.

On Aug. 6 the Yankees started a four-game series against Boston with a 2.5-game lead in the division and a 5.5-game lead in the wild card. Their probability to make the playoffs was 85 percent and the Champ LI of that game was 1.43, making it a relatively important game. One four-game sweep later and a Yankees playoff berth was nearly assured with a probability of 95 percent. Correspondingly, their Champ LI fell to .50 and steadily dropped the rest of the year until it fell to zero upon clinching the playoffs.

Considerations And Caveats

The Championship Leverage Index quantifies just how important each game of the season is to each team. At this point you may be wondering why each game should have a different value at all. After all, aren't all games created equal, since they are all worth just one game in the standings? Why was game No. 162 of the Detroit Tigers season (Champ LI 10.4) any more important than the Tigers' opening day game (Champ LI 1.0)? In some sense, you would be right—they do all count for one game in the standings. After all, had the Tigers won on opening day, that would have given them the AL Central crown. In retrospect, *every* game on the Tigers schedule was a must-win, do-or-die game, the outcome of which would alter their playoff fate. Therefore, in hindsight, all games do have the same value.

The thing is, on opening day, nobody *knew* that the Tigers would end up tied for the AL Central title on the final day of the season. In all likelihood, the division would be decided by more than just one game, rendering the outcome of any particular one ballgame irrelevant. That one game would only be relevant if changing the outcome would alter the playoff picture, and on opening day the probability of that being the case was quite low—the Champ LI reflects that.

Fast forward to game No. 162. Because of the standings, we *knew* that the outcome of the game would be of the utmost importance. In this case, it was *very* likely that the outcome of the game would play a deciding role in the Tigers' playoff hopes. And it is this knowledge that gives certain games a "big game" feel and certain other games a meaningless feel.

The considerations here closely parallel the issues surrounding the single game Leverage Index. Within the context of one game, each inning is equally important—runs count the same no matter when they are scored and one inning of scoreless pitching is worth the same whether it comes in the first or in the ninth. By this logic it's true that the ninth inning is no more important than the first inning, and on average, both will indeed have the same Leverage Index.

However, when given the knowledge of the score in the ninth inning, this changes the importance of the situation. In a 7-0 game, the events of the ninth inning are very likely to be inconsequential to the game's outcome, but in a tie-game, the events of the ninth are likely to be *very* consequential. Hence the situations are given very different Leverage Indices. The very same properties hold true for the Championship Leverage Index as well.

While the description of Champ LI that I provided at the beginning of the article is probably the easiest way to think about it, another way of describing it is that it essentially measures the probability that the outcome of one game will decide a playoff berth. At the beginning of the season, this probability is fairly low, while for teams in a September pennant race, this probability becomes much higher. For teams that are out of contention, the probability of one game deciding its playoff fate is close to zero. In essence it is this probability that Championship Leverage Index is measuring.

Championship WPA

Some of you are probably also familiar with the statistic called Win Probability Added. As a refresher, WPA for an event is calculated by taking the probability of winning the game *after* an event has occurred and subtracting it by the probability of winning *before* the event occurred. If a player homers and increases his team's chances to win from 50 percent to 70 percent, then the event is worth .20 WPA. A WPA value for each player over the course of a season can be calculated by summing up the WPA of all events that a player contributed.

Here I'll introduce Championship WPA. As you might imagine, Champ WPA measures the increase in a team's probability of winning a championship. Adding the Championship WPA of all teams together will sum to zero. Championship WPA takes into account the relative importance of each game as well as the players' impact on those games.

The Nuts And Bolts Of Championship Leverage WPA

To calculate Champ WPA, we simply find the increase or decrease in the probability of winning a World Series after each event occurs. In game No. 162, Jason Kubel hit a three-run homer in the bottom of the first inning to give the Twins a 3-0 lead. So how much did Kubel's blast contribute to a championship with that one swing?

With a victory in that game, the Twins' chances of making the playoffs would increase from 50 percent to 75 percent. And of course, once in the playoffs, they would have to win the World Series, meaning we have to multiply this difference by one-eighth. Knowing this, we can calculate that winning the game would increase the chances of the Twins winning the World Series by 3.125 percent, while a loss would decrease the Twins' chances by 3.125 percent.

Of course, Kubel's homer didn't win the game all by itself. After Kubel's dinger, the probability of the Twins winning the game increased from 58.5 percent to 79.4 percent giving the event a WPA of .209. Therefore, to get Kubel's contribution to a championship with that one swing, we multiply .03125 x 2 x .209 and get 1.3 percent championships won. For such a big home run, 1.3 percent of a World Series title may seem awfully small, but it is actually an extremely large percentage for a regular season at-bat. The same home run in an average game would have had less than one-tenth of that impact.

We can also report this number in terms of the number of games won, weighted by the games' importance. To do this, we simply multiply the play's WPA by the Champ LI. For Kubel's homer, we find that his HR in game No. 162 was worth the equivalent of winning 2.2 average MLB games (10.4 x .209).

Of the most important plays of the season, the top five most important plays came in the final showdown between Detroit and Minnesota. No. 1 is Orlando Cabrera's two-run homer giving Minnesota the lead in the bottom of the seventh inning. That homer alone was worth 4.90 percent of a World Series championship. It's followed closely by Brandon Inge's 10th-inning go-ahead double which gave Detroit 4.88 percent of a championship. Because these were huge plays coming in the biggest game of the year, it's no surprise that they had the biggest impact on their team's championship fate.

Championship WPA For Players

Of course, we can also calculate Champ WPA for individual players over the course of the season. How much of a championship did each player win or lose, when factoring in the importance of each game? Champ WPA rewards players for coming up big in big games. Therefore, those playing in key games and performing well have a major advantage.

One would be tempted to think of Champ WPA as the ultimate "MVP-stat", rewarding players on good teams who come up big in pennant races. Chipper Jones won his 1999 MVP largely on the basis of having a huge September and powering the Braves to a playoff berth over the Mets. Championship WPA would certainly reward him for his clutch performance. However, I wouldn't really recommend using it to award an MVP, and closer examination reveals that Champ WPA doesn't correlate particularly well with MVP voters' preferences.

First of all, players on *really* good teams don't rate particularly highly since they play in a lot of meaningless games after their team has locked up a playoff berth. While MVP voters clearly have a preference for players on good teams, they don't tend to punish those on teams that ran away with their division. Second of all, Champ WPA puts *enormous* stock in players' performances in huge games—far more than average MVP voter does (or should).

Consider that above we determined that Cabrera's game No. 163 homer won 4.90 percent of a championship. Now consider that over the course of the entire season, Albert Pujols won 4.84 percent of a championship. Indeed, one clutch home run in a one-game tiebreaker is worth as much as an entire season of spectacular play. But that does not mean that the player who came through with one big play should be the MVP over the guy who hit 47 homers. The fact that Cabrera hit the homer does not mean he was a more valuable player than Pujols, and it certainly does not mean he was a *better* player than Pujols.

It *is* saying that Pujols' play over the course of the season and Cabrera's homer both increased the chances of their respective team winning the World Series by about the same amount. It is also saying that if someone offered you a choice between (1) one future regular season of Albert Pujols' 2009 production, or (2) next time your team is in a one-game tiebreaker, you get to automatically increase your chances of winning by 40 percent (the homer's WPA), that both of those choices yield approximately the same value.

Viewed this way, we see that both Pujols's season and Cabrera's homer provided their teams with extraordinary value. However, Pujols' value came from being an incredibly talented player who won a lot of games for the Cardinals, while Cabrera's value came from getting relatively lucky and hitting a home run in the right place at the right time.

Below I'll present the Top 20 leaders in Championship WPA for both the American and National Leagues.

In the NL, the Champ WPA leaderboard looks fairly normal, with Prince Albert leading the pack at 4.84 percent of a championship won. This 4.84 percent translates to about 8.06 games won in the standings, a number very similar to his regular 7.71 WPA.

The other players on the list are, predictably, players who played on good teams in pennant races. They usually had high WPA's that were made even more meaningful since their teams were playing important games. In all, this list is not a bad approximation of how the MVP voting is likely to go. It's dominated by great players who also played on great teams. The exception is the Reds' Joey Votto, who managed to rack up 2.55 percent of a championship before the Reds fell out of the race.

The American League list, on the other hand, is a mix of great players and players who came up big for the Twins and Tigers in the final days of the season.

National League Champ WPA Leaders

Team	Player	Champ WPA	Weighted WPA	WPA
STL	A. Pujols	4.84%	8.06	7.71
STL	C. Carpenter	4.21%	7.02	5.79
MIL	P. Fielder	4.20%	7.01	7.92
PHI	C. Utley	3.69%	6.15	4.39
PHI	R. Howard	3.69%	6.15	6.07
SFG	T. Lincecum	3.66%	6.11	4.57
STL	A. Wainwright	3.25%	5.42	4.26
SFG	P. Sandoval	2.79%	4.65	4.49
COL	H. Street	2.65%	4.41	3.28
SFG	M. Cain	2.55%	4.25	3.50
CIN	J. Votto	2.55%	4.24	5.87
FLA	H. Ramirez	2.43%	4.04	3.34
ATL	J. Jurrjens	2.42%	4.03	4.32
COL	U. Jimenez	2.38%	3.97	3.12
PHI	R. Ibanez	2.36%	3.93	3.54
SFG	B. Wilson	2.27%	3.78	1.49
LAD	A. Ethier	2.08%	3.47	5.18
LAD	J. Broxton	2.05%	3.41	2.90
COL	J. Affeldt	2.01%	3.35	3.08
STL	R. Franklin	2.01%	3.34	2.27

At 6.81 percent of a title, the Twins' Joe Nathan is the player who provided the most value to his team given the context of his performance. Nathan was a good player, racking up 47 saves with a 2.10 ERA, but he's not at the top of the list for that reason. He's at the top because of his great performances during the final week of the season when he saved three games and turned in a clutch performance in game No. 163. While his regular WPA is only 3.58, his value more than triples when accounting for the context of the games.

Also on the list is Alexi Casilla, the Twins' infielder who hit .202 in 80 games for Minnesota. However, despite a half season's worth of poor play, he singled in the game-winning run in the bottom of the 12th inning of game No. 163. That hit alone was hugely valuable and it vaulted him to the leaderboard.

Now, the assertion that Casilla is a more valuable player to the Twins than Joe Mauer is, of course, laughable. Without Mauer the Twins are nothing, while without Casilla they are, well, pretty much the same since he wasn't even on the roster for half the season. However, you can make the assertion that the sum of the value of Casilla's performances *at the time they were*

American League Champ WPA Leaders

Team	Player	Champ WPA	Weighted WPA	WPA
MIN	J. Nathan	6.81%	11.35	3.58
DET	J. Verlander	6.50%	10.83	4.71
BOS	J. Papelbon	4.56%	7.60	4.88
TEX	S.Feldman	3.83%	6.38	3.06
MIN	J. Kubel	3.74%	6.23	2.61
BOS	J. Bay	3.68%	6.13	4.64
MIN	A. Casilla	3.53%	5.88	-0.49
MIN	M. Tolbert	3.00%	5.00	0.40
DET	M. Cabrera	2.99%	4.98	1.27
DET	E. Jackson	2.91%	4.85	3.38
NYY	J. Damon	2.88%	4.80	4.15
DET	R. Porcello	2.75%	4.58	1.36
MIN	J. Mauer	2.74%	4.56	3.84
NYY	M. Teixeira	2.58%	4.30	4.03
DET	D. Kelly	2.53%	4.21	0.07
LAA	B. Abreu	2.46%	4.10	3.10
NYY	M. Rivera	2.43%	4.05	3.62
SEA	F. Gutierrez	2.40%	4.00	3.50
NYY	A. Rodriguez	2.37%	3.95	3.94
DET	C. Granderson	2.36%	3.94	-0.02

performed were more valuable than the sum of the value of Mauer's performances *at the time they were performed.*

With the benefit of hindsight of course, we see that Mauer's performance all season long was instrumental in allowing the Twins to make the playoffs. However, when he was getting all those hits in August, there was little chance that they would have an impact on the Twins' playoff hopes. Meanwhile, when Casilla had his moment, everybody knew that the effect on the Twins' championship prospects was huge. The fact that Casilla came through in the biggest game of the year is reflected in his Champ WPA.

If Casilla has some kind of "big game" skill that is repeatable, he would indeed be a hugely valuable player. However, big game performance is largely *not* repeatable, and therein lies the "problem" with Champ WPA. While Champ WPA accurately measures the importance of each event as it happens, it is not at all useful in player evaluation.

Of course, player evaluation is not the point. Champ WPA is, I believe, most useful for looking at the impact of particular plays. It's a lot of fun to see what percentage of a championship was won or lost by a particular play and which players should earn the credit. However it, by definition, does not treat players equally, since not every player gets a chance to play in big games. While the lists above are fun, it's important to realize what it is measuring, and remember that much of a player's Champ WPA is out of his control.

Conclusion

Both Championship Leverage Index and Championship WPA can be useful tools when examining the importance of a game or a play to a team's championship hopes. While Championship Leverage Index doesn't exactly tell you anything new, it can be a fun and informative stat that quanitifies games in their larger context. Fans can feel when a game has great importance and when games are likely to be meaningful. Hopefully you'll find the graphs found elsewhere in this book interesting as you look back upon your favorite team's season. As you do, you will probably be able pick out the key games from the graph and see that they match up to your intuition of which games were the turning points in the season.

Championship WPA can also be a useful retrospective tool to look back and quantify key moments in the season. While it shouldn't be taken as a predictive measure or as a measure of talent or performance, it does measure the value of each event within the context of the situation. While everyone knows that Alexi Casilla provided huge value to his team by knocking in the winning run to clinch the A.L. Central, Championship WPA is there to quantify the event and measure how much it meant to the team (3.6 percent of a championship). I wouldn't choose an MVP by the stat, but it is a fun an informative way to measure performance.

As an addendum to the book, I'll be reviewing Championship Leverage Index and Championship WPA as it pertains to the postseason. The addendum will be available for download on the THT Annual 2010 download page (see the introduction to the Statistics section for details).

Hit Tracker 2009

by Greg Rybarczyk

In 2009, there were 5,042 home runs hit in 2,430 games, or 2.07 per game (this compares with 2.01 per game in 2008, 2.04 per game in 2007 and 2.22 per game in 2006) and Hit Tracker tracked them all. I'd like to share our results with you.

The New York Yankees led all teams with 244, home runs followed by the Phillies and Rangers with 224 each. The Red Sox (212), Blue Jays (209) and Rays (199) gave the AL East four of the top six totals in baseball, perhaps in part because each of those three clubs got to play nine games at the new Yankee Stadium. The Yankees' new park surrendered 237 total homers in 81 games, the most in MLB and 22 more than Rangers Ballpark in Arlington. Unsurprisingly, due to the unbalanced schedule, the only AL East team we haven't mentioned yet, the Baltimore Orioles, allowed the most home runs in 2009 (218). The Milwaukee Brewers followed close behind with 207 to lead the National League.

The Atlanta Braves were the stingiest team in terms of giving up the long ball, allowing only 119 homers. Their home park, Turner Field, saw 124 homers, second fewest in MLB to the Cardinals' home park, Busch Stadium (120). The injury-decimated New York Mets totaled only 95 home runs on offense, fewest in the league, and joined the 2008 San Francisco Giants as one of only two major league teams in the last 16 years to hit fewer than 100 home runs in a full season. The Mets' NL East rivals hit 42 home runs in 36 games at the Mets' new park, Citi Field, nearly as many as the Mets hit in their entire 81-game home schedule (49).

Albert Pujols of the St. Louis Cardinals led MLB with a career-high 47 homers, while four other NL sluggers (Prince Fielder, Ryan Howard, Mark Reynolds and Adrian Gonzalez) topped 40. Mark Teixeira and Carlos Peña topped the AL list with 39 home runs each. St. Louis' Colby Rasmus led all ML rookies with 16 home runs, closely followed by Baltimore's Nolan Reimold (15), Gordon Beckham (14) from the White Sox and Pittsburgh's Andrew McCutchen (12).

Milwaukee's Braden Looper gave up a league-leading 39 home runs, including 21 at Miller Park, while Baltimore's Jeremy Guthrie served up 35 long balls to pace the AL. Among ERA qualifiers, St. Louis' Chris Carpenter was the toughest to homer off, allowing only seven home runs in 192.2 innings.

Home Run Distances: How Far They Really Went In 2009

The average home run in 2009 covered just short of 399 feet, about two feet farther than the previous season, which fits well with the 3.4 percent increase in home runs from 2008 to 2009.

Only five percent of all home runs are hit farther than 440 feet, so this serves as a good milestone: anyone who hits a ball 440 feet or farther can be considered among the most powerful hitters in the league. In 2009, 135 different hitters achieved this distinction, and 55 did it more than once. A handful of players hit seven of their home runs at least 440 feet: Nelson Cruz, Adam Dunn, Ryan Howard, Chris Iannetta and Albert Pujols. These notable sluggers were all tied for second place in this list, however, because Arizona's Mark Reynolds put himself in his own league with an amazing 17 home runs of at least 440 feet!

Some sluggers distinguished themselves by not making the list: among the AL home run leaders, neither Aaron Hill nor Jason Bay, who each hit 36 home runs, qualified. Chase Utley knocked 31 pitches over the wall, but none went as far as 440 feet, and none of 30-home run hitter Curtis Granderson's long balls were long enough to make the list.

Mark Reynolds's outstanding power performance allowed him to claim the prestigious Golden Sledgehammer award for 2009; he led MLB with an average standard distance (i.e. with weather and altitude factored out) of 416 feet on his career-high 44 home runs. Reynolds knocked the second- and seventh-longest home runs of the year, and hit the season's longest homer in three different parks: a 481-foot blast on July 28 at Chase Field, a 471-footer on Aug.27 at AT&T Park and a 462-footer on Aug. 1 at Citi Field. Quite a performance for the young hitter, who figures to light up the Hit Tracker leader board for years to come!

Washington's newly acquired slugger Adam Dunn continued his prodigious home-run-hitting ways in 2009 as well, smashing home runs number five, 11 and 13 on the distance list, including a 473-footer at Miller Park that flew all the way out that park's open window in deep right-center field. Dunn's new home, Nationals Park, proved to his liking as well, as he knocked 19 balls over the fence there, six into the upper deck in right field. The only negative aspect of Dunn's power in 2009 was that for the first time since the 2004 season, Dunn did not total exactly 40 home runs, coming up with "only" 38.

Along with the well-known long-distance hitters like Reynolds and Dunn, several less likely players made their mark in 2009 with unexpected bursts of power.

- On April 7, Detroit's Brandon Inge blasted a 460-foot home run at Rogers Centre, his longest in more than three seasons dating back to at least 2005.
- On May 22, Philadelphia's Raul Ibañez hit the longest home run in the short history of the new Yankee Stadium, a 477-foot blast deep into the right-center field bleachers above the home bullpen.
- On July 10, San Francisco's Pablo Sandoval launched a 462-foot homer to deep right-center field at AT&T Park, although this feat was rather overshadowed by fellow Giant Jonathan Sanchez's no-hitter in the same game. Sandoval also hit home runs of 450 and 456 feet among his 25 round-trippers in his breakout first full season in the majors.
- On Oct. 2, two different young power hitters went *very* deep:
    - At Tropicana Field, Yankees rookie callup Juan Miranda hammered a 469-foot home run to the back wall in right field for his first career MLB home run.
    - In Cincinnati, 25-year-old Wladimir Balentien hit the longest home run of the year, a 495-foot bomb to the top of the left field upper deck at Great American Ball Park.

Ballparks

Different playing fields are a unique element of baseball among major team sports. Different field configurations often have an under-appreciated, but profound, impact on the games being played there. In the following section, we'll examine several major league ballparks through the lens of Hit Tracker, and discover some fascinating things you might never have known without closely following (and analyzing) the flight of the baseball through the air.

Citi Field

On April 13, 2009, the Mets hosted their first game at their new home ballpark, Citi Field. While others have written extensively about the many improvements and amenities of the new ballpark, my interest naturally focused on the comparative differences between the home run fences in the two parks.

Even before the 2009 season started, it was well known that there was a big difference between Shea Stadium and the new Citi Field. The home run fences at Citi are considerably more distant than those at Shea: on average, the fences are nine feet farther from home plate, and in one place in front of the bullpen in right-center field, the Citi Field fence is 27 feet deeper than the corresponding spot in Shea. Only in the right field corner is the new park's home run fence closer to home plate, and thus more favorable for home runs. The fences are also taller at Citi Field everywhere except the right field corner and in front of the bullpen; sections in left field, in straightaway center field, and in parts of right field are twice as high as the fence at Shea (16 feet vs. eight feet).

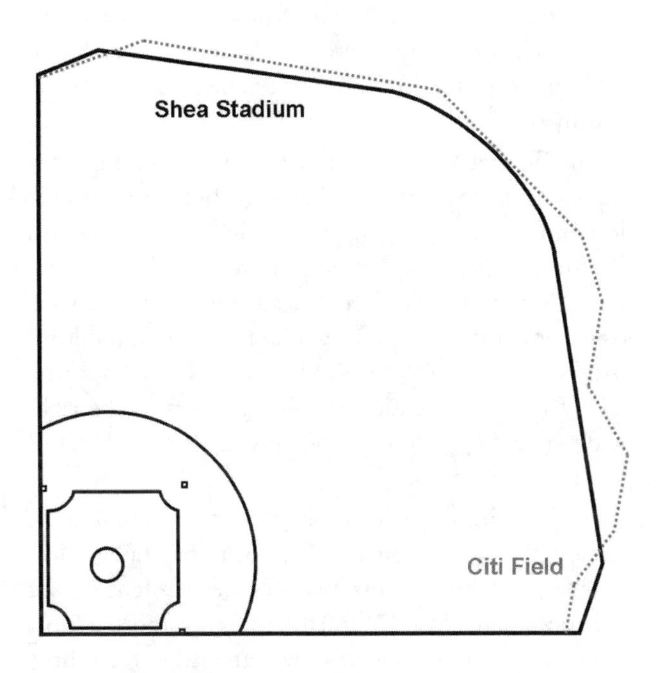

Naturally, with such a big difference "on paper," it is interesting to try to quantify the actual impact of the new park's configuration after a season's worth of games there. Detailed analysis of long fly balls hit at Citi Field during the 2009 season, using Hit Tracker, allows us to "project" those fly balls into the now-demolished Shea Stadium, and to compare each actual result in Citi Field with the hypothetical result in Shea. The difference between the two venues is remarkable!

During the 81 Mets home games in 2009, the new park's deeper and taller home run fences led to a total of 64 fly balls which were not home runs in Citi Field but which would have cleared the fences in Shea Stadium. These 64 "stolen" home runs were offset by a total of only four batted balls that were home runs in Citi Field but which would not have cleared Shea's fences; all of these four "gift" homers were hit close to the right field corner, the only place where Citi's fences are easier to clear than Shea's. At the end of the article, there is a list of all "would be" home runs affected by Citi Field.

The most negatively affected hitter was New York's David Wright, who lost nine home runs to the combination of deeper and taller fences. The impact was primarily to Wright's slugging percentage, however, and not his batting average, because those nine balls that would have been homers in Shea Stadium became two triples, five doubles, one single and just one fly out. Those extra 19 bases would have pushed Wright's home slugging percentage from .434 up to .508, and his overall number from .447 to .482.

Wright's teammate Johan Santana benefitted the most from the change, with nine potential Shea Stadium home runs turned into four doubles, one triple and four fly outs.

The Florida Marlins suffered the worst among visiting teams, losing seven of their own home runs to the deeper fences, while only three Mets homers against the Marlins were kept inside the new park, for a net of -4. The Philadelphia Phillies came out way ahead, losing only three of their own homers, while the Mets lost six against the Phillies, with Chase Utley knocking two of the aforementioned "gift" homers in the right field corner of Citi, giving the Phillies an overall net of plus-five home runs.

Despite the damage to their home run numbers, overall, the impact on the Mets was favorable. The Mets lost 27 home runs to Citi's deeper fences, but their opponents lost 37. Furthermore, of those 27 lost homers, visiting outfielders only managed to turn three into fly outs (11 percent), while of the opponents' 37 lost homers, Mets outfielders were able to run down and catch 13 (35 percent); this difference is statistically significant. Certainly the Mets' lost season of 2009 can't be blamed on their new ballpark, and with the return of their many injured stars, the Mets' fortunes should rebound significantly in 2010.

New Yankee Stadium

The New York Yankees also opened a new ballpark in 2009, kicking off their inaugural season at the new Yankee Stadium on April 16. The new park's home run fences was advertised as being essentially the same as that of the prior Yankee Stadium, but in fact the new fence line was a bit shallower in right field, and a bit deeper in dead center field, than was its predecessor. The difference in right field, about 4.5 feet on average, ranges to as much as nine feet in one spot, making the fence in right field the closest in MLB: from the foul line to the home bullpen, the New Yankee Stadium fence averages just under 19 feet closer to home plate than the fences in the other 29 MLB parks.

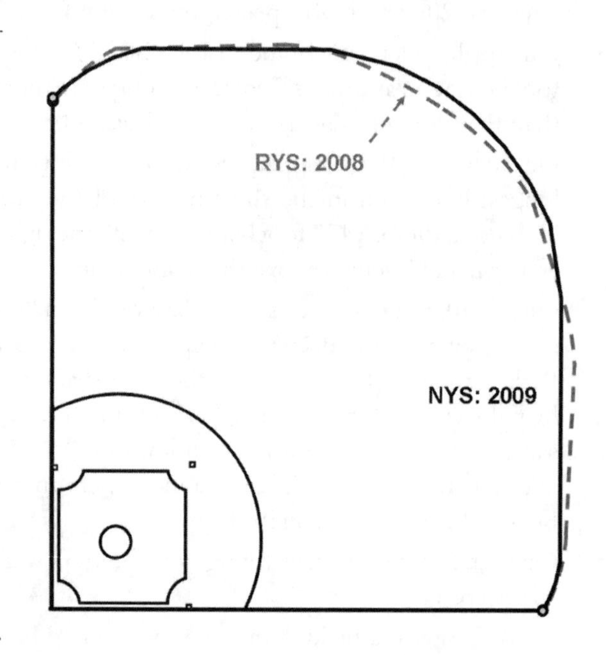

While the rest of the home run fences at new Yankee Stadium, from center field to the left field corner, averages about three feet deeper than the rest of MLB overall, the dimensions of the new park make it very favorable for home runs. The results from the 2009 season bear this out. In 81 games at the new Yankee Stadium, there were 237 home runs, or 2.93 per game, which was tops in MLB.

Hit Tracker analysis of all the long fly balls hit at the New Yankee Stadium in 2009 finds that of the 237 home runs hit during the regular season, 28 would not have been home runs in the old Yankee Stadium, due to having been hit in places where the new park's fences are shallower. There were also 12 non-homers hit in the new park (five doubles, one triple, six fly outs) that would have been home runs in the old park. (These were all hit to center and left-center field, where the new park is slightly deeper than the old.) Overall, the net difference due to the dimension changes is plus-16 home runs for the new ballpark.

This observed difference, 16 home runs, is entirely insufficient to explain the jump in home runs in the Bronx, where in 2008 only 160 home runs were hit (1.98 per game). Some, including myself, have speculated that the wind may move through the new park differently than it did through the old park, perhaps providing some extra distance to fly balls on some days, and anecdotes from a variety of sources suggest this may be true. However, a study by renowned baseball physicist Dr. Alan Nathan found no significant disproportionate overall wind effect at New Yankee Stadium. A more likely explanation for the dramatic rise in home runs there concerns the team that plays half their games in the new ballpark.

The right-to-left asymmetry of the dimensions of the home run fences at New Yankee Stadium has led to a corresponding asymmetry of results in terms of home runs; 143 of the 237 home runs hit there in 2009 (60 percent) were hit to right or right-center field, while in the other 29 MLB parks, the rest of MLB averaged 61 of 166 homers, or 37 percent, in those same directions. There is more asymmetry in who hit those homers to right and right-center field: the Yankees, featuring a lineup filled with powerful left-handed and switch-hitters, hit 99 of these 143 home runs (69 percent), while the New York pitchers held their visiting opponents to only 44 homers to the same area of the stadium (far fewer than Yankees hitters, and in fact far fewer than they would have been expected to hit in an average MLB park, much less the shortest right field in baseball).

To summarize, homers to right and right-center field are more than twice as frequent at the new Yankee Stadium as in the rest of MLB, and the Yankees hit twice as many of those home runs as their opponents. The precise impact on the Yankees' success at home from their prowess at hitting and denying home runs to right and right-center field is impossible to know, but there can be no doubt that the scoring differential driven by this home run differential was significant. Consider the following data which show home runs at new Yankee Stadium hit to right and right-center field, with the season split into two periods, before and after June 1:

Period	NYY HR's	VIS HR's	% NYY	Home Record	Win %
Before June 1st	32	20	61.5%	14-9	.609
After June 1st	67	24	73.6%	43-15	.741
Entire Season	99	44	69.2%	57-24	.704

The Yankees' home winning percentage is remarkably correlated with the Yankees' relative performance at hitting home runs into the right field seats at new Yankee Stadium. Early in the year, the Yankees had a small edge in home runs to right and right-center and a correspondingly small edge in home winning percentage. After June 1, the Yankees maintained their home run hitting to that area of the field but clamped down tightly on opposing hitters doing the same, and their overall performance at home went from good to phenomenal!

Whether by design or happenstance, it is clear that the Yankees built an extreme home run environment in right and right-center field in their new ballpark, and then proceeded to utterly dominate their opponents in the exploitation of that environment. Visiting teams who wish to do well in the Bronx in 2010 and beyond will need to find a way to compete with the Yankees in the contest for control of the right field seats.

Target Field

In April 2010, the Twins will open their home schedule outdoors for the first time since 1981 at Target Field in downtown Minneapolis. How will the new park play with respect to power hitting, compared to the previous 28 seasons in the Hubert H. Humphrey Metrodome?

The dimensions of the new park are fairly similar to those of the old park, with the fences taller in right field, but shorter in left. The exact layouts of the new and old park are shown on the overlay diagram.

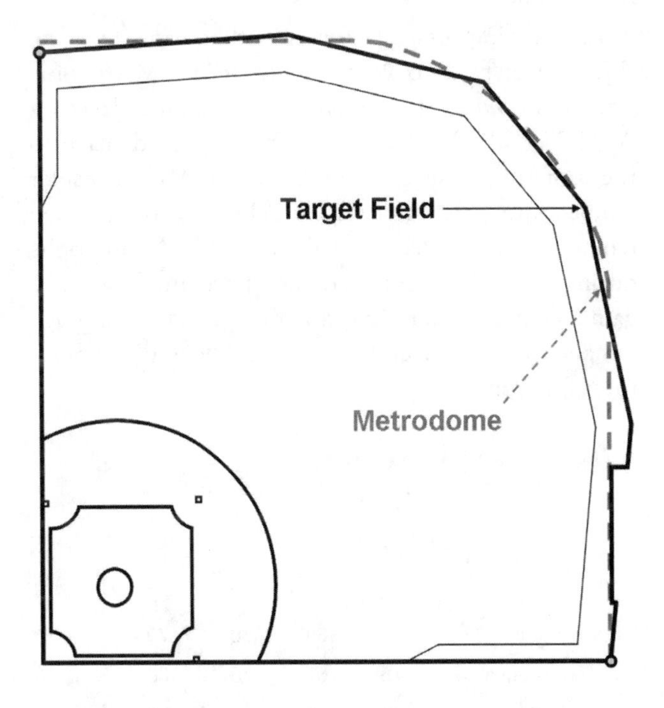

In the overlay diagram, the arrows indicate the location in each ballpark where the right field fence transitions from 23 feet high to the lower height that extends around to the left field line. (This is eight feet high in Target Field and seven feet high in the Metrodome.)

Target Field has an area in right field, just to the left of the overhanging sections 136-138, that is deeper than the corresponding area in the Metrodome. There is another area in left center field, in front of the bullpens, where Target Field's fence is several feet closer than that of the Metrodome. Analysis of the 189 home runs hit in the Metrodome in 2009 suggests that these two differences should essentially cancel each other out.

There is, however, one major difference between the fence lines of the two parks: this is the length of the 23-foot-high wall in right field that each park features. The Metrodome "baggie" fence extended for just over 200 feet away from the right field pole, while the Target Field wall drops from 23 to eight feet at a point about 250 feet from the right field line. There is, therefore, a segment of right-center field about 6.5 degrees wide, where the fence at Target Field is dramatically higher than it used to be in the Metrodome. Analysis of the 189 home runs hit at the Metrodome in 2009 reveals that six homers that cleared the short home run fence just to the left of the "baggie" would have hit the "extended" 23-foot-high wall at Target Field and stayed in the field of play. Based on dimensions alone, thus, Target Field should slightly suppress home runs compared to the Metrodome.

Another important factor is weather, something the Twins haven't had to worry about since the Metrodome opened in 1982 (apart from a nine-minute delay on April 27, 1986 due to a loss of power and damage to the roof from a severe thunderstorm). We'll consider temperature first: in the table below are the average temperatures (in degrees Fahrenheit) in Minneapolis during baseball season and the approximate average game temperatures for day and night games (the "day" temperatures are given for 2 pm, and "night" temperatures for 8 pm):

Month	Avg. High	Avg. Low	Day	Night
April	54	33	54	44
May	66	43	66	57
June	75	53	75	65
July	80	60	80	70
August	75	57	75	66
September	71	50	71	60
October	58	33	58	42

The temperature data suggest that early- and late-season games will typically be played in cooler temperatures than the thermostat setting at the Metrodome, about 68 degrees. Night games in April and, if the Twins are successful, October, will be particularly cool, perhaps 20 to 25 degrees cooler than dome games have been in the recent past. The cooler, more dense air will offer more resistance to fly balls, taking 10 to 12 feet off a canonical 400-foot fly ball. Since Hit Tracker data show that about 30 percent of all MLB home runs clear the fence by 10 feet or less, we can estimate that night games at Target Field in April or October should see home runs reduced by about one-third.

Mid-summer day games will most often be warmer than dome games, and the warmer, less dense air will offer less resistance to fly balls. A typical 400-foot fly ball struck on a pleasant, 80-degree summer day at Target Field should fly about four feet farther than it would have inside the Metrodome. Using the same conversion factor as before, we can predict that games played in these conditions should see home runs increased by 10 to 15 percent.

Night games at Target Field during high summer, and day games in May or September, should typically be played at similar temperatures to dome games, and thus home run rates in these games should be unchanged.

Overall, on a weighted-average basis, game temperatures at Target Field should be slightly lower than they were in the Metrodome, and thus home run rates in the new park should be lower; however, this effect is (1) relatively small, and (2) subject not only to lots of variation in game temperatures, but also to the effects of wind.

The impact of wind at Target Field will necessarily be different than was the case inside the Metrodome, where, notwithstanding any conspiracy theories about adjustable ventilation ducts or strategically switched fans, wind had no impact on Twins games. However, it is difficult to predict how the wind flow on a macroscopic scale outside Target Field will translate to the movement of air on a more micro-scale inside the stadium walls.

Prevailing winds in Minneapolis during baseball season tend to come from the northwest: these winds should be interdicted by the third-base side of the main grandstand, but there is a gap between the left field (fair territory) seating area and the main grandstand, and another even larger gap between the first base side of the main grandstand and the center field upper deck. Just how the wind will behave over the field in each type of weather, in each season, and how that wind will impact fly balls, will bear close observation during early season games at Target Field. The long-term impact of wind on Twins home games will not be well understood, and thus predictable to any significant extent, for some time.

Situational Home Run Data

Sportvision's PITCHf/x data has revolutionized the analysis of pitching, and to a lesser extent, hitting. The publicly available data include pitch type for about 90 percent of all home runs hit in 2009; analysis of this data, combined with Hit Tracker data on home runs and home run distance, reveals some interesting information.

Average Home Run Distance By Pitch Type, 2009

A common assumption is that pitches that are thrown harder will be hit harder, and thus will fly farther; we might therefore expect to see the longest average distance for the fastest pitch, the four-seam fastball. However, this turns out to not be true.

Here is a table showing pitch types, the average distance of homers hit off them, and the percentage of home runs hit off that pitch type across MLB:

Pitch Name	Avg. Dist.	% of HRs
Sinker	400.0	1.4%
Fastball	399.6	4.7%
4-seam Fastball	399.4	53.3%
2-seam Fastball	399.2	3.7%
Slider	398.7	15.5%
Curve	398.5	5.7%
Cutter	398.4	2.7%
Changeup	397.5	12.7%
Knuckleball	387.6	0.4%
Total	398.9	100.0%

In the table, we have a very interesting result, or perhaps "non-result." Aside from the lower average distance on the very small sample (16) of home runs hit off knuckleballs, there is scarcely any significant difference between any of the pitches. The same lack of difference persists when we examine only longer homers: in aggregate, no pitch gets hit any farther than any other pitch.

In retrospect, this outcome is perhaps unsurprising, if one considers game theory as applied to pitch selection. If any type of pitch, thrown at its typical relative frequency, were hit a lot farther than the other pitches, going forward pitchers would choose to throw it less frequently. Hitters would gradually learn to expect the pitch less often and would become slightly less effective at hitting it. Pitches that proved to be difficult to hit a long way would see the opposite trend: pitchers would choose to throw them more often, hitters would come to expect more of them and gradually become more adept at hitting them over the fence. Over time (and there has been plenty of that since baseball got started in the nineteenth century), the different pitch types and corresponding outcomes would naturally reach an equilibrium, where the frequency of pitch selection would even out the "value" of each pitch type (here represented by average home run distance).

That theory makes sense overall, but for individual players, we can't expect performance on all pitch types to even out. The data bear this out: for example, Milwaukee's Braden Looper surrendered 17 home runs (out of 39 total for the year) off his changeup, with average distance of 408 feet, but only eight home runs off his fastball, with average distance of 389 feet. As an aside, Looper must be getting a lot of value out of his changeup in other ways (e.g. strikeouts, weak grounders), to be willing to endure this degree of abuse via the home run. (But that's someone else's article!)

Individual hitters also often have their own particular preferences: Yankees second baseman Robinson Cano hit eight home runs off fastballs, averaging 382 feet, but also hammered six home runs off curveballs that averaged 407 feet. MLB hitters as a group hit 63 percent of all homers off fastballs, and only 6 percent off curveballs, but Cano squared up the curve quite well in 2009. Some hitters show a distinct tendency to hit most of their homers off one type of pitch: Minnesota's Joe Mauer hit 24 of his 28 home runs off fastballs, 20 of them off four-seam fastballs. Other hitters hit home runs off just about any pitch they see: Milwaukee's Prince Fielder hit 19 homers off fastballs, 12 off changeups, and 10 off sliders, among his 46 total home runs.

More Situations: Count And Outs

Average Home Run Distance by Count, 2009

Count	Avg. Dist.	% HR
2-1	401.5	8.9%
3-1	400.7	5.1%
1-0	400.1	11.6%
0-2	399.7	3.2%
1-1	399.7	12.1%
3-0	399.7	0.4%

Count	Avg. Dist.	% HR
0-0	399.2	18.0%
3-2	398.0	9.4%
0-1	398.0	9.3%
2-0	397.5	6.0%
2-2	396.1	8.3%
1-2	396.1	7.7%

This seems to be another "non-result", or at least the results don't seem to follow any discernable pattern. The difference in average distance between hitter's counts like 2-1 and 3-1 and pitcher's counts like 0-1 or 1-2 is quite small, and the average distance for 2-0 pitches is near the bottom. And who would have guessed that the average of 0-2 home runs would be the same as for 1-1 counts?

Average Home Run Distance by Outs, 2009

Outs	Avg. Dist.	% HR
0	399.6	36.7%
1	397.8	33.2%
2	399.1	30.1%

Again, there's nothing interesting to see here. No matter the number of outs, home runs, on average, fly about the same distance.

In summary, the distance a home run travels is not strongly influenced by the type of pitch thrown, or by such situational factors as the count or the number of outs. The key factors in how far a home run flies, and to a great extent whether or not a long fly ball becomes a home run, remain the pitcher and the hitter.

Here's one final interesting tidbit from the PITCHf/x data: who hit a home run off the fastest pitch in 2009?

Hitter	Pitcher	Speed	Distance
Gomes, Jonny	Jimenez, Ubaldo	99.8	438
Teixeira, Mark	Zumaya, Joel	99.0	386
Branyan, Russell	Jimenez, Ubaldo	99.0	427
Martinez, Victor	League, Brandon	98.8	388
Konerko, Paul	Zumaya, Joel	98.8	376
Smith, Seth	Zumaya, Joel	98.6	387
Berkman, Lance	MacDougal, Mike	98.2	385
Kouzmanoff, Kevin	Motte, Jason	98.2	413
Hart, Corey	Paulino, Felipe	98.1	413
Gerut, Jody	Paulino, Felipe	98.1	407

Cincinnati's Jonny Gomes claims the honor by having turned the hardest fastball around for a homer, in this case lining a 99.8 mph fastball from Colorado's Ubaldo Jimenez off the facing of the upper deck in left-center field at Great American Ball Park in Cincinnati on Aug. 1. Impressive!

Acknowledgements

I would like to once again acknowledge the outstanding efforts of my assistants Brenton Blair and Norm Chouinard, without whose help I could not have made it through another season with Hit Tracker. My sincere thanks and appreciation go out to Mark Zimmerman for all his hard work over the past two seasons. I extend my warmest regards to the many people I have met in person, over the phone and via e-mail because of Hit Tracker this year, particularly the regulars on the Book Blog who have shared their thoughts with me at length. I am honored to have gotten to know you all.

Special thanks also go to Dan Brooks for his help with PITCHf/x data.

The Lost Flies of Citi Field

Date	Hitter	Team	Pitcher	Team	At Citi	At Shea
4/18/2009	Hardy, J.J.	MIL	Santana, Johan	NYM	FLY OUT	HR
4/25/2009	Maxwell, Justin	WAS	Stokes, Brian	NYM	Double	HR
4/26/2009	Willingham, Josh	WAS	Perez, Oliver	NYM	FLY OUT	HR
4/27/2009	Carroll, Brett	FLA	Green, Sean	NYM	FLY OUT	HR
4/27/2009	Wright, David	NYM	Pinto, Renyel	FLA	Triple	HR
4/28/2009	Sheffield, Gary	NYM	Nolasco, Ricky	FLA	Triple	HR
4/29/2009	Maybin, Cameron	FLA	Santana, Johan	NYM	Triple	HR
5/8/2009	Bixler, Brian	PIT	Green, Sean	NYM	Double	HR
5/10/2009	Beltran, Carlos	NYM	Grabow, John	PIT	Double	HR
5/10/2009	Delgado, Carlos	NYM	Snell, Ian	PIT	Double	HR
5/11/2009	Wright, David	NYM	Lowe, Derek	ATL	Double	HR
5/12/2009	Jones, Chipper	ATL	Pelfrey, Mike	NYM	FLY OUT	HR
5/12/2009	Wright, David	NYM	Jurrjens, Jair	ATL	Triple	HR
5/13/2009	Johnson, Kelly	ATL	Putz, J.J.	NYM	Double	HR
5/13/2009	Jones, Chipper	ATL	Niese, Jonathon	NYM	Double	HR
5/13/2009	Reyes, Jose	NYM	Gonzalez, Mike	ATL	Double	HR
5/25/2009	Kearns, Austin	WAS	Maine, John	NYM	FLY OUT	HR
5/27/2009	Dunn, Adam	WAS	Santana, Johan	NYM	FLY OUT	HR
5/27/2009	Murphy, Daniel	NYM	Colome, Jesus	WAS	Double	HR
5/30/2009	Cantu, Jorge	FLA	Redding, Tim	NYM	Double	HR
5/30/2009	Carroll, Brett	FLA	Takahashi, Ken	NYM	Double	HR
5/31/2009	Ramirez, Hanley	FLA	Maine, John	NYM	Double	HR
5/31/2009	Uggla, Dan	FLA	Maine, John	NYM	Double	HR
6/9/2009	Feliz, Pedro	PHI	Santana, Johan	NYM	Double	HR
6/9/2009	Sheffield, Gary	NYM	Happ, J.A.	PHI	Single	HR
6/9/2009	Tatis, Fernando	NYM	Happ, J.A.	PHI	Double	HR
6/9/2009	Utley, Chase	PHI	Santana, Johan	NYM	HR	Double
6/10/2009	Pelfrey, Mike	NYM	Hamels, Cole	PHI	Double	HR
6/10/2009	Utley, Chase	PHI	Pelfrey, Mike	NYM	HR	Double
6/10/2009	Werth, Jayson	PHI	Pelfrey, Mike	NYM	Single	HR
6/11/2009	Castillo, Luis	NYM	Moyer, Jamie	PHI	Double	HR
6/11/2009	Wright, David	NYM	Moyer, Jamie	PHI	Single	HR
6/19/2009	Longoria, Evan	TB	Nieve, Fernando	NYM	FLY OUT	HR
6/19/2009	Wright, David	NYM	Sonnanstine, Andy	TB	Double	HR
6/19/2009	Zobrist, Ben	TB	Nieve, Fernando	NYM	FLY OUT	HR
6/21/2009	Longoria, Evan	TB	Pelfrey, Mike	NYM	Double	HR
6/21/2009	Wright, David	NYM	Cormier, Lance	TB	Double	HR
6/24/2009	Church, Ryan	NYM	Thompson, Brad	STL	Double	HR
6/27/2009	Teixeira, Mark	NYY	Redding, Tim	NYM	Double	HR
6/28/2009	Cabrera, Melky	NYY	Hernandez, Livan	NYM	FLY OUT	HR
6/28/2009	Jeter, Derek	NYY	Hernandez, Livan	NYM	Double	HR
7/7/2009	Blake, Casey	LAD	Redding, Tim	NYM	FLY OUT	HR

Date	Hitter	Team	Pitcher	Team	At Citi	At Shea
7/8/2009	Ramirez, Manny	LAD	Rodriguez, Francisco	NYM	HR	Double
7/11/2009	Encarnacion, Edwin	CIN	Santana, Johan	NYM	Double	HR
7/11/2009	Gomes, Jonny	CIN	Santana, Johan	NYM	FLY OUT	HR
7/28/2009	Wright, David	NYM	Marquis, Jason	COL	Double	HR
7/30/2009	Hawpe, Brad	COL	Santana, Johan	NYM	FLY OUT	HR
7/30/2009	Pagan, Angel	NYM	De la Rosa, Jorge	COL	FLY OUT	HR
7/30/2009	Wright, David	NYM	Rincon, Juan	COL	Double	HR
8/3/2009	Pagan, Angel	NYM	Haren, Dan	ARI	Triple	HR
8/4/2009	Ludwick, Ryan	STL	Santana, Johan	NYM	Double	HR
8/5/2009	Ankiel, Rick	STL	Figueroa, Nelson	NYM	FLY OUT	HR
8/5/2009	Berroa, Angel	NYM	Thompson, Brad	STL	FLY OUT	HR
8/5/2009	Pujols, Albert	STL	Niese, Jonathon	NYM	Double	HR
8/5/2009	Pujols, Albert	STL	Figueroa, Nelson	NYM	Double	HR
8/15/2009	Schierholtz, Nate	SF	Santana, Johan	NYM	Double	HR
8/17/2009	Schierholtz, Nate	SF	Hernandez, Livan	NYM	Double	HR
8/18/2009	McCann, Brian	ATL	Dessens, Elmer	NYM	Single	HR
8/20/2009	Tatis, Fernando	NYM	Kawakami, Kenshin	ATL	Double	HR
8/22/2009	Werth, Jayson	PHI	Feliciano, Pedro	NYM	Double	HR
8/24/2009	Murphy, Daniel	NYM	Lee, Cliff	PHI	Double	HR
9/8/2009	Pagan, Angel	NYM	Badenhop, Burke	FLA	Triple	HR
9/9/2009	Johnson, Nick	FLA	Broadway, Lance	NYM	Double	HR
9/18/2009	Francoeur, Jeff	NYM	Martin, J.D.	WAS	Double	HR
9/18/2009	Wright, David	NYM	Martin, J.D.	WAS	FLY OUT	HR
9/18/2009	Zimmerman, Ryan	WAS	Pelfrey, Mike	NYM	HR	Double
9/20/2009	Murphy, Daniel	NYM	Mock, Garrett	WAS	Double	HR
9/21/2009	Prado, Martin	ATL	Misch, Pat	NYM	Double	HR

And the MVP Goes To...

by David Gassko

Who was the most valuable player of the 2009 season? It's a question that can be answered in a variety of ways using a variety of methods, but ultimately, the official answer belongs to the Baseball Writers Association of America (BWAA). Though much has been said about how the BWAA does its job (and many of those things have been unflattering), the official MVP vote still garners a ton of interest from baseball fans, and so long as the award is of interest, then *predicting* who will win the award (as opposed to who deserves it) will be of interest as well.

For example, it is my belief, as this is written in the last weeks of the season, that Joe Mauer and Albert Pujols will win the American League and National League MVP awards, respectively, while Felix Hernandez and Adam Wainwright take the AL and NL Cy Young awards this season. By the time you read this, you'll be able to see if those predictions came true, but even if they don't, I hope you will agree that the process that led to those calls was very reasonable and works pretty darn well.

Predicting the MVP

So how do we go about projecting who will win the MVP? Well, we can ask a psychic, flip a coin, or ... we can build a model. Having considered the first two methods, for the purposes of this article I have decided on the third, as I consider it to be more accurate and more interesting, though perhaps a psychic would have something to say about that (a coin most certainly would not).

The model I built was based on all MVP votes since 1967, which is the first year that both the MVP and Cy Young award were handed out to players in each league. (Due to an error in my database, the model did not include results from 2008.) That gives us a sample size of more than 40 years, which makes for a pretty stable sample. Only players who were on at least one MVP ballot were included in the sample.

I figured the share of points each player got out of the maximum possible. (A first-place vote is worth 14 points. These days, a player garnering all 28 first place votes, two for each team, in the American League will get 392 points. A player getting all 32 first place votes in the National League will end up with 448 points.) I put each of these on a 1,000 point scale.

For example: Jimmy Rollins received 353 points in the 2007 NL MVP vote, which is equal to 78.8 percent of the maximum he could have had. On a 1,000 point scale, that would be 788 points. This procedure puts every player from every year and every league on the same scale

I then observed that MVP points were not distributed normally, but log-normally, meaning that there were a lot of players with a few votes, but very few with a ton (as should be expected). To correct for that, I took the natural logarithm of each player's adjusted vote share, so that the statistical tests I performed would be valid.

I then gathered every potentially pertinent statistic for each player, adjusted it for the offensive level of the league (with pitchers removed, of course), and ran regressions until my face turned blue trying to predict the number of MVP votes a player should be expected to received. So as not to have the same effect on another part of your body, I'll get straight to my results, listing the categories that voters seem to look at in order of importance:

1. **Home runs** It is probably no surprise that writers love power hitters, but I was surprised to see that they care even more about power than they do, say, RBIs (of course, the two are highly correlated and therefore somewhat difficult to disentangle, but I'm fairly confident that this is correct). They say that chicks dig the long ball, but it looks like baseball writers do, too.
2. **Hits** Well, it's no surprise that baseball writers care about batting average; the only challenge is trying to figure out how to model that. After all, it seems intuitive that writers care more about the batting average of a put-it-in-play type of hitter than a big bopper who strikes out 150 times a year. It turns out that the model works best if instead of using straight hits (one extreme) or straight batting average (the other), we use hits above average, calculated as hits minus the number of hits an average player would have gathered in the same number of at-bats.
3. **Playoffs** That this ranks below home runs and hits goes to show that writers will consider voting for a player on a losing team, but that it ranks above everything else still means that they won't actually choose a player on a non-contender unless his numbers are head-and-shoulders above everyone else.
4. **Runs or RBIs** I'm not the first person to try to build a model for predicting the MVP, and my work definitely was informed by previous attempts. One of those is a 2006 article by Jacob Wheatley-

Schaller, who observed that in his first tests, runs proved to be statistically insignificant. The author was able to make runs significant only by including runs totals just for leadoff-type hitters. I ran into a similar problem, and my solution was to create a category which was equal to a player's runs scored if that number was greater than his RBIs and equal to his RBIs if the situation was reversed. As you can see, it's a very important variable.

5. **Stolen bases** Voters care about speed, though I do believe that this category functions in part as a stand-in for a player's fielding ability (which cannot be easily modeled with traditional statistics).
6. **RBIs** Though runs scored matter only for those leadoff-type hitters, RBIs are important for all. If we add together the weight on this category and the Runs or RBIs variable, we find that RBIs get slightly more weight in the model than making the playoffs, though the two numbers are basically equal. That surprised me.
7. **Position** Shortstops and catchers get a boost in MVP voting, and by a similar amount.
8. **Caught stealing** The flip side of stolen bases. These two variables were probably more important in the '80s, when hitters like Rickey Henderson and Tim Raines were running wild.
9. **Coors Field** Colorado hitters get penalized big time in MVP voting—though this category is relatively unimportant due to the small number of Colorado players in the sample, playing at Coors actually accords a significantly larger penalty than making the playoffs provides a benefit.
10. **Strikeouts** Last, and well, least. Voters don't like strikeouts, though as their selection of Ryan Howard in 2006 demonstrated, they're willing to get over it.

That's the model. Ten variables in all, and for the statistically minded readers among us, those 10 account for about 50 percent of the variation in MVP voting among hitters (an adjusted r^2 of 0.463 to be exact). More importantly, in conjunction with my model for pitchers (which takes as its inputs the predicted number of Cy Young points based on the model described below, as well as whether the pitcher's team made the playoffs), this algorithm correctly predicts 53 of the 82 MVP races in my database, or 65 percent in all.

While that's far from perfect, it's pretty good for a model that knows only the numbers, and nothing of the storylines that abound in a given year. After all, there is no way of slicing and dicing the numbers that would have told you that Shannon Stewart would be a serious MVP contender in 2003.

Predicting the Cy Young

The model for projecting the Cy Young follows much the same form as the MVP algorithm. Again, I built a database with all Cy Young votes since 1967 (though there was once more a strange error in my database that resulted in American League 2008 results not being included), and again I adjusted each pitcher's vote total based on his share of the maximum, taking the natural logarithm so that the numbers were normally distributed.

Again, only players who were listed on at least one Cy Young ballot that year were included in the sample. Numbers were once more adjusted for league averages (with an innings-pitched adjustment added in), and then I was ready to run as many statistical tests as necessary. Luckily, projecting the Cy Young proved to be a far easier task than building the MVP model. Here is what I found, with the variables again listed in order of importance:

1. **Wins** In case you thought that there was anything writers cared more about than wins, well, I'm sorry to burst your bubble, but there isn't. Winning a lot of games is definitely the best way to get a Cy Young.
2. **Outs** Like batting average, it's unclear what is the best way to include ERA. We know that writers (correctly) prefer a low ERA when it is accomplished over a lot of innings, but how do we model that? In this case, we can include outs and earned runs as two separate variables and allow the model to tell us what baseline the writers use. We find that writers give a lot of credit to guys who pitch a bunch of innings, choosing a baseline that corresponds to a 6.30 ERA (meaning that a pitcher gets 0 "Cy Young points" in the model if he posts a 6.30 ERA), which is well below average as well as most estimates of replacement level. In other words, getting outs and pitching innings are more important relative to preventing runs than they should be, in the minds of the writers.
3. **Saves** Each save is like a third of a win to the writers. So 20 wins is the same thing as 60 saves. Makes sense.
4. **Earned Runs** See No. 2.
5. **Losses** Writers seem to overvalue durability in general; in the same way they set a very low ERA baseline (meaning that innings pitched get more weight than they should, and a good ERA gets

less weight than it should), the writers seem to give significantly more merit to an extra win than demerit for an extra loss, even though one is just the flip side of the other.

6. **Strikeouts** This is not a hugely important variable, but if all else is equal, writers will prefer the higher strikeout guys. That's neither surprising nor incorrect.
7. **Shutouts** Makes sense.

All in all, none of this should be too surprising. In fact, these are (though in slightly different form) the same variables that are included in Bill James' Cy Young predictor. (James also includes a bonus for pitchers whose teams make the playoffs, but I found that variable to be insignificant in Cy Young voting, though it is a significant determinant in a pitcher's MVP support). I do believe, however, that my model is a bit more accurate, and a bit more rigorous.

Like the MVP algorithm, the Cy Young model explains almost half the variation in actual Cy Young voting totals (with an adjusted r^2 of 0.448), and overall, it is able to correctly project 60 out of the 83 Cy Young races in my database, or 72 percent. That's a bit better than the MVP model, though I must admit no more accurate than the James' formula (though no less accurate, either. I also believe that my model is better on the whole, though clearly, if the two are equally good at predicting winners any advantage must necessarily be slight).

What It All Means

So we have a model—two, actually—and we have some predictions, but where do we go from here? The future value of this model is obvious: It can help us predict who will win the major awards before they are actually awarded, or before the season is even over if we'd like. The explanatory value is also clear: Though regression analysis is imperfect—it does not allow us to read the writers' minds—it does provide pretty good insight into what the writers are thinking and what they look at. I, for example, was surprised to see how important home runs were, or which positions the writers give extra credit to, or how much they debit Colorado hitters. If we're going to complain or argue about MVP (or Cy Young) voting, it makes sense to know what actually goes into the writers' decisions.

Personally, I find a bad decision a lot less objectionable if it is consistent with past results than if it seems that the writers have established a whole new set of standards for that particular vote. I don't insist that you agree with me, but that's my opinion. Still, there is one more thing our model allows us to do that I think is of great interest, and that is to revisit past results, see where it missed, and why. I'll dedicate the rest of this article to that pursuit, and hope we'll learn a little more about how baseball writers think on the way.

MVP Misses

Let's start with 2006, where the model managed to whiff on both leagues. Surprisingly, the model agreed with the sabermetric consensus at the time, which makes me wonder if the writers departed from their established standards in part as a backlash against sabermetrics. In the National League, the writers chose Ryan Howard over Albert Pujols, even though Pujols' Cardinals made the playoffs (Howard's Phillies didn't), and even though Pujols mostly managed to match Howard's insane triple crown stats (.313 BA, 58 HR, 149 RBIs for Howard, versus a .331 BA, 49 HR, 137 RBIs for Pujols) with 131 fewer strikeouts.

In the American League, the voters went with Justin Morneau over Derek Jeter. This was a contentious race in 2006, and it's no easier to proclaim a winner today—Jeter barely ekes out a victory in the model. His higher batting average and stolen bases total and his position outweigh Morneau's huge home run and RBI advantages, though actually the voters settled on the opposite. This is perhaps the hardest type of race to judge within the confines of the model (in terms of actual value, Jeter was far ahead of Morneau, and Joe Mauer was even better) just because the two players produced in such different ways.

Then there's the National League in 2001-2004, years when in actual MVP voting, players not named Bonds didn't stand a chance. In the model, Bonds wins in only one of those years, 2002; Luis Gonzalez, Gary Sheffield and Albert Pujols win in the others. Though my statistical tests indicated that voters do not consider walks in MVP voting, Bonds is an obvious exception to the rule.

A few guys have been screwed out of at least a couple MVPs, according to the model: Mike Piazza (1995, 1997, 2000), Albert Belle (1995, 1996) and Don Mattingly (1984, 1986). Let's take them one by one, starting with Piazza, who was really underappreciated by MVP voters. In 1995, he was beaten out by Barry Larkin, who had more impressive numbers in only two categories: stolen bases (51 versus one) and strikeouts (49 versus 80). Piazza wins in batting average (.346 versus .319), home runs (32 versus 15), and RBIs (93 versus 66). The steals are nice, but it's difficult to make the case that Larkin was the more deserving candidate. In 1997, Piazza lost to Larry Walker, even though Piazza more or less matched his numbers (.362 BA, 40 HR, 124 RBI for Piazza, .366 BA, 49 HR, 130 RBI for Walker) while playing a much tougher position and without playing at Coors Field. In 2000, Piazza again had more or less the same batting line as the MVP winner (Jeff Kent), and again, the voters gave him no credit for playing catcher. Steroid rumors aside, I really believe Piazza is the most underappreciated player from the 1990s. His (unjustified) lack of MVPs is a big reason for that.

I'm not sure why Piazza had such a tough time in MVP voting (was his poor defensive reputation really such a big deal?), but I do have a pretty good idea when it comes to Albert Belle. Simply put, the writers hated the man. Belle's failure to win in 1995, however, is especially bad because, among the 10 categories that matter to the writers, Belle trailed the winner (Mo Vaughn) in only one—stolen bases—and I can tell you right now that no one was voting for Vaughn because of his speed on the base paths. In 1996, Belle's numbers were almost exactly the same as the winner's (Juan Gonzalez), so at least that vote was justifiable.

Mattingly, meanwhile, is proof that the media have a lot less East Coast or Yankees bias than it is often accused of harboring. If the writers had not decided to start giving MVPs to pitchers for the first time in over a decade, Mattingly could have had three straight MVP awards and a much stouter Hall of Fame case. It's difficult to compare his numbers to those of Willie Hernandez (1984) or Roger Clemens (1986), but in my opinion, the Clemens MVP is much easier to understand than the Hernandez selection.

Cy Young Slights

The Cy Young award has not seen the kind of systematic misses we observe with the MVP. No player has been denied contrary to the model's predictions more than once. No player has "beaten" the model more than once, either. The Cy Young is a much easier race to call, relative to the MVP. Pitchers are judged on fewer categories, and all those categories are related. It's extraordinarily rare for a pitcher to win a lot of games, but post a mediocre ERA, whereas with the MVP you might be comparing one guy with a great average to another with a ton of home runs, and who knows who the writers will favor? (Well, the model knows to some extent, but obviously it doesn't always guess right.)

The only consistent problem I've been able to locate is that the model does not think much of closers—of the nine who have won Cy Young awards since 1967, the model correctly called only four, and none since the mid-80s. The early closers who won Cy Young awards won primarily not due to their save totals, but because they pitched a lot of innings (and gave up few runs) in addition to saving a good number of games. The last four closers to win a Cy Young, on the other hand, have averaged 86 innings pitched, and save totals be damned, the model just can't name a winner who has thrown so few innings.

Wrapping Up

When I conceived of this article, I thought that the predictions my models generated would be hugely enlightening. They would show that the writers had changed their standards over the year, or mistreated certain players, or been totally predictable. Instead, minus the second point to some extent, none of these theories have really come true. The writers have worked with a pretty stable set of standards over the years, if you don't count their special treatment of Barry Bonds's walk totals. The MVP model has missed a bit more often in the past decade than it previously had, but the Cy Young model has conversely been better. How much of this is random variation is difficult to tell. A few players do seem to have been screwed over by the writers, but I did not find any more bias than I expected. And in terms of being predictable, well, the models we developed do a very good job, but there's definitely an element of randomness in the writers' decisions as well.

Overall, though, I'm happy with the results. The models we developed proved to be both accurate and intuitive, as well as enlightening. They hold a significant amount of value for future historical analyses; baseball researchers will be able to look at past races and tell us why they turned out the way they did, or for that matter, why they deviated from the model's predictions. Going even further back, we will be able to make educated guesses as to who would have won these awards before they ever existed. How many MVPs would Babe Ruth have had? How many Cy Youngs could be awarded to Cy Young? We'll be able to do more than just say, "a lot." And of course, in future seasons we will be able to calculate who is in the running for these awards before even the writers have started talking about it.

But I leave all these analyses for another day. For now, I am content to end with my steadfast predictions of Joe Mauer and Albert Pujols for MVP and Felix Hernandez and Adam Wainwright for the Cy Young. They're locks to win. Or not.

Appendix: Award Winners and Predicted Winners, 1967-2007.

Year	League	MVP	Predicted Winner	Cy Young	Predicted Winner
1967	AL	Carl Yastrzemski		Jim Lonborg	Joe Horlen
1967	NL	Orlando Cepeda		Mike McCormick	
1968	AL	Denny McLain		Denny McLain	
1968	NL	Bob Gibson	Willie McCovey	Bob Gibson	
1969	AL	Harmon Killebrew		Denny McLain	
1969	NL	Willie McCovey		Tom Seaver	
1970	AL	Boog Powell	Carl Yastrzemski	Jim Perry	Dave McNally
1970	NL	Johnny Bench		Bob Gibson	
1971	AL	Vida Blue	Bobby Murcer	Vida Blue	
1971	NL	Joe Torre		Fergie Jenkins	Tom Seaver
1972	AL	Dick Allen		Gaylord Perry	
1972	NL	Johnny Bench	Billy Williams	Steve Carlton	
1973	AL	Reggie Jackson		Jim Palmer	
1973	NL	Pete Rose	Joe Morgan	Tom Seaver	
1974	AL	Jeff Burroughs	Reggie Jackson	Catfish Hunter	
1974	NL	Steve Garvey		Mike Marshall	
1975	AL	Fred Lynn		Jim Palmer	
1975	NL	Joe Morgan		Tom Seaver	
1976	AL	Thurman Munson		Jim Palmer	Bill Campbell
1976	NL	Joe Morgan		Randy Jones	
1977	AL	Rod Carew		Sparky Lyle	Jim Palmer
1977	NL	George Foster		Steve Carlton	
1978	AL	Jim Rice		Ron Guidry	
1978	NL	Dave Parker		Gaylord Perry	
1979	AL	Don Baylor		Mike Flanagan	Jim Kern
1979	NL	Willie Stargell	Dave Winfield	Bruce Sutter	J.R. Richard
1980	AL	George Brett		Steve Stone	Mike Norris
1980	NL	Mike Schmidt		Steve Carlton	
1981	AL	Rollie Fingers		Rollie Fingers	
1981	NL	Mike Schmidt		Fernando Valenzuela	Steve Carlton
1982	AL	Robin Yount		Pete Vuckovich	Dan Quisenberry
1982	NL	Dale Murphy		Steve Carlton	
1983	AL	Cal Ripken		La Marr Hoyt	Richard Dotson
1983	NL	Dale Murphy		John Denny	
1984	AL	Willie Hernandez	Don Mattingly	Willie Hernandez	
1984	NL	Ryne Sandberg		Rick Sutcliffe	Bruce Sutter
1985	AL	Don Mattingly		Bret Saberhagen	Ron Guidry
1985	NL	Willie McGee	Pedro Guerrero	Dwight Gooden	
1986	AL	Roger Clemens	Don Mattingly	Roger Clemens	
1986	NL	Mike Schmidt		Mike Scott	
1987	AL	George Bell	Alan Trammell	Roger Clemens	
1987	NL	Andre Dawson		Steve Bedrosian	Bob Welch

Year	League	MVP	Predicted Winner	Cy Young	Predicted Winner
1988	AL	Jose Canseco		Frank Viola	
1988	NL	Kirk Gibson	Kevin McReynolds	Orel Hershiser	
1989	AL	Robin Yount	Bret Saberhagen	Bret Saberhagen	
1989	NL	Kevin Mitchell		Mark Davis	Mike Scott
1990	AL	Rickey Henderson		Bob Welch	
1990	NL	Barry Bonds		Doug Drabek	
1991	AL	Cal Ripken		Roger Clemens	
1991	NL	Terry Pendleton	Barry Bonds	Tom Glavine	
1992	AL	Dennis Eckersley	Mark McGwire	Dennis Eckersley	Mike Mussina
1992	NL	Barry Bonds		Greg Maddux	
1993	AL	Frank Thomas		Jack McDowell	Randy Johnson
1993	NL	Barry Bonds		Greg Maddux	
1994	AL	Frank Thomas		David Cone	
1994	NL	Jeff Bagwell		Greg Maddux	
1995	AL	Mo Vaughn	Albert Belle	Randy Johnson	
1995	NL	Barry Larkin	Mike Piazza	Greg Maddux	
1996	AL	Juan Gonzalez	Albert Belle	Pat Hentgen	
1996	NL	Ken Caminiti		John Smoltz	
1997	AL	Ken Griffey		Roger Clemens	
1997	NL	Larry Walker	Mike Piazza	Pedro Martinez	Greg Maddux
1998	AL	Juan Gonzalez		Roger Clemens	
1998	NL	Sammy Sosa		Tom Glavine	Kevin Brown
1999	AL	Ivan Rodriguez	Rafael Palmeiro	Pedro Martinez	
1999	NL	Chipper Jones		Randy Johnson	Mike Hampton
2000	AL	Jason Giambi	Frank Thomas	Pedro Martinez	
2000	NL	Jeff Kent	Mike Piazza	Randy Johnson	
2001	AL	Ichiro Suzuki	Bret Boone	Roger Clemens	Mark Mulder
2001	NL	Barry Bonds	Luis Gonzalez	Randy Johnson	
2002	AL	Miguel Tejada		Barry Zito	
2002	NL	Barry Bonds		Randy Johnson	
2003	AL	Alex Rodriguez	Manny Ramirez	Roy Halladay	
2003	NL	Barry Bonds	Gary Sheffield	Eric Gagne	Jason Schmidt
2004	AL	Vladimir Guerrero		Johan Santana	
2004	NL	Barry Bonds	Albert Pujols	Roger Clemens	
2005	AL	Alex Rodriguez		Bartolo Colon	
2005	NL	Albert Pujols		Chris Carpenter	
2006	AL	Justin Morneau	Derek Jeter	Johan Santana	
2006	NL	Ryan Howard	Albert Pujols	Brandon Webb	
2007	AL	Alex Rodriguez		C.C. Sabathia	
2007	NL	Jimmy Rollins		Jake Peavy	
2008	AL	Dustin Pedroia	Cliff Lee	Cliff Lee	
2008	NL	Albert Pujols		Tim Lincecum	Brandon Webb

What the Heck is PITCHf/x?

by Mike Fast

There is a revolution underway in baseball. It is a quiet revolution, not as controversial perhaps as 100-pitch limits for starting pitchers, but in the end, the changes it brings may be more influential.

The revolution debuted on Oct. 4, 2006, in an American League Division Series game between the Oakland Athletics and Minnesota Twins at the Metrodome. Most of us had no idea that, as Esteban Loaiza threw a first pitch strike to Twins leadoff batter Jason Kendall, Sportvision's PITCHf/x cameras were tracking the trajectory of the pitch, identifying its speed, break and location in real time and transmitting this information for use by broadcasters and Major League Baseball's Gameday web application.

Sportvision is a TV sports broadcast effects company based in Mountain View, Calif. Its engineers are most famous for creating the glowing FoxTrax hockey puck and the yellow first-down line superimposed on football broadcast video. Its current bread and butter product is GPS tracking of race cars during NASCAR races, and it provides this information to broadcasters and online to race fan subscribers. So when Sportvision turned its attention to baseball, it brought a strong pedigree in applying technology to sports broadcasts to bring fans new insight into their sports.

To track the flight of each major league pitch precisely, Sportvision has installed a pair of cameras in each stadium, in the stands above home plate and first base. Twenty-eight of these installations occurred during the 2007 season, and the other two, in Baltimore and Washington, were completed before the 2008 season. Detailed tracking data were recorded for about a third of the pitches thrown in the major leagues in 2007 and more than 95 percent of the pitches in 2008 and 2009. Sportvision made these data available in real-time to Major League Baseball Advanced Media (MLBAM) for use in its online Gameday application and to broadcasters such as ESPN for its K-Zone strike zone graphic.

How Do We Get The Data?

Sportvision's tracking software takes the approximately 20 images of the baseball acquired during its flight from the pitcher's hand to home plate, determines the 3-D ball location on the baseball field from each image, and finds the pitch trajectory that best fits these 20 or so points along the path of the pitch. The software assumes that the baseball experiences constant acceleration; i.e., that the forces on the ball do not change in any meaningful way during its flight. This is a good assumption for rapidly spinning baseball pitches, and almost all pitches fit this criterion. The notable exception is the knuckleball, which spins very slowly, causing the drag force on the baseball to change depending on the seam orientation. However, it turns out that the PITCHf/x constant-acceleration model works fairly well for knuckleballs, too, with only slightly larger errors than for other pitch types.

What information does Sportvision and MLBAM collect about the game? We already mentioned that the PITCHf/x tracking software calculates the position, velocity and acceleration of the pitched baseball in three dimensions. It also puts a date-time stamp on each pitch. The PITCHf/x operator is a Sportvision employee on site at each baseball game. The operator is responsible for monitoring the calibration of the system during the game and for recording the top and bottom of the strike zone for every batter from the center field camera video.

Other information is entered in real time by a stringer, an MLBAM employee also at the game, into software for transmission to Gameday. That person records the result of each pitch (for example, ball, called strike, swinging strike, foul ball or in play). The stringer notes any pinch hitters or defensive substitutions and records the result of each at-bat (for example, single or fly out), the movement of baserunners, and the location on the playing field where the batted ball is fielded. MLBAM software attempts to classify the type of pitch that was thrown (for example, fastball or slider).

All of this data is available free on the MLBAM Gameday website. As a result, between the PITCHf/x data on the trajectory of the pitch and the MLBAM stringer's record of game events, we have a wealth of information on every baseball game.

Differences Between Coarse And Fine Data

With this abundance of fine-grained data, particularly the detailed record of the speed and movement of every pitch, a new analytical approach must be crafted and new common language developed for discussion among fans and analysts. Our current language of baseball has its roots in the 19th century with Henry

Chadwick, inventor of the box score. Games have been described in terms of hits and outs, bases and runs. These are very clear but coarse measuring sticks, but they are the ones we have come to understand. We can converse in that language without needing to explain the context. Debates about the merits of various analytical approaches do not require arguments about foundational principles. Instead, the validity of the base-out counting system and much of the long analytical history built atop it is assumed.

Within the last decade, the availability of detailed fielding data has begun to shift this paradigm, if only perhaps at the margin. It is widely recognized that fielding is not well measured by simply recording which fielder recorded each out. More detailed data on the path of the batted ball are desirable for determining which fielder should be assigned credit or blame for fielding or not fielding a ball and how much credit or blame he should get based on the difficulty of the play. However, since most of this data is proprietary, the impact on the language of the game has so far been small.

With the wide availability of PITCHf/x data, however, a seismic shift in the language of baseball and its analysis is beginning. The description of a pitch is now on a continuum between fast and slow, breaking left or right, up or down. How do we make sense of these detailed data? Where is the context?

Radar gun readings have established some context for the speed of a pitch; as a result, that information from PITCHf/x has been the most quickly adopted and easily understood, although no one really knows yet what difference one mph of speed on his fastball means to a pitcher's effectiveness. These fundamental concepts will have to be investigated, understood and communicated over time. Almost every baseball fan has an intuitive understanding of the difference between a .260 hitter, a .290 hitter and a .320 hitter. One is average, one is good, and one is among the best in the game. I suspect some day we will have a similar intuitive understanding about pitch speeds. However, that context is only now emerging. We have so much new information that it is difficult to assimilate it quickly. We should remember that our current analytical framework of understanding was developed over more than a century.

The new detail we have about pitch movement is particularly challenging in that we have almost no common lexicon or understanding to draw from. What does it mean, if anything, when the movement on a pitcher's fastball changes by a few inches from one game to another? What does "movement on a pitcher's fastball" even mean? This context, too, must be developed over time.

Spin Deflection

I'm not a fan of the term "movement" to describe a pitch. How a ball moves depends on its initial velocity and the forces on the ball in flight, which include gravity, drag, and the Magnus, or spin, force. It has become popular for analysts to use the term "movement" to refer to the deflection of the ball due to the spin force. I prefer to refer to it as spin deflection.

Speed and the spin characteristics of a pitch are our primary ways to identify what type of pitch a pitcher threw. A pitcher's grip and wrist motion on release apply spin to the baseball, and this spin produces force on the baseball that causes it to veer. The topspin on a curveball causes it to veer downward more than it would from gravity alone. The backspin on a fastball causes it to drop less than it would due to gravity. Most pitches also have some sidespin, which causes the ball to veer to the left or right.

The Physics Of Baseball

One of the more fascinating results of the PITCHf/x data set is the extent to which it has expanded our knowledge of the physics of baseball. Dr. Robert Adair is well known for his excellent book, *The Physics of Baseball*, which he wrote in 1987 as the result of research he undertook at the behest of then National League president Bart Giamatti. In fact, Adair served as an adviser to Sportvision in the early days of PITCHf/x development.

However, our understanding of the physics of pitched and batted baseballs has improved immensely simply through the availability of such a large, high-quality data set. We have learned a great deal about the drag and spin forces on a baseball. Dr. Alan Nathan has led the investigation into many topics of interest, along with a crowd of others, and you can read more at his Physics of Baseball website (see References section).

Gameday Application

Many people's first exposure to PITCHf/x is through MLBAM's Gameday application. (For those who are unfamiliar with Gameday, it lets fans follow the game online. It falls somewhere between a TV broadcast and box score, attempting to model and describe the game in detail without showing actual game video or audio.)

At the center of the Gameday application is a display of pitch trajectories from the pitcher to the batter for the current at-bat. These pitch trajectories are based on the data taken in real time from PITCHf/x. Below the pitch trajectory display, Gameday gives additional information about each pitch, including the speed, BRK (break), PFX (spin deflection) and the pitch type.

The speed of the pitch 50 feet from home plate is displayed here. This is not the maximum speed of the pitch. That occurs as the ball leaves the pitcher's hand, which typically happens around 55 feet from home plate. However, the 50-foot distance for reporting pitch speed was chosen so that the PITCHf/x speeds would match most closely to typical radar gun readings.

The most confusing aspects of the PITCHf/x data displayed in Gameday are the two parameters, BRK and PFX, each measured in inches. Break refers to the maximum bend in the pitch. The arc of a curveball bends much more than a fastball. Break is useful in that sense, and perhaps that sense only, but it has found little use in the analytical community.

PFX is related closely to the parameters preferred by the analytical community for describing and identifying pitches, but it has a fatal shortcoming. PFX, as presented on Gameday, refers to the total amount of spin deflection, but it tells the viewer nothing about the direction of the spin deflection, which is a critical piece of information. Totally different pitches may have similar PFX values. I recommend ignoring the PFX value while watching Gameday.

The pitch type displayed on Gameday is produced by a neural-net algorithm MLBAM developed to attempt to identify pitch types in real time. It's correct much more often than it's wrong, but it's far from perfect. Consider it sufficient for entertainment value and even for surface-level analysis of pitchers. Deeper and more accurate analysis usually requires more accurate pitch types.

The Strike Zone

One of the most popular uses of PITCHf/x data is to evaluate umpires' ball-strike calls. Fans love to blame the umpire when he hurts their team with a call at a critical juncture of the game. Now PITCHf/x, by identifying the exact location where the ball crossed the plate, gives them the ammunition they need to fire off a half-educated missive against the men in blue.

A common misconception among novice umpire evaluators is that a strike call a couple of inches past the outside edge is a sure sign that the umpire was out to get the batter and his team. In an ideal world, umpires might be able to call the exact zone described in the official rules. In reality, it's a complex classification task, one that umpires typically address by setting up behind the inside edge of home plate. This helps them call the inside edge of the strike zone fairly accurately but at the expense of inaccuracy on the outside edge. A typical strike zone called by most umpires will include strike calls a few inches off the outside edge of the plate.

Major League Baseball uses a human-audited version of the PITCHf/x data to grade the umpires, but this version of the data is not available publicly.

Pitch Classification

An important area of ongoing research is in the classification of pitch types. As previously mentioned, MLBAM classifies pitch types based on its own algorithm for use in Gameday; it's been doing this classification since the beginning of the 2008 season. One approach that is suitable for much research that requires pitch types is to use the MLBAM classifications. It is accurate enough for most work that involves differentiating between fastballs and off-speed pitches. Another approach is to group the pitches into bins by speed and spin deflection and use these bins without regard to a particular label, such as "two-seam fastball" or "slider." Both approaches have merit in ease of use and probably do a decent job of approximating what the hitter sees, particularly at the season level.

However, in examining pitching strategies, evaluating pitchers or examining a single game in detail, pitch classifications need to be more attuned to what the pitcher is actually doing rather than taking a "close enough" approach. It can be fascinating to attempt to get inside the pitcher's head and understand his craft. His various pitch types are his tools, and correctly identifying them is key to understanding his strategy, his strengths, and his weaknesses.

How does one identify pitch types? Because pitchers are so different, there's no perfect one-size-fits-all approach, but there are some helpful guidelines. The graphs of Luke Hochevar's pitches from his September 23rd start against the Red Sox on the next page illustrate some useful guidelines.

I am a strong advocate of looking at a pitcher's data at the game level rather than the season level when classifying pitches. Due to inconsistencies (usually small but sometimes big) between PITCHf/x systems at different parks and sometimes at the same park at different points in the season, it can be difficult to distinguish

(continued on page 157)

The Graphs of Hochevar

Two ways of looking at the pitch data are particularly useful when classifying pitches into types. The first is to plot pitch speed versus horizontal spin deflection. Speed helps us separate fastballs from off-speed pitches. The horizontal spin deflection helps us separate fastballs and change-ups, which break in toward a same-handed batter, from curveballs and sliders, which break away from a same-handed batter. The slower speed of change-ups, curves and sliders causes them to "sink," since gravity has more time to act on them.

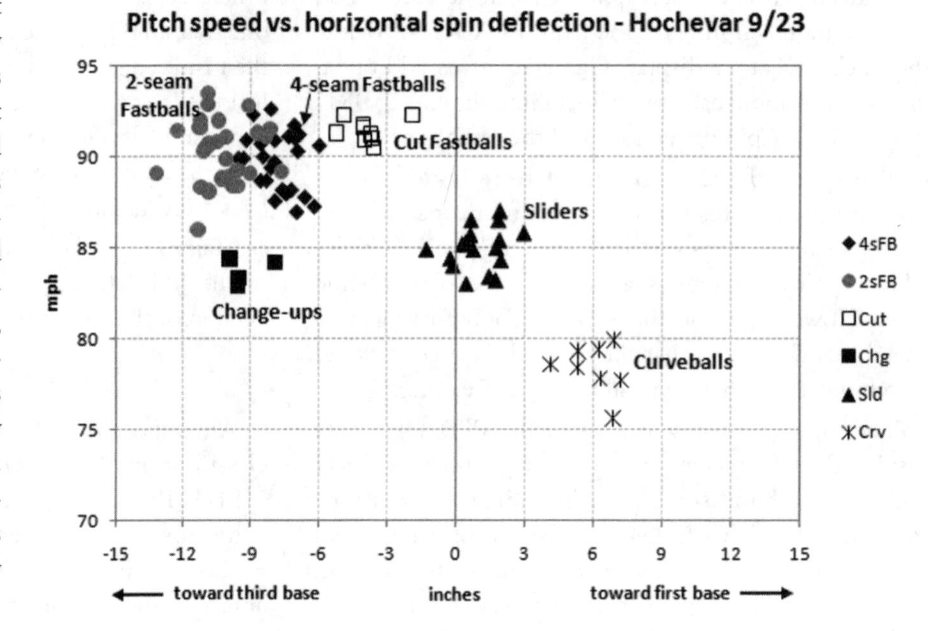

It is also often useful to plot spin deflection in both the vertical and horizontal dimensions. For example, this can help us separate four-seam fastballs from two-seam fastballs. Two-seam fastballs have less vertical spin deflection (i.e., they "sink" relative to the four-seamer), and they break in more toward a same-handed batter.

Due to inconsistencies between PITCHf/x systems at different parks (and sometimes at the same park at different points in the season), it can be difficult to distinguish between pitch types on a season-level graph That's why I prefer to identify pitches on a game level.

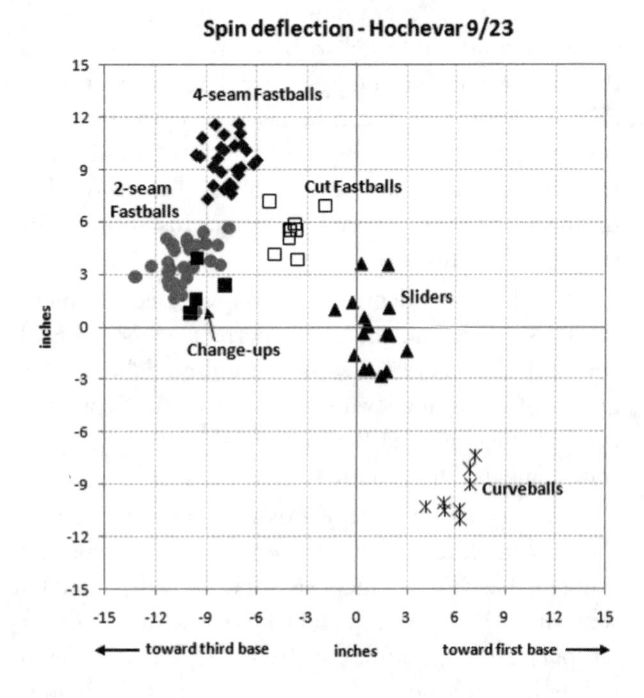

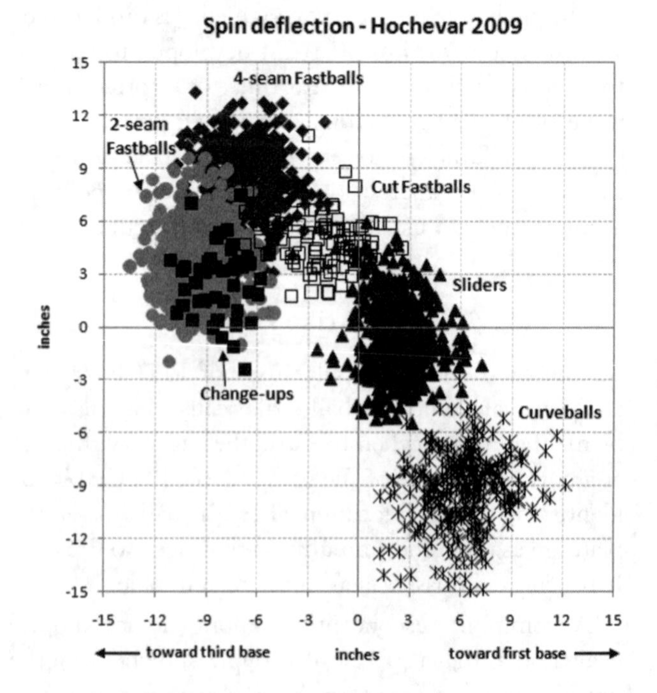

(continued from page 155)
between pitch types on a season-level graph, whereas the distinctions between pitches may be obvious at the game level.

Some pitchers' pitch types may be particularly difficult to distinguish, but in those cases there are additional tools in the classifier's arsenal. For example, pitchers often throw a few pitch types primarily to one handedness of batter. Change-ups and split-finger fastballs tend to be thrown to opposite-handed hitters. Sliders are thrown more frequently to same-handed hitters. So handedness of the batter can be one clue.

Pitch location is another place to look for help. Some pitchers tend to throw their four-seam fastball to one side of the plate and their two-seam fastball to the other side of the plate. It also may be useful to graph pitches in terms of spin axis and spin rate to tease out subtle differences between pitch types. Sometimes something as simple as looking at the sequence of pitch speeds over the course of a game may help identify the boundary between fastballs and change-ups.

Really, the tools for pitch classification are as endless as your understanding of the game of baseball and the tendencies of the pitcher in question. The discipline of pitch classification is as fine a way as any to increase your understanding of the art of pitching.

HITf/x, FIELDf/x and Trackman

The growing success of PITCHf/x has only increased the thirst for similarly detailed knowledge about additional parts of the game. In May 2008, Sportvision held its First Annual PITCHf/x Summit for analysts, scientists and team personnel. At the summit, Peter Jensen presented a proposal for using existing PITCHf/x camera footage to track batted balls coming off the bat. By spring 2009, Sportvision had brought this HITf/x system to fruition, and participants in the Second Annual PITCHf/x Summit in July 2009 were given access to a month's worth of HITf/x data.

This HITf/x data set contained the initial velocity (speed and direction) for nearly all the batted balls hit in every major league game during April 2009. Ground balls that hit the dirt area near home plate proved to be difficult to track in the PITCHf/x video, although Sportvision provided some trajectory data based on the flight of the ball after the first bounce for these grounders.

Analysis of the HITf/x data is still in its nascent stages. Sportvision is fine-tuning its data production procedures and is considering whether or how to make additional HITf/x data available to the public. Nonetheless, this data holds considerable promise for evaluation not only of hitting and pitching but also a better system of fielding evaluation. Knowing exactly how hard and in what direction each ball was hit allows us to distinguish between a screaming line drive into the hole at short and a Texas Leaguer dropping just over the shortstop's glove. Most of our currently available data sets consider both of those batted balls simply as singles to left field.

This past summer, Sportvision and MLBAM announced their plans to take the digital tracking of game events to another level altogether. Sportvision has installed a camera system in AT&T Park in San Francisco that allows it to track the movement of the players and the baseball across the whole field throughout the game. Plans are to install and test this system in the other parks around the league during the 2010 season, similar to the test and installation phase for PITCHf/x in 2007. This system, popularly labeled FIELDf/x, promises to give us an unprecedented window into baserunning, defensive positioning, full batted ball trajectories, and detailed assessments of fielder capabilities.

Sportvision has not announced plans to share any of this data publicly, although it can be expected that MLBAM will want to incorporate much of the information from FIELDf/x into its Gameday application to make the viewer's experience even more immersive. Other broadcasters likely will want to make use of this fascinating storehouse of information, and many major league clubs will no doubt want to tap this analytical gold mine. It will be interesting to see how FIELDf/x unfolds and how far-reaching its impacts on the game will be.

Another tracking technology that has gotten less press but is no less interesting is Trackman Baseball, a portable phased array Doppler radar system for tracking pitched and batted balls. Trackman is widely used for tracking golf shots, and the parent company, Interactive Sports Games, has adapted the technology for baseball. The Trackman Baseball system is able to reconstruct the full trajectory of batted balls. Its portability makes it promising for scouting and coaching applications, where the fixed nature and expense of the PITCHf/x and FIELDf/x systems prevent their use.

Conclusions

Baseball and baseball analysis is undergoing exciting transitions due to these new tracking technologies. The wide availability and discussion of much of this information among the online sabermetric community is leading to an explosion in our understanding of the game at a much deeper level than previously possible.

Thanks to a number of enterprising individuals, it is now possible for a baseball fan or researcher to interact with this data at any number of levels. Several of them are listed in the References section. I hope this article will help you engage at a level that interests you and increase your enjoyment of the game.

References

Several websites present PITCHf/x data in graphical format. Brooks Baseball (http://www.BrooksBaseball.net), created by Dan Brooks, offers a variety of detailed pitcher and umpire charts for each game, available in real time. Fangraphs (http://www.fangraphs.com—look for the PitchFx tab under each pitcher's page) offers basic speed, spin deflection and release point graphs for every pitcher, usually within a couple days after the game. Texas Leaguers (http://pitchfx.texasleaguers.com), created by Trip Somers, also has basic spin deflection and release points graphs, usually available the day after the game, but offers useful flexibility in graphing between dates of the user's choice.

If you are interested in further reading or resources on PITCHf/x and related topics, you may find the following websites useful. Dan Brooks has created a PITCHf/x tutorial at the Sons of Sam Horn discussion board (http://www.sonsofsamhorn.net/wiki/index.php/Pitchfx). My Fastballs blog contains a glossary of XML fields in the Gameday data (http://fastballs.wordpress.com/2007/08/02/glossary-of-the-gameday-pitch-fields/). Dr. Alan Nathan has a site with all manner of information about the physics of baseball (http://webusers.npl.illinois.edu/~a-nathan/pob/).

If you want to get your hands dirty, you can find the data in raw XML format at the MLB Gameday website (http://gd2.mlb.com/components/game/mlb). If you want to build your own database, you can download the necessary files from Baseball on a Stick, or you can get your hands even a little dirtier and build it using the instructions from my Fastballs blog (http://fastballs.wordpress.com/2007/08/23/how-to-build-a-pitch-database). For those who don't want the headache of Python or Perl code, Jeff and Darrell Zimmerman have provided a database of PITCHf/x data for download, and they appreciate donations for the bandwidth needed (http://www.wantlinux.net/category/baseball-data/).

Acknowledgments

Special thanks go to Alan Nathan and Marv White for their support, encouragement, and willingness to share time and data; to Dave Studenmund and the team at Hardball Times for providing a platform that fosters good baseball research and specifically for encouraging me in my work; and to the other PITCHf/x analysts, too many to list here, for sharing so much of their work and ideas.

Where Was That Pitch?

by Dave Allen

Consider the pitcher. He wants to throw strikes but he doesn't want to give up hits. He wants to throw the pitch in the strike zone, but not to the center of the plate where batters make the best contact. It's a difficult balancing act, so germane to the game that it even has its own lingo. Pitchers talk about finding the "black" of the plate, outside the hitter's "wheelhouse."

This has probably been the pitcher's fundamental task for as long as baseball has been played. Warren Spahn talked about it when he said "Home plate is 17 inches wide, but I ignore the middle 12 inches. I pitch to the two-and-a-half inches on each side." Ted Williams took the idea further in his book *The Science of Hitting*, creating a map showing what he thought his batting average was in each location in the strike zone.

And now we have PITCHf/x. The PITCHf/x system records the trajectory of every pitch thrown in a major league game (for a longer background on the system, read Mike Fast's article in this Annual). Thus we have the exact location where every pitch either crossed the plate or would have crossed it (most hits are contacted in front of the plate). With this data we can examine exactly how the location of a pitch affects the outcome.

What follows is a detailed examination of the value of each type of pitch by its location. A lot has already been written about this subject, so I've pulled together the best research I could find and added my own graphical take. Hopefully, this will serve as a useful resource for you. There is also a detailed list of sources at the end of the article, for those who want to research the topic further.

The Value Of A Pitch

Thanks to PITCHf/x, we have pitch locations, but we need some way of valuing a pitch. For pitches that end an at-bat, in an out or a hit, we have a good idea of the value, but what about the 80 percent of pitches that do not end an at-bat? We don't want to just throw those data away. Luckily, John Walsh developed a way to value all pitches. He built on the idea of batting runs (or linear weights) developed by Pete Palmer, which gave a value to every at-bat-ending event. Palmer calculated the average number of runs scored in an inning from each base/out state over a number of years (e.g., how many runs does an offense score in an inning when it has, say, one out and a runner on second?). He called this value the run expectancy. The "batting runs" of any event on the field is simply the change in run expectancy from before to after the event.

Walsh took the same approach with a pitch. The value of any pitch is the change in run expectancy from before the pitch to after it. In the same way that Palmer calculated the run expectancy in each base/out state, Walsh calculated the run expectancy in at-bats that pass through each count. In this case he called the change in expectancy the run value of a pitch.

The run value of a first pitch strike is the difference between the average batting runs of outcomes of all at-bats (all at bats start at 0-0 count) and the average batting runs of outcomes of at-bats that pass through the 0-1 count, which is about –0.04 runs. This definition means that the run value of a pitch is count dependent. For example, the value of a pitch fouled off on a count with two strikes is zero, while it is negative in other counts.

Finally the value of the last pitch in an at-bat is the batting runs of the outcome of the at-bat minus the run expectancy in the count it was thrown. So a pitch hit for a home run in a 0-2 count has a different value than one in a 3-0 count. That's necessary for the sum of the value of the pitches in an at-bat to equal the batting runs of the event ending the at-bat. Negative run values denote pitches that result in fewer runs scored. They're good for the pitcher; positive ones are good for the batter.

With this definition in hand and the PITCHf/x data, we can ask a host of additional questions. How does the difference in speed between a pitcher's fastball and change-up affect the success of his change-up? More generally, how is a pitch influenced by the one that precedes it? What are the platoon splits for each pitch type? What is the relative importance of speed, movement and location in determining the success of a fastball?

But, returning to the task at hand: how the run value of a pitch is affected by its location as it crosses the plane of the plate. Joe Sheehan was the first to look at this with the PITCHf/x data by breaking the pitch location into bins. Nine bins were placed in the strike zone and 16 outside it. Not surprisingly, all 16 outside bins had positive run values; these pitches tend to be taken for balls. The eight bins along the edge of the strike zone had negative run values, while the one in the center of the zone had a positive run value. Pitching in the strike zone is good for the pitcher unless he hits the heart of the plate. The results were fairly intuitive.

Sheehan noted that the analysis could be improved by taking a spatially continuous approach rather than binning the data and by separating the analysis by pitch type (a good location for a fastball might not be good for a curveball). Fortunately for him, unfortunately for us, he was hired away by a major league team before he could release such an analysis, but I continued that work a year later. Here I will review and expand this work.

Explaining The Graphs

For each pitch type and handedness combination (e.g., right-handed batter vs. left-handed pitcher) I show the run value based on pitch location. I take a Loess regression approach. Loess regression is a modern regression analysis that fits a series of low-degree polynomials to a set of data and then splices them together. This allows for maximum flexibility in the form of the fit curve (or in this case surface). Here I fit a surface in x-z space (location of the pitch as it crosses the plate) to the run value of that pitch, just as you would fit a curve to a set of points varying across one dimension. In the plots I display just the surface, not the actual pitches it is fit to, as if you fit a line to a set of points and then just displayed the line and not the points.

Since I am displaying how run value varies against two variables and the page is only two-dimensional, the third dimension (the dependent one, run value) is displayed as the intensity on a gray scale. The color scale goes from -0.04 runs (black) to 0.04 runs (white). Remember, negative is good for the pitcher. For context, –0.04 runs is about the value of a strike in a 0-0 count and 0.04 runs about the value of a ball in a 0-0 count. I added a white contour line where the location shifts from having a negative to a positive run value. In some graphs, there are multiple contour lines—for example, one circle inside a larger one. This means that the area outside the largest circle has a positive run value (usually outside the strike zone), the area between the two has a negative (along the edges of the zone) and then inside the smallest circle back to positive (the center of the zone).

On top of that in each plot, I show the location of the strike zone for context. I use the larger two-foot wide one described by Walsh. I take the top and bottom of the zone as roughly the average top and bottom, at 1.5 and 3.5 feet, and scale the pitch height accordingly as described by Tom Tango. To make the strike zone box stand out, it is white if the value of a pitch in that location is negative (as these areas are darker) and black if it is positive (as these areas are lighter).

Finally, I cut off the values shown to include just the locations where there are enough pitches to get a good estimate of the value. The result is that I show just the areas of highest pitch density. For all the graphs, that covers roughly 90 percent of the pitches thrown. This also serves to show roughly where the different pitches are thrown in each handedness combination.

Each of the images is from the catcher's perspective. So right-handed batters stand to the left of the zone at about -2 and negative x-valued pitches are inside. Left-handed batters stand to the right of the zone at about 2 and positive x-valued pitches are inside.

Don't Throw Down The Middle

There are some broad trends that apply to all pitch types. Generally, pitches outside the strike zone have a positive run value and those inside the strike zone a negative run value, although this is not universally so. This is not surprising; pitches outside the zone are most often taken as balls that have a positive run value, while those in the zone are more likely to result in strikes.

Within the zone there are some relatively consistent patterns across most of the pitch types. Right down the middle generally has a positive run value; pitches in this location are swung at often (it is good for batters to swing at pitches in the zone), hit at a high rate and have a high slugging rate on contacted pitches. The lowest run value is generally on pitches up and in, as these pitches have a low slugging rate on balls in play (many infield flies), and on pitches down-and-away, which have a low slugging average on balls in play (many ground balls) and a low contact rate. Pitches up and away and down and in tend to have intermediate run values and vary by pitch type. Additionally, there is considerable variation in the run value pattern outside the zone based on pitch type.

Pitch Types

In the following pages, we'll look at four-seam fastballs, two-seam fastballs, change-ups, sliders and curveballs. The pitches are based on my own post-hoc pitch classification. Unfortunately there were not enough splitters, cutters or knuckleballs to produce these images, as the technique requires a large number of pitches across many locations to be meaningful. Pitch speed and horizontal and vertical spin deflection

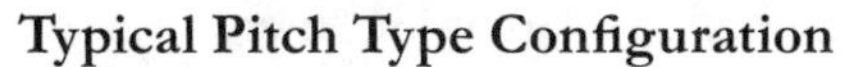

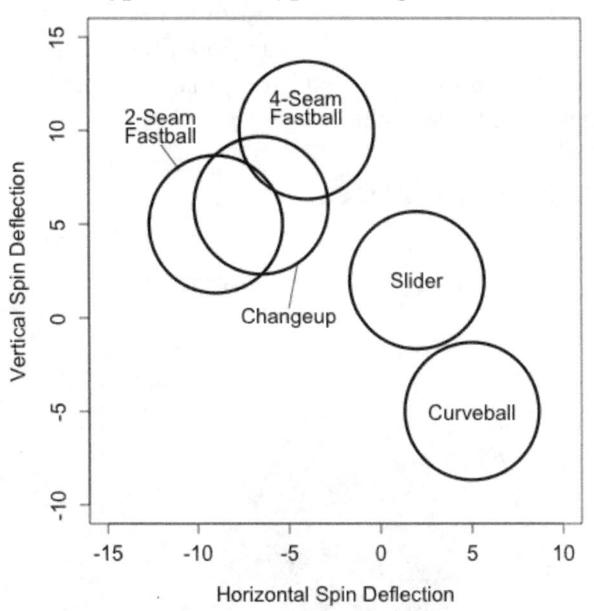

are the factors that determine pitch type in my classification algorithm. The spin deflection is the deflection of the ball due to the spin on it. (See Mike Fast's article in this Annual for a more thorough discussion). It is typically broken into two components: vertical (if a pitch drops less than expected by gravity due to backspin, as a four-seam fastball does, or drops more than expected from gravity due to topspin, like a curveball) and horizontal (if a pitch veers to the left or right due to side spin). I include a figure on the left that shows the typical spin deflection for these pitch types thrown by a right-handed pitcher.

For a lefty, flip the graph over the y-axis.

You'll find run value graphs for most of these pitch types on the next several pages. You will find some interesting things in each one, but these are the findings that jump out at me.

Change-ups are thrown most often in opposite-handed at-bats and have no platoon split. So here I show the images just for those at-bats.

Change-ups are generally successful on the outside edge of the plate or low in the zone. Interestingly, the up-and-in area that is usually good for the pitcher is not good with change-ups. The negative region extending down and away out of the zone is present, but not as large as with sliders.

Remember that these are averages for all pitchers, across all pitch speeds and movement within a particular pitch type. These trends do not hold for all pitchers. In fact, Walsh profiled Ted Lilly showing how he throws his change-up inside more often than outside, and often up-and-in, and gets good results with it.

Four-seam fastballs are the fastest pitch and have the most upward vertical horizontal deflection. That is,

Changeup Run Values

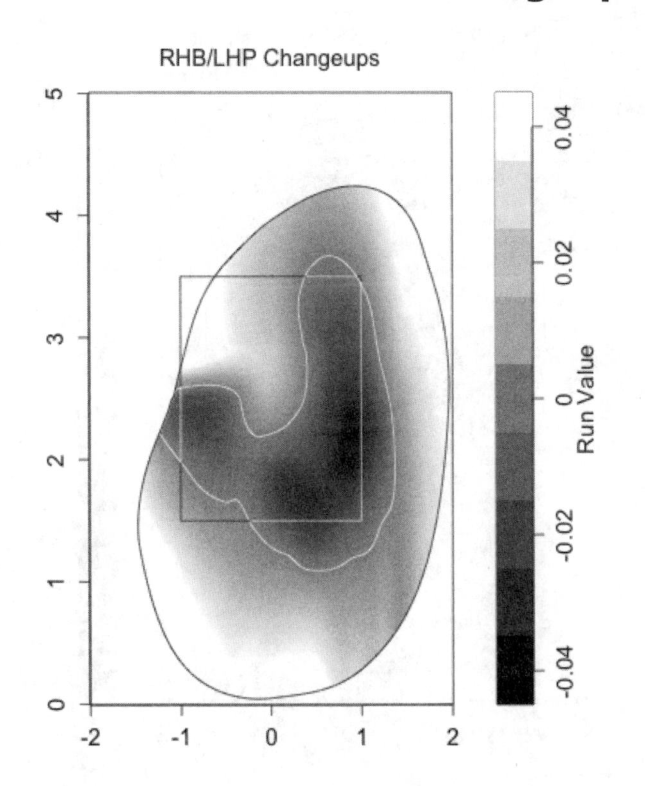

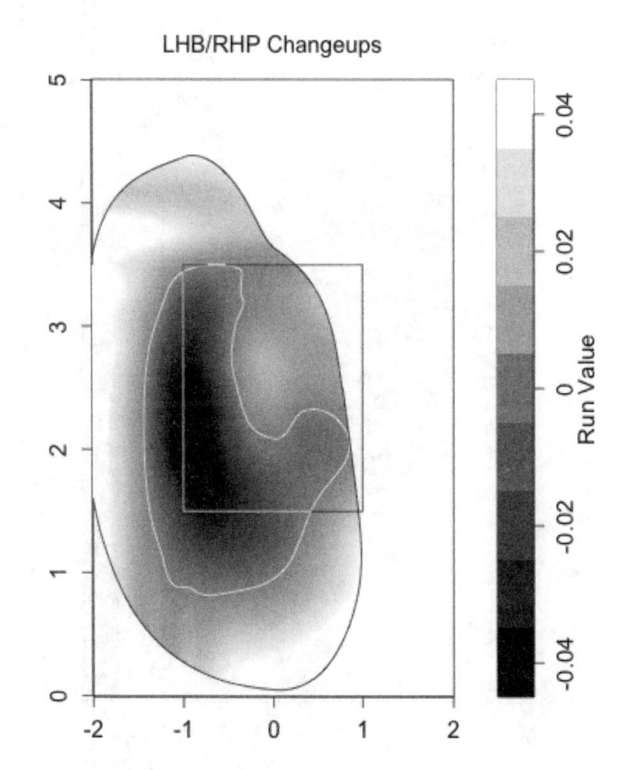

their backspin causes them to drop about 10 inches less than expected from gravity as they move toward the plate, and thus they appear to "rise."

The most noticeable trend with four-seam fastballs is that there is a large section above the strike zone of negative run value—larger and more negative than for other pitch types. These four-seam fastballs above the strike zone are swung at much more often than other pitches in this location and batters make little and poor contact on these pitches.

Four-Seam Fastball Run Values

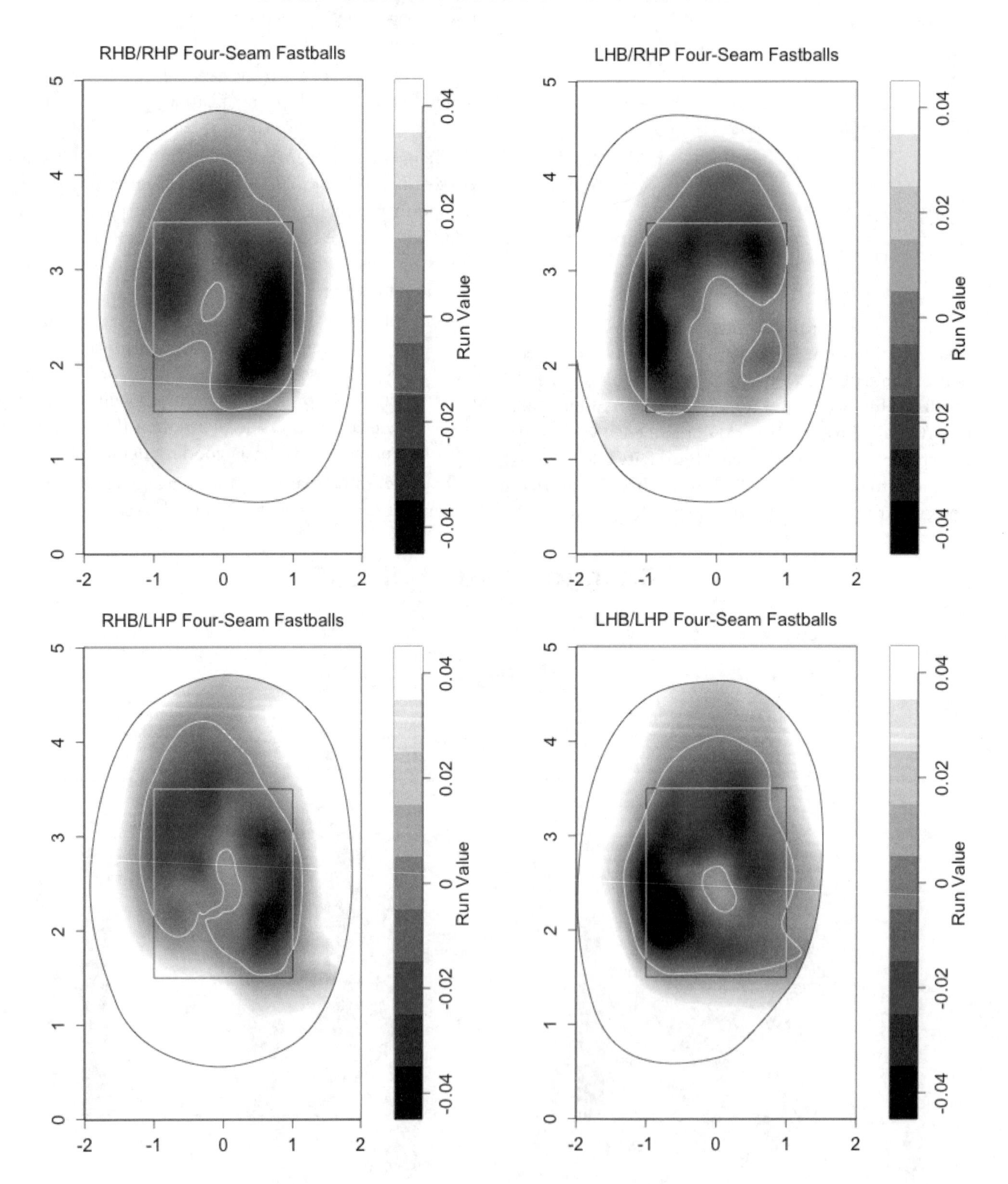

On the other hand, four-seam fastballs low in the zone do quite poorly. Compared to other pitches, there is a very small portion (if any, depending on the handedness combination) of the bottom of the zone where these pitches have a negative run value. Not unrelated: Four-seam fastballs are thrown higher than any other pitch.

Two-seam fastballs are generally slower than four-seam fastballs, tail in more to the pitcher's throwing arm side (in to same-handed batters) and have less "rise."

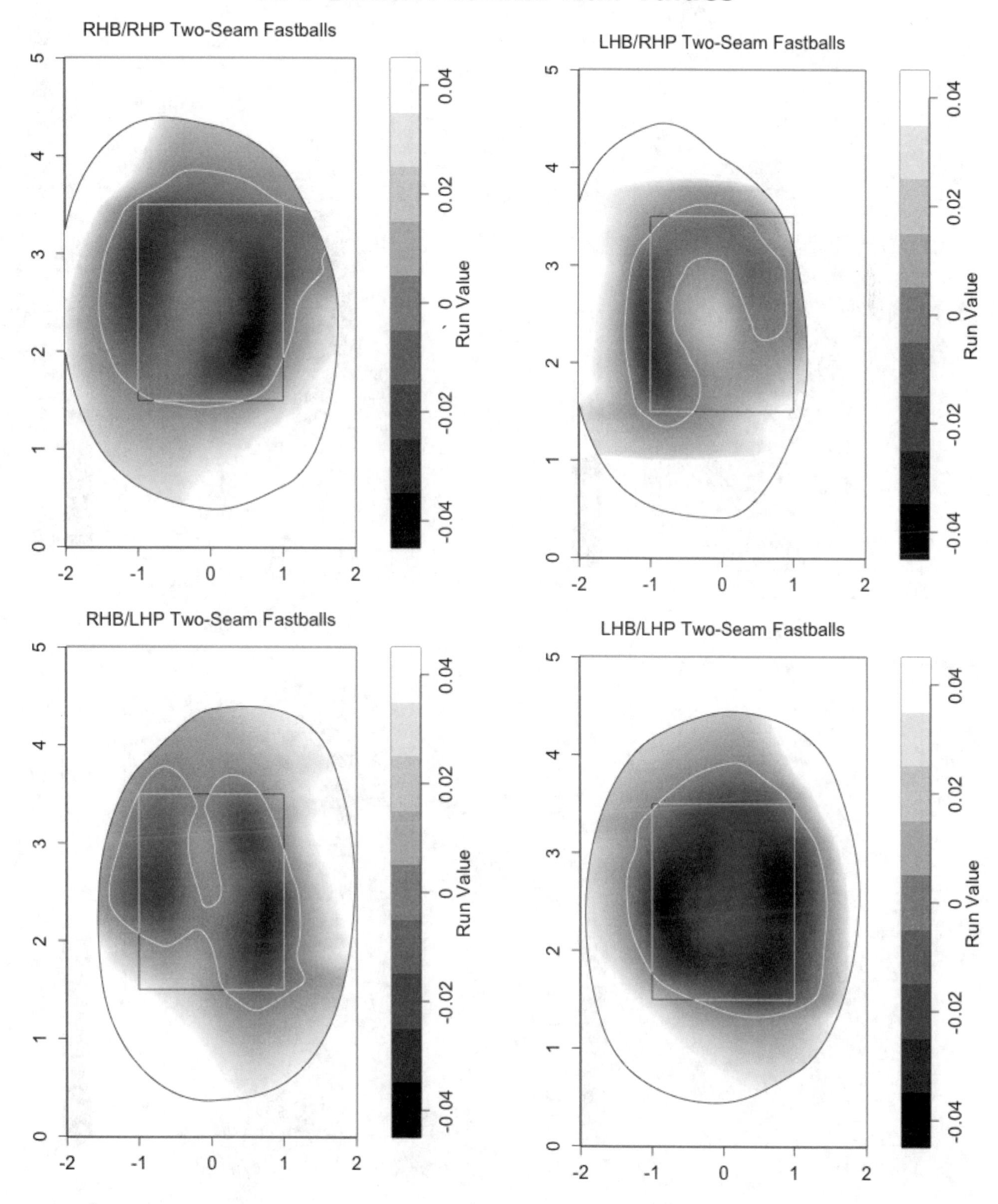

Because they rise less than four-seam fastballs (which are thrown more often), two-seam fastballs appear to sink. Some pitchers' two-seam fastballs are called sinkers.

Note that the same-handed images are much darker than the opposite-handed ones. This shows the extreme platoon split of this pitch type; they do very well in same-handed at-bats and poorly in opposite-handed ones.

This extreme platoon split makes comparison a bit harder, but generally, compared to four-seam fastballs, the region above the zone has a higher run value and the

Curveball Run Values

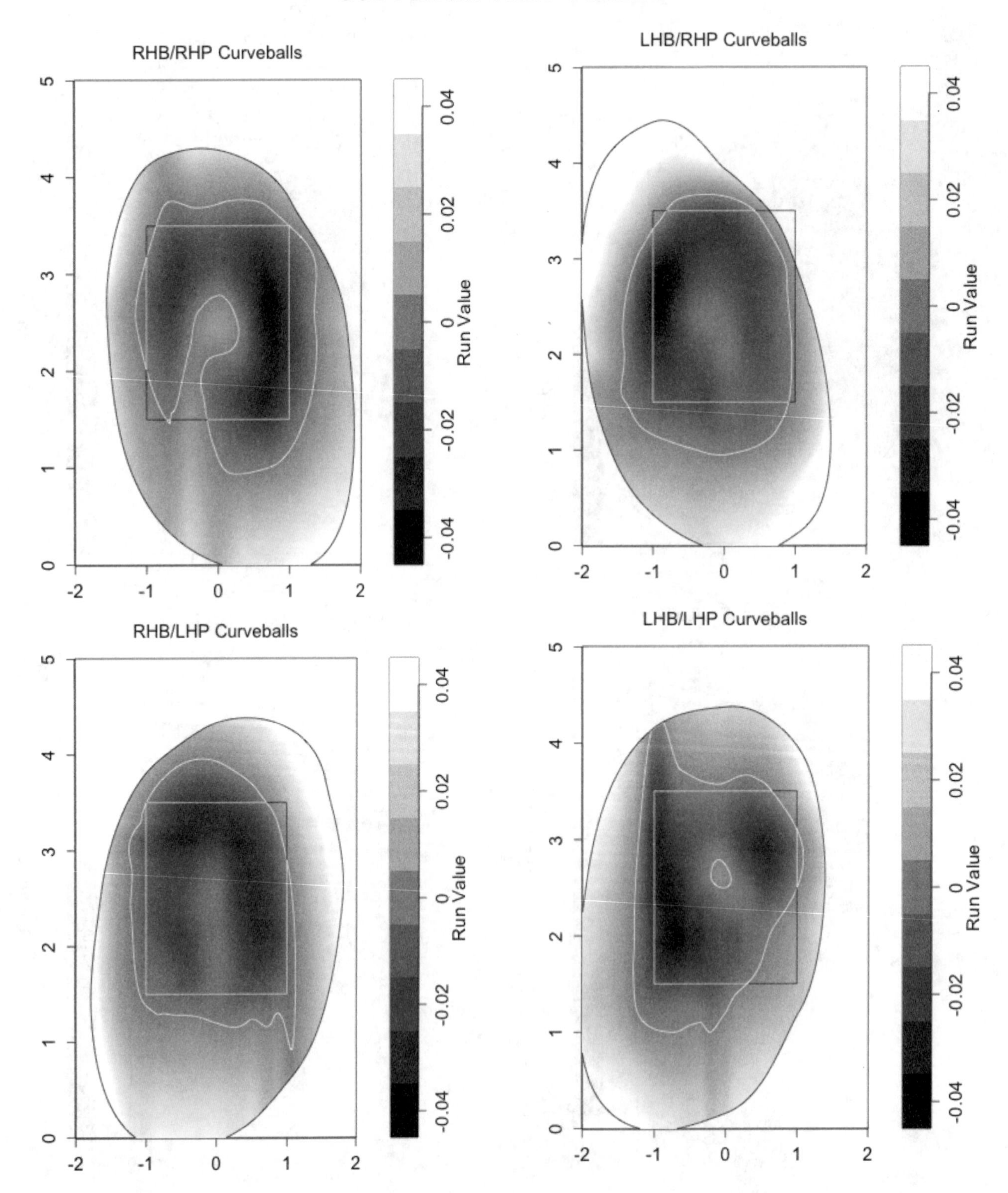

region at the bottom and below the zone has a lower run value. This should not be terribly surprising—four-seam fastballs succeed by inducing whiffs and pop-ups (which occur more on pitches up in the zone), while two-seam fastballs succeed by inducing grounders (which occur more on pitches down in the zone).

Curveballs, Walsh found, do not show a platoon split, but still are thrown in the same proportion in opposite- and same-handed at-bats. So I show all four images.

These are the most surprising ones to me. There is much less contrast and structure in these images than the other ones. This means there is less variation in the run value of a curveball based on its location, which would suggest that location does not play as big a role in curveball success as in other pitches. Particularly surprising is that curveballs up in the zone, where I thought "hanging curves" would have a large positive run value, show results similar to those lower in the zone.

Sliders are thrown mostly in same-handed at-bats; not surprisingly Walsh found that they show an extreme platoon split. For that reason, here I just show the sliders in same-handed at-bats.

The negative run value area extends far away and below the zone for sliders. This is because batters swing at these pitches at a relatively high rate, but make little and poor contact. Sliders generally have very little horizontal or vertical spin deflection. This means in same-handed at-bats relative to fastballs they sink and tail away. Consider a situation in which a batter initially thought a pitch was a fastball that looked headed for the heart of the plate, so he swung at it. But the pitch was really a slider, so its spin deflection relative to a fastball took it down and away from the heart of the plate. I think this is why we see the negative valued region extending so far below and outside of the strike zone.

Conclusion

The data make Spahn's point, as Max Marchi has noted, that pitching to the edges of the plate is better. And the images show some similarity to Ted Williams's zone. So even without the PITCHf/x data these guys knew what they were talking about. Beyond that, though, the new information gives us a more complete picture of where pitches are successful and how that changes by pitch type. More work is being done to look at pitch success based not only on location, but also on speed, movement and sequencing and how these factors interact.

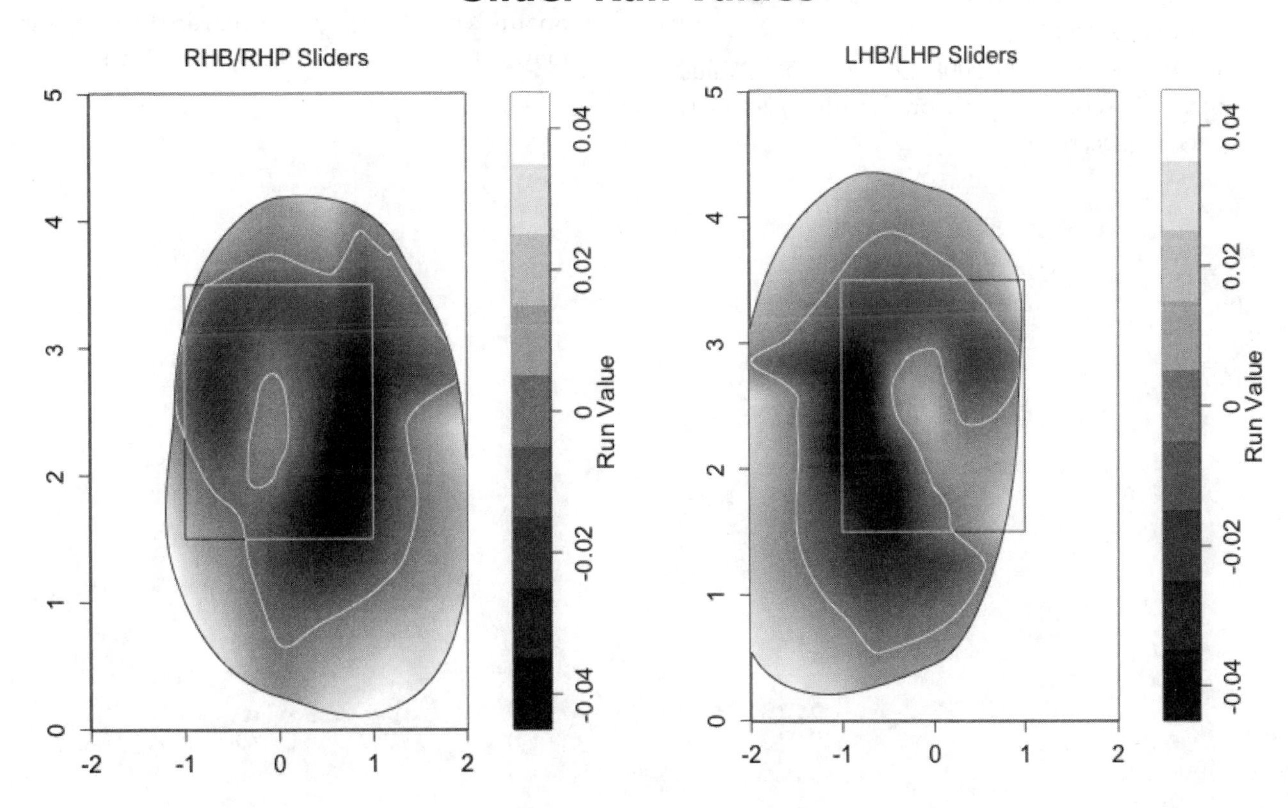

Related Articles On The Web

- John Walsh, *The Hardball Times Baseball Annual 2008*, The Origin of the Platoon Advantage, p. 163.
- John Walsh. Feb. 26, 2008. Searching for the Game's Best Pitch. http://www.hardballtimes.com/main/article/searching-for-the-games-best-pitch/
- Josh Kalk. July 1, 2008. Anatomy of a Pitch: Change Up. http://www.hardballtimes.com/main/article/anatomy-of-a-pitch-change-up/
- Dave Allen. May 22, 2009. Optimal Fastball-Change-up Speed Separation. http://baseballanalysts.com/archives/2009/05/optimal_fastbal.php
- Jonathan Hale. May 28, 2009. Inside the Change-Up. http://www.hardballtimes.com/main/article/inside-the-changeup/
- Max Marchi. July 3, 2009. Master of Fooling http://www.hardballtimes.com/main/article/master-of-fooling/
- Josh Kalk. Feb. 10, 2009. Pitch Sequencing. http://www.hardballtimes.com/main/article/pitch-sequencing/
- Chris Moore. Sept. 21, 2009. Best Fastballs in Baseball. http://baseballanalysts.com/archives/2009/09/best_pitch_in_b.php
- Jeremy Greenhouse. Sept. 9, 2009. On That Stuff. http://baseballanalysts.com/archives/2009/09/on_that_stuff.php
- Joe Sheehan. Feb. 29, 2008. Locational Run Values. http://baseballanalysts.com/archives/2008/02/lwts_by_locatio.php
- Dave Allen. March 16, 2009. Run Value by Pitch Location. http://baseballanalysts.com/archives/2009/03/run_value_by_pi.php
- Dave Allen. March 16, 2009. Run Value by Pitch Type and Location. http://baseballanalysts.com/archives/2009/03/run_value_by_pi_1.php
- John Walsh. July 11, 2007. Strike Zone: Fact vs Fiction. http://www.hardballtimes.com/main/article/strike-zone-fact-vs-fiction
- Tom Tango. June 5, 2009. Scaling PITCHf/x. http://www.insidethebook.com/ee/index.php/site/article/scaling_pitchf_x/
- Dave Allen. March 23, 2009. Deconstructing the Fastball Run Value Map. http://baseballanalysts.com/archives/2009/03/deconstructing.php
- Dave Allen. March 30, 2009. Deconstructing the Non-Fastball Run Maps. http://baseballanalysts.com/archives/2009/03/deconstructing_1.php
- John Walsh, *The Hardball Times Baseball Annual 2008*, The Origin of the Platoon Advantage, p. 163.
- John Walsh. July 28, 2008. The Inside Change-Up: Courage or Folly? http://www.hardballtimes.com/main/article/the-inside-changeup-courage-or-folly/
- Max Marchi. April 24, 2009. What Did Warren Spahn Know? http://www.hardballtimes.com/main/article/what-did-warren-spahn-know/

Miles Per Starter

by Tom M. Tango

You had to build a foundation to work off of, and you had to develop stamina because my intent was to pitch a lot of innings. ... The better conditioned you are, you lessen your chances of injuries more.
—Nolan Ryan, April 5, 2009, *Dallas Morning News*

To listen to all the pitch count talk, you'd think that pitcher arms were hanging by a thread. Nolan Ryan thinks differently. He believes that if you are conditioned to pitch a lot, you will be able to pitch a lot. Is this true?

We can think of a car. Each car has a certain amount of mileage in its lifetime. If you use the car regularly, you can lengthen its mileage life. However, what if you use the car regularly, but not as often? Can you still get the same amount of mileage, albeit spread out over more years? That is, if you drive a car for 12,000 miles for 15 years, you'll get 180,000 miles out of the car. What if you drive it for 9,000 miles a year? Can you drive it for 20 years (and also get 180,000 miles)? Or is the lack of miles driven really only buying you a couple of years, so that you can drive it for 17 years for a total of 150,000 miles?

Ferguson Jenkins faced 4,927 batters from the age of 25 through 28. Among pitchers born since 1932 for that age group, he ranks first. Here are the top 10:

Most Batters Faced, Ages 25-28, Born in 1932 or later

Pitcher	Born	Batters Faced
Jenkins, Fergie	1942	4,927
Drysdale, Don	1936	4,866
Ryan, Nolan	1947	4,765
Palmer, Jim	1945	4,706
Blue, Vida	1949	4,701
Marichal, Juan	1937	4,613
Carlton, Steve	1944	4,576
Coleman, Joe	1947	4,541
Hunter, Catfish	1946	4,537
McDowell, Sam	1942	4,535

Nolan Ryan was third. Had we looked at pitch counts, the young Ryan would have topped the chart. And Nolan Ryan had a very long career. Is he an exception, or just an exception to the rule?

You will note that the top 10 were all born between 1936 and 1949. Had we extended the listing, Dave Stieb (born 1957) would pop in at No. 11. If we look at the 35 most-used pitchers for this age group, the earliest was Drysdale, born in 1936, and the latest was Roger Clemens, born in 1962. That is a span of 27 years. But in a 10-year span, we find 23 of these 35 pitchers born between 1942 and 1951. If we had to narrow down a decade where young pitchers were the most heavily used, this would be the time period.

Did their arms fall off? Considering the abundance of Hall of Famers, the answer seems self-evident. Is this standard though? After all, we expect Hall of Famers to be pitching a lot in the prime of their careers. Let's construct a list of the top 10 most-used pitchers for each decade, starting with pitchers born in 1922, for the age group 25 through 28.

Most Batters Faced, Ages 25-28, Born Between 1922 and 1931

Pitcher	Born	Batters Faced	Batters Faced Next 4 years	Batters Faced Rest of Career
Roberts, Robin	1926	5,327	4,633	6,449
Friend, Bob	1930	4,422	4,230	3,571
Lary, Frank	1930	4,363	3,569	1,158
Kellner, Alex	1924	3,991	2,745	1,180
Antonelli, Johnny	1930	3,976	1,906	0
Brewer, Tom	1931	3,971	1,020	0
Sullivan, Frank	1930	3,945	2,376	49
Pierce, Billy	1927	3,809	4,145	2,849
Erskine, Carl	1926	3,793	2,308	117
Rush, Bob	1925	3,788	3,830	1,161

I added two additional columns: the number of batters faced in the next four years (meaning ages 29-32) and the number of batters faced for the rest of their career beyond that point (meaning from age 33 to retirement). We see that five of the young pitchers still pitched a lot at ages 29-32, with three others pitching a fair amount. Two of them would have their careers end before the age of 33. And even starting at age 33, only three pitchers would build up much of a career. This decade was not kind to starting pitchers. Had I extended the list to the top 20 young workhorses, we'd also find Whitey Ford and Jim Bunning.

These top 20 starters averaged 3,785 batters faced at age 25-28. From ages 29-32, they averaged 2,795 batters faced. And from age 33 to the end of their careers, they faced an average of 2,194. Let's see what happened to pitchers in future decades.

Most Batters Faced, Ages 25-28, Born Between 1932 and 1941

Pitcher	Born	Batters Faced	Batters Faced Next 4 years	Batters Faced Rest of Career
Drysdale, Don	1936	4,866	4,502	267
Marichal, Juan	1937	4,613	4,502	4,024
Stottlemyre, Mel	1941	4,472	4,437	485
Osteen, Claude	1939	4,431	4,500	3,619
Kaat, Jim	1938	4,115	3,974	8,698
Monbouquette, Bill	1936	4,090	2,346	0
Fisher, Jack	1939	3,957	1,252	0
Ramos, Pedro	1935	3,904	1,440	364
Koufax, Sandy	1935	3,775	3,441	0
Chance, Dean	1941	3,760	1,093	0

We see that six of those young workhorses continued to pitch at the same pace in the next four years. But four of them simply plummeted, with their careers cut short very early. And starting from age 33, only three of them kept going (Marichal, Osteen, and Kaat). When we extend the list to the top 20 starters, we add Jim Perry and Mickey Lolich. These top 20 average 3,917 batters faced as youngsters, which is 130 more batters than the top workhorses of the previous decade. So, the move toward working starters harder had begun. And from ages 29-32, these workhorses faced 2,764 batters, just a smidge less than the starters from the previous decade.

From this limited sample, giving these pitchers more to do did not have an effect of making them pitch less than they otherwise would have. And from age 33 onward, they faced 1,823 batters, which is substantially less then the prior decade's starters. So, perhaps what happened is that working them harder as youngsters cut their careers short in the long-term, with no short-term effect.

Let's see if this is just a blip. Perhaps we are just reading what we can in the numbers, or perhaps future decades will exhibit different patterns.

Most Batters Faced, Ages 25-28, Born between 1942 and 1951

Pitcher	Born	Batters Faced	Batters Faced Next 4 years	Batters Faced Rest of Career
Jenkins, Fergie	1942	4,927	4,899	7,776
Ryan, Nolan	1947	4,765	4,413	11,171
Palmer, Jim	1945	4,706	4,563	4,666
Blue, Vida	1949	4,701	3,510	2,392
Carlton, Steve	1944	4,576	4,583	10,441
Coleman, Joe	1947	4,541	1,643	0
Hunter, Catfish	1946	4,537	3,589	460
McDowell, Sam	1942	4,535	2,492	149
Leonard, Dennis	1951	4,442	2,858	828
Seaver, Tom	1944	4,425	4,297	8,530

Wow. First, notice that the No. 10 guy in batters faced, Tom Seaver, faced 4,425 batters. This would put him No. 5 in the previous decade, and No. 2 20 years earlier. Not only did these pitchers face an enormous number of batters as youngsters, they continued to face a large number the following four years, with only Joe Coleman as a major exception. And then we have several of them posting exceptionally long careers beyond that (Ryan, Carlton, Seaver, Jenkins).

When we consider the top 20 most-worked starters, we also find Don Sutton, Bert Blyleven, Rick Reuschel and Steve Rogers. Averaging these 20, they faced 4,425 batters as youngsters, 3,200 at ages 29-32, and an astounding 3,891 from age 33 onward. If the theory was that a starter's arm needs some pampering, the starters from this decade proved otherwise. Yes, we have four starters of the top 10 that didn't do anything after age 33, but this is true of every decade's top 10 workhorses.

Let's continue with the next decade.

Most Batters Faced, Ages 25-28, Born Between 1952 and 1961

Pitcher	Born	Batters Faced	Batters Faced Next 4 years	Batters Faced Rest of Career
Stieb, Dave	1957	4,500	3,402	1,855
Witt, Mike	1960	4,265	1,461	183
Morris, Jack	1955	4,183	4,285	6,188
Viola, Frank	1960	4,180	4,077	1,137
Moore, Mike	1959	4,118	3,643	3,235

Pitcher	Born	Batters Faced	Batters Faced Next 4 years	Batters Faced Rest of Career
Valenzuela, Fern.	1960	3,953	1,788	2,505
Browning, Tom	1960	3,891	3,357	723
Darling, Ron	1960	3,872	3,169	1,959
Langston, Mark	1960	3,864	3,920	3,813
Soto, Mario	1956	3,835	2,021	0

Having witnessed great success by sending out their young workhorses to the wolves, what did managers do the next decade? They reverted back to their original pattern! This chart looks like those prior to the Nolan Ryan era. Extend the list to the top 20, and no pitcher of real note jumps out. We have Dennis Eckersley (future reliever), Jimmy Key, Jim Clancy, and Bruce Hurst. The average workhorse among the top 20 faced 3,820 batters from age 25-28, and followed that up with 2,826 batters, which is pretty much what the pre-Ryan era did. And for their age-33 and onward years? They averaged 1,864 batters, which is again in-line with the pre-Ryan era.

Finally, we come to the just- or soon-to-be-retired generation of starters.

Most Batters Faced, Ages 25-28, Born Between 1962 and 1971

Pitcher	Born	Batters Faced	Batters Faced Next 4 years	Batters Faced Rest of Career
Clemens, Roger	1962	4,184	3,566	10,511
Maddux, Greg	1966	3,969	3,643	8,904
McDowell, Jack	1966	3,929	2,288	93
Brown, Kevin	1965	3,800	3,348	5,467
Cone, David	1963	3,672	3,759	4,225
Hentgen, Pat	1968	3,667	3,595	1,404
Glavine, Tom	1966	3,653	3,720	8,454
Martinez, Pedro	1971	3,634	2,809	2,917
Gubicza, Mark	1962	3,616	2,106	1,440
Swindell, Greg	1965	3,568	1,979	1,321

This decade continued the pattern of reducing the workload on young starters even more. Roger Clemens, the most-worked young starter of his generation, would rank 18th in the Ryan era for most batters faced. Clearly the hope here is that by driving your car less, you will get more miles in the later years. Again, extend to the top 20, and we add John Smoltz, Steve Trachsel, and Doug Drabek. Overall, our gang of 20 faced only 3,616 batters as youngsters, and followed that up with 2,728 batters faced at ages 29-32, a number indistinguishable from all the other decades (except, of course, the Ryan era). But, for the rest of their career from age 33, they faced a healthy 2,928 batters and counting (Pedro Martinez and John Smoltz are the only active pitchers remaining. If we give them each 1,000 more batters faced for their careers, the overall average will increase by 100 batters for the group.)

Let's show the averages for each decade of top 20 young starters.

Most Batters Faced, Ages 25-28, Top 20 Starters

Born	Batters Faced	Batters Faced Next 4 years	Batters Faced Rest of Career
1922 to 1931	3,785	2,795	2,194
1932 to 1941	3,917	2,764	1,823
1942 to 1951	4,425	3,200	3,891
1952 to 1961	3,820	2,826	1,864
1962 to 1971	3,616	2,728	2,928

There are three major points of interest in this chart. The first is that the Ryan-led era stands head-and-shoulders above each decade. If the idea is that pitching to a lot of batters will curtail your career, these pitchers proved otherwise. They simply kept going and going and going.

The second is that the other four decades each had roughly 2,800 batters faced at ages 29-32. That is, regardless of how much or how little they were used as youngsters, they all faced roughly the same number of batters in the following four years. Extra rest didn't help in being able to face more batters in later years.

The third point of interest is that the Clemens/Maddux-led era was able to sustain itself from age 33 onward. While not as much as the Ryan-led era, it was clearly far above all the other decades. So, limiting the number of batters faced in their youth (ages 25-28) by about 200 batters each, allowed them to face an extra 1,000 batters in their old age (from age 33 onward).

This sets up an interesting decision for teams. In order to give a pitcher the best chance at a long life, they either have to severely curtail his usage when he is young or they have to pitch him very hard. It is the indecisive in-between that is the worst of all worlds.

However, teams do not control the contract of a pitcher in perpetuity. In fact, it would behoove the teams to not think of the pitcher's arm after age 33, if the pitcher is only 25. And if he's a young pitcher, the

Ryan era data would indicate that they should pitch him hard.

This chart shows the total number of pitchers who faced at least 3,000 batters from the ages of 25-28, along with their averages at each age class. As you can see, in the era prior to the Ryan-led one, and the two decades following it, teams have established a pretty set pattern: They send about 36-38 starters out there to face at least 3,000 batters. The overall averages of each group are more or less similar, including the Ryan-led era. Except of course, during Ryan's time, they sent out 63 pitchers to work hard as youngsters. Had this really been devastating, we would have seen a big drop in the averages. And we don't see that.

Minimum 3,000 Batters Faced, Ages 25-28

Born	Number	Batters Faced	Batters Faced Next 4 years	Batters Faced Rest of Career
1922 to 1931	26	3,634	2,704	2,064
1932 to 1941	38	3,599	2,591	2,051
1942 to 1951	63	3,772	2,741	2,490
1952 to 1961	36	3,553	2,585	1,518
1962 to 1971	38	3,407	2,563	2,271

So far, all we've talked about is the quantity, the mileage on the pitcher's arm. But, what about the quality? Perhaps the babying of an arm lets a pitcher get more out of it? Does it make the engine run more efficiently?

Let's focus on all those pitchers with at least 3,000 batters faced between the ages of 25-28. There are 201 of these pitchers. At that age range, Pedro Martinez allowed a total of 3.01 runs per nine innings pitched (both earned and unearned). The league average during his time was 4.92. Pedro allowed runs at 61 percent of the league average. We'll call this metric the Runs Allowed (RA) Index. Pedro's figure is the lowest for the time period we're discussing. Tom Seaver is next at 65 percent, followed by Greg Maddux also at 65 percent. Fourth in line is Kevin Appier (!) at 67 percent. Rounding out the top 10: Whitey Ford, Robin Roberts, Jose Rijo, Roger Clemens, Jim Palmer, and Billy Pierce.

The best performance among these 201 pitchers at age 29-32 is, once again, Pedro, who allowed runs at 48 percent of league average. Following him were Greg Maddux and Sandy Koufax at 53 percent. No one else was close. Seaver was next at 66 percent. Finally, among the old pitchers (ages 33 and later), the best RA Index was a two-way race with John Smoltz and Dennis Eckersley. Of course, they had the advantage of pitching in relief. Among full-time starters, the leaders were Roger Clemens and Kevin Brown at 72 percent, with Whitey Ford and Bob Gibson at 76 percent. Where are our young heroes: Pedro, Maddux, and Seaver? When they got old, they allowed runs at 86 percent to 88 percent of the league average.

Now, let's get to it. Here is the average RA Index, by decade.

Minimum 3,000 Batters Faced, Ages 25-28

Born	No.	RA Index 25 to 28	RA Index 29 to 32	RA Index 33 onward
1922 to 1931	26	88.4%	96.4%	93.6%
1932 to 1941	38	92.8%	94.6%	95.3%
1942 to 1951	63	91.8%	96.5%	96.9%
1952 to 1961	36	94.9%	99.0%	106.0%
1962 to 1971	38	88.1%	90.2%	90.0%

Here we see something interesting. The babying of the pitchers in the Clemens/Maddux era leads to the best performance for the young pitchers, at 88.1% runs allowed of the league average. And those pitchers (who managed to survive) did get slightly worse in the years that followed, with a 2 percentage point increase. The Drysdale era (1932-1941) showed a similar 2 percentage point increase in RA Index. However, we see in the Ryan era that pitchers' RA Index increased by 5 percentage points. So, while they were able to pitch far more, they were also a bit less effective in doing so. The Dave Stieb-led era was a mess. Even though they worked at normal capacity compared to the Drysdale and Robin Roberts eras, their performance took a nose dive from age 33 onwards. The only pitchers of the 1952-1961 decade to allow runs at 95 percent of the league average or better were Eck, Stieb, Jimmy Key, and Frank Viola. That's it. It was an enormous collapse.

Note that we have survivor bias. The only pitchers left in the age 33 and older group are those good enough or strong enough to last that long. As an example, if we look at the RA Index for pitchers ages 29 to 32 for those in the Ryan-era, the average was 96.5 percent, if weighted by innings, but it's 100 percent if we take the simple average. And for those age 33 and older, the median is 110 percent of the league average. As you can see, the jump in runs allowed from each age class is roughly 10 percentage points, which certainly sounds better than the fairly flat numbers we see in the chart above.

What's a manager to do? Let's presume that the two choices we have are the Ryan era type of pitcher handling and the Clemens/Maddux era type of pitcher handling. In the Ryan era, a top 20 starter faced 1,100 batters a year, and gave up runs at 92 percent of league average. In the Clemens/Maddux era, an equivalent starter faced 900 batters and gave up runs at 88 percent of league average. Which is better?

Facing 1,100 batters means having around 28 decisions. When you give up runs at 92 percent of league average, your win percentage is around .540. So, a .540 record on 28 decisions sets your won-loss record to 15-13.

Facing 900 batters means having around 23 decisions. When you give up runs at 88 percent of league average, your win percent is around .560. So, a .560 record on 23 decisions sets your won-loss record to 13-10.

This is the likely choice facing the manager: Do you want a 13-10 pitcher or a 15-13 pitcher? In order to get those two extra wins, can you live with three extra losses?

That's for the 25-28 age group. When you move to the 29-32 age group, the net effect is to choose between a 10-10 pitcher, or a 9-8 pitcher. That is, to get one extra win, you have to take two extra losses.

Overall, for the age 25-32 eight-year time period, the Ryan era usage gives you 102 wins and 93 losses, while the Clemens/Maddux era usage gives you 90 wins and 75 losses. That's 12 more wins in the Ryan era, with 18 more losses, or a win percentage of .400. For those of you familiar with the concept of replacement level, you will realize that this is a wash! That is, in order to give the Clemens/Maddux-era pitchers such little workload, you then have to overuse your No. 5 and No. 6 starters. Those guys will be pretty close to be .400 pitchers. In the end, you end up at the same spot.

This becomes the balancing act that managers face. If you allow a pitcher to pace himself, like the pre-Clemens/Maddux-era pitchers were more inclined to do, then they can pitch longer, but less effectively. If you want your pitcher to throw harder every pitch, then you have to pitch them less (and they'll be more effective on a pitch-for-pitch level). If you try something in between, like the Stieb-led era, you risk losing on both ends.

In the current era, where home runs are a big weapon, a pitcher pacing is not much of an option. So, the conditions of the era really force the manager's hand. And, he seems to be deploying his starters as effectively as possible. It's either we continue with the careful handling as is happening, or we go back to the all-out era of Ryan's time. Both have worked.

The Red Sox own my arm. They can do what they want with it.

-Pedro Martinez, early on in his six-year contract

Appendix: Stats for All Pitchers in the Study

Birth Class	Pitcher	Born	Batters Faced	Batters Faced Next 4 years	Batters Faced Rest of Career	RA Index 25 to 28	RA Index 29 to 32	RA Index 33 onward
1922	Roberts, Robin	1926	5,327	4,633	6,449	68%	96%	96%
1922	Friend, Bob	1930	4,422	4,230	3,571	88%	89%	92%
1922	Lary, Frank	1930	4,363	3,569	1,158	83%	97%	104%
1922	Kellner, Alex	1924	3,991	2,745	1,180	110%	111%	95%
1922	Antonelli, Johnny	1930	3,976	1,906	0	85%	93%	
1922	Brewer, Tom	1931	3,971	1,020	0	96%	121%	
1922	Sullivan, Frank	1930	3,945	2,376	49	83%	115%	140%
1922	Pierce, Billy	1927	3,809	4,145	2,849	69%	79%	89%
1922	Erskine, Carl	1926	3,793	2,308	117	90%	100%	191%
1922	Rush, Bob	1925	3,788	3,830	1,161	96%	90%	86%
1922	Ford, Whitey	1928	3,702	3,085	5,784	68%	74%	76%
1922	Garver, Ned	1925	3,687	2,683	2,356	92%	94%	100%
1922	Parnell, Mel	1922	3,458	3,295	794	80%	89%	126%
1922	Turley, Bob	1930	3,432	2,055	575	79%	104%	118%
1922	Stobbs, Chuck	1929	3,395	1,535	0	114%	113%	
1922	Shantz, Bobby	1925	3,366	1,701	2,441	87%	93%	79%
1922	Simmons, Curt	1929	3,364	2,257	4,458	93%	94%	103%
1922	Gray, Ted	1924	3,331	1,209	0	99%	135%	

Birth Class	Pitcher	Born	Batters Faced	Batters Faced Next 4 years	Batters Faced Rest of Career	RA Index 25 to 28	RA Index 29 to 32	RA Index 33 onward
1922	Law, Vern	1930	3,286	3,025	3,131	101%	82%	100%
1922	Bunning, Jim	1931	3,286	4,288	7,803	85%	87%	87%
1922	Nuxhall, Joe	1928	3,281	2,559	3,576	93%	109%	98%
1922	Foytack, Paul	1930	3,173	2,791	391	88%	114%	139%
1922	Jackson, Larry	1931	3,154	4,253	5,411	88%	92%	96%
1922	Blackwell, Ewell	1922	3,122	1,617	18	79%	104%	151%
1922	Houtteman, Art	1927	3,052	296	0	107%	187%	
1922	Meyer, Russ	1923	3,009	2,895	403	94%	101%	139%
1932	Drysdale, Don	1936	4,866	4,502	267	78%	83%	120%
1932	Marichal, Juan	1937	4,613	4,502	4,024	73%	75%	107%
1932	Stottlemyre, Mel	1941	4,472	4,437	485	88%	89%	105%
1932	Osteen, Claude	1939	4,431	4,500	3,619	86%	91%	95%
1932	Kaat, Jim	1938	4,115	3,974	8,698	98%	102%	99%
1932	Monbouquette, Bill	1936	4,090	2,346	0	95%	112%	
1932	Fisher, Jack	1939	3,957	1,252	0	115%	121%	
1932	Ramos, Pedro	1935	3,904	1,440	364	97%	113%	142%
1932	Koufax, Sandy	1935	3,775	3,441	0	75%	53%	
1932	Chance, Dean	1941	3,760	1,093	0	94%	113%	
1932	Pascual, Camilo	1934	3,732	3,253	1,944	80%	94%	109%
1932	Cardwell, Don	1935	3,709	1,994	1,605	106%	105%	108%
1932	Perry, Jim	1935	3,673	2,249	7,195	102%	82%	95%
1932	Pappas, Milt	1939	3,666	3,219	1,486	91%	97%	97%
1932	Maloney, Jim	1940	3,664	986	0	87%	101%	
1932	Broglio, Ernie	1935	3,650	1,255	0	85%	137%	
1932	Lolich, Mickey	1940	3,634	5,212	4,725	104%	86%	102%
1932	Kralick, Jack	1935	3,575	1,493	0	87%	110%	
1932	Short, Chris	1937	3,533	3,083	2,044	79%	89%	109%
1932	Terry, Ralph	1936	3,515	1,053	0	86%	111%	
1932	Jay, Joey	1935	3,511	1,871	0	94%	111%	
1932	O'Toole, Jim	1937	3,467	839	0	97%	99%	
1932	Ellsworth, Dick	1940	3,459	965	0	116%	113%	
1932	Podres, Johnny	1932	3,447	2,716	1,565	85%	97%	103%
1932	Gibson, Bob	1935	3,370	4,246	8,119	93%	79%	76%
1932	Grant, Mudcat	1935	3,355	3,511	1,845	102%	103%	84%
1932	Tiant, Luis	1940	3,299	2,515	8,039	79%	96%	91%
1932	Barber, Steve	1938	3,209	1,837	1,096	84%	128%	108%
1932	Shaw, Bob	1933	3,176	2,976	1,389	95%	79%	125%
1932	Kline, Ron	1932	3,176	1,771	1,840	106%	96%	93%
1932	Lemaster, Denny	1939	3,173	2,956	93	105%	94%	200%
1932	O'Dell, Billy	1932	3,172	3,054	1,316	79%	98%	95%
1932	Ortega, Phil	1939	3,145	565	0	107%	175%	
1932	Sadecki, Ray	1940	3,141	2,181	1,497	114%	97%	105%
1932	Cloninger, Tony	1940	3,136	2,023	0	113%	117%	
1932	Pizarro, Juan	1937	3,135	1,792	991	82%	115%	112%
1932	Perry, Gaylord	1938	3,055	5,018	13,685	92%	81%	88%
1932	Jarvis, Pat	1941	3,002	2,339	0	97%	101%	

Birth Class	Pitcher	Born	Batters Faced	Batters Faced Next 4 years	Batters Faced Rest of Career	RA Index 25 to 28	RA Index 29 to 32	RA Index 33 onward
1942	Jenkins, Fergie	1942	4,927	4,899	7,776	83%	88%	95%
1942	Ryan, Nolan	1947	4,765	4,413	11,171	80%	86%	88%
1942	Palmer, Jim	1945	4,706	4,563	4,666	69%	69%	86%
1942	Blue, Vida	1949	4,701	3,510	2,392	84%	92%	104%
1942	Carlton, Steve	1944	4,576	4,583	10,441	78%	95%	92%
1942	Coleman, Joe	1947	4,541	1,643	0	110%	109%	
1942	Hunter, Catfish	1946	4,537	3,589	460	76%	87%	124%
1942	McDowell, Sam	1942	4,535	2,492	149	87%	109%	69%
1942	Leonard, Dennis	1951	4,442	2,858	828	90%	96%	105%
1942	Seaver, Tom	1944	4,425	4,297	8,530	65%	66%	88%
1942	Richard, J.R.	1950	4,354	1,613	0	86%	69%	
1942	Holtzman, Ken	1945	4,324	3,547	857	90%	99%	135%
1942	Rogers, Steve	1949	4,311	3,706	3,158	95%	80%	90%
1942	Stoneman, Bill	1944	4,266	740	0	102%	165%	
1942	Wise, Rick	1945	4,257	2,773	2,961	94%	102%	102%
1942	Sutton, Don	1945	4,235	4,251	9,194	76%	81%	91%
1942	Blyleven, Bert	1951	4,189	2,300	7,469	81%	94%	93%
1942	Reuschel, Rick	1949	4,176	3,762	5,420	98%	93%	89%
1942	Slaton, Jim	1950	4,150	1,956	2,354	104%	92%	112%
1942	Jones, Randy	1950	4,075	2,503	0	86%	115%	
1942	Goltz, Dave	1949	4,068	3,032	683	95%	93%	124%
1942	Medich, Doc	1948	4,044	3,010	1,413	89%	103%	102%
1942	Bahnsen, Stan	1944	4,001	3,499	2,041	99%	106%	106%
1942	Barr, Jim	1948	3,985	2,838	915	87%	105%	100%
1942	Burris, Ray	1950	3,913	2,153	2,749	112%	119%	101%
1942	Drago, Dick	1945	3,890	1,657	1,504	97%	94%	94%
1942	Reuss, Jerry	1949	3,883	2,588	5,554	94%	90%	104%
1942	McNally, Dave	1942	3,855	4,034	358	85%	85%	141%
1942	Matlack, Jon	1950	3,807	2,409	330	88%	98%	117%
1942	John, Tommy	1943	3,797	2,270	10,751	93%	82%	93%
1942	Wilson, Don	1945	3,788	875	0	83%	85%	
1942	Montefusco, John	1950	3,755	2,176	873	90%	108%	89%
1942	Hooton, Burt	1950	3,713	2,817	1,693	78%	89%	111%
1942	Peterson, Fritz	1942	3,705	3,636	882	89%	104%	114%
1942	Forsch, Bob	1950	3,698	3,235	4,374	101%	97%	111%
1942	Messersmith, Andy	1945	3,670	3,749	372	85%	76%	138%
1942	Bonham, Bill	1948	3,620	2,347	0	113%	101%	
1942	Flanagan, Mike	1951	3,577	3,066	4,999	88%	94%	99%
1942	Splittorff, Paul	1946	3,563	3,412	3,803	104%	96%	107%
1942	Merritt, Jim	1943	3,480	896	0	108%	104%	
1942	Bosman, Dick	1944	3,443	2,237	0	93%	117%	
1942	Grimsley, Ross	1950	3,391	1,473	0	96%	147%	
1942	Tidrow, Dick	1947	3,361	2,312	1,739	107%	86%	110%
1942	Halicki, Ed	1950	3,344	825	0	92%	135%	
1942	Cleveland, Reggie	1948	3,342	2,042	274	103%	104%	140%
1942	Phoebus, Tom	1942	3,312	981	0	94%	116%	

Birth Class	Pitcher	Born	Batters Faced	Batters Faced Next 4 years	Batters Faced Rest of Career	RA Index 25 to 28	RA Index 29 to 32	RA Index 33 onward
1942	May, Rudy	1944	3,297	3,179	3,881	96%	100%	89%
1942	Ellis, Dock	1945	3,272	3,136	1,227	89%	94%	132%
1942	Singer, Bill	1944	3,262	3,591	288	90%	102%	179%
1942	McGlothlin, Jim	1943	3,252	1,008	0	94%	130%	
1942	Alexander, Doyle	1950	3,190	2,428	6,503	87%	110%	91%
1942	Ruthven, Dick	1951	3,163	3,216	1,001	103%	116%	131%
1942	Lee, Bill	1946	3,160	2,844	1,868	85%	110%	100%
1942	Blass, Steve	1942	3,157	2,503	0	102%	105%	
1942	Rau, Doug	1948	3,124	2,015	45	83%	94%	213%
1942	Pattin, Marty	1943	3,062	3,228	2,211	98%	102%	92%
1942	Krausse, Lew	1943	3,051	582	0	109%	145%	
1942	Renko, Steve	1944	3,039	3,497	4,168	113%	102%	101%
1942	Morton, Carl	1944	3,034	4,079	0	108%	98%	
1942	Briles, Nelson	1943	3,028	2,605	1,588	107%	97%	102%
1942	Curtis, John	1948	3,017	1,937	1,370	103%	109%	117%
1942	Brett, Ken	1948	3,016	1,692	144	91%	105%	109%
1942	Koosman, Jerry	1942	3,004	3,575	9,417	74%	91%	95%
1952	Stieb, Dave	1957	4,500	3,402	1,855	72%	93%	93%
1952	Witt, Mike	1960	4,265	1,461	183	89%	114%	120%
1952	Morris, Jack	1955	4,183	4,285	6,188	89%	80%	110%
1952	Viola, Frank	1960	4,180	4,077	1,137	85%	89%	94%
1952	Moore, Mike	1959	4,118	3,643	3,235	103%	87%	120%
1952	Valenzuela, Fernando	1960	3,953	1,788	2,505	89%	114%	104%
1952	Browning, Tom	1960	3,891	3,357	723	102%	106%	107%
1952	Darling, Ron	1960	3,872	3,169	1,959	89%	107%	111%
1952	Langston, Mark	1960	3,864	3,920	3,813	100%	88%	95%
1952	Soto, Mario	1956	3,835	2,021	0	83%	109%	
1952	Gross, Kevin	1961	3,774	2,969	2,191	107%	104%	103%
1952	Langford, Rick	1952	3,741	1,984	498	93%	107%	124%
1952	Clancy, Jim	1955	3,686	3,414	2,202	99%	93%	129%
1952	Gullickson, Bill	1959	3,588	1,800	2,139	100%	103%	114%
1952	Petry, Dan	1958	3,565	2,110	454	92%	117%	139%
1952	Hurst, Bruce	1958	3,555	3,816	2,047	94%	87%	101%
1952	Barker, Len	1955	3,509	1,061	0	105%	123%	
1952	Waits, Rick	1952	3,475	1,629	220	98%	121%	154%
1952	Key, Jimmy	1961	3,429	3,361	2,788	80%	82%	82%
1952	Eckersley, Dennis	1954	3,411	3,245	3,136	91%	106%	69%
1952	Cox, Danny	1959	3,402	794	916	93%	116%	103%
1952	Terrell, Walt	1958	3,388	3,519	1,565	98%	109%	115%
1952	McGregor, Scott	1954	3,364	3,664	475	89%	97%	157%
1952	Bannister, Floyd	1955	3,364	3,491	1,416	90%	100%	114%
1952	Vuckovich, Pete	1952	3,327	1,660	650	89%	89%	124%
1952	Hawkins, Andy	1960	3,280	1,999	0	101%	128%	
1952	Knepper, Bob	1954	3,256	3,890	2,466	108%	95%	122%
1952	Leal, Luis	1957	3,225	0	0	100%		
1952	Sorensen, Lary	1955	3,208	1,389	78	108%	127%	181%

Birth Class	Pitcher	Born	Batters Faced	Batters Faced Next 4 years	Batters Faced Rest of Career	RA Index 25 to 28	RA Index 29 to 32	RA Index 33 onward
1952	Sutcliffe, Rick	1956	3,175	3,283	3,557	95%	97%	115%
1952	Welch, Bob	1956	3,165	3,717	4,397	90%	80%	98%
1952	Smith, Zane	1960	3,164	2,976	1,850	111%	92%	105%
1952	McCatty, Steve	1954	3,112	1,901	0	90%	109%	
1952	Boyd, Oil Can	1959	3,027	2,354	0	97%	102%	
1952	Keough, Matt	1955	3,022	315	0	106%	106%	
1952	Dotson, Richard	1959	3,022	1,579	0	102%	127%	
1962	Clemens, Roger	1962	4,184	3,566	10,511	68%	73%	72%
1962	Maddux, Greg	1966	3,969	3,643	8,904	65%	53%	86%
1962	McDowell, Jack	1966	3,929	2,288	93	76%	97%	152%
1962	Brown, Kevin	1965	3,800	3,348	5,467	95%	72%	72%
1962	Cone, David	1963	3,672	3,759	4,225	84%	73%	85%
1962	Hentgen, Pat	1968	3,667	3,595	1,404	84%	95%	104%
1962	Glavine, Tom	1966	3,653	3,720	8,454	80%	69%	86%
1962	Martinez, Pedro	1971	3,634	2,809	2,917	61%	48%	86%
1962	Gubicza, Mark	1962	3,616	2,106	1,440	82%	108%	92%
1962	Swindell, Greg	1965	3,568	1,979	1,321	96%	104%	79%
1962	Hamilton, Joey	1970	3,547	1,762	57	94%	122%	273%
1962	Fernandez, Alex	1969	3,545	812	0	79%	79%	
1962	Drabek, Doug	1962	3,513	3,646	2,798	83%	81%	118%
1962	Rijo, Jose	1965	3,491	1,028	420	68%	85%	114%
1962	Karl, Scott	1971	3,472	424	0	103%	154%	
1962	Benes, Andy	1967	3,455	3,555	1,636	97%	91%	114%
1962	Erickson, Scott	1968	3,434	3,465	1,161	107%	95%	133%
1962	Smoltz, John	1967	3,425	3,465	3,980	85%	70%	68%
1962	Hanson, Erik	1965	3,415	2,339	243	92%	101%	123%
1962	Trachsel, Steve	1970	3,339	3,243	3,527	101%	102%	103%
1962	Stottlemyre, Todd	1965	3,328	3,230	1,895	105%	90%	97%
1962	Mussina, Mike	1968	3,326	3,569	6,392	80%	73%	86%
1962	Abbott, Jim	1967	3,314	1,182	0	88%	144%	
1962	Appier, Kevin	1967	3,290	2,841	3,056	67%	84%	93%
1962	Jones, Bobby	1970	3,275	2,283	0	95%	120%	
1962	Alvarez, Wilson	1970	3,235	1,042	985	89%	103%	79%
1962	Martinez, Ramon	1968	3,227	1,682	77	88%	99%	181%
1962	Hitchcock, Sterling	1971	3,213	1,191	91	102%	114%	135%
1962	Navarro, Jaime	1967	3,207	3,514	174	99%	123%	229%
1962	Baldwin, James	1971	3,196	2,253	274	104%	103%	115%
1962	Bosio, Chris	1963	3,132	2,927	278	86%	94%	120%
1962	Gooden, Dwight	1964	3,132	1,804	2,051	95%	97%	104%
1962	Witt, Bobby	1964	3,084	3,219	2,550	114%	102%	119%
1962	Harnisch, Pete	1966	3,074	2,341	1,567	88%	94%	94%
1962	Fernandez, Sid	1962	3,034	2,005	685	87%	80%	92%
1962	Jackson, Danny	1962	3,033	2,904	942	98%	105%	155%
1962	Finley, Chuck	1962	3,025	3,679	6,736	82%	89%	90%
1962	Hibbard, Greg	1964	3,013	1,192	0	96%	122%	

Relievers Yesterday And Today

by Sean Smith

Sept. 13, 2008, Anaheim, Calif. – The Angels lead the Seattle Mariners 5-2 in the top of the ninth inning. Francisco Rodriguez enters the game in search of his 58th save. He has a little trouble, allowing the first two men reach base. With one out and runners on second and third he strikes out Wladimir Balentien and Raul Ibanez to end the game. Rodriguez breaks Bobby Thigpen's record to become the major league's single-season saves leader.

Rodriguez recorded 58 saves while pitching in 76 games, working only 68.1 innings. The modern day closer pitches only one inning (if that), almost always in save situations. It wasn't always this way.

In the early years of professional baseball, pitchers were expected to complete what they started. As time went on, relief pitching, especially in tight, late-game situations, was something ace starters did between starts. In 1930, for instance, Lefty Grove led the American League in wins with 28 and in saves with nine. Eventually, the role of the relief specialist became a part of the game.

Firpo Marberry, pitching in the late 1920s, and Clint Brown, in the late 1930s, had a few seasons that would have fit right in with the relief usage of the 1950s or 1960s, but it wasn't until after World War II that the relief ace became common. By a happy coincidence, the rise of the relief ace occurred during a time we currently call the "Retrosheet era" (1953 to the present), which means that we have detailed play-by-play information for virtually the entire reliever revolution.

During the Retrosheet era, the relief ace has increasingly pitched less often and for shorter duration, specialized in more important situations, and pitched more effectively in the relatively fewer situations he was called on to pitch.

The question at hand is: Has this been a good thing? Has the evolution of the reliever and the ace been a benefit to their teams? I am going to take advantage of the Retrosheet era data and use two sophisticated baseball statistics—Wins Above Replacement and Win Probability Added—to answer our question.

Allow me to start with a couple of case studies, two very similar relievers who pitched in very different times.

Radatz And Gagne

Dick Radatz and Eric Gagne shined for only brief moments as bullpen stars, 40 years apart. Both had three consecutive great seasons after failing to impress as starting pitchers. Both hold strikeout records that are reflective of the era in which they pitched.

Called "The Monster," Radatz stood 6-foot-5, 235 pounds. The 1964 season was his third in the majors, his third of dominant relief, and his best. He pitched 157 innings, struck out 181, saved 29 games and won 16. It was also his last truly dominant year.

Radatz's 181 strikeouts in 1964 are a single-season record for a relief pitcher. This is a record that will stand unless the game changes drastically. It is almost impossible for a modern relief pitcher, throwing as few innings as they do, to come anywhere close to that record. Troy Percival was a full-time closer from 1999 to 2004, and would not have broken that record even if every single one of his outs had been a strikeout. Brad Lidge came closest in recent years, striking out 157 in 94 innings during the 2004 season (and 20 more in the playoffs). But he still finished 27 short.

Radatz had decent numbers in the minor leagues in 1960, mostly as a starter. He went 12-4 with a 3.69 ERA in two leagues. That ERA was about 10 points better than his league's average. From Radatz's own words on the matter: "When Johnny Pesky first told me I was going to the bullpen, I was shocked. I felt I was being pushed aside—that I had gone down in the organization's estimation[1]."

Of the eight pitchers with the most starts on the Triple-A Minneapolis team, he had the sixth-best ERA. While I don't know for sure what they were thinking back then, it appears that he was moved to the bullpen because the team did not expect him to make it as a major league starter, or felt that it had better options. The move worked immediately. The following season, Radatz pitched entirely in relief in the minors, posting a 2.28 ERA and allowing only 50 hits in 71 minor league innings.

Radatz made the big league roster in 1962 and immediately became one of the most dominant relievers the game had seen. He didn't even allow a run in April. Radatz dominated for three seasons, but his 1965 performance was not quite as good due to a shoulder injury. He never recovered his form.

Another interesting item from the March 1964 article is this quote: "It's my job to walk out there and save ballgames. There isn't a greater challenge in the game." While the save didn't become an official statistic until 1969, Jerome Holtzman invented the statistic in 1960 and kept track of it in his *Sporting News* columns. Whether Radatz paid attention to the save statistic or not, saving ballgames was how he defined his job.

Forty years later, Eric Gagne was considered a top prospect as a starter. From 1998 to 2001 he was exclusively a starter in the minor leagues, with more than three times as many strikeouts as walks. He even made it to the big leagues as a starter before the Dodgers decided to try him in a different role.

In the 2000 and 2001 seasons, Gagne made 43 major league starts with a 10-13 record and a 4.91 ERA. He struck out his share of hitters, but his biggest problem was allowing too many home runs (44 in 253 innings). Moved to the bullpen in 2002, Gagne found a home.

From 2002 to 2004, he pitched exactly 82.1 innings each year, saved 152 games in total, struck out 13.3 batters per nine innings, and won a Cy Young award. Gagne was hurt in 2005 and never regained his effectiveness (despite pitching well for Texas in the first half of 2007, he wasn't the dominant pitcher he had been).

Gagne holds a strikeout record of his own. In 2003 he struck out 14.98 batters per nine innings, and 45 percent of the batters he faced. Both are records for pitchers with at least 50 innings pitched, though I would not put either record in the same unbreakable category as Radatz's 181 strikeouts, given current reliever workloads.

Wins Above Replacement

Wins above replacement, or WAR (as calculated by baseballprojection.com), is primarily a context-neutral way to measure the impact of pitcher seasons. It is based on the pitcher's runs allowed compared to what a replacement level pitcher would allow, given that pitcher's innings pitched and situation.

For starting pitchers, allowing 25 percent more runs than the league average is considered replacement level. Relief pitchers, however, are compared to a stricter replacement level, just 5 percent worse than league average, because a starting pitcher has a tougher job than a relief pitcher.

A starter normally has to face a lineup at least three times, and has to pace himself to some extent in order to be able to throw 100 or more pitches. A reliever can throw with maximum effort, knowing he has to pitch to only a few batters, and rarely more than two innings these days. You can see the difference in the data.

Pitchers who have pitched in both roles (such as Dennis Eckersley or John Smoltz) have historically pitched better as relievers. From 1993 to 2008, pitchers in dual roles struck out 15 percent more batters in relief, allowed 13 percent fewer home runs and allowed slightly fewer hits on balls in play. They walked batters at about the same rate in both roles. I checked all the earlier seasons in the Retrosheet data and found that these starter/reliever differences have been relatively consistent since 1953.

Back to WAR: The estimate of runs relative to replacement level is adjusted for the pitcher's ballpark. It is then adjusted for the quality of opponents he faced—in 2009 you would expect a pitcher to allow more runs facing the Yankees than when facing the Royals, and with unbalanced schedules things don't always even out over the season.

Another adjustment is for defensive support. If a pitcher pitched in front of a poor defense, he should be expected to allow a few more runs. After all of these adjustments, the total runs above replacement are converted to wins. Typically, 10 runs converts to a win, but the exact number is dependent on the pitcher's run environment.

Finally, WAR accounts for pitcher leverage. Leverage Index, invented by Tom Tango, is a measure of the criticality of a situation. Starting pitchers and position players pitch or hit in a mix of varying game situations. Their leverage over the course of a season will be very close to 1.0 (in other words, average).

On the other hand, the job of a relief specialist is to pitch only in those situations in which runs have a high impact on wins and losses. A relief ace typically will have a Leverage Index of 1.6 to 2.0, and I believe it is necessary to factor this into any estimation of his value.

In the WAR calculation however, I do not give a pitcher credit for the entire leverage he faced, but instead half of the leverage above 1.0. This is because the relief ace's innings will not be filled in with a replacement level (i.e., the first guy up from Triple-A) pitcher. Instead, the setup man will take over the closer role, moving from a 1.5 leverage to a 2.0, and the No. 3 guy in the pen will take over the setup man's innings, and so on. Giving a reliever half credit for the leverage above one very closely approximates the overall impact of this "chaining" replacement.

Another way to look at it is this: Part of that extra leverage comes from a team's decision to use the pitcher in those situations, and part of it comes from the pitcher's talent, which is best suited for the most important game situations. In a very simplistic example, is a team better off with (1) two relief pitchers with 4.00 ERAs, or (2) one with a 2.50 and another with a 5.50? (Assume you can't replace them and have to give them equal innings.) The answer is certainly (2), since you can use the 2.50 pitcher to win close games and use the other guy in a mop-up role or to finish blowouts. Both teams will allow the same number of runs over the season, but the team with a star and scrub will win more games than the one with two average Joes.

By WAR, here are the 12 best relief seasons since 1953:

Wins above replacement, 1953 to 2008

Pitcher	WAR
1. Rich Gossage, 1975	7.0
2. John Hiller, 1973	6.9
3. Mark Eichhorn, 1986	6.4
4. Bruce Sutter, 1977	6.3
5. Doug Corbett, 1980	5.9
6. Ted Abernathy, 1967	5.8
6. Rich Gossage, 1977	5.8
8. Greg Minton, 1982	5.7
9. Mariano Rivera, 1996	5.4
10. Sid Monge, 1979	5.3
10. Dan Quisenberry, 1983	5.3
12. Dick Radatz, 1964	5.2

Of the top 12 seasons, only one (Rivera's amazing 1996) was posted during the last two decades. The key reason these pitchers added so much more value than today's pitchers is that they simply pitched a lot more. Every one of the "old-timers" on the list pitched at least 100 innings, and they averaged around 130.

Gossage, now in the Hall of Fame, probably had the best career of any relief pitcher before Rivera—he's the only one with two spots on the top 12. John Hiller saved 38 games in 1973, a record that stood for a decade until Dan Quisenberry broke it.

Eichhorn and Rivera made the list for seasons in which they did not pitch as closers (John Wetteland was still the Yankees closer in 1996). Eichhorn, a submariner, was only five innings short of qualifying for the ERA title in 1986, his rookie season, while winning 14 games and striking out 166. He had other good years, but would never come close to his 1986 level of dominance. In 1996, Rivera pitched 27 more innings than he ever would again once he became the closer, and added 14 more (with one run allowed) during that year's championship run.

Radatz has the earliest season on the top dozen list, 1964. He was over four wins above replacement during his 1962 and 1963 seasons as well. Gagne's best season by WAR was 4.3 in 2003.

Win Probability Added

Another stat used to measure the impact of relief pitching is WPA, Win Probability Added, as published by Fangraphs. WPA looks at the probability that a team will win the game given the inning, number of outs, base runners and run environment. A pitcher's WPA measures how much he increases or decreases this win probability for each batting event while he's on the mound. Using WPA, the list of top 12 pitchers appears to be more evenly distributed among time periods.

By WPA (1974-2008 only)

Pitcher	WPA
1. Willie Hernandez, 1984	8.6
2. Doug Corbett, 1980	7.6
3. Dan Quisenberry, 1980	7.1
4. Goose Gossage, 1975	6.9
5. Keith Foulke, 2000	6.6
6. Troy Percival, 1996	6.5
7. Aurelio Lopez, 1979	6.2
8. J.J. Putz, 2007	6.0
9. Trevor Hoffman, 1998	5.9
10. Jose Mesa, 1995	5.8
11. Kent Tekulve, 1979	5.7
12. Bill Caudill, 1982	5.7
12. Mark Davis, 1989	5.7

Fangraphs has WPA only for 1974 to the present, so to get a sense of Radatz's WPA I looked at Jeff Sagarin's Player Win Averages (available at http://www.kiva.net/~jsagarin/mills/seasons.htm), which is essentially the same thing except for the scale. (To correct the scale, divide Sagarin's points by 2,000). Radatz logged his best WPA total in 1963, at 5.8—he had only 3.4 WPA points in 1964. Gagne contributed between 5.4 and 5.6 in each of his three big years.

There are a few seasons on both the top WPA and WAR lists, such as Gossage's 1975 and Corbett's 1980, but WPA and WAR measure different things. WAR is a semi-context neutral measure. Say a pitcher pitches in two games, the first a one-run game, and the other a 10-run blowout. He pitches a 1-2-3 inning for a save in the first, and gives up a two-run homer in the second. Another pitcher gets to pitch in the exact same situations, but blows the save with a two-run homer, and pitches a perfect inning to close out the blowout.

WAR will value the pitchers equally. Both pitched two innings, allowed two runs, and faced the same average leverage. WPA, on the other hand, will rank the first pitcher more highly since he protected a lead and gave up runs only when they had no impact on wins or losses. In other words, WPA measures clutch pitching, and WAR does not. That is the biggest reason why the two measures differ. Which you prefer depends on what you want to measure.

Dan Quisenberry's 1980 season illustrates the difference. While he pitched very well, it is only his fifth-best season by WAR, yet his best in WPA and the third best of any reliever since 1974. His ERA was 3.09–good but nowhere close to his 1.94 ERA in 1983, when he also pitched 10 more innings.

One difference between the metrics is leverage, Quiz had a career high 2.2 leverage index in 1980 and WPA gives full credit for leverage, unlike the half credit given by WAR.

Another difference is he must have pitched his best when the game was on the line, and given up a greater-than-normal share of runs in less important situations. Indeed, according to Baseball Reference, batters had a .588 OPS against Quisenberry in high-leverage situations, and .793 in low-leverage situations.

Digging deeper, Quiz did have two bad games in which he allowed a total of 10 runs. Those games add negative WPA to his total, but once you've lost it doesn't matter that much how much you lose by. He seems to have had a lot of games in which he entered in the eighth inning with runners on base, stranded them, and went on to win or save the game. Situations like that really add to WPA.

Workload

I looked at the pitchers who had the greatest relief seasons, defined as those having a season WAR of 3.0 or better. To qualify as a reliever in this study, he must relieve in 90 percent or more of his appearances. Here is the average workload, by year grouping:

Year grouping	Games	Innings
1954-1969	64	116
1970-1974	65	124
1975-1979	69	120
1980-1984	67	114
1985-1989	65	98
1990-1994	68	89
1995-1999	70	82
2000-2004	72	81
2005-2008	67	73

There has been some fluctuation in games pitched, but no clear trend. Relief aces pitch about as often now as they have for the last 50 years. However, their innings have dropped tremendously. A relief ace used to pitch two innings much of the time, though there were a number of three-or-four inning appearances mixed in too.

With starters pitching many fewer complete games and relief aces being used less often and for more specialized situations, a lot of innings are now put in the hands of inferior pitchers. The effect this has had on the game will be explored later.

Leverage

Leverage is a measure of how important game situations seem, at that particular time, in terms of the impact hits and outs would have on the win expectancy of the game. Leverage was developed by Tom Tango from Insidethebook.com, and used by my site, baseballprojection.com, in the evaluation of pitcher value. An average leverage value is 1.0, and almost all starting pitchers average around 1.0 in a full season.

A relief pitcher pitching the most important innings, such as protecting ninth-inning leads, may post a Leverage Index of 2.0 or more. Relief pitchers used in mop-up roles will have the lowest leveraged innings, with middle relievers somewhere in between. In recent

The Stats of Gagne and Radatz

Eric Gagne

Year	G	IP	Wins	Saves	ERA	ERA+	Lev	WAR	WPA
2002	77	82.3	4	52	1.97	192	1.9	3.2	5.4
2003	77	82.3	2	55	1.20	335	1.9	4.3	5.6
2004	70	82.3	7	45	2.19	187	1.9	2.5	5.5
3 year total								10.0	16.5

Dick Radatz

Year	G	IP	Wins	Saves	ERA	ERA+	Lev	WAR	WPA
1962	62	124.7	9	24	2.24	184	1.6	4.4	2.8
1963	66	132.3	15	25	1.97	191	1.7	4.7	5.8
1964	79	157	16	29	2.29	168	1.7	5.2	3.4
3 year total								14.3	12.0

years some eighth-inning setup men have had leverage indices that approach those of closers. Scot Shields had a Leverage Index of 2.0 in 2005, and at least 1.6 each year from 2005 to 2008.

A pitcher's Leverage Index changes with every out recorded, baserunner allowed or run scored. Here are some examples of what Leverage Index would be in certain situations, assuming a run environment of 4.5 runs, from the perspective of the home team taking the mound:

- Seventh inning, tie game, start of inning: 1.54
- Eighth inning, tie game, start of inning: 1.85
- Eighth inning, one-run lead, start of inning: 2.16
- Ninth inning, tie game, start of inning: 2.32
- Ninth inning, one-run lead, start of inning: 2.87
- Ninth inning, three-run lead, start of inning: 0.75

Let's look at the workload table again, adding in the Leverage Index of the top relievers:

Relievers with 3.0 WAR seasons, 1954-2008

Year grouping	Games	Innings	Leverage
1954-1969	64	116	1.58
1970-1974	65	124	1.64
1975-1979	69	120	1.73
1980-1984	67	114	1.73
1985-1989	65	98	1.81
1990-1994	68	89	1.75
1995-1999	70	82	1.81
2000-2004	72	81	1.74
2005-2008	67	73	1.77

Looking at the most valuable relief pitchers in each era, their Leverage Index has increased slightly over time. Relief aces are better leveraged than they were before 1975, but there has been no recognizable trend since. The key difference is that ace relievers pitched more innings before 1975, and mixed more low leverage innings into their workload. There are high leverage situations in the seventh and eighth innings, to be sure, but holding other factors (score, baserunners, outs) equal, the ninth inning always will be the inning with the highest leverage.

Using these stats to compare Gagne and Radatz (see the top of the page), both were incredibly dominant during their three-year stretch, though their usage was drastically different. While Gagne comes out ahead in WPA, Radatz comes out ahead in WAR, and if you average the two metrics, they are almost equal. The number of games the two aces pitched was similar, but Radatz pitched 50 percent more innings than Gagne in 1962, and almost twice as many in 1964. On average, Gagne did pitch in higher leverage situations.

Survival Rate

We've seen many pitchers have brief flashes of glory only to quickly fade from the scene. We've also seen pitchers from different eras last a long time, whether it's Rich Gossage, Rollie Fingers, Trevor Hoffman or Mariano Rivera. Given that a pitcher has an outstanding season in year one, defined as 3.0 WAR or higher, what are the odds that he remains at least an effective pitcher, defined as 1.0 WAR, in year two?

Time period	Pitchers	Survivors	Survival Rate
1954-1965	18	10	56%
1966-1970	14	7	50%
1971-1975	19	11	58%
1976-1980	31	19	61%
1981-1985	30	20	67%
1986-1990	28	21	75%
1991-1995	18	11	61%
1996-2000	30	22	73%
2001-2005	32	21	66%

It does appear that relief pitchers are less likely to disappear after a great season than they used to be, which should increase the chances that one is able to put together a long career. Given today's baseball economy, this may not always be to the advantage of the team, though it is obviously better for the pitcher.

It might be in a team's self-interest to work the pitcher as hard as it can, up to the point of diminishing effectiveness, before he leaves as a free agent. On the other hand, a player should want a steady, moderate workload, since that allows him to pitch for more seasons and maximize his career earnings. The presence of player agents to protest against extreme workloads (if they were to reappear), combined with the fact that no team wants to be viewed as responsible for injuring a pitcher regardless of contract status, means pitcher usage patterns predominantly favor the pitcher these days.

That's the case, at least, during the regular season. In the playoffs, the desire for a championship can push both the pitcher and the team to stretch workload limits. Rivera did this for years with no ill effects. Keith Foulke and Brad Lidge may have been worked a bit too hard during playoff runs. Coming back to Francisco Rodriguez, he holds the record with 18.2 innings in the Angels' 2002 playoff run–after appearing in only five regular-season innings.

This is a crude analysis of the effects of workload. Such studies are very difficult as you can't tell how much of a pitcher's decline is due to injury, a decrease in ability from overuse, or an age-related drop in skill that would have happened anyway. The results aren't conclusive, but suggest that lighter workloads have some positive effect on pitcher longevity.

Neither Radatz nor Gagne had a very long career. Assuming he's done, Gagne pitched 10 seasons. In the last four, he unsuccessfully tried to regain his pre-injury effectiveness. Radatz pitched for seven years, the last three ineffectively. Both had their last season at age 32, unless Gagne is planning a comeback.

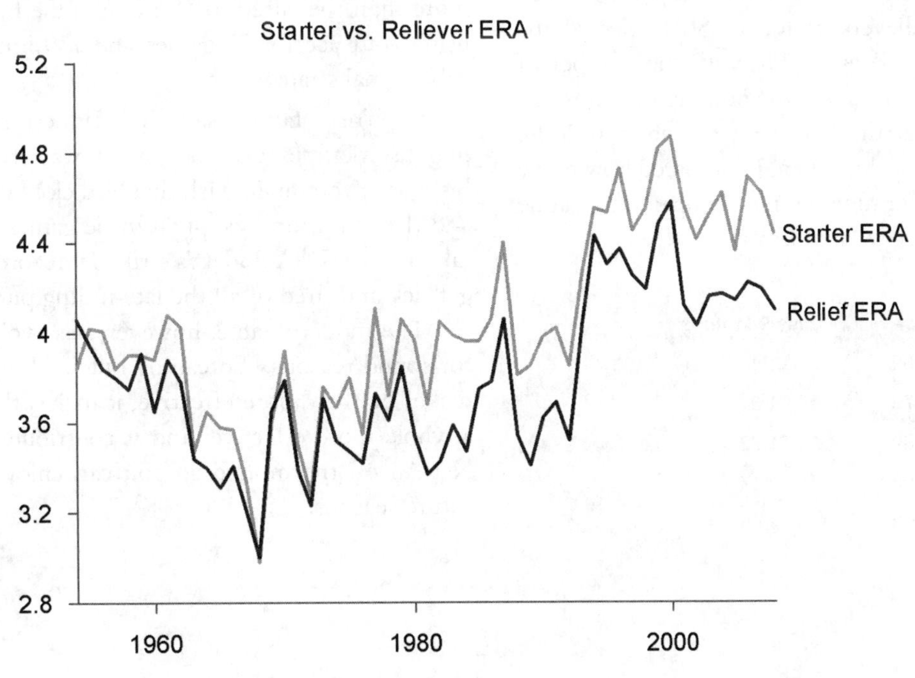

Effectiveness

Modern relief aces are more effective than ever, as judged by run rates compared to the league average. From 1954 to 1979, bullpens accounted for 26 to 30 percent of all innings pitched every year. From 1995 to 2008, bullpens pitched between 33 and 35 percent of all innings. Relief aces have pitched fewer innings, so more innings than ever before are going to middle relievers. Modern bullpens often have seven or more pitchers, compared to the four- or five-man bullpens of the past.

How have bullpens fared over time, compared to starting pitchers in the same seasons?

From 1954 to 1976, relievers as a group had ERAs 0.12 runs per nine innings better than starters. From 1977 to 2008, the relief advantage has been 0.34 runs. The graph on the previous page compares the two.

Even with more innings going to pitchers further down the bullpen hierarchy, and fewer to the pitchers considered the best, bullpen ERAs actually have improved over time relative to starting pitchers. In 1975, bullpens pitched 27 percent of total innings; a relief ace would pitch 120 of them, or roughly 30 percent of bullpen innings. Today, with bullpens handling 35 percent of innings and closers pitching only 75, the ace is responsible for only 15 percent of a bullpen's innings. This suggests that limiting workloads and/or increasing the number of times your pitchers have the platoon advantage has had beneficial effects on relief effectiveness.

Another way to look at this is to pick apart how well the league's top relievers perform. So I selected the best relievers by WAR each year, with the number of pitchers selected equal to half the number of teams. In 1960, I'm looking at the best eight relievers; in 2008, I'm looking at the top 15. Then, I compared how many runs they allowed per nine innings compared to league average. The results, by decade:

Decade	Runs+/9 Innings
1960-69	1.43
1970-79	1.51
1980-89	1.72
1990-99	2.17
2000-08	2.45

As you can see, these relief aces have improved tremendously.

And finally, instead of selecting by WAR, I selected the top pitchers on each team based on their "total leverage," which I defined as innings pitched times Leverage Index. This tells you who the manager thought was his best pitcher, regardless of the results that pitcher produced. This chart shows that over time, the most leveraged pitchers have allowed fewer runs per nine innings compared to league average, and the relative effectiveness of these pitchers has increased over time.

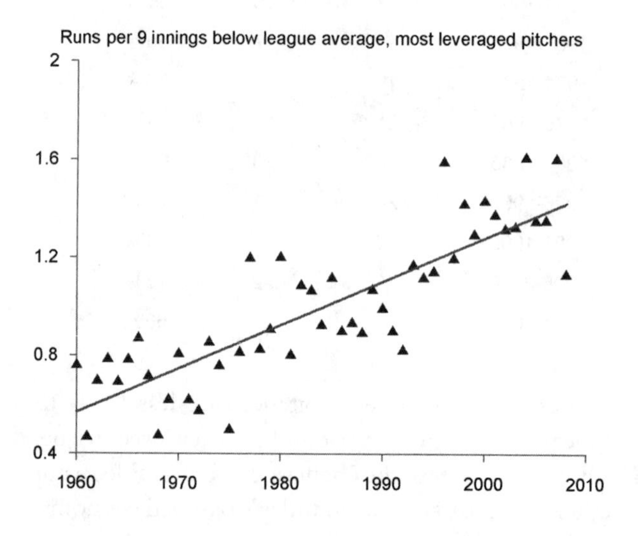

Relief aces are now more effective in the innings they pitch, bullpens as a group are more effective in the innings they pitch, and bullpens are pitching a lot more than they used to. So don't pine for the days of using your ace for 75 games and 130 innings. It is a suboptimal strategy.

If you're a fan of say, the Minnesota Twins, you might sometimes wish Joe Nathan was on the mound a bit more. You might wish that he'd close out the eighth and the ninth innings, pitch in tie games, maybe even take a run at Dick Radatz's strikeout record. You might get sick and tired of all the late-inning pitching changes. The modern game, however, has evolved this way for sound reasons. Spreading out the bullpen innings makes Nathan more effective, it makes the bullpen as a whole more effective, and it contributes to keeping Nathan on the mound so you can enjoy his work in future seasons.

A New Approach to MLE's

by Jeff Sackmann

Major league equivalencies (MLEs) are estimates of how a non-Major League player would have performed in the Major Leagues in a given period of time. For instance, we might be interested in an MLE for 1936 Josh Gibson (Negro League), 1999 Ichiro Suzuki (Japan) or 2009 Pedro Alvarez (minors). None of those players appeared in the majors in the respective season, but for a variety of reasons, it would be educational to have an idea how they would have performed.

In any of those cases, we would take the player's actual statistics, apply some algorithm based on what we know about the environment in which he played, and estimate what he would have done if he was a member of, say, the Pittsburgh Pirates. Alvarez slugged .590 in Double-A Altoona in 2009; one commonly used algorithm sees that as equivalent to a .444 mark in the big leagues.

Most techniques for generating MLEs are based around league "factors." We might say that a pitcher's strikeout rate will decrease by 19 percent if he moved from the Double-A Texas League to the National League. While the factors differ from league to league and from stat to stat, they are in one sense universal: The algorithm is the same for any player, a 19-year-old or a 26-year-old, a flamethrower or a soft-tosser.

These factors, in turn, come from careful analysis of those players who moved between leagues in a single season. For instance, in 2009, Mat Gamel split time between Triple-A and the majors. In Nashville, he reached base at a .367 rate. For Milwaukee, that number declined to .338. If that was all the information we had about the Pacific Coast League and the N.L., we could estimate that all hitters would lose about 8 percent of their OBP upon promotion.

Of course, we have a lot more data. In a single year, hundreds of players spend substantial time at more than one level. The difficulty level of each league doesn't change much from year to year, so we aren't limited to 2009 data when creating MLEs for 2009 minor leaguers. To generate these factors, we can use the experiences of hundreds of league changers and get an aggregate picture of what happens to players when they are promoted or demoted.

The Major League Curveball

One common complaint about MLEs is that they are built from a biased sample. The Triple-A players who appear in the majors are not selected at random. Clubs usually select the players who they think have the best chance at major-league success, and sometimes those evaluations are based on nonstatistical data. If MLEs are derived largely from observations of prospects and fringe major leaguers, perhaps they shouldn't be applied with much confidence to players who don't fit into one of those two categories.

In other words, MLEs treat all players equally. It is almost a truism among baseball analysts that minor leaguers are more than the sum of their stats.

It's almost certainly true that hitting in the big leagues is harder than hitting in the minors. Is it equally more difficult for all players? That's a more complicated question, and I suspect that most baseball fans would be inclined to say "no." For every Chris Coghlan who arrives ready to hit the cover off the ball, there's a Cameron Maybin who doesn't enjoy immediate success, despite solid minor-league numbers.

Much of the difference between the players who have successful transitions and those who don't could be explained by chance—after all, some rookies are bound to be lucky out of the gate, while others are doomed to be unlucky. But that explanation doesn't strike me as particularly satisfying. While chance plays a role, it seems intuitively true that some players are better-suited to major-league success than others, even if their minor-league stats are identical.

So perhaps there is something that separates the guys who will successfully move up from those who will struggle. Some of those guys get pegged as "Quad-A" players—performers who excel in the minors, but aren't good enough for the majors. If you talk to enough baseball commentators, you'll eventually hear something like "so-and-so can't hit a major league curveball" to explain why a player can't make the jump. As an explanation, it's probably overused, but again, it's more appealing than writing everything off to luck.

Quantify The Magic

Talking about something like the "major league curveball" might seem to move us into the realm of scouting. But I don't think it has to.

Let's stipulate that there is a qualitative difference between the pitchers in Triple-A and those in the bigs. Maybe it's a little extra bite on the fastball or finesse in painting the corners. Maybe it's that curveball. Perhaps you disagree that there's any such thing; that's okay, but as it turns out, making this assumption generates some interesting conclusions, some of which support the notion that this qualitative difference exists.

Whatever it is, the presence of such a quality suggests that we may be barking up the wrong tree by calculating MLEs the way we do. Hundreds of data points for 2009 Triple-A hitters come from matchups with Willie Collazo, but Collazo's last three organizations seem convinced that the 29-year-old isn't big-league material. He's about as close to the definition of "Quad-A" as you can get. So perhaps all those Collazo-influenced data points—along with those having to do with all the other Triple-A pitchers who don't have that big league stuff—shouldn't be considered if we want to know how a hitter will fare against major-league pitching.

For every Collazo, there is a pitcher in Triple-A who is viewed as major-league material. Some, like Tommy Hanson, are big-time prospects making their last stop on the way to the show; others, such as Kyle Davies, are on the line between big leaguer and bush leaguer, and they split time across levels accordingly.

In other words, when a hitter is in Triple-A, he's facing some of the same pitchers he'll face in the big leagues. Even if they aren't the exact same arms, at-bats against the likes of Hanson and Davies surely tell us something about how a player will face other major leaguers. They may not tell us much about how that hitter would handle Zack Greinke, but they get us closer.

Let me restate this in a different way. The object of an MLE is to estimate how a hitter would have performed against major-league competition. Even if he's not in the major leagues, he's facing some major-league competition (if not technically, something very close to it). If there is truly a qualitative difference between Triple-A and MLB pitching, we should be focusing much more heavily on those more relevant matchups.

Introducing pMLE

Given play-by-play data on minor leaguers, we can break down their plate appearances into two groups. The first group is made up of PAs against the Hansons and Davieses of the world—pitchers who also appeared in the big leagues. We're basically using personnel decisions as a proxy for that major-league magic. If a pitcher inspires a GM to put him on the big-league roster, he has something going for him that some of his teammates don't. Sometimes you can see it in the numbers; other times you can't.

The second group is made up of matchups against the Collazos of the world. They may have some predictive value, but again, we're using the proxy of personnel decisions. There's a reason GMs aren't recalling those pitchers, and maybe those reasons have something to do with the padded numbers that minor-league vets are able to post in Triple-A.

I call the MLEs that result from analysis of that first group pMLEs. The "p" is for "play-by-play." Let's see how it works.

Garrett Jones, a 28-year-old first baseman/outfielder for the Pirates, finally got a chance in 2009 to show that he could hit major-league pitching. He's a fascinating test case. He has languished in the high minors for years, posting the sort of big-power/high-strikeout numbers that scream "Quad-A all-star." Yet given the chance, he had a great half season in the majors. He's even more attractive as a demonstration case for pMLE since he split the 2009 season about halfway between Triple-A and the majors, giving us decent samples for both of his stops.

To steer clear of issues such as park factors, batted-ball luck and differences between defensive skill across levels, this study focuses on the most fundamental aspects of the batter-pitcher matchup: walk rate and strikeout rate. Here are three sets of rates for Jones' 2009 season: his minor-league performance, a traditional MLE based on that performance and his actual major-league performance:

Level	PA	W/PA	K/PA
AAA	299	6.0%	15.7%
MLE	299	4.7%	16.7%
MLB	358	11.2%	21.2%

The traditional MLE hints at Jones' increased strikeout rate in the bigs, though not nearly to a sufficient degree. It misses the increase in walk rate as well, which is understandable, since there's little reason to believe someone will walk more when facing better pitching. (Oddly, it turns out that Jones's situation isn't at all unique. We'll discuss some possible reasons for that later on.)

Enter pMLE. Here's how Jones's minor-league record breaks down if we separate his plate appearances against pitchers who appeared in the majors last year:

	PA	W/PA	K/PA
MLBers	176	5.7%	17.0%
Others	123	6.5%	13.8%

No surprises here. On the reasonable assumption that pitchers who spent time in the majors are better than those who didn't, it stands to reason that Jones had a tougher time against the first group. If anything, we might expect the difference in walk rate to be a bit more pronounced.

We're not done yet. We need to know more about the guys who faced Jones in those 176 PAs. If we weigh them according to major-league playing time and the number of times they faced Jones in Triple-A, we get the following composite profile:

	W/PA	K/PA
Jones guys	8.7%	14.8%
MLB average	8.9%	18.0%

While the level jumpers walked big leaguers at about the same rate as the average MLB pitcher, they struck out fewer batters. This makes sense: For every Tommy Hanson, there are several Clayton Mortensens and Jeff Grays making the jump. These are mostly fringe-level performers, and their numbers reflect that.

We're just about done, then, with walk rate. If Jones walked 5.7 percent of the time against pitchers who were roughly league average, that's equivalent to about the same rate. Strikeout rate is trickier. Given the strikeout rate of the composite level jumper, Jones's strikeout rate against them, and league average, we can use the Odds Ratio method to calculate Jones's strikeout rate against MLB average. I'll spare you the arithmetic; the formula spits out a 20.7 percent strikeout rate for Jones.

Let's revisit Jones's overall numbers and add a row for pMLE:

Level	PA	W/PA	K/PA
AAA	299	6.0%	15.7%
MLE	299	4.7%	16.7%
pMLE		**5.8%**	**20.7%**
MLB	358	11.2%	21.2%

It's just one example, but the improvement is striking. There isn't a big difference in the estimate of walk rate; as noted, that came out of left field. But Jones is a power-and-strikeouts guy—the type of player who is easy to write off as a low-rent Russell Branyan. The pMLE translation reflects the fact that, when Jones faces better stuff, his strikeouts rise quite a bit. It also puts that increase in perspective. If we had looked at these numbers in June, we could've reached the conclusion that Jones would keep his strikeout rate at a manageable level.

More Than Just Garrett?

It's all well and good that this algorithm does a better job of analyzing Jones's Triple-A performance, but the object of a translation system is to do the same thing for everybody.

Before we can test pMLE, we need a baseline for comparison purposes. We need to know how effectively traditional MLEs predict same-season major-league strikeout and walk rates.

I put together a group of the 20 players who spent the most plate appearances in both Triple-A and the minors. (The cutoff was about 175 PA at both levels.) That gives us a sample of players like Jones, Matt Tolbert, Will Venable and Travis Snider—a decent mix of bona fide prospects and fringe big leaguers.

On average, traditional MLEs predicted strikeout rates within 24 percent of the actual MLB strikeout rate and a walk rate within about 38 percent of the actual MLB walk rate. A better measure may be the median walk rate: It's within 25 percent of the MLB rate. The median isn't skewed by a few players who, like Jones, suddenly discovered how to take ball four upon promotion to the big leagues.

Interestingly, quite a few players in this sample profile like Jones: reasonably high strikeout rates in the minors and major-league strikeout rates that far exceed their MLEs. Kyle Blanks is among the more dramatic examples. His 22.5 percent strikeout rate in Triple-A traditionally translates to 24.6 percent; he struck out in 32.7 percent of his major-league plate appearances. Steve Pearce's minor-league numbers translate to a 16 percent strikeout rate; he struck out 23 percent of the time in the big leagues.

Traditional MLEs are doing a pretty good job, but there's plenty of room for improvement. pMLE appears to cover some of that ground.

The results for walk rate are unimpressive, as pMLE is roughly as accurate as the traditional method. For strikeouts, though, pMLE rates are within about 14 percent of actual MLB rates. Of the 20 players in this sample, pMLE is better than traditional MLEs for 13. Here are the five for which pMLE makes the most improvement over the traditional method (abbreviated as tMLE in the following tables):

Player	MLB K%	tMLE K%	pMLE K%
Carlos Gonzalez	22.4%	16.2%	22.3%
Andrew McCutchen	16.8%	11.9%	15.6%
Steve Pearce	23.1%	15.9%	19.5%
Will Venable	27.6%	22.3%	27.8%
Cameron Maybin	25.6%	18.5%	22.0%

Here are the five for which the traditional method proved most accurate in comparison to pMLE:

Player	MLB K%	tMLE K%	pMLE K%
Jake Fox	19.4%	17.7%	16.2%
Andy Marte	17.2%	16.9%	19.4%
Clete Thomas	24.9%	26.3%	28.7%
Tony Gwynn	14.3%	13.3%	16.8%
Daric Barton	13.1%	14.8%	15.6%

Strikeouts, Not Walks?

It would certainly be great if, as the data suggest, pMLE does a better job than the traditional method of translating Triple-A strikeouts. It's a bit of a concern, though, that pMLE doesn't make any improvement on walk rate.

One possible reason for the discrepancy is sample size. It may be that we just don't have enough data to properly tease out walk rates with an approach like this. Strikeouts are about twice as common as walks, and for the players in this sample, the ratio is closer to 2.5 to 1. We're already working with worryingly small samples—200 or so plate appearances at each of two levels for most of these players—and pMLE shrinks those totals even more by discarding some of the minor-league data.

Two other causes spring to mind. pMLE is based on the supposition that there is some fundamental difference between major-league pitchers (including has-beens and will-bes) and everybody else. That may be true, but it doesn't have to be true for all pitching skills. Plenty of guys can throw 80-mph strikes. My poster boy for "everybody else," Willie Collazo, has a very respectable career rate of 2.4 walks per nine innings. If MLB-quality walk prevention isn't limited to MLB-quality pitchers, there's no reason why pMLE would be better than the traditional method. In fact, it should be worse, since it applies the same sort of reasoning to a smaller pool of plate appearances.

A final problem may be a difference between major-league and minor-league strike zones. That such a difference exists is based largely on anecdotal data, but if it does, that would also endanger the premise of pMLE. If a Pearce-Davies matchup in Triple-A is played with different rules than a Pearce-Davies matchup in the majors, it stands to reason one couldn't accurately predict the other. This would presumably have some effect on strikeout rate, as well, but since a swing-and-a-miss is the same at any level, the effect would be smaller.

Putting pMLE To Work

Whether due to small samples or something inherent in certain types of ballplayers, we can expect that sometimes pMLE will be more accurate than a traditional MLE, and vice versa. Even if one of the algorithms "wins" a majority of the time, it doesn't mean the other is worthless.

A good comparison is to defensive evaluation. While many fielding stats attempt to measure the entirety of a player's defensive skill, sabermetricians are aware of the differences and may see one stat as more reliable for a certain type of player (or team). It is also provocative when different credible stats vary wildly in estimating the defensive value of a certain player.

The same may be true of MLEs. For those who take the time to calculate pMLEs, they may serve as a sort of red flag. For instance, in 197 Triple-A plate appearances last year, Eugenio Velez walked 13 times. Using the traditional multiplier, that suggests 10 walks, or a 5.1 percent walk rate. That's low, but not alarmingly so. In the 79 PA that pMLE uses, Velez walked only once: a 1.2 percent rate. As it turned out, Velez walked about 5 percent of the time for San Francisco, but if scouts had expressed concern that Velez's modest plate discipline couldn't stand up against top-tier competition, pMLE would confirm those doubts.

With that in mind, here are traditional translations and pMLEs for the 2009 Triple-A performances of 10 noteworthy prospects:

Player	tMLE K%	tMLE W%	pMLE K%	pMLE W%
Reid Brignac	16.7%	4.5%	18.0%	5.3%
Alcides Escobar	15.0%	4.8%	16.8%	5.5%
Jesus Guzman	18.0%	5.6%	24.1%	8.2%
Austin Jackson	24.4%	5.8%	29.7%	6.3%
Kila Ka'aihue	17.0%	13.7%	18.4%	15.9%
Matt LaPorta	16.0%	7.9%	17.6%	8.3%
Sean Rodriguez	28.4%	9.3%	28.8%	8.3%
Drew Stubbs	24.4%	8.2%	24.8%	10.0%
Brett Wallace	19.1%	4.7%	26.0%	6.7%
Eric Young	15.9%	7.7%	21.0%	9.1%

Interestingly, pMLE walk and strikeout rates are both higher than traditional translations for almost all of these players. The same was true of strikeout rates for many of the players we looked at earlier. (Walk rates were split about evenly for the earlier sample of players.)

The numbers that pop out to me are the pMLE strikeout rates for Jackson and Wallace. Neither comes as a big surprise; to me, the pMLE red flag is akin to watching a hitter flail, Francoeur-style, at a 1-2 curveball off the plate. The player who pMLE seems to endorse most strongly is Ka'aihue, whose modest walk rate and manageable strikeout rate weren't accumulated solely against minor-league journeymen.

Moving On And Stepping Back

While it's encouraging to see results that appear to have unique predictive value, it's important to recognize the limits of pMLE. First and foremost is the limited availability of relevant data. Of the 10 prospects highlighted a moment ago, only three had more than 250 PA for pMLE to consider; two of them had fewer than 200 despite playing much of their season in Triple-A. Essentially, then, we're extrapolating major-league performance based on two months of playing time against back-of-the-rotation starters, middle relievers and the occasional prospect.

Further, it's tough to imagine applying this algorithm to any translation problem other than Triple-A to MLB. While traditional translations work in part by "chaining" relationships between levels (e.g., finding the relationship between Double-A and Triple-A, then the relationship between Triple-A and the majors), there's no way to chain your way to Double-A pMLEs. It's equally far-fetched to use the method for players in leagues outside of North America.

Despite these limitations, there's plenty that can be done with the pMLE algorithm. It doesn't have to be limited to strikeouts and walks, and it can analyze pitchers as well. (My first foray into pMLE focused on R.J. Swindle and showed that he retired MLB-quality hitters at the same rate as others. His major-league experience thus far hasn't exactly given me a vote of confidence.)

There are almost certainly ways to improve the algorithm, as well. Given the reasoning behind filtering out pitchers who didn't appear in the major leagues, it may be useful to eliminate plate appearances against rehabbing pitchers and/or those who didn't cross a given playing-time threshold in the majors. I experimented a bit with parameters like those and got mixed results.

In the upcoming months, I'll explore some of these avenues at The Hardball Times Website. There are always new ways to evaluate prospects and find diamonds in the minor-league rough. I'm encouraged that this tool is one of them.

Better Than We Thought

by John Walsh

Baseball has always had its over- and underrated players. For various reasons, the public perception of a player's abilities does not always line up with his true value. This is not a bad thing, necessarily, because it gives us fans endless hours of lively discussion about just who these players are. One group of fans who especially like to debate this issue are the analytical types.

Bill James himself wrote frequently about under- and overrated players in his *Baseball Abstracts* 30 years ago. That makes sense of course: The more we study the game, the more we understand what makes players valuable and the better we are able to measure that value. "Oh, so walks are more valuable than we thought? I guess that means Eddie Yost was a better player than we give him credit for."

Players can be under appreciated for different reasons, but often it boils down to one of two situations. Sometimes, we simply are not using the best criteria when judging the player's performance. We might look at a player's batting average or RBI total, when his on-base abilities and power numbers will give us a better measure of the player. Or maybe we look at stolen base totals, without taking into account the times caught stealing. But, hey, you're reading an article in the *Hardball Times Baseball Annual*, you already know this.

Another reason that we may under- (or over-) estimate a player is that we might not fully consider all the important aspects of his game. Look at any discussion of the upcoming MVP awards and who might win the hardware. You hear talk of home runs, RBIs and sure, why not, OBP and Isolated Power. Maybe, just maybe, defensive position will be mentioned. But, what about all the rest, especially defensive play? Not just range, but also throwing. And there's more: baserunning, by which I don't just mean stolen bases, but also advancing on hits and outs, and not getting thrown out on the basepaths. Even something as seemingly minor as avoiding the double play is important.

This all seems pretty obvious, so why don't we consider this stuff when we evaluate players? The answer is simple: We haven't had ready access to reliable information on these nonhitting categories.

Until now, that is. A smart and industrious guy by the name of Sean Smith over at BaseballProjection.com has put together a valuable tool for evaluating players going back to the mid-1950s. Sean, who is a friend of THT and has contributed articles to the Annual and website, has produced state-of-the-art measures of hitting, defense and other minor categories and put them all into his WAR Database. ("WAR" stands for Wins Above Replacement.) Each player is rated on the following categories (when relevant):

- Batting
- Baserunning
- Avoidance of grounding into double plays
- Defensive range
- Catcher defense
- Defensive arm for outfielders
- Double-play proficiency for infielders

You can read about how Sean measures these aspects on his site BaseballProjection.com, but I wanted to make special mention of Sean's Total Zone system, which he uses to measure defensive range. After hitting, defensive range is the biggest aspect of a player's value. Total Zone uses Retrosheet play-by-play data to evaluate defensive range for all players of the last 55 years or so. It's a clever system that squeezes just about every bit of relevant information out of the Retrosheet data, data that is not as complete as modern data from professional stats providers such as Baseball Info Solutions or STATS, Inc. The data I am using covers the period from 1955 through 2008.

So, let's reach down into the WAR Database and pick out a name. Here's one—Mark Belanger. Do you remember Belanger? He was the regular shortstop on Earl Weaver's Baltimore Orioles. He started on three pennant-winners, including the World Series champs in 1970. One thing about Belanger: He could not hit. In 18 major league seasons Belanger compiled a slash line of .228/.300/.280 for an OPS+ of 68. From 1968 until 1978, the years Belanger was a full-time player, 74 major leaguers came to the plate at least 4,500 times. Of those, Belanger was last in batting average and slugging percentage. He did take an occasional walk, however, and managed to rank 69th in on-base percentage.

Belanger was clearly one of the two worst hitters in baseball during that period (the other was Sandy Alomar, Sr.). Yet Belanger started on the juggernaut Orioles—and not just one year when the O's had a hole

The Value of Belanger

Name	PA	BatRuns	Bsr	GIDP	Range	Arm	PosAdj	Other
Mark Belanger	6402	-248	15	15	236	5	113	384

Legend
PA - plate appearances
BatRuns - hitting
Bsr - baserunning
GIDP – Double Play avoidance (as hitter)
Range - defensive range
Arm - arm rating (or Double Play proficiency for infielders)
PosAdj - value of defensive position played
Other - sum of everything except BatRuns

at short, but year in and year out, pennant after pennant. Of course, if you know anything about Belanger, you probably know that he was a genius with the glove. He is widely considered one of the best ever defensive shortstops and won eight Gold Glove awards.

Just how good was Belanger, overall? Did the slick leather make up for the diseased wood? This is where the WAR data can help out. The table up top shows Belanger's contribution to his teams. (Note: Smith's Plate Appearance totals did not include sacrifice hits and flies. Further discrepancies may be noticed in players whose careers predate 1955.)

There's a lot of information there so let's go through it, step-by-step. BatRuns shows the batting contribution, expressed as runs above (or below) average. We've already seen that Belanger was a very weak hitter—that value of minus-248 batting runs is the ninth worst mark of the Retrosheet era. On the other hand, those 236 runs for defensive range is the second most of the Retrosheet era, behind Brooks Robinson's total of 268 range runs above average. (Brooks earned his runs in a lot more playing time, though.)

So, yes, we see that Belanger's glove really did offset the weak bat: Belanger rates as an essentially average player when you consider his hitting and defensive range. But wait, there's more. Belanger was an above average baserunner, saving his team 15 runs with his legs. He did not steal many bases, he was usually around 10-15 steals per year and his career success rate was 69 percent, i.e. nothing special. But he was adept at taking the extra base and avoiding outs on the bases. He saved an additional 15 runs by grounding into fewer double plays than the average batter would have, given the same opportunities. The "Arm" category for infielders (plus-5 for "The Blade") measures double play proficiency (on defense). The PosAdj (position adjustment) column in the table above gives the value (in Belanger's case) of playing shortstop, a premium defensive position. All these values are expressed in runs above an average player.

I'm going to call "Other" the sum of everything except hitting. Belanger's mark of 384 is very high—he is surpassed only by Ozzie Smith and Luis Aparicio, who both had much longer careers. Think about this: If you were to look just at Belanger's hitting, you'd conclude that he was one of the very worst players in baseball history. If you look at everything except hitting, you'd say he's one of the very best. Adding it all up, Belanger was a well above average player. Over his career he contributed 32 wins above replacement (WAR), and was about as valuable such players from recent memory as Shawn Green, Garret Anderson or Ray Durham.

Many of the players near Belanger on the career WAR ranking had longer careers than he did, however. If we consider WAR/year or WAR per 650 plate appearances, Belanger comes in at 3.2 WAR/year. That's a good player. A free agent in today's game that produces 3.2 WAR is worth about $14 million. Here are some other players who averaged or are averaging 3.2 WAR/year for their careers: Felipe Alou, Chone Figgins, Johnny Damon, Mike Lowell, Fred McGriff, Paul O'Neill, Amos Otis, Jimmy Rollins, Juan Gonzalez, Andre Dawson, Jim Rice and Dave Winfield. Now, these WAR values are not perfect (no stat is) and maybe Belanger comes out a little high and maybe Winfield and some of these others come out a bit low. I'm not saying Belanger was as good as all these guys. But WAR has been shown to work very well in general and while that doesn't prove anything specifically, I'm thinking that Belanger was a lot better ballplayer than many of us believed.

So who else has been underrated because much of their value comes from the non-hitting categories, the column labeled "Other"? Who are these "Other" guys?

There are, of course, many ways that you could define "Other guys", but I did the following: First I

The "Others"—Most Value Other than Batting

Name	PA	BatRuns	Bsr	GIDP	Range	Arm	PosAdj	Other	Other_650	WAR	WAR_650
Ozzie Smith	10,501	-140	82	27	214	25	147	495	30.6	67.5	4.2
Luis Aparicio	10,993	-235	95	18	144	5	164	426	25.2	50.4	3.0
Brooks Robinson	11,567	20	0	-35	268	26	69	328	18.4	69.9	3.9
Cal Ripken	12,746	181	-8	-24	141	40	143	292	14.9	91.2	4.7
Omar Vizquel	10,757	-198	10	10	127	4	140	291	17.6	45.3	2.7
Andruw Jones	7,445	90	10	1	180	58	23	272	23.7	57.8	5.0
Ivan Rodriguez	9,169	105	3	-19	151	0	128	263	18.6	67.9	4.8
Bert Campaneris	9,366	-114	51	20	59	3	128	261	18.1	44.6	3.1
Larry Bowa	8,909	-320	47	44	22	8	137	258	18.8	18.7	1.4
Kenny Lofton	9,097	125	81	26	79	34	26	246	17.6	67.2	4.8
Alan Trammell	9,175	124	21	19	59	17	118	234	16.6	66.7	4.7
Barry Larkin	8,931	189	85	8	37	-10	114	234	17.0	69.9	5.1
Willie Wilson	8,218	-88	121	29	112	-3	-31	228	18.0	40.8	3.2
Devon White	7,972	-52	39	19	148	-11	17	212	17.3	41.5	3.4
Gary Carter	8,887	146	-10	-10	107	5	118	210	15.4	64.7	4.7
Bill Russell	7,837	-190	25	8	78	-4	100	207	17.2	24.5	2.0
Willie Randolph	9,299	122	39	-10	74	40	58	201	14.0	63.0	4.4
Willie Mays	11,089	748	71	-13	107	45	-12	198	11.6	140.2	8.2
Dave Concepcion	9,480	-139	28	-13	30	20	133	198	13.6	33.9	2.3
Bill Mazeroski	8,222	-206	-6	-3	110	37	57	195	15.4	25.3	2.0

split players into short, medium and long careers, with 4,000 and 7,000 plate appearances being the dividing lines between the groups. For each group, I looked for the players with the highest total of "Other" runs above average. Remember, "Other" includes defensive range and arm, baserunning, avoiding grounding into double plays and positional adjustment. For infielders "Arm" is a measure of double-play proficiency. For catchers, "Range" measures overall defense, including throwing out basestealers. "Arm" for catchers is not used for anything (it appears as zero in the tables).

The Top 20 "Other Guys" among players with long careers (more than 7,000 PA), ranked by "Other" runs above average, are listed at the top. I've added a few columns:

- Other_650—"Other" runs per 650 PA
- WAR—career Wins Above Replacement
- WAR_650—WAR per 650 PA

Wow, that's a list of some pretty good players. Too good, actually, if you're looking for underrated guys. I count seven Hall of Famers and a few others who got close or will go in at some point—it's hard to claim that a guy with a plaque in Cooperstown is underrated. What we're seeing here is that players with long careers are generally good players. And if you're going to lead in anything, including "Other" runs above average, it helps to have a long career.

Smith is not underrated, but his "Other" stats are very impressive. We knew about the defensive wizardry, but Ozzie was just superb at everything (except hitting). Smith is the only below-average hitter with 60 or more career WAR. (Only one other 60-WAR player had fewer than 100 batting runs—Robinson, third on the above list.)

Sometimes players (especially if they had long careers) have such great defensive reputations that we tend to give them a pass on the hitting. They end up being overrated by many. I would put Mazeroski, Aparicio, Concepcion and Vizquel in this group. They were all fine players—about as good as Belanger on a per-year basis (admittedly in longer careers). Maz was undeniably a fabulous defensive player, but he was a poor hitter and was also below average as a baserunner and double-play avoider. Aparicio, though a fine player (three WAR per year), may be somewhat overrated due to his defense and speed. They were excellent, but the bat was very bad.

Lofton, Trammell and Larkin make for a nice trio in the middle of this list. They are all very close in career WAR, WAR per year and "Other" runs, although they came by their "Other" runs a little differently. Lofton was excellent in every category, but did not enjoy the upward positional adjustment that the shortstops did, Larkin had more speed and Trammell was stronger

The "Others"—Short Careers

Name	PA	BatRuns	Bsr	GIDP	Range	Arm	PosAdj	Other	Other_650	WAR	WAR_650
Gary DiSarcina	3,934	-182	-1	3	60	4	64	130	21.5	9.2	1.5
Steve Yeager	3,953	-93	-7	-6	70	0	71	128	21.0	14.4	2.4
Dal Maxvill	3,821	-195	-3	-4	58	6	67	124	21.1	3.7	0.6
Adam Everett	2,448	-101	5	10	65	3	31	114	30.3	8.4	2.2
Ron Karkovice	2,856	-82	0	2	62	0	50	114	25.9	13.2	3.0
Mike Benjamin	2,057	-117	7	3	78	4	20	112	35.4	5.4	1.7
Pokey Reese	3,082	-141	21	1	63	3	22	110	23.2	5.9	1.2
Rey Ordonez	3,314	-203	1	3	44	12	50	110	21.6	0.2	0.0
Clay Dalrymple	3,451	-58	-17	3	62	0	59	107	20.2	16.2	3.1
Jose Reyes	3,452	8	30	12	31	-5	35	103	19.4	21.0	4.0
Gil McDougald	3,126	39	3	2	56	9	27	97	20.2	22.9	4.8
Mike Gallego	3,289	-71	-6	0	60	14	28	96	19.0	13.4	2.6
Brandon Inge	3,588	-78	-8	-2	73	4	29	96	17.4	14.4	2.6
Johnny Logan	3,783	-7	9	-6	51	-6	48	96	16.5	22.2	3.8
Frank Duffy	2,844	-108	-2	-3	45	5	50	95	21.7	7.0	1.6
Hal Lanier	3,843	-240	-4	-8	57	-7	52	90	15.2	-5.2	-0.9
Cesar Izturis	3,347	-155	-2	13	33	7	38	89	17.3	2.8	0.5
Charlie O'Brien	2,501	-73	-7	-7	58	0	44	88	22.9	9.3	2.4
Bobby Knoop	3,941	-90	-2	-6	53	13	28	86	14.2	9.9	1.6
Jose Uribe	3,324	-112	-5	15	16	6	53	85	16.6	6.4	1.3

on the double play. It's interesting that many believe Larkin will be inducted into the Hall of Fame, while Trammel and Lofton appear to have little chance.

Let's go to the short-career guys now, the players with fewer than 4,000 plate appearances. The top 20 are listed above, ranked by runs above average in the nonhitting categories.

Ah, this is more like it—a bunch of guys you have mostly never heard of. Well, maybe you should have heard of some of them. Ron Karkovice was a catcher who played 12 seasons with the Chicago White Sox. Like many of these players, he couldn't really hit, but man was he good at the "other" stuff. Karkovice was a marvelous defender and was a good baserunner (for a catcher), too. Karkovice averaged three WAR per full season—about the same as the career marks of Maury Wills or Edgardo Alfonzo.

You probably don't remember Mike Benjamin—he was a thoroughly forgettable utility player from the 1990s. I remember him, though, because I hated to see him come to the plate for my Boston Red Sox. He really sucked. Or did he? Turns out that Benjamin was not that bad of a ballplayer. Couldn't hit at all, but he was above average in everything else: baserunning, avoiding the GIDP, defensive range and turning the double play. Put it all together and you have a major-league average player. Maybe he should have gotten *more* playing time.

Many of these players are like Benjamin—weak-hitting middle infielders whose defense and base-running elevated them to league average or close to it. Adam Everett, Pokey Reese, Mike Gallego, Frank Duffy and Bobby Knoop fall into this group. And some middle infielders are so terrible with the bat that the best glove and legs in the world will not pull them much above replacement level: Dal Maxvill, Rey Ordonez, Hal Lanier and Cesar Izturis really were as bad as we thought, maybe worse.

Johnny Logan and Gil McDougald most definitely do *not* belong in the group of middle infielders with feeble bats—they could actually hit some, especially McDougald. During his 10-year career, McDougald played in eight World Series (think about that) and could actually hit a lot. He was a super-utility guy (before the term had been invented) for the great Yankees teams of the 1950s. He played all over the infield and was excellent defensively everywhere he played. Good baserunner, too. His career began in 1951, so the first few years are not included in the WAR data (which starts with the 1955 season), but I think these numbers give us a good picture of his career. McDougald was chosen by the Washington Senators in the 1961 expansion draft and he retired rather than leave the Yankees, despite being only 32 years old. His 4.8 WAR per year, which is admittedly inflated because of his early retirement,

The "Others"—Medium Length Careers

Name	PA	BatRuns	Bsr	GIDP	Range	Arm	PosAdj	Other	Other_650	WAR	WAR_650
Mark Belanger	6,402	-248	15	15	236	5	113	384	39.0	32.0	3.2
Ozzie Guillen	6,932	-303	9	22	106	0	107	244	22.9	17.5	1.6
Rey Sanchez	5,119	-212	14	3	129	12	54	212	26.9	16.3	2.1
Jim Sundberg	6,742	-80	-13	-8	115	0	117	211	20.3	34.7	3.3
Brad Ausmus	6,809	-228	-3	-8	100	0	116	205	19.6	18.0	1.7
Clete Boyer	6,275	-113	-7	-5	146	12	49	195	20.2	26.4	2.7
Ed Brinkman	6,529	-277	-1	-8	74	5	110	180	17.9	6.4	0.6
Greg Gagne	6,080	-148	-9	2	83	3	98	177	18.9	22.6	2.4
Jose Valentin	6,198	-42	25	11	58	16	66	176	18.5	34.0	3.6
Freddie Patek	6,084	-157	46	9	-2	16	98	167	17.8	20.5	2.2
Jimmy Rollins	5,725	-35	46	7	42	6	62	163	18.5	29.2	3.3
Scott Fletcher	5,829	-86	7	1	80	20	54	162	18.1	27.0	3.0
Craig Counsell	4,526	-121	1	13	113	6	28	161	23.1	16.8	2.4
Paul Blair	6,514	-57	2	1	140	34	-17	160	16.0	30.4	3.0
Scott Rolen	6,775	221	15	-4	128	1	19	159	15.3	58.0	5.6
Nellie Fox	6,583	-29	25	13	80	2	38	158	15.6	32.1	3.2
Lance Johnson	5,738	-40	43	16	99	-17	16	157	17.8	30.4	3.4
Tim Foli	6,347	-287	0	8	34	16	96	154	15.8	3.6	0.4
Mike Bordick	6,333	-131	-6	-3	66	6	87	150	15.4	24.4	2.5
Mike Cameron	6,726	62	37	5	90	0	17	149	14.4	42.6	4.1

is comparable to the yearly production of stars such as Derek Jeter, Tony Gwynn and Will Clark.

Let's turn finally to the guys with medium-length careers. I saved this group for last, because I have this feeling that maybe some of these players could have had longer careers, maybe even Hall-of-Fame-type careers had all their contributions been fully appreciated. Once again, the table is up top.

Well, not much potential Hall of Fame material except Nellie Fox, who's actually *in* the Hall and Scott Rolen who seems to be on his way. But look how many three-WAR players we have here. I've already listed a number of three-WAR players in my comments on Belanger and Karkovice. I can't resist, here are a few more in the three to 3.5 WAR range: Mark Grace, Frank Howard, Craig Biggio, Tim Salmon and Pete Rose. Now I realize I'm being provocative when I mention guys with very long careers like Biggio and Grace. If Jose Valentin had played as long as Biggio, there's no way he'd keep that WAR per year number up around 3.5. The same may be true for someone like Lance Johnson and, yes, Belanger, too. Defense ages just like anything else, after all. But, I'm saying that several of these guys were playing at an All-Star level and maybe weren't recognized for it.

Let's look at Valentin, who has long been a favorite of the sabermetrically inclined. Valentin is one of those players dismissed, perhaps, by the casual fan for his low batting average (.243 career), but he would take a walk and had above-average power. In addition to the power, the stat heads have known for a while about Valentin's great range (plus-58 runs by the Total Zone estimate we are using here). And look at his other contributions: plus-25 in baserunning, plus-11 in avoiding the GIDP, plus-16 in turning (or starting) the double play, all of it at the premium positions of shortstop and second base.

Lance Johnson was a speedy center fielder for the Cubs and Mets in the '90s. I remember him as one of the five post-1940s players to hit at least 20 triples in a season. Johnson was a decent hitter (league-average OBP), but he had little power. With his speed, he was an excellent base runner and he rarely hit into double plays. And although he had a weak arm (minus-17 runs), he was a top-notch fly-catcher. The complete package is impressive: 3.4 WAR per year. Who knew?

Only one player on this list is average or better in every category: Mike Cameron. Cameron is very underrated by the average fan and mainstream media, and probably by baseball insiders, too: He's played for six different teams in his impressive career. He is widely regarded as a good defensive center fielder, but I'm not sure people realize just how good he has been in the field, nor do they appreciate his baserunning skills. Well, you probably know (or could easily find out) that he has stolen almost 300 bases at a good success rate. But did you know that he successfully takes the extra base on hits 56 percent of the time, while the major league average is 39 percent? It works out to plus-37 runs in baserunning.

Cameron's hitting is also underrated because he hits for a low average (.250 lifetime) and strikes out a lot (he's 11th on the career strikeout list with 1,798). But he is willing to take a walk and has some power, making him an above average hitter. Together with the other stuff, it adds up to a four WAR per year player. There are lots of four WAR players in the Hall of Fame. For example: Robin Yount, Ernie Banks, Harmon Killebrew, Kirby Puckett, Brooks Robinson and Billy Williams. Cameron will never sniff the Hall of Fame and I don't think he should. But, over the years, Cameron has provided more value to his teams each year than many other players who enjoy much better reputations.

If you are still with me, you may be asking yourself, "Does all this make any sense?" Or you might be thinking, "This guy's a nut job! Belanger as good as Winfield? Mike Cameron compared to Ernie Banks? Mike Freakin' Cameron?" OK, OK, you have a point. Of course, I've been simplifying things. I'm using a single number (average WAR per year) to compare players, without taking into account peak value (WAR in best years) and career value (total WAR). Banks topped 6.5 WAR in five seasons and Cameron has never reached that level. That makes a big difference. A *big* difference. And I'm only half-serious in comparing Karkovice to Wills. It's just a device I use to drive home my point: Some of these guys really were better than we thought. A lot better.

Oh Lucky Men!

by Dave Studenmund

Yet today I consider myself the luckiest man on the face of the earth.

- Lou Gehrig, who had nothing on Lucky Lohrke.

Lucky Lohrke died this year. Lohrke was a relatively nondescript middle infielder in the late 1940s and early 1950s who totaled about 1,000 plate appearances in seven seasons and batted .242 for the Giants and Phillies. Yet the story behind those numbers is one of the most remarkable in baseball history.

As chronicled by Craig Wright's excellent "A Page from Baseball's Past," Lohrke just missed being involved in the greatest tragedy in the history of professional baseball. It involved the Spokane Indians, who were run off the road by an oncoming car en route to Bremerton on June 11, 1946. Six people were killed and several others severely injured when their bus crashed through a guard rail and plummeted 300 feet into a canyon.

Fifty minutes earlier, Lohrke had been with the team during a pit stop in Ellensburg when he received some happy news: He was being promoted to the Pacific Coast League San Diego Padres. Since he had to report to San Diego immediately, Lohrke decided to hitchhike back to Spokane and grab a plane. When the bus resumed its fateful journey, Lohrke headed in the opposite direction.

Lohrke had returned from the service in World War II the previous November. He originally was going to return home on an Army transport plane from New Jersey to California, but a colonel pulled rank at the last minute and took his place. That colonel was killed along with 19 other returning soldiers when the plane crashed outside Kansas City. Lohrke made it home a little later, alive.

Lohrke had been in some of the fiercest battles of the war, including Normandy and the Battle of the Bulge. It is said that, on two occasions, soldiers on either side of him were killed in battle while he remained alive.

It is also said that Lucky Lohrke didn't like his nickname. Perhaps you can see why.

His real name was Jack and, as Craig has pointed out, Jack's luck manifested itself on the baseball field as well.

Lohrke batted .303 in his half-season at San Diego and the Giants drafted him to be their third baseman. The Giants had gone 61-93 in 1946 but with Lohrke on board in 1947 they finished fourth in the National League with a 81-73 tally. Lohrke actually helped—his offense was an improvement over the previous third baseman, Bill Rigney—but the Giants also had big seasons from Johnny Mize (51 home runs), Walker Cooper, Willard Marshall and newcomer Bobby Thomson.

The Giants won 78 games in 1948, though Lohrke lost his regular third base job to Sid Gordon. Foolishly, the Giants sent Lohrke to the minors for part of the 1949 season and their win total decreased to 73.

Lohrke returned to the big club in 1950 and stayed on the roster all season, though he played in only 30 games. Still, Lohrke's luck held and the Giants bounced back to win 86 games and finish third. That team had turned over significantly from the Giants of a few years earlier. Alvin Dark was the shortstop and Eddie Stanky the second baseman (Stanky batted .300 with 144 walks). Hank Thompson, Whitey Lockman, Monte Irvin and Don Mueller were all young players who had recently joined the team.

You may be familiar with the Giants of 1951. A kid named Willie Mays was brought up to the big club after batting .477 in 139 at-bats for Minneapolis, Sal Maglie and Larry Jansen both won 23 games and Lohrke stayed with the club all year long, though he played in only 23 games. The Giants won 98 games, including a three-game playoff against the Dodgers, and lost the World Series to the Yankees, 4-2. Lohrke was hitless in two World Series at-bats.

It is well known that Mays was on deck when Bobby Thomson hit the Shot Heard 'Round the World that won the series against the Dodgers. It is less well known that Lohrke was warming up to take over third base if the game had gone into extra innings.

The Giants traded Lohrke after the season (predictably, the Giants finished second the next year). He went to the Phillies, who had finished 73-81 in 1951. Naturally, the Phillies improved to 87-67 with Lohrke on board, though he played in only 25 games. The next year, with Lohrke on the roster again, they were 83-71.

Unfortunately, during the year Lohrke again was shipped to the minors, where he batted only .194. His baseball skills had seemingly deteriorated to the point at which he wasn't even a useful utility player anymore. The Phillies let him go after the season.

They didn't have another winning season for the next eight years.

There is one last postscript to Lohrke's story, courtesy of Craig Wright. The next year (1954), Lohrke tried out for the Pirates and didn't make the club. He was assigned to their Triple-A team, the Hollywood Stars. Quoting Craig, "Without Lohrke, Pittsburgh finished in last place with 101 losses. Jack spent the whole year with the ... Stars, and they won 101 games!"

Jack Lohrke may have been the luckiest man in baseball history, both on and off the field.

Or was he? Being curious, and having lots of baseball data at hand, I decided to search for the luckiest and unluckiest major leaguers ever. What follows are several investigations into the players most favored by Lady Fortune on the field. Even if we don't settle on the Luckiest Player Ever, we're sure to find some interesting quirks of fate.

There are many ways to define and quantify luck. You may be familiar with the concept of a team's "Pythagorean Record." That's the record a team could be expected to post based on its runs scored and allowed.

Teams' actual records tend to be close to their Pythagorean records, but there are some famous exceptions. The 1905 Detroit Tigers, for example, allowed 90 more runs than they scored, but they still managed to finish above .500 with a 79-74 record. That's a remarkable achievement—a "Pythagorean variance" of 14 more wins than expected, the greatest in baseball history—and I have no idea how they did it.

Most Pythagorean variances are the result of things that players and teams (and managers) can't consistently control. The team's record in close games, for instance, or clutch hitting. Clutch pitching. Losing a lot of blowout games but not winning any blowouts. Luck, actually. When baseball analysts like me find things that tend to be random instead of predictable, we call that luck.

We've looked into baseball's past and chronicled which teams have been the luckiest and unluckiest with their Pythagorean variances, but what about the players? Are there some player who played on more teams with favorable Pythagorean variances than not?

The answer is yes, of course. And the winner of our first "You can be lucky like Lohrke" search is Ruben Sierra. It helps to have played for nine different teams over 20 seasons, sometimes playing for more than one team in a year. But give Sierra some "credit." When you add up all the Pythagorean variances of the teams that Ruben Sierra played for, you find that they finished 59 games better than "expected." That is eight more than the second-luckiest player.

The interesting quirk is that Sierra came into this talent late in his career.

Sierra played his first six years with the Rangers, who finished a total of 10 games above their Pythagorean records during that time, although they never won the division. In his seventh year, he started with the Rangers but was traded to the first-place A's in August. The Rangers finished three games above their projected record and the A's finished seven above theirs. A double hit worth 10 "lucky wins" in one year.

That was a pretty good start. Sierra had a few ups and downs in the middle of his career, occasionally displaying his talent for Pythagoras and hitting sometimes too. But his last five years, for the Yankees, Rangers and Twins, was when he made his mark. Those teams combined to finish a staggering 26 games better than their Pythagorean records. The 2004 Yankees, in particular, were nearly 12 games better than their projected record, the fourth-best variance ever.

Sierra played on first-place teams (mostly the Yankees) the last four years of his career, including the Twins in his final year when he batted only .179 in 28 at bats before being released in early July. It was a remarkable run. Ruben Sierra was sometimes accused of being moody and self-centered, but it turns out that he wasn't that bad a guy to have in the clubhouse.

The top 20 players in positive career Pythagorean variances have been:

Player	Team Games	Pyth Var	Pct.
Ruben Sierra	3,965	59	1.5%
Dennis Martinez	3,755	51	1.4%
Pete Rose	3,982	51	1.3%
Dave Winfield	3,601	48	1.3%
Davey Concepcion	3,012	48	1.6%
Joe Coleman	2,899	47	1.6%
Early Wynn	3,558	46	1.3%
George Foster	3,176	45	1.4%
Johnny Podres	2,532	45	1.8%
Bobby Tolan	2,257	45	2.0%
Duke Snider	2,802	44	1.6%
Ray Knight	2,212	44	2.0%
Jim Fregosi	3,227	43	1.3%
Jim Gilliam	2,200	42	1.9%
Johnny Bench	2,690	40	1.5%
Todd Zeile	3,317	40	1.2%

Player	Team Games	Pyth Var	Pct.
Joe Nolan	1,879	39	2.1%
Rich Dauer	1,557	39	2.5%
Jim Spencer	2,635	39	1.5%
Marquis Grissom	2,684	39	1.4%

There are some well-known, successful players on this list. You've got to play a lot of games with a lot of good teams to do well here. You probably noticed a lot of Reds: Pete Rose, Johnny Bench, Dave Concepcion, George Foster, Bobby Tolan. From 1970 to 1981, the Reds won 1,108 games but were projected to win "only" 1,070. That 37-game difference was one of the best extended streaks in baseball history.

A few other players of note:

- The Baltimore Orioles had positive Pythagorean variances every year from 1976 to 1984. Dennis Martinez and Rich Dauer were Orioles each one of those years. Dauer retired a year later, but Martinez had the same effect on several other teams later in his career. Dauer stands out, however, by virtue of having a short but very "lucky" career with the Orioles.
- Joe Nolan was a vagabond backup catcher who played on two standout Pythagorean teams: the 1972 Mets (ninth-best all-time variance of 11 games; Nolan had just a cup of coffee with the Mets) and the 1981 Reds (a whopping nine-game variance in the strike-shortened season. Much has been made of the fact that the Reds had the best record in the majors but didn't make the postseason due to the split season. Perhaps it was the Pythagorean baseball gods wreaking justice.)
- Joe Coleman won a lot of games pitching for the Tigers in the early 1970s. The Tigers also had a pretty good Pythagorean streak those years, including the AL's best variances in both 1973 and 1974.

The least lucky player in this category was Lee Mazzilli, who spent 13 years with some staggeringly unlucky teams in New York and Pittsburgh. The 1984 Pirates team, in particular, was 12 games worse than its projected Pythagorean record—the fourth-worst variance in major league history.

By the way, Jack Lohrke was a unlucky Pythagorean player, too. His teams actually finished 14 games under their projected record—of all the teams Lohrke joined, only the '51 Giants had a winning record significantly higher than their Pythagorean record.

Jack Lohrke's specialty, remember, was improving teams just by being on their roster. Of course, lots of teams get better and worse as players switch between them. So I combed my data and associated all the players on a team's roster with that team's record vs. its record the previous year.

Is there a player whose teams seem to do better just because he's there?

This is the sort of thing a loyal player won't do well in. If you stay with one team your entire major league career, or even most of it, chances are that all the improvements and declines will even out over the years. However, if you switch teams often, you have a chance to rack up some improvement points. And if you're traded in midseason to contenders, you might do very, very well in this stat.

Here are major league history's top 20 "team improvers:"

Player	Team Games	Games Improved	Rate
Dennis Cook	2,996	128	4%
Jack O'Connor	3,135	112	4%
Mike Difelice	2,429	111	5%
Darren Holmes	2,366	105	4%
Brian Johnson	1,397	104	7%
Cliff Floyd	2,849	101	4%
Gene Moore	2,157	101	5%
Danny Heep	2,055	98	5%
Rusty Staub	3,822	98	3%
Armando Reynoso	1,881	96	5%
Kenny Lofton	3,172	95	3%
Rich Bordi	1,403	94	7%
Tris Speaker	3,361	92	3%
Alex Johnson	2,259	89	4%
Mike Donlin	1,956	89	5%
Dan Brouthers	2,411	88	4%
Aaron Sele	2,365	88	4%
Ray Benge	2,006	87	4%
Vinny Castilla	2,851	85	3%
Jay Johnstone	3,340	85	3%

I remember Dennis Cook as a durable left-handed reliever, the type who was in demand by contending teams late in his career. But Cook traveled across the baseball continent throughout his baseball career. Overall, he pitched for nine different teams in 15 seasons. And his presence had a positive effect on almost all of them.

- In just his second season (1989), Cook was traded from the Giants to the Phillies in June. The Giants were in the middle of a nine-win improvement from 1988 en route to winning the NL West. The Phillies were improving a bit, though they still finished sixth.
- Starting the 1990 season on Phillies' roster, Cook worked his magic and the Phillies improved 10 wins over 1989, finishing fourth. Cook himself didn't finish with the Phils, as he was traded to the Dodgers in September. The Dodgers were in the middle of a nine-game improvement themselves. So twice in his early career, Cook got an "improvement boost" from midseason deals.
- Cook spent a lot of time in the minors in 1991, but he did pitch 20 innings for the Dodgers, who improved another 10 games and finished second in the National League West.
- Traded to Cleveland during the offseason, Cook did it again for the Indians, who improved their record by 19 wins in 1992. Alas, they had gone 57-105 the year before, so they still finished only fourth in '92. The next year, the Indians didn't improve at all, became disenchanted with their good luck charm and released him.
- Cook signed on with the White Sox for the strike-shortened 1994 season. The Sox won "only" 67 games but that was enough to take the division. If you prorate their victories over a 162-game season, the Sox actually gained two wins over their 1993 season.
- The Indians must have realized their mistake, grabbing Cook off waivers from the Sox in the offseason. Even though they had finished first in 1994, the Indians improved to 100 wins (a prorated improvement of six wins) in 1995. Once again, Cook was nowhere near when the season ended, traded to the Rangers in June. Predictably, the Rangers were also a prorated seven games better in 1995.

And so it went. Cook also pitched for the 1997 Marlins (who improved by 12 wins and won the World Series), the 1999 Mets (eight games and the postseason), the 2001 Phillies (improved by 21 wins over the previous year) and 2002 Angels (24-game improvement).

You can argue that Cook was lucky or you can argue that his teams were lucky. Perhaps it was good old American stick-to-it-ivness. Whomever or whatever you want to credit, luck and Cook went together like a horse and carriage. It was just hard to tell which one went first.

I'm not going to talk too much about the number-two guy on the list, Jack O'Connor. O'Connor played at the end of the 19th century, when owners sometimes owned more than one team and moved players between them indiscriminately. For instance, O'Connor was one of the players moved when the owners of the Cleveland Spiders bought the St. Louis Browns and decided to move all their best players there in 1899. The Browns improved by 44 wins and the Spiders had the worst season in baseball history.

The two unluckiest players in this regard, the two players whose teams got worse when they were there, were Fred Jacklitsch and John Candelaria.

Fred Jacklitsch, who was not related to Pat Listach, was a backup catcher from the early 1900s who played for some memorable clunkers, including the 1915 Baltimore Terrapins of the Federal League (which won only 47 games after winning 84 in 1914). These were the same Terrapins that lured Chief Bender to the FL only to see him post a 4-16 record. That was bad luck, indeed.

Jacklitsch also played for 1902 Phillies (who declined some 25 wins because they lost most of their best players to the American League), the 1904 Brooklyn Superbas (21 wins worse than the year before; their No. 1 catcher was the infamous Bill Bergen), the 1905 Yankees (a decline of 20 wins) and the 1917 Braves. Jacklitsch had only one at-bat for the Braves, who were just three years removed from their miracle year but declined 17 wins from their 1916 record. Fred Jacklitsch wasn't a bad player. But he was not a guy you wanted on your roster.

And how about the Candy Man? This one surprised me. John Candelaria was an unlucky teammate? It seems that Candelaria was sort of the opposite of Ruben Sierra; he got unluckier as he aged.

Candelaria pitched his first 10 years in Pittsburgh, so his improvements and declines from those years even out. Once he started switching teams, however, things went downhill. Actually, things started out poorly his last year in Pittsburgh, 1984, when the Pirates sank 18 wins to a 57-104 record.

Candelaria was then traded to the Angels who lost 17 wins in his third year there. During that year (1987), the Angels moved him onto the Mets, who were busy with a 16-win decline of their own. He was granted free agency during the offseason and he signed with the Yankees for 1988, probably figuring he could break the curse. Unfortunately (or unluckily), the Yankees declined by three wins in '88 and another 11 wins in '89. The Yankees traded him away.

You can probably guess the rest of the story. The cappers were his last two years, when he signed with the Dodgers, who declined from 93 to 63 wins in his second year there (1992), and when he returned home to the 1993 Pirates, who had just let Barry Bonds walk. Their win total fell from 96 to 75.

The parallels between the Candy Man and Cook are pretty interesting. Both were left handers for hire late in their careers. But Cook was a lucky charm; Candelaria was an accidental step on the foul line.

Jack Lohrke's teams improved by 47 games in his short career, an improvement rate of 4 percent. Lohrke was lucky, though he didn't have Cook's longevity. Someday we'll have to talk about Brian Johnson, whose 7 percent improvement rate is the highest since 1900. In a seven-year career, Johnson played for six teams that improved by 10 games or more.

Let me run one more idea by you. I hope you know a little bit about a stat called Win Shares. Win Shares were invented by Bill James as a way to attribute a team's wins to individual players, kind of like the number of shares a stock owner owns in a company.

The approach is very complex, taking more than 100 pages of explanation in the *Win Shares* book, but it includes each player's contribution to his team in terms of hitting, fielding and pitching. The greatest year in baseball history was Hoss Radbourn's 89 in 1884. After 1900, the highest total was Honus Wagner's 59 in 1908.

Those are way out there, however. In most years, a total of 30 or more Win Shares is enough to gain MVP consideration and 40 is only reached every few years by a great player.

For individual players, Win Shares are a predictable stat, just like home runs and strikeouts. But sometimes players outperform their history of Win Shares and other times they clunk out. Think there are some teammates that are associated with Win Shares streaks and slumps?

I calculated the "predicted Win Shares" of each player in each major league season, based primarily on how he had performed before that season and how much he played during the season in question (I don't want to bog you down with details; I'll put the full explanation at the end of this article). I then linked them to each player's teammates—same as the previous two exercises—and calculated which teammate most boosted the individual play of those around him.

The top 20:

Player	Win Shares	Predicted Win Shares	Diff	%
Smoky Joe Wood	3,639	3,349	290	9%
Mort Cooper	3,393	3,115	278	9%
Tom Prince	4,482	4,213	269	6%
Gene Moore	3,519	3,252	267	8%
Tris Speaker	5,517	5,255	262	5%
Bobby Tolan	3,729	3,470	260	7%
Dixie Walker	5,259	5,000	259	5%
Frankie Frisch	5,037	4,779	258	5%
Frank Crosetti	4,866	4,611	255	6%
Nellie Fox	4,719	4,465	254	6%
Johnny Hopp	4,713	4,459	254	6%
Clyde Engle	2,481	2,245	236	11%
Larry Gardner	4,302	4,066	236	6%
Pedro Martinez	3,459	3,226	233	7%
Armando Reynoso	3,069	2,836	233	8%
Ed Cicotte	3,528	3,298	230	7%
Buck Martinez	4,257	4,028	230	6%
Lew Riggs	2,616	2,386	230	10%
Pinch Thomas	2,718	2,493	225	9%
Lefty Gomez	4,038	3,816	222	6%

Hey, this is a fascinating list, starting at the very top. Smoky Joe Wood was a great pitcher who spent 11 seasons with the Red Sox and Indians, and his teammates almost always outperformed their predicted Win Shares. Of course, Wood contributed to that type of luck, too. In his best year, 1912, he was 34-5 with a 1.91 ERA. He had 44 Win Shares while my system predicted he would have "only" 26.

The year that Wood apparently most inspired his teammates was 1912. Tris Speaker (who is also on our list) accrued 51 Win Shares, nearly 20 more than predicted. Larry Gardner (a fine third baseman) had perhaps his finest year with 29 Win Shares, 11 more than predicted. Altogether, the 1912 Red Sox won 105 games and the World Series.

Wood was also quite inspirational in Cleveland, circa 1920, when Tris Speaker had another big year (39 Win Shares) and Steve O'Neill had his best year ever. Actually, so did Stan Coveleski, Jim Bagby and Elmer Smith. Smoky Joe Wood was quite the teammate.

I kind of like this approach. It captures the notion of players who managed to reach a peak in their careers and isolates which teammates were there most often. There's no "Jack O'Connor" effect, because teammates carry their past history with them, even if they switch teams.

Here's something else I like about this list. Remember all the Reds from our first list, the one that had the top Pythagorean variances? Well, the only one of them to make this list is perhaps the least well-known Red of the era, outfielder Bobby Tolan. The only Yankees to appear are Lefty Gomez and Frank Crosetti. No Pete Rose, Johnny Bench, Babe Ruth or Mickey Mantle. There are stars on the list, big ones, but the presence of Crosetti and Tolan makes me feel that we've found the really key links.

Of course, you might say that Crosetti and Tolan were only lucky in that they played with great players. And you'd be right about that. But great players don't typically stay great. Most return to earth at some point; few sustain greatness the way Ruth or Mantle did. If there was a teammate associated with truly sustained greatness, I don't have a problem giving him credit for that.

Crosetti played for the Yankees for 16 years. In four of those years, 1932, 1936, 1939 and 1943, his teammates outperformed their predicted Win Shares by 40 or more Win Shares. In 1932, Red Ruffing jumped from 11 and 15 Win Shares the two previous years to 26 Win Shares, the highest total of his career. Tony Lazzeri jumped from 19 and 15 the two previous years to 27, the second-best season of his career.

The 1939 Yankees were perhaps the greatest team in history, and Crosetti was there. Charlie Keller had a great rookie year and Red Rolfe had his best year. So did George Selkirk.

That's how it ran for Crosseti, Tolan and others on our list. Great teammates, yes, but great teammates having their best years. That's what I would call luck.

There are some obscure names on the list, too.

- Gene Moore is the only player on both this list and the "improved teams" list. Moore was an outfielder—a spare one, usually—from 1931 to 1945. He played for the Cardinals, Braves, Dodgers, Yankees and Senators and he seemed to inspire his teammates everywhere he went. Most notably, he was with the Browns the only time they reached the postseason, in 1944. That was Vern Stephens' best year: 34 Win Shares and third in MVP voting. It was also pitcher Jack Kramer's best year by far. Dizzy Dean also had his best year when Moore was his teammate. So did Paul Dean, Ripper Collins, Pepper Martin, Jim Turner, Lou Fette and George Case.
- Johnny Hopp was a pretty good first baseman/outfielder from 1940 to 1952. He made most of his impact with the Cardinals during World War II, when it was easier for established major leaguers to reach new performance heights.
- Clyde Engle was an all-purpose player, good hitter who spent two years in the Federal League. He was on the same 1912 Red Sox team as Joe Wood, but he also spent a little time with the 1910 Yankees (who finished second despite having only won 51 games two years before).
- Pinch Thomas—what a great name—was a light-hitting catcher who was smart enough to be Smoky Joe Wood's teammate for a number of years. Second degree luck, you might say.

The unluckiest player in our Win Shares methodology, the guy you just didn't want to see in the clubhouse, was Frank Tanana. Tanana was a fireballing youngster who morphed into a crafty lefty in his old age and managed to have a very good 21-year career. But boy, did he bring down his teammates.

One of his real downer years was 1980. Teammate Don Baylor batted only .250 with a .341 slugging percentage. The year before he had been the league's MVP. Nearly every Angel had a below-average year and no one was significantly better than predicted.

He killed the Tigers in 1989. Alan Trammell had only 13 Win Shares. Chet Lemon had 10, Jack Morris had four, Doyle Alexander had eight. Among the regulars, only Lou Whitaker was better than predicted. Want to blame someone for the Tigers' 59-103 record that year, two years after winning 98? Blame Frank Tanana.

There are so many great stories embedded in our research that it's hard to know where to stop. What's Tom Prince's story, for instance? (Hint: focus on the Pirates in the early 1990s and the Twins in the early 2000s). Or Dixie Walker's? Nellie Fox? Wonderful stories to be uncovered, but I doubt that any of them can match our original inspiration.

Jack Lohrke is 173rd on this list, with a positive variance of 138 actual Win Shares over predicted Win Shares—at a rate of almost 9 percent. That is a pretty good rate, right up there with Smoky Joe, but Lohrke's career was much shorter.

A lot of players have been nominated to be "Lucky like Lohrke," and I don't know which one to choose. Ruben Sierra, Dennis Martinez, Rich Dauer, Dennis Cook, Smoky Joe Wood, Frank Crosetti, Bobby Tolan? You've seen the research, but none of these guys make a compelling case equal to Lohrke's remarkable "backstory." It says here that the crown is still his. Lucky Lohrke truly was the luckiest player in baseball history.

A few notes about the methodologies in this article:

- For those of you who care, I used the "Pythagen-Pat" approach to the Pythagorean Variances. You can find a definition of PythgenPat in the Hardball Times statistical glossary (http://www.hardball-times.com/statpages/glossary/.
- To calculate each team's improvement scale, I had to average the number of games played between the two seasons involved (this made a big impact on the strike years). The calculation was (Winning Percent in Year Two divided by Winning Percent in Year One) times (The number of games played in both years divided by two).
- To calculate predicted Win Shares…
    - I first calculate each player's "expected Win Shares," which are the number of Win Shares an average player would have accrued that season, given that specific player's playing time.
    - I then calculate Win Shares Above Average for the three prior years, if available. Win Shares Above Average (or, WSAA) equals Win Shares minus expected Win Shares.
- Finally, I calculate Predicted Win Shares …
    - For rookies, I take 80 percent of the year's expected Win Shares to set predicted Win Shares. In the history of baseball, rookies have delivered at about that level.
    - For second-year players, I take 95 percent of the current year's expected Win Shares and add 50 percent of the previous year's WSAA.
    - For third-year players, I add 45 percent of the previous year's WSAA and 20 percent of the WSAA from the season before, and add them to the current season's expected Win Shares.
    - For all other players, I add 45 percent of the previous year's WSAA, plus 30 percent of WSAA from two years earlier, plus 15 percent of WSAA from three years earlier to the current season's expected Win Shares.

Statistics

It's the Hardball Times Statistics

Welcome to where the numbers are. From this point on (that is, once you've slogged through this introduction), you'll see nothing but graphs and numbers. Oh, there may be a few words—names of players and that sort of thing—but mostly numbers until we run out of space.

There is one tiny exception: We've snuck a bonus article into our stats. John Dewan has contributed his cutting-edge fielding figures to the Annual, including both his plus/minus range figures and Defensive Runs Saved. So the first part of our stats section is actually an article from John describing his system, followed by three years of position-by-position fielding stats. You'll see a wealth of data on those pages. In fact, you may want to spend all your time just nudging those figures around in your head.

Don't stop there, however. There is a lot more to see. On the other side of Dewan, we've got the old-fashioned stats section, a review of the season just past, organized by league and team. Here is how the numbers fall out…

League Stats

First up is an overview of each league (basically, team-level stats grouped by league). We already showed you division race graphs in our Division View articles, but back here you'll find graphs and stats that lay out the factors behind each team's success or lack thereof.

You'll also find some miscellaneous team stats, things like stolen bases and pitches per plate appearances and home/road splits. Also some "win" stats, like WPA and Win Shares, for each team. I'm not going to explain all of them; there is a Glossary at the back of the book. Stick your thumb there and leave it there, just in case.

Team Stats

After a few pages of league stats, you get to the core of our stats section: team and player stats organized by teams, in alphabetical order. Arizona is first, not the A's. Four pages per team (usually).

There's a graph at the beginning of each team's section, and I've copied the Tigers' graph onto the next page to give you a preview. Turn the page and take a look. I know it's a bunch of lines and stuff, a lot of information packed into one graph. So let me explain.

First, the gray area represents the number of wins each team garnered over the previous 10 games. In fact, the graph doesn't start until the 10th game of the season. Accompanying the running 10-game win total are two lines. One shows the average number of runs scored over the 10 games, and the other shows the average number of runs allowed during that time. These are included to give you a sense of whether each team's record was a function of scoring runs, allowing runs or both.

There's another line, toward the bottom of the graph. That represents each team's Championship Leverage Index, as invented and discussed by Sky Andrecheck a little earlier in the book. Championship LI is driven by each team's standing in the pennant race—the more intense the battle, the higher the LI.

You can see these dynamics on the Tigers' graph. First of all, note that streak in mid-May when they won eight of 10 games? Both the Tigers' offense and defense did well, spurring the attack. However, the reasons for that eight-game spike at the end of June are a little unclear; both offense and defense were about average. They probably had a few breaks go their way.

The spike in Championship LI near the end of July is telling—that's when they played a key three-game series with the White Sox, taking two of three behind some very strong pitching.

The Tigers had one other eight-of-10 streak, a key one, in early September. They really boosted their lead in the A.L. Central and their Championship LI went down during the streak because things seemed to be well in hand.

But those things quickly turned as the Tigers went into a brief slump and won only three of 10 in mid-September. The Championship LI tells the story as it rebounds quickly and then zooms to 10 on the last Sunday of the season. It literally went "off the charts" on playoff day. The Championship LI of that game with the Twins was 20 and we just couldn't fit it into the graph.

The stats in the Team sections should make sense to you. Most of them are traditional baseball stats, their presentation aligned to help you pick out the key numbers. However, there are a few funky sabermetric stats that I should point out.

First of all, we use a couple of cutting-edge offensive stats called Base Runs and Gross Production Average. They're our favorite "runs created" stats because they're pretty easy to understand and one is an "absolute" stat while the other is a "rate" stat. Definitions are in the Glossary.

For pitchers, we've included Pitching Runs Created, which is the interpretation of a pitcher's season from a hitter's point of view. In other words, Pitching Runs Created represents the impact a pitcher had but from a hitter's perspective. You can directly compare a hitter's Base Runs with a pitcher's Runs Created to get a sense of their relative worth. The definition of Pitching Runs Created is also in the Glossary.

Split Stats

There are two types of splits embedded in each table of "traditional" stats:

- Home/Away splits (labeled "H-A"), and
- Lefty/Righty splits (labeled "L^R" for batters and "R^L" for pitchers)

Both statistics are simply computed as the difference in Gross Production Average (GPA—it's in the Glossary) for each split. The Home/Away splits are computed as each player's home GPA minus his GPA on the road.

The lefty/right splits are a little more difficult to present in a simple table, but we were determined to make it work. Here's how we did it:

- We put a "handedness" label next to each batter and pitcher in the table. Each left-handed batter or pitcher has an asterisk (*) next to his name, while

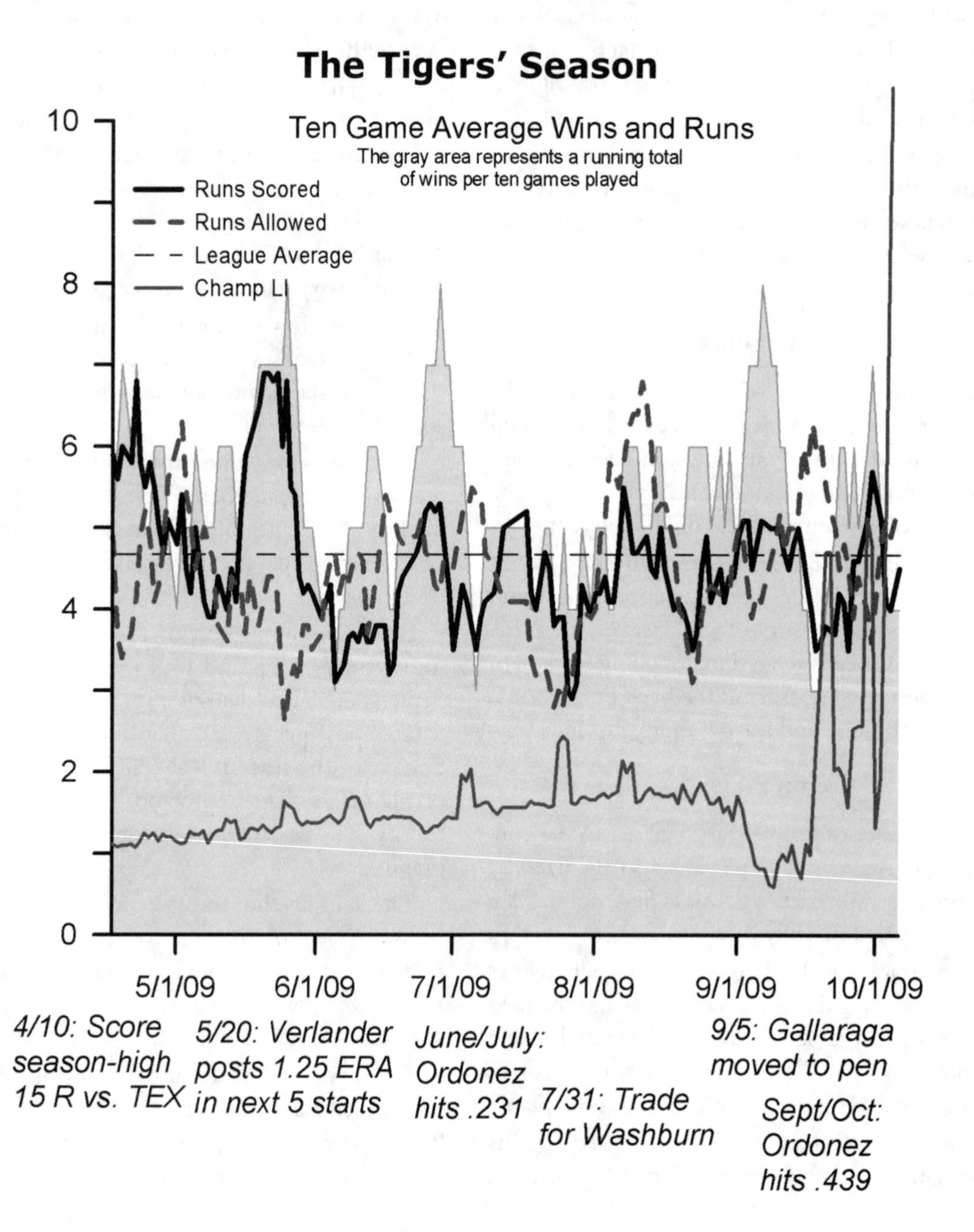

switch hitters have a plus sign (+) next to theirs. Right-handed players have no label.

- We vary the lefty/righty calculation according to the player's handedness. For righty batters, the calculation is L-R (average versus left-handed pitchers minus average versus right-handed pitchers). For lefty batters, the calculation is R-L. For switch hitters, we stuck to the more conventional L-R.
- For pitchers, we switched the calculations—for right-handed pitchers, it's R-L, for southpaws, it's L-R.

This is why we use the label "L^R." The exact calculation depends on the player's natural handedness and whether he was a pitcher or batter.

Why do we do this? To make the tables easier to read. Remember this rule: Natural splits for batters are positive, and natural splits for pitchers are negative (said another way: more offense is good for batters, and less offense is good for pitchers).

Use these guidelines for judging splits: On average, batters batted .012 points (in GPA) better at home last year. Obviously, pitchers were -.012 points better at home. Righty batters were .016 points better against lefty pitchers, and lefty batters were .030 points better against right-handers. Switch hitters were slightly better against right-handed pitchers.

Our splits may take a little getting used to, but this approach allows us to pack a lot of information into a little space.

Batted Ball Stats

Along with the traditional batting and pitching stats, we've included some unique tables of "Batted Ball Stats." I wrote about these stats extensively during the season, and you can download a PDF file of my weekly Batted Ball Reports from the THT Annual download page (details at the end of these ramblings).

As a quick summary, take a gander at the Batted Ball Stats of the Giants' breakout player, Pablo Sandoval. The best way to read this info is probably to start on the right, where we display Pablo's strengths as a hitter in four categories:

- Not In Play (NIP on the table) balls, or strikeouts, walks and Hit by Pitches.
- Ground Balls (GB)
- Line Drives (LD)
- Fly Balls (FB)

On the far right, we list each player's output relative to the league average. Sandoval, for instance, was above average in all four categories: Two runs for NIP, 13 runs on ground balls (turns out that the big guy had quite the "ground ball stroke"), 13 runs on line drives and 15 runs on fly balls.

Most hitters have a particular strength or two. Sandoval hit on all four cylinders in 2009, and that was the secret to his success.

When you move to the left on the table, you can see breakdowns of each batted ball type. For instance, the "Runs Per Event" columns show exactly that: how many runs each player created for each type of batted ball. Home run hitters, for instance, create more runs per fly ball.

The next two columns over show the "out rate" (basically, the inverse of batting average) on two types of batted balls: ground balls and outfield flies that aren't home runs. Sandoval had an average out rate in the latter category, but his out rate on ground balls was only 68 percent, seven points lower than the major league average.

The next two columns are two of my favorites. They break down fly balls into infield flies (one of the best indicators of a good hitter in my book) and proportion of outfield flies that were home runs. Sandoval, for instance, had somewhat favorable rates in both categories. His infield-fly rate was below the major league average and his home run rate was above it.

Finally, the left-hand columns are "frequency" columns. They show the percent of plate appearances in which the batter either struck out or walked/hit by pitch (Sandoval didn't walk a lot, but he did make contact and didn't strike out a lot) and the percent of batted balls broken into each type. Sandoval had a slight inclination toward the ground ball—he hit a slightly higher percentage of them than the major league average.

Batted Ball Batting Stats

	% of PA		% of Batted Balls					Out %		Runs Per Event				Total Runs vs. Avg.				
Player	**K%**	**BB%**	**GB%**	**LD%**	**FB%**	**IF/F**	**HR/OF**	**GB**	**OF**	**NIP**	**GB**	**LD**	**OF**	**NIP**	**GB**	**LD**	**FB**	**Tot**
Sandoval Pa	13	9	45	19	36	.08	.15	68	83	.07	.09	.48	.25	2	13	13	15	43
MLB Average	**18**	**10**	**43**	**19**	**38**	**.10**	**.11**	**75**	**83**	**.05**	**.04**	**.39**	**.19**	--	--	--	--	--

We feel that the Batted Ball stats, in conjunction with the traditional baseball stats, offer a deep view into the action on the diamond. It's relatively easy to say that Sandoval had a fine year, for instance, but now you know that the key to his success was a well-rounded game. This has implications for his future performance, by the way, if you tend to think his ground ball batting average was fluky.

Our Fielding Stats

You'll find fielding stats on the last page of each team's section. As in the batting and pitching sections, most of these stats are traditional and straightforward. There are two exceptions, however: Revised Zone Rating (RZR) and plays made Out Of Zone (OOZ).

John Dewan invented and Baseball Info Solutions provided these fielding stats. As we say in the Glossary, RZR measures how often a fielder successfully fields a ball that is hit into his zone. A zone is defined as all areas of the field in which that fielding position successfully converts at least 50 percent of chances into outs, on average. RZR differs from the original Zone Rating by removing plays made out of zone and listing them separately.

To help you get acquainted with RZR, here is the average RZR and total plays made out of zone for each position in 2009:

POS	BIZ	Plays	RZR	OOZ
1B	6,094	4,765	.782	1,484
2B	12,482	10,148	.813	1,189
3B	9,746	6,944	.712	1,796
SS	13,071	10,472	.801	1,656
LF	8,139	7,273	.894	2,178
CF	10,324	9,608	.931	2,939
RF	8,326	7,561	.908	2,257

(BIZ stands for "Balls in Zone")

Because these stats may be new to you, they're presented in a slightly different format in our stats. For Zone Rating, we've got "ZRDif" for each player who played at least 100 innings at any position. ZRDif is the difference between that player's RZR and the average RZR at that position. It's a "relative rate" stat, if you will, much like WPA or the Batted Ball Stats.

We also list each player's plays made out of zone along with something we've simply called "Dif." (You can spot the point at which our marketing budget ran out of money.) Dif is the average difference between that player's plays made out of zone and the average plays made out of zone at that position, per 1,000 innings.

Remember, these are both rate stats, and they're intended to complement the fielding stats you'll find in Dewan's article.

By the way, you get some funky results when you look at rate stats for players who played just 100 innings at a position. Mike Jacobs, who is no John Olerud, played just over 100 innings at first base for the Royals. His RZR Difference was -.139, which is just terrible. But his OOZ Diff was +64.

Don't trust every number you crunch.

Each team section, by the way, has a list of "Stat Facts" in the beginning, contributed by THT's Steve Treder. They highlight some of the most interesting stats for each team.

Appendix and Downloads

There is also an Appendix of win-based stats: the Win Shares, WAR and WPA stats of most players on every team are listed in our Appendix. What's more, you can download these stats in an Excel spreadsheet.

Yes, part of the value of purchasing the THT Annual includes access to a special Downloads webpage. On the Downloads page, you'll be able to download these bonus features:

- Sky Andrecheck's coverage of the postseason
- A master PDF file of all Dave Studenmund's weekly 2009 Batted Ball Reports
- An Excel spreadsheet of all batted ball stats for all batters and pitchers
- A "Win Stats" spreadsheet that includes the most popular win-based stats (WAR, WPA and Win Shares) for all players

The URL of the Downloads webpage is...

http://www.hardballtimes.com/THT2010Annual/

...the username is "tht10" and the password is "hanley".

So enjoy the numbers. And remember, pitchers and catchers report in February.

The Tiger and the Mariner

by John Dewan

Here is the story of two teams that learned an important lesson in 2009.

The Tigers

Two years ago, in 2008, the Detroit Tigers were going to set the world on fire. There was talk of scoring 1,000 runs as a team, a feat accomplished only twice in the last 70 years. They were supposed to be an offensive juggernaut. They threw defense to the wind. To bolster the offense, they moved their slick-fielding third baseman (Brandon Inge) to catcher. This made room for the newly acquired basher Miguel Cabrera. At that point Cabrera already had proven with his previous team (Marlins) that he was woeful at third, but the idea was that his offense would more than make up for his defense.

That particular experiment lasted exactly 14 games.

Cabrera made five errors and lost three runs defensively in those 14 games. The Tigers then threw everything and everybody but the kitchen sink at the third base position. It was like tee-ball. (You know: Everyone gets a chance to try out at every position.) Seven different players played third for the Tigers that season, and every single one of them lost runs defensively for the club. Except Inge, the guy they could have been playing all along:

Defensive Runs Saved – 2008 Detroit Tigers Third Base

Carlos Guillen	-9
Miguel Cabrera	-3
Jeff Larish	-3
Ramon Santiago	-3
Ryan Raburn	-2
Mike Hessman	-2
Brandon Inge	1

This motley third-base crew lost 21 runs defensively for the Tigers, their worst defensive position in 2008.

The thing is, in 2007 the Tigers were a very good defensive club. They had 58 defensive runs saved as a team, fourth best in baseball, and they won 88 games. And third base was their strongest defensive position with 20 runs saved, thanks to Inge.

In 2008 the Tigers lost 88 games, and third base was their weakest defensive position.

In 2009 the Tigers rediscovered defensive religion. They realized that what they tried in 2008 simply doesn't work in major league baseball. All offense and no defense doesn't cut it. A team needs balance. Inge went back to third base, and the Tigers brought in one of the best defensive catchers in baseball, Gerald Laird, to take his place behind the plate. At shortstop, the offensive-minded but mediocre defensively Edgar Renteria was sent packing. He was replaced by the best defensive shortstop of the 21st^{rrd} century so far, Adam Everett. (That is my assessment based on my defensive metrics outlined in *The Fielding Bible* and *The Fielding Bible, Volume II.)*

What happened? The Tigers improved by 41 runs defensively at third base. They improved by 17 runs at shortstop. They improved their win total by 12 games and won 86 games for the season. They just missed the playoffs by losing the 163rd game of the year to the Twins, but they spent more time in first place in 2009 than any other team in the American League.

The Mariners

The Seattle Mariners were the most improved team in baseball in 2009. They improved their record from 61-101 in 2008 to 85-77. That's an increase of 24 wins in one year.

The Seattle Mariners also were the most improved defensive team in baseball this past season. This is not a coincidence. They improved their Defensive Runs Saved as a team from 17 runs saved in 2008 to 109 runs saved in 2009. That's an increase of 92 runs in one year.

The rule of thumb among stat-heads is that 10 runs is about equal to a win. Using this, we can estimate that Seattle's defensive improvement gained the Mariners about nine additional wins in 2009 over the 2008 club. That certainly doesn't account for the entire 24-win improvement. After all, hitting and pitching are also essential, but it does show how much defense matters. Nine games out of the 24-win gain are significant. Give any team in major league baseball 92 more runs and see how far it moves up in the standings.

How did the Mariners do it? Outfield defense is the main answer. In 2008 they had only 11 runs saved defensively from their entire outfield. Defensively, all

Components of Defensive Runs Saved

Component	Applicable Positions	2009 Leader	Top 2009 Runs Saved Total
Plus/Minus Runs Saved	All except Catchers	Chone Figgins	30
Earned Runs Saved	Catchers	Jason Varitek	8
Stolen Base Runs Saved	Catchers	Kenji Johjima	9
Stolen Base Runs Saved	Pitchers	Buehrle/Kershaw/ Verlander	4
Bunt Runs Saved	Corner Infielders	Nick Johnson/ Adrian Gonzalez	3
Double Play Runs Saved	Middle Infielders	Placido Polanco/ Ian Kinsler	5
Outfield Arm Runs Saved	Outfielders	Adam Jones	12
Home Run Saving Catch Runs Saved	Outfielders	Adam Jones	6

they had was Ichiro. He split time between right field and center field. In right field he saved 15 runs defensively, but in center field he was pretty much average (-1 run saved). In 2009 the team brought in two of the best defensive outfielders in the game to join Suzuki. Franklin Gutierrez had just completed two seasons playing right field for the Indians, where he saved a total of 32 runs defensively. Endy Chavez saved 23 runs playing all three outfield positions in the previous two years for the Mets. And neither player was a regular on his team those years; neither started as many as 100 games in either season.

On the 2009 Mariners, Ichiro was moved back to right field and Gutierrez became the center fielder. Chavez didn't play full time, but played most in left field. The results were spectacular. The outfield saved 56 runs defensively, the best in baseball.

Don't like defense? Then you would be clueless in Seattle.

Description of the Team Defensive Charts

Defensive Runs Saved (Runs Saved, for short) is the innovative metric introduced by John Dewan in *The Fielding Bible—Volume II.* The Runs Saved value indicates how many runs a player saved or hurt his team in the field compared to the average player at his position. A player near zero Runs Saved is about average; a positive number of runs saved indicates above-average defense, below-average fielders post negative Runs Saved totals. There are eight components of Runs Saved, listed above with the 2009 leaders as seen in the *Bill James Handbook 2010.* The definition of each component is:

- Plus Minus Runs Saved evaluates the fielder's range and ability to convert a batted ball to an out.
- Earned Runs Saved measures a catcher's influence on his pitching staff.
- Stolen Base Runs Saved gives the catcher credit for throwing out runners and preventing them from attempting steals in the first place.
- Stolen Base Runs Saved measures the pitcher's contributions to controlling the running game.
- Bunt Runs Saved evaluates a fielder's handling of bunted balls in play.
- Double Play Runs Saved credits infielders for turning double plays as opposed to getting one out on the play.
- Outfield Arm Runs Saved evaluates an outfielder's throwing arm based on how often runner advance on base hits and are thrown out trying to take extra bases.
- Home Run Saving Catch Runs credits the outfielder 1.6 runs per robbed home run.

In the top chart on each of the three following pages, we break down each team's defense by Runs Saved at each position to isolate that team's strengths and weaknesses. As you can see, Mariners centerfielders (primarily Gutierrez) played the strongest defense of any position in baseball last year, while the Athletics were crippled by a poor defensive showing from the team's shortstops.

The second chart on each page rates each team's performance in four categories. Plus/Minus is broken down into Middle Infield, Corner Infield and Outfield. Ground DP tells you how often the team turned double plays given its opportunities (ground ball with a man on first and fewer than two outs). A team's overall handling of Bunts is rated on the A through F grade scale. The Throwing section rates how often outfielders gun out opposing baserunners and how often they prevent runners from trying for extra bases in the first place.

Team Defensive Runs by Position - 2009

Team	Pitcher	Catcher	First Base	Second Base	Third Base	Shortstop	Left Field	Center Field	Right Field	Total
Seattle Mariners	12	12	1	5	28	-5	8	35	13	109
Los Angeles Angels	-1	-3	10	14	28	-4	23	-1	-1	65
Tampa Bay Rays	-11	-4	-11	13	15	5	26	-1	27	59
Toronto Blue Jays	7	6	-1	22	11	14	-4	-11	8	52
Cincinnati Reds	11	1	-4	-3	-3	10	16	14	7	49
Texas Rangers	2	3	-8	21	-16	18	6	5	12	43
Detroit Tigers	-3	2	-2	5	8	4	13	17	-5	39
Arizona Diamondbacks	-6	3	-13	14	-4	9	15	3	12	33
San Francisco Giants	7	-4	11	-4	-5	-8	12	5	19	33
Pittsburgh Pirates	4	0	-1	-9	0	16	13	0	9	32
Los Angeles Dodgers	0	5	3	8	15	6	-4	-3	2	32
St Louis Cardinals	11	5	12	-8	-8	13	-5	4	6	30
New York Mets	13	-1	12	-12	-11	-8	7	11	7	18
Chicago Cubs	3	7	3	-1	-3	3	-2	0	7	17
Colorado Rockies	5	-2	-2	2	3	13	15	-9	-9	16
Philadelphia Phillies	-5	2	-1	14	7	-5	-1	-7	12	16
Atlanta Braves	4	2	7	-11	2	19	-11	-10	7	9
Washington Nationals	8	-1	-20	0	21	-3	-3	11	-6	7
New York Yankees	4	-7	1	6	-13	1	0	3	7	2
Houston Astros	3	2	-1	-4	-12	-15	-3	10	19	-1
Cleveland Indians	-4	-9	5	2	-7	4	-7	-1	13	-4
San Diego Padres	4	2	11	-20	2	-15	-1	16	-4	-5
Chicago White Sox	16	0	-4	1	-11	2	-8	5	-10	-9
Baltimore Orioles	7	-8	-12	-5	-4	14	0	0	-3	-11
Oakland Athletics	1	2	-8	-10	-7	-32	18	13	10	-13
Milwaukee Brewers	-10	-7	-1	20	-8	2	-14	0	-5	-23
Florida Marlins	-12	-4	-8	-7	-5	4	-19	5	18	-28
Minnesota Twins	-4	-5	1	-22	9	-24	-1	16	-5	-35
Boston Red Sox	-17	-8	10	9	-18	-19	-1	-10	2	-52
Kansas City Royals	3	-5	-3	-13	-13	-17	5	-1	-20	-64

Team Totals and Rankings - 2009

	PLUS/MINUS					GROUND DP				BUNTS				THROWING				
Team	Middle Infield	Corner Infield	Outfield	Total	Rank	GDP Opps	GDP	Pct	Rank	Opps	Score	Grade	Rank	Opps To Advance	Extra Bases	Kills	Pct	Rank
Seattle Mariners	-8	+38	+76	+106	1	284	128	.451	3	31	.587	B	7	404	169	15	.418	4
Tampa Bay Rays	+28	+8	+57	+93	2	273	113	.414	11	39	.503	C+	24	418	181	24	.433	10
Arizona Diamondbacks	+30	-23	+46	+53	3	317	117	.369	25	51	.509	C+	21	457	220	10	.481	26
Los Angeles Angels	+1	+52	-2	+51	4	313	154	.492	1	31	.505	C+	22	452	196	19	.434	11
Texas Rangers	+41	-28	+38	+51	4	289	138	.478	2	28	.430	D+	29	434	208	17	.479	23
San Francisco Giants	-6	+1	+39	+34	6	299	111	.371	24	72	.593	B	4	360	157	19	.436	12
Pittsburgh Pirates	+12	0	+17	+29	7	342	140	.409	15	55	.537	C+	15	428	189	18	.442	14
Los Angeles Dodgers	+20	+19	-14	+25	8	299	114	.381	23	45	.593	B	3	369	177	16	.480	24
Cincinnati Reds	+8	-14	+27	+21	9	336	135	.402	17	46	.620	B+	1	434	169	23	.389	1
Detroit Tigers	+6	+14	0	+20	10	319	140	.439	5	32	.433	D+	28	439	184	20	.419	5
Toronto Blue Jays	+42	+27	-51	+18	11	345	145	.420	9	33	.342	F	30	456	181	16	.397	2
New York Mets	-19	+2	+25	+8	12	332	113	.340	30	46	.538	C+	14	460	208	15	.452	15
Colorado Rockies	+21	0	-13	+8	12	334	120	.359	28	57	.534	C+	17	440	213	18	.484	27
San Diego Padres	-40	+18	+29	+7	14	318	117	.368	26	61	.588	B	6	428	236	15	.551	30
New York Yankees	+11	-12	+8	+7	14	290	112	.386	21	28	.511	C+	20	423	180	11	.426	7
St Louis Cardinals	+3	+6	-15	-6	16	366	149	.407	16	43	.566	B-	8	425	182	13	.428	9
Cleveland Indians	-2	-2	-6	-10	17	337	150	.445	4	49	.541	B-	13	532	256	15	.481	25
Chicago Cubs	+8	-4	-15	-11	18	346	118	.341	29	65	.565	B-	9	374	175	16	.468	20
Atlanta Braves	+12	+5	-29	-12	19	354	138	.390	19	43	.592	B	5	418	195	14	.467	19
Philadelphia Phillies	+9	+5	-34	-20	20	271	108	.399	18	48	.558	B-	10	426	181	27	.425	6
Washington Nationals	-4	-2	-15	-21	21	330	127	.385	22	54	.553	B-	11	455	207	16	.455	17
Milwaukee Brewers	+24	-12	-35	-23	22	312	135	.433	6	45	.518	C+	19	424	202	9	.476	22
Oakland Athletics	-53	-20	+44	-29	23	301	129	.429	7	36	.504	C+	23	464	203	17	.438	13
Florida Marlins	-7	-19	-6	-32	24	319	115	.361	27	55	.525	C+	18	424	192	14	.453	16
Minnesota Twins	-59	+17	+9	-33	25	281	116	.413	13	33	.480	C	27	447	222	11	.497	29
Houston Astros	-26	-19	+7	-38	26	347	143	.412	14	40	.609	B+	2	472	202	21	.428	8
Boston Red Sox	-15	-11	-19	-45	27	251	97	.386	20	41	.537	C+	16	459	217	14	.473	21
Chicago White Sox	+1	-16	-46	-61	28	314	130	.414	10	45	.493	C	26	413	189	22	.458	18
Baltimore Orioles	+6	-22	-73	-89	29	312	132	.423	8	27	.544	B-	12	483	195	22	.404	3
Kansas City Royals	-46	-17	-42	-105	30	317	131	.413	12	40	.499	C	25	481	238	22	.495	28

Team Defensive Runs by Position - 2008

Team	Pitcher	Catcher	First Base	Second Base	Third Base	Shortstop	Left Field	Center Field	Right Field	Total
Philadelphia Phillies	1	-3	2	33	3	16	4	14	9	79
St Louis Cardinals	3	4	14	16	7	20	2	-8	18	76
Oakland Athletics	14	5	6	23	10	-17	-9	17	15	64
Toronto Blue Jays	9	1	5	3	29	-4	-7	-3	23	56
Milwaukee Brewers	8	10	-9	-3	3	17	11	14	2	53
New York Mets	13	-2	-6	-18	2	-4	25	21	13	44
Atlanta Braves	-2	7	5	-3	15	14	-2	7	-5	36
Cleveland Indians	1	-3	-6	7	-4	-3	12	3	24	31
Tampa Bay Rays	-8	-4	15	8	13	-13	14	1	0	26
Washington Nationals	2	1	-6	-13	11	12	12	-4	10	25
Houston Astros	-2	0	13	-19	3	8	3	7	11	24
Boston Red Sox	-5	2	2	9	12	1	0	0	-1	20
Seattle Mariners	-1	-3	0	-2	25	-13	-6	0	17	17
Florida Marlins	-8	-3	-21	6	-1	4	7	22	3	9
Chicago Cubs	13	0	4	-3	-6	4	8	-11	0	9
Los Angeles Dodgers	3	-2	0	-17	14	1	5	5	-5	4
Arizona Diamondbacks	0	-3	-12	6	-8	-1	11	7	-4	-4
San Diego Padres	-14	-2	0	-7	0	-6	6	7	11	-5
Los Angeles Angels	-13	-4	16	2	4	6	-8	4	-13	-6
San Francisco Giants	-12	3	5	-13	-6	1	7	-4	12	-7
Pittsburgh Pirates	9	4	-3	2	-3	10	-11	-17	2	-7
Minnesota Twins	4	-2	-2	-3	-15	-3	-14	17	9	-9
Colorado Rockies	9	1	-3	15	-6	6	0	-6	-25	-9
Cincinnati Reds	-1	-2	16	9	-25	-11	-12	18	-4	-12
Detroit Tigers	20	8	-8	9	-21	-13	-3	-3	-4	-15
Baltimore Orioles	-13	0	-7	-3	-13	-30	11	20	19	-16
Texas Rangers	-5	1	-1	-6	-26	-5	1	-4	18	-27
Chicago White Sox	-7	-9	-8	-7	6	1	3	-5	-8	-34
New York Yankees	-2	-1	-18	-13	-10	-10	10	12	-6	-38
Kansas City Royals	8	-5	-10	-6	-12	9	-7	-8	-11	-42

Team Totals and Rankings - 2008

	PLUS/MINUS					GROUND DP				BUNTS				THROWING				
Team	Middle Infield	Corner Infield	Outfield	Total	Rank	GDP Opps	GDP	Pct	Rank	Opps	Score	Grade	Rank	Opps To Advance	Extra Bases	Kills	Pct	Rank
Philadelphia Phillies	+70	+7	0	+77	1	338	127	.376	22	45	.559	B-	11	406	163	27	.401	2
St Louis Cardinals	+43	+26	-3	+66	2	330	135	.409	11	37	.634	A-	3	456	202	20	.443	8
Toronto Blue Jays	+4	+47	0	+51	3	293	111	.379	21	35	.499	C	24	373	167	21	.448	12
New York Mets	-21	-12	+79	+46	4	341	113	.331	29	47	.640	A-	2	446	203	20	.455	16
Milwaukee Brewers	+25	-5	+25	+45	5	374	132	.353	25	68	.504	C+	23	389	175	15	.450	15
Oakland Athletics	-5	+26	+24	+45	5	273	142	.520	1	34	.529	C+	17	419	188	20	.449	13
Washington Nationals	-1	+3	+35	+37	7	310	119	.384	19	39	.549	B-	14	465	227	12	.488	27
Tampa Bay Rays	-12	+33	+11	+32	8	303	134	.442	8	45	.622	B+	4	392	179	19	.457	17
Atlanta Braves	+22	+24	-19	+27	9	390	132	.338	28	34	.566	B-	10	416	187	13	.450	14
Boston Red Sox	+16	+18	-8	+26	10	299	119	.398	15	42	.577	B	7	422	202	14	.479	25
Florida Marlins	+17	-28	+36	+25	11	313	100	.319	30	54	.512	C+	20	448	207	20	.462	19
San Diego Padres	-16	-7	+46	+23	12	324	127	.392	17	53	.692	A+	1	424	216	14	.509	29
Houston Astros	-18	+24	+15	+21	13	296	120	.405	12	30	.532	C+	16	398	178	20	.447	11
Cleveland Indians	-10	-5	+33	+18	14	330	159	.482	2	47	.447	C-	27	489	203	23	.415	3
Arizona Diamondbacks	+6	-25	+30	+11	15	324	114	.352	26	52	.513	C+	19	415	199	13	.480	26
Seattle Mariners	-23	+35	-20	-8	16	336	138	.411	10	44	.572	B	8	510	215	20	.422	4
San Francisco Giants	-10	-8	+10	-8	16	283	104	.367	23	53	.607	B+	6	441	207	12	.469	22
Los Angeles Angels	0	+28	-41	-13	18	315	141	.448	4	31	.555	B-	13	407	206	16	.506	28
Los Angeles Dodgers	-11	+12	-14	-13	18	362	124	.343	27	50	.613	B+	5	452	210	19	.465	21
Baltimore Orioles	-38	-21	+37	-22	20	368	142	.386	18	44	.473	C	26	501	199	24	.397	1
Chicago Cubs	+6	-4	-26	-24	21	266	97	.365	24	49	.558	B-	12	361	161	17	.446	10
Cincinnati Reds	+2	-11	-24	-33	22	340	130	.382	20	50	.567	B-	9	442	187	18	.423	5
Chicago White Sox	-13	+3	-25	-35	23	311	138	.444	6	37	.435	D+	28	432	203	10	.470	23
Colorado Rockies	+21	-12	-48	-39	24	359	144	.401	14	43	.535	C+	15	519	241	15	.464	20
Minnesota Twins	-13	-21	-8	-42	25	327	142	.434	9	28	.511	C+	21	467	208	23	.445	9
Pittsburgh Pirates	+14	-4	-53	-43	26	391	157	.402	13	68	.524	C+	18	505	233	15	.461	18
Detroit Tigers	-8	-34	-22	-64	27	341	153	.449	3	36	.411	D+	30	503	237	14	.471	24
Texas Rangers	-22	-37	-7	-66	28	361	160	.443	7	44	.506	C+	22	549	240	19	.437	7
New York Yankees	-29	-33	-8	-70	29	280	110	.393	16	36	.419	D+	29	447	191	22	.427	6
Kansas City Royals	-4	-24	-49	-77	30	301	134	.445	5	31	.474	C	25	463	238	15	.514	30

Team Defensive Runs by Position - 2007

Team	Pitcher	Catcher	First Base	Second Base	Third Base	Shortstop	Left Field	Center Field	Right Field	Total
Toronto Blue Jays	-10	-1	9	22	5	23	7	5	10	70
Atlanta Braves	8	-1	-2	-3	4	0	18	23	20	67
Philadelphia Phillies	5	7	-1	14	4	5	-9	12	29	66
Detroit Tigers	4	5	1	10	20	-5	3	16	4	58
St Louis Cardinals	12	7	28	-1	22	-15	3	-4	4	56
Kansas City Royals	-1	-5	15	9	2	16	8	0	11	55
Colorado Rockies	21	4	8	12	-19	31	1	-2	-10	46
New York Mets	-5	0	-1	-4	14	12	12	18	-3	43
Arizona Diamondbacks	-1	-1	-6	19	-5	0	21	3	13	43
Minnesota Twins	6	1	-1	-8	12	19	1	1	1	32
Oakland Athletics	-9	10	2	16	3	0	1	0	2	25
San Francisco Giants	-6	5	17	-13	23	12	-6	-17	10	25
Chicago Cubs	-14	-15	-6	-1	16	5	21	15	-2	19
Cleveland Indians	3	4	-8	1	-4	1	15	-1	7	18
Texas Rangers	4	2	1	3	-10	-9	17	-4	11	15
San Diego Padres	3	-13	-3	-3	2	4	6	10	2	8
New York Yankees	4	-6	7	21	3	-25	7	-4	-5	2
Washington Nationals	4	-3	-22	-5	20	-17	8	11	6	2
Boston Red Sox	-12	-4	4	2	7	2	-16	10	6	-1
Los Angeles Angels	-20	-2	22	9	-2	2	7	-14	-5	-3
Baltimore Orioles	-11	-3	-6	0	3	0	3	5	4	-5
Los Angeles Dodgers	-1	10	-11	-15	-1	9	-12	4	8	-9
Milwaukee Brewers	-1	-7	-11	-6	-21	6	12	2	13	-13
Seattle Mariners	11	-8	-16	1	4	-7	-9	6	0	-18
Pittsburgh Pirates	-6	0	4	-6	-18	10	-11	-5	14	-18
Houston Astros	9	-4	2	-19	-16	8	6	-7	-9	-30
Cincinnati Reds	-4	4	-9	8	-14	-1	-18	3	0	-31
Florida Marlins	-10	0	-10	-11	-20	-27	4	22	12	-40
Chicago White Sox	4	3	-3	-21	-11	-8	7	8	-25	-46
Tampa Bay Devil Rays	-14	-3	-1	-9	-15	-29	-3	1	4	-69

Team Totals and Rankings - 2007

	PLUS/MINUS					GROUND DP				BUNTS				THROWING				
Team	Middle Infield	Corner Infield	Outfield	Total	Rank	GDP Opps	GDP	Pct	Rank	Opps	Score	Grade	Rank	Opps To Advance	Extra Bases	Kills	Pct	Rank
Toronto Blue Jays	+56	+25	+16	+97	1	348	148	.425	8	22	.461	C-	30	416	187	18	.450	13
New York Mets	+15	+11	+42	+68	2	319	110	.345	29	54	.622	B+	2	400	203	16	.508	29
Kansas City Royals	+25	+24	+14	+63	3	296	139	.470	1	25	.466	C-	26	448	211	21	.471	22
Atlanta Braves	-5	+4	+62	+61	4	334	123	.368	27	59	.529	C+	17	432	179	21	.414	2
Arizona Diamondbacks	+19	-18	+43	+44	5	330	141	.427	6	41	.562	B-	10	409	191	18	.467	20
Detroit Tigers	0	+29	+15	+44	5	297	125	.421	10	24	.515	C+	19	452	203	18	.449	12
Chicago Cubs	+3	+13	+23	+39	7	303	117	.386	26	61	.534	C+	14	402	173	27	.430	6
St Louis Cardinals	-17	+58	-11	+30	8	338	135	.399	22	35	.734	A+	1	477	211	19	.442	9
Oakland Athletics	+14	+8	-1	+21	9	318	135	.425	9	33	.480	C	22	453	222	12	.490	26
San Diego Padres	0	-6	+25	+19	10	326	128	.393	24	67	.612	B+	4	418	207	14	.495	27
Cleveland Indians	+5	-9	+22	+18	11	335	137	.409	17	49	.530	C+	16	458	214	14	.467	21
Philadelphia Phillies	+25	-2	-5	+18	11	341	137	.402	21	55	.589	B	6	473	192	29	.406	1
Boston Red Sox	+3	+14	-4	+13	13	278	117	.421	11	31	.577	B	8	380	180	13	.474	23
San Francisco Giants	+1	+46	-34	+13	13	328	130	.396	23	63	.618	B+	3	445	201	9	.452	15
Minnesota Twins	+14	+16	-23	+7	15	298	127	.426	7	29	.469	C-	25	426	182	18	.427	4
Texas Rangers	-9	-14	+25	+2	16	366	143	.391	25	37	.470	C	24	487	232	20	.476	24
Washington Nationals	-33	-8	+40	-1	17	318	132	.415	14	55	.580	B	7	451	216	13	.479	25
Colorado Rockies	+46	-16	-33	-3	18	346	156	.451	4	44	.518	C+	18	442	199	12	.450	14
Los Angeles Angels	+8	+27	-40	-5	19	296	135	.456	3	30	.465	C-	27	449	204	18	.454	16
Baltimore Orioles	+3	-5	-6	-8	20	333	135	.405	19	49	.462	C-	28	508	227	19	.447	10
Milwaukee Brewers	-5	-41	+36	-10	21	298	124	.416	13	51	.545	B-	12	479	220	15	.459	18
Los Angeles Dodgers	-8	-20	+14	-14	22	338	142	.420	12	46	.593	B	5	439	242	9	.551	30
New York Yankees	-20	+17	-39	-42	23	333	153	.459	2	39	.462	C-	29	458	196	25	.428	5
Pittsburgh Pirates	-4	-18	-26	-48	24	369	164	.444	5	52	.575	B	9	514	235	21	.457	17
Houston Astros	-5	-17	-28	-50	25	334	114	.341	30	52	.547	B-	11	436	219	19	.502	28
Seattle Mariners	-11	-14	-28	-53	26	339	140	.413	16	34	.472	C	23	498	215	16	.432	7
Cincinnati Reds	+7	-29	-41	-63	27	319	132	.414	15	49	.490	C	21	476	213	17	.447	11
Florida Marlins	-54	-44	+18	-80	28	346	127	.367	28	56	.530	C+	15	545	237	26	.435	8
Chicago White Sox	-38	-15	-29	-82	29	345	139	.403	20	55	.536	C+	13	515	239	15	.464	19
Tampa Bay Devil Rays	-51	-17	-39	-107	30	314	128	.408	18	49	.491	C	20	528	220	24	.417	3

American League Team Stats

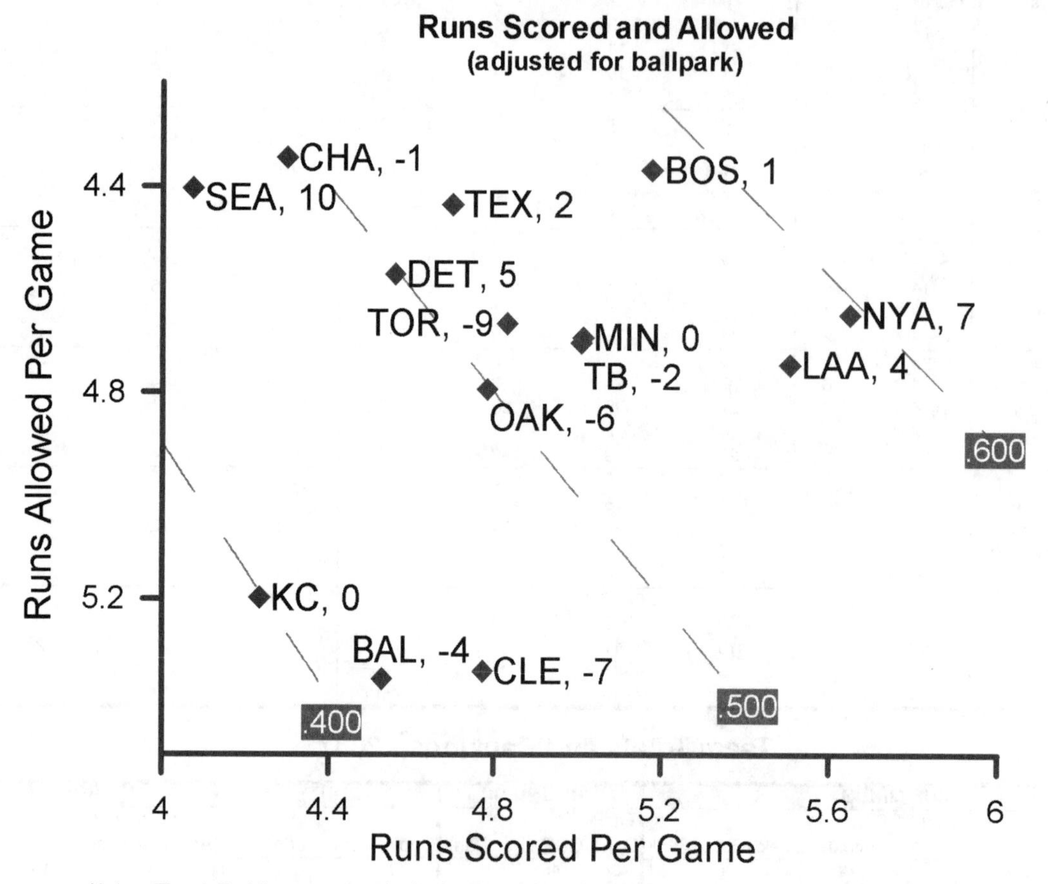

Notes: The dotted lines represent winning percentage based on run differential. The number after each team name represents the difference between the team's actual record and its run differential record.

Team Record						Scoring Runs			Preventing Runs				Projection	
Team	**W**	**L**	**RS**	**RA**	**RS-RA**	**AB/RSP**	**BA/RSP**	**HR**	**ERA**	**HRA**	**K**	**DER**	**PWINS**	**VAR**
LAA	97	65	883	761	122	1,509	.297	173	4.45	180	1,062	.691	93	4
BAL	64	98	741	876	-135	1,340	.284	160	5.15	218	933	.683	68	-4
BOS	95	67	872	736	136	1,427	.283	212	4.36	167	1,230	.681	94	1
CHA	79	83	724	732	-8	1,342	.265	184	4.15	169	1,119	.692	80	-1
CLE	65	97	773	865	-92	1,432	.261	161	5.06	183	986	.682	72	-7
DET	86	77	743	745	-2	1,355	.261	183	4.29	182	1,102	.697	81	5
KC	65	97	686	842	-156	1,340	.260	144	4.83	166	1,153	.677	65	0
MIN	87	76	817	765	52	1,441	.278	172	4.50	185	1,052	.693	87	0
NYA	103	59	915	753	162	1,542	.272	244	4.26	181	1,260	.699	96	7
OAK	75	87	759	761	-2	1,450	.272	135	4.26	156	1,124	.685	81	-6
SEA	85	77	640	692	-52	1,275	.235	160	3.87	172	1,043	.715	75	10
TB	84	78	803	754	49	1,438	.269	199	4.33	183	1,125	.699	86	-2
TEX	87	75	784	740	44	1,326	.268	224	4.38	171	1,016	.701	85	2
TOR	75	87	798	771	27	1,416	.257	209	4.47	181	1,181	.684	84	-9
Average	**82**	**80**	**781**	**771**	**10**	**1,402**	**.269**	**183**	**4.45**	**178**	**1,099**	**.691**	**81**	**1**

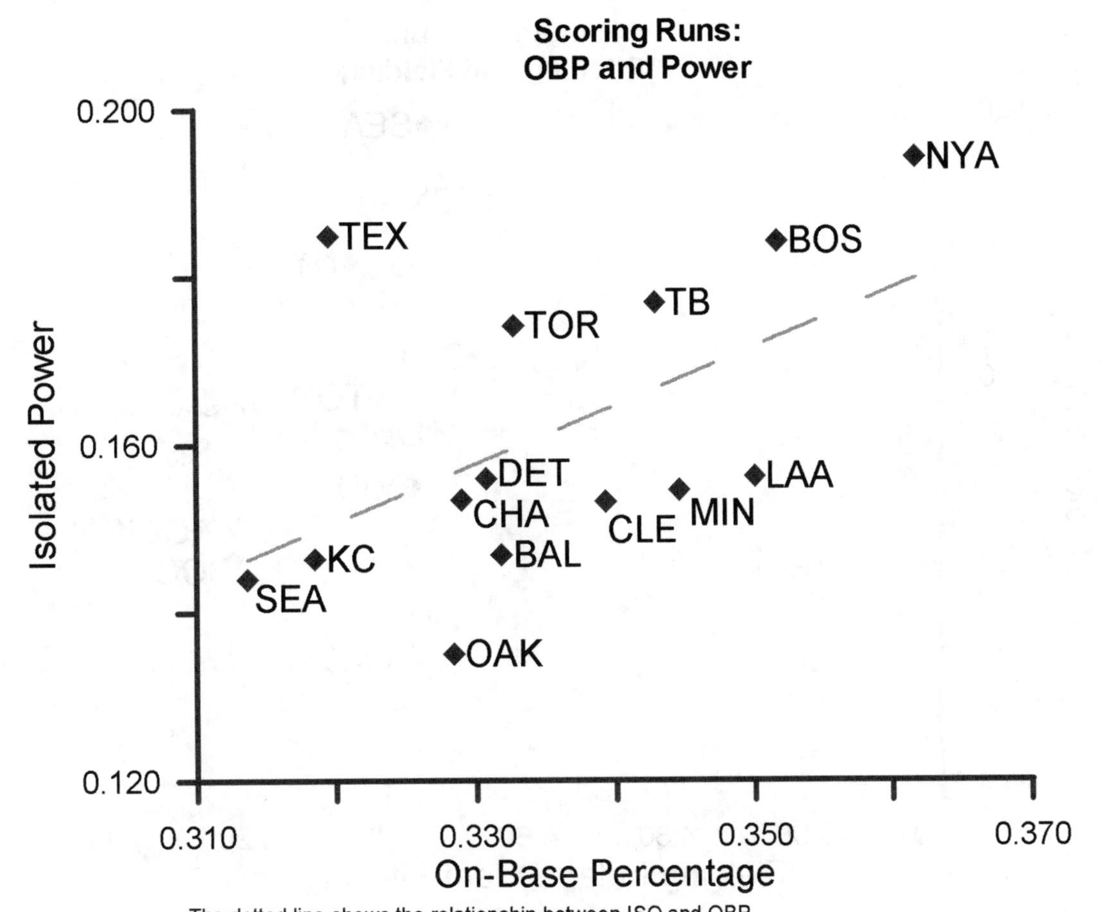

The dotted line shows the relationship between ISO and OBP.

Team	Runs	PA	H	1B	2B	3B	HR	TB	SO	BB	HBP	SH	SF	BA	OBP	SLG	GPA	ISO
LAA	883	6,305	1,604	1,105	293	33	173	2,482	1,054	547	41	43	52	.285	.350	.441	.268	.156
BAL	741	6,233	1,508	1,022	307	19	160	2,333	1,013	517	39	13	46	.268	.332	.415	.253	.147
BOS	872	6,344	1,495	923	335	25	212	2,516	1,120	659	70	19	51	.270	.352	.454	.272	.184
CHA	724	6,132	1,410	960	246	20	184	2,248	1,022	534	62	34	39	.258	.329	.411	.251	.153
CLE	773	6,320	1,468	965	314	28	161	2,321	1,211	582	81	39	50	.264	.339	.417	.257	.153
DET	743	6,234	1,443	980	245	35	183	2,307	1,114	540	61	53	39	.260	.331	.416	.253	.156
KC	686	6,103	1,432	961	276	51	144	2,242	1,091	457	42	38	32	.259	.318	.405	.245	.146
MIN	817	6,346	1,539	1,056	271	40	172	2,406	1,021	585	45	51	57	.274	.345	.429	.262	.155
NYA	915	6,449	1,604	1,014	325	21	244	2,703	1,014	663	54	31	39	.283	.362	.478	.282	.194
OAK	759	6,247	1,464	1,001	307	21	135	2,218	1,046	527	50	31	54	.262	.328	.397	.247	.135
SEA	640	6,113	1,430	971	280	19	160	2,228	1,093	421	49	56	44	.258	.314	.402	.242	.144
TB	803	6,223	1,434	902	297	36	199	2,400	1,229	642	49	25	45	.263	.343	.439	.264	.177
TEX	784	6,127	1,436	889	296	27	224	2,458	1,253	472	37	40	51	.260	.320	.445	.255	.185
TOR	798	6,362	1,516	955	339	13	209	2,508	1,028	548	45	24	49	.266	.333	.440	.260	.174
Average	**781**	**6,253**	**1,485**	**979**	**295**	**28**	**183**	**2,384**	**1,094**	**550**	**52**	**36**	**46**	**.267**	**.338**	**.428**	**.259**	**.161**

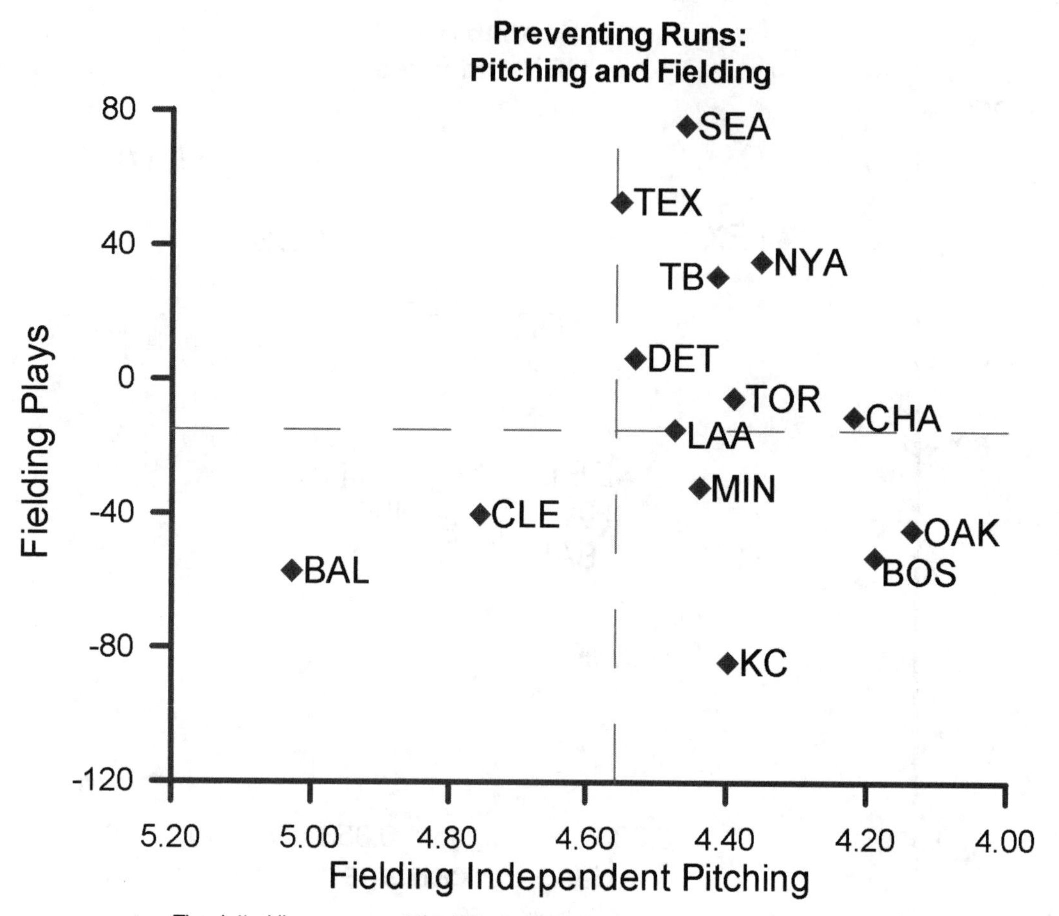

The dotted lines represent the league averages.

Team	RA	IP	BFP	H	HRA	TBA	K	BB	ShO	Sv	Op	%Save	Holds	ERA	FIP	UERA	DER
LAA	761	1445.0	6,252	1,513	180	2,401	1,062	523	13	51	70	73%	79	4.45	4.47	0.29	.691
BAL	876	1429.0	6,359	1,633	218	2,699	933	546	3	31	53	58%	61	5.15	5.03	0.37	.683
BOS	736	1436.0	6,283	1,494	167	2,361	1,230	530	11	41	59	69%	72	4.36	4.19	0.26	.681
CHA	732	1439.0	6,155	1,438	169	2,282	1,119	507	11	36	54	67%	55	4.15	4.22	0.43	.692
CLE	865	1434.0	6,354	1,570	183	2,484	986	598	6	25	43	58%	49	5.06	4.76	0.37	.682
DET	745	1447.0	6,240	1,449	182	2,328	1,102	594	9	42	66	64%	67	4.29	4.53	0.34	.697
KC	842	1426.0	6,265	1,486	166	2,333	1,153	600	9	34	56	61%	50	4.83	4.40	0.49	.677
MIN	765	1453.0	6,274	1,542	185	2,441	1,052	466	7	48	64	75%	82	4.50	4.44	0.24	.693
NYA	753	1450.0	6,247	1,386	181	2,251	1,260	574	8	51	66	77%	74	4.26	4.35	0.41	.699
OAK	761	1447.0	6,243	1,486	156	2,315	1,124	523	10	38	50	76%	68	4.26	4.14	0.47	.685
SEA	692	1452.0	6,159	1,359	172	2,166	1,043	534	10	49	77	64%	82	3.87	4.46	0.42	.715
TB	754	1427.0	6,146	1,421	183	2,305	1,125	515	5	41	63	65%	79	4.33	4.41	0.43	.699
TEX	740	1434.0	6,172	1,432	171	2,292	1,016	531	11	45	58	78%	77	4.38	4.55	0.26	.701
TOR	771	1451.0	6,281	1,509	181	2,427	1,181	551	10	25	41	61%	50	4.47	4.39	0.32	.684
Average	**771**	**1,440.7**	**6,245**	**1,480**	**178**	**2,363**	**1,099**	**542**	**9**	**40**	**59**	**68%**	**68**	**4.45**	**4.45**	**0.36**	**.691**

Running and Miscellaneous Batting Stats

Team	SB	CS	SB%	GDP	P/PA	BABIP	H-A	L-R
LAA	148	63	70%	128	3.89	.322	.008	-.004
BAL	76	37	67%	131	3.80	.300	.036	-.026
BOS	126	39	76%	137	3.94	.301	.032	.004
CHA	113	49	70%	139	3.80	.285	.001	.027
CLE	84	31	73%	140	3.93	.308	-.023	.004
DET	72	33	69%	131	3.76	.294	.019	.010
KC	88	29	75%	136	3.79	.298	.029	.004
MIN	85	32	73%	147	3.87	.306	.014	.004
NYA	111	28	80%	144	3.89	.306	.012	.003
OAK	133	48	73%	130	3.83	.298	.006	-.012
SEA	89	33	73%	124	3.78	.293	-.000	.003
TB	194	61	76%	104	3.96	.303	.020	.006
TEX	149	36	81%	97	3.83	.296	.032	-.003
TOR	73	23	76%	130	3.76	.290	-.003	-.006
Average	**110**	**39**	**74%**	**130**	**3.85**	**.300**	**.013**	**.013**

	Win Probability Added				Win Shares			
Tm	Bat	Start	Bullpen	LI	Bat	Pitch	Field	WSAge
BAL	-10.2	-7.5	0.7	0.93	97	64	32	28.4
BOS	4.0	2.8	7.2	1.10	137	102	45	29.7
CHA	-5.1	2.3	0.8	0.96	91	102	43	29.8
CLE	-4.6	-7.3	-4.1	0.92	112	54	29	27.6
DET	-0.7	4.3	0.8	1.05	108	101	49	28.1
KC	-10.7	-2.3	-3.0	0.94	86	73	36	27.1
LAA	9.5	2.9	3.6	1.08	152	95	45	29.5
MIN	0.8	-1.3	6.1	0.97	131	89	41	27.8
NYA	12.8	-0.4	9.6	0.97	167	98	44	30.7
OAK	-5.5	-5.6	5.1	0.93	111	80	34	28.0
SEA	-0.2	2.2	2.0	1.24	89	114	52	29.1
TB	1.4	1.8	-0.2	1.03	130	83	39	27.6
TEX	0.6	0.7	4.7	0.93	115	100	46	27.9
TOR	-3.1	-2.7	-0.2	1.04	115	75	35	29.6
Average	**-0.8**	**-0.7**	**2.4**	**1.01**	**117**	**88**	**41**	**28.6**

Leverage Index (LI) for bullpen only.

Miscellaneous Pitching and Fielding Stats

Team	DER	Fld %	UER	SBA	CS	%CS	PO	E	TE	FE	DP	GIDP	H-A	R-L
LAA	.691	.986	46	167	39	23%	12	85	36	48	174	155	.003	-.029
BAL	.683	.985	59	152	33	22%	11	90	46	44	151	132	-.010	-.013
BOS	.681	.986	41	174	23	13%	8	82	43	39	120	96	-.015	-.007
CHA	.692	.981	69	174	42	24%	28	113	47	65	158	131	.001	-.014
CLE	.682	.984	59	144	33	23%	7	97	40	57	170	149	-.020	-.014
DET	.697	.985	55	138	50	36%	5	88	47	40	164	140	-.022	.001
KC	.677	.981	77	153	39	25%	15	116	60	55	160	130	.005	.011
MIN	.693	.987	39	139	32	23%	19	76	32	40	135	115	-.009	.003
NYA	.699	.985	66	177	52	29%	19	86	43	43	131	110	-.003	.004
OAK	.685	.983	76	130	38	29%	15	105	48	54	154	129	-.019	-.039
SEA	.715	.982	67	111	44	40%	10	105	42	60	150	128	-.016	-.014
TB	.699	.983	68	118	28	24%	6	98	51	45	135	114	-.022	.005
TEX	.701	.982	42	142	43	30%	9	106	54	51	168	136	.006	-.011
TOR	.684	.988	51	135	46	34%	10	76	44	32	168	143	-.022	-.006
Average	**.691**	**.984**	**58**	**147**	**39**	**26%**	**12**	**95**	**45**	**48**	**153**	**129**	**-.010**	**-.009**

Batted Ball Batting Stats

	% of PA		% of Batted Balls					Out %		Runs Per Event				Total Runs vs. Avg.				
Team	K%	BB%	GB%	LD%	FB%	IF/F	HR/OF	GB	OF	NIP	GB	LD	OF	NIP	GB	LD	FB	Tot
BAL	16	9	44	18	38	.10	.10	74	83	.05	.04	.39	.17	-6	10	5	-10	-1
BOS	18	11	39	19	42	.10	.12	74	81	.07	.04	.39	.22	44	-1	8	90	141
CHA	17	10	43	17	39	.11	.12	75	84	.06	.04	.38	.19	8	-11	-22	4	-21
CLE	19	10	44	20	36	.08	.11	76	82	.05	.03	.40	.19	9	-15	29	-3	19
DET	18	10	42	18	40	.11	.12	74	86	.05	.05	.39	.18	-2	13	-12	-9	-9
KC	18	8	46	18	37	.10	.10	75	81	.03	.04	.37	.19	-34	-1	-27	-3	-66
LAA	17	9	44	19	37	.09	.11	72	82	.05	.06	.40	.20	2	45	28	23	98
MIN	16	10	46	18	36	.10	.11	74	82	.06	.04	.39	.20	19	21	2	10	52
NYA	16	11	43	20	37	.10	.15	75	82	.08	.03	.39	.25	51	-8	39	117	198
OAK	17	9	41	19	39	.10	.08	75	83	.05	.04	.38	.15	-3	-3	8	-49	-47
SEA	18	8	44	17	38	.10	.10	75	84	.03	.04	.39	.17	-45	9	-23	-28	-87
TB	20	11	41	20	40	.09	.13	74	84	.05	.04	.39	.21	18	5	12	42	77
TEX	20	8	40	19	41	.08	.14	73	85	.02	.05	.39	.21	-49	12	-1	58	20
TOR	16	9	39	18	43	.10	.11	75	85	.05	.04	.42	.18	4	-12	28	27	47
MLB Average	***18***	***10***	***43***	***19***	***38***	***.10***	***.11***	***75***	***83***	***.05***	***.04***	***.39***	***.19***	--	--	--	--	--

Batted Ball Pitching Stats

	% of PA		% of Batted Balls					Out %		Runs Per Event				Total Runs vs. Avg.				
Team	K%	BB%	GB%	LD%	FB%	IF/F	HR/OF	GB	OF	NIP	GB	LD	OF	NIP	GB	LD	FB	Tot
BAL	15	9	42	19	40	.10	.13	74	82	.07	.04	.41	.22	19	3	48	93	164
BOS	20	10	41	19	40	.11	.10	74	79	.04	.04	.39	.21	-16	5	-6	34	16
CHA	18	9	44	18	37	.10	.11	75	84	.04	.04	.40	.19	-20	10	-4	-6	-21
CLE	16	10	43	19	38	.09	.11	73	82	.07	.05	.40	.20	28	20	20	33	101
DET	18	10	43	18	39	.09	.11	75	83	.05	.03	.39	.19	12	-10	-1	12	13
KC	18	10	44	18	38	.10	.11	71	83	.05	.06	.39	.19	13	39	-7	9	54
LAA	17	9	42	19	40	.10	.11	76	83	.05	.03	.41	.19	-2	-19	25	19	22
MIN	17	8	41	18	41	.10	.11	74	83	.04	.05	.39	.18	-22	15	-6	19	7
NYA	20	10	42	19	38	.10	.12	76	84	.04	.03	.38	.20	-3	-14	-11	2	-26
OAK	18	9	44	18	38	.09	.10	73	83	.04	.05	.40	.17	-17	29	3	-24	-9
SEA	17	9	41	19	40	.09	.10	75	87	.05	.04	.36	.15	-3	-8	-17	-48	-76
TB	18	9	41	19	40	.09	.11	74	85	.04	.04	.37	.19	-16	3	-15	14	-15
TEX	16	10	42	20	38	.09	.11	76	85	.06	.03	.39	.17	11	-15	22	-16	2
TOR	19	10	45	20	35	.09	.12	77	81	.04	.02	.41	.22	-6	-23	33	33	37
MLB Average	***18***	***10***	***43***	***19***	***38***	***.10***	***.11***	***75***	***83***	***.05***	***.04***	***.39***	***.19***	--	--	--	--	--

National League Team Stats

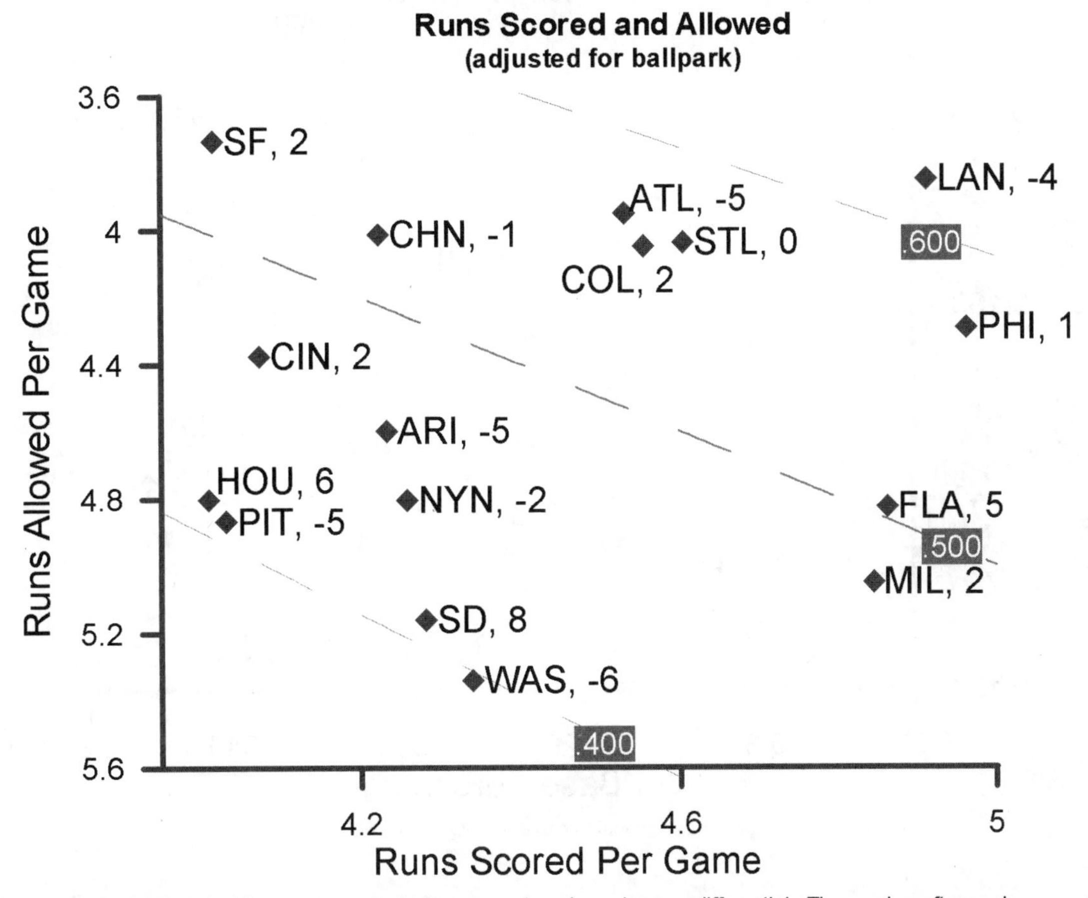

Notes: The dotted lines represent winning percentage based on run differential. The number after each team name represents the difference between the team's actual record and its run differential record.

Team Record					Scoring Runs			Preventing Runs				Projection	
Team	**W**	**L**	**RS**	**RA**	**RS-RA**	**AB/RSP**	**BA/RSP**	**HR**	**ERA**	**HRA**	**K**	**DER**	**PWINS**	**VAR**
ARI	70	92	720	782	-62	1,356	.240	173	4.42	168	1,158	.689	75	-5
ATL	86	76	735	641	94	1,416	.278	149	3.58	119	1,232	.689	91	-5
CHN	83	78	707	672	35	1,395	.241	161	3.84	160	1,272	.704	84	-1
CIN	78	84	673	723	-50	1,347	.250	158	4.18	188	1,069	.707	76	2
COL	92	70	804	715	89	1,403	.259	190	4.22	141	1,154	.692	90	2
FLA	87	75	772	766	6	1,434	.272	159	4.30	160	1,248	.686	82	5
HOU	74	88	643	770	-127	1,302	.267	142	4.54	176	1,144	.679	68	6
LAN	95	67	780	611	169	1,526	.259	145	3.41	127	1,272	.715	99	-4
MIL	80	82	785	818	-33	1,428	.262	182	4.83	207	1,104	.691	78	2
NYN	70	92	671	757	-86	1,432	.277	95	4.45	158	1,031	.696	72	-2
PHI	93	69	820	709	111	1,385	.255	224	4.16	189	1,153	.695	92	1
PIT	62	99	636	768	-132	1,352	.251	125	4.59	152	919	.692	67	-5
STL	91	71	730	640	90	1,376	.264	160	3.66	123	1,049	.696	91	0
SD	75	87	638	769	-131	1,352	.242	141	4.37	167	1,187	.696	67	8
SF	88	74	657	611	46	1,345	.245	122	3.55	140	1,302	.709	86	2
WAS	59	103	710	874	-164	1,403	.255	156	5.00	173	911	.687	65	-6
Average	**80**	**82**	**718**	**727**	**-9**	**1,391**	**.258**	**155**	**4.19**	**159**	**1,138**	**.695**	**81**	**-1**

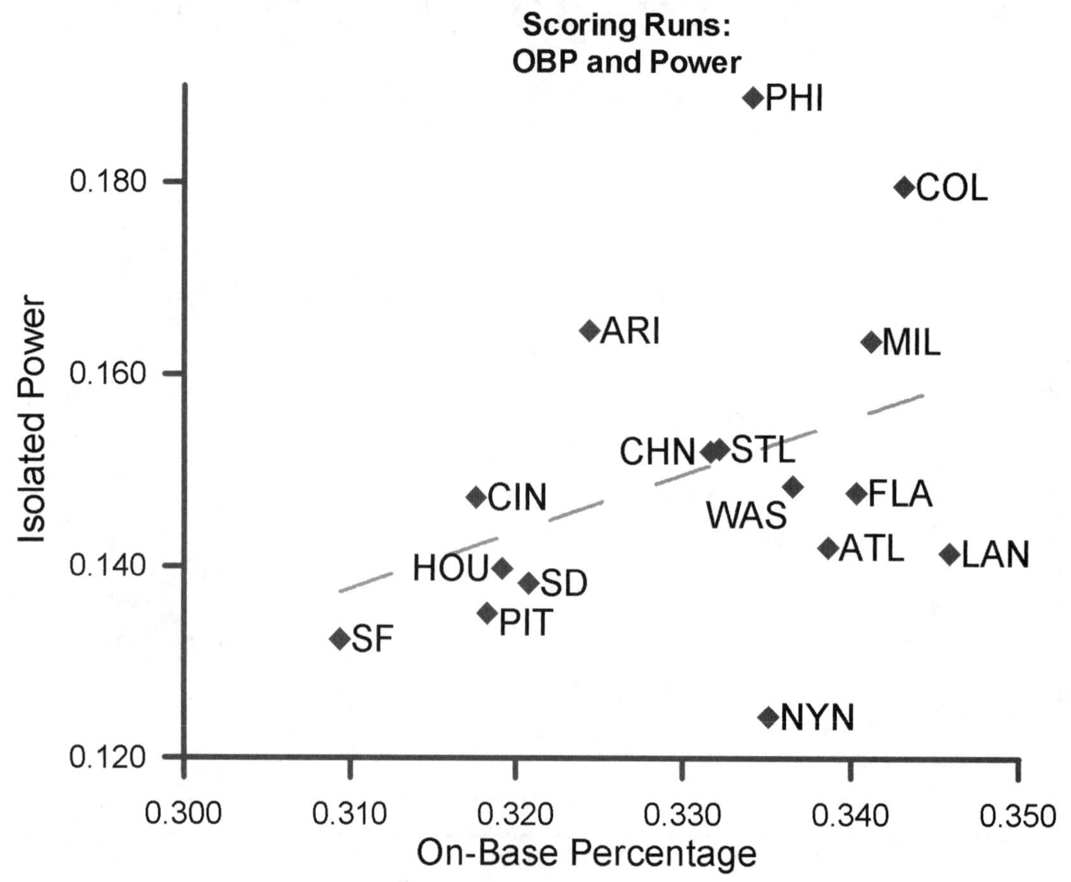

The dotted line shows the relationship between ISO and OBP.

Team	Runs	PA	H	1B	2B	3B	HR	TB	SO	BB	HBP	SH	SF	BA	OBP	SLG	GPA	ISO
ARI	720	6,269	1,408	883	307	45	173	2,324	1,298	571	37	54	41	.253	.324	.418	.250	.165
ATL	735	6,335	1,459	990	300	20	149	2,246	1,064	602	52	95	47	.263	.339	.405	.254	.142
CHN	707	6,244	1,398	915	293	29	161	2,232	1,185	592	59	65	42	.255	.332	.407	.251	.152
CIN	673	6,187	1,349	886	280	25	158	2,153	1,129	531	53	100	41	.247	.318	.394	.241	.147
COL	804	6,241	1,408	868	300	50	190	2,378	1,277	660	47	76	60	.261	.343	.441	.265	.180
FLA	772	6,312	1,493	1,013	296	25	159	2,316	1,226	568	63	70	39	.268	.340	.416	.257	.148
HOU	643	6,040	1,415	971	270	32	142	2,175	990	448	43	66	45	.260	.319	.400	.244	.140
LAN	780	6,385	1,511	1,049	278	39	145	2,302	1,068	607	63	78	44	.270	.346	.412	.259	.141
MIL	785	6,296	1,447	947	281	37	182	2,348	1,231	610	71	58	47	.263	.341	.426	.260	.164
NYN	671	6,159	1,472	1,033	295	49	95	2,150	928	526	36	88	55	.270	.335	.394	.249	.124
PHI	820	6,338	1,439	868	312	35	224	2,493	1,155	589	71	55	45	.258	.334	.447	.262	.189
PIT	636	6,058	1,364	916	289	34	125	2,096	1,142	499	46	60	36	.252	.318	.387	.240	.135
STL	730	6,168	1,436	953	294	29	160	2,268	1,041	528	61	68	43	.263	.332	.415	.253	.152
SD	638	6,179	1,315	878	265	31	141	2,065	1,182	586	57	74	36	.242	.321	.381	.240	.138
SF	657	6,057	1,411	971	275	43	122	2,138	1,158	392	50	67	55	.257	.309	.389	.237	.132
WAS	710	6,273	1,416	951	271	38	156	2,231	1,208	617	56	64	42	.258	.337	.406	.253	.148
Average	**718**	**6,221**	**1,421**	**943**	**288**	**35**	**155**	**2,245**	**1,143**	**558**	**54**	**71**	**45**	**.259**	**.331**	**.409**	**.251**	**.150**

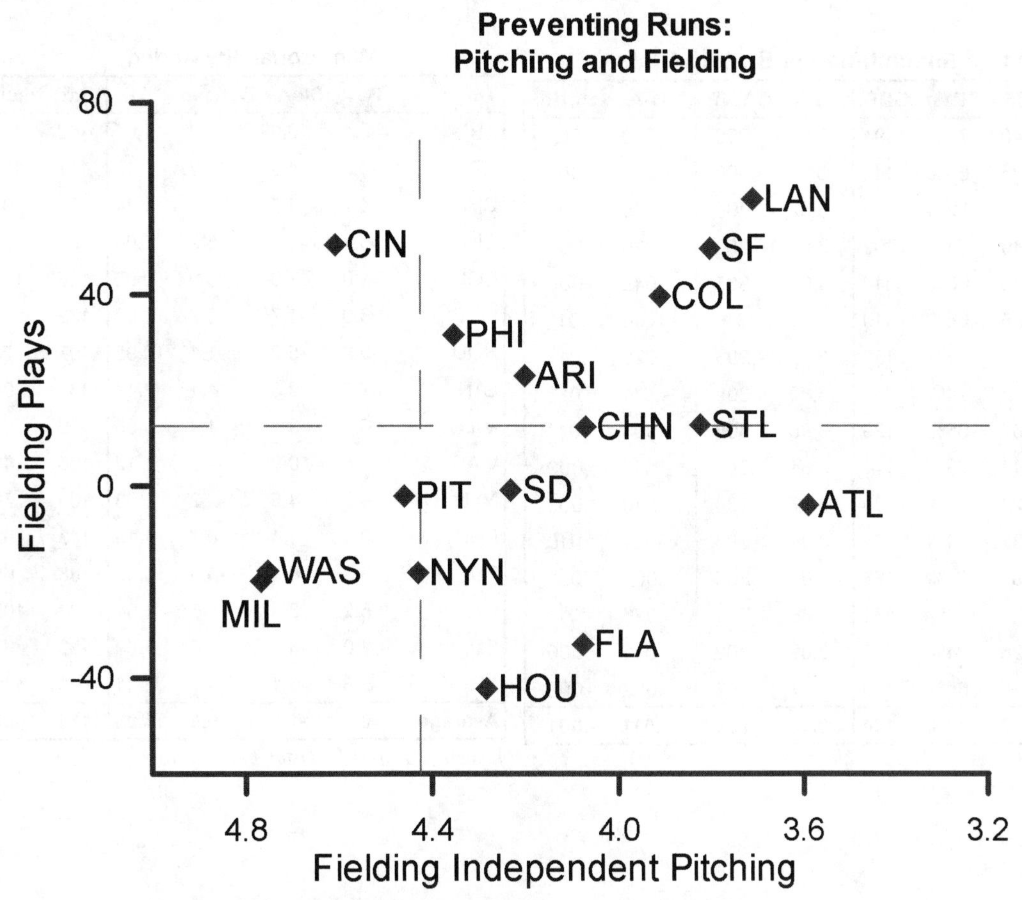

The dotted lines represent the league averages.

Team	RA	IP	BFP	H	HR	TBA	K	BB	ShO	Sv	Op	%Save	Holds	ERA	FIP	UERA	DER
ARI	782	1447.0	6,267	1,470	168	2,343	1,158	525	12	36	55	65%	46	4.42	4.20	0.44	.689
ATL	641	1462.0	6,208	1,399	119	2,149	1,232	530	10	38	59	64%	71	3.58	3.59	0.37	.689
CHN	672	1445.0	6,177	1,329	160	2,110	1,272	586	8	40	58	69%	75	3.84	4.07	0.35	.704
CIN	723	1458.0	6,253	1,420	188	2,303	1,069	577	12	41	53	77%	80	4.18	4.61	0.28	.707
COL	715	1438.0	6,171	1,427	141	2,215	1,154	528	7	45	61	74%	73	4.22	3.91	0.25	.692
FLA	766	1446.0	6,299	1,425	160	2,260	1,248	601	5	45	69	65%	93	4.30	4.08	0.47	.686
HOU	770	1430.0	6,237	1,521	176	2,430	1,144	546	10	39	65	60%	83	4.54	4.28	0.30	.679
LAN	611	1473.0	6,182	1,265	127	1,961	1,272	584	9	44	70	63%	77	3.41	3.71	0.32	.715
MIL	818	1435.0	6,352	1,498	207	2,515	1,104	607	8	44	66	67%	89	4.83	4.77	0.30	.691
NYN	757	1426.0	6,284	1,452	158	2,293	1,031	616	12	39	60	65%	75	4.45	4.43	0.33	.696
PHI	709	1455.0	6,263	1,479	189	2,390	1,153	489	9	44	66	67%	81	4.16	4.35	0.22	.695
PIT	768	1418.0	6,144	1,491	152	2,390	919	563	7	28	45	62%	62	4.59	4.46	0.29	.692
STL	640	1440.0	6,087	1,407	123	2,110	1,049	460	11	43	57	75%	72	3.66	3.83	0.34	.696
SD	769	1450.0	6,273	1,422	167	2,239	1,187	603	9	45	68	66%	92	4.37	4.23	0.40	.696
SF	611	1446.0	6,103	1,268	140	1,997	1,302	584	18	41	58	71%	70	3.55	3.80	0.25	.709
WAS	874	1424.0	6,349	1,533	173	2,495	911	629	3	33	58	57%	62	5.00	4.75	0.52	.687
Average	**727**	**1443.3**	**6,228**	**1,425**	**159**	**2,263**	**1,138**	**564**	**9**	**40**	**61**	**67%**	**75**	**4.19**	**4.19**	**0.34**	**.695**

Running and Miscellaneous Batting Stats

Team	SB	CS	SB%	GDP	P/PA	BABIP	H-A	L-R
ARI	102	40	72%	94	3.83	.299	.032	.001
ATL	58	26	69%	142	3.70	.300	-.008	.002
CHN	56	34	62%	134	3.82	.296	.019	-.006
CIN	96	40	71%	103	3.82	.282	.020	.005
COL	106	55	66%	112	4.00	.305	.042	-.009
FLA	75	35	68%	110	3.89	.316	.014	-.011
HOU	113	44	72%	153	3.75	.293	.020	.012
LAN	116	48	71%	141	3.89	.309	-.011	.013
MIL	68	37	65%	129	3.85	.305	.003	.017
NYN	122	44	73%	144	3.84	.307	.012	.009
PHI	119	28	81%	90	3.87	.286	.010	.002
PIT	90	32	74%	124	3.84	.296	.031	-.010
STL	75	31	71%	128	3.67	.296	-.003	-.031
SD	82	29	74%	131	3.86	.284	-.026	-.011
SF	78	28	74%	115	3.62	.302	.025	-.006
WAS	73	40	65%	133	3.87	.302	.002	.008
Average	**89**	**37**	**71%**	**124**	**3.82**	**.299**	**.011**	**-.001**

	Win Probability Added				Win Shares			
Tm	Bat	Start	Bullpen	LI	Bat	Pitch	Field	WSAge
ARI	-8.1	-0.6	-2.3	1.01	92	82	37	26.5
ATL	-0.0	4.8	0.2	1.16	117	101	41	28.6
CHN	-4.4	4.0	2.9	1.14	95	104	50	29.7
CIN	-5.4	-2.7	5.2	1.06	97	90	47	28.3
COL	1.0	7.0	3.0	0.95	125	107	44	28.0
FLA	3.9	-1.7	3.7	1.08	132	89	40	26.8
HOU	-0.9	-5.0	-1.1	0.95	107	78	37	31.2
LAN	7.6	2.3	4.1	1.17	135	104	46	29.1
MIL	6.2	-8.6	1.4	0.95	152	56	31	28.9
WAS	-7.8	-10.0	-4.3	1.12	105	46	27	27.7
NYN	-4.3	-4.5	-2.2	1.03	106	70	33	29.8
PHI	9.9	1.4	0.7	1.13	143	92	44	30.7
PIT	-8.3	-4.3	-5.9	0.93	88	65	33	26.7
STL	5.2	3.3	1.5	1.04	128	102	43	29.2
SD	2.0	-8.6	0.6	1.00	132	61	32	27.4
SF	-3.5	6.1	4.4	1.11	93	119	52	28.3
Average	**-0.4**	**-1.1**	**0.8**	**1.05**	**115**	**85**	**40**	**28.6**

Leverage Index (LI) for bullpen only.

Miscellaneous Pitching and Fielding Stats

Team	DER	Fld %	UER	SBA	CS	%CS	PO	E	TE	FE	DP	GIDP	H-A	R-L
ARI	.689	.980	71	138	33	24%	14	124	63	61	133	116	.006	-.012
ATL	.689	.985	60	143	46	32%	11	96	36	56	159	138	-.016	-.014
CHN	.704	.983	56	132	43	33%	4	105	42	60	144	119	-.004	-.017
CIN	.707	.985	46	126	47	37%	15	89	38	51	161	135	-.007	.003
COL	.692	.986	40	142	27	19%	14	87	40	47	146	119	.012	-.011
FLA	.686	.982	75	171	42	25%	6	106	56	49	129	114	.006	-.008
HOU	.679	.987	48	94	29	31%	9	78	31	46	161	142	-.016	-.004
LAN	.715	.986	53	128	39	30%	14	83	36	46	134	110	-.020	.002
MIL	.691	.984	48	103	21	20%	8	98	45	53	149	135	-.018	-.011
NYN	.696	.984	52	100	34	34%	11	97	41	52	134	116	-.028	-.001
PHI	.695	.987	36	132	37	28%	17	76	28	48	132	107	.001	.007
PIT	.692	.988	45	150	43	29%	23	73	37	35	171	138	-.031	-.009
STL	.696	.985	54	72	28	39%	10	96	36	58	167	147	-.013	-.023
SD	.696	.984	65	142	42	30%	12	94	44	49	146	119	-.048	-.023
SF	.709	.985	40	149	42	28%	8	88	39	47	138	112	-.019	.011
WAS	.687	.977	83	127	38	30%	16	143	63	76	155	126	-.025	-.019
Average	**.695**	**.985**	**55**	**128**	**37**	**29%**	**12**	**96**	**42**	**52**	**147**	**125**	**-.014**	**-.008**

Batted Ball Batting Stats

	% of PA		% of Batted Balls					Out %		Runs Per Event				Total Runs vs. Avg.				
Team	**K%**	**BB%**	**GB%**	**LD%**	**FB%**	**IF/F**	**HR/OF**	**GB**	**OF**	**NIP**	**GB**	**LD**	**OF**	**NIP**	**GB**	**LD**	**FB**	**Tot**
ARI	21	10	43	18	39	.11	.12	72	83	.03	.06	.39	.20	-21	23	-26	5	-20
ATL	17	10	44	20	36	.07	.10	76	83	.06	.03	.38	.17	22	-24	20	-34	-17
CHN	19	10	43	20	37	.09	.11	76	82	.05	.03	.38	.19	8	-25	-1	-1	-20
CIN	18	9	43	19	38	.11	.10	76	84	.04	.04	.37	.17	-11	-8	-32	-40	-90
COL	20	11	41	19	39	.09	.13	75	82	.05	.04	.41	.22	18	-6	9	45	65
FLA	19	10	42	20	38	.10	.11	72	83	.04	.06	.39	.18	-4	28	6	-11	19
HOU	16	8	48	18	34	.10	.10	75	83	.04	.04	.37	.18	-24	5	-26	-35	-81
LAN	17	10	45	21	34	.08	.10	76	82	.06	.03	.38	.18	27	-14	38	-25	27
MIL	20	11	43	18	38	.11	.12	72	85	.05	.06	.41	.20	13	20	-3	4	35
NYN	15	9	47	20	33	.10	.07	76	80	.06	.03	.38	.16	7	-14	24	-63	-46
PHI	18	10	40	20	40	.09	.14	76	83	.05	.04	.36	.23	13	-22	-8	84	68
PIT	19	9	45	18	37	.10	.09	75	82	.04	.04	.39	.17	-23	-8	-15	-51	-97
SD	19	10	44	19	38	.11	.10	77	84	.05	.03	.38	.17	4	-31	-27	-51	-104
SF	19	7	45	19	36	.10	.09	75	82	.01	.04	.38	.17	-62	-4	-18	-45	-129
STL	17	10	45	18	37	.10	.10	74	84	.05	.05	.39	.18	4	12	-8	-19	-11
WAS	19	11	45	19	36	.09	.11	74	85	.05	.04	.40	.18	13	4	-5	-32	-20
MLB Average	**18**	**10**	**43**	**19**	**38**	**.10**	**.11**	**75**	**83**	**.05**	**.04**	**.39**	**.19**	**--**	**--**	**--**	**--**	**--**

Batted Ball Pitching Stats

	% of PA		% of Batted Balls					Out %		Runs Per Event				Total Runs vs. Avg.				
Team	**K%**	**BB%**	**GB%**	**LD%**	**FB%**	**IF/F**	**HR/OF**	**GB**	**OF**	**NIP**	**GB**	**LD**	**OF**	**NIP**	**GB**	**LD**	**FB**	**Tot**
ARI	18	9	43	20	37	.08	.11	74	84	.04	.05	.38	.18	-15	14	6	-8	-3
ATL	20	9	46	19	34	.09	.09	75	81	.03	.04	.38	.18	-23	-10	-8	-44	-86
CHN	21	10	43	18	39	.12	.11	75	83	.04	.04	.38	.19	-4	-16	-39	-20	-79
CIN	17	10	42	19	39	.10	.12	75	85	.06	.04	.37	.18	17	-10	-12	-1	-6
COL	19	9	47	20	33	.08	.10	78	80	.04	.02	.39	.21	-15	-30	4	-10	-50
FLA	20	10	43	19	38	.09	.11	73	81	.04	.05	.36	.20	-2	20	-34	9	-7
HOU	18	10	46	19	35	.08	.12	74	82	.04	.04	.40	.22	-6	9	18	32	54
LAN	21	10	44	18	38	.11	.09	76	84	.04	.03	.37	.15	-7	-26	-48	-78	-159
MIL	17	11	43	19	39	.09	.13	74	83	.06	.04	.40	.22	24	4	14	58	101
NYN	16	11	43	19	39	.11	.10	74	82	.07	.05	.38	.18	33	5	-4	-5	29
PHI	18	9	41	21	39	.11	.12	76	83	.04	.03	.38	.20	-19	-18	20	16	-1
PIT	15	10	44	19	37	.09	.10	74	83	.07	.05	.40	.18	26	14	28	-6	62
SD	19	10	44	18	38	.10	.11	73	83	.05	.05	.38	.19	6	11	-29	-10	-22
SF	21	10	43	19	38	.10	.10	77	85	.04	.03	.39	.16	-15	-29	-22	-68	-134
STL	17	8	50	18	32	.10	.09	75	83	.04	.04	.39	.17	-24	1	-6	-69	-99
WAS	14	11	44	19	36	.10	.11	74	82	.08	.05	.39	.20	49	24	29	28	131
MLB Average	***18***	***10***	***43***	***19***	***38***	***.10***	***.11***	***75***	***83***	***.05***	***.04***	***.39***	***.19***	***--***	***--***	***--***	***--***	***--***

Arizona Diamondbacks

Stat Facts:

- Mark Reynolds put the ball in play in just 54% of his PAs
- Reynolds produced an XBH 21% of the time he put the ball in play
- 29% of Reynolds's outfield flies were home runs
- Reynolds's H-A was exactly .000
- Danny Haren's total of -43 runs below average was sixth-best in the majors
- Chris Young's GB% (26%) was lowest in the majors
- Young's FB % (56%) was highest of anyone with at least 500 PAs
- 22% of Young's flyballs were infield pop-ups
- Doug Davis allowed the most walks (103) in the majors
- Juan Gutierrez allowed 11 SBs in 12 attempts
- Justin Upton committed 10 fielding errors, the most by any outfielder
- The Diamondbacks -23 middle infield plus/minus ranked last in the majors

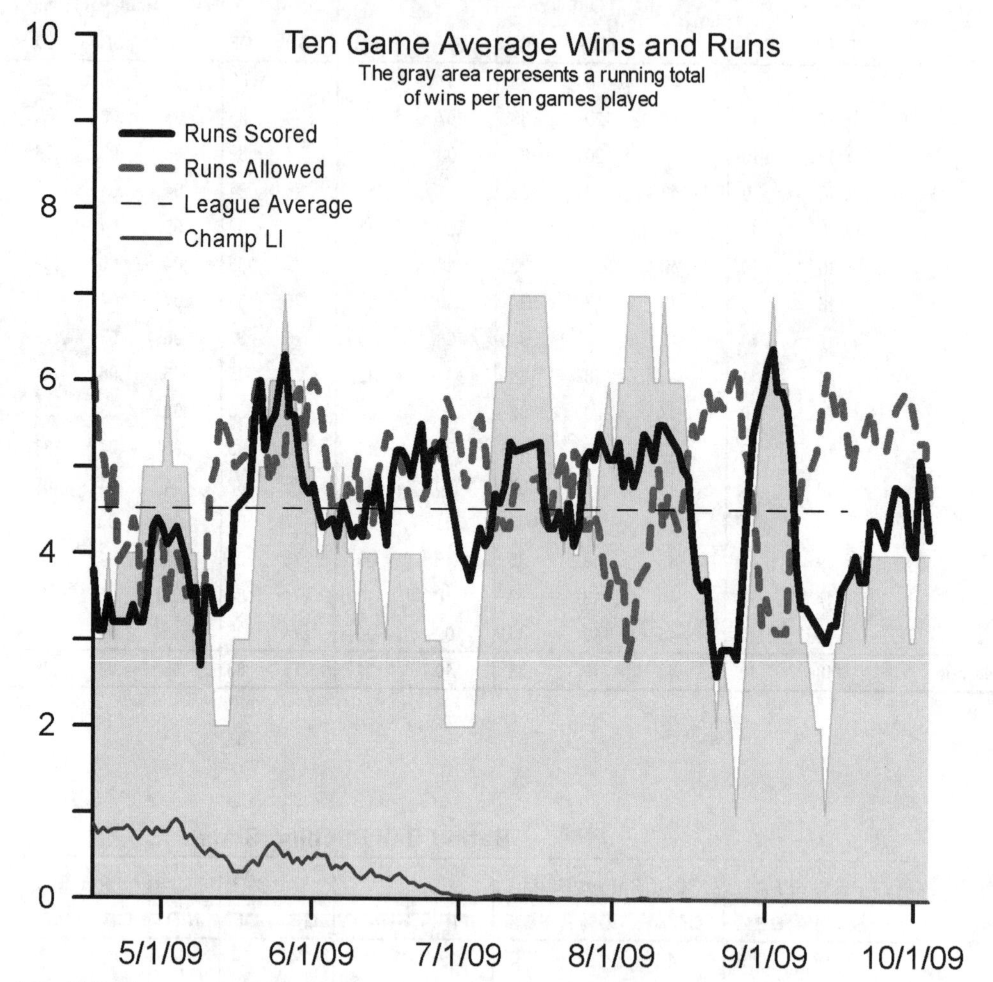

4/6: Webb makes only start of year

5/6: Upton moved into #3 slot

7/18: Haren is 10-5, 1.96; goes 4-5, 4.95 rest of year

7/26-8/9: Reynolds goes 20-for-53 with 11 HR, 19 K

8/10: Young demoted to minors

9/22: Reynolds breaks own strikeout record

Team Batting and Pitching/Fielding Stats by Month

	April	May	June	July	Aug	Sept/Oct
Wins	9	13	9	14	15	10
Losses	13	16	17	12	14	20
RS/G	3.8	4.6	4.8	4.5	5.0	3.9
RA/G	4.8	5.1	4.9	4.1	4.7	5.2
OBP	.308	.319	.332	.334	.340	.310
SLG	.394	.414	.406	.442	.451	.394
FIP	4.27	4.45	4.01	3.72	4.41	4.57
DER	.698	.674	.687	.687	.707	.686

Batting Stats

Player	BR	Runs	RBI	PA	Outs	H	2B	3B	HR	TB	K	BB	IBB	HBP	SH	SF	SB	CS	GDP	H-A	L^R	BA	OBP	SLG	GPA
Reynolds M	*99*	98	102	662	445	150	30	1	44	314	223	76	3	5	0	3	24	9	8	-.000	.016	.260	.349	.543	*.279*
Upton J	*88*	84	86	588	383	158	30	7	26	280	137	55	3	2	1	4	20	5	10	.028	.121	.300	.366	.532	*.284*
Drew S *	*65*	71	65	595	400	139	29	12	12	228	87	49	7	1	5	7	5	1	5	.056	.082	.261	.320	.428	*.239*
Montero M *	*60*	61	59	470	308	125	30	0	16	203	78	38	5	3	2	2	1	2	6	-.002	-.004	.294	.355	.478	*.266*
Young C	*52*	54	42	501	348	92	28	4	15	173	133	59	2	4	3	2	11	4	3	-.025	.096	.212	.311	.400	*.229*
Parra G *	*46*	59	60	491	348	132	21	8	5	184	89	25	1	1	4	6	5	7	18	.033	.102	.290	.324	.404	*.235*
Lopez F +	*45*	44	25	383	246	104	18	1	6	142	59	34	3	1	1	2	6	3	2	.078	-.003	.301	.364	.412	*.254*
Roberts R	*42*	41	25	351	225	85	17	2	7	127	55	40	1	3	2	1	7	3	2	.046	.082	.279	.367	.416	*.256*
Ojeda A +	*28*	38	16	310	204	65	17	3	1	91	28	32	3	6	6	1	3	1	4	.053	-.018	.246	.340	.345	*.228*
Tracy C *	*27*	29	39	288	199	61	15	0	8	100	38	26	7	1	0	4	1	0	3	.094	.076	.237	.306	.389	*.224*
Byrnes E	*23*	26	31	258	192	54	14	1	8	94	30	12	0	3	2	2	9	3	4	.025	.040	.226	.270	.393	*.209*
Snyder C	*19*	20	22	202	137	33	7	0	6	58	47	32	4	2	1	2	0	0	5	.003	.024	.200	.333	.352	*.227*
Romero A *	*12*	14	18	157	116	36	6	2	1	49	23	11	1	1	0	0	2	0	7	-.029	.066	.248	.306	.338	*.211*
Whitesell J	*11*	7	14	133	89	21	7	0	1	31	29	24	4	1	0	0	0	0	2	.023	.026	.194	.346	.287	*.217*
Ryal R	*11*	11	9	68	43	16	6	2	3	35	21	6	1	2	0	1	0	0	0	.265	.010	.271	.353	.593	*.293*
Allen B *	*10*	13	14	116	87	21	7	0	4	40	40	12	2	0	0	0	0	0	4	-.003	.110	.202	.284	.385	*.213*
Clark T +	*8*	7	11	78	57	12	4	0	4	28	24	11	0	0	0	1	0	0	3	.028	.051	.182	.295	.424	*.227*
Oeltjen T *	*8*	11	4	73	54	17	4	1	3	32	13	1	0	0	1	1	3	1	0	.044	.141	.243	.250	.457	*.216*
Jackson C	*7*	8	14	110	82	18	4	0	1	25	16	11	0	0	0	0	5	0	1	.059	-.040	.182	.264	.253	*.173*
Haren D	*6*	6	10	87	57	18	5	0	1	26	22	3	0	0	9	2	0	0	2	-.010	.125	.247	.269	.356	*.200*
Hester J	*3*	4	4	30	21	7	2	0	1	12	7	2	0	0	0	0	0	0	0	.297	-.256	.250	.300	.429	*.231*
Scherzer M	*3*	4	3	61	42	12	2	0	0	14	17	3	0	0	5	0	0	0	1	.113	.002	.226	.268	.264	*.178*
Wilson J	*2*	1	2	30	22	6	1	0	0	7	3	3	0	1	0	0	0	0	2	-.009	-.150	.231	.333	.269	*.207*
Buckner B	*1*	0	6	23	17	5	2	0	0	7	8	0	0	0	2	0	0	0	1	.230	-.211	.238	.238	.333	*.181*
Carlin L +	*1*	3	1	21	15	3	0	0	0	3	3	3	0	0	0	0	0	0	0	.136	-.136	.167	.286	.167	*.162*

Only includes batters with at least one Base Run. Italicized stats have been adjusted for home park.

Batted Ball Batting Stats

	% of PA		% of Batted Balls					Out %		Runs Per Event				Total Runs vs. Avg.				
Player	K%	BB%	GB%	LD%	FB%	IF/F	HR/OF	GB	OF	NIP	GB	LD	OF	NIP	GB	LD	FB	Tot
Reynolds M	34	12	35	17	47	.09	.29	64	80	.01	.10	.40	.46	-6	5	-8	41	31
Upton J	23	10	45	19	36	.14	.20	65	81	.02	.10	.47	.34	-3	12	5	14	27
Montero M	17	9	44	20	36	.09	.14	74	78	.05	.05	.40	.27	-1	3	4	10	16
Lopez F	15	9	53	22	25	.03	.09	71	78	.06	.07	.35	.19	1	6	3	-2	8
Roberts R	16	12	38	19	43	.06	.07	70	82	.09	.08	.37	.14	4	3	0	-1	7
Drew S	15	8	39	19	42	.08	.07	72	85	.05	.06	.40	.14	-1	3	3	-4	1
Snyder C	23	17	37	17	46	.19	.14	75	82	.08	.04	.28	.22	4	-1	-5	0	-2
Whitesell J	22	19	46	20	34	.15	.04	81	82	.10	.00	.35	.11	4	-2	-1	-3	-3
Allen B	34	10	44	17	39	.12	.18	79	89	-.01	.01	.49	.26	-2	-1	-1	0	-5
Tracy C	13	9	35	18	48	.08	.08	79	87	.08	.02	.36	.11	1	-2	-1	-3	-5
Ojeda A	9	12	46	15	38	.11	.01	78	88	.15	.04	.49	.01	6	-0	1	-13	-6
Young C	27	13	26	18	56	.22	.12	71	84	.03	.07	.38	.21	-0	-1	-6	1	-7
Parra G	18	5	53	18	29	.05	.05	72	76	-.01	.05	.41	.17	-8	3	2	-4	-7
Romero A	15	8	55	18	26	.19	.04	71	92	.04	.05	.40	.02	-1	1	0	-7	-7
Jackson C	15	10	41	18	41	.18	.04	79	93	.07	.02	.35	.01	0	-1	-1	-5	-7
Byrnes E	12	6	40	15	45	.25	.11	75	86	.04	.04	.34	.17	-2	-0	-4	-2	-8
MLB Average	***18***	***10***	***43***	***19***	***38***	***.10***	***.11***	***75***	***83***	***.05***	***.04***	***.39***	***.19***	--	--	--	--	--

Pitching Stats

Player	PRC	IP	BFP	G	GS	K	BB	IBB	HBP	H	HR	DP	DER	SB	CS	PO	W	L	Sv	Op	Hld	H-A	R^L	RA	ERA	FIP
Haren D	*123*	229.3	909	33	33	223	38	2	4	192	27	14	.721	18	6	0	14	10	0	0	0	-.030	-.032	3.26	3.14	3.26
Davis D *	*76*	203.3	889	34	34	146	103	1	4	203	25	23	.699	11	6	7	9	14	0	0	0	-.001	.015	4.47	4.12	4.88
Scherzer M	*62*	170.3	741	30	30	174	63	1	10	166	20	11	.677	10	6	1	9	11	0	0	0	-.001	-.033	4.97	4.12	3.90
Garland J	*54*	167.7	728	27	27	83	52	5	6	188	19	26	.692	8	2	0	8	11	0	0	0	.024	.027	4.83	4.29	4.58
Gutierrez J	*30*	71.0	307	65	0	66	30	5	3	67	2	5	.680	11	1	1	4	3	9	10	7	.029	-.081	4.18	4.06	2.84
Petit Y	*24*	89.7	407	23	17	74	34	1	0	102	19	2	.682	9	1	0	3	10	0	0	0	.066	-.006	6.22	5.82	5.36
Zavada C *	*24*	51.0	221	49	0	52	24	2	3	45	5	2	.701	2	2	2	3	3	0	0	4	-.069	.061	3.88	3.35	3.86
Qualls C	*23*	52.0	217	51	0	45	7	2	2	53	5	6	.665	3	0	0	2	2	24	29	0	-.016	-.037	3.98	3.63	3.07
Vasquez E	*20*	53.0	238	53	0	45	29	2	3	52	4	5	.682	6	1	1	3	3	0	4	4	.125	.046	4.58	4.42	4.13
Rauch J	*20*	54.3	235	58	0	35	17	0	1	57	5	5	.701	5	0	0	2	2	2	3	12	.022	-.025	4.47	4.14	4.05
Buckner B	*19*	77.3	342	16	13	64	29	0	3	94	12	14	.637	4	2	2	4	6	0	0	0	.088	-.072	6.63	6.40	4.75
Rosales L	*16*	45.3	186	33	0	31	12	2	0	40	5	3	.739	1	0	0	2	1	0	0	2	-.054	.015	4.76	4.76	3.88
Boyer B	*12*	37.0	160	30	0	18	12	0	3	39	0	5	.669	4	1	0	0	1	0	0	2	.016	.003	4.86	2.68	3.39
Pena T	*11*	34.0	153	37	0	26	11	0	1	41	3	3	.652	1	2	0	5	3	1	2	8	-.073	-.095	5.29	4.24	3.83
Mulvey K	*5*	23.0	104	6	4	18	12	0	2	23	5	1	.731	1	1	0	0	3	0	0	0	.073	.179	7.04	7.04	6.24
Schlereth D	*5*	18.3	86	21	0	22	15	1	1	15	1	0	.702	0	0	0	1	4	0	3	0	-.036	.062	6.38	5.89	3.91
Schoeneweis	*5*	24.0	117	45	0	14	13	1	2	29	6	1	.695	7	0	0	1	2	0	3	6	-.120	-.027	7.50	7.13	6.98
Cabrera D	*3*	11.0	51	6	1	7	7	0	2	11	0	2	.657	0	1	0	0	1	0	0	0	-.170	.156	6.55	6.55	4.33
Augenstein B	*3*	17.0	81	7	2	6	6	2	2	23	2	2	.677	1	0	0	0	1	0	0	0	-.041	.089	8.47	7.94	5.03
Slaten D *	*1*	6.3	30	11	0	4	1	0	0	10	1	0	.625	1	0	0	0	0	0	0	0	-.059	.078	7.11	7.11	4.41

Italicized stats have been adjusted for home park.

Batted Ball Pitching Stats

	% of PA		% of Batted Balls					Out %		Runs Per Event				Total Runs vs. Avg.				
Player	K%	BB%	GB%	LD%	FB%	IF/F	HR/OF	GB	OF	NIP	GB	LD	OF	NIP	GB	LD	FB	Tot
Haren D	25	5	43	20	37	.06	.12	78	87	-.04	.02	.37	.18	-24	-7	-5	-7	-43
Gutierrez J	21	11	40	20	39	.09	.03	68	90	.04	.08	.40	.03	-0	4	0	-12	-9
Rosales L	17	6	34	19	47	.12	.07	83	81	.01	-.01	.36	.14	-2	-2	-1	-1	-6
Zavada C	23	13	28	21	51	.09	.08	73	84	.05	.05	.38	.13	1	-1	-1	-2	-4
Qualls C	21	4	57	20	23	.08	.15	77	83	-.04	.03	.44	.24	-5	0	3	-1	-4
Boyer B	11	9	61	18	22	.08	.00	71	67	.09	.06	.21	.19	1	3	-4	-2	-2
Rauch J	15	8	37	20	43	.14	.08	76	84	.04	.04	.37	.14	-1	0	1	-2	-2
Pena A	17	8	46	21	33	.05	.09	71	84	.03	.06	.41	.14	-1	1	2	-2	1
Vasquez E	19	13	43	17	40	.06	.07	72	82	.08	.06	.39	.14	3	1	-1	-2	1
Scherzer M	23	10	42	18	40	.08	.11	74	82	.02	.06	.44	.20	-4	3	0	2	1
Mulvey K	17	13	46	26	29	.10	.22	75	93	.09	.04	.35	.29	1	-0	1	1	3
Schoeneweis S	12	13	44	20	36	.13	.22	71	86	.12	.06	.32	.30	2	1	-0	3	6
Garland J	11	8	46	19	35	.07	.10	74	83	.08	.04	.38	.18	1	1	4	0	7
Davis D	16	12	43	22	35	.09	.13	75	85	.08	.04	.33	.21	9	-1	-2	1	8
Buckner W	19	9	49	21	30	.06	.18	69	80	.04	.07	.37	.29	-0	4	2	5	11
Petit Y	18	8	31	20	49	.09	.14	68	85	.03	.10	.39	.21	-2	4	3	9	14
MLB Average	***18***	***10***	***43***	***19***	***38***	***.10***	***.11***	***75***	***83***	***.05***	***.04***	***.39***	***.19***	--	--	--	--	--

Fielding Stats

Name	INN	SBA/G	CS%	ERA	WP+PB/G	PO	A	TE	FE
Catchers									
Montero M	924.7	0.83	21%	4.11	0.506	733	60	8	1
Snyder C	436.0	0.64	16%	4.62	0.619	363	21	0	0
Hester J	53.0	1.19	14%	5.60	0.509	45	3	0	0
Carlin L	34.0	1.59	0%	9.26	0.529	24	1	0	0

Name	Inn	PO	A	TE	FE	FPct	DPS	DPT	ZRDif	OOZ	Dif
First Base											
Tracy C	501.0	471	37	1	1	.996	3	1	.015	19	4
Allen B	254.7	260	11	0	2	.993	1	0	-.143	7	-7
Whitesell J	250.3	246	12	1	0	.996	0	0	-.004	5	-14
Reynolds M	218.0	186	11	0	5	.975	3	0	-.127	4	-16
Clark T	131.0	128	13	0	3	.979	1	0	.036	5	4
Ryal R	45.7	39	5	0	1	.978	0	0	--	0	--
Jackson C	43.0	42	1	0	1	.977	0	0	--	1	--
Snyder C	4.0	1	0	0	0	1.000	0	0	--	--	--
Second Base											
Lopez F	715.3	138	243	3	6	.977	23	31	.006	26	9
Roberts R	407.3	99	117	0	2	.991	4	14	-.015	14	7
Ojeda A	247.7	44	93	0	0	1.000	4	15	.048	14	29
Ryal R	77.3	9	27	0	0	1.000	3	4	--	4	--
Shortstop											
Drew S	1142.0	173	362	7	4	.980	32	34	.008	45	1
Ojeda A	241.7	31	74	2	1	.972	9	6	.008	14	20
Wilson J	64.0	12	27	1	1	.951	6	1	--	4	--
Third Base											
Reynolds M	1125.0	88	240	9	10	.945	27	2	-.051	53	6
Ojeda A	143.0	14	25	3	2	.886	5	0	-.057	4	-14
Roberts R	132.0	14	24	2	1	.927	3	0	.048	5	-4
Tracy C	47.0	5	9	0	0	1.000	0	0	--	0	--

Name	Inn	PO	A	TE	FE	FPct	DPS	DPT	ZRDif	OOZ	Dif
Left Field											
Parra G	577.0	129	4	3	0	.978	0	0	.025	28	-2
Byrnes E	385.7	92	3	0	3	.969	0	0	.061	29	25
Jackson C	179.3	35	0	0	1	.972	0	0	.010	7	-11
Roberts R	114.0	22	0	1	0	.957	0	0	-.047	11	46
Romero A	111.7	29	0	0	0	1.000	0	0	.023	7	12
Oeltjen T	80.0	20	1	1	0	.955	0	0	--	6	--
Center Field											
Young C	1020.0	287	3	0	2	.993	1	0	.018	66	-3
Parra G	328.0	89	3	1	2	.968	0	0	-.061	22	-1
Byrnes E	38.3	14	0	0	0	1.000	0	0	--	5	--
Oeltjen T	34.3	6	0	0	0	1.000	0	0	--	1	--
Romero A	26.7	11	1	0	0	1.000	0	0	--	1	--
Right Field											
Upton J	1180.0	294	4	2	10	.961	1	0	.011	66	4
Romero A	142.0	24	1	0	1	.962	0	0	.039	6	-10
Parra G	60.7	11	1	0	0	1.000	0	0	--	2	--
Byrnes E	40.0	12	0	0	0	1.000	0	0	--	3	--
Oeltjen T	25.0	10	1	0	0	1.000	0	0	--	5	--

Atlanta Braves

Stat Facts:

- Javier Vaquez led the majors with 20 sacrifice hits
- Vazquez 's total of -47 runs below average was tied for third-best in the majors
- Peter Moylan allowed zero home runs in 73 IP
- Moylan induced 14 DPs
- Kenshin Kawakami allowed just 6 SBs in 11 attempts
- Dave Ross threw out 43% of runners attempting to steal
- Jeff Francoeur had the lowest GPA (.214) of any corner outfielder with at least 300 PAs
- Derek Lowe's Out/GB rate was 72%, lowest of ML pitchers with at least 162 IP
- Chipper Jones had the lowest ZR (.664) of any regular third baseman
- Diory Hernandez drew 6 walks, 3 of them IBBs
- Hernandez's GPA was .142
- Brian McCann had the second-most Base Runs (79) of any catcher

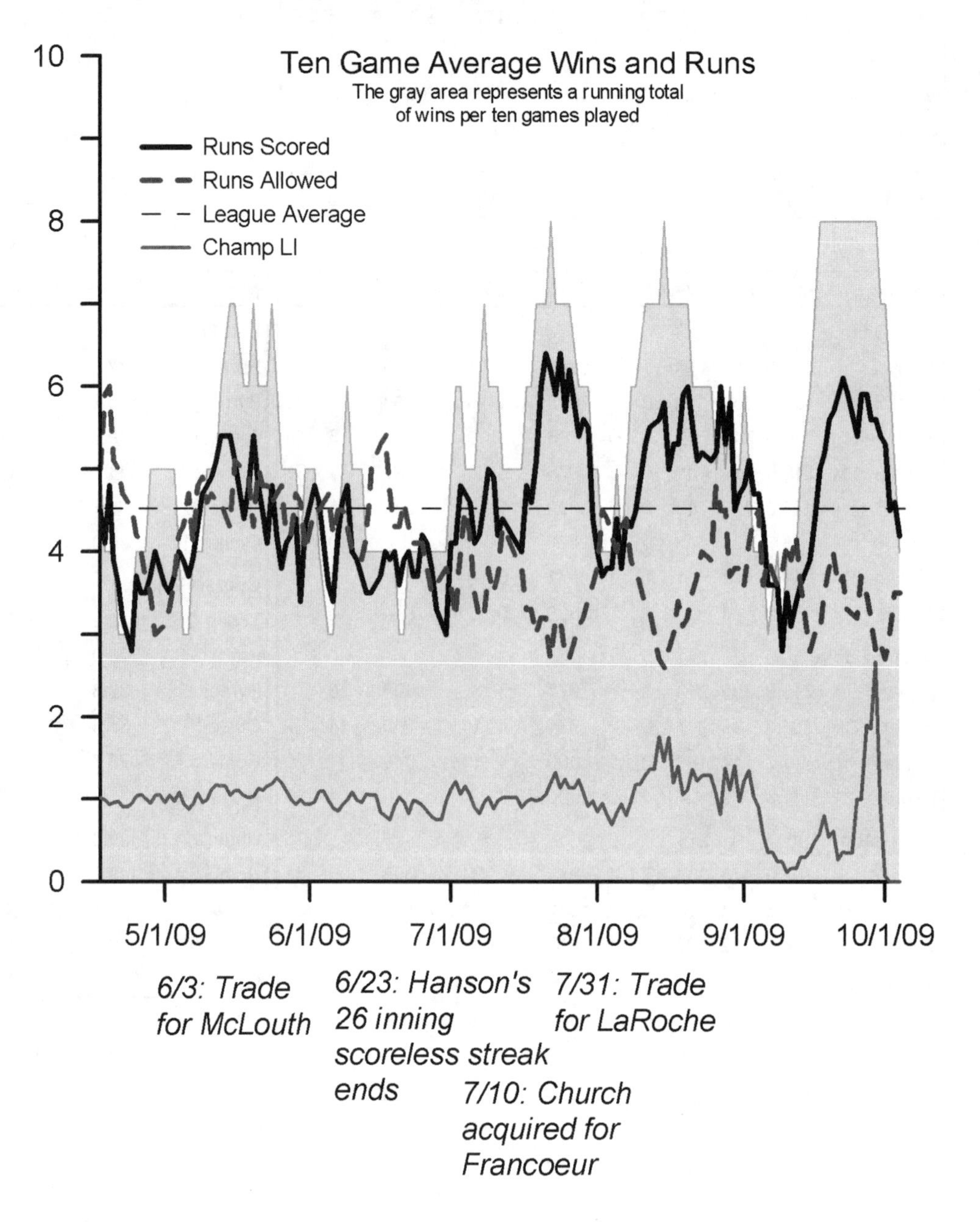

Team Batting and Pitching/Fielding Stats by Month

	April	May	June	July	Aug	Sept/Oct
Wins	10	15	11	16	17	17
Losses	11	14	15	11	11	14
RS/G	4.0	4.7	3.6	5.1	5.1	4.5
RA/G	4.3	4.6	4.2	3.5	3.6	3.6
OBP	.343	.332	.309	.362	.350	.335
SLG	.409	.384	.378	.466	.425	.377
FIP	3.33	3.62	4.08	3.59	3.50	3.65
DER	.674	.687	.696	.706	.669	.696

Batting Stats

Player	*BR*	Runs	RBI	PA	Outs	H	2B	3B	HR	TB	K	BB	IBB	HBP	SH	SF	SB	CS	GDP	H-A	L^R	BA	OBP	SLG	*GPA*
Jones C +	82	80	71	596	374	129	23	2	18	210	89	101	18	1	0	6	4	1	14	-.014	.031	.264	.388	.430	.281
Escobar Y	81	89	76	604	395	158	26	2	14	230	62	57	3	10	7	2	5	4	21	-.006	-.053	.299	.377	.436	.278
McCann B *	79	63	94	551	369	137	35	1	21	237	83	49	3	5	3	6	4	1	17	.007	.086	.281	.349	.486	.278
Prado M	68	64	49	503	332	138	38	0	11	209	59	36	1	2	11	4	1	3	17	.002	.048	.307	.358	.464	.277
Diaz M	66	56	58	425	274	116	18	4	13	181	90	35	2	13	5	1	12	5	14	.001	.111	.313	.390	.488	.297
Anderson G *	58	52	61	534	374	133	27	0	13	199	73	27	2	2	0	9	1	0	11	-.003	-.004	.268	.303	.401	.236
McLouth N *	52	59	36	396	264	87	20	1	11	142	70	47	1	5	3	2	12	6	6	-.064	.091	.257	.354	.419	.263
LaRoche A *	44	30	40	242	144	69	11	1	12	118	59	28	6	0	0	2	0	0	1	.024	.064	.325	.401	.557	.319
Kotchman C *	42	28	41	336	221	84	20	0	6	122	28	32	6	3	0	3	0	0	7	-.017	.045	.282	.354	.409	.261
Johnson K *	38	47	29	346	241	68	20	3	8	118	54	32	1	3	6	2	7	2	4	-.017	-.111	.224	.303	.389	.233
Infante O	28	24	27	229	146	62	9	1	2	79	28	19	0	1	2	4	2	0	5	.009	-.003	.305	.361	.389	.259
Francoeur J	28	32	35	324	239	76	12	2	5	107	46	12	2	3	1	4	5	1	10	.059	.045	.250	.282	.352	.214
Ross D	25	18	20	151	94	35	9	0	7	65	39	21	0	1	1	0	0	0	1	-.042	-.096	.273	.380	.508	.297
Church R *	17	20	18	144	98	33	12	0	2	51	22	16	2	1	0	0	0	0	4	-.043	-.062	.260	.347	.402	.256
Schafer J *	16	18	8	195	136	34	8	0	2	48	63	27	3	0	0	1	2	1	2	-.027	-.006	.204	.313	.287	.212
Norton G +	6	3	7	97	66	11	2	0	0	13	20	20	0	1	0	0	0	0	1	.066	.120	.145	.330	.171	.191
Conrad B +	6	7	8	58	44	11	1	2	2	22	14	3	1	1	0	0	0	0	1	-.234	.067	.204	.259	.407	.218
Hudson T	3	2	2	15	8	4	0	0	1	7	1	2	0	0	1	0	0	0	0	-.200	.391	.333	.429	.583	.338
Lowe D	3	6	1	70	43	12	0	0	0	12	16	4	0	0	12	0	0	0	1	.003	-.117	.222	.276	.222	.179
Blanco G *	3	5	1	48	36	8	0	1	0	10	9	4	0	0	1	0	2	0	1	.030	.115	.186	.255	.233	.173
Jones B *	2	2	1	17	9	4	0	0	0	4	3	4	0	0	0	0	0	0	0	-.281	-.441	.308	.471	.308	.288
Vazquez J	2	6	3	91	56	12	3	0	0	15	14	3	0	0	20	0	0	0	0	-.128	.070	.176	.211	.221	.150
Jurrjens J	2	7	4	80	57	8	2	0	0	10	24	8	0	0	7	0	0	0	0	-.071	.075	.123	.219	.154	.137
Gorecki R	1	6	3	27	20	5	0	0	0	5	12	1	0	0	0	1	1	0	0	-.075	.161	.200	.222	.200	.150
Canizares B	1	1	0	21	17	4	1	0	0	5	6	0	0	0	0	0	0	0	0	-.093	.123	.190	.190	.238	.145
Hernandez D	1	6	6	93	78	12	3	0	1	18	22	6	3	0	2	0	0	1	4	.088	-.095	.141	.198	.212	.142

Only includes batters with at least one Base Run. Italicized stats have been adjusted for home park.

Batted Ball Batting Stats

	% of PA		% of Batted Balls					Out %		Runs Per Event				Total Runs vs. Avg.				
Player	**K%**	**BB%**	**GB%**	**LD%**	**FB%**	**IF/F**	**HR/OF**	**GB**	**OF**	**NIP**	**GB**	**LD**	**OF**	**NIP**	**GB**	**LD**	**FB**	**Tot**
Diaz M	21	11	48	25	27	.03	.18	70	75	.05	.06	.38	.34	1	4	6	8	19
Jones C	15	17	45	20	35	.04	.13	78	86	.13	.02	.35	.21	18	-4	0	5	18
LaRoche A	24	12	30	24	46	.03	.17	63	77	.03	.13	.41	.30	0	3	4	11	18
McCann B	15	10	38	21	41	.08	.14	79	82	.07	.00	.40	.24	2	-6	6	13	15
Escobar Y	10	11	50	20	30	.04	.10	79	78	.13	.00	.41	.21	9	-7	9	3	13
Prado M	12	8	44	20	37	.09	.08	67	87	.07	.08	.42	.13	-0	8	8	-6	10
Ross D	26	15	30	22	49	.05	.17	81	85	.05	.01	.54	.26	1	-2	3	4	7
Kotchman C	8	10	51	19	30	.12	.08	76	79	.14	.03	.35	.18	5	1	1	-2	5
McLouth N	18	13	40	18	43	.12	.11	74	88	.08	.05	.44	.15	5	1	1	-3	4
Infante O	12	9	32	27	41	.07	.01	72	82	.08	.05	.36	.06	1	1	6	-5	2
Church R	15	12	44	17	38	.05	.03	74	86	.09	.05	.57	.06	2	1	3	-4	1
Johnson K	16	10	39	18	43	.08	.08	85	85	.07	-.02	.42	.14	1	-6	-0	-3	-8
Schafer J	32	14	44	18	39	.10	.06	80	76	.02	.01	.39	.16	-1	-1	-3	-4	-9
Anderson G	14	5	41	20	38	.07	.07	79	82	.02	.02	.38	.13	-6	-4	5	-6	-11
Francoeur J	14	5	41	18	41	.08	.04	73	87	.00	.04	.37	.06	-5	-0	-1	-10	-16
MLB Average	**18**	**10**	**43**	**19**	**38**	**.10**	**.11**	**75**	**83**	**.05**	**.04**	**.39**	**.19**	**--**	**--**	**--**	**--**	**--**

Pitching Stats

Player	PRC	IP	BFP	G	GS	K	BB	IBB	HBP	H	HR	DP	DER	SB	CS	PO	W	L	Sv	Op	Hld	H-A	R^L	RA	ERA	FIP
Vazquez J	*121*	219.3	874	32	32	238	44	2	4	181	20	13	.708	7	5	0	15	10	0	0	0	.007	-.038	3.08	2.87	2.80
Jurrjens J	*111*	215.0	884	34	34	152	75	1	3	186	15	23	.718	14	7	1	14	10	0	0	0	-.038	-.048	2.97	2.60	3.72
Hanson T	*70*	127.7	522	21	21	116	46	1	5	105	10	15	.710	18	8	1	11	4	0	0	0	-.011	-.065	2.96	2.89	3.53
Kawakami K	*59*	156.3	669	32	25	105	57	6	6	153	15	15	.712	6	5	0	7	12	1	1	0	-.031	.035	4.20	3.86	4.15
Lowe D	*59*	194.7	855	34	34	111	63	7	4	232	16	29	.666	13	4	2	15	10	0	0	0	.003	.013	5.04	4.67	4.00
Soriano R	*45*	75.7	307	77	0	102	27	4	1	53	6	4	.708	3	0	0	1	6	27	31	6	-.079	-.097	2.97	2.97	2.44
Gonzalez M *	*39*	74.3	315	80	0	90	33	8	7	56	7	6	.708	7	2	2	5	4	10	17	17	.028	-.046	3.39	2.42	3.25
Moylan P	*33*	73.0	309	87	0	61	35	8	2	65	0	14	.668	11	3	1	6	2	0	5	25	-.036	-.112	3.58	2.84	2.67
Medlen K	*26*	67.7	294	37	4	72	30	2	2	65	5	6	.670	1	1	1	3	5	0	2	1	-.058	.100	4.52	4.26	3.31
O'Flaherty E	*24*	56.3	236	78	0	39	18	4	6	52	2	7	.690	4	3	1	2	1	0	2	15	.002	-.050	3.67	3.04	3.29
Hudson T	*19*	42.3	180	7	7	30	13	0	0	49	4	5	.654	1	4	0	2	1	0	0	0	-.051	-.028	3.61	3.61	3.88
Bennett J	*15*	34.0	163	33	0	23	21	4	3	42	2	6	.623	3	1	1	2	4	0	0	2	-.004	-.040	3.44	3.18	4.33
Acosta M	*14*	37.3	174	36	0	32	19	2	2	45	4	4	.632	4	1	0	1	1	0	0	2	.070	-.008	4.58	4.34	4.36
Reyes J *	*5*	27.0	119	6	5	21	13	3	1	27	4	5	.688	1	0	0	0	2	0	0	0	-.127	-.161	8.33	7.00	4.74
Logan B *	*4*	17.3	82	20	0	10	9	3	1	21	1	2	.656	4	0	0	1	1	0	0	1	.144	-.102	6.23	5.19	3.96
Parr J	*4*	14.0	66	8	0	12	5	0	1	17	1	0	.638	0	0	0	0	0	0	0	0	.095	-.175	5.79	5.79	3.65
Carlyle B	*3*	21.3	107	16	0	12	12	4	0	35	5	5	.603	0	0	0	0	1	0	0	2	-.119	.053	9.70	8.86	6.20
Campillo J	*1*	4.3	21	5	0	3	3	0	0	7	0	0	.533	0	2	1	1	0	0	1	0	-.105	-.214	6.23	4.15	3.84

Italicized stats have been adjusted for home park.

Batted Ball Pitching Stats

	% of PA		% of Batted Balls					Out %		Runs Per Event				Total Runs vs. Avg.				
Player	K%	BB%	GB%	LD%	FB%	IF/F	HR/OF	GB	OF	NIP	GB	LD	OF	NIP	GB	LD	FB	Tot
Vazquez J	27	5	42	24	35	.09	.11	78	86	-.04	.03	.33	.17	-23	-7	-6	-12	-47
Jurrjens J	17	9	43	18	39	.09	.06	77	82	.04	.03	.38	.13	-3	-5	-5	-13	-27
Soriano R	33	9	31	21	48	.07	.08	69	89	-.01	.06	.41	.11	-6	-2	-3	-7	-18
Hanson T	22	10	40	18	42	.11	.07	77	83	.03	.02	.42	.14	-3	-5	-1	-7	-16
Gonzalez M	29	13	38	18	44	.14	.11	72	85	.03	.05	.45	.17	-1	-1	-3	-4	-9
Moylan P	20	12	62	18	20	.10	.00	76	69	.06	.03	.35	.18	2	0	-3	-7	-8
O'Flaherty E	17	10	55	17	28	.04	.04	72	86	.06	.06	.30	.06	1	3	-3	-8	-8
Medlen K	24	11	41	23	36	.11	.09	73	81	.03	.06	.37	.17	-1	1	1	-4	-3
Kawakami K	16	9	42	19	39	.07	.09	78	83	.06	.03	.41	.17	1	-3	2	-1	-1
Hudson T	17	7	62	18	20	.11	.17	69	80	.03	.08	.32	.30	-1	4	-2	-1	1
Reyes J	18	12	50	15	35	0.00	.14	80	67	.07	.00	.42	.37	1	-1	-1	6	4
Bennett J	14	15	55	23	23	.12	.09	68	85	.12	.06	.45	.16	4	1	4	-3	6
Acosta M	18	12	44	19	37	.11	.10	63	74	.07	.12	.34	.24	2	4	-1	2	6
Lowe D	13	8	56	18	26	.05	.10	76	72	.06	.03	.39	.26	-1	1	4	6	10
Carlyle E	11	11	36	23	41	.15	.18	66	83	.12	.06	.46	.30	2	1	4	5	11
MLB Average	***18***	***10***	***43***	***19***	***38***	***.10***	***.11***	***75***	***83***	***.05***	***.04***	***.39***	***.19***	--	--	--	--	--

Fielding Stats

Name	INN	SBA/G	CS%	ERA	WP+PB/G	PO	A	TE	FE
Catchers									
McCann B	1078.7	0.81	22%	3.65	0.334	924	58	6	5
Ross D	354.0	0.94	43%	3.43	0.229	314	37	1	0
Sammons C	30.0	0.60	0%	2.40	0.900	23	2	0	0

Name	Inn	PO	A	TE	FE	FPct	DPS	DPT	ZRDif	OOZ	Dif
First Base											
Kotchman C	703.3	674	61	0	0	1.000	2	0	.034	30	8
LaRoche A	515.7	520	43	0	1	.998	2	0	-.053	25	14
Prado M	182.7	160	14	0	1	.994	3	0	.042	6	-1
Canizares B	43.0	33	2	0	0	1.000	0	0	--	3	--
Norton G	18.0	21	2	0	0	1.000	0	0	--	1	--
Second Base											
Johnson K	655.7	135	222	2	8	.973	14	39	.003	13	-8
Prado M	513.3	116	162	0	4	.986	10	25	-.005	9	-10
Infante O	199.0	42	62	0	2	.981	5	6	-.013	2	-17
Conrad B	84.0	22	31	0	0	1.000	3	7	--	2	--
Hernandez D	10.7	4	5	0	0	1.000	0	0	--	1	--
Shortstop											
Escobar Y	1208.0	191	409	6	7	.979	47	33	.037	52	5
Hernandez D	181.0	26	61	1	0	.989	11	7	-.033	8	6
Infante O	73.0	11	21	0	0	1.000	1	1	--	6	--
Third Base											
Jones C	1136.0	85	208	7	14	.930	27	1	-.072	50	2
Prado M	266.0	14	65	0	2	.975	7	1	.042	16	19
Infante O	45.0	1	14	1	0	.938	0	0	--	2	--
Hernandez D	13.0	1	5	0	0	1.000	2	0	--	1	--
Conrad B	2.0	0	0	0	0	0.000	0	0	--	--	--

Name	Inn	PO	A	TE	FE	FPct	DPS	DPT	ZRDif	OOZ	Dif
Left Field											
Anderson G	1026.0	193	4	2	0	.980	0	0	-.044	41	-10
Diaz M	301.0	67	0	0	1	.985	0	0	-.007	20	16
Gorecki R	56.0	15	0	0	1	.938	0	0	--	2	--
Infante O	36.3	11	0	0	0	1.000	0	0	--	4	--
Jones B	35.0	5	0	0	0	1.000	0	0	--	3	--
Blanco G	8.0	0	1	0	1	.500	0	0	--	0	--
Center Field											
McLouth N	740.3	196	4	0	1	.995	2	0	-.001	51	1
Schafer J	432.0	127	4	0	0	1.000	1	0	.006	39	22
Church R	127.0	31	0	0	0	1.000	0	0	-.046	8	-5
Blanco G	72.0	20	0	0	0	1.000	0	0	--	2	--
Infante O	49.3	7	0	0	0	1.000	0	0	--	4	--
Gorecki R	36.0	9	1	0	0	1.000	0	0	--	2	--
Diaz M	6.0	1	0	0	0	1.000	0	0	--	--	--
Right Field											
Francoeur J	701.0	157	6	0	0	1.000	0	0	-.005	36	-1
Diaz M	540.7	89	2	0	2	.978	0	0	-.025	21	-13
Church R	173.0	36	3	1	0	.975	2	0	.052	12	17
Infante O	33.0	6	0	0	0	1.000	0	0	--	2	--
Blanco G	10.0	1	0	0	0	1.000	0	0	--	--	--
Barton B	2.0	1	0	0	0	1.000	0	0	--	0	--
Prado M	2.0	0	0	0	0	0.000	0	0	--	--	--
Gorecki R	1.0	1	0	0	0	1.000	0	0	--	0	--

Baltimore Orioles

Stat Facts:

- The Orioles' outfield throwing ranked 3rd in the majors
- The Orioles' -73 outfield plus/minus ranked last in the majors
- Nick Markakis made the fewest OOZ plays (34) of any right fielder with at least 1,000 innings
- Markakis tied for the AL lead with 10 sacrifice flies
- Aubrey Huff was 0-for-6 in stolen base attempts
- Mark Hendrickson allowed 15 SBs in 15 attempts
- Adam Eaton allowed 9 SBs in 9 attempts
- Jeremy Guthrie led the AL in home runs allowed (35)
- David Hernandez allowed 27 homers in 101 IP
- Hernandez's FIP (6.70) was highest of any ML pitcher with at least 50 IP
- Alfredo Simon faced 28 batters, and allowed 5 home runs
- Cesar Izturis had the most PAs (412) of anyone in the majors with 0 sacrifice flies

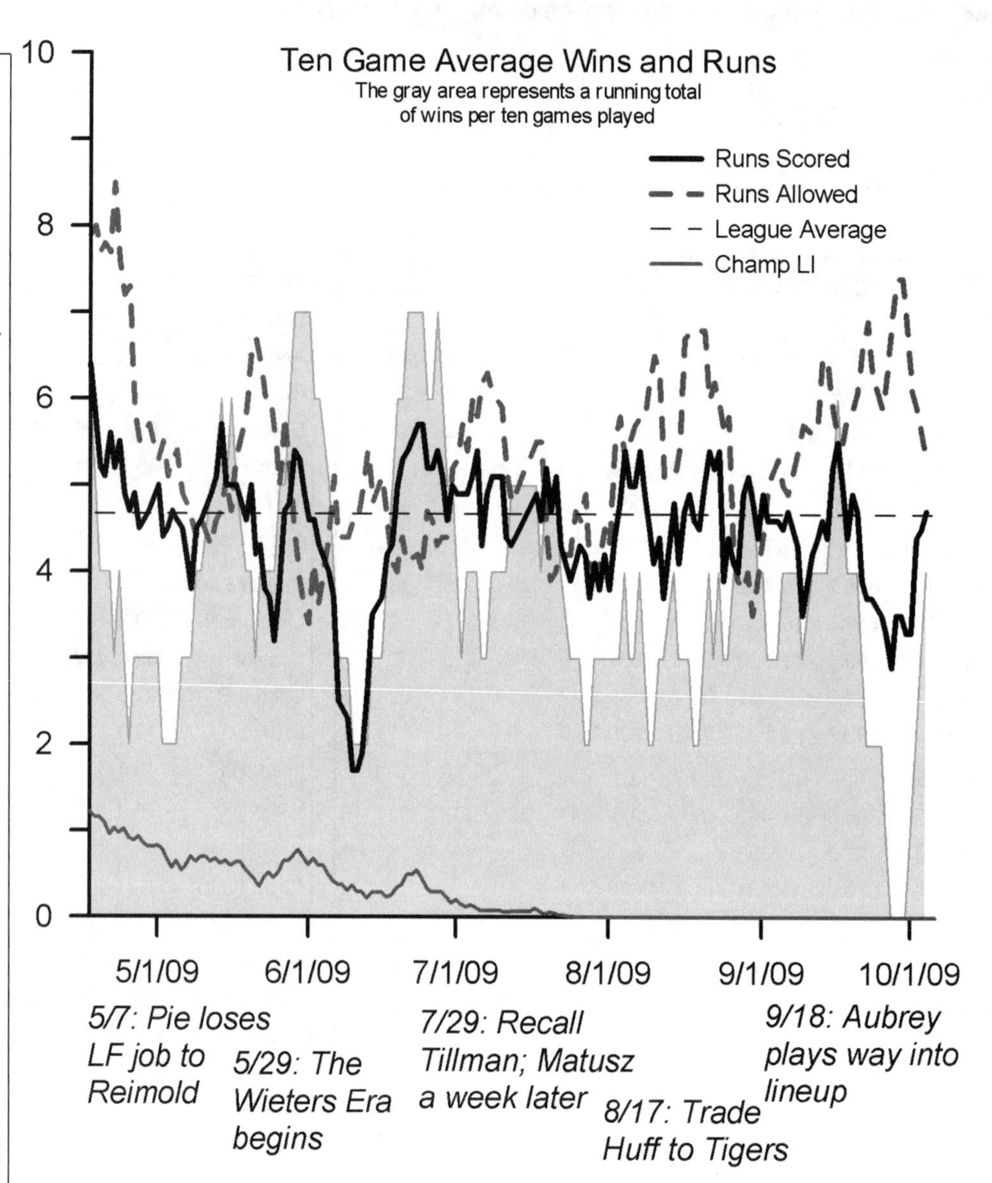

Team Batting and Pitching/Fielding Stats by Month

	April	May	June	July	Aug	Sept/Oct
Wins	9	14	12	9	10	10
Losses	13	15	14	16	20	20
RS/G	5.27	4.62	4.23	4.48	4.63	4.33
RA/G	6.55	4.97	4.77	4.76	5.47	6.03
OBP	.352	.322	.337	.318	.335	.330
SLG	.416	.454	.399	.390	.431	.397
FIP	5.45	4.71	4.47	4.77	5.05	5.76
DER	.660	.701	.690	.706	.666	.676

Batting Stats

Player	*BR*	Runs	RBI	PA	Outs	H	2B	3B	HR	TB	K	BB	IBB	HBP	SH	SF	SB	CS	GDP	H-A	L^R	BA	OBP	SLG	*GPA*
Roberts B +	*102*	110	79	717	467	179	56	1	16	285	112	74	3	2	1	8	30	7	7	-.024	-.005	.283	.356	.451	*.270*
Markakis N *	*95*	94	101	711	468	188	45	2	18	291	98	56	0	3	0	10	6	2	12	.008	.064	.293	.347	.453	*.267*
Scott L *	*73*	61	77	506	337	116	26	1	25	219	104	55	5	1	0	1	0	0	4	.059	.003	.258	.340	.488	*.272*
Jones A	*67*	83	70	519	359	131	22	3	19	216	93	36	3	7	0	3	10	4	13	.008	-.058	.277	.335	.457	*.262*
Reimold N	*59*	49	45	411	268	100	18	2	15	167	77	47	1	3	0	3	8	2	8	.027	-.004	.279	.365	.466	*.278*
Huff A *	*50*	51	72	480	339	109	24	1	13	174	74	41	7	4	0	5	0	6	12	.070	.035	.253	.321	.405	*.243*
Mora M	*48*	44	48	496	349	117	20	0	8	161	60	34	1	8	1	3	3	3	13	.085	.006	.260	.321	.358	*.232*
Wigginton T	*45*	44	41	436	316	112	19	0	11	164	57	23	1	2	0	1	1	2	16	.035	-.024	.273	.314	.400	*.239*
Wieters M +	*45*	35	43	385	263	102	15	1	9	146	86	28	2	1	0	2	0	0	11	.036	-.042	.288	.340	.412	*.254*
Izturis C +	*34*	34	30	412	303	99	14	4	2	127	38	18	0	3	4	0	12	4	11	.100	.038	.256	.294	.328	*.212*
Pie F *	*33*	38	29	281	194	67	10	3	9	110	58	24	1	0	2	3	1	3	6	.040	.054	.266	.326	.437	*.253*
Zaun G +	*23*	23	13	197	129	41	10	0	4	63	30	27	0	2	0	0	0	0	2	-.072	-.048	.244	.355	.375	*.251*
Aubrey M *	*13*	12	14	95	66	26	7	0	4	45	10	5	0	0	0	0	0	0	2	-.009	.159	.289	.326	.500	*.269*
Andino R	*13*	31	10	215	163	44	7	0	2	57	47	15	1	0	0	2	3	3	6	.066	.002	.222	.274	.288	*.194*
Moeller C	*11*	6	10	100	69	23	8	1	2	39	16	7	0	1	1	2	0	0	3	.080	-.145	.258	.313	.438	*.248*
Fiorentino J	*7*	8	8	75	47	18	1	0	0	19	16	8	0	0	1	2	2	0	1	.085	-.058	.281	.351	.297	*.230*
Salazar O	*6*	4	6	33	20	13	0	0	2	19	4	2	0	0	0	0	0	0	2	.162	.141	.419	.455	.613	*.354*
Montanez L	*5*	5	6	91	68	15	5	0	1	23	16	5	0	2	1	1	0	1	0	.099	-.144	.183	.244	.280	*.178*
Freel R	*1*	2	1	20	13	2	0	0	0	2	4	5	0	0	0	0	0	0	0	.055	-.281	.133	.350	.133	*.189*
Turner J	*1*	2	3	22	16	3	0	0	0	3	3	4	0	0	0	0	0	0	1	-.125	.236	.167	.318	.167	*.183*

Only includes batters with at least one Base Run. Italicized stats have been adjusted for home park.

Batted Ball Batting Stats

	% of PA		% of Batted Balls					Out %		Runs Per Event				Total Runs vs. Avg.				
Player	K%	BB%	GB%	LD%	FB%	IF/F	HR/OF	GB	OF	NIP	GB	LD	OF	NIP	GB	LD	FB	Tot
Roberts B	16	11	36	22	42	.07	.08	74	80	.07	.05	.36	.18	4	2	5	4	15
Markakis N	14	8	43	17	41	.07	.09	69	86	.06	.08	.45	.14	0	10	6	-2	15
Reimold N	19	12	48	14	37	.16	.16	69	77	.07	.07	.43	.30	3	5	-3	8	14
Scott L	21	11	40	17	43	.13	.18	78	85	.05	.03	.46	.29	1	-3	1	14	13
Jones A	18	8	55	17	28	.06	.19	76	78	.03	.04	.35	.33	-3	2	-4	11	6
Zaun G	15	15	41	19	40	.07	.08	79	87	.11	.02	.42	.11	4	-1	1	-3	1
Moeller C	16	8	33	21	45	.15	.07	72	89	.04	.05	.46	.10	-0	-0	2	-2	-1
Wieters M	22	8	42	19	40	.07	.09	70	77	.00	.06	.39	.19	-5	2	-0	2	-1
Pie F	21	9	41	21	38	.11	.14	77	84	.02	.02	.42	.23	-2	-3	2	2	-1
Huff A	15	9	47	16	37	.12	.11	78	82	.06	.01	.40	.20	1	-3	-3	1	-4
Wigginton T	13	6	43	18	39	.13	.08	74	87	.03	.04	.43	.11	-4	-0	4	-8	-8
Andino R	22	7	53	17	30	.04	.05	76	76	-.00	.02	.36	.14	-3	-1	-3	-4	-11
Mora M	12	8	43	19	38	.10	.06	77	86	.08	.02	.36	.09	1	-3	0	-11	-13
Izturis C	9	5	49	20	30	.13	.02	76	87	.05	.03	.32	.04	-3	1	0	-16	-18
MLB Average	***18***	***10***	***43***	***19***	***38***	***.10***	***.11***	***75***	***83***	***.05***	***.04***	***.39***	***.19***	--	--	--	--	--

Pitching Stats

Player	*PRC*	IP	BFP	G	GS	K	BB	IBB	HBP	H	HR	DP	DER	SB	CS	PO	W	L	Sv	Op	Hld	H-A	R^L	RA	ERA	FIP
Guthrie J	*65*	200.0	874	33	33	110	60	1	9	224	35	17	.705	9	2	4	10	17	0	0	0	.005	-.034	5.40	5.04	5.39
Bergesen B	*56*	123.3	519	19	19	65	32	4	5	126	11	12	.702	1	3	0	7	5	0	0	0	-.044	-.011	3.79	3.43	4.10
Hendrickson	*37*	105.0	457	53	11	61	33	4	2	116	16	9	.696	15	0	0	6	5	1	3	2	.040	-.033	5.06	4.37	4.90
Hernandez D	*34*	101.3	462	20	19	68	46	0	1	118	27	7	.709	8	2	0	4	10	0	0	0	.053	-.000	5.51	5.42	6.70
Johnson J	*31*	70.0	300	64	0	49	23	3	3	73	8	12	.687	4	1	0	4	6	10	16	14	.011	-.007	4.11	4.11	4.26
Sherrill G *	*31*	41.3	171	42	0	39	13	2	2	34	3	3	.719	3	0	0	0	1	20	23	0	-.011	-.118	2.40	2.40	3.19
Berken J	*29*	119.7	560	24	24	66	44	2	6	164	19	16	.645	12	3	0	6	12	0	0	0	-.025	-.006	6.92	6.54	5.36
Bass B	*29*	86.3	400	48	0	54	44	5	5	106	11	13	.657	5	5	3	5	3	0	0	1	.043	-.014	5.42	4.90	5.13
Baez D	*28*	71.7	295	59	0	40	22	3	5	59	8	10	.759	4	0	0	4	6	0	2	15	-.099	-.044	4.52	4.02	4.53
Uehara K	*28*	66.7	279	12	12	48	12	1	0	71	7	4	.689	4	0	1	2	4	0	0	0	-.029	.004	4.46	4.05	3.61
Albers M	*21*	67.0	309	56	0	49	36	3	2	80	3	9	.639	9	3	0	3	6	0	4	10	-.013	-.077	5.78	5.51	3.88
Tillman C	*21*	65.0	285	12	12	39	24	1	2	77	15	7	.693	1	5	0	2	5	0	0	0	-.026	.046	5.54	5.40	6.14
Matusz B *	*18*	44.7	196	8	8	38	14	0	0	52	6	4	.659	9	2	0	5	2	0	0	0	-.057	-.064	4.84	4.63	4.18
Meredith C	*13*	28.7	118	29	0	17	12	4	2	26	3	7	.726	3	0	0	0	0	0	0	3	-.024	.073	3.77	3.77	4.41
Hill R *	*12*	57.7	275	14	13	46	40	2	1	68	7	5	.652	11	2	2	3	3	0	0	0	.062	.016	8.27	7.80	5.20
Ray C	*11*	43.3	214	46	0	39	23	7	1	64	8	5	.601	6	1	0	0	4	0	3	6	.012	-.144	7.48	7.27	4.97
Mickolio K	*10*	13.7	59	11	0	14	7	1	0	11	0	0	.711	0	0	0	0	2	0	0	2	.182	.158	2.63	2.63	2.46
Eaton A	*8*	41.0	194	8	8	28	19	1	0	56	9	3	.652	9	0	0	2	5	0	0	0	-.072	-.086	8.56	8.56	6.00
Sarfate D	*8*	23.0	101	20	0	20	14	0	1	21	3	3	.698	3	1	0	0	1	0	0	1	-.071	.009	5.87	5.09	5.10
Castillo A *	*7*	12.0	49	20	0	8	4	1	1	12	0	3	.667	0	1	1	0	0	0	0	5	.064	-.037	3.00	2.25	2.86
Walker J *	*4*	12.3	55	22	0	9	0	0	1	19	5	1	.625	1	1	0	0	0	0	1	2	-.040	.210	5.84	5.11	7.25
Waters C *	*4*	11.7	49	5	1	5	5	0	0	9	3	0	.833	1	0	0	1	0	0	0	0	.031	-.014	5.40	5.40	6.96
Lambert C	*3*	5.7	26	4	0	7	1	0	0	8	2	0	.625	0	0	0	0	0	0	0	0	-.020	-.173	4.76	4.76	5.84
Simon A	*1*	6.3	28	2	2	3	2	0	0	8	5	0	.833	1	1	0	0	1	0	0	0	-.461	-.048	9.95	9.95	
Henn S *	*1*	3.0	19	6	0	6	4	0	0	6	0	0	.333	0	0	0	0	0	0	1	0	-.174	-.395	9.00	9.00	3.19

Italicized stats have been adjusted for home park.

Batted Ball Pitching Stats

	% of PA		% of Batted Balls					Out %		Runs Per Event				Total Runs vs. Avg.				
Player	K%	BB%	GB%	LD%	FB%	IF/F	HR/OF	GB	OF	NIP	GB	LD	OF	NIP	GB	LD	FB	Tot
Baez D	14	9	61	13	26	.05	.15	84	87	.07	-.02	.44	.20	1	-7	-3	-3	-12
Sherrill G	23	9	33	15	51	.17	.06	77	85	.01	.03	.45	.11	-2	-1	-1	-3	-7
Bergesen B	13	7	50	18	32	.06	.09	80	83	.05	.01	.44	.16	-2	-5	4	-3	-5
Uehara K	17	4	30	17	53	.19	.08	71	81	-.02	.06	.43	.17	-5	1	1	1	-2
Meredith C	14	12	64	12	24	.05	.15	75	76	.09	.05	.26	.29	1	1	-4	1	-1
Johnson J	16	9	52	18	30	.05	.13	74	82	.05	.04	.37	.21	-1	1	-1	0	-0
Sarfate D	20	15	34	11	55	.14	.10	68	81	.08	.07	.53	.21	2	0	-1	2	2
Matusz B	19	7	31	21	48	.12	.10	68	77	.01	.09	.35	.22	-2	2	0	4	4
Albers M	16	12	48	20	31	.12	.05	73	75	.09	.05	.44	.16	4	1	5	-4	6
Hendrickson M	13	8	45	20	35	.06	.14	79	77	.05	.02	.36	.26	-1	-3	2	11	9
Tillman C	14	9	37	18	45	.05	.16	73	87	.07	.05	.44	.22	1	0	3	9	13
Hill R	17	15	31	21	48	.16	.10	70	83	.10	.06	.54	.17	6	-0	8	0	14
Eaton A	14	10	33	23	44	.09	.14	71	78	.07	.06	.45	.26	1	0	6	7	14
Bass B	14	12	61	15	23	.06	.17	72	75	.11	.05	.41	.33	6	5	-1	5	15
Ray C	18	11	41	21	38	.04	.15	65	80	.06	.11	.47	.26	1	4	5	6	15
Guthrie J	13	8	35	19	47	.14	.13	77	83	.06	.02	.41	.22	-0	-6	9	18	21
Hernandez D	15	10	29	18	53	.13	.16	68	89	.07	.09	.43	.22	3	4	3	14	23
Berken J	12	9	39	24	37	.06	.12	72	78	.08	.05	.38	.23	3	2	13	12	31
MLB Average	***18***	***10***	***43***	***19***	***38***	***.10***	***.11***	***75***	***83***	***.05***	***.04***	***.39***	***.19***	***--***	***--***	***--***	***--***	***--***

Fielding Stats

Name	INN	SBA/G	CS%	ERA	WP+PB/G	PO	A	TE	FE
Catchers									
Wieters M	738.3	1.01	22%	5.03	0.232	489	35	4	1
Zaun G	435.3	0.79	24%	5.13	0.186	294	17	4	1
Moeller C	239.3	0.98	4%	5.68	0.376	194	6	0	0
Rodriguez G	16.0	0.00	0%	4.50	0.563	10	0	0	0

Name	Inn	PO	A	TE	FE	FPct	DPS	DPT	ZRDif	OOZ	Dif
First Base											
Huff A	826.0	822	59	0	4	.995	9	1	.006	20	-10
Wigginton T	333.0	315	30	0	4	.989	3	0	-.077	12	2
Aubrey M	191.0	189	17	0	0	1.000	1	0	.075	9	13
Scott L	63.0	54	3	0	1	.983	0	0	--	1	--
Salazar O	16.0	20	1	0	0	1.000	0	0	--	1	--
Second Base											
Roberts B	1340.0	249	432	5	6	.984	32	70	-.024	45	6
Wigginton T	39.3	8	11	0	0	1.000	0	2	--	2	--
Andino R	39.0	12	8	0	0	1.000	1	2	--	0	--
Turner J	6.0	3	3	0	0	1.000	0	1	--	0	--
Freel R	4.0	0	1	0	0	1.000	0	0	--	0	--
Shortstop											
Izturis C	934.7	171	337	3	5	.984	35	28	.029	39	3
Andino R	478.3	76	163	4	4	.968	27	9	.006	20	4
Wigginton T	13.0	3	8	0	0	1.000	0	1	--	2	--
Salazar O	3.0	0	2	1	0	.667	0	0	--	0	--
Third Base											
Mora M	1050.0	113	254	8	3	.971	19	1	.020	40	-3
Wigginton T	317.7	24	54	0	4	.951	4	0	-.133	11	-7
Turner J	34.0	3	7	0	0	1.000	1	0	--	2	--
Salazar O	17.0	4	0	0	0	1.000	0	0	--	0	--
Andino R	7.0	0	1	0	0	1.000	0	0	--	1	--
Freel R	3.0	0	0	0	0	0.000	0	0	--	--	--

Name	Inn	PO	A	TE	FE	FPct	DPS	DPT	ZRDif	OOZ	Dif
Left Field											
Reimold N	732.3	172	7	4	1	.973	0	1	-.032	35	-3
Pie F	272.0	85	3	1	0	.989	0	0	.050	18	16
Scott L	199.0	53	0	0	0	1.000	0	0	.013	14	20
Montanez L	135.7	34	0	0	0	1.000	0	0	.065	11	31
Fiorentino J	51.0	9	1	0	0	1.000	0	0	--	3	--
Freel R	31.0	8	0	0	0	1.000	0	0	--	0	--
Wigginton T	6.0	1	0	0	0	1.000	0	0	--	0	--
Salazar O	1.0	0	0	0	0	0.000	0	0	--	--	--
Andino R	1.0	0	0	0	0	0.000	0	0	--	--	--
Center Field											
Jones A	1005.0	349	9	3	2	.986	1	0	-.009	91	23
Pie F	311.7	112	2	0	1	.991	0	0	-.025	26	15
Fiorentino J	101.3	26	1	0	0	1.000	0	0	-.046	3	-38
Montanez L	9.0	2	0	0	0	1.000	0	0	--	0	--
Andino R	2.0	1	0	0	0	1.000	0	0	--	0	--
Right Field											
Markakis N	1402.0	298	13	2	4	.981	1	0	-.004	34	-28
Montanez L	12.0	1	0	0	0	1.000	0	0	--	0	--
Reimold N	9.0	1	0	0	0	1.000	0	0	--	0	--
Freel R	3.0	0	0	0	0	0.000	0	0	--	--	--
Fiorentino J	3.0	1	0	0	0	1.000	0	0	--	0	--

Boston Red Sox

Stat Facts:

- Jacoby Ellsbury led the majors with 70 steals
- Jacoby is the first AL player to steal 70 bags since 1997
- Dustin Pedroia was the toughest hitter in the majors to strike out
- Pedroia's BB% (11%) was nearly double his K% (6%)
- Brad Penny allowed 27 SB (most in the majors) in 29 attempts
- With SF, Penny allowed 1 SB in 2 attempts in 42 IP
- Tim Wakefield allowed 23 SBs in 26 attempts
- Wakefield's IF/F rate (.18) was highest of any ML pitcher with at least 100 IP
- Boston's ERA with Jason Varitek catching (3.87) was nearly 1.5 runs lower than their other catchers
- Jon Lester tied for 2nd in the AL with 6 pickoffs
- Jason Bay played the most innings (1279) of any player with zero errors
- J.D. Drew had the highest ZR (.952) of any regular right fielder

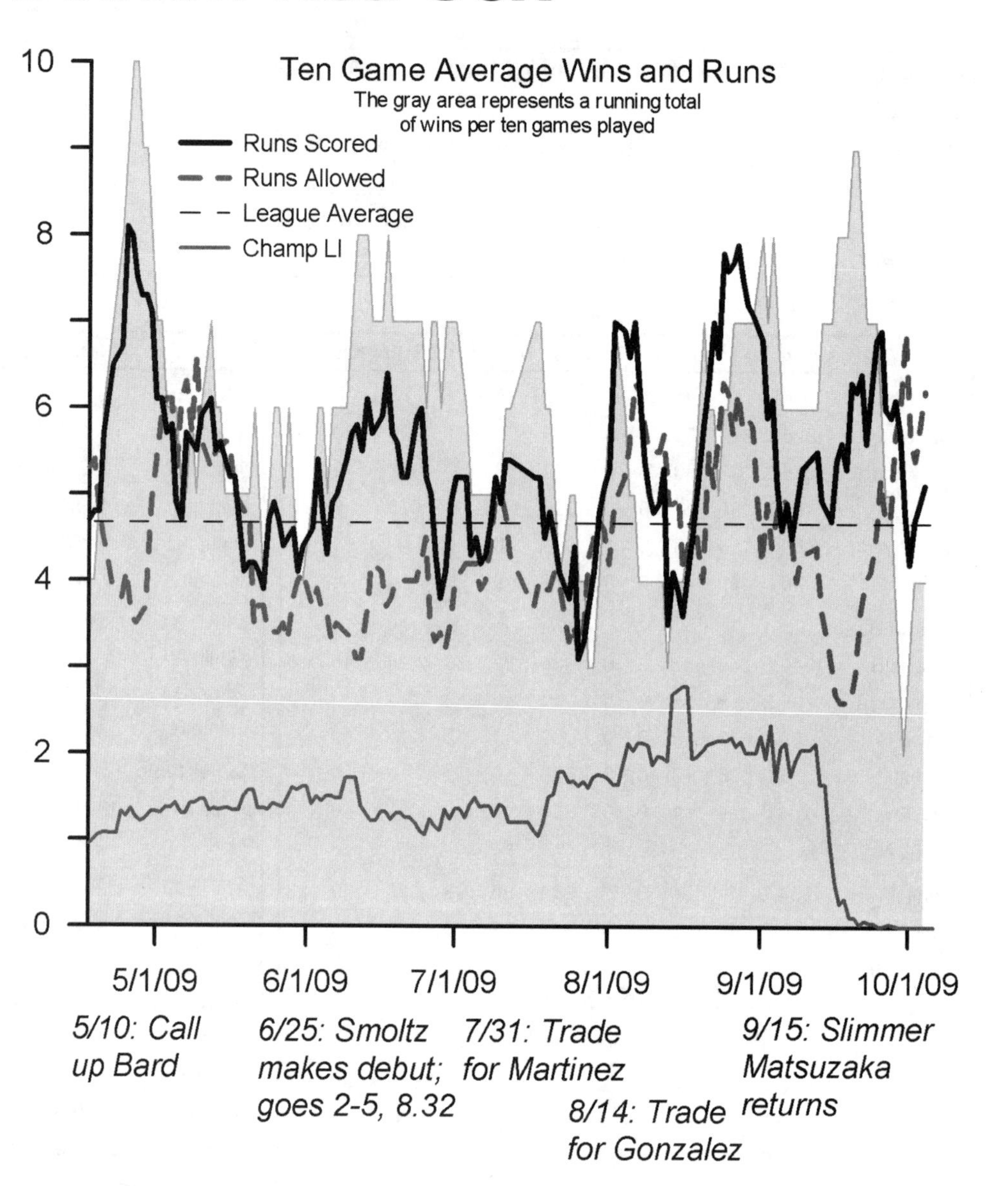

Team Batting and Pitching/Fielding Stats by Month

	April	May	June	July	Aug	Sept/Oct
Wins	14	15	18	13	16	19
Losses	8	14	8	12	12	13
RS/G	5.7	4.9	5.3	4.8	5.9	5.7
RA/G	4.9	4.4	3.7	4.4	5.1	4.7
OBP	.364	.350	.348	.328	.356	.362
SLG	.463	.452	.433	.419	.494	.456
FIP	4.57	4.04	3.53	3.37	5.01	4.56
DER	.685	.671	.690	.670	.695	.677

Batting Stats

Player	*BR*	Runs	RBI	PA	Outs	H	2B	3B	HR	TB	K	BB	IBB	HBP	SH	SF	SB	CS	GDP	H-A	L^R	BA	OBP	SLG	*GPA*
Bay J	*106*	103	119	638	401	142	29	3	36	285	162	94	4	9	0	4	13	3	9	.017	.026	.267	.384	.537	*.295*
Youkilis K	*103*	99	94	588	352	150	36	1	27	269	125	77	6	16	0	4	7	2	9	.018	.004	.305	.413	.548	*.311*
Pedroia D	*96*	115	72	714	468	185	48	1	15	280	45	74	3	5	3	6	20	8	19	.048	-.020	.296	.371	.447	*.268*
Ellsbury J *	*93*	94	60	693	461	188	27	10	8	259	74	49	3	6	6	6	70	12	13	.018	-.011	.301	.355	.415	*.253*
Drew J *	*86*	84	68	539	338	126	30	4	24	236	109	82	5	3	1	1	2	6	6	.047	.020	.279	.392	.522	*.295*
Ortiz D *	*80*	77	99	627	423	129	35	1	28	250	134	74	5	5	0	7	0	2	9	.051	.038	.238	.332	.462	*.255*
Lowell M	*59*	54	75	484	341	129	29	1	17	211	61	33	5	1	0	5	2	1	24	.057	.028	.290	.337	.474	*.260*
Varitek J +	*44*	41	51	425	294	76	24	0	14	142	90	54	6	3	0	4	0	0	6	.070	.043	.209	.313	.390	*.229*
Martinez V +	*38*	32	41	237	146	71	12	0	8	107	23	24	0	1	0	1	1	0	6	-.090	-.003	.336	.405	.507	*.297*
Green N	*27*	35	35	309	225	65	18	0	6	101	69	20	1	8	2	3	1	4	10	.053	-.013	.236	.303	.366	*.219*
Gonzalez A	*19*	26	15	159	110	42	10	0	5	67	29	5	0	2	4	0	2	0	4	.088	-.122	.284	.316	.453	*.246*
Baldelli R	*18*	23	23	164	118	38	4	1	7	65	37	11	0	2	0	1	1	0	6	-.009	.043	.253	.311	.433	*.239*
Lugo J	*15*	16	8	123	78	31	4	1	1	40	18	12	0	0	1	1	3	0	0	-.088	.071	.284	.352	.367	*.241*
Kottaras G *	*11*	15	10	107	72	22	11	0	1	36	25	11	0	0	0	3	0	0	1	.102	.114	.237	.308	.387	*.226*
Bailey J	*10*	14	9	91	66	16	3	2	3	32	21	10	0	4	0	0	0	0	5	.086	.227	.208	.330	.416	*.243*
Kotsay M *	*6*	4	5	79	57	19	2	0	1	24	12	4	1	0	0	1	2	1	1	.044	.083	.257	.291	.324	*.204*
Kotchman C *	*6*	9	7	95	72	19	3	0	1	25	14	7	0	1	0	0	1	0	4	-.041	.041	.218	.284	.287	*.192*
Reddick J *	*4*	5	4	62	49	10	4	0	2	20	17	2	0	1	0	0	0	0	0	-.069	-.078	.169	.210	.339	*.172*
Anderson B	*3*	7	5	21	14	5	0	0	2	11	5	3	0	0	0	1	0	0	2	.227	-.026	.294	.381	.647	*.320*
Lowrie J +	*3*	5	11	76	58	10	2	0	2	18	20	6	0	0	0	2	0	0	0	-.024	.104	.147	.211	.265	*.155*
Van Every J	*3*	1	3	13	7	4	0	0	1	7	5	2	0	0	0	0	0	0	0	.198	.400	.364	.462	.636	*.353*
LaRoche A *	*2*	2	3	19	15	5	2	0	1	10	2	0	0	0	0	0	0	0	1	--	.012	.263	.263	.526	*.240*
Bates A	*2*	2	2	12	7	4	2	0	0	6	4	1	0	0	0	0	0	0	0	--	-.008	.364	.417	.545	*.311*
Brown D	*2*	1	1	4	2	1	0	0	1	4	0	1	0	0	0	0	0	0	0	.558	.500	.333	.500	1.333	*.537*
Gathright J	*1*	7	0	17	13	5	0	0	0	5	2	1	0	0	0	0	1	0	2	-.280	.081	.313	.353	.313	*.228*
Beckett J	*1*	1	1	5	4	1	0	0	1	4	3	0	0	0	0	0	0	0	0	-.290	.483	.200	.200	.800	*.279*
Woodward C	*1*	0	0	16	11	1	0	0	0	1	4	2	0	2	0	0	0	0	0	.062	-.173	.083	.313	.083	*.155*

Only includes batters with at least one Base Run. Italicized stats have been adjusted for home park.

Batted Ball Batting Stats

	% of PA		% of Batted Balls					Out %		Runs Per Event				Total Runs vs. Avg.				
Player	K%	BB%	GB%	LD%	FB%	IF/F	HR/OF	GB	OF	NIP	GB	LD	OF	NIP	GB	LD	FB	Tot
Youkilis K	21	16	35	21	44	.05	.17	70	83	.08	.07	.49	.27	11	2	12	19	44
Bay J	25	16	33	18	49	.11	.21	74	74	.07	.04	.41	.38	10	-2	-3	35	40
Drew D	20	16	39	20	41	.10	.19	77	81	.09	.04	.42	.33	10	-1	3	19	31
Pedroia D	6	11	39	20	41	.10	.07	71	86	.18	.06	.39	.12	13	5	11	-6	23
Martinez V	10	11	39	23	38	.04	.12	70	80	.13	.07	.36	.20	3	2	5	5	15
Ortiz D	21	13	32	17	50	.09	.14	83	78	.06	-.01	.34	.27	4	-9	-8	23	10
Ellsbury J	11	8	50	18	32	.09	.05	70	80	.08	.07	.37	.14	2	13	1	-7	9
Lowell M	13	7	39	21	41	.12	.12	79	82	.05	.00	.40	.20	-2	-6	7	6	6
Baldelli R	23	8	46	18	36	.15	.17	67	79	.01	.07	.35	.28	-2	2	-1	2	1
Lugo J	15	10	38	23	39	.20	.04	74	85	.07	.06	.36	.09	1	1	1	-3	-0
Gonzalez A	18	4	37	14	49	.19	.11	74	66	-.02	.04	.33	.29	-3	1	-3	5	-1
Kottaras G	23	10	30	23	48	.15	.03	86	75	.03	-.03	.38	.17	-1	-2	0	-0	-3
Varitek J	21	13	38	15	47	.16	.12	77	82	.06	.03	.32	.21	4	-2	-9	2	-5
Green N	22	9	38	18	44	.12	.08	74	85	.02	.03	.48	.12	-2	-2	2	-5	-8
MLB Average	***18***	***10***	***43***	***19***	***38***	***.10***	***.11***	***75***	***83***	***.05***	***.04***	***.39***	***.19***	--	--	--	--	--

Pitching Stats

Player	*PRC*	IP	BFP	G	GS	K	BB	IBB	HBP	H	HR	DP	DER	SB	CS	PO	W	L	Sv	Op	Hld	H-A	R^L	RA	ERA	FIP
Lester J *	*118*	203.3	843	32	32	225	64	0	3	186	20	17	.682	19	6	6	15	8	0	0	0	-.018	.018	3.54	3.41	3.25
Beckett J	*102*	212.3	883	32	32	199	55	1	7	198	25	16	.700	15	3	0	17	6	0	0	0	-.036	-.010	4.20	3.86	3.71
Papelbon J	*61*	68.0	285	66	0	76	24	1	4	54	5	1	.722	10	1	0	1	1	38	41	0	.010	.023	1.99	1.85	3.10
Wakefield T	*50*	129.7	572	21	21	72	50	0	10	137	12	15	.701	23	3	0	11	5	0	0	0	.012	-.002	4.65	4.58	4.67
Buchholz C	*41*	92.0	399	16	16	68	36	1	2	91	13	7	.714	6	0	0	7	4	0	0	0	-.014	-.028	4.30	4.21	4.76
Penny B	*40*	131.7	590	24	24	89	42	0	5	160	17	12	.666	27	2	0	7	8	0	0	0	-.021	.021	6.08	5.61	4.59
Saito T	*40*	55.7	240	56	0	52	25	2	5	50	6	3	.711	7	2	0	3	3	2	4	3	-.017	.120	2.59	2.43	4.23
Ramirez R	*39*	69.7	301	70	0	52	32	4	4	61	7	10	.714	6	0	0	7	4	0	4	12	.078	-.050	3.36	2.84	4.38
Okajima H *	*35*	61.0	258	68	0	53	21	3	2	56	8	5	.713	0	0	1	6	0	0	2	23	.040	-.143	3.39	3.39	4.14
Masterson J	*31*	72.0	312	31	6	67	25	2	6	72	7	5	.667	8	4	1	3	3	0	1	6	-.040	-.071	4.75	4.50	3.80
Bard D	*25*	49.3	212	49	0	63	22	3	3	41	5	4	.655	4	0	0	2	2	1	4	13	-.086	-.103	4.38	3.65	3.29
Delcarmen M	*22*	59.7	278	64	0	44	34	3	4	64	5	3	.675	9	1	0	5	2	0	3	6	-.086	.085	5.13	4.53	4.57
Matsuzaka D	*21*	59.3	283	12	12	54	30	1	2	81	10	9	.615	7	0	0	4	6	0	0	0	-.012	-.036	5.76	5.76	5.13
Byrd P	*9*	34.0	155	7	6	11	11	0	0	47	4	4	.667	2	1	0	1	3	0	0	0	-.071	-.155	5.82	5.82	5.04
Wagner B *	*9*	13.7	56	15	0	22	7	0	1	8	1	1	.720	1	0	0	1	1	0	0	6	-.070	-.068	3.29	1.98	2.68
Smoltz J	*9*	40.0	186	8	8	33	9	1	3	59	8	4	.609	1	0	0	2	5	0	0	0	-.054	-.198	8.33	8.33	4.97
Tazawa J	*5*	25.3	130	6	4	13	9	0	3	43	4	2	.604	1	0	0	2	3	0	0	0	-.060	.155	8.17	7.46	5.64
Bowden M	*3*	16.0	75	8	1	12	6	0	0	23	3	1	.630	1	0	0	1	1	0	0	1	.135	-.081	9.56	9.56	5.25
Jones H *	*2*	12.7	63	11	0	9	7	1	1	16	3	0	.674	1	0	0	0	0	0	0	1	.081	-.158	9.24	9.24	6.51
Lopez J *	*2*	11.7	64	14	0	5	9	0	2	20	1	1	.574	1	0	0	0	2	0	0	0	.091	.028	10.03	9.26	6.28
Cabrera F	*1*	5.3	28	6	0	8	4	1	1	7	0	0	.533	2	0	0	0	0	0	0	1	-.015	-.202	8.44	8.44	2.44
Gonzalez E	*1*	3.7	18	2	0	1	2	0	0	5	1	0	.714	0	0	0	0	0	0	0	0	-.175	.583	4.91	4.91	7.83

Italicized stats have been adjusted for home park.

Batted Ball Pitching Stats

	% of PA		% of Batted Balls					Out %		Runs Per Event				Total Runs vs. Avg.				
Player	K%	BB%	GB%	LD%	FB%	IF/F	HR/OF	GB	OF	NIP	GB	LD	OF	NIP	GB	LD	FB	Tot
Lester J	27	8	48	18	34	.10	.11	77	80	-.01	.02	.43	.21	-14	-4	-4	-5	-27
Beckett J	22	7	47	21	32	.08	.14	77	86	-.00	.04	.36	.21	-13	-2	-1	-5	-20
Papelbon J	27	10	27	21	52	.16	.06	75	86	.01	.05	.34	.10	-3	-2	-3	-7	-14
Saito T	22	13	31	17	52	.18	.07	83	76	.06	-.02	.43	.17	1	-4	-1	-1	-4
Okajima H	21	9	30	16	54	.16	.09	68	81	.03	.09	.32	.16	-2	2	-5	0	-4
Buchholz C	17	10	54	18	29	.02	.15	78	80	.05	.02	.31	.26	0	-1	-5	3	-3
Bard D	30	12	45	19	36	.14	.14	69	88	.02	.08	.44	.20	-1	2	-1	-3	-2
Ramirez R	17	12	35	18	48	.16	.08	76	79	.07	.02	.40	.17	3	-3	-1	-0	-1
Masterson J	21	10	50	18	32	.03	.11	73	79	.03	.05	.39	.23	-1	1	-2	1	-1
Wakefield T	13	10	36	17	47	.18	.07	74	80	.10	.04	.36	.16	5	-0	-2	-1	2
Byrd P	7	7	34	16	50	.11	.07	75	76	.12	.04	.53	.17	1	-1	3	3	6
Delcarmen M	16	14	42	17	40	.12	.07	71	80	.10	.07	.40	.18	5	2	-0	1	7
Tazawa J	10	9	25	23	53	.04	.08	64	71	.11	.10	.33	.23	1	1	2	7	11
Smoltz J	18	6	43	18	39	.06	.16	66	72	.01	.09	.43	.33	-2	4	2	9	13
Penny B	15	8	41	19	40	.07	.10	72	78	.05	.07	.38	.21	-1	6	3	9	17
Matsuzaka D	19	11	34	23	43	.08	.13	66	78	.06	.09	.42	.26	2	3	6	8	18
MLB Average	***18***	***10***	***43***	***19***	***38***	***.10***	***.11***	***75***	***83***	***.05***	***.04***	***.39***	***.19***	--	--	--	--	--

Fielding Stats

Name	INN	SBA/G	CS%	ERA	WP+PB/G	PO	A	TE	FE
Catchers									
Varitek J	924.0	1.15	8%	3.87	0.214	856	37	3	0
Martinez V	257.0	0.67	11%	5.22	0.280	215	8	4	0
Kottaras G	243.7	1.11	13%	5.36	0.813	196	8	1	0
Brown D	12.0	0.00	0%	3.00	0.000	6	2	0	0

Name	Inn	PO	A	TE	FE	FPct	DPS	DPT	ZRDif	OOZ	Dif
First Base											
Youkilis K	647.0	565	52	1	0	.998	5	1	.073	24	3
Kotchman C	190.0	185	19	0	0	1.000	1	0	.068	6	-3
Martinez V	189.3	160	3	0	0	1.000	0	0	-.146	7	3
Bailey J	180.0	158	11	1	1	.988	1	0	.088	4	-12
Kotsay M	125.3	103	11	0	0	1.000	3	0	-.098	7	22
Ortiz D	39.0	42	6	0	1	.980	0	0	--	4	--
LaRoche A	36.0	29	6	0	0	1.000	1	0	--	1	--
Bates A	30.0	35	0	0	1	.972	0	0	--	1	--
Second Base											
Pedroia D	1346.0	253	404	1	5	.991	42	45	.029	34	-2
Green N	58.0	12	17	0	0	1.000	0	1	--	0	--
Woodward	27.0	5	6	0	0	1.000	0	0	--	0	--
Lowrie J	5.0	0	0	0	0	0.000	0	0	--	--	--
Shortstop											
Green N	644.3	104	198	8	6	.956	19	16	-.019	32	11
Gonzalez A	361.0	51	107	1	0	.994	7	9	.048	13	-2
Lugo J	243.3	39	51	4	3	.928	2	6	-.118	2	-30
Lowrie J	163.7	22	52	0	1	.987	7	9	.129	1	-32
Woodward	12.7	0	2	0	1	.667	0	0	--	0	--
Velazquez G	11.7	3	3	0	0	1.000	0	1	--	1	--
Third Base											
Lowell M	895.0	82	174	4	5	.966	13	1	-.011	17	-23
Youkilis K	494.3	52	99	1	3	.974	5	0	.027	24	7
Green N	19.3	4	4	1	0	.889	0	0	--	1	--
Lowrie J	10.0	1	4	0	0	1.000	0	0	--	2	--
Woodward	7.0	1	1	0	0	1.000	0	0	--	0	--
Velazquez G	4.0	0	3	1	0	.750	0	0	--	0	--
Kottaras G	4.0	0	2	0	0	1.000	0	0	--	0	--
Baldelli R	3.0	0	0	0	0	0.000	0	0	--	--	--

Name	Inn	PO	A	TE	FE	FPct	DPS	DPT	ZRDif	OOZ	Dif
Left Field											
Bay J	1279.0	310	15	0	0	1.000	2	0	-.024	49	-12
Reddick J	81.3	20	0	0	0	1.000	0	0	--	7	--
Youkilis K	14.0	3	1	0	1	.800	0	0	--	0	--
Bailey J	13.0	2	0	0	0	1.000	0	0	--	0	--
Gathright J	12.0	4	0	0	0	1.000	0	0	--	1	--
Baldelli R	11.0	3	0	0	0	1.000	0	0	--	0	--
Anderson B	11.0	0	0	0	0	0.000	0	0	--	--	--
Kotsay M	8.0	2	0	0	0	1.000	0	0	--	0	--
Green N	7.0	3	0	0	1	.750	0	0	--	0	--
Center Field											
Ellsbury J	1302.0	357	5	1	1	.995	1	0	-.037	71	-13
Baldelli R	51.0	14	1	0	0	1.000	1	0	--	2	--
Kotsay M	28.0	5	0	0	0	1.000	0	0	--	0	--
Gathright J	20.0	5	0	0	0	1.000	0	0	--	2	--
Van Every J	15.0	2	0	0	0	1.000	0	0	--	0	--
Anderson B	12.0	2	0	0	0	1.000	0	0	--	0	--
Reddick J	8.0	1	0	0	0	1.000	0	0	--	1	--
Right Field											
Drew J	1083.0	242	5	1	1	.992	2	0	.044	64	7
Baldelli R	228.7	49	2	2	1	.944	0	0	-.024	11	-4
Anderson B	41.0	4	0	0	0	1.000	0	0	--	2	--
Reddick J	35.0	9	0	0	1	.900	0	0	--	3	--
Van Every J	14.3	4	0	0	0	1.000	0	0	--	1	--
Gathright J	11.0	4	0	0	0	1.000	0	0	--	0	--
Kotsay M	8.7	1	0	0	0	1.000	0	0	--	--	--
Bailey J	8.0	2	0	0	0	1.000	0	0	--	0	--
Carter C	6.0	2	0	0	0	1.000	0	0	--	0	--
Lopez J	0.7	0	0	0	0	0.000	0	0	--	0	--

Chicago Cubs

Stat Facts:

- Kosuke Fukudome was thrown out in 10 of 16 stolen base attempts
- Fukudome made the fewest OOZ plays (45) of any center fielder with at least 900 innings
- The Cubs' GDP defense ranked 29th in the majors
- Sam Fuld walked 16% of the time, and struck out just 9%
- Koyie Hill hit zero infield pop-ups
- Derek Lee made the fewest OOZ plays (27) of any regular first baseman
- Carlos Zambrano had a higher ISO (.246) than any hitter on the team except Lee
- Zambrano allowed just 5 SBs in 13 attempts
- Carlos Marmol hit 12 batters in 74 IP
- Marmol struck out or walked 51% of the batters he faced
- Ted Lilly's FB% (51%) was highest of ML pitchers with at least 162 IP
- Alfonso Soriano committed 9 fielding errors, the most by any left fielder

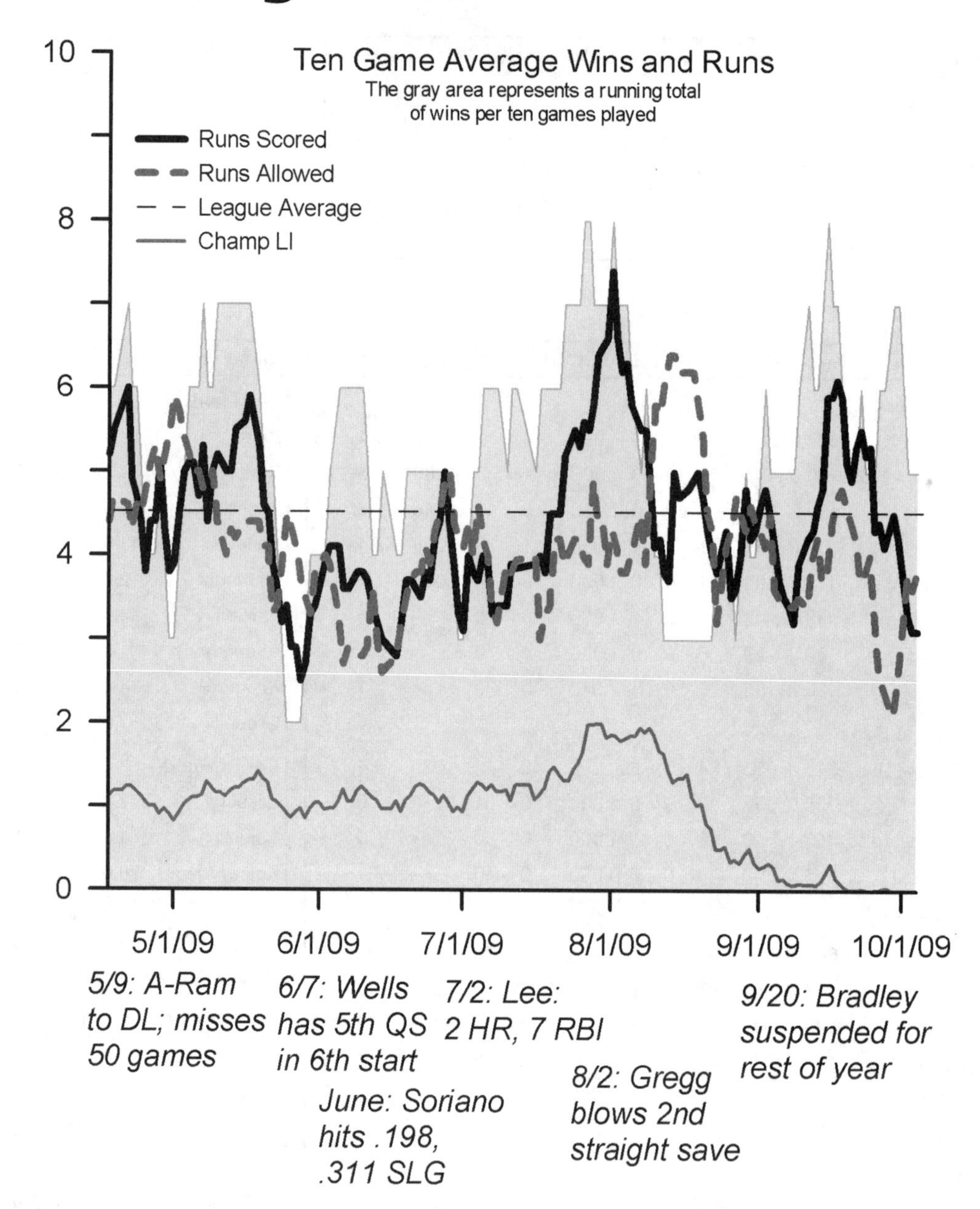

Team Batting and Pitching/Fielding Stats by Month

	April	May	June	July	Aug	Sept/Oct
Wins	10	15	11	18	11	18
Losses	11	13	14	9	17	14
RS/G	4.6	4.3	3.6	5.2	4.4	4.2
RA/G	5.0	3.9	3.8	3.9	5.0	3.7
OBP	.331	.330	.303	.348	.340	.335
SLG	.396	.420	.364	.468	.416	.377
FIP	4.64	4.16	4.33	4.25	4.22	3.38
DER	.695	.714	.719	.709	.692	.693

Batting Stats

Player	*BR*	Runs	RBI	PA	Outs	H	2B	3B	HR	TB	K	BB	IBB	HBP	SH	SF	SB	CS	GDP	H-A	L^R	BA	OBP	SLG	*GPA*
Lee D	*105*	91	111	615	381	163	36	2	35	308	109	76	6	3	0	4	1	0	12	.040	-.009	.306	.393	.579	*.309*
Fukudome K *	*73*	79	54	603	395	129	38	5	11	210	112	93	3	3	3	5	6	10	15	-.047	.096	.259	.375	.421	*.263*
Theriot R	*69*	81	54	677	454	171	20	5	7	222	93	51	1	6	13	5	21	10	13	.030	.032	.284	.343	.369	*.237*
Soriano A	*58*	64	55	522	371	115	25	1	20	202	118	40	6	3	0	2	9	2	7	-.012	-.055	.241	.303	.423	*.233*
Bradley M +	*56*	61	40	473	305	101	17	1	12	156	95	66	4	11	2	1	2	3	10	.073	.020	.257	.378	.397	*.259*
Ramirez A	*52*	46	65	342	218	97	14	1	15	158	43	28	3	8	0	0	2	1	8	.085	.068	.317	.389	.516	*.292*
Fontenot M *	*40*	38	43	419	296	89	22	2	9	142	83	35	4	2	0	5	4	1	7	-.009	.049	.236	.301	.377	*.221*
Soto G	*37*	27	47	389	278	72	19	1	11	126	77	50	3	3	0	5	1	0	19	.055	.034	.218	.321	.381	*.231*
Fox J	*29*	23	44	241	165	56	12	0	11	101	47	14	1	5	0	6	0	0	5	-.070	-.044	.259	.311	.468	*.247*
Baker J	*29*	27	21	224	146	62	15	1	4	91	46	17	0	2	0	2	0	0	5	-.015	.008	.305	.362	.448	*.264*
Hoffpauir M	*29*	28	35	257	181	56	12	1	10	100	46	20	1	1	0	2	1	0	3	.063	.061	.239	.300	.427	*.232*
Hill K +	*22*	26	24	284	202	60	12	2	2	82	78	27	6	1	2	1	0	0	9	.060	.025	.237	.312	.324	*.213*
Johnson R	*20*	23	22	186	129	42	10	2	4	68	27	13	0	6	1	1	2	1	5	.046	.094	.255	.330	.412	*.242*
Fuld S *	*16*	17	2	115	70	29	6	1	1	40	10	17	1	1	0	0	2	1	1	.034	-.025	.299	.409	.412	*.276*
Scales B +	*14*	15	15	138	99	30	8	2	3	51	32	11	1	2	0	1	0	0	5	.008	-.030	.242	.312	.411	*.234*
Blanco A +	*10*	15	12	138	98	31	8	0	1	42	14	8	3	1	6	0	0	2	4	-.000	-.008	.252	.303	.341	*.213*
Zambrano C +	*8*	7	11	72	54	15	5	0	4	32	28	1	0	0	1	1	0	0	0	.064	.023	.217	.225	.464	*.209*
Miles A +	*6*	17	5	170	132	29	7	1	0	38	21	8	1	0	5	0	3	0	4	.001	.028	.185	.224	.242	*.155*
Wells R	*2*	5	2	61	39	9	3	0	0	12	7	2	0	0	12	0	0	0	1	.013	-.076	.191	.224	.255	*.159*
Taguchi S	*1*	1	0	12	8	3	1	0	0	4	4	1	0	0	0	0	0	0	0	-.317	-.132	.273	.333	.364	*.232*
Harden R *	*1*	3	0	48	35	8	1	0	0	9	15	1	0	0	4	0	0	0	0	.089	-.002	.186	.205	.209	*.139*
Samardzija J	*1*	1	1	6	4	1	0	0	1	4	1	0	0	0	1	0	0	0	0	-.363	1.450	.200	.200	.800	*.279*
Marshall S *	*1*	2	2	15	10	3	0	0	0	3	5	1	0	0	1	0	0	0	0	.016	.201	.231	.286	.231	*.179*
Colvin T *	*1*	1	2	20	14	3	0	0	0	3	5	2	0	0	0	1	0	0	0	.024	.054	.176	.250	.176	*.151*
Freel R	*1*	1	1	32	25	4	0	0	0	4	7	2	0	1	1	0	1	0	1	-.023	.104	.143	.226	.143	*.132*

Only includes batters with at least one Base Run. Italicized stats have been adjusted for home park.

Batted Ball Batting Stats

	% of PA		% of Batted Balls					Out %		Runs Per Event				Total Runs vs. Avg.				
Player	K%	BB%	GB%	LD%	FB%	IF/F	HR/OF	GB	OF	NIP	GB	LD	OF	NIP	GB	LD	FB	Tot
Lee D	18	13	35	19	46	.05	.19	69	79	.08	.07	.41	.32	8	4	5	35	52
Ramirez A	13	11	35	21	44	.13	.15	67	85	.10	.08	.38	.22	3	3	5	7	20
Fukudome K	19	16	46	24	30	.08	.10	74	82	.10	.04	.36	.21	13	0	4	-3	14
Bradley M	20	16	47	20	33	.08	.13	80	77	.09	.01	.39	.24	10	-3	-0	2	8
Fuld S	9	16	47	25	28	.04	.04	73	86	.18	.07	.42	.06	4	1	4	-3	6
Baker J	21	8	44	20	36	.09	.08	66	75	.02	.10	.37	.21	-1	4	1	1	5
Johnson R	15	10	50	17	33	.14	.11	78	68	.08	.03	.31	.29	1	-0	-2	2	1
Fox J	20	8	34	19	47	.13	.15	75	85	.02	.04	.34	.23	-2	-1	-2	5	0
Hoffpauir J	18	8	28	21	52	.13	.12	79	89	.03	.02	.44	.15	-2	-3	3	0	-1
Scales B	23	9	46	14	40	.05	.09	79	75	.02	-.00	.47	.23	-1	-2	-1	2	-3
Soriano A	23	8	33	19	48	.09	.12	78	82	.01	.03	.40	.19	-6	-3	-1	4	-5
Blanco A	10	7	53	19	28	.17	.04	87	74	.07	-.03	.39	.16	-0	-3	0	-3	-7
Soto G	20	14	41	18	41	.07	.10	81	83	.07	-.02	.31	.19	4	-7	-6	1	-8
Fontenot M	20	9	44	18	38	.09	.09	77	83	.03	.04	.40	.16	-2	-1	-1	-3	-8
Hill K	27	10	51	21	28	.00	.04	74	74	.01	.03	.37	.16	-3	-1	-1	-5	-10
Theriot R	14	8	50	20	30	.05	.05	75	85	.06	.04	.40	.09	0	3	4	-17	-10
Miles A	12	5	50	20	30	.15	.00	88	85	.01	-.03	.30	.02	-2	-5	-2	-8	-18
MLB Average	***18***	***10***	***43***	***19***	***38***	***.10***	***.11***	***75***	***83***	***.05***	***.04***	***.39***	***.19***	--	--	--	--	--

Pitching Stats

Player	PRC	IP	BFP	G	GS	K	BB	IBB	HBP	H	HR	DP	DER	SB	CS	PO	W	L	Sv	Op	Hld	H-A	R^L	RA	ERA	FIP
Lilly T *	89	177.0	706	27	27	151	36	2	2	151	22	16	.729	12	4	1	12	9	0	0	0	-.058	-.004	3.36	3.10	3.67
Dempster R	82	200.0	842	31	31	172	65	4	6	196	22	23	.692	16	11	0	11	9	0	0	0	-.018	-.049	4.23	3.65	3.87
Wells R	72	165.3	694	27	27	104	46	4	6	165	14	24	.695	14	4	0	12	10	0	0	0	.009	-.077	3.65	3.05	3.86
Zambrano C	71	169.3	733	28	28	152	78	6	9	155	10	14	.688	5	8	2	9	7	0	0	0	.041	-.021	4.15	3.77	3.56
Harden R	56	141.0	609	26	26	171	67	5	6	122	23	10	.702	8	4	0	9	9	0	0	0	.050	-.010	4.72	4.09	4.29
Marmol C	39	74.0	335	79	0	93	65	3	12	43	2	7	.736	2	0	1	2	4	15	19	27	.036	.044	3.53	3.41	3.99
Guzman A	33	61.0	245	55	0	47	23	4	1	41	8	6	.771	2	4	0	3	3	1	1	15	-.032	-.002	2.95	2.95	4.30
Marshall S *	32	85.3	373	55	9	68	32	4	1	91	10	7	.683	3	1	0	3	7	0	0	7	-.024	-.029	4.54	4.32	4.10
Heilman A	30	72.3	313	70	0	65	34	4	1	68	9	9	.706	3	2	0	4	4	1	7	10	-.021	.050	4.23	4.11	4.26
Gregg K	25	68.7	298	72	0	71	30	2	3	60	13	6	.724	1	0	0	5	6	23	30	1	-.103	.079	4.98	4.72	4.90
Berg J	16	12.0	46	11	0	7	1	0	0	10	0	1	.737	1	0	0	0	0	0	0	0	.064	-.074	0.75	0.75	2.23
Caridad E	15	19.3	74	14	0	17	3	0	3	15	0	4	.706	0	1	0	1	0	0	0	2	-.132	.038	1.86	1.40	2.32
Hart K	15	27.7	120	8	4	13	18	1	2	23	3	5	.762	6	1	0	3	1	0	0	0	-.034	-.115	2.60	2.60	5.68
Grabow J *	12	25.0	105	30	0	16	12	1	1	19	1	3	.747	2	0	0	0	0	0	0	7	.011	-.081	3.24	3.24	3.83
Gorzelanny T	12	38.3	168	13	7	40	13	0	1	39	6	2	.685	1	0	0	4	2	0	0	1	.022	-.083	5.87	5.63	4.19
Ascanio J	8	15.3	73	14	0	18	9	2	2	18	1	0	.605	2	1	0	0	1	0	0	1	-.042	-.219	3.52	3.52	3.41
Samardzija J	7	34.7	161	20	2	21	15	1	1	46	7	3	.658	3	1	0	1	3	0	0	0	.085	-.099	7.53	7.53	5.86
Patton D	6	27.7	134	20	0	23	19	2	0	31	4	0	.682	6	0	0	3	1	0	0	0	-.051	-.042	7.16	6.83	5.21
Stevens J	3	12.7	59	11	0	9	8	1	1	14	2	1	.692	1	1	0	1	0	0	0	0	.108	.032	7.11	7.11	5.68
Cotts N *	2	11.0	55	19	0	9	9	0	1	14	3	2	.636	1	0	0	0	2	0	1	2	.080	.140	7.36	7.36	7.79
Waddell J *	1	1.7	8	3	0	2	0	0	0	3	0	0	.500	0	0	0	0	0	0	0	1	.300	-.117	5.40	5.40	0.75

Italicized stats have been adjusted for home park.

Batted Ball Pitching Stats

	% of PA		% of Batted Balls					Out %		Runs Per Event				Total Runs vs. Avg.				
Player	K%	BB%	GB%	LD%	FB%	IF/F	HR/OF	GB	OF	NIP	GB	LD	OF	NIP	GB	LD	FB	Tot
Lilly T	21	5	32	17	51	.10	.10	76	86	-.02	.04	.36	.15	-14	-2	-9	-2	-27
Wells R	15	7	48	19	33	.15	.09	75	85	.04	.03	.38	.13	-3	0	1	-12	-15
Zambrano C	21	12	45	18	37	.15	.07	76	78	.05	.04	.38	.17	3	-2	-5	-9	-12
Guzman A	19	9	48	13	39	.09	.14	81	88	.04	-.00	.40	.19	-1	-4	-5	-1	-10
Dempster R	20	8	47	18	34	.13	.13	74	80	.02	.04	.39	.23	-6	-1	-4	1	-10
Marmol C	28	23	36	16	48	.21	.03	75	88	.10	.02	.49	.04	12	-3	-4	-13	-8
Harden R	28	12	38	18	44	.15	.17	69	85	.02	.07	.37	.25	-2	1	-8	4	-5
Grabow J	15	13	47	14	38	.14	.04	78	83	.10	.01	.33	.09	2	-1	-2	-3	-4
Heilman A	21	11	41	21	39	.13	.13	72	84	.05	.05	.35	.20	1	-0	-2	-1	-2
Hart K	11	17	40	14	45	.08	.09	79	91	.17	-.00	.36	.09	4	-1	-2	-2	-1
Gorzelanny T	24	8	40	22	39	.09	.15	80	82	.01	.01	.36	.26	-2	-1	-0	2	-1
Gregg K	24	11	38	18	44	.11	.17	78	84	.03	.02	.31	.28	-1	-2	-5	7	-1
Marshall S	18	9	49	23	28	.06	.15	79	83	.04	.01	.43	.24	-1	-4	7	-0	2
Patton D	17	14	55	16	29	.00	.15	73	77	.09	.06	.34	.27	2	1	-2	2	3
Samardzija J	13	10	41	18	40	.06	.16	80	68	.09	.01	.44	.36	1	-1	2	9	11
MLB Average	***18***	***10***	***43***	***19***	***38***	***.10***	***.11***	***75***	***83***	***.05***	***.04***	***.39***	***.19***	--	--	--	--	--

Fielding Stats

Name	INN	SBA/G	CS%	ERA	WP+PB/G	PO	A	TE	FE
Catchers									
Soto G	811.0	0.91	28%	4.00	0.433	720	50	3	1
Hill K	627.3	0.72	40%	3.69	0.373	573	46	3	0
Fox J	7.0	0.00	0%	0.00	0.000	6	1	0	0

Name	Inn	PO	A	TE	FE	FPct	DPS	DPT	ZRDif	OOZ	Dif
First Base											
Lee D	1231.0	1088	94	0	5	.995	7	2	.022	27	-12
Hoffpauir	167.0	136	10	0	1	.993	0	0	.165	3	-16
Fox J	40.0	40	1	1	1	.953	0	1	--	1	--
Baker J	7.0	8	0	0	0	1.000	0	0	--	--	--
Second Base											
Fontenot	529.3	112	149	1	2	.989	12	20	.044	12	-5
Baker J	368.7	103	116	0	1	.995	14	15	.072	8	-6
Miles A	253.7	71	69	1	1	.986	4	16	-.047	4	-12
Blanco A	224.3	52	71	0	0	1.000	6	13	.017	6	-1
Scales B	67.7	14	19	0	1	.971	1	3	--	0	--
Soriano A	1.7	0	0	0	0	.000	0	0	--	--	--
Shortstop											
Theriot R	1311.0	206	411	5	10	.976	45	40	.027	47	-2
Blanco A	90.3	15	31	1	2	.939	5	2	--	0	--
Miles A	44.0	7	13	0	0	1.000	0	2	--	0	--
Third Base											
Ramirez A	683.7	45	137	3	7	.948	10	3	-.050	25	-5
Fontenot	360.0	26	77	0	3	.963	6	0	-.071	14	-3
Fox J	195.3	8	38	1	1	.958	2	0	.013	7	-6
Baker J	84.0	6	18	0	1	.960	0	0	--	5	--
Scales B	58.3	6	11	0	1	.944	1	0	--	0	--
Freel R	50.7	2	10	1	0	.923	1	0	--	3	--
Miles A	12.0	1	1	0	0	1.000	0	0	--	0	--
Hill K	1.0	0	0	0	0	.000	0	0	--	--	--
Soriano A	0.3	0	0	0	0	.000	0	0	--	--	--

Name	Inn	PO	A	TE	FE	FPct	DPS	DPT	ZRDif	OOZ	Dif
Left Field											
Soriano A	1004.0	201	7	2	9	.950	2	0	-.073	47	-4
Fox J	140.7	34	1	1	2	.921	0	0	.073	5	-15
Scales B	113.3	32	0	0	0	1.000	0	0	.065	9	29
Fuld S	79.3	24	1	1	0	.962	0	0	--	6	--
Hoffpauir	64.3	12	0	0	0	1.000	0	0	--	2	--
Johnson R	25.0	5	0	0	0	1.000	0	0	--	1	--
Taguchi S	15.0	1	1	0	0	1.000	0	0	--	1	--
Freel R	3.0	0	0	0	0	0.000	0	0	--	--	--
Marshall S	0.3	0	0	0	0	0.000	0	0	--	--	--
Center Field											
Fukudome	903.0	226	4	1	1	.991	1	0	.022	45	-18
Johnson R	305.3	74	3	0	1	.987	1	0	.019	17	-12
Fuld S	161.7	39	0	0	0	1.000	0	0	-.166	13	12
Colvin T	45.0	16	0	0	0	1.000	0	0	--	6	--
Gathright J	22.3	6	0	0	0	1.000	0	0	--	2	--
Freel R	7.0	1	0	0	0	1.000	0	0	--	0	--
Bradley M	1.0	0	0	0	0	0.000	0	0	--	--	--
Right Field											
Bradley M	914.0	197	5	0	3	.985	4	0	.009	42	-6
Fukudome	263.3	79	1	0	0	1.000	1	0	.061	17	12
Hoffpauir	187.0	43	1	0	1	.978	0	0	.038	8	-9
Johnson R	37.0	4	0	0	0	1.000	0	0	--	1	--
Scales B	18.0	3	0	0	0	1.000	0	0	--	1	--
Fox J	17.0	2	0	0	0	1.000	0	0	--	0	--
Freel R	4.0	0	0	0	0	0.000	0	0	--	--	--
Taguchi S	3.0	1	0	0	0	1.000	0	0	--	--	--
Fuld S	2.0	2	0	0	0	1.000	0	0	--	1	--

Chicago White Sox

Stat Facts:

- Gavin Floyd had the lowest H-A (-.062) of any ML pitcher with at least 162 IP
- John Danks had the lowest LD% (15%) of any ML pitcher with at least 162 IP
- Chris Getz stole 25 bases in 27 attempts
- 29% of Jim Thome's outfield flies were home runs
- Bobby Jenks allowed 9 SBs in 9 attempts
- Mark Buerhle allowed just 4 SBs in 8 attempts
- Buerhle tied for the ML lead with 8 pickoffs
- Clayton Richard had 6 pickoffs in 89 IP
- Wilson Betemit committed 4 errors in 8 chances at third base
- Josh Fields had nearly as many strikeouts (76) as total bases (83)
- Scott Podsednik was tied for 11th in the majors with 30 steals
- Podsednik was 4th in the majors in caught stealing (13)

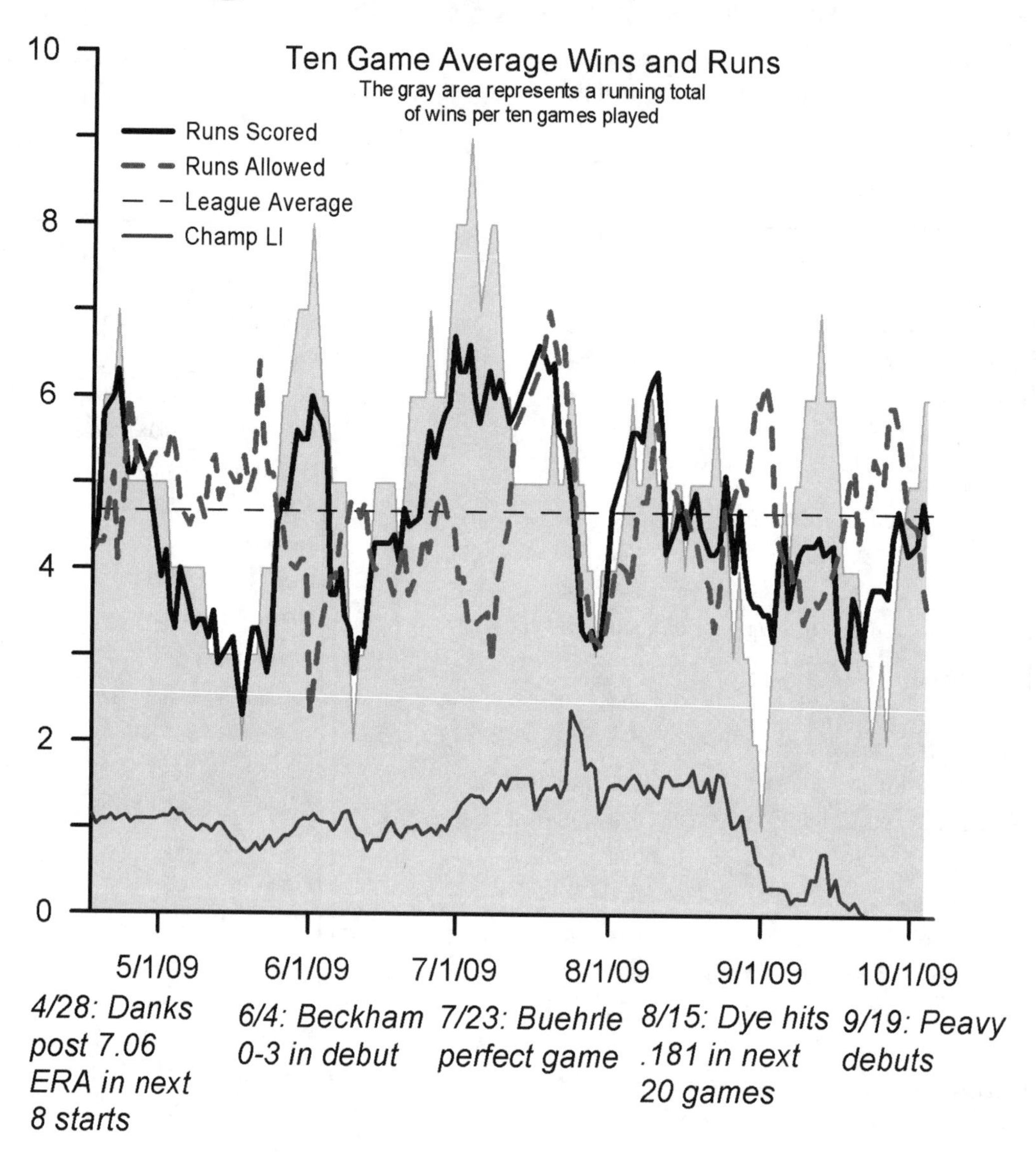

Team Batting and Pitching/Fielding Stats by Month

	April	May	June	July	Aug	Sept/Oct
Wins	11	13	15	14	11	15
Losses	10	15	13	13	17	15
RS/G	4.6	4.1	4.7	4.8	4.5	4.1
RA/G	4.7	4.6	4.3	4.5	5.1	4.0
OBP	.337	.315	.341	.331	.325	.327
SLG	.413	.390	.445	.428	.415	.382
FIP	4.13	4.08	4.43	4.14	4.65	3.94
DER	.672	.683	.727	.697	.670	.702

Batting Stats

Player	*BR*	Runs	RBI	PA	Outs	H	2B	3B	HR	TB	K	BB	IBB	HBP	SH	SF	SB	CS	GDP	H-A	L^R	BA	OBP	SLG	*GPA*
Konerko P	*87*	75	88	621	410	151	30	1	28	267	89	58	4	10	0	7	1	0	15	.018	.077	.277	.353	.489	*.270*
Dye J	*73*	78	81	574	394	126	19	1	27	228	108	64	2	5	0	2	0	2	15	.011	.047	.250	.340	.453	*.256*
Podsednik S	*73*	75	48	587	395	163	25	6	7	221	74	39	1	3	6	2	30	13	8	.007	.013	.304	.353	.412	*.252*
Ramirez A	*66*	71	68	606	412	150	14	1	15	211	66	49	3	1	6	8	14	5	15	.004	.106	.277	.333	.389	*.238*
Thome J *	*62*	55	74	417	267	86	15	0	23	170	116	69	3	0	0	3	0	0	8	.032	.045	.249	.372	.493	*.279*
Pierzynski A	*60*	57	49	535	372	151	22	1	13	214	52	24	6	1	3	3	1	1	18	-.018	.037	.300	.331	.425	*.245*
Beckham G	*57*	58	63	430	290	102	28	1	14	174	65	41	0	6	1	4	7	4	10	-.068	.036	.270	.347	.460	*.261*
Quentin C	*50*	47	56	399	279	83	14	0	21	160	52	31	2	15	0	2	3	0	11	.056	-.019	.236	.323	.456	*.249*
Getz C *	*45*	49	31	415	283	98	18	4	2	130	54	30	1	6	1	3	25	2	4	-.016	.013	.261	.324	.347	*.223*
Nix J	*33*	36	32	290	205	57	11	0	12	104	64	28	1	4	1	2	10	2	5	-.051	.057	.224	.308	.408	*.231*
Fields J	*24*	29	30	268	194	53	5	2	7	83	76	25	0	2	2	0	2	3	5	-.000	.058	.222	.301	.347	*.214*
Anderson B	*17*	25	13	210	151	44	9	0	2	59	49	20	0	3	2	0	3	6	4	-.070	-.031	.238	.322	.319	*.216*
Kotsay M *	*15*	12	18	127	86	33	7	0	3	49	9	11	2	0	1	2	1	1	5	.037	.116	.292	.349	.434	*.255*
Wise D *	*12*	17	11	153	116	32	8	3	2	52	27	3	0	4	4	0	4	5	1	.066	-.134	.225	.262	.366	*.201*
Rios A	*8*	11	9	154	126	29	6	0	3	44	29	6	0	0	1	1	5	2	7	.116	.056	.199	.229	.301	*.171*
Castro R	*8*	8	12	84	63	14	3	0	4	29	23	8	0	0	0	0	0	0	1	-.185	.148	.184	.262	.382	*.205*
Lillibridge	*5*	9	3	112	85	15	2	0	0	17	26	14	0	1	2	0	6	3	2	-.080	.009	.158	.273	.179	*.161*
Betemit W +	*3*	2	3	50	38	9	5	0	0	14	13	5	0	0	0	0	0	0	2	-.021	.013	.200	.280	.311	*.196*
Miller C	*3*	5	5	42	32	8	3	0	0	11	9	3	0	0	0	0	0	0	1	.006	.210	.205	.262	.282	*.181*
Flowers T	2	3	0	20	14	3	1	0	0	4	8	3	0	1	0	0	0	0	1	-.036	.108	.188	.350	.250	*.212*
Buehrle M *	*1*	1	1	5	3	1	0	0	1	4	1	0	0	0	1	0	0	0	0	-.363	--	.250	.250	1.000	*.349*
Richard C *	*1*	1	0	3	2	1	1	0	0	2	1	0	0	0	0	0	0	0	0	-.317	--	.333	.333	.667	*.304*

Only includes batters with at least one Base Run. Italicized stats have been adjusted for home park.

Batted Ball Batting Stats

	% of PA		% of Batted Balls					Out %		Runs Per Event				Total Runs vs. Avg.				
Player	K%	BB%	GB%	LD%	FB%	IF/F	HR/OF	GB	OF	NIP	GB	LD	OF	NIP	GB	LD	FB	Tot
Konerko P	14	11	36	19	46	.08	.14	78	85	.09	.01	.41	.22	5	-5	4	15	19
Thome J	28	17	44	20	36	.11	.29	77	81	.06	.02	.39	.46	5	-3	-2	17	17
Beckham G	15	11	40	17	43	.12	.11	77	81	.08	.02	.49	.21	3	-4	4	5	8
Dye J	19	12	40	17	44	.13	.17	77	88	.07	.02	.40	.24	4	-4	-3	9	6
Podsednik S	13	7	53	18	30	.10	.06	70	84	.05	.08	.43	.11	-1	12	5	-12	3
Quentin C	13	12	37	16	47	.10	.16	79	92	.10	.01	.31	.20	5	-4	-6	8	3
Kotsay M	7	9	45	19	36	.08	.09	77	81	.14	.01	.37	.16	1	-1	1	-0	1
Pierzynski A	10	5	47	20	33	.07	.09	74	82	.04	.03	.35	.17	-4	0	4	-1	-1
Nix J	22	11	39	13	48	.18	.16	67	84	.04	.10	.23	.24	-0	3	-10	4	-3
Ramirez A	11	8	46	16	38	.15	.09	75	79	.08	.04	.37	.16	2	1	-4	-3	-4
Getz C	13	9	47	19	33	.11	.02	77	76	.07	.03	.39	.10	1	-0	2	-9	-7
Wise D	18	5	36	17	47	.08	.04	73	89	-.02	.07	.41	.07	-3	1	-1	-4	-8
Anderson B	23	11	47	13	40	.17	.04	70	79	.03	.07	.40	.12	-0	2	-4	-5	-8
Fields J	28	10	41	18	41	.06	.11	76	89	.01	.03	.42	.16	-3	-2	-2	-3	-10
Lillibridge B	23	13	47	19	34	.09	.00	81	95	.05	.01	.28	-.07	1	-2	-3	-7	-11
Rios A	19	4	47	11	42	.08	.07	75	90	-.03	.03	.47	.06	-4	-1	-3	-5	-12
MLB Average	***18***	***10***	***43***	***19***	***38***	***.10***	***.11***	***75***	***83***	***.05***	***.04***	***.39***	***.19***	--	--	--	--	--

Pitching Stats

Player	PRC	IP	BFP	G	GS	K	BB	IBB	HBP	H	HR	DP	DER	SB	CS	PO	W	L	Sv	Op	Hld	H-A	R^L	RA	ERA	FIP
Danks J *	*96*	200.3	839	32	32	149	73	1	5	184	28	24	.719	18	7	6	13	11	0	0	0	.031	.012	4.00	3.77	4.67
Buehrle M *	*91*	213.3	874	33	33	105	45	3	5	222	27	33	.711	4	4	8	13	10	0	0	0	.013	.037	4.09	3.84	4.51
Floyd G	*88*	193.0	797	30	30	163	59	4	2	178	21	25	.701	14	4	0	11	11	0	0	0	-.062	.002	4.34	4.06	3.80
Thornton M *	*53*	72.3	291	70	0	87	20	2	1	58	5	4	.697	4	5	1	6	3	4	9	24	-.044	-.006	2.74	2.74	2.47
Carrasco D	*43*	93.3	405	49	1	62	29	4	2	103	5	11	.661	1	3	2	5	1	0	1	0	.004	-.086	4.05	3.76	3.43
Dotel O	*35*	62.3	268	62	0	75	36	1	0	54	7	6	.673	14	5	1	3	3	0	3	16	-.056	-.112	3.75	3.32	3.93
Richard C *	*34*	89.0	387	26	14	66	37	0	3	94	10	12	.675	8	5	6	4	3	0	0	0	.052	-.063	5.06	4.65	4.52
Contreras J	*34*	114.7	513	21	21	89	45	3	6	121	11	10	.671	19	3	0	5	13	0	0	0	-.048	.031	6.51	5.42	4.14
Jenks B	*26*	53.3	228	52	0	49	16	1	2	52	9	6	.691	9	0	0	3	4	29	35	0	-.029	-.083	4.05	3.71	4.50
Garcia F	*24*	56.0	229	9	9	37	12	0	0	56	4	5	.699	10	1	0	3	4	0	0	0	.024	.072	4.34	4.34	3.44
Peavy J	*22*	20.0	75	3	3	18	6	0	0	11	1	3	.780	0	0	0	3	0	0	0	0	.123	.096	1.35	1.35	2.94
Linebrink S	*21*	56.0	259	57	0	55	23	6	3	70	9	5	.621	11	1	0	3	7	2	4	7	-.008	-.007	5.46	4.66	4.39
Colon B	*19*	62.3	276	12	12	38	21	3	2	69	13	4	.708	0	0	1	3	6	0	0	0	.016	-.065	6.06	4.19	5.65
Pena T	*17*	36.0	159	35	0	29	9	3	1	40	4	1	.681	6	0	0	1	2	1	2	5	.034	-.048	4.25	3.75	3.61
Torres C	*9*	28.3	130	8	5	22	17	2	2	30	5	3	.702	4	1	0	1	2	0	0	0	.093	.022	6.35	6.04	5.73
Poreda A *	*8*	11.0	49	10	0	12	8	1	1	9	0	2	.643	1	1	1	1	0	0	0	0	.001	.134	2.45	2.45	3.19
Williams R *	*8*	17.7	80	25	0	22	12	4	3	13	2	0	.707	5	2	2	0	1	0	0	3	-.039	-.113	4.58	4.58	4.04
Hudson D	*8*	18.7	82	6	2	14	9	0	1	16	3	1	.745	1	0	0	1	1	0	0	0	-.086	.058	4.34	3.38	5.39
Broadway L	*5*	16.0	76	8	0	9	9	1	0	19	0	1	.655	1	0	0	0	1	0	0	0	.139	-.081	5.63	5.06	3.57
Gobble J *	*3*	12.0	59	12	0	10	7	1	2	14	3	0	.703	0	0	0	0	0	0	0	0	.237	-.085	7.50	7.50	6.77
Nunez J	*1*	5.7	29	7	0	3	2	0	0	10	1	0	.609	0	0	0	0	0	0	0	0	.370	-.262	9.53	9.53	5.49

Italicized stats have been adjusted for home park.

Batted Ball Pitching Stats

	% of PA		% of Batted Balls					Out %		Runs Per Event				Total Runs vs. Avg.				
Player	K%	BB%	GB%	LD%	FB%	IF/F	HR/OF	GB	OF	NIP	GB	LD	OF	NIP	GB	LD	FB	Tot
Floyd G	20	8	44	22	33	.07	.12	82	84	.01	-.01	.38	.20	-8	-12	5	-3	-19
Thornton M	30	7	46	17	36	.09	.08	75	81	-.02	.05	.40	.16	-7	-0	-4	-5	-16
Danks J	18	9	44	15	41	.12	.13	74	84	.04	.05	.33	.21	-1	4	-15	5	-8
Buehrle M	12	6	45	19	36	.10	.12	76	83	.04	.03	.33	.20	-7	-2	-3	4	-7
Garcia F	16	5	45	14	41	.11	.06	78	79	-.00	.02	.45	.16	-3	-1	-1	-1	-6
Carrasco D	15	8	47	20	33	.14	.06	73	81	.04	.05	.41	.13	-2	2	4	-7	-2
Pena A	18	6	45	25	29	.14	.13	76	92	.00	.05	.39	.15	-2	0	3	-3	-1
Jenks R	21	8	49	18	33	.06	.16	74	88	.01	.05	.42	.22	-2	1	0	0	-1
Dotel O	28	13	30	19	51	.12	.10	84	73	.04	-.02	.46	.26	0	-4	-0	5	1
Richard C	17	10	48	18	34	.12	.11	68	88	.06	.08	.41	.14	1	6	1	-5	3
Torres C	17	15	38	18	45	.05	.14	72	90	.10	.08	.47	.17	2	0	1	1	4
Contreras J	17	10	48	15	37	.07	.09	71	83	.05	.07	.51	.16	1	6	2	-3	6
Colon B	14	8	44	16	40	.15	.17	75	90	.06	.05	.55	.23	0	2	3	3	9
Linebrink S	21	10	37	24	39	.09	.14	65	78	.03	.11	.33	.28	-0	5	2	7	12
MLB Average	***18***	***10***	***43***	***19***	***38***	***.10***	***.11***	***75***	***83***	***.05***	***.04***	***.39***	***.19***	--	--	--	--	--

Fielding Stats

Name	INN	SBA/G	CS%	ERA	WP+PB/G	PO	A	TE	FE
Catchers									
Pierzynski A	1104.0	0.97	17%	4.10	0.416	879	50	3	2
Castro R	220.7	1.06	12%	4.57	0.245	163	7	3	0
Miller C	88.0	0.92	11%	3.38	0.307	68	3	0	0
Flowers T	27.0	0.67	0%	5.67	1.000	20	0	0	0

Name	Inn	PO	A	TE	FE	FPct	DPS	DPT	ZRDif	OOZ	Dif
First Base											
Konerko P	1141.0	1159	79	0	4	.997	5	3	.068	36	-3
Kotsay M	158.7	155	12	0	0	1.000	2	0	-.076	4	-9
Fields J	94.0	100	4	0	0	1.000	1	0	--	3	--
Betemit W	46.0	41	7	0	1	.980	0	0	--	2	--
Second Base											
Getz C	896.3	196	298	2	5	.986	25	44	.013	15	-11
Nix J	406.0	81	137	4	1	.973	14	19	.026	11	-0
Lillibridge B	137.3	29	43	0	2	.973	0	5	.012	3	-6
Shortstop											
Ramirez A	1293.0	220	410	6	14	.969	44	42	.014	56	5
Nix J	111.0	19	39	2	4	.906	3	7	-.125	6	16
Lillibridge B	35.0	8	7	0	1	.938	2	0	--	0	--
Third Base											
Beckham G	885.0	73	205	5	9	.952	21	0	.006	39	3
Fields J	421.7	27	101	4	4	.941	8	0	-.054	17	-1
Nix J	89.0	2	20	1	0	.957	2	0	--	4	--
Betemit W	43.0	0	4	3	1	.500	0	0	--	0	--
Lillibridge B	1.0	0	0	0	0	.000	0	0	--	--	--

Name	Inn	PO	A	TE	FE	FPct	DPS	DPT	ZRDif	OOZ	Dif
Left Field											
Quentin C	753.0	157	6	0	2	.988	2	0	-.036	32	-8
Podsednik	615.7	139	3	0	0	1.000	1	0	.043	20	-18
Nix J	22.0	4	0	0	0	1.000	0	0	--	0	--
Kotsay M	18.0	3	0	0	0	1.000	0	0	--	0	--
Wise D	18.0	0	0	0	0	.000	0	0	--	--	--
Owens J	13.0	4	0	0	0	1.000	0	0	--	0	--
Center Field											
Anderson B	438.0	108	2	0	2	.982	1	0	.003	23	-15
Podsednik	397.0	115	3	0	1	.992	1	0	.002	32	13
Rios A	285.0	82	0	0	2	.976	0	0	.016	11	-29
Wise D	215.7	72	2	0	1	.987	1	0	.049	25	48
Lillibridge B	79.0	15	1	0	1	.941	1	0	--	5	--
Owens J	16.0	7	0	0	0	1.000	0	0	--	2	--
Kotsay M	9.0	2	0	0	0	1.000	0	0	--	0	--
Right Field											
Dye J	1120.0	238	9	1	4	.980	3	0	-.031	46	-11
Wise D	137.7	24	4	0	0	1.000	2	0	.092	5	-16
Rios A	67.3	11	0	0	0	1.000	0	0	--	2	--
Kotsay M	54.0	13	1	0	0	1.000	0	0	--	5	--
Anderson B	28.0	10	1	0	0	1.000	0	0	--	0	--
Podsednik	18.0	4	0	0	1	.800	0	0	--	0	--
Nix J	14.0	7	0	0	0	1.000	0	0	--	4	--

Cincinnati Reds

Stat Facts:

- Willy Taveras had the lowest GPA (.191) of any player in the majors with at least 400 PAs
- Jay Bruce's LD% of 13% was lowest of any player in the majors with at least 300 PAs
- Johnny Cueto was second in the majors with 14 hit batsmen
- Cueto allowed just 2 SBs in 7 attempts
- Mike Lincoln allowed 7 home runs in 23 IP
- Lincoln struck out 8% of the batters he faced, and walked 20%
- The DER behind Aaron Harang (.659) was lowest of any ML pitcher with at least 162 IP
- Harang's LD% (24%) was highest of any ML pitcher with at least 162 IP
- The Reds earned the fifth-most defensive runs (49) in the majors
- The Reds' bunt defense and outfield throwing each ranked 1st in the majors
- Joey Votto's GPA (.321) was 5th in the NL

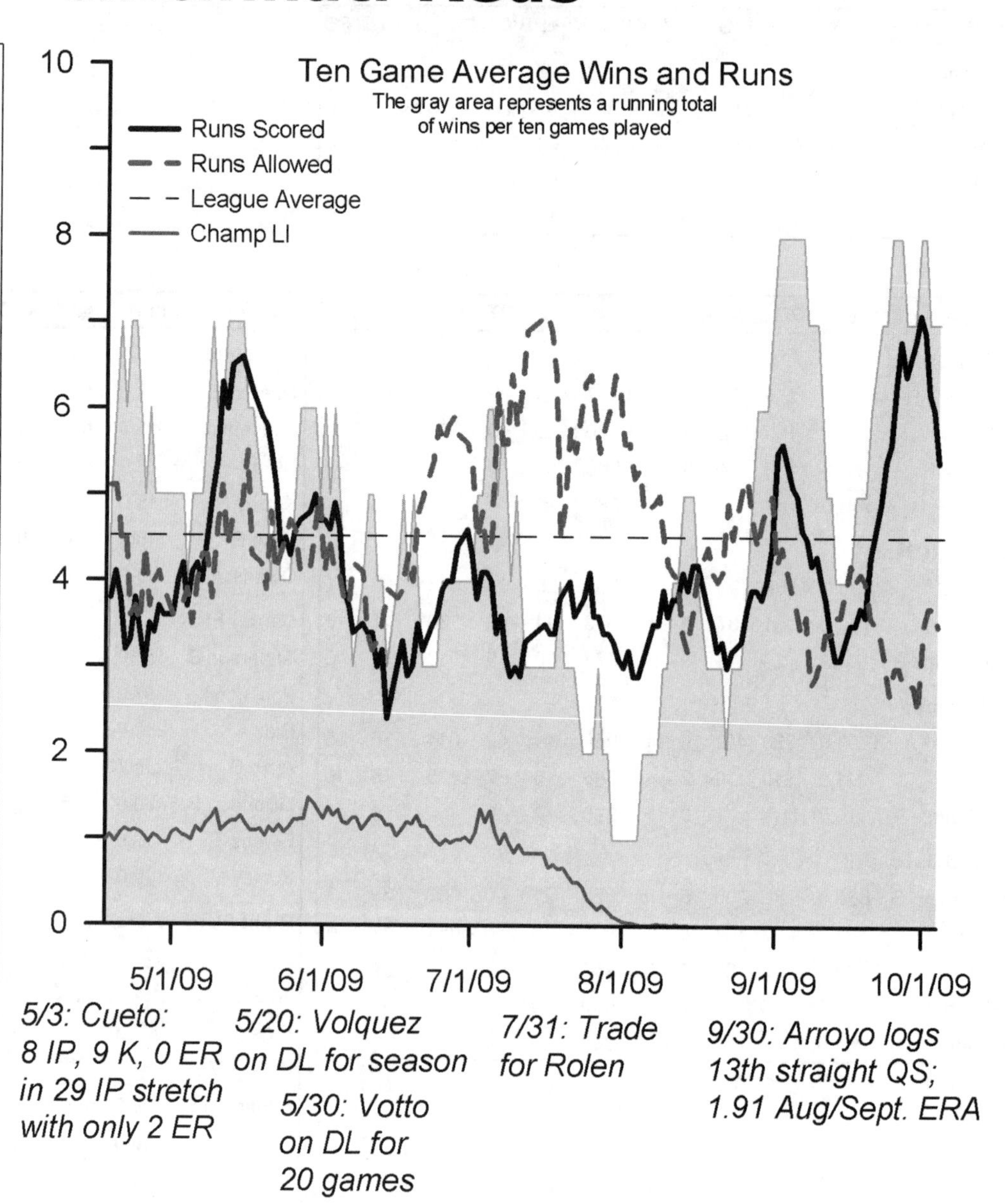

Team Batting and Pitching/Fielding Stats by Month

	April	May	June	July	Aug	Sept/Oct
Wins	11	15	11	8	13	20
Losses	10	13	15	19	16	11
RS/G	3.7	5.1	3.7	3.3	3.9	4.9
RA/G	4.4	4.4	4.5	5.8	4.4	3.4
OBP	.315	.340	.300	.292	.308	.343
SLG	.371	.444	.349	.375	.375	.435
FIP	4.66	4.56	4.92	5.18	4.44	4.29
DER	.714	.714	.710	.674	.707	.725

Batting Stats

Player	*BR*	Runs	RBI	PA	Outs	H	2B	3B	HR	TB	K	BB	IBB	HBP	SH	SF	SB	CS	GDP	H-A	L^R	BA	OBP	SLG	*GPA*
Votto J *	*96*	82	84	544	327	151	38	1	25	266	106	70	10	4	0	1	4	1	8	-.011	.022	.322	.414	.567	*.321*
Phillips B	*80*	78	98	644	453	161	30	5	20	261	75	44	3	6	2	8	25	9	21	.041	.039	.276	.329	.447	*.255*
Bruce J *	*49*	47	58	387	276	77	15	2	22	162	75	38	2	2	1	1	3	3	5	.088	.043	.223	.303	.470	*.249*
Gomes J	*48*	39	51	314	215	75	17	0	20	152	85	26	2	5	0	2	3	1	8	.035	.024	.267	.338	.541	*.282*
Nix L *	*42*	42	46	337	241	74	26	1	15	147	81	22	3	2	0	4	0	1	5	-.035	.105	.239	.291	.476	*.245*
Hairston J	*37*	47	27	340	234	78	18	1	8	122	46	21	0	3	6	3	7	3	2	.042	.010	.254	.305	.397	*.232*
Dickerson C	*36*	31	15	299	191	70	13	3	2	95	66	39	1	1	2	2	11	3	3	-.025	.046	.275	.370	.373	*.255*
Hernandez R	*34*	25	37	331	220	74	13	1	5	104	34	33	2	3	4	4	1	0	7	.047	.020	.258	.336	.362	*.237*
Taveras W	*32*	56	15	437	315	97	11	2	1	115	58	18	0	2	11	2	25	6	2	.024	-.027	.240	.275	.285	*.191*
Hanigan R	*28*	22	11	293	194	66	6	1	3	83	31	37	7	2	2	1	0	0	9	.053	.022	.263	.361	.331	*.240*
Stubbs D	*25*	27	17	196	137	48	5	1	8	79	49	15	0	0	1	0	10	4	1	.134	.026	.267	.323	.439	*.250*
Rosales A	*23*	23	19	266	185	49	10	1	4	73	46	26	0	5	2	3	1	2	2	.000	.026	.213	.303	.317	*.211*
Janish P	*22*	36	16	292	210	54	21	0	1	78	40	26	1	5	5	0	2	0	8	-.019	-.007	.211	.296	.305	*.205*
Rolen S	*20*	24	24	162	104	37	7	1	3	55	20	19	0	3	0	3	1	2	2	.005	.195	.270	.364	.401	*.259*
Encarnacion	*18*	10	16	165	114	29	6	1	5	52	38	24	0	2	0	0	1	1	3	.072	.067	.209	.333	.374	*.239*
Gonzalez A	*17*	16	26	270	196	51	12	0	3	72	36	15	4	2	6	4	0	1	3	-.037	-.011	.210	.258	.296	*.186*
Balentien W	*16*	12	11	125	83	29	7	1	3	47	27	15	0	0	0	0	1	1	1	-.045	-.140	.264	.352	.427	*.260*
McDonald D	*11*	12	10	111	81	28	6	1	2	42	31	5	0	1	0	0	1	0	4	.062	.156	.267	.306	.400	*.233*
Owings M	*8*	7	10	58	40	14	4	1	3	29	19	1	0	1	1	1	0	0	0	.257	-.128	.259	.281	.537	*.255*
Sutton D +	*6*	10	9	76	55	14	4	1	1	23	20	7	0	1	2	0	0	2	1	-.096	-.010	.212	.297	.348	*.217*
Francisco J	*6*	4	7	25	12	9	1	0	1	13	7	3	0	1	0	0	0	0	0	.000	.094	.429	.520	.619	*.381*
Miller C	*5*	4	10	69	47	10	1	0	1	14	14	9	0	1	2	1	0	0	1	.019	-.001	.179	.299	.250	*.193*
Tatum C	*4*	3	6	77	57	11	1	0	1	15	10	7	1	1	1	0	0	0	0	.081	-.100	.162	.250	.221	*.164*
Barker K *	*3*	2	3	36	25	9	3	0	0	12	9	3	1	0	0	1	0	0	2	-.054	.267	.281	.333	.375	*.239*
Harang A	*1*	1	6	54	40	7	1	0	1	11	12	1	0	0	6	0	0	0	0	-.014	.009	.149	.167	.234	*.131*
Maloney M *	*1*	1	0	15	9	3	0	0	0	3	5	1	0	0	2	0	0	0	0	-.068	.239	.250	.308	.250	*.197*
Castillo W +	*1*	0	1	3	1	2	0	0	0	2	0	0	0	0	0	0	0	0	0	.350	.350	.667	.667	.667	*.458*
Richar D *	*1*	1	0	9	6	2	0	0	0	2	1	1	0	0	0	0	0	0	0	.068	.213	.250	.333	.250	*.208*

Only includes batters with at least one Base Run. Italicized stats have been adjusted for home park.
Batted ball stats are listed after fielding stats.

Pitching Stats

Player	PRC	IP	BFP	G	GS	K	BB	IBB	HBP	H	HR	DP	DER	SB	CS	PO	W	L	Sv	Op	Hld	H-A	R^L	RA	ERA	FIP
Arroyo B	*83*	220.3	923	33	33	127	65	6	9	214	31	26	.724	12	6	1	15	13	0	0	0	.005	-.033	4.13	3.84	4.75
Harang A	*61*	162.3	703	26	26	142	43	6	4	186	24	15	.659	13	5	2	6	14	0	0	0	-.047	.010	4.55	4.21	4.08
Cueto J	*60*	171.3	740	30	30	132	61	0	14	172	24	19	.701	2	5	2	11	11	0	0	0	.038	-.007	4.73	4.41	4.74
Masset N	*47*	76.0	292	74	0	70	24	0	0	54	6	12	.745	2	2	0	5	1	0	2	20	.021	-.026	2.61	2.37	3.28
Bailey H	*39*	113.3	496	20	20	86	52	1	3	115	12	9	.694	10	5	1	8	5	0	0	0	-.030	-.024	4.84	4.53	4.44
Cordero F	*38*	66.7	276	68	0	58	30	2	0	58	2	9	.694	3	4	1	2	6	39	43	0	-.040	.004	2.84	2.16	3.06
Owings M	*32*	119.7	542	26	19	68	64	3	6	126	18	12	.715	7	2	0	7	12	1	1	0	-.032	-.003	5.64	5.34	5.65
Rhodes A *	*32*	53.3	215	66	0	48	20	3	1	37	3	4	.741	2	2	1	1	1	0	2	25	-.071	-.108	2.70	2.53	3.09
Herrera D *	*23*	61.7	262	70	0	44	24	2	2	63	5	14	.668	1	2	0	4	4	0	0	9	-.014	-.142	4.38	3.06	3.95
Burton J	*22*	59.3	265	53	0	45	23	6	4	61	5	4	.681	4	0	1	1	0	0	0	7	-.013	.062	4.55	4.40	3.79
Fisher C	*20*	52.3	226	39	0	48	31	2	1	50	4	9	.676	1	5	2	1	1	0	1	2	.042	-.042	4.47	4.47	4.03
Volquez E	*19*	49.7	218	9	9	47	32	0	5	34	6	2	.766	2	0	0	4	2	0	0	0	-.026	.028	4.53	4.35	5.06
Weathers D	*18*	38.0	160	43	0	27	17	1	0	27	7	1	.798	1	0	0	3	3	1	4	13	.081	-.029	3.32	3.32	5.39
Lehr J	*18*	65.3	286	11	11	33	28	1	3	72	14	7	.716	6	1	2	5	3	0	0	0	-.044	.049	5.37	5.37	6.30
Wells K	*15*	46.3	197	10	7	25	22	0	5	37	5	4	.764	7	2	0	2	3	0	0	0	-.029	-.031	4.66	4.66	5.22
Maloney M *	*14*	40.7	170	7	7	28	8	1	3	43	9	4	.705	2	3	1	2	4	0	0	0	.081	-.021	4.87	4.87	5.39
Roenicke J	*8*	13.3	54	11	0	14	4	0	0	13	0	3	.639	3	0	0	0	0	0	0	0	-.073	-.066	2.70	2.70	1.95
Ramirez R	*5*	12.3	48	11	0	8	4	0	1	8	2	2	.818	1	0	0	0	0	0	0	3	.038	-.128	3.65	3.65	5.18
Lincoln M	*4*	23.0	115	19	0	9	19	2	4	29	7	4	.711	0	2	1	1	1	0	0	1	.178	-.133	8.22	8.22	9.06
Viola P *	*2*	7.0	30	9	0	5	3	0	0	7	2	1	.750	0	0	0	0	0	0	0	0	-.143	-.347	5.14	5.14	6.72

Italicized stats have been adjusted for home park.

Batted Ball Pitching Stats

	% of PA		% of Batted Balls					Out %		Runs Per Event				Total Runs vs. Avg.				
Player	K%	BB%	GB%	LD%	FB%	IF/F	HR/OF	GB	OF	NIP	GB	LD	OF	NIP	GB	LD	FB	Tot
Masset N	24	8	54	14	32	.10	.09	79	87	.00	.01	.45	.13	-4	-3	-5	-7	-19
Rhodes A	22	10	41	17	42	.09	.06	73	96	.03	.06	.42	.02	-1	1	-2	-10	-12
Cordero F	21	11	41	23	36	.09	.03	79	88	.04	.00	.42	.03	0	-4	3	-11	-11
Arroyo B	14	8	45	19	37	.12	.13	77	86	.06	.03	.36	.19	-1	-4	-2	1	-7
Wells K	13	14	49	19	32	.13	.10	78	91	.13	.03	.27	.12	4	-0	-3	-5	-4
Weathers D	17	11	43	13	44	.13	.17	78	91	.06	.02	.37	.23	1	-2	-4	1	-4
Volquez E	22	17	45	21	34	.07	.15	86	85	.09	-.03	.32	.24	5	-4	-3	-0	-3
Bailey D	17	11	43	21	37	.05	.09	70	91	.07	.07	.35	.11	3	5	0	-8	-1
Fisher C	21	14	44	18	38	.09	.08	75	78	.07	.03	.36	.18	3	-0	-2	-1	-0
Herrera D	17	10	50	20	30	.07	.10	78	85	.06	.01	.48	.17	1	-3	5	-3	0
Burton L	17	10	43	15	42	.05	.07	72	79	.06	.06	.44	.17	1	1	-1	1	3
Maloney M	16	6	34	13	53	.07	.14	70	81	.02	.07	.43	.25	-2	0	-2	8	4
Cueto J	18	10	42	18	41	.09	.12	74	82	.05	.05	.37	.22	1	-0	-4	9	6
Harang A	20	7	35	24	41	.11	.13	68	81	.00	.08	.35	.23	-9	4	4	10	9
Owings M	13	13	37	21	42	.14	.12	73	88	.12	.04	.33	.16	10	1	1	-2	10
Lehr J	12	11	40	20	40	.08	.17	72	91	.11	.05	.32	.23	3	1	-0	6	10
Lincoln M	8	20	44	19	38	.10	.26	83	85	.22	.00	.51	.38	6	-1	3	6	13
MLB Average	***18***	***10***	***43***	***19***	***38***	***.10***	***.11***	***75***	***83***	***.05***	***.04***	***.39***	***.19***	--	--	--	--	--

Fielding Stats

Name	INN	SBA/G	CS%	ERA	WP+PB/G	PO	A	TE	FE
Catchers									
Hanigan R	670.3	0.63	40%	4.27	0.349	494	44	1	0
Hernandez R	451.0	0.88	25%	4.41	0.279	353	26	1	0
Tatum C	173.0	0.52	30%	4.32	0.260	137	10	1	0
Miller C	164.0	0.82	27%	3.02	0.220	125	12	0	0

Name	Inn	PO	A	TE	FE	FPct	DPS	DPT	ZRDif	OOZ	Dif
First Base											
Votto J	1097.0	960	101	3	7	.991	8	2	.022	41	3
Hernandez R	251.7	238	12	1	3	.984	4	1	-.097	6	-10
Rosales A	84.7	68	11	0	0	1.000	0	0	--	6	--
Barker K	25.0	32	1	0	0	1.000	0	0	--	1	--
Second Base											
Phillips B	1332.0	307	409	6	3	.988	35	61	.016	38	1
Hairston J	75.0	16	22	0	1	.974	2	3	--	0	--
Sutton D	39.0	9	11	0	0	1.000	1	1	--	1	--
Rosales A	11.0	2	3	0	0	1.000	0	1	--	0	--
Richar D	1.0	0	0	0	0	.000	0	0	--	--	--
Shortstop											
Janish P	592.3	110	212	1	2	.991	31	21	.060	20	-5
Gonzalez A	587.3	97	163	2	4	.977	24	18	-.005	18	-8
Hairston J	217.3	47	56	2	0	.981	5	1	-.019	12	17
Rosales A	33.0	4	12	0	0	1.000	1	1	--	1	--
Sutton D	28.3	7	16	0	0	1.000	1	3	--	0	--
Third Base											
Rosales A	419.3	37	81	1	6	.944	7	0	-.009	19	4
Encarnacion	362.3	25	69	3	1	.959	6	0	-.068	11	-11
Rolen S	339.3	29	64	0	0	1.000	3	0	.054	13	-3
Hairston J	275.3	33	40	4	3	.913	6	0	-.157	13	6
Francisco J	30.0	1	8	0	1	.900	2	0	--	3	--
Richar D	19.7	1	2	1	0	.750	0	0	--	0	--
Janish P	6.0	1	3	0	0	1.000	0	0	--	0	--
Sutton D	5.3	1	1	0	0	1.000	0	0	--	0	--
Hernandez R	1.0	1	0	0	0	1.000	0	0	--	--	--

Name	Inn	PO	A	TE	FE	FPct	DPS	DPT	ZRDif	OOZ	Dif
Left Field											
Nix L	558.0	118	2	0	1	.992	2	0	.095	33	9
Gomes J	253.0	46	3	1	0	.980	1	0	-.094	6	-27
Dickerson C	251.7	58	1	1	2	.952	0	0	-.007	19	25
Balentien W	155.7	39	1	0	1	.976	0	0	.071	12	27
McDonald D	124.0	27	1	0	1	.966	1	0	.015	7	6
Hairston J	80.0	24	0	0	0	1.000	0	0	--	5	--
Sutton D	36.0	11	0	0	0	1.000	0	0	--	1	--
Center Field											
Taveras W	839.0	266	7	2	2	.986	2	0	-.004	65	10
Stubbs D	368.7	111	4	0	0	1.000	0	0	-.020	29	11
Dickerson C	170.7	57	4	0	0	1.000	3	0	.049	9	-15
Nix L	34.0	9	0	0	1	.900	0	0	--	2	--
McDonald D	29.0	10	0	0	1	.909	0	0	--	3	--
Hairston J	17.0	5	0	0	0	1.000	0	0	--	0	--
Right Field											
Bruce J	810.3	200	11	0	2	.991	2	0	-.008	47	6
Gomes J	269.3	57	2	0	0	1.000	0	0	-.101	11	-11
Dickerson C	122.0	31	0	0	0	1.000	0	0	-.024	8	13
Balentien W	110.0	28	0	0	0	1.000	0	0	-.028	6	2
McDonald D	66.7	24	1	0	0	1.000	0	0	--	6	--
Nix L	63.0	14	0	0	0	1.000	0	0	--	4	--
Hairston J	14.0	6	0	0	0	1.000	0	0	--	2	--
Sutton D	3.0	0	0	0	0	.000	0	0	--	--	--

Batted Ball Batting Stats

	% of PA		% of Batted Balls					Out %		Runs Per Event				Total Runs vs. Avg.				
Player	**K%**	**BB%**	**GB%**	**LD%**	**FB%**	**IF/F**	**HR/OF**	**GB**	**OF**	**NIP**	**GB**	**LD**	**OF**	**NIP**	**GB**	**LD**	**FB**	**Tot**
Votto J	19	14	39	22	39	.01	.18	76	69	.08	.04	.40	.37	7	-0	7	31	46
Gomes J	27	10	34	20	46	.10	.23	72	89	.01	.05	.45	.33	-3	-0	2	12	10
Phillips B	12	8	50	17	33	.08	.13	75	81	.07	.03	.34	.23	0	-0	-4	7	3
Dickerson C	22	13	49	22	29	.06	.04	71	78	.06	.07	.40	.15	3	3	2	-5	2
Rolen S	12	14	46	16	38	.15	.08	75	86	.13	.05	.47	.12	3	1	1	-3	2
Stubbs R	25	8	42	21	37	.06	.18	63	92	-.01	.11	.36	.24	-3	4	-0	2	2
Bruce J	19	10	39	13	49	.08	.17	74	89	.05	.05	.32	.24	-0	1	-10	11	2
Balentien W	22	12	47	18	35	.07	.11	79	75	.05	.02	.45	.26	0	-1	0	1	1
Encarnacion E	23	16	41	14	46	.13	.13	85	74	.07	-.03	.34	.28	2	-3	-4	3	-1
Nix L	24	7	38	20	43	.14	.16	77	85	-.01	.03	.41	.26	-6	-2	0	6	-2
Hanigan R	11	13	48	24	27	.07	.05	81	87	.14	-.00	.34	.06	6	-3	4	-9	-2
McDonald D	28	5	47	18	35	.15	.09	66	80	-.04	.08	.45	.19	-3	1	-0	-1	-3
Hairston J	14	7	34	24	42	.12	.07	74	87	.04	.06	.34	.10	-2	3	3	-7	-3
Hernandez R	10	11	49	19	32	.16	.06	77	86	.12	.02	.37	.09	4	-2	1	-9	-6
Rosales A	17	12	45	16	40	.12	.05	75	85	.07	.05	.31	.09	2	0	-6	-7	-11
Janish P	14	11	37	19	44	.16	.01	76	92	.09	.03	.42	-.01	2	-1	1	-16	-15
Gonzalez A	13	6	36	18	46	.11	.03	78	92	.03	.03	.31	.02	-2	-1	-4	-12	-19
Taveras W	13	5	47	17	36	.19	.01	71	90	.00	.08	.37	-.01	-6	9	-5	-23	-26
MLB Average	***18***	***10***	***43***	***19***	***38***	***.10***	***.11***	***75***	***83***	***.05***	***.04***	***.39***	***.19***	--	--	--	--	--

Cleveland Indians

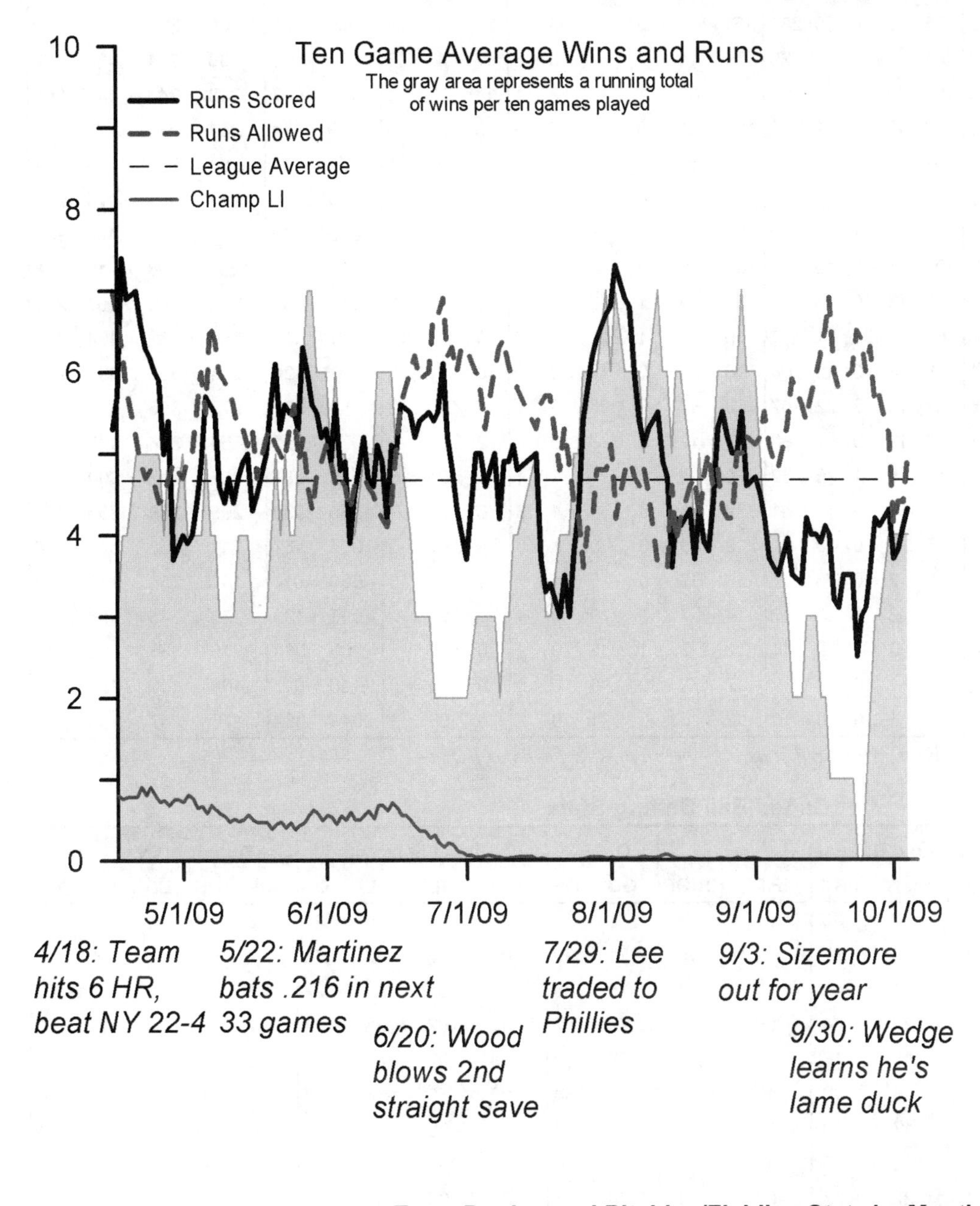

Stat Facts:

- In just 327 PAs, Kelly Shoppach led the AL with 18 HBPs
- Shin-Soo Choo was second with 17
- Choo stole 21 bases in 23 attempts
- Choo was 3rd in the AL in Base Runs (117)
- Tomakazu Ohka allowed 18 home runs in 71 IP
- Asdrubal Cabrera started 50 DPs in just 870 innings at shortstop
- Luis Valbuena turned 46 DPs in just 652 innings at second base
- Kerry Wood allowed 10 SBs in 10 attempts
- Jhonny Peralta's GPA (.236) was 5th-lowest of players with at least 600 PAs
- The DER behind Aaron Laffey (.665) was 3rd-lowest of any AL pitcher with at least 120 IP
- The DER behind Carl Pavano (.666) was 4th-lowest
- The DER behind Fausto Carmona (.669) was 6th-lowest

Team Batting and Pitching/Fielding Stats by Month

	April	May	June	July	Aug	Sept/Oct
Wins	8	14	9	12	15	7
Losses	14	16	18	12	12	25
RS/G	5.3	5.2	4.8	5.2	4.6	3.8
RA/G	5.9	5.3	5.6	5.0	4.5	5.7
OBP	.358	.356	.321	.357	.336	.313
SLG	.441	.412	.402	.462	.427	.373
FIP	5.30	4.42	4.92	4.81	4.24	5.01
DER	.673	.681	.688	.698	.691	.663

Batting Stats

Player	BR	Runs	RBI	PA	Outs	H	2B	3B	HR	TB	K	BB	IBB	HBP	SH	SF	SB	CS	GDP	H-A	L^R	BA	OBP	SLG	GPA
Choo S *	117	87	86	685	419	175	38	6	20	285	151	78	5	17	0	7	21	2	9	-.039	.028	.300	.394	.489	.300
Cabrera A +	81	81	68	581	379	161	42	4	6	229	89	44	1	1	10	3	17	4	13	-.024	-.016	.308	.361	.438	.272
Sizemore G *	71	73	64	503	340	108	20	6	18	194	92	60	1	4	2	1	13	8	4	-.009	.037	.248	.343	.445	.266
Peralta J	67	57	83	645	456	148	35	1	11	218	134	51	0	4	2	6	0	2	20	-.023	-.014	.254	.316	.375	.236
Martinez V +	64	56	67	435	281	107	21	1	15	175	51	51	3	2	0	5	0	0	11	-.023	-.012	.284	.368	.464	.282
Hafner T *	56	46	49	383	253	92	19	0	16	159	67	41	6	3	0	1	0	0	7	.039	.060	.272	.355	.470	.277
Francisco B	46	48	33	355	245	77	21	1	10	130	59	33	0	8	4	2	13	3	11	-.010	.040	.250	.336	.422	.257
Valbuena L *	45	52	31	398	287	92	25	3	10	153	83	26	0	0	2	2	2	3	8	-.005	.031	.250	.298	.416	.238
DeRosa M	44	47	50	314	210	75	13	0	13	127	63	29	1	3	1	3	1	1	6	.045	.103	.270	.342	.457	.268
Garko R	40	29	39	273	177	68	10	0	11	111	40	20	1	10	2	2	0	0	6	-.001	.056	.285	.362	.464	.279
Shoppach K	40	33	40	327	221	58	14	0	12	108	98	33	0	18	2	3	0	0	8	-.101	.120	.214	.335	.399	.251
Carroll J	39	53	26	358	238	87	10	2	2	107	63	36	0	3	3	1	4	2	8	-.052	.004	.276	.355	.340	.245
LaPorta M	25	29	21	198	141	46	13	0	7	80	37	12	0	3	0	2	2	0	6	-.026	-.022	.254	.308	.442	.249
Marte A	18	20	25	175	124	36	6	1	6	62	30	14	1	1	1	4	0	0	5	-.033	-.087	.232	.293	.400	.232
Crowe T +	17	22	17	202	147	43	9	3	1	61	39	11	0	1	4	3	6	0	7	-.033	.030	.235	.278	.333	.208
Brantley M *	13	10	11	121	84	35	4	0	0	39	19	8	0	0	1	0	4	4	3	-.029	-.167	.313	.358	.348	.248
Gimenez C	7	12	7	130	99	16	2	0	3	27	36	17	0	0	1	1	1	1	3	-.096	-.017	.144	.256	.243	.176
Marson L	6	6	4	52	35	11	6	0	0	17	14	7	0	0	0	1	0	0	2	-.065	-.133	.250	.346	.386	.252
Dellucci D *	5	3	1	45	30	11	3	0	0	14	12	2	1	2	0	1	0	0	1	-.263	.069	.275	.333	.350	.238
Barfield J	3	5	2	20	13	8	1	0	0	9	7	0	0	0	0	0	0	1	0	-.198	-.017	.400	.400	.450	.293
Toregas W	3	1	6	60	43	9	1	0	0	10	12	6	0	1	0	2	0	0	1	-.044	.082	.176	.267	.196	.169

Only includes batters with at least one Base Run. Italicized stats have been adjusted for home park.

Batted Ball Batting Stats

	% of PA		% of Batted Balls					Out %		Runs Per Event				Total Runs vs. Avg.				
Player	K%	BB%	GB%	LD%	FB%	IF/F	HR/OF	GB	OF	NIP	GB	LD	OF	NIP	GB	LD	FB	Tot
Choo S	22	14	42	22	36	.04	.13	75	77	.06	.04	.46	.27	8	1	11	14	33
Cabrera A	15	8	48	22	30	.02	.05	71	78	.04	.06	.43	.16	-2	6	12	-4	12
Hafner T	17	11	39	21	40	.13	.15	75	85	.07	.05	.42	.22	3	1	5	4	12
Martinez V	12	12	46	20	34	.09	.15	78	87	.12	.02	.38	.21	7	-3	4	3	12
Sizemore G	18	13	36	16	48	.09	.12	79	82	.08	.02	.48	.20	5	-3	1	7	9
Garko R	15	11	44	16	40	.10	.15	73	84	.08	.05	.38	.23	2	0	-1	5	6
DeRosa M	20	10	44	17	39	.08	.17	81	77	.04	-.00	.38	.32	-0	-4	-2	10	4
Francisco B	17	12	40	16	43	.12	.11	77	80	.08	.02	.38	.21	3	-1	-3	4	2
Shoppach K	30	16	41	22	37	.08	.20	76	85	.04	.03	.35	.30	2	-3	-4	4	-0
LaPorta M	19	8	40	18	42	.10	.13	76	85	.02	.02	.43	.19	-2	-1	1	1	-1
Brantley M	16	7	47	26	27	.08	.00	60	91	.02	.12	.29	-.03	-1	4	1	-6	-2
Carroll J	18	11	46	24	30	.04	.03	76	79	.06	.03	.37	.10	2	-1	4	-8	-4
Marte A	17	9	31	16	53	.10	.10	85	89	.04	-.04	.46	.13	-1	-4	-0	-1	-6
Valbuena L	21	7	41	22	37	.14	.10	74	88	-.00	.05	.43	.15	-6	0	5	-6	-7
Crowe T	19	6	56	16	27	.13	.03	76	76	-.01	.03	.38	.13	-3	-0	-2	-5	-11
Gimenez C	28	13	41	19	40	.03	.10	94	96	.03	-.07	.34	.08	-0	-4	-3	-4	-11
Peralta J	21	9	50	19	31	.09	.09	75	79	.02	.03	.41	.17	-5	-2	2	-7	-12
MLB Average	***18***	***10***	***43***	***19***	***38***	***.10***	***.11***	***75***	***83***	***.05***	***.04***	***.39***	***.19***	--	--	--	--	--

Pitching Stats

Player	PRC	IP	BFP	G	GS	K	BB	IBB	HBP	H	HR	DP	DER	SB	CS	PO	W	L	Sv	Op	Hld	H-A	R^L	RA	ERA	FIP
Lee C *	*85*	152.0	641	22	22	107	33	1	3	165	10	14	.676	7	2	1	7	9	0	0	0	.008	-.088	3.14	3.14	3.33
Laffey A *	*40*	121.7	539	25	19	59	57	1	2	140	9	28	.665	1	4	0	7	9	1	1	0	-.016	-.063	5.10	4.44	4.61
Pavano C	*40*	125.7	534	21	21	88	23	0	3	150	19	17	.666	20	6	0	9	8	0	0	0	-.014	.041	5.73	5.37	4.38
Huff D *	*38*	128.3	574	23	23	65	41	1	1	159	16	15	.672	7	1	0	11	8	0	0	0	-.029	.030	5.75	5.61	4.76
Sowers J *	*38*	123.3	545	23	22	51	52	3	3	134	11	14	.703	5	3	2	6	11	0	0	0	-.016	-.005	5.33	5.25	4.79
Carmona F	*31*	125.3	596	24	24	79	70	0	8	151	16	10	.669	8	4	0	5	12	0	0	0	-.027	-.086	6.97	6.32	5.46
Wood K	*26*	55.0	241	58	0	63	28	0	3	48	7	4	.700	10	0	0	3	3	20	26	0	-.070	-.016	4.25	4.25	4.25
Lewis J	*26*	66.3	285	47	0	62	29	3	2	62	13	6	.715	2	0	0	2	4	1	5	4	-.075	-.106	5.02	4.61	5.14
Sipp T *	*23*	40.0	168	46	0	48	25	2	0	27	5	5	.733	3	0	0	2	0	0	0	9	-.055	-.005	3.60	2.93	4.14
Masterson J	*20*	57.3	256	11	10	52	35	1	2	56	5	10	.667	7	2	0	1	7	0	0	0	-.091	-.125	5.49	4.55	4.39
Ohka T	*19*	71.0	306	18	6	31	19	1	4	77	18	6	.748	3	0	0	1	5	0	0	0	-.039	.004	5.96	5.96	6.54
Perez C	*16*	33.3	133	32	0	38	12	0	3	24	5	4	.747	6	2	0	0	1	1	3	4	-.020	.020	4.32	4.32	4.21
Smith J	*15*	34.0	142	37	0	30	13	0	0	30	4	4	.705	1	0	0	0	0	0	1	10	.031	-.123	4.24	3.44	4.10
Betancourt R	*14*	30.7	129	29	0	32	15	4	0	25	3	3	.709	4	1	0	1	2	1	3	8	.002	-.161	4.40	3.52	3.45
Herges M	*13*	25.3	107	21	0	18	6	0	0	24	3	2	.700	2	0	0	2	1	0	1	1	-.019	-.044	3.55	3.55	4.02
Perez R *	*10*	48.0	230	54	0	32	25	6	2	66	5	9	.608	4	2	0	4	3	0	1	6	.032	.098	7.69	7.31	4.52
Reyes A	*9*	38.3	176	8	8	22	23	0	2	40	5	4	.710	7	2	0	1	1	0	0	0	.060	-.030	7.04	6.57	5.70
Veras J	*8*	24.7	107	22	0	22	14	0	2	19	3	3	.727	3	1	0	1	2	0	0	3	-.049	-.037	5.84	4.38	4.93
Gosling M *	*8*	25.0	114	15	0	13	11	1	0	30	5	3	.694	0	0	0	0	0	0	0	0	.048	-.056	5.40	5.04	5.95
Aquino G	*6*	16.0	74	10	0	11	15	3	0	13	1	2	.723	1	0	1	1	2	0	0	1	.129	.022	4.50	4.50	4.88
Todd J	*5*	20.7	99	19	0	18	7	1	0	31	3	2	.592	0	0	0	0	1	0	0	1	-.033	-.103	7.40	7.40	4.21
Chulk V	*4*	12.0	55	8	0	4	10	0	0	10	1	2	.750	0	0	0	0	1	0	1	0	-.111	.219	4.50	3.75	6.11
Vizcaino L	*4*	11.7	56	11	0	9	12	2	0	8	2	0	.758	5	0	0	1	3	1	1	1	-.138	.189	5.40	5.40	6.45
Carrasco C	*3*	22.3	112	5	5	11	11	1	0	40	6	1	.571	3	3	3	0	4	0	0	0	-.173	.054	9.27	8.87	7.04
Kobayashi M	2	9.7	45	10	0	4	4	0	1	12	2	2	.676	0	0	0	0	0	0	0	0	.358	.021	8.38	8.38	6.60
Jackson Z *	*1*	8.7	47	3	1	10	4	0	2	14	2	0	.552	1	0	0	0	0	0	0	1	.077	.020	10.38	9.35	5.96
Lewis S *	*1*	4.3	20	1	1	3	1	0	0	7	2	0	.643	0	0	0	0	0	0	0	0	--	.388	8.31	8.31	8.50

Italicized stats have been adjusted for home park.
Batted ball stats are listed after fielding stats.

Fielding Stats

Name	INN	SBA/G	CS%	ERA	WP+PB/G	PO	A	TE	FE
Catchers									
Shoppach K	672.0	0.83	21%	4.67	0.442	476	31	4	0
Martinez V	430.0	0.94	13%	5.78	0.356	285	14	0	0
Toregas W	153.0	0.71	17%	5.00	0.353	119	9	0	0
Marson L	123.0	1.10	40%	5.27	0.146	95	8	1	0
Gimenez C	56.0	0.80	20%	4.18	0.161	36	4	0	0

Name	Inn	PO	A	TE	FE	FPct	DPS	DPT	ZRDif	OOZ	Dif
First Base											
Garko R	407.0	418	36	2	1	.993	3	0	.091	18	10
Marte A	390.3	380	23	1	4	.988	5	0	-.058	15	4
Martinez V	385.7	348	17	1	2	.992	2	0	.043	13	-1
Gimenez C	123.0	133	4	0	1	.993	0	0	-.032	6	14
LaPorta M	78.0	78	4	0	2	.976	0	0	--	4	--
DeRosa M	41.0	41	1	0	1	.977	0	0	--	2	--
Romero N	9.0	7	0	0	0	1.000	0	0	--	--	--
Second Base											
Valbuena L	652.0	162	228	3	3	.985	15	46	-.061	24	9
Carroll J	467.0	89	137	1	0	.996	9	14	.039	14	2
Cabrera A	244.0	59	82	1	0	.993	10	19	-.060	4	-11
Barfield J	36.0	12	12	0	0	1.000	2	2	--	0	--
Graffanino T	35.0	10	10	1	0	.952	1	2	--	0	--
Shortstop											
Cabrera A	870.0	143	288	3	6	.980	50	23	.002	29	-5
Peralta J	334.0	62	123	3	1	.979	18	18	.013	18	16
Valbuena L	205.0	37	73	2	3	.957	2	4	-.032	9	6
Romero N	25.0	1	6	0	0	1.000	1	0	--	1	--
Third Base											
Peralta J	902.0	78	211	7	8	.951	16	3	-.046	39	2
DeRosa M	355.0	25	74	2	6	.925	11	0	-.068	15	1
Carroll J	156.0	11	37	1	1	.960	6	1	-.007	12	35
Graffanino T	18.0	0	8	0	0	1.000	0	0	--	2	--
Valbuena L	2.0	0	1	0	0	1.000	0	0	--	0	--
Romero N	1.0	0	0	0	0	.000	0	0	--	--	--

Name	Inn	PO	A	TE	FE	FPct	DPS	DPT	ZRDif	OOZ	Dif
Left Field											
Francisco B	393.0	97	0	0	1	.990	0	0	.002	11	-22
LaPorta M	256.7	53	2	1	0	.982	0	0	.023	9	-15
Crowe T	251.0	50	4	0	2	.964	0	0	-.098	15	9
Choo S	164.0	37	0	0	0	1.000	0	0	-.079	15	41
DeRosa M	130.0	22	1	0	0	1.000	0	0	.106	4	-20
Gimenez C	81.0	20	0	0	0	1.000	0	0	--	3	--
Brantley M	63.3	13	0	0	0	1.000	0	0	--	2	--
Garko R	48.0	10	1	0	1	.917	0	0	--	0	--
Carroll J	35.0	7	0	0	1	.875	0	0	--	2	--
Dellucci D	8.0	1	0	0	0	1.000	0	0	--	0	--
Barfield J	4.0	0	0	0	0	.000	0	0	--	--	--
Center Field											
Sizemore G	806.3	259	1	0	0	1.000	0	0	-.022	59	5
Francisco B	260.7	71	5	0	0	1.000	3	0	.007	11	-26
Crowe T	193.0	68	0	1	0	.986	0	0	-.003	17	20
Brantley M	166.0	46	0	0	1	.979	0	0	-.028	9	-14
Choo S	8.0	1	0	0	0	1.000	0	0	--	--	--
Right Field											
Choo S	1084.0	279	11	3	4	.976	2	0	.022	78	20
LaPorta M	82.3	24	1	1	0	.962	0	0	--	5	--
Francisco B	74.0	15	0	0	0	1.000	0	0	--	2	--
DeRosa M	68.0	16	0	0	0	1.000	0	0	--	4	--
Carroll J	35.0	10	0	0	0	1.000	0	0	--	2	--
Gimenez C	34.0	8	0	0	0	1.000	0	0	--	0	--
Crowe T	28.0	12	0	0	1	.923	0	0	--	3	--
Garko R	28.0	6	0	0	0	1.000	0	0	--	0	--

Batted Ball Pitching Stats

	% of PA		% of Batted Balls					Out %		Runs Per Event				Total Runs vs. Avg.				
Player	K%	BB%	GB%	LD%	FB%	IF/F	HR/OF	GB	OF	NIP	GB	LD	OF	NIP	GB	LD	FB	Tot
Lee C	17	6	43	21	36	.10	.06	73	86	.00	.05	.38	.11	-8	4	5	-14	-13
Perez C	29	11	35	14	51	.10	.14	86	75	.02	-.04	.30	.27	-1	-3	-4	3	-5
Wood K	26	13	40	15	45	.06	.11	66	85	.04	.09	.37	.16	0	2	-4	-1	-4
Sipp T	29	15	35	14	51	.11	.12	78	75	.04	.00	.33	.26	1	-3	-5	3	-3
Betancourt R	25	12	31	12	57	.04	.07	68	83	.03	.06	.40	.14	-0	-0	-3	0	-3
Smith J	21	9	55	17	28	.04	.15	76	86	.03	.03	.44	.23	-1	-1	-0	-1	-2
Herges M	17	6	46	14	40	.13	.11	78	76	.00	.02	.49	.25	-1	-1	-0	2	-1
Veras E	21	15	41	12	47	.16	.12	70	78	.08	.06	.27	.23	2	0	-3	1	-1
Masterson J	20	14	58	12	30	.14	.12	68	74	.08	.07	.29	.26	4	4	-7	-0	1
Lewis J	22	11	37	16	48	.09	.16	69	82	.04	.07	.31	.29	-0	0	-6	10	4
Gosling M	11	10	33	20	47	.12	.14	69	88	.10	.06	.38	.19	1	1	1	2	5
Reyes A	13	14	33	20	47	.12	.10	80	81	.13	.01	.37	.18	4	-2	1	2	5
Sowers J	9	10	38	19	43	.08	.07	73	87	.12	.05	.40	.11	6	0	4	-6	5
Pavano C	16	5	45	19	36	.09	.13	70	82	-.01	.06	.41	.22	-8	6	4	6	7
Ohka T	10	8	38	17	45	.16	.18	83	85	.08	-.01	.42	.28	0	-4	2	10	8
Laffey A	11	11	49	21	30	.07	.08	72	84	.12	.04	.37	.12	7	3	6	-8	8
Perez R	14	12	49	24	27	.04	.09	74	67	.10	.04	.45	.26	3	-0	7	2	13
Carrasco C	10	10	48	27	25	.00	.27	74	69	.12	.05	.43	.51	1	2	6	7	16
Huff D	11	7	38	20	42	.11	.09	73	83	.07	.05	.43	.17	-0	3	12	2	17
Carmona F	13	13	55	18	27	.03	.14	74	78	.12	.05	.39	.27	11	5	2	7	25
MLB Average	***18***	***10***	***43***	***19***	***38***	***.10***	***.11***	***75***	***83***	***.05***	***.04***	***.39***	***.19***	--	--	--	--	--

Colorado Rockies

Stat Facts:

- Ubaldo Jimenez's total of -39 runs below average was seventh-best in the majors
- Clint Barmes was thrown out in 10 of 22 stolen base attempts
- Barmes had the lowest GPA (.222) of any player with more than 510 PAs
- 69% of Brad Hawpe's outfield flies were outs, tied for lowest rate among ML regulars
- Todd Helton's 17 line drive runs tied for the major league lead
- Jason Hammel allowed 18 SBs in 20 attempts
- Hammel had the highest H-A (.072) of any ML pitcher with at least 162 IP
- Yorvit Torrealba threw out 8% of runners attempting to steal
- Aaron Cook allowed just 4 SBs in 8 attempts

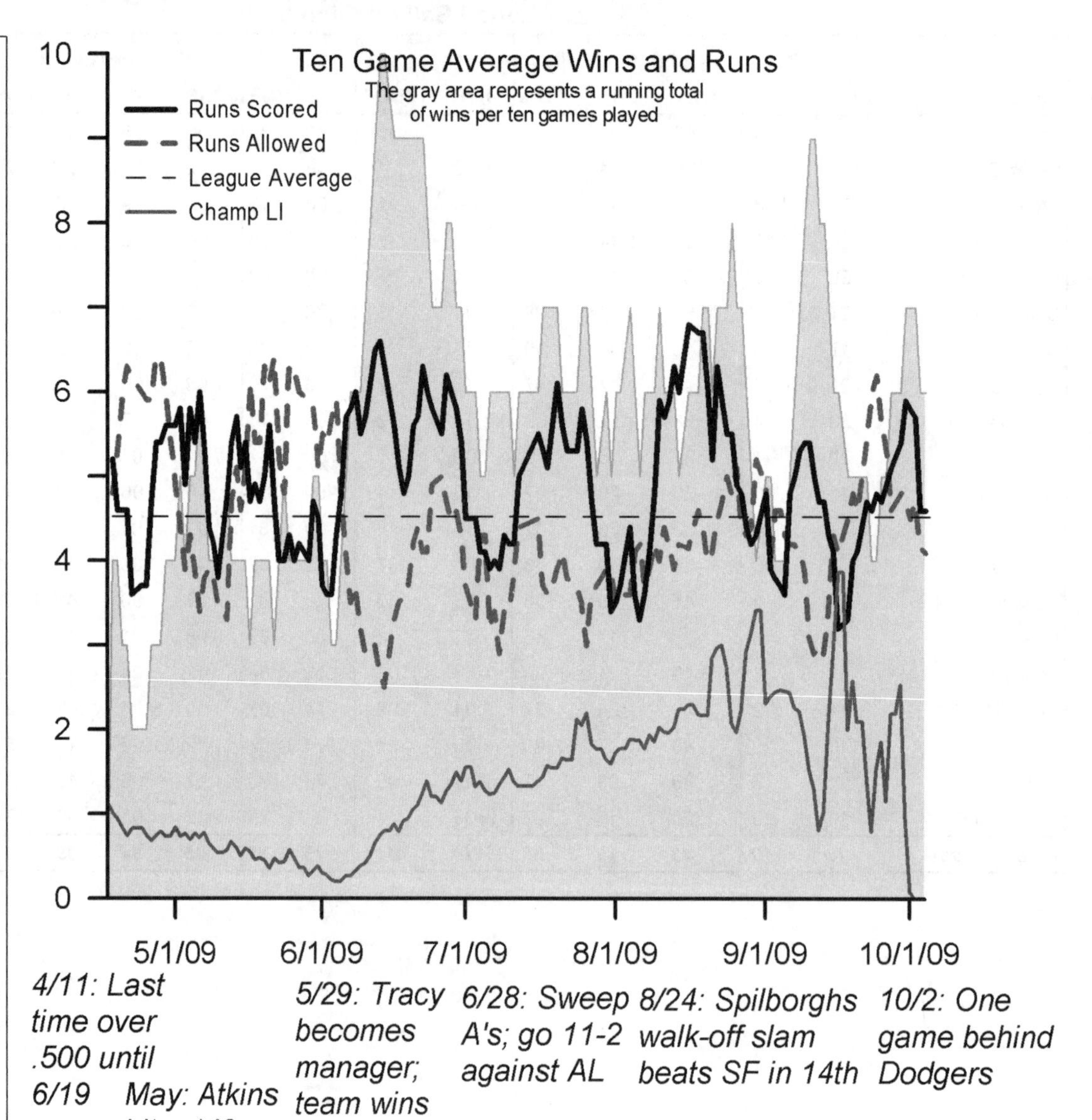

Team Batting and Pitching/Fielding Stats by Month

	April	May	June	July	Aug	Sept/Oct
Wins	8	12	21	15	16	20
Losses	12	17	7	11	12	11
RS/G	5.4	4.5	5.5	4.5	5.2	4.8
RA/G	5.4	5.1	3.8	3.8	4.4	4.3
OBP	.347	.320	.350	.344	.353	.345
SLG	.444	.406	.470	.426	.465	.431
FIP	5.16	3.49	3.94	3.56	4.21	3.77
DER	.669	.671	.713	.705	.690	.703

Batting Stats

Player	BR	Runs	RBI	PA	Outs	H	2B	3B	HR	TB	K	BB	IBB	HBP	SH	SF	SB	CS	GDP	H-A	L^R	BA	OBP	SLG	GPA
Tulowitzki T	96	101	92	628	413	161	25	9	32	300	112	73	4	3	0	9	20	11	20	.045	-.009	.297	.377	.552	.283
Helton T *	95	79	86	645	383	177	38	3	15	266	73	89	5	2	0	10	0	1	15	.032	.075	.325	.416	.489	.284
Hawpe B *	85	82	86	588	379	143	42	3	23	260	145	79	7	4	0	4	1	3	18	.012	.058	.285	.384	.519	.278
Barmes C	64	69	76	604	431	135	32	3	23	242	121	31	2	10	6	7	12	10	6	.068	.031	.245	.294	.440	.222
Fowler D +	62	73	34	518	332	115	29	10	4	176	116	67	1	1	14	3	27	10	4	.038	.037	.266	.363	.406	.243
Stewart I *	59	74	70	491	339	97	19	3	25	197	138	56	3	5	0	5	7	4	7	.029	.051	.228	.322	.464	.239
Smith S *	57	61	55	387	243	98	20	4	15	171	67	46	3	2	1	3	4	1	5	.100	.009	.293	.378	.510	.273
Gonzalez C *	47	53	29	317	206	79	14	7	13	146	70	28	3	3	5	3	16	4	3	.036	.024	.284	.353	.525	.266
Iannetta C	44	41	52	350	228	66	15	2	16	133	75	43	3	11	1	6	0	1	4	.095	.080	.228	.344	.460	.248
Spilborghs R	38	55	48	393	281	85	24	3	8	139	79	34	0	2	3	2	9	5	9	.041	.025	.241	.310	.395	.219
Atkins G	34	37	48	399	282	80	12	1	9	121	58	41	2	2	0	2	0	0	8	.018	.076	.226	.308	.342	.206
Torrealba Y	25	27	31	242	156	62	11	1	2	81	42	21	5	1	3	4	1	1	4	-.003	-.060	.291	.351	.380	.232
Phillips P	7	5	9	54	31	14	2	0	1	19	3	7	1	0	1	1	0	0	0	.013	-.144	.311	.396	.422	.260
Murton M	6	7	6	56	39	13	5	0	1	21	14	4	0	0	0	0	2	0	0	-.079	-.028	.250	.304	.404	.218
Giambi J *	6	4	11	31	17	7	1	0	2	14	8	7	0	0	0	0	0	0	0	-.056	-.239	.292	.452	.583	.320
Young Jr. E	4	7	1	61	48	14	1	0	1	18	12	4	0	0	0	0	4	4	1	.190	.075	.246	.295	.316	.194
Quintanilla	3	7	2	69	48	10	2	0	0	12	27	8	0	0	3	0	0	0	0	.102	.072	.172	.273	.207	.160
Jimenez U	3	5	2	77	48	13	0	0	0	13	15	6	0	0	12	0	0	0	2	.061	-.074	.220	.292	.220	.171
Marquis J *	2	7	8	75	53	11	3	0	0	14	14	2	0	0	9	0	0	0	0	-.003	-.013	.172	.197	.219	.131
Cook A	1	3	6	58	39	5	1	0	0	6	14	7	0	1	5	1	0	0	0	-.004	-.024	.114	.245	.136	.133
Rusch G *	1	0	0	6	4	2	1	0	0	3	2	0	0	0	0	0	0	0	0	.113	.413	.333	.333	.500	.252
Morales F *	1	0	1	5	3	2	0	0	0	2	2	0	0	0	0	0	0	0	0	-.467	.117	.400	.400	.400	.257
Bellorin E	1	1	0	9	6	2	0	0	0	2	1	1	1	0	0	0	0	0	0	--	-.083	.250	.333	.250	.195

Only includes batters with at least one Base Run. Italicized stats have been adjusted for home park.

Batted Ball Batting Stats

	% of PA		% of Batted Balls					Out %		Runs Per Event				Total Runs vs. Avg.				
Player	K%	BB%	GB%	LD%	FB%	IF/F	HR/OF	GB	OF	NIP	GB	LD	OF	NIP	GB	LD	FB	Tot
Helton T	11	14	40	25	36	.05	.09	73	82	.14	.05	.39	.18	16	3	17	4	39
Tulowitzki T	18	12	42	18	40	.12	.20	72	85	.07	.05	.44	.31	6	4	5	21	35
Hawpe B	25	14	43	20	36	.02	.18	78	69	.05	.01	.42	.38	5	-5	3	26	29
Smith G	17	12	39	19	42	.05	.13	71	87	.08	.07	.50	.20	4	2	7	5	19
Gonzalez C	22	10	38	23	39	.12	.16	74	81	.03	.05	.50	.26	-1	2	8	4	11
Fowler D	22	13	42	21	37	.05	.04	72	77	.06	.08	.49	.14	4	4	5	-7	6
Iannetta C	21	15	32	16	52	.09	.14	77	89	.08	.03	.45	.20	6	-2	-2	5	6
Stewart I	28	12	40	14	46	.09	.21	85	77	.03	-.02	.41	.37	-1	-8	-9	22	4
Torrealba Y	17	9	50	23	28	.10	.05	70	83	.04	.07	.38	.12	-0	4	3	-5	1
Barmes C	20	7	31	20	49	.17	.13	73	88	.00	.06	.39	.18	-8	1	1	1	-6
Spilborghs R	20	9	46	18	36	.04	.08	76	77	.03	.03	.34	.20	-2	-1	-5	1	-6
Atkins G	15	11	42	16	42	.09	.08	71	91	.08	.06	.30	.09	3	2	-7	-9	-11
MLB Average	***18***	***10***	***43***	***19***	***38***	***.10***	***.11***	***75***	***83***	***.05***	***.04***	***.39***	***.19***	--	--	--	--	--

Pitching Stats

Player	PRC	IP	BFP	G	GS	K	BB	IBB	HBP	H	HR	DP	DER	SB	CS	PO	W	L	Sv	Op	Hld	H-A	R^L	RA	ERA	FIP
Jimenez U	*109*	218.0	914	33	33	198	85	6	10	183	13	19	.719	15	6	2	15	12	0	0	0	.007	-.037	3.59	3.47	3.33
Marquis J	*81*	216.0	921	33	33	115	80	6	4	218	15	30	.707	18	4	0	15	13	0	0	0	-.010	-.019	4.33	4.04	4.07
de la Rosa J	*76*	185.0	799	33	32	193	83	3	9	172	20	16	.684	16	3	2	16	9	0	0	0	.024	-.074	4.62	4.38	3.91
Hammel J	*65*	176.7	771	34	30	133	42	6	9	203	17	13	.660	18	2	1	10	8	0	0	0	.072	-.010	4.79	4.33	3.66
Cook A	*58*	158.0	675	27	27	78	47	2	2	175	19	21	.699	4	4	3	11	6	0	0	0	-.008	-.018	4.33	4.16	4.62
Street H	*36*	61.7	240	64	0	70	13	4	0	43	7	2	.753	9	0	0	4	1	35	37	2	.026	.035	3.21	3.06	2.79
Daley M	*23*	51.0	211	57	0	55	18	2	2	43	6	4	.708	2	0	0	1	1	0	3	12	.013	-.047	4.24	4.24	3.58
Betancourt R	*23*	25.3	98	32	0	29	5	1	0	17	1	2	.730	4	0	0	3	1	1	3	12	.011	-.057	1.78	1.78	1.85
Fogg J	*19*	45.7	187	24	1	27	20	1	1	32	7	5	.788	3	0	1	0	2	0	0	1	.061	-.092	3.94	3.74	5.28
Contreras J	*16*	17.0	76	7	2	17	8	1	0	20	2	2	.633	4	0	0	1	0	0	1	1	.025	-.009	1.59	1.59	3.92
Morales F *	*15*	40.0	179	40	2	41	23	4	1	38	4	3	.673	1	1	1	3	2	7	8	7	-.057	-.047	4.95	4.50	3.90
Corpas M	*10*	33.7	146	35	0	24	7	0	1	44	3	5	.631	1	1	0	1	3	1	3	7	.031	-.102	5.88	5.88	3.60
Belisle M	*9*	31.0	133	24	0	22	5	1	1	35	6	4	.677	4	0	0	3	1	0	0	1	-.012	.028	6.10	5.52	4.73
Peralta J	*7*	24.7	113	27	0	22	12	2	3	27	3	2	.671	2	0	1	0	3	0	1	6	.010	-.153	6.20	6.20	4.53
Beimel J *	*7*	15.7	68	26	0	11	4	1	0	19	2	1	.667	2	0	0	0	1	0	1	3	-.046	.008	4.02	4.02	3.98
Grilli J	*6*	19.3	99	22	0	22	13	2	0	29	2	1	.548	3	1	1	0	1	1	1	3	.049	-.089	6.05	6.05	3.93
Embree A *	*6*	24.7	111	36	0	12	12	2	1	28	3	5	.675	3	3	2	2	2	0	3	6	-.055	.034	6.57	5.84	5.10
Rincon J	*6*	26.3	116	26	0	25	20	4	1	18	2	3	.750	2	0	0	3	2	0	0	1	-.145	.002	7.86	7.52	4.18
Flores R *	*4*	12.0	52	27	0	14	2	0	0	14	2	0	.647	1	0	0	0	1	0	0	10	-.002	-.053	5.25	5.25	3.48
Chacin J	*4*	11.0	48	9	1	13	11	0	0	6	1	1	.783	3	1	0	0	1	0	0	0	-.083	-.091	4.91	4.91	4.97
Herges M	*4*	9.3	40	9	0	8	2	0	0	10	2	2	.643	0	1	0	1	0	0	0	0	.263	-.062	3.86	2.89	4.87
Rusch G *	*4*	18.7	92	11	0	13	3	1	0	35	3	3	.548	0	0	0	2	0	0	0	1	-.047	-.082	7.23	6.75	4.17
Eaton A	*3*	8.0	41	4	0	7	8	2	0	9	1	0	.680	0	0	0	1	0	0	0	0	.019	.043	5.63	5.63	5.28
Speier R	*2*	5.7	25	5	0	2	3	0	1	6	0	1	.684	0	0	0	0	0	0	0	0	.342	.184	4.76	4.76	4.56
Rogers E	*2*	4.0	16	1	1	3	2	0	0	3	0	1	.727	0	0	0	0	0	0	0	0	--	.080	4.50	4.50	3.15

Italicized stats have been adjusted for home park.

Batted Ball Pitching Stats

	% of PA		% of Batted Balls					Out %		Runs Per Event				Total Runs vs. Avg.				
Player	K%	BB%	GB%	LD%	FB%	IF/F	HR/OF	GB	OF	NIP	GB	LD	OF	NIP	GB	LD	FB	Tot
Jimenez U	22	10	53	20	28	.11	.08	80	81	.04	.01	.35	.17	-2	-11	-9	-17	-39
Street H	29	5	38	19	43	.08	.11	86	85	-.04	-.02	.34	.18	-7	-5	-5	-2	-18
Marquis J	12	9	56	17	27	.04	.08	80	81	.08	.00	.42	.17	4	-9	2	-8	-12
Fogg J	14	11	48	10	42	.19	.13	76	88	.09	.04	.35	.20	2	-0	-5	-0	-4
de la Rosa J	24	12	45	21	34	.08	.12	76	82	.04	.04	.41	.21	-1	-2	2	-2	-3
Daley M	26	9	34	11	55	.17	.10	84	63	.01	-.01	.43	.33	-2	-4	-5	9	-2
Rincon J	22	18	48	18	34	.09	.10	91	74	.10	-.06	.44	.24	3	-4	-1	-0	-2
Morales F	23	13	27	23	50	.07	.08	63	81	.06	.09	.27	.14	1	0	-2	-1	-1
Corpas M	16	5	49	22	30	.12	.10	70	77	.00	.06	.38	.23	-2	2	2	0	2
Belisle M	17	5	40	21	40	.08	.16	78	81	-.01	.02	.35	.28	-2	-0	0	4	2
Cook A	12	7	57	19	25	.01	.14	79	79	.06	.01	.37	.26	-1	-5	2	6	2
Embree A	11	12	41	23	36	.10	.11	71	83	.13	.06	.35	.18	2	1	1	0	4
Peralta J	19	13	25	26	49	.06	.09	89	71	.07	-.05	.32	.28	1	-2	1	5	5
Hammel J	17	7	46	23	31	.08	.11	75	83	.01	.05	.41	.19	-8	4	13	-4	6
MLB Average	***18***	***10***	***43***	***19***	***38***	***.10***	***.11***	***75***	***83***	***.05***	***.04***	***.39***	***.19***	--	--	--	--	--

Fielding Stats

Name	INN	SBA/G	CS%	ERA	WP+PB/G	PO	A	TE	FE
Catchers									
Iannetta C	763.7	0.77	23%	4.21	0.306	542	59	5	0
Torrealba Y	545.3	0.87	8%	4.37	0.363	505	27	0	0
Phillips P	111.3	1.37	6%	4.12	0.485	95	8	1	0
Bellorin E	18.0	0.00	0%	2.00	0.000	11	0	0	0

Name	Inn	PO	A	TE	FE	FPct	DPS	DPT	ZRDif	OOZ	Dif
First Base											
Helton T	1275.0	1349	96	2	1	.998	8	0	.009	34	-8
Atkins G	126.3	124	5	0	1	.992	0	0	.068	3	-11
Giambi J	34.0	29	2	0	0	1.000	1	0	--	1	--
Baker J	3.0	3	0	0	0	1.000	0	0	--	--	--
Second Base											
Barmes C	1147.0	241	413	4	8	.982	37	47	.032	30	-1
Stewart I	152.3	36	43	0	3	.963	3	5	-.146	5	5
Quintanilla	75.7	23	28	0	1	.981	4	6	--	1	--
Young Jr. E	44.0	8	10	0	0	1.000	0	1	--	0	--
Baker J	17.0	4	5	1	0	.900	1	0	--	2	--
McCoy M	2.0	0	0	0	0	0.000	0	0	--	--	--
Shortstop											
Tulowitzki T	1294.0	215	433	3	6	.986	40	44	-.001	42	-6
Barmes C	103.3	13	49	0	1	.984	3	3	.110	5	10
Quintanilla	41.0	13	15	0	1	.966	3	2	--	2	--
Third Base											
Stewart I	831.0	43	176	3	4	.969	9	1	.045	36	2
Atkins G	577.0	37	137	1	7	.956	13	0	.009	24	0
Quintanilla	16.0	1	6	0	0	1.000	0	0	--	1	--
Baker J	14.3	0	2	0	0	1.000	0	0	--	0	--

Name	Inn	PO	A	TE	FE	FPct	DPS	DPT	ZRDif	OOZ	Dif
Left Field											
Smith S	627.3	135	4	0	1	.993	1	0	.024	35	5
Spilborghs	415.0	83	5	1	0	.989	1	0	.027	25	10
Gonzalez C	294.3	67	2	0	0	1.000	0	0	.021	24	31
Murton M	74.7	12	0	0	0	1.000	0	0	--	5	--
Stewart I	27.0	4	1	0	0	1.000	0	0	--	3	--
Center Field											
Fowler D	977.7	247	5	0	4	.984	2	0	-.010	62	-5
Gonzalez C	309.7	82	3	1	1	.977	0	0	.016	30	29
Spilborghs	113.0	30	2	1	1	.941	0	0	-.105	11	29
Young Jr. E	38.0	4	0	0	0	1.000	0	0	--	0	--
Right Field											
Hawpe B	1195.0	213	4	2	3	.977	1	0	-.032	44	-15
Spilborghs	192.3	37	1	1	0	.974	0	0	-.015	12	10
Gonzalez C	28.7	3	1	0	0	1.000	0	0	--	0	--
Murton M	10.3	1	0	0	0	1.000	0	0	--	0	--
Stewart I	10.0	1	0	0	0	1.000	0	0	--	0	--
McCoy M	1.3	1	0	0	0	1.000	0	0	--	--	--

Detroit Tigers

Stat Facts:

- Justin Verlander led the majors with 269 strikeouts
- Verlander faced the most batters (982) of any pitcher in the majors
- Verlander had the most caught stealing (16) in the majors, and allowed only 9 SBs
- In 390 PAs, Adam Everett led the AL with 15 sacrifice hits
- Curtis Granderson grounded into 1 double play in 710 PAs
- Granderson's L-R of .126 was highest among AL regulars
- The Tigers' bunt defense ranked 28th in the majors
- 91% of Brandon Inge's fly balls were outs, highest rate among ML regulars
- Jarrod Washburn allowed 12 home runs in 43 IP
- Eddie Bonine allowed zero SBs in 4 attempts
- Fernando Rodney's LD% (11%) was lowest of any ML pitcher with at least 75 IP
- Placido Polanco committed zero fielding errors, and just 2 total errors

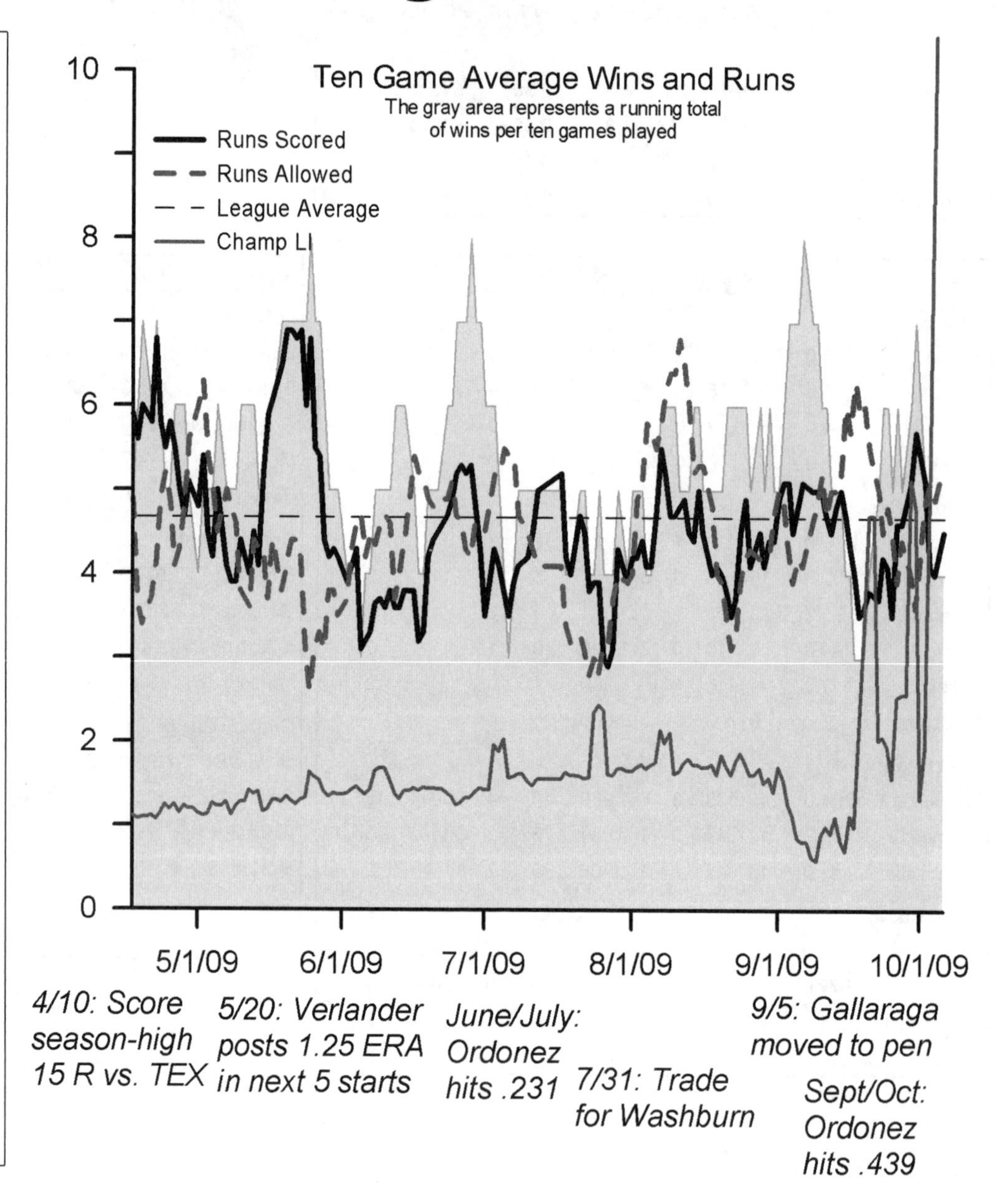

Team Batting and Pitching/Fielding Stats by Month

	April	May	June	July	Aug	Sept/Oct
Wins	11	17	15	10	16	17
Losses	10	11	13	14	13	16
RS/G	5.3	5.1	4.0	4.3	4.3	4.4
RA/G	5.0	3.8	4.8	4.0	5.0	4.8
OBP	.339	.335	.319	.317	.319	.350
SLG	.417	.430	.417	.405	.420	.409
FIP	4.72	3.83	4.90	4.45	4.86	4.52
DER	.705	.711	.686	.693	.699	.691

Batting Stats

Player	BR	Runs	RBI	PA	Outs	H	2B	3B	HR	TB	K	BB	IBB	HBP	SH	SF	SB	CS	GDP	H-A	L^R	BA	OBP	SLG	GPA
Cabrera M	115	96	103	685	437	198	34	0	34	334	107	68	14	5	0	1	6	2	22	.047	.018	.324	.396	.547	.315
Granderson C	98	91	71	710	481	157	23	8	30	286	141	72	4	2	3	2	20	6	1	-.049	.126	.249	.327	.453	.260
Polanco P	76	82	72	676	459	176	31	4	10	245	46	36	2	9	7	5	7	2	15	.022	-.004	.285	.331	.396	.248
Inge B	72	71	84	637	450	129	16	1	27	228	170	54	1	17	1	3	2	5	12	.014	.058	.230	.314	.406	.243
Ordonez M	68	54	50	518	341	144	24	2	9	199	65	51	2	0	0	2	3	1	19	.042	.058	.310	.376	.428	.276
Raburn R	46	44	45	291	195	76	11	2	16	139	60	26	2	2	1	1	5	4	6	-.031	.054	.291	.359	.533	.295
Laird G	41	49	33	477	331	93	23	2	4	132	68	40	0	10	10	4	5	0	11	.044	.050	.225	.306	.320	.218
Guillen C +	39	36	41	322	220	67	10	3	11	116	56	39	2	3	0	3	1	3	7	-.019	.005	.242	.339	.419	.257
Thames M	37	33	36	294	200	65	11	1	13	117	72	29	2	1	0	6	0	2	5	-.045	.020	.252	.323	.453	.259
Thomas C *	36	46	39	310	212	66	13	3	7	106	77	33	0	1	1	0	3	0	3	.050	.016	.240	.324	.385	.242
Santiago R +	31	29	35	296	197	70	6	2	7	101	57	17	1	4	10	3	1	2	3	.058	-.035	.267	.318	.385	.240
Everett A	31	43	44	390	274	82	21	0	3	112	61	22	0	4	15	4	5	2	9	.068	.052	.238	.288	.325	.211
Anderson J *	15	22	16	175	131	40	4	4	0	52	22	8	0	1	1	0	13	2	4	.024	.027	.242	.282	.315	.206
Avila A *	13	9	14	72	44	17	4	0	5	36	18	10	0	0	0	1	0	0	0	.172	-.105	.279	.375	.590	.316
Larish J *	11	13	7	90	63	16	3	1	4	33	25	15	0	0	0	1	0	1	4	-.177	.168	.216	.344	.446	.266
Huff A *	8	8	13	117	89	20	6	0	2	32	13	10	0	1	0	0	0	0	3	-.010	.031	.189	.265	.302	.195
Kelly D *	6	8	3	62	42	14	3	1	0	19	10	4	0	1	1	0	1	0	0	.057	.123	.250	.311	.339	.225
Ramirez W	3	6	3	13	8	4	0	1	1	9	3	1	0	0	0	1	0	0	1	-.342	.036	.364	.385	.818	.378
Porcello R	1	0	2	5	3	2	0	0	0	2	1	0	0	0	0	0	0	0	0	-.280	--	.400	.400	.400	.280
Ryan D	1	1	4	30	25	4	1	0	0	5	12	4	0	0	0	0	0	1	2	.098	-.051	.154	.267	.192	.168

Only includes batters with at least one Base Run. Italicized stats have been adjusted for home park.

Batted Ball Batting Stats

	% of PA		% of Batted Balls					Out %		Runs Per Event				Total Runs vs. Avg.				
Player	K%	BB%	GB%	LD%	FB%	IF/F	HR/OF	GB	OF	NIP	GB	LD	OF	NIP	GB	LD	FB	Tot
Cabrera M	15	11	43	20	37	.08	.19	71	78	.07	.06	.41	.33	5	4	10	28	48
Raburn R	21	10	38	15	48	.14	.20	72	77	.03	.05	.41	.36	-1	1	-3	16	13
Ordonez M	13	10	51	21	28	.07	.09	72	81	.09	.06	.38	.16	4	5	7	-5	11
Granderson C	20	10	29	21	49	.13	.14	81	87	.04	.02	.38	.22	-0	-6	2	11	6
Thames M	24	10	35	18	47	.18	.17	69	94	.02	.08	.42	.21	-2	2	-1	2	1
Guillen C	17	13	36	20	44	.07	.12	79	88	.08	.01	.34	.18	4	-4	-2	1	-0
Polanco P	7	7	43	20	37	.08	.05	73	87	.11	.05	.38	.07	1	5	8	-17	-2
Thomas C	25	11	48	16	36	.10	.11	75	80	.03	.05	.41	.22	-1	1	-4	-0	-4
Inge B	27	11	41	15	44	.10	.17	67	91	.02	.08	.37	.22	-3	5	-11	5	-5
Huff A	11	9	52	15	33	.06	.07	79	93	.10	.03	.22	.07	1	-0	-4	-4	-7
Anderson J	13	5	58	15	26	.11	.00	80	84	.02	.01	.57	.03	-2	-1	3	-7	-7
Santiago R	19	7	46	18	36	.10	.11	71	88	.01	.07	.32	.17	-3	3	-5	-3	-8
Laird G	14	10	41	14	44	.14	.03	74	85	.08	.05	.38	.07	3	2	-8	-15	-18
Everett A	16	7	43	18	40	.12	.03	73	92	.02	.06	.40	.02	-4	1	-2	-18	-22
MLB Average	*18*	*10*	*43*	*19*	*38*	*.10*	*.11*	*75*	*83*	*.05*	*.04*	*.39*	*.19*	--	--	--	--	--

Pitching Stats

Player	*PRC*	IP	BFP	G	GS	K	BB	IBB	HBP	H	HR	DP	DER	SB	CS	PO	W	L	Sv	Op	Hld	H-A	R^L	RA	ERA	FIP
Verlander J	*130*	240.0	982	35	35	269	63	5	6	219	20	15	.675	9	16	3	19	9	0	0	0	-.030	-.012	3.71	3.45	2.83
Jackson E	*101*	214.0	890	33	33	161	70	3	5	200	27	21	.715	23	9	0	13	9	0	0	0	.002	.021	3.91	3.62	4.34
Porcello R	*68*	170.7	720	31	31	89	52	0	3	176	23	26	.712	8	2	1	14	9	0	0	0	-.004	-.011	4.27	3.96	4.87
Lyon B	*48*	78.7	314	65	0	57	31	9	2	56	7	8	.770	3	2	0	6	5	3	6	15	-.044	-.011	2.86	2.86	3.81
Galarraga A	*44*	143.7	642	29	25	95	67	1	6	158	24	15	.698	3	5	0	6	10	0	0	0	-.028	-.059	5.83	5.64	5.54
Miner Z	*35*	92.3	409	51	5	62	45	1	2	101	11	15	.675	4	2	0	7	5	1	5	8	.005	.058	4.78	4.29	4.89
Rodney F	*32*	75.7	330	73	0	61	41	4	2	70	8	13	.702	2	0	0	2	5	37	38	0	-.068	.000	4.52	4.40	4.50
Perry R	*28*	61.7	273	53	0	60	38	5	1	56	7	8	.689	10	3	0	0	1	0	3	6	-.065	-.061	4.38	3.79	4.37
Seay B *	*21*	48.7	208	67	0	37	17	3	3	46	3	3	.709	0	1	0	6	3	0	4	28	.011	-.002	4.25	4.25	3.52
Ni F *	*20*	31.0	121	36	0	21	11	2	1	20	3	3	.788	1	1	1	0	0	0	2	3	-.058	-.108	2.61	2.61	4.06
Robertson N	*15*	49.7	234	28	6	35	28	3	2	59	4	6	.648	5	1	0	2	3	0	0	0	-.086	-.022	5.98	5.44	4.46
French L *	*13*	29.3	133	7	5	19	11	1	1	33	2	2	.670	1	0	0	1	2	0	0	0	-.041	-.060	3.99	3.38	3.91
Bonine E	*12*	34.3	145	10	4	19	12	1	1	40	7	7	.679	0	4	0	1	1	0	0	0	.046	.044	4.98	4.46	5.78
Zumaya J	*12*	31.0	149	29	0	30	22	3	1	34	5	2	.670	2	0	0	3	3	1	7	7	-.041	-.155	5.23	4.94	5.29
Washburn J *	*9*	43.0	193	8	8	21	16	0	2	51	12	3	.725	2	1	0	1	3	0	0	0	.043	-.114	7.33	7.33	7.10
Willis D *	*7*	33.7	160	7	7	17	28	0	1	37	4	8	.691	4	0	0	1	4	0	0	0	-.167	.068	7.49	7.49	6.31
Figaro A	*5*	17.0	83	5	3	16	10	0	1	23	3	1	.623	6	0	0	2	2	0	0	0	.047	-.202	6.88	6.35	5.54
Rincon J	*4*	10.3	49	7	0	10	6	0	0	12	2	1	.645	2	0	0	1	0	0	0	0	-.142	-.174	5.23	5.23	5.51
Dolsi F	*3*	10.7	47	6	0	3	4	0	0	13	0	3	.600	1	1	0	1	0	0	1	0	.013	-.134	5.06	1.69	3.75
Fien C	*2*	11.3	53	9	0	9	6	0	0	13	2	1	.694	0	0	0	0	1	0	0	0	-.230	.065	8.74	7.94	5.49
Bonderman J	*2*	10.3	53	8	1	5	8	0	1	16	4	2	.657	1	1	0	0	1	0	0	0	-.059	.127	8.71	8.71	9.87
Rapada C *	*1*	3.3	16	3	0	2	2	1	0	4	1	0	.727	0	0	0	0	0	0	0	0	--	-.061	5.40	5.40	6.79

Italicized stats have been adjusted for home park.

Batted Ball Pitching Stats

	% of PA		% of Batted Balls					Out %		Runs Per Event				Total Runs vs. Avg.				
Player	K%	BB%	GB%	LD%	FB%	IF/F	HR/OF	GB	OF	NIP	GB	LD	OF	NIP	GB	LD	FB	Tot
Verlander J	27	7	36	21	43	.09	.08	70	87	-.02	.07	.44	.11	-20	3	5	-20	-32
Lyon B	18	11	47	17	36	.14	.11	87	81	.06	-.04	.39	.18	0	-8	-3	-4	-15
Jackson E	18	8	39	18	42	.12	.11	75	85	.03	.04	.36	.18	-5	-1	-4	1	-9
Ni F	17	10	31	13	56	.23	.08	78	91	.05	.01	.52	.09	-0	-2	-1	-4	-6
Seay B	18	10	37	16	47	.07	.05	81	77	.05	.01	.43	.13	0	-3	-1	-1	-5
Porcello R	12	8	54	17	29	.05	.14	78	82	.06	.02	.36	.22	-1	-3	-3	3	-4
Rodney F	18	13	58	11	31	.09	.11	73	80	.08	.04	.48	.21	4	1	-5	-1	-2
Perry R	22	14	42	19	39	.07	.11	75	89	.07	.03	.47	.15	3	-2	2	-3	0
French L	14	9	28	22	50	.12	.04	62	84	.06	.16	.36	.10	0	3	1	-2	3
Zumaya J	20	15	34	14	52	.06	.11	72	80	.08	.05	.46	.21	2	0	-1	3	5
Robertson N	15	13	41	18	41	.07	.06	72	81	.10	.05	.47	.11	4	1	3	-3	5
Bonine E	13	9	56	16	28	.03	.23	78	74	.07	.02	.34	.41	1	-0	-1	6	6
Willis D	11	18	52	17	31	.12	.13	79	69	.18	.00	.35	.28	6	-1	-1	2	6
Miner Z	15	11	45	19	36	.10	.11	76	81	.08	.03	.41	.20	4	-1	3	2	7
Washburn J	11	9	42	15	44	.08	.20	73	83	.10	.07	.30	.30	1	2	-3	10	10
Galarraga A	15	11	40	22	39	.09	.15	76	84	.09	.03	.35	.24	6	-1	3	11	19
MLB Average	***18***	***10***	***43***	***19***	***38***	***.10***	***.11***	***75***	***83***	***.05***	***.04***	***.39***	***.19***	--	--	--	--	--

Fielding Stats

Name	INN	SBA/G	CS%	ERA	WP+PB/G	PO	A	TE	FE
Catchers									
Laird G	1090.3	0.82	40%	4.23	0.371	844	78	2	1
Avila A	153.3	0.88	27%	5.52	0.528	101	7	0	0
Sardinha D	92.7	1.17	17%	3.50	0.486	90	7	0	0
Ryan D	78.7	0.69	33%	3.89	0.229	60	6	0	0
Treanor M	32.0	1.13	0%	5.91	0.563	28	0	0	0

Name	Inn	PO	A	TE	FE	FPct	DPS	DPT	ZRDif	OOZ	Dif
First Base											
Cabrera M	1315.0	1215	105	5	2	.995	10	4	-.026	52	5
Larish J	67.0	68	5	0	0	1.000	0	0	--	3	--
Raburn R	36.0	35	2	0	0	1.000	0	0	--	1	--
Guillen C	18.0	19	0	0	0	1.000	0	0	--	0	--
Kelly D	7.0	7	0	0	0	1.000	0	0	--	1	--
Thames M	3.0	3	0	0	0	1.000	0	0	--	--	--
Laird G	1.0	1	0	0	0	1.000	0	0	--	--	--
Second Base											
Polanco P	1289.0	290	439	2	0	.997	43	62	.012	39	3
Santiago R	156.7	33	52	0	0	1.000	2	13	-.018	5	4
Kelly D	1.0	0	0	0	0	0.000	0	0	--	--	--
Shortstop											
Everett A	942.7	161	282	6	8	.969	39	27	.037	39	3
Santiago R	502.3	78	159	2	4	.975	15	20	.031	12	-14
Dlugach B	2.0	0	0	0	0	0.000	0	0	--	0	--
Third Base											
Inge B	1387.0	143	281	13	7	.955	34	1	.049	55	-2
Raburn R	33.0	2	4	2	2	.600	0	0	--	2	--
Kelly D	14.0	2	5	0	0	1.000	1	0	--	1	--
Larish J	6.0	1	1	0	0	1.000	0	0	--	1	--
Dlugach B	5.0	1	3	0	0	1.000	0	0	--	1	--
Santiago R	2.0	0	0	0	0	0.000	0	0	--	--	--

Name	Inn	PO	A	TE	FE	FPct	DPS	DPT	ZRDif	OOZ	Dif
Left Field											
Raburn R	437.7	112	9	0	4	.960	2	0	-.062	33	25
Guillen C	322.7	79	0	0	2	.975	0	0	-.026	20	12
Anderson J	305.3	66	3	0	2	.972	0	0	.032	16	2
Thomas C	142.0	38	0	2	0	.950	0	0	-.019	10	20
Thames M	125.0	19	0	0	0	1.000	0	0	-.051	3	-26
Kelly D	97.3	23	0	0	0	1.000	0	0	--	4	--
Ramirez W	17.0	3	1	0	0	1.000	0	0	--	0	--
Center Field											
Granderson	1384.0	400	4	2	1	.993	2	0	.005	108	10
Raburn R	33.0	14	0	0	0	1.000	0	0	--	2	--
Thomas C	25.0	8	0	0	0	1.000	0	0	--	1	--
Anderson J	5.0	0	0	0	0	0.000	0	0	--	--	--
Right Field											
Ordonez M	796.3	149	6	1	1	.987	1	0	.017	26	-20
Thomas C	502.3	127	5	1	1	.985	3	0	-.019	31	10
Anderson J	87.7	13	1	0	0	1.000	1	0	--	3	--
Raburn R	43.7	10	0	0	0	1.000	0	0	--	1	--
Kelly D	14.0	6	1	0	0	1.000	0	0	--	1	--
Ramirez W	3.0	1	0	0	0	1.000	0	0	--	0	--

Florida Marlins

Stat Facts:

- Dan Uggla played the most innings (1401) of any middle infielder
- Uggla had the lowest ZR (.774) of any regular second baseman
- Nick Johnson walked in 28% of his PAs
- 58% of Hanley Ramirez's ground balls were outs, lowest rate in the majors
- Ramirez's GBR of .14 was highest among ML regulars
- Josh Johnson's total of -38 runs below average was eighth-best in the majors
- Johnson's GPA (.212) was 3rd-highest of any pitcher
- Rick VandenHurk went 0-for-21 with 17 strikeouts
- 18% of the flyballs allowed by Chris Volstad were home runs
- Chris Coghlan made the fewest OOZ plays (33) of any left fielder with at least 900 innings
- Kiko Calero had 4 pickoffs in 60 IP
- Ricky Nolasco's FIP (3.29) was far better than his ERA (5.06)

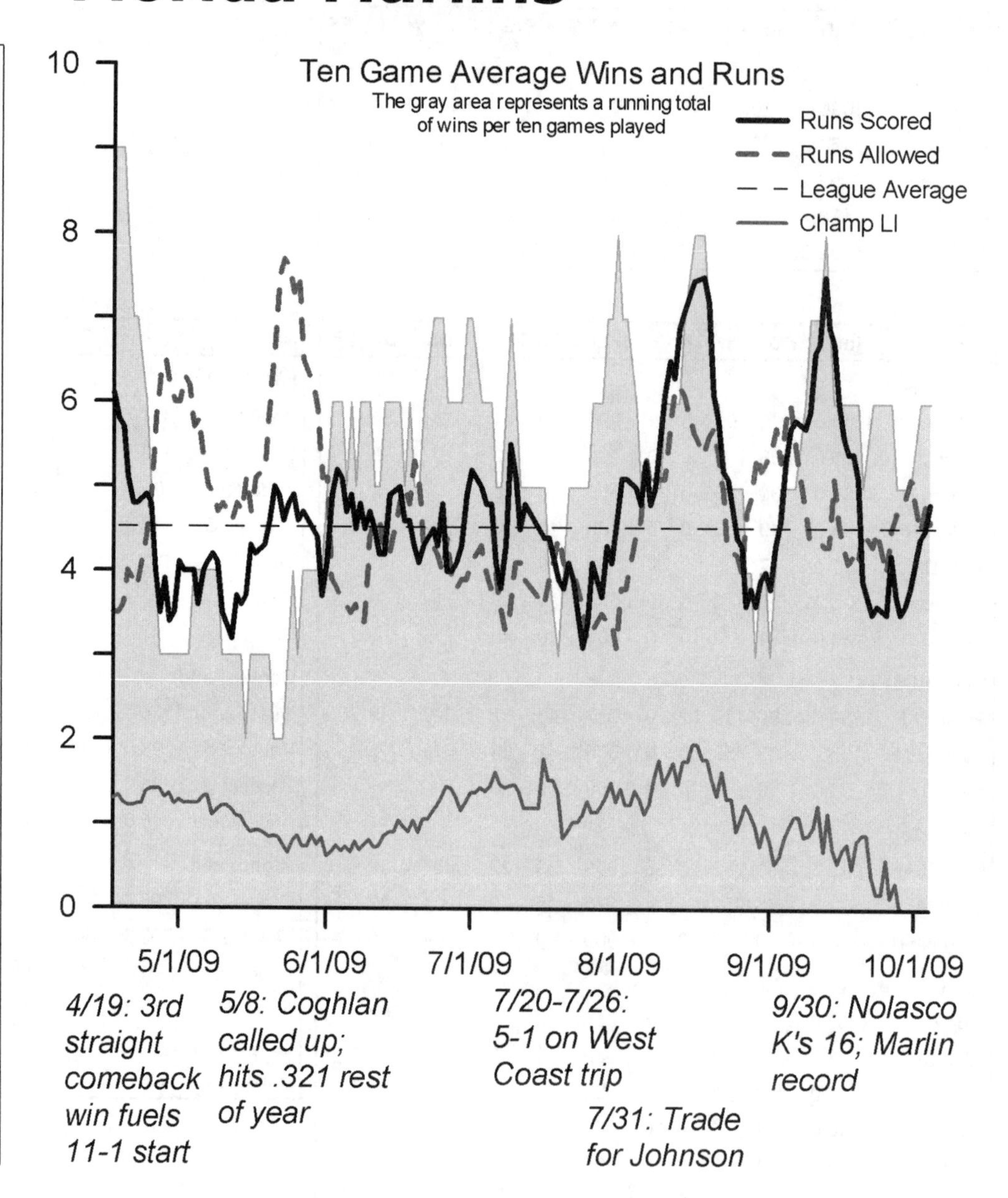

Team Batting and Pitching/Fielding Stats by Month

	April	May	June	July	Aug	Sept/Oct
Wins	14	9	17	14	14	19
Losses	8	20	11	10	14	12
RS/G	5.1	4.1	4.7	4.3	5.3	5.1
RA/G	4.8	5.6	4.3	3.7	5.5	4.5
OBP	.328	.313	.338	.330	.375	.353
SLG	.398	.372	.432	.399	.451	.436
FIP	3.90	4.60	3.81	4.00	4.21	4.15
DER	.694	.679	.690	.712	.666	.682

Batting Stats

Player	*BR*	Runs	RBI	PA	Outs	H	2B	3B	HR	TB	K	BB	IBB	HBP	SH	SF	SB	CS	GDP	H-A	L^R	BA	OBP	SLG	*GPA*
Ramirez H	*118*	101	106	652	396	197	42	1	24	313	101	61	14	9	1	5	27	8	9	.013	-.064	.342	.410	.543	*.327*
Uggla D	*94*	84	90	668	438	137	27	1	31	259	150	92	4	7	1	4	2	1	10	.055	-.023	.243	.354	.459	*.280*
Coghlan C *	*86*	84	47	565	350	162	31	6	9	232	77	53	2	4	3	1	8	5	3	-.050	.014	.321	.390	.460	*.296*
Cantu J	*84*	67	100	643	432	169	42	0	16	259	81	47	4	6	0	5	3	1	15	.043	.046	.289	.345	.443	*.271*
Ross C	*79*	73	90	604	428	151	37	1	24	262	122	34	1	9	0	2	5	2	18	.022	.062	.270	.321	.469	*.267*
Hermida J *	*60*	48	47	491	326	111	14	2	13	168	101	56	4	4	0	2	5	2	6	-.014	.062	.259	.348	.392	*.260*
Baker J *	*51*	59	50	423	282	101	25	0	9	153	89	41	5	5	2	2	0	0	10	.013	.046	.271	.349	.410	*.265*
Bonifacio E	*44*	72	27	509	359	116	11	6	1	142	95	34	0	2	8	4	21	9	5	.018	.044	.252	.303	.308	*.218*
Paulino R	*32*	24	27	266	182	65	10	1	8	101	48	25	2	0	1	1	1	0	8	.032	.023	.272	.340	.423	*.264*
Gload R *	*30*	33	30	259	173	60	10	2	6	92	30	23	4	2	1	3	0	0	3	.055	.117	.261	.329	.400	*.253*
Johnson N *	*24*	24	18	150	81	29	8	0	2	43	18	36	1	6	1	3	0	2	4	-.047	.090	.279	.477	.413	*.324*
Maybin C	*22*	30	13	199	137	44	12	2	4	72	51	17	1	1	4	1	1	3	2	-.038	-.038	.250	.318	.409	*.250*
Helms W	*22*	18	33	234	167	58	11	0	3	78	54	13	1	3	1	3	1	1	10	-.072	-.009	.271	.318	.364	*.239*
Carroll B	*17*	18	18	158	110	33	8	2	3	54	33	11	1	4	1	1	0	0	2	.080	.046	.234	.306	.383	*.238*
Johnson J *	*6*	8	10	77	50	12	1	0	3	22	33	6	0	0	9	0	0	0	0	.042	.093	.194	.265	.355	*.212*
Amezaga A +	*4*	6	5	75	55	15	3	0	0	18	16	5	2	0	0	1	1	1	0	-.043	-.067	.217	.267	.261	*.189*
Sanchez G	*3*	2	3	23	17	5	0	0	2	11	3	2	0	0	0	0	0	0	1	.105	.126	.238	.304	.524	*.273*
De Aza A *	*3*	6	3	27	15	5	1	0	0	6	5	5	0	0	1	1	0	0	0	.023	.284	.250	.385	.300	*.253*
Hayes B	*2*	5	2	12	9	3	1	0	1	7	4	0	0	1	0	0	0	0	1	.028	.240	.273	.333	.636	*.315*

Only includes batters with at least one Base Run. Italicized stats have been adjusted for home park.

Batted Ball Batting Stats

	% of PA		% of Batted Balls					Out %		Runs Per Event				Total Runs vs. Avg.				
Player	**K%**	**BB%**	**GB%**	**LD%**	**FB%**	**IF/F**	**HR/OF**	**GB**	**OF**	**NIP**	**GB**	**LD**	**OF**	**NIP**	**GB**	**LD**	**FB**	**Tot**
Ramirez H	15	11	39	20	42	.10	.13	58	80	.07	.14	.41	.23	5	20	10	14	49
Coghlan C	14	10	48	23	30	.07	.08	71	77	.08	.07	.41	.19	4	8	13	-1	24
Uggla D	22	15	37	17	46	.10	.18	75	86	.07	.04	.37	.26	9	-2	-8	16	15
Cantu J	13	8	36	21	43	.12	.08	72	86	.07	.05	.42	.13	1	2	14	-4	12
Johnson N	12	28	46	19	35	.10	.07	73	77	.21	.04	.25	.19	11	0	-2	1	10
Ross C	20	7	33	19	48	.14	.13	72	83	.01	.05	.40	.22	-7	-1	2	11	4
Hermida J	21	12	41	20	39	.14	.12	67	90	.06	.09	.36	.15	3	6	-1	-6	2
Paulino R	18	9	39	21	39	.08	.12	68	92	.04	.07	.39	.14	-0	2	2	-2	2
Baker J	21	11	49	20	31	.04	.11	79	72	.04	.02	.40	.26	0	-3	1	4	2
Gload R	12	10	40	21	39	.08	.08	75	88	.10	.04	.36	.12	2	-0	2	-3	1
Maybin C	26	9	55	17	28	.06	.13	73	79	.01	.07	.48	.26	-2	3	-1	-1	-0
Carroll B	21	9	39	19	42	.11	.08	79	81	.03	.02	.39	.16	-1	-1	-0	-1	-3
Helms W	23	7	43	18	39	.09	.05	70	76	-.01	.05	.38	.15	-4	0	-2	-2	-7
Bonifacio E	19	7	53	19	28	.04	.01	75	80	.01	.04	.36	.06	-5	7	-4	-18	-21
MLB Average	***18***	***10***	***43***	***19***	***38***	***.10***	***.11***	***75***	***83***	***.05***	***.04***	***.39***	***.19***	--	--	--	--	--

Pitching Stats

Player	PRC	IP	BFP	G	GS	K	BB	IBB	HBP	H	HR	DP	DER	SB	CS	PO	W	L	Sv	Op	Hld	H-A	R^L	RA	ERA	FIP
Johnson J	102	209.0	855	33	33	191	58	6	6	184	14	20	.700	18	8	0	15	5	0	0	0	-.029	.007	3.32	3.23	3.03
Nolasco R	58	185.0	785	31	31	195	44	7	2	188	23	8	.666	13	4	1	13	9	0	0	0	.010	.004	5.40	5.06	3.29
Calero K	47	60.0	239	67	0	69	30	4	1	36	1	2	.746	7	3	4	2	2	0	5	12	-.004	-.049	1.95	1.95	2.42
Volstad C	43	159.0	682	29	29	107	59	3	3	169	29	22	.694	21	10	1	9	13	0	0	0	.018	.014	5.66	5.21	5.29
Sanchez A	34	86.0	383	16	16	71	46	5	1	84	10	8	.702	11	1	0	4	8	0	0	0	-.011	.030	4.08	3.87	4.48
Sanches B	31	56.3	248	47	0	51	26	8	6	50	5	3	.706	6	3	0	4	2	0	3	9	-.086	-.006	2.88	2.56	3.77
West S *	29	103.3	467	20	20	70	44	0	3	115	11	12	.667	3	0	0	8	6	0	0	0	-.046	.033	5.40	4.79	4.54
Badenhop B	29	72.0	303	35	2	57	24	4	1	71	5	11	.685	4	0	0	7	4	0	1	2	-.016	-.032	4.00	3.75	3.35
Pinto R *	28	61.3	275	73	0	58	45	2	2	53	4	8	.693	2	4	0	4	1	0	4	13	.042	.058	3.67	3.23	4.31
Meyer D *	26	58.3	242	71	0	56	21	2	1	47	7	5	.720	3	0	0	3	2	2	2	20	.077	.017	3.70	3.09	3.82
Nunez L	26	68.7	293	75	0	60	27	5	4	59	13	5	.735	8	1	0	4	6	26	33	14	.052	.002	4.33	4.06	5.00
VandenHurk R	21	58.7	256	11	11	49	21	3	4	57	11	3	.725	4	1	0	3	2	0	0	0	-.006	-.059	4.45	4.30	5.04
Miller A *	21	80.0	366	20	14	59	43	1	2	85	7	6	.671	13	3	0	3	5	0	0	1	-.012	.038	5.85	4.84	4.46
Donnelly B	14	25.3	104	30	0	25	9	1	1	22	1	4	.662	2	0	0	3	0	2	2	9	.054	-.039	2.84	1.78	2.76
Lindstrom M	11	47.3	219	54	0	39	24	2	2	54	5	4	.651	5	2	0	2	1	15	17	8	.067	-.031	6.65	5.89	4.40
Wood T	11	22.3	97	18	0	16	10	1	1	22	2	3	.706	1	0	0	1	0	0	0	1	.008	.012	3.22	2.82	4.23
Martinez C	7	26.3	112	15	0	18	8	1	0	27	2	2	.679	0	0	0	1	1	0	1	0	-.070	.263	5.47	5.13	3.57
Penn H	2	22.0	120	16	1	27	20	2	2	30	3	0	.559	4	1	0	1	0	0	0	1	.189	-.057	11.05	7.77	5.20
Martinez C	1	2.3	13	2	0	2	2	0	1	3	1	0	.714	1	0	0	0	0	0	0	1	-.070	.263	3.86	3.86	10.87
Kensing L	1	7.3	40	6	0	7	5	0	0	14	1	1	.519	2	0	0	0	1	0	0	0	-.031	-.077	9.82	9.82	5.06
Taylor G *	1	11.0	63	3	3	5	12	0	1	16	0	0	.622	0	0	0	0	2	0	0	0	.144	.098	11.45	8.18	5.79
Ayala L	1	7.7	42	10	0	7	6	3	1	12	1	0	.556	1	1	0	0	3	0	1	2	.005	-.337	11.74	11.74	4.59
Leroux C	1	6.7	35	5	0	2	4	0	0	11	0	0	.621	0	0	0	0	0	0	0	0	.067	-.049	10.80	10.80	4.35

Italicized stats have been adjusted for home park.

Batted Ball Pitching Stats

	% of PA		% of Batted Balls					Out %		Runs Per Event				Total Runs vs. Avg.				
Player	K%	BB%	GB%	LD%	FB%	IF/F	HR/OF	GB	OF	NIP	GB	LD	OF	NIP	GB	LD	FB	Tot
Johnson J	22	7	50	18	32	.12	.09	73	80	.00	.05	.31	.18	-12	1	-14	-13	-38
Calero K	29	13	32	16	52	.13	.02	72	90	.03	.07	.35	.01	-1	0	-6	-11	-18
Badenhop B	19	8	54	20	26	.09	.10	77	76	.03	.02	.33	.21	-2	-2	-2	-3	-8
Meyer D	23	9	36	16	48	.12	.10	67	87	.02	.08	.31	.14	-2	1	-5	-2	-8
Nolasco C	25	6	38	22	40	.08	.12	72	79	-.03	.06	.37	.24	-17	3	-0	9	-6
Sanches B	21	13	33	17	50	.10	.07	70	87	.06	.07	.39	.10	2	1	-2	-4	-3
Donnelly B	24	10	39	20	41	.07	.04	58	83	.02	.12	.26	.12	-1	2	-2	-2	-3
Nunez L	20	11	41	15	44	.07	.16	69	85	.04	.07	.23	.25	-0	1	-9	7	-1
Pinto R	21	17	43	14	42	.10	.06	74	82	.09	.04	.44	.15	6	-1	-3	-3	-0
Martinez C	16	7	56	13	31	.08	.08	74	77	.03	.05	.49	.19	-1	1	-0	-1	-0
Sanchez A	19	12	42	20	38	.10	.11	77	83	.07	.03	.37	.19	3	-1	-0	-1	1
VandenHurk H	19	10	27	23	50	.08	.13	73	90	.04	.07	.37	.17	-0	0	1	2	3
Lindstrom M	18	12	45	20	35	.11	.08	67	70	.07	.09	.33	.24	2	3	-1	2	6
Miller A	16	12	48	22	30	.07	.09	77	77	.09	.03	.42	.21	4	-0	5	-1	8
Penn H	23	18	51	19	30	.15	.18	68	57	.09	.09	.56	.39	3	2	2	2	10
West S	15	10	40	19	41	.09	.09	67	85	.07	.07	.39	.16	2	6	2	1	11
Volstad C	16	9	49	17	34	.05	.18	77	78	.06	.02	.35	.32	0	-1	-5	21	15
MLB Average	***18***	***10***	***43***	***19***	***38***	***.10***	***.11***	***75***	***83***	***.05***	***.04***	***.39***	***.19***	--	--	--	--	--

Fielding Stats

Name	INN	SBA/G	CS%	ERA	WP+PB/G	PO	A	TE	FE
Catchers									
Baker J	864.0	1.01	19%	4.43	0.417	748	42	6	0
Paulino R	582.3	1.07	28%	4.16	0.417	511	46	2	0

Name	Inn	PO	A	TE	FE	FPct	DPS	DPT	ZRDif	OOZ	Dif
First Base											
Cantu J	850.0	829	38	2	3	.993	5	0	-.022	24	-6
Gload R	294.7	266	20	0	1	.997	2	0	.057	10	-0
Johnson N	260.7	192	24	0	5	.977	0	0	-.115	11	8
Helms W	31.0	33	5	0	1	.974	0	0	--	0	--
Sanchez G	8.0	12	0	0	0	1.000	0	0	--	0	--
Hayes B	2.0	2	0	0	0	1.000	0	0	--	--	--
Second Base											
Uggla D	1401.0	264	426	10	6	.977	36	56	-.039	39	0
Bonifacio E	38.0	6	13	0	0	1.000	1	3	--	2	--
Coghlan C	7.0	2	0	0	0	1.000	0	0	--	--	--
Shortstop											
Ramirez H	1259.0	221	349	5	5	.983	34	39	.007	46	-2
Bonifacio E	135.3	11	32	2	1	.935	3	2	-.095	7	13
Amezaga A	42.0	5	15	0	0	1.000	0	0	--	3	--
Gonzalez A	10.0	0	2	0	0	1.000	0	0	--	0	--
Third Base											
Bonifacio E	717.7	48	151	8	6	.934	13	0	-.036	28	-3
Helms W	365.7	31	70	5	2	.935	10	1	.038	8	-20
Cantu J	355.0	26	45	3	4	.910	8	0	-.155	13	-5
Gonzalez A	8.0	0	1	0	0	1.000	0	0	--	0	--

Name	Inn	PO	A	TE	FE	FPct	DPS	DPT	ZRDif	OOZ	Dif
Left Field											
Coghlan C	1039.0	209	3	0	5	.977	1	0	-.017	33	-19
Hermida J	340.0	61	0	0	1	.984	0	0	-.046	11	-18
Carroll B	32.0	11	0	0	0	1.000	0	0	--	2	--
Bonifacio E	21.3	3	0	0	0	1.000	0	0	--	0	--
De Aza A	10.0	2	0	0	0	1.000	0	0	--	1	--
Amezaga A	3.0	1	0	0	0	1.000	0	0	--	0	--
Gload R	0.7	1	0	0	0	1.000	0	0	--	0	--
Center Field											
Ross C	858.3	233	4	1	1	.992	2	0	-.008	53	-6
Maybin C	416.0	124	1	0	1	.992	0	0	-.007	39	26
Amezaga A	81.3	27	0	0	0	1.000	0	0	--	11	--
Bonifacio E	58.7	20	0	0	0	1.000	0	0	--	6	--
De Aza A	30.0	17	0	0	1	.944	0	0	--	4	--
Carroll B	2.0	1	1	0	0	1.000	1	0	--	--	--
Right Field											
Hermida J	620.3	140	3	0	0	1.000	1	0	-.005	38	9
Ross C	450.0	104	2	0	1	.991	1	0	.005	30	14
Carroll B	319.3	85	4	0	0	1.000	0	0	.044	25	26
Gload R	46.7	10	0	0	1	.909	0	0	--	1	--
Amezaga A	10.0	5	0	0	0	1.000	0	0	--	1	--

Houston Astros

Stat Facts:

- Hunter Pence was thrown out in 11 of 25 steal attempts, and grounded into 25 double plays
- Miguel Tejada led the majors with 29 GIDPs
- Tejada put the ball in play 89% of the time
- Defensively, Tejada started 51 DPs, most by any player in the majors
- Michael Bourn had 1 GIDP in 678 PAs
- Bourn tied for the most OOZ plays (113) by any center fielder
- Brian Moehler issued the most IBBs (12) in the majors
- Felipe Paulino allowed 20 home runs in 98 IP
- The DER behind Tim Byrdak (.786) was highest of any ML pitcher with at least 60 IP
- The Astros' bunt defense ranked 2nd in the majors
- Kaz Matsui committed zero throwing errors
- Mike Hampton's GPA (.268) was by far the highest of any pitcher

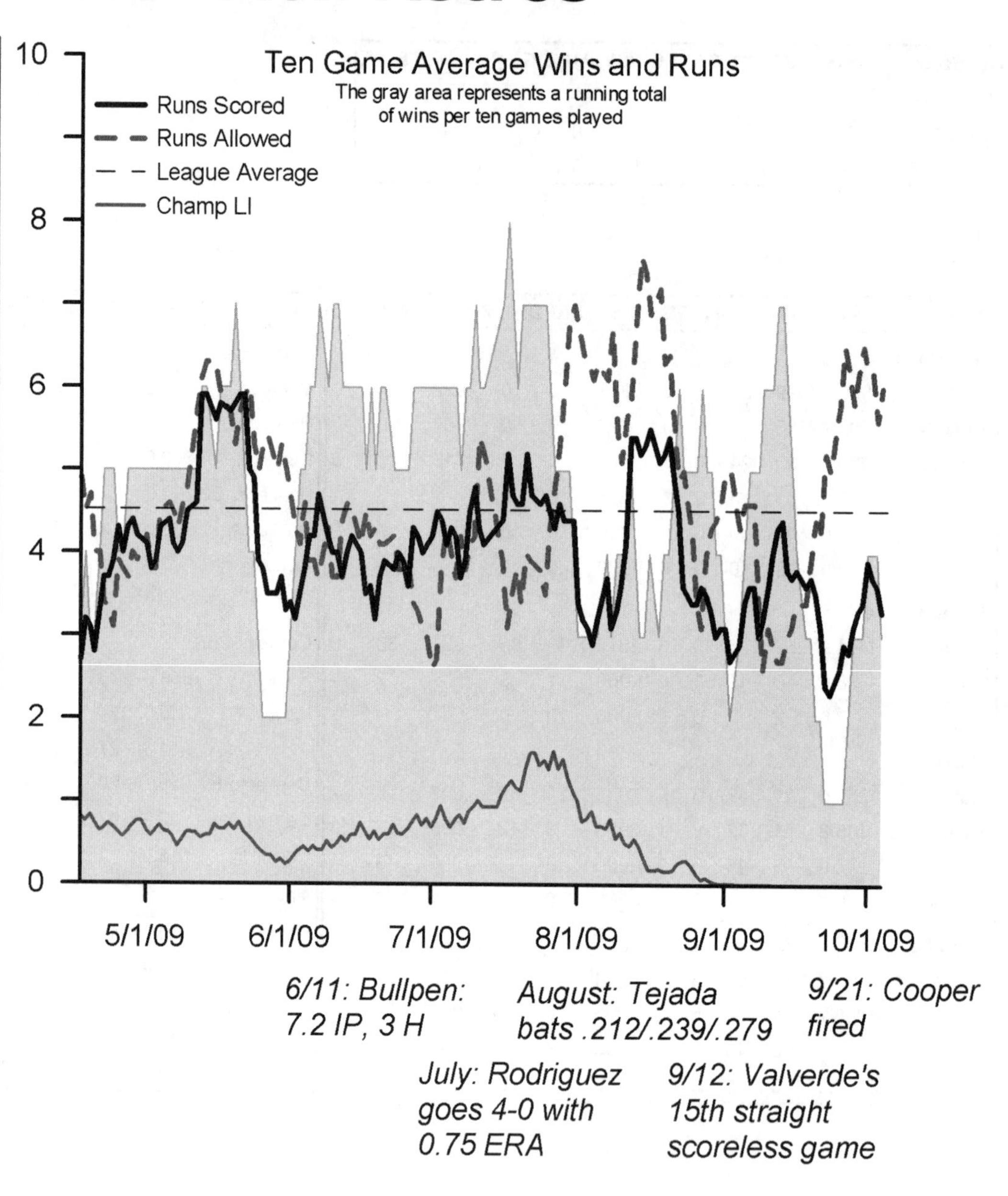

Team Batting and Pitching/Fielding Stats by Month

	April	May	June	July	Aug	Sept/Oct
Wins	9	11	16	15	12	11
Losses	13	15	11	13	16	20
RS/G	3.5	4.7	4.0	4.4	4.0	3.2
RA/G	4.2	5.5	3.7	5.1	5.3	4.5
OBP	.315	.347	.323	.332	.299	.298
SLG	.381	.429	.400	.413	.395	.380
FIP	4.54	4.64	4.31	4.19	4.25	4.14
DER	.683	.675	.718	.676	.660	.665

Batting Stats

Player	*BR*	Runs	RBI	PA	Outs	H	2B	3B	HR	TB	K	BB	IBB	HBP	SH	SF	SB	CS	GDP	H-A	L^R	BA	OBP	SLG	*GPA*
Lee C	*90*	65	102	662	451	183	35	1	26	298	51	41	5	3	0	8	5	3	21	.053	.030	.300	.343	.489	*.279*
Berkman L +	*87*	73	80	563	351	126	31	1	25	234	98	97	14	1	0	4	7	4	13	.032	-.097	.274	.399	.509	*.310*
Bourn M *	*87*	97	35	678	446	173	27	12	3	233	140	63	1	2	5	2	61	12	1	-.015	.012	.285	.354	.384	*.258*
Pence H	*85*	76	72	647	456	165	26	5	25	276	109	58	1	1	0	3	14	11	25	.012	.025	.282	.346	.472	*.277*
Tejada M	*82*	83	86	674	467	199	46	1	14	289	48	19	2	11	0	8	5	2	29	.053	.014	.313	.340	.455	*.270*
Matsui K +	*52*	56	46	533	364	119	20	2	9	170	85	34	2	3	16	4	19	3	4	.013	.042	.250	.302	.357	*.227*
Blum G +	*42*	34	49	427	297	94	14	1	10	140	61	33	4	7	0	6	0	1	9	.061	.085	.247	.314	.367	*.235*
Keppinger J	*33*	35	29	344	242	78	13	3	7	118	33	27	3	3	7	2	0	2	13	-.063	.047	.256	.320	.387	*.243*
Rodriguez I	*30*	41	34	344	260	82	15	2	8	125	74	13	0	1	1	2	0	2	13	-.010	.056	.251	.280	.382	*.224*
Michaels J	*18*	17	16	152	107	32	12	1	4	58	38	16	0	1	0	0	1	2	2	.118	.003	.237	.322	.430	*.255*
Quintero H	*14*	11	14	168	128	37	8	1	4	59	41	7	1	4	0	0	0	0	8	.067	.058	.236	.286	.376	*.225*
Erstad D *	*11*	13	11	150	112	26	8	2	2	44	31	14	3	0	1	1	0	2	2	.014	.105	.194	.268	.328	*.205*
Maysonet E	*8*	9	7	79	50	20	2	0	1	25	19	5	0	0	4	1	0	0	1	-.095	-.005	.290	.333	.362	*.243*
Coste C	*6*	3	10	112	85	21	5	0	0	26	28	8	0	0	0	1	0	0	3	.038	.016	.204	.259	.252	*.181*
Hampton M	*5*	6	7	41	25	12	1	0	1	16	8	2	0	0	1	1	0	0	0	.016	.214	.324	.350	.432	*.268*
Towles J	*4*	7	3	53	40	9	2	0	2	17	16	3	1	1	1	0	0	0	1	-.180	.108	.188	.250	.354	*.203*
Ortiz R	*1*	2	2	31	24	5	0	0	1	8	9	1	0	0	2	0	0	0	1	.061	-.146	.179	.207	.286	*.166*
Kata M +	*1*	2	5	52	43	10	1	0	0	11	5	0	0	1	0	1	1	0	3	.023	-.058	.200	.212	.220	*.152*
Fulchino J	*1*	0	0	3	2	1	1	0	0	2	0	0	0	0	0	0	0	0	0	-.475	.950	.333	.333	.667	*.320*
Norris B	*1*	1	0	18	13	3	0	0	0	3	4	0	0	1	1	0	0	0	0	-.162	-.201	.188	.235	.188	*.154*

Only includes batters with at least one Base Run. Italicized stats have been adjusted for home park.

Batted Ball Batting Stats

	% of PA		% of Batted Balls					Out %		Runs Per Event				Total Runs vs. Avg.				
Player	**K%**	**BB%**	**GB%**	**LD%**	**FB%**	**IF/F**	**HR/OF**	**GB**	**OF**	**NIP**	**GB**	**LD**	**OF**	**NIP**	**GB**	**LD**	**FB**	**Tot**
Berkman L	17	17	43	18	39	.08	.19	78	80	.12	.02	.38	.32	16	-3	-1	20	32
Lee C	8	7	36	20	44	.11	.11	72	84	.10	.05	.37	.18	1	1	8	8	18
Pence H	17	9	53	15	33	.11	.17	70	84	.05	.06	.42	.28	-0	6	-3	10	12
Tejada M	7	4	49	20	31	.13	.08	71	82	.06	.06	.36	.16	-4	9	9	-6	8
Bourn M	21	10	58	21	22	.04	.03	70	78	.03	.08	.41	.14	-2	19	3	-16	5
Michaels J	25	11	31	21	48	.23	.11	83	75	.03	-.02	.43	.27	-1	-2	1	2	-0
Keppinger J	10	9	53	18	29	.05	.09	81	87	.11	-.01	.42	.14	2	-6	3	-5	-6
Quintero H	24	7	57	10	32	.11	.12	82	66	-.02	-.01	.51	.34	-3	-3	-3	3	-7
Erstad D	21	9	56	15	29	.03	.07	79	81	.03	.03	.26	.17	-1	-1	-5	-2	-9
Coste C	25	7	45	16	39	.23	.00	82	78	-.01	-.02	.49	.04	-2	-2	-1	-5	-10
Blum G	14	9	36	18	46	.14	.08	77	84	.07	.03	.29	.13	1	-2	-5	-4	-10
Rodriguez I	22	4	54	19	27	.06	.12	77	76	-.04	.02	.30	.27	-8	-2	-5	1	-15
Matsui K	16	7	48	19	33	.13	.07	73	85	.03	.06	.31	.12	-4	5	-7	-13	-20
MLB Average	***18***	***10***	***43***	***19***	***38***	***.10***	***.11***	***75***	***83***	***.05***	***.04***	***.39***	***.19***	--	--	--	--	--

Pitching Stats

Player	PRC	IP	BFP	G	GS	K	BB	IBB	HBP	H	HR	DP	DER	SB	CS	PO	W	L	Sv	Op	Hld	H-A	R^L	RA	ERA	FIP
Rodriguez W	101	205.7	849	33	33	193	63	5	5	192	21	25	.691	3	4	1	14	12	0	0	0	-.052	-.078	3.37	3.02	3.52
Oswalt R	71	181.3	757	30	30	138	42	4	8	183	19	21	.691	2	1	0	8	6	0	0	0	.015	-.007	4.12	4.12	3.75
Hawkins L	40	63.3	259	65	0	45	16	2	2	60	7	7	.714	5	3	1	1	4	11	15	19	.043	.093	2.27	2.13	3.92
Moehler B	39	154.7	694	29	29	91	51	12	4	187	21	17	.676	12	3	0	8	12	0	0	0	.019	.008	5.88	5.47	4.57
Fulchino J	37	82.0	336	61	0	71	27	3	3	70	7	5	.719	4	2	1	6	4	0	3	12	-.015	-.030	3.62	3.40	3.52
Valverde J	35	54.0	219	52	0	56	21	1	2	40	5	5	.726	5	3	0	4	2	25	29	1	-.030	-.093	2.50	2.33	3.50
Byrdak T *	30	61.3	261	76	0	58	36	0	3	39	10	3	.786	2	4	2	1	2	0	2	9	.017	.020	3.38	3.23	5.29
Hampton M *	30	112.0	494	21	21	74	46	6	2	128	13	16	.674	5	2	0	7	10	0	0	0	.020	-.071	5.71	5.30	4.46
Paulino F	23	97.7	448	23	17	93	37	2	4	126	20	9	.633	2	2	3	3	11	0	1	0	-.050	-.102	6.73	6.27	5.11
Ortiz R	23	85.7	387	23	13	65	48	2	4	95	8	13	.660	6	3	0	3	6	0	0	1	-.061	.007	5.88	5.57	4.60
Norris B	20	55.7	249	11	10	54	25	1	3	59	9	4	.677	1	0	1	6	3	0	0	0	.030	.091	4.69	4.53	4.77
Arias A	18	45.7	209	42	0	39	19	4	6	49	1	8	.632	3	0	0	2	1	0	2	9	.009	-.029	4.14	3.35	3.11
Gervacio S	16	21.0	83	29	0	25	8	3	1	16	1	4	.667	3	1	0	1	1	0	1	6	-.014	-.108	2.14	2.14	2.25
Sampson C	15	55.3	248	49	0	33	21	6	0	66	2	5	.661	1	0	0	4	2	3	6	15	-.131	.003	5.53	5.04	3.24
Wright W *	14	44.7	204	49	0	47	25	3	0	53	9	7	.642	5	0	0	3	4	0	2	6	-.075	.036	5.44	5.44	5.14
Brocail D	6	17.7	84	20	0	9	13	0	0	21	4	3	.672	2	1	0	1	0	0	1	3	-.154	-.128	4.58	4.58	7.28
Bazardo Y	5	32.0	154	10	6	17	22	0	1	37	2	4	.652	2	0	0	1	3	0	0	0	.027	-.014	8.72	7.88	5.06
Geary G	3	20.0	97	16	0	12	10	1	1	30	4	3	.614	0	0	0	1	3	0	2	2	-.081	-.067	8.55	8.10	6.05
Lopez W	2	19.3	97	8	2	9	8	0	1	32	4	1	.627	1	0	0	0	2	0	1	0	-.093	.014	9.78	8.38	6.31
Backe B	2	13.0	65	5	1	10	6	1	0	21	5	1	.636	1	0	0	0	0	0	0	0	-.040	.004	10.38	10.38	7.77
Paronto C	1	6.7	36	6	0	3	1	0	0	15	4	0	.607	0	0	0	0	0	0	0	0	.293	.106	12.15	12.15	10.50

Italicized stats have been adjusted for home park.

Batted Ball Pitching Stats

	% of PA		% of Batted Balls					Out %		Runs Per Event				Total Runs vs. Avg.				
Player	K%	BB%	GB%	LD%	FB%	IF/F	HR/OF	GB	OF	NIP	GB	LD	OF	NIP	GB	LD	FB	Tot
Rodriguez W	23	8	45	18	37	.06	.11	76	83	.01	.03	.39	.18	-10	-3	-6	-3	-21
Fulchino J	21	9	47	14	38	.09	.09	78	81	.02	.03	.40	.19	-2	-1	-5	-1	-10
Oswalt R	18	7	43	21	36	.13	.11	75	81	.01	.03	.39	.20	-9	-4	5	-2	-10
Valverde J	26	11	41	13	46	.09	.05	70	82	.02	.07	.43	.11	-1	1	-4	-4	-9
Hawkins L	17	7	45	24	31	.10	.13	80	85	.02	-.00	.29	.21	-2	-4	-0	-1	-8
Byrdak T	22	15	42	14	45	.08	.15	81	91	.07	.01	.34	.20	3	-2	-6	1	-4
Arias A	19	12	61	16	23	.13	.04	69	81	.07	.07	.50	.12	2	3	1	-6	1
Sampson C	13	8	52	20	28	.04	.04	75	74	.07	.04	.38	.19	0	1	2	-1	2
Norris B	22	11	37	20	43	.19	.16	69	85	.04	.08	.36	.25	0	1	-1	3	4
Bazardo Y	11	15	46	24	30	.00	.06	72	87	.15	.07	.38	.10	4	2	3	-3	7
Wright D	23	12	43	23	34	.02	.18	63	92	.05	.11	.38	.24	1	3	2	2	8
Hampton M	15	10	51	20	29	.02	.13	75	79	.07	.03	.39	.24	2	0	3	4	9
Ortiz R	17	13	48	22	30	.13	.12	75	75	.09	.04	.37	.26	6	-0	4	1	10
Moehler B	13	8	44	20	36	.08	.12	76	82	.06	.03	.46	.22	-0	-2	14	7	19
Paulino F	21	9	42	19	39	.06	.18	65	81	.03	.10	.39	.30	-2	8	0	15	21
MLB Average	***18***	***10***	***43***	***19***	***38***	***.10***	***.11***	***75***	***83***	***.05***	***.04***	***.39***	***.19***	--	--	--	--	--

Fielding Stats

Name	INN	SBA/G	CS%	ERA	WP+PB/G	PO	A	TE	FE
Catchers									
Rodriguez I	748.0	0.58	29%	4.48	0.373	618	41	4	0
Quintero H	427.0	0.48	39%	4.34	0.358	358	36	5	0
Coste C	141.0	0.45	0%	4.66	0.255	116	5	0	0
Towles J	114.0	0.87	9%	5.61	0.158	83	8	0	0

Name	Inn	PO	A	TE	FE	FPct	DPS	DPT	ZRDif	OOZ	Dif
First Base											
Berkman L	1141.0	1107	116	2	4	.995	9	0	-.026	46	6
Coste C	115.7	118	7	0	1	.992	0	0	.051	5	9
Erstad D	98.7	94	7	0	0	1.000	2	0	--	2	--
Blum G	59.3	58	3	0	0	1.000	0	0	--	1	--
Boone A	10.0	9	1	0	0	1.000	0	0	--	0	--
Kata M	4.0	5	0	0	0	1.000	0	0	--	--	--
Lee C	1.0	2	0	0	0	1.000	0	0	--	--	--
Second Base											
Matsui K	1101.0	279	373	0	6	.991	37	58	.003	23	-7
Keppinger J	138.7	33	48	0	1	.988	4	7	-.053	2	-13
Maysonet E	112.0	22	46	1	1	.971	3	6	.044	3	-1
Kata M	47.0	9	24	0	0	1.000	2	2	--	2	--
Smith J	31.0	4	8	0	0	1.000	3	2	--	0	--
Shortstop											
Tejada M	1371.0	214	475	7	14	.970	51	52	-.029	51	-1
Keppinger J	38.7	5	13	0	0	1.000	0	2	--	2	--
Maysonet E	9.0	1	1	0	0	1.000	0	0	--	0	--
Manzella T	8.0	1	3	0	0	1.000	1	0	--	0	--
Smith J	2.0	0	0	0	0	0.000	0	0	--	--	--
Blum G	1.0	0	0	0	0	0.000	0	0	--	--	--
Third Base											
Blum G	830.3	45	164	2	1	.986	15	0	.027	20	-17
Keppinger J	507.7	38	110	4	3	.955	15	0	-.021	18	-6
Johnson C	48.0	2	5	0	0	1.000	0	0	--	0	--
Maysonet E	35.0	1	8	0	0	1.000	0	0	--	1	--
Boone A	8.0	0	2	0	0	1.000	0	0	--	--	--
Smith J	1.0	0	1	0	0	1.000	0	0	--	0	--

Name	Inn	PO	A	TE	FE	FPct	DPS	DPT	ZRDif	OOZ	Dif
Left Field											
Lee C	1272.0	211	9	0	2	.991	0	0	-.081	51	-10
Michaels J	90.3	18	0	0	0	1.000	0	0	--	4	--
Erstad D	61.3	7	0	0	0	1.000	0	0	--	4	--
Keppinger J	3.3	0	1	0	0	1.000	0	0	--	0	--
Kata M	2.7	0	0	0	0	0.000	0	0	--	--	--
Center Field											
Bourn M	1326.0	371	11	0	3	.992	0	0	.018	113	17
Michaels J	102.0	30	0	0	0	1.000	0	0	.000	3	-39
Erstad D	2.0	0	0	0	0	0.000	0	0	--	--	--
Right Field											
Pence H	1375.0	316	16	0	4	.985	2	0	-.004	81	7
Erstad D	34.0	8	0	0	0	1.000	0	0	--	3	--
Michaels J	20.3	4	0	0	0	1.000	0	0	--	2	--

Kansas City Royals

Stat Facts:

- The Royals earned the fewest defensive runs (-64) in the majors
- The Royals' -46 middle infield plus/minus ranked 28th in the majors
- Zack Greinke led the majors with 167 PRC, 22 more than second-best
- Greinke allowed 5 SBs in 14 attempts
- David DeJesus was thrown out in 9 of 13 stolen base attempts
- DeJesus had the highest ZR (.927) of any regular left fielder, and committed zero errors
- Billy Butler had the highest H-A (.109) of any regular in the majors
- Kyle Davies had the highest H-A (.116) of any pitcher with at least 60 IP
- Miguel Olivo was 6.6 times more likely to strike out than to walk
- John Buck committed 8 throwing errors in 367 innings
- Brian Bannister and Gil Meche each allowed 15 SBs in 16 attempts

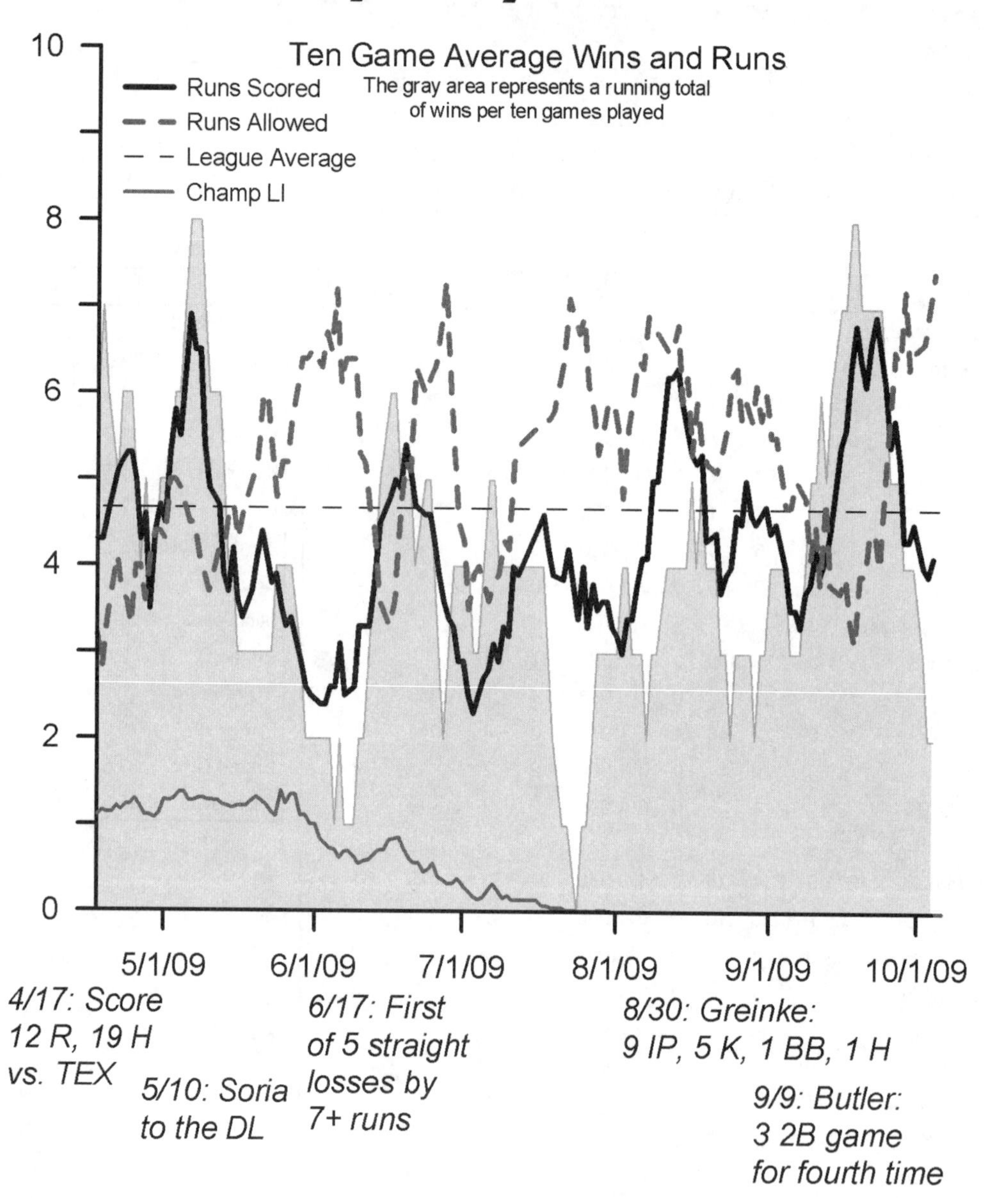

Team Batting and Pitching/Fielding Stats by Month

	April	May	June	July	Aug	Sept/Oct
Wins	12	11	10	7	10	15
Losses	10	17	16	19	19	16
RS/G	4.4	4.0	3.7	3.5	4.8	4.9
RA/G	3.7	5.3	5.0	5.6	5.9	5.3
OBP	.331	.321	.288	.305	.317	.344
SLG	.429	.388	.393	.374	.423	.424
FIP	3.69	3.59	4.90	4.77	4.73	4.65
DER	.699	.651	.723	.659	.671	.672

Batting Stats

Player	*BR*	Runs	RBI	PA	Outs	H	2B	3B	HR	TB	K	BB	IBB	HBP	SH	SF	SB	CS	GDP	H-A	L^R	BA	OBP	SLG	*GPA*
Butler B	*95*	78	93	672	445	183	51	1	21	299	103	58	3	2	0	4	1	0	20	.109	.055	.301	.362	.492	*.286*
Callaspo A +	*83*	79	73	634	419	173	41	8	11	263	51	52	4	1	0	5	2	1	15	.054	.046	.300	.356	.457	*.275*
DeJesus D *	*77*	74	71	627	420	157	28	9	13	242	87	51	0	8	5	5	4	9	10	.027	.039	.281	.347	.434	*.265*
Teahen M *	*65*	69	50	571	395	142	34	1	12	214	123	37	4	6	2	2	8	1	12	.006	-.005	.271	.325	.408	*.248*
Olivo M	*53*	51	65	416	305	97	15	5	23	191	126	19	0	5	1	1	5	2	10	-.024	-.009	.249	.292	.490	*.254*
Jacobs M *	*50*	46	61	478	344	99	16	1	19	174	132	41	2	2	0	1	0	0	9	.077	.076	.228	.297	.401	*.234*
Bloomquist W	*47*	52	29	468	332	115	11	8	4	154	73	27	1	1	4	2	25	6	7	-.061	.006	.265	.308	.355	*.227*
Maier M *	*39*	42	31	397	266	83	15	3	3	113	76	43	2	4	7	2	9	2	6	.039	-.081	.243	.333	.331	*.233*
Guillen J	*30*	30	40	312	226	68	8	0	9	103	50	22	1	8	0	1	1	0	13	.040	-.068	.242	.314	.367	*.233*
Buck J	*26*	16	36	202	143	46	12	4	8	90	55	13	0	1	1	1	1	1	2	.049	-.050	.247	.299	.484	*.255*
Crisp C +	*25*	30	14	215	145	41	8	5	3	68	23	29	1	1	4	1	13	2	4	-.004	-.021	.228	.336	.378	*.246*
Betancourt Y	*21*	25	27	263	197	59	10	5	4	91	26	11	0	0	3	3	0	2	8	.053	.075	.240	.269	.370	*.214*
Pena B +	*21*	17	18	183	125	45	10	0	6	73	18	12	2	0	4	2	0	0	5	-.024	-.039	.273	.318	.442	*.254*
Gordon A *	*21*	28	22	189	131	38	6	0	6	62	43	21	0	2	1	1	5	0	5	.007	.040	.232	.324	.378	*.241*
Anderson J *	*9*	20	8	123	96	28	3	0	1	34	21	5	0	0	0	0	12	3	3	.016	.057	.237	.268	.288	*.193*
Aviles M	*5*	10	8	127	101	22	3	1	1	30	26	4	0	0	2	1	1	0	3	.026	.048	.183	.208	.250	*.156*
Freel R	*4*	8	3	51	34	11	2	0	0	13	12	4	0	0	0	0	0	0	0	.066	-.053	.244	.306	.289	*.210*
Hernandez L	*3*	4	4	81	60	15	1	0	0	16	18	4	0	1	3	0	1	0	2	.049	.064	.205	.256	.219	*.170*
Chen B *	*1*	0	0	2	0	1	0	0	0	1	0	1	0	0	0	0	0	0	0	-.700	--	1.000	1.000	1.000	*.700*

Only includes batters with at least one Base Run. Italicized stats have been adjusted for home park.

Batted Ball Batting Stats

	% of PA		% of Batted Balls					Out %		Runs Per Event				Total Runs vs. Avg.				
Player	K%	BB%	GB%	LD%	FB%	IF/F	HR/OF	GB	OF	NIP	GB	LD	OF	NIP	GB	LD	FB	Tot
Butler B	15	9	47	18	35	.08	.12	75	75	.06	.04	.43	.27	0	1	6	15	22
Callaspo A	8	8	41	17	42	.04	.05	74	79	.12	.05	.39	.15	4	2	4	4	15
DeJesus D	14	9	46	20	34	.09	.09	77	81	.07	.03	.39	.18	2	0	4	-1	5
Buck J	27	7	37	18	45	.15	.16	73	81	-.02	.06	.46	.29	-4	0	0	5	1
Pena B	10	7	51	22	28	.07	.13	79	79	.07	.02	.35	.22	-0	-1	1	-0	-1
Teahen M	22	8	51	20	29	.09	.11	76	75	.01	.03	.44	.25	-7	-0	5	1	-1
Olivo M	30	6	45	14	40	.08	.23	75	77	-.04	.04	.39	.40	-12	-1	-8	19	-2
Crisp C	11	14	48	18	34	.06	.06	81	78	.15	.00	.26	.19	5	-3	-4	-0	-2
Gordon A	23	12	44	14	42	.08	.13	73	88	.05	.04	.33	.18	1	0	-4	-0	-4
Guillen J	16	10	46	14	40	.15	.11	70	93	.06	.06	.37	.12	1	2	-4	-6	-7
Anderson J	17	4	64	17	19	.00	.07	81	79	-.02	.01	.34	.16	-2	-1	-2	-3	-9
Jacobs M	28	9	37	17	46	.17	.17	73	81	-.00	.04	.37	.27	-7	-2	-7	7	-9
Maier M	19	12	42	18	40	.10	.03	73	78	.06	.06	.29	.12	2	0	-7	-7	-11
Bloomquist W	16	6	46	21	33	.11	.04	69	84	.01	.08	.30	.09	-5	8	-2	-12	-11
Betancourt Y	10	4	43	16	41	.15	.05	73	89	.02	.05	.33	.08	-3	1	-3	-8	-13
Aviles M	20	3	45	19	36	.12	.03	84	90	-.05	-.02	.37	.03	-4	-3	-1	-6	-13
MLB Average	***18***	***10***	***43***	***19***	***38***	***.10***	***.11***	***75***	***83***	***.05***	***.04***	***.39***	***.19***	--	--	--	--	--

Pitching Stats

Player	PRC	IP	BFP	G	GS	K	BB	IBB	HBP	H	HR	DP	DER	SB	CS	PO	W	L	Sv	Op	Hld	H-A	R^L	RA	ERA	FIP
Greinke Z	167	229.3	915	33	33	242	51	0	4	195	11	19	.685	5	9	2	16	8	0	0	0	-.003	-.026	2.51	2.16	2.42
Bannister B	50	154.0	668	26	26	98	50	4	4	161	15	16	.693	15	1	0	7	12	0	0	0	-.020	.020	5.49	4.73	4.16
Soria J	42	53.0	222	47	0	69	16	1	2	44	5	4	.654	0	1	0	3	2	30	33	0	.053	.037	2.38	2.21	2.78
Meche G	42	129.0	581	23	23	95	58	0	3	144	17	16	.669	15	1	0	6	10	0	0	0	.001	.024	5.65	5.09	4.85
Tejeda R	41	73.7	313	35	6	87	50	2	3	43	4	5	.751	11	3	1	4	2	0	0	2	.021	-.091	3.67	3.54	3.61
Davies K	40	123.0	538	22	22	86	66	1	4	122	18	17	.709	17	4	1	8	9	0	0	0	.116	.025	5.56	5.27	5.38
Hochevar L	37	143.0	631	25	25	106	46	0	8	167	23	16	.658	19	4	4	7	13	0	0	0	-.040	-.031	6.86	6.55	4.93
Wright J	25	79.0	350	65	0	60	44	5	7	73	8	14	.684	7	3	2	3	5	0	3	12	.038	.047	5.81	4.33	4.74
Chen B *	19	62.3	279	17	9	45	25	3	4	74	12	5	.674	4	4	4	1	6	0	0	0	-.016	-.079	6.06	5.78	5.50
Colon R	18	50.3	220	43	0	29	22	1	2	50	7	4	.725	7	1	0	2	3	0	3	6	-.012	.015	4.83	4.83	5.22
Cruz J	15	50.3	219	46	0	38	29	1	1	46	6	6	.724	2	3	0	3	4	2	6	7	.095	.011	6.08	5.72	4.96
Farnsworth K	14	37.3	168	41	0	42	14	2	1	43	3	2	.611	2	2	0	1	5	0	2	5	.006	-.019	5.30	4.58	3.03
Mahay R *	14	41.3	200	41	0	34	19	1	2	55	9	4	.640	0	0	0	1	1	0	0	4	.002	-.091	5.66	4.79	5.83
Ponson S	12	58.7	273	14	9	32	25	1	2	79	6	9	.644	1	0	0	1	7	0	1	0	-.171	-.075	7.67	7.36	4.76
Bale J *	9	28.3	136	43	0	24	18	2	1	34	3	6	.644	4	0	0	0	1	1	5	10	.138	-.094	6.04	5.72	4.67
Ramirez H *	6	22.7	104	19	1	13	11	3	0	27	3	3	.688	1	0	0	0	2	0	1	2	.097	-.166	6.35	5.96	4.82
Rosa C	5	10.7	43	7	0	4	3	0	0	10	1	2	.743	0	0	0	0	0	1	1	0	.171	.090	3.38	3.38	4.50
Hughes D *	5	14.0	63	8	1	15	8	0	2	13	2	2	.667	0	1	1	0	2	0	0	2	-.149	-.097	5.79	5.14	5.05
Lerew A	4	13.3	62	3	2	7	8	0	0	14	4	3	.698	1	0	0	0	1	0	0	0	.032	-.078	5.40	4.05	7.84
DiNardo L *	2	21.3	117	5	5	8	15	0	1	41	2	4	.549	1	0	0	0	3	0	0	0	-.022	.045	11.81	10.13	5.91
Marte V	2	12.0	58	8	0	7	12	1	0	13	2	2	.703	0	2	0	0	0	0	0	0	-.168	.071	9.00	8.25	6.94
Yabuta Y	1	14.0	77	12	0	9	7	0	0	29	3	1	.552	2	0	0	2	1	0	1	0	-.108	-.079	13.50	13.50	6.19
Waechter D	1	5.3	28	5	0	3	3	0	0	9	2	0	.650	0	0	0	0	0	0	0	0	-.451	.247	8.44	8.44	8.63

Italicized stats have been adjusted for home park.

Batted Ball Pitching Stats

	% of PA		% of Batted Balls					Out %		Runs Per Event				Total Runs vs. Avg.				
Player	K%	BB%	GB%	LD%	FB%	IF/F	HR/OF	GB	OF	NIP	GB	LD	OF	NIP	GB	LD	FB	Tot
Greinke Z	26	6	40	19	41	.10	.05	72	81	-.03	.06	.38	.12	-22	0	-8	-18	-47
Tejeda R	28	17	35	15	50	.13	.05	66	94	.06	.09	.36	.03	4	1	-8	-13	-16
Soria J	31	8	40	18	42	.09	.10	66	80	-.02	.09	.38	.18	-5	1	-3	-1	-7
Bannister B	15	8	50	17	34	.09	.10	72	83	.05	.06	.32	.17	-1	7	-8	-4	-6
Farnsworth K	25	9	46	21	34	.14	.10	57	93	.01	.16	.39	.09	-2	6	0	-5	0
Colon R	13	11	42	15	43	.10	.11	74	86	.09	.05	.33	.18	2	1	-3	1	1
Cruz J	17	14	24	22	54	.13	.09	66	90	.09	.09	.36	.10	3	1	0	-3	1
Ramirez H	13	11	42	18	40	.06	.10	76	81	.10	.03	.41	.21	1	0	1	2	3
Wright J	17	15	59	17	24	.05	.15	77	80	.10	.02	.42	.27	7	-2	-1	-0	4
Bale J	18	14	45	21	34	.00	.10	78	85	.09	.02	.48	.15	2	1	3	-1	5
Davies K	16	13	42	17	41	.13	.13	77	83	.09	.02	.38	.21	8	-2	-3	4	6
Ponson S	12	10	49	22	29	.05	.09	70	85	.10	.07	.45	.17	2	3	8	-1	12
Chen B	16	10	31	17	51	.16	.14	73	77	.07	.06	.42	.26	1	0	1	9	12
Mahay R	17	11	39	18	43	.15	.17	64	79	.06	.09	.42	.31	1	3	1	8	13
DiNardo L	7	14	57	20	23	.10	.11	60	82	.19	.12	.49	.20	3	5	5	-0	13
Meche G	16	10	49	17	34	.07	.13	72	80	.07	.05	.40	.24	3	6	-1	8	16
Hochevar L	17	9	47	18	36	.08	.15	72	79	.04	.06	.46	.27	-1	6	6	13	24
MLB Average	***18***	***10***	***43***	***19***	***38***	***.10***	***.11***	***75***	***83***	***.05***	***.04***	***.39***	***.19***	--	--	--	--	--

Fielding Stats

Name	INN	SBA/G	CS%	ERA	WP+PB/G	PO	A	TE	FE
Catchers									
Olivo M	845.7	0.78	23%	4.49	0.692	718	47	6	2
Buck J	366.7	1.20	16%	5.18	0.417	309	14	8	0
Pena B	213.7	0.88	19%	5.56	0.885	168	7	0	0

Name	Inn	PO	A	TE	FE	FPct	DPS	DPT	ZRDif	OOZ	Dif
First Base											
Butler B	1248.0	1141	92	4	5	.992	11	2	-.046	49	5
Jacobs M	112.0	94	14	0	2	.982	1	0	-.139	11	64
Teahen M	60.0	60	3	0	0	1.000	0	0	--	2	--
Bloomquist	6.0	3	0	0	0	1.000	0	0	--	--	--
Second Base											
Callaspo A	1240.0	233	379	5	12	.973	43	51	-.005	27	-6
Bloomquist	107.0	24	35	0	2	.967	3	7	.020	3	1
Hernandez	36.0	3	7	0	0	1.000	0	0	--	1	--
Teahen M	23.0	5	6	0	0	1.000	0	1	--	0	--
Hulett T	18.0	2	7	0	0	1.000	0	1	--	0	--
Freel R	2.0	0	0	0	0	0.000	0	0	--	--	--
Shortstop											
Betancourt	611.0	111	181	5	4	.970	18	19	-.111	24	1
Aviles M	269.3	51	92	3	1	.973	14	13	-.008	10	-1
Bloomquist	237.7	51	80	5	1	.956	11	9	-.009	8	-5
Pena T	166.0	29	44	5	0	.936	7	2	-.066	5	-8
Hernandez	139.0	20	52	1	0	.986	5	8	-.061	4	-10
Callaspo A	2.0	1	0	0	0	1.000	0	0	--	--	--
Hulett T	1.0	0	0	0	0	0.000	0	0	--	--	--
Third Base											
Teahen M	869.0	66	171	4	7	.956	10	0	-.041	28	-9
Gordon A	406.0	21	94	2	8	.920	7	0	-.024	15	-5
Callaspo A	99.0	11	13	0	0	1.000	1	0	--	4	--
Bloomquist	21.0	2	5	0	0	1.000	0	0	--	1	--
Hernandez	19.0	4	2	0	0	1.000	0	0	--	0	--
Aviles M	10.0	0	0	0	0	0.000	0	0	--	--	--
Hulett T	2.0	0	0	0	1	0.000	0	0	--	--	--

Name	Inn	PO	A	TE	FE	FPct	DPS	DPT	ZRDif	OOZ	Dif
Left Field											
DeJesus D	1204.0	294	13	0	0	1.000	3	0	.033	78	14
Maier M	108.7	23	0	0	0	1.000	0	0	.006	5	-4
Bloomquist	69.0	24	0	0	0	1.000	0	0	--	4	--
Guillen J	33.0	2	0	0	0	1.000	0	0	--	0	--
Freel R	9.0	2	1	0	0	1.000	0	0	--	0	--
Anderson J	1.0	0	0	0	0	0.000	0	0	--	--	--
Hulett T	1.0	0	0	0	0	0.000	0	0	--	--	--
Center Field											
Maier M	593.0	181	10	0	0	1.000	4	0	-.005	31	-16
Crisp C	412.0	120	0	2	1	.976	0	0	.007	30	5
Anderson J	199.7	55	2	0	0	1.000	0	0	.022	15	7
Bloomquist	164.3	34	0	0	0	1.000	0	0	.069	4	-44
Freel R	32.0	5	0	0	0	1.000	0	0	--	1	--
DeJesus D	25.0	10	0	0	0	1.000	0	0	--	0	--
Right Field											
Guillen J	504.0	96	4	1	3	.962	0	0	-.124	16	-20
Bloomquist	329.0	76	3	1	1	.975	1	0	-.019	20	9
Teahen M	251.0	39	0	0	1	.975	0	0	-.151	11	-8
Maier M	178.0	46	1	0	0	1.000	1	0	.065	10	4
Anderson J	87.0	38	0	0	1	.974	0	0	--	5	--
Freel R	64.0	9	0	0	0	1.000	0	0	--	1	--
DeJesus D	10.0	6	0	0	0	1.000	0	0	--	0	--
Hulett T	3.0	2	0	0	0	1.000	0	0	--	0	--

Los Angeles Angels of Anaheim

Stat Facts:

- The Angels earned the second-most defensive runs (65) in the majors
- The Angels' +52 corner infield plus/minus was best in the majors
- The Angels' GDP defense ranked first in the majors
- Chone Figgins had the most PAs (729) of anyone in the majors with zero IBBs
- Figgins led the majors with 17 times caught stealing
- 8 of the 22 walks Darren Oliver allowed were intentional
- Mike Napoli allowed .534 WP+PB per game
- Jered Weaver's GB% (31%) was lowest of any ML pitcher with at least 162 IP
- Kendry Morales tied for the ML lead with 18 DPs started at first base
- Howie Kendrick made 36 OOZ plays in just 806 innings
- The Angels had 10 batters with 400 or more PAs, and .264 was the lowest GPA among them
- Jeff Mathis had 73 total bases, and 73 strikeouts

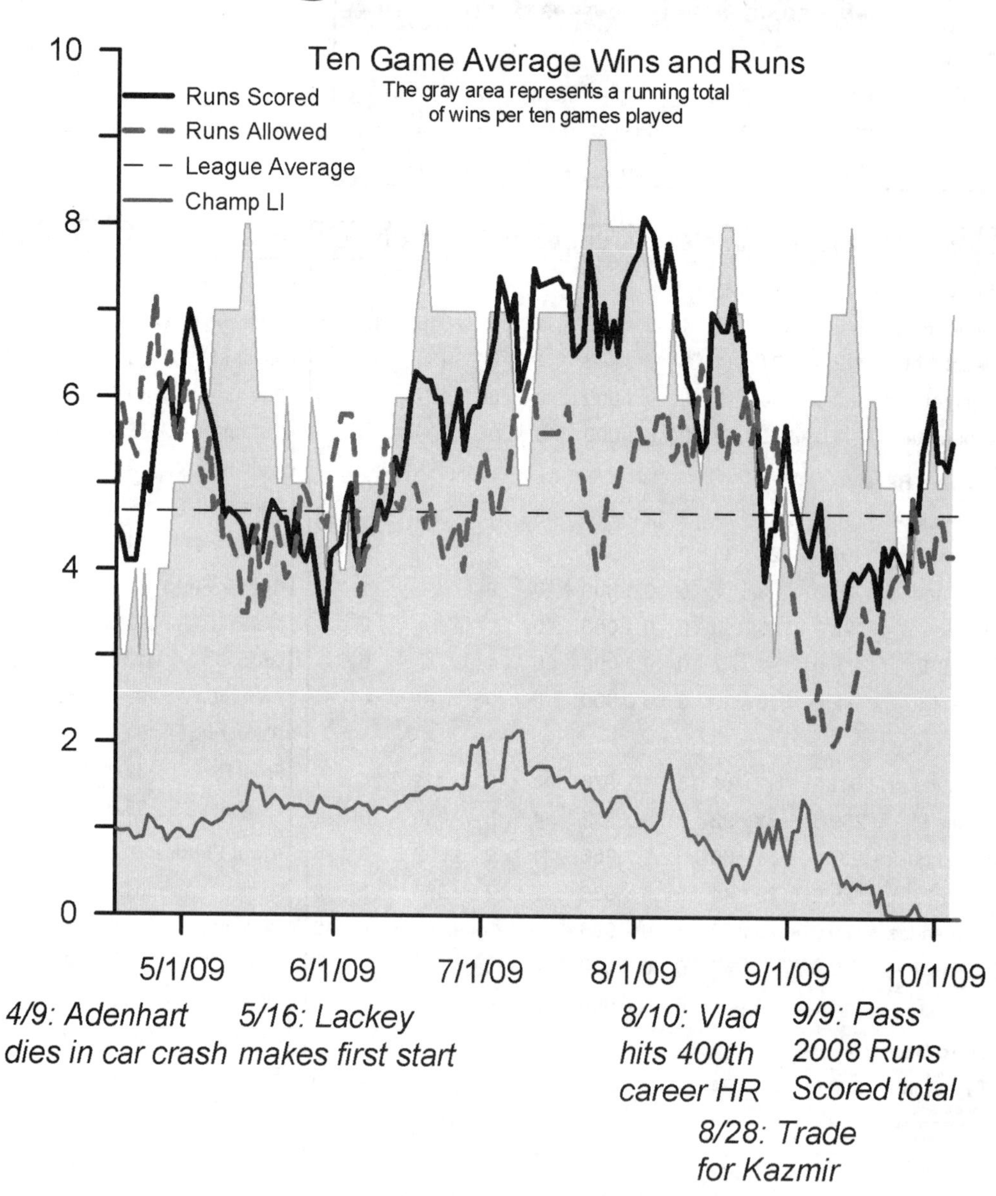

Team Batting and Pitching/Fielding Stats by Month

	April	May	June	July	Aug	Sept/Oct
Wins	9	16	17	19	17	19
Losses	12	12	9	7	12	13
RS/G	5.0	4.6	5.7	7.1	6.2	4.3
RA/G	5.4	4.7	4.6	5.3	5.2	3.4
OBP	.341	.338	.345	.379	.360	.337
SLG	.427	.394	.466	.495	.473	.397
FIP	4.50	4.42	4.67	4.84	4.80	3.79
DER	.666	.706	.680	.697	.687	.700

Batting Stats

Player	*BR*	Runs	RBI	PA	Outs	H	2B	3B	HR	TB	K	BB	IBB	HBP	SH	SF	SB	CS	GDP	H-A	L^R	BA	OBP	SLG	*GPA*
Figgins C +	*110*	114	54	729	457	183	30	7	5	242	114	101	0	1	8	4	42	17	8	.006	-.079	.298	.395	.393	*.279*
Morales K +	*107*	86	108	622	415	173	43	2	34	322	117	46	10	2	0	8	3	7	15	.069	-.050	.306	.355	.569	*.305*
Abreu B *	*105*	96	103	667	421	165	29	3	15	245	113	94	7	1	0	9	30	8	15	-.006	.045	.293	.390	.435	*.287*
Hunter T	*86*	74	90	506	329	135	26	1	22	229	92	47	4	3	0	5	18	4	9	.008	.044	.299	.366	.508	*.294*
Rivera J	*80*	72	88	572	397	152	24	1	25	253	57	36	1	2	0	5	0	1	19	-.027	.089	.287	.332	.478	*.272*
Aybar E +	*76*	70	58	556	363	157	23	9	5	213	54	30	1	5	12	5	14	7	9	-.039	.012	.312	.353	.423	*.267*
Napoli M	*68*	60	56	432	287	104	22	1	20	188	103	40	1	7	0	3	3	3	6	-.027	.078	.272	.350	.492	*.283*
Izturis M +	*63*	74	65	437	283	116	22	3	8	168	41	35	2	5	3	7	13	5	7	.036	.079	.300	.359	.434	*.273*
Kendrick H	*55*	61	61	400	277	109	21	3	10	166	71	20	1	4	2	0	11	4	8	.045	.021	.291	.334	.444	*.264*
Guerrero V	*54*	59	50	407	287	113	16	1	15	176	56	19	3	4	0	1	2	1	16	-.048	-.052	.295	.334	.460	*.268*
Matthews Jr.	*43*	44	50	360	242	79	19	2	4	114	74	40	2	2	0	2	4	1	4	.041	-.000	.250	.336	.361	*.244*
Mathis J	*22*	26	28	272	192	50	8	0	5	73	73	22	0	4	8	1	2	3	2	.065	.013	.211	.288	.308	*.209*
Quinlan R	*10*	13	14	120	91	28	5	0	2	39	30	5	0	0	0	0	1	1	3	-.029	.032	.243	.275	.339	*.211*
Willits R +	*6*	16	6	92	64	17	2	0	0	19	17	5	0	0	6	1	5	1	0	-.024	-.031	.213	.256	.238	*.176*
Rodriguez S	*3*	4	4	29	22	5	0	0	2	11	7	3	0	0	0	1	0	0	2	.011	-.043	.200	.276	.440	*.237*
Wood B	*3*	5	3	46	36	8	1	0	1	12	19	3	0	1	1	0	0	0	3	.100	.015	.195	.267	.293	*.195*
Evans T	*1*	2	1	7	5	2	0	0	0	2	2	0	0	0	0	0	0	0	0	.233	.583	.286	.286	.286	*.202*

Only includes batters with at least one Base Run. Italicized stats have been adjusted for home park.

Batted Ball Batting Stats

	% of PA		% of Batted Balls					Out %		Runs Per Event				Total Runs vs. Avg.				
Player	K%	BB%	GB%	LD%	FB%	IF/F	HR/OF	GB	OF	NIP	GB	LD	OF	NIP	GB	LD	FB	Tot
Morales K	19	8	42	17	41	.06	.19	71	81	.02	.06	.41	.33	-5	4	1	31	31
Abreu B	17	14	48	19	33	.03	.10	68	82	.10	.08	.34	.20	12	9	-1	2	21
Figgins C	16	14	41	24	36	.07	.03	70	83	.10	.07	.43	.08	14	8	16	-17	20
Hunter T	18	10	47	16	36	.11	.19	69	80	.05	.08	.36	.33	0	7	-4	15	19
Napoli M	24	11	38	19	43	.10	.18	69	82	.03	.08	.41	.30	-1	4	0	14	16
Rivera J	10	7	44	18	38	.10	.15	75	86	.07	.03	.43	.21	-1	-1	7	8	13
Izturis M	9	9	43	19	38	.12	.07	74	84	.11	.05	.44	.12	4	3	8	-4	10
Kendrick H	18	6	54	19	27	.01	.12	72	77	.00	.06	.41	.26	-5	5	3	4	6
Guerrero V	14	6	42	18	40	.14	.13	77	77	.02	.01	.39	.25	-4	-3	3	9	5
Aybar E	10	6	46	21	33	.12	.03	76	83	.07	.04	.46	.08	-1	7	12	-15	3
Matthews Jr. G	21	12	42	19	39	.11	.04	72	82	.05	.07	.39	.10	1	3	-0	-8	-5
Quinlan R	25	4	55	18	27	.09	.10	76	74	-.05	.03	.37	.20	-3	0	-1	-2	-6
Mathis J	27	10	37	17	46	.18	.08	68	88	.01	.09	.33	.11	-3	1	-6	-7	-15
MLB Average	***18***	***10***	***43***	***19***	***38***	***.10***	***.11***	***75***	***83***	***.05***	***.04***	***.39***	***.19***	--	--	--	--	--

Pitching Stats

Player	PRC	IP	BFP	G	GS	K	BB	IBB	HBP	H	HR	DP	DER	SB	CS	PO	W	L	Sv	Op	Hld	H-A	R^L	RA	ERA	FIP
Weaver J	*101*	211.0	882	33	33	174	66	3	4	196	26	7	.721	19	6	3	16	8	0	0	0	-.056	-.063	3.88	3.75	4.10
Lackey J	*77*	176.3	748	27	27	139	47	1	9	177	17	18	.690	13	3	0	11	8	0	0	0	.023	-.025	4.29	3.83	3.80
Saunders J *	*65*	186.0	805	31	31	101	64	2	6	202	29	32	.701	18	7	4	16	7	0	0	0	-.016	-.038	4.94	4.60	5.23
Palmer M	*51*	121.3	505	40	13	69	55	2	4	105	12	22	.737	12	4	0	11	2	0	0	0	-.061	-.063	4.08	3.93	4.75
Santana E	*48*	139.7	614	24	23	107	47	4	10	159	24	22	.674	15	5	0	8	8	0	0	1	.061	-.055	5.35	5.03	5.03
Oliver D *	*48*	73.0	293	63	1	65	22	8	5	61	5	10	.714	9	3	2	5	1	0	1	20	-.024	.022	2.71	2.71	3.08
Bulger J	*36*	65.7	262	64	0	68	30	1	1	46	7	11	.744	3	0	0	6	1	1	4	9	.039	-.022	3.56	3.56	3.88
Kazmir S *	*29*	36.3	143	6	6	26	10	0	1	28	1	5	.724	1	2	2	2	2	0	0	0	.053	-.034	1.98	1.73	3.03
Fuentes B *	*26*	55.0	242	65	0	46	24	2	5	53	6	4	.708	1	1	1	1	5	48	55	0	.070	-.059	3.93	3.93	4.41
Jepsen K	*19*	54.7	237	54	0	48	19	2	0	63	2	6	.637	3	0	0	6	4	1	2	17	-.059	-.129	5.43	4.94	2.84
Speier J	*15*	40.0	182	41	0	39	15	2	4	44	7	2	.675	3	0	0	4	2	0	1	8	.047	-.112	5.18	5.18	4.79
O'Sullivan S	*15*	51.7	227	12	10	29	16	1	1	60	12	7	.710	5	0	0	4	2	0	0	0	.014	.037	5.92	5.92	6.02
Arredondo J	*15*	45.0	202	43	0	47	23	2	0	47	6	4	.667	2	1	0	2	3	0	1	16	.052	.043	6.00	6.00	4.24
Loux S	*13*	58.3	271	18	6	19	19	0	4	84	4	10	.636	7	3	0	2	3	0	0	0	.063	-.090	6.48	5.86	4.61
Thompson R	*8*	19.3	92	13	0	21	7	0	1	27	6	1	.632	6	0	0	0	0	0	0	0	.092	-.055	5.12	5.12	6.29
Rodriguez R	*7*	30.7	145	18	0	10	9	1	1	47	4	3	.628	2	1	0	0	1	0	2	2	-.038	-.057	6.46	5.58	5.11
Moseley D	*5*	14.7	65	3	3	8	3	1	0	20	3	1	.667	2	1	0	1	0	0	0	0	-.123	.085	4.91	4.30	5.17
Shields S	*4*	17.7	83	20	0	12	15	0	0	16	1	3	.709	2	0	0	1	3	1	4	6	-.055	.008	7.13	6.62	5.12
Escobar K	*3*	5.0	23	1	1	5	4	0	1	4	0	1	.692	2	1	0	0	1	0	0	0	--	.389	3.60	3.60	4.19
Bell T	*2*	20.3	110	8	4	14	11	2	0	40	3	2	.524	1	1	0	1	2	0	0	0	.061	-.107	11.07	9.74	5.06
Ortega A	*2*	12.7	62	3	3	7	6	0	0	19	4	2	.644	1	0	0	0	2	0	0	0	.127	.143	10.66	9.24	7.61

Italicized stats have been adjusted for home park.

Batted Ball Pitching Stats

	% of PA		% of Batted Balls					Out %		Runs Per Event				Total Runs vs. Avg.				
Player	K%	BB%	GB%	LD%	FB%	IF/F	HR/OF	GB	OF	NIP	GB	LD	OF	NIP	GB	LD	FB	Tot
Weaver J	20	8	31	19	50	.14	.10	79	86	.02	.03	.44	.15	-8	-5	4	-4	-13
Oliver D	22	9	44	14	41	.05	.07	77	79	.02	.03	.34	.15	-2	-1	-6	-3	-12
Lackey J	19	7	45	20	35	.05	.10	80	82	.02	.01	.40	.18	-7	-7	4	-2	-12
Palmer J	14	12	51	16	34	.10	.11	80	80	.10	-.00	.33	.20	6	-8	-7	-1	-10
Bulger J	26	12	43	14	43	.09	.11	79	80	.03	-.00	.38	.23	-1	-4	-6	1	-10
Kazmir S	18	8	26	18	56	.17	.02	68	83	.02	.05	.32	.05	-1	-1	-2	-5	-9
Jepsen K	20	8	57	16	27	.11	.05	66	87	.02	.09	.44	.05	-2	6	-0	-8	-5
Fuentes B	19	12	36	17	47	.12	.09	69	87	.06	.07	.37	.12	2	1	-2	-3	-3
Arredondo J	23	11	44	18	38	.04	.13	68	85	.04	.08	.41	.19	-0	1	-1	0	1
Speier J	21	10	35	21	44	.08	.14	71	88	.04	.06	.44	.18	-0	-0	2	1	2
Rodriguez R	7	7	52	25	23	.03	.14	75	75	.12	.04	.42	.28	1	1	6	2	10
O'Sullivan S	13	7	37	20	44	.05	.16	77	81	.06	.02	.35	.29	-0	-2	1	11	10
Saunders J	13	9	47	17	36	.13	.14	78	82	.07	.02	.43	.23	2	-4	5	8	10
Bell T	13	10	36	31	33	.14	.13	61	86	.09	.12	.49	.19	1	3	8	0	12
Loux S	7	8	47	21	33	.07	.06	75	75	.14	.03	.43	.19	3	1	8	2	14
Santana E	17	9	38	20	42	.11	.14	72	81	.05	.05	.38	.25	-0	-0	3	14	16
MLB Average	***18***	***10***	***43***	***19***	***38***	***.10***	***.11***	***75***	***83***	***.05***	***.04***	***.39***	***.19***	--	--	--	--	--

Fielding Stats

Name	INN	SBA/G	CS%	ERA	WP+PB/G	PO	A	TE	FE
Catchers									
Napoli M	758.0	1.03	15%	4.86	0.534	526	48	5	2
Mathis J	657.0	0.95	25%	3.99	0.438	507	58	5	2
Wilson B	24.0	0.38	0%	3.00	0.375	19	1	0	0
Budde R	6.0	1.50	0%	10.50	0.000	7	1	0	0

Name	Inn	PO	A	TE	FE	FPct	DPS	DPT	ZRDif	OOZ	Dif
First Base											
Morales K	1279.0	1274	86	1	7	.994	18	0	.022	50	5
Quinlan R	126.0	119	16	0	0	1.000	1	1	.028	7	21
Wood B	34.0	35	5	0	0	1.000	2	0	--	4	--
Wilson B	6.0	5	0	0	0	1.000	0	0	--	1	--
Second Base											
Kendrick H	805.7	156	271	0	4	.991	29	40	-.016	36	17
Izturis M	567.3	114	180	1	1	.993	21	27	.050	14	-3
Rodriguez	36.0	5	6	0	0	1.000	2	2	--	1	--
Sandoval F	22.0	4	8	0	0	1.000	0	1	--	0	--
Figgins C	14.0	2	2	0	0	1.000	0	0	--	1	--
Shortstop											
Aybar E	1189.0	240	378	5	6	.983	38	58	.016	37	-7
Izturis M	224.7	33	52	1	1	.977	6	5	-.036	11	11
Wood B	31.0	6	8	1	2	.824	2	1	--	1	--
Third Base											
Figgins C	1339.0	109	314	6	8	.968	34	3	.037	96	30
Wood B	41.0	6	1	0	0	1.000	0	0	--	0	--
Quinlan R	31.0	2	4	0	1	.857	0	0	--	1	--
Izturis M	25.0	3	4	0	0	1.000	0	0	--	0	--
Sandoval F	9.0	0	3	0	0	1.000	0	0	--	1	--

Name	Inn	PO	A	TE	FE	FPct	DPS	DPT	ZRDif	OOZ	Dif
Left Field											
Rivera J	1032.0	231	10	0	2	.992	3	0	.007	59	7
Willits R	132.3	19	0	0	0	1.000	0	0	.040	5	-13
Abreu B	85.0	20	0	0	0	1.000	0	0	--	5	--
Matthews	84.0	25	0	0	1	.962	0	0	--	5	--
Quinlan R	79.0	16	1	0	0	1.000	0	0	--	3	--
Rodriguez	19.0	2	0	0	0	1.000	0	0	--	1	--
Evans T	10.0	2	0	0	0	1.000	0	0	--	1	--
Pettit C	3.0	1	0	0	0	1.000	0	0	--	--	--
Izturis M	0.3	0	0	0	0	0.000	0	0	--	--	--
Figgins C	0.0	0	0	0	0	0.000	0	0	--	--	--
Center Field											
Hunter T	977.3	308	2	1	0	.997	0	0	-.018	69	3
Matthews	435.7	125	1	0	1	.992	0	0	-.039	26	-8
Willits R	26.0	8	0	0	0	1.000	0	0	--	1	--
Evans T	4.0	1	0	0	0	1.000	0	0	--	0	--
Rodriguez	2.0	1	0	0	0	1.000	0	0	--	--	--
Right Field											
Abreu B	1081.0	249	10	1	7	.970	4	0	-.035	36	-19
Matthews	218.0	43	1	0	1	.978	0	0	-.026	13	7
Rivera J	42.0	6	1	0	0	1.000	0	0	--	1	--
Willits R	39.0	9	0	0	0	1.000	0	0	--	3	--
Pettit C	18.0	3	0	0	0	1.000	0	0	--	0	--
Guerrero V	16.0	4	0	0	0	1.000	0	0	--	0	--
Quinlan R	15.0	4	0	0	0	1.000	0	0	--	1	--
Evans T	12.0	3	0	0	0	1.000	0	0	--	0	--
Rodriguez	4.0	0	0	0	0	0.000	0	0	--	--	--

Los Angeles Dodgers

Stat Facts:

- James Loney had the most PAs (652) of anyone in the majors with 0 HBPs
- Loney had the lowest H-A (-.068) of any NL regular
- Andre Ethier had the highest H-A (.079) of any NL regular
- Jonathan Broxton had the lowest H-A (-.170) of any ML pitcher with at least 60 IP
- Broxton's FIP (1.98) was lowest of any ML pitcher with at least 40 IP
- Broxton struck out 38% of the batters he faced, highest rate in the majors
- Juan Pierre's K% of 6% was lowest in the NL
- The DER behind Randy Wolf (.741) was highest of any ML pitcher with at least 162 IP
- Just 5% of the outfield flies allowed by Clayton Kershaw were home runs
- Kershaw allowed just 6 SBs in 13 attempts, and picked off 7 runners

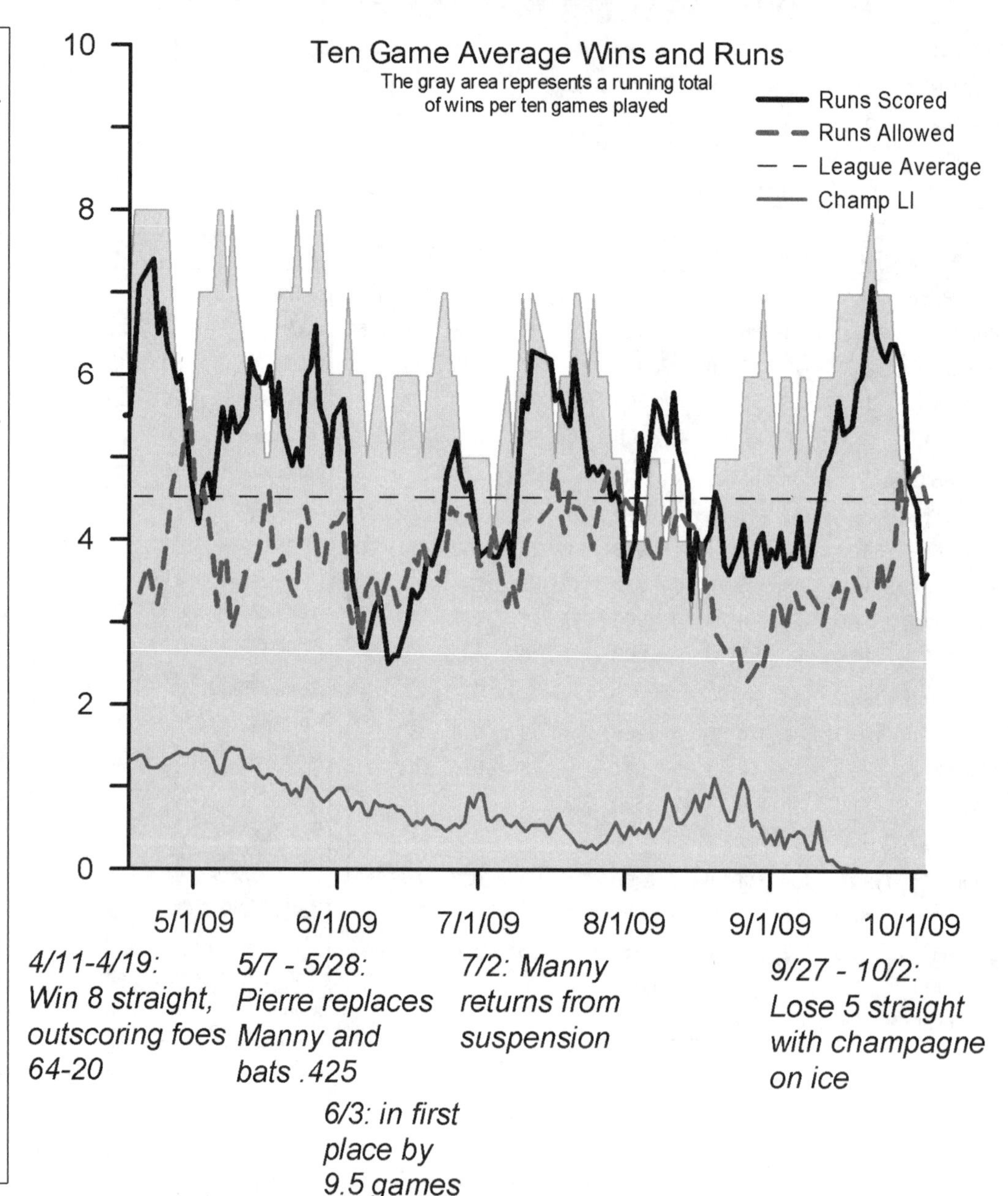

Team Batting and Pitching/Fielding Stats by Month

	April	May	June	July	Aug	Sept/Oct
Wins	15	20	14	15	14	17
Losses	8	9	12	10	15	13
RS/G	5.7	5.4	3.6	5.0	4.5	4.8
RA/G	4.2	3.6	3.7	4.2	3.4	3.7
OBP	.381	.361	.308	.359	.329	.339
SLG	.445	.395	.369	.446	.417	.404
FIP	3.87	3.86	3.84	3.91	3.73	3.41
DER	.715	.707	.726	.726	.716	.702

Batting Stats

Player	BR	Runs	RBI	PA	Outs	H	2B	3B	HR	TB	K	BB	IBB	HBP	SH	SF	SB	CS	GDP	H-A	L^R	BA	OBP	SLG	GPA
Ethier A *	108	92	106	685	457	162	42	3	31	303		72	10	13	0	4	6	4	19	.079	.104	.272	.361	.508	.295
Kemp M	107	97	101	667	448	180	25	7	26	297		52	6	3	0	6	34	8	14	-.036	.085	.297	.352	.490	.287
Hudson O +	84	74	62	631	412	156	35	6	9	230	99	62	4	4	9	5	8	1	16	.019	.028	.283	.357	.417	.270
Blake C	83	84	79	565	365	136	25	6	18	227		63	8	6	1	10	3	4	12	-.012	.076	.280	.363	.468	.286
Loney J *	82	73	90	652	433	162	25	2	13	230	68	70	10	0	1	4	7	3	16	-.068	-.010	.281	.357	.399	.266
Furcal R +	80	92	47	680	465	165	28	5	9	230	89	61	2	1	3	2	12	6	11	-.026	.042	.269	.335	.375	.250
Ramirez M	77	62	63	431	258	102	24	2	19	187	81	71	21	7	0	1	0	1	7	-.039	-.027	.290	.418	.531	.327
Martin R	61	63	53	588	403	126	19	0	7	166	80	69	9	11	2	1	11	6	18	.017	.040	.250	.352	.329	.245
Pierre J *	57	57	31	425	282	117	16	8	0	149	27	27	3	8	9	1	30	12	7	-.043	-.033	.308	.365	.392	.268
Belliard R	18	13	17	83	53	27	7	0	5	49	16	6	0	0	0	0	1	0	3	.025	.149	.351	.398	.636	.345
Loretta M	15	19	25	204	146	42	8	0	0	50	21	20	2	1	0	2	1	1	6	-.085	.061	.232	.309	.276	.212
Ausmus B	12	9	9	107	68	28	4	0	1	35	21	5	0	2	5	0	1	0	1	-.071	-.023	.295	.343	.368	.252
Castro J	12	18	9	121	82	31	4	0	1	38	25	6	1	0	2	1	0	0	1	-.069	-.004	.277	.311	.339	.229
DeWitt B *	5	4	4	53	41	10	3	0	2	19	7	3	0	0	0	1	0	0	2	-.049	.019	.204	.245	.388	.212
Billingsley	3	2	4	67	47	10	2	0	1	15	24	4	0	0	7	0	0	0	1	.094	-.193	.179	.233	.268	.175
Wolf R *	3	5	11	81	58	11	4	0	1	18	22	2	0	1	9	1	1	0	1	.058	.203	.162	.194	.265	.157
Mientkiewicz	3	0	3	20	12	6	1	0	0	7	6	1	0	1	0	0	0	0	0	.464	.052	.333	.400	.389	.283
Jones M	2	1	0	15	9	4	1	0	0	5	6	0	0	2	0	0	0	0	0	.006	.074	.308	.400	.385	.282
Paul X *	2	3	1	16	13	3	1	0	1	7	4	2	0	0	0	0	0	1	1	-.314	.190	.214	.313	.500	.271
Hoffmann J	1	2	7	24	20	4	2	0	1	9	5	0	0	0	0	2	0	0	2	.142	-.054	.182	.167	.409	.181
Abreu T +	1	0	1	11	7	2	0	0	0	2	2	3	0	0	0	0	0	1	0	--	.238	.250	.455	.250	.272
Hu C	1	2	2	6	4	2	1	0	0	3	2	0	0	0	0	1	0	0	1	.413	-.330	.400	.333	.600	.306
Thome J *	1	0	3	17	13	4	0	0	0	4	7	0	0	0	0	0	0	0	0	-.060	.200	.235	.235	.235	.168
Weaver J	1	1	0	15	10	3	0	0	0	3	6	0	0	0	2	0	0	0	0	-.093	-.210	.231	.231	.231	.165
Padilla V	1	0	2	14	10	3	0	0	0	3	7	0	0	0	1	0	0	0	0	.193	.019	.231	.231	.231	.165

Only includes batters with at least one Base Run. Italicized stats have been adjusted for home park.

Batted Ball Batting Stats

	% of PA		% of Batted Balls					Out %		Runs Per Event				Total Runs vs. Avg.				
Player	K%	BB%	GB%	LD%	FB%	IF/F	HR/OF	GB	OF	NIP	GB	LD	OF	NIP	GB	LD	FB	Tot
Ramirez M	19	18	33	25	42	.08	.17	78	90	.11	.03	.47	.23	13	-2	13	7	31
Ethier A	17	12	38	20	42	.04	.16	79	77	.08	.00	.33	.29	8	-8	-1	27	26
Kemp M	21	8	40	21	38	.05	.15	68	79	.02	.07	.37	.27	-5	7	4	18	24
Blake C	21	12	42	23	35	.05	.14	74	83	.06	.04	.39	.24	4	-0	7	7	17
Loney J	10	11	43	22	35	.09	.07	80	83	.12	.01	.40	.13	8	-7	14	-8	7
Hudson O	16	10	56	19	26	.04	.08	80	72	.07	.01	.48	.24	3	-7	8	-1	5
Pierre J	6	8	51	24	24	.05	.00	73	79	.15	.06	.33	.08	4	4	6	-11	3
Ausmus B	20	7	39	26	35	.04	.04	72	83	.00	.05	.38	.09	-1	-0	2	-2	-3
Furcal R	13	9	53	19	28	.12	.07	72	87	.08	.06	.35	.12	2	12	-2	-16	-3
Castro J	21	5	34	23	43	.14	.03	79	84	-.02	.01	.49	.06	-2	-2	3	-4	-5
Martin R	14	14	49	21	31	.15	.06	73	88	.12	.04	.33	.07	11	2	-1	-18	-6
Loretta M	10	10	41	20	39	.06	.00	82	88	.12	-.01	.38	-.01	2	-4	1	-10	-10
MLB Average	***18***	***10***	***43***	***19***	***38***	***.10***	***.11***	***75***	***83***	***.05***	***.04***	***.39***	***.19***	--	--	--	--	--

Pitching Stats

Player	*PRC*	IP	BFP	G	GS	K	BB	IBB	HBP	H	HR	DP	DER	SB	CS	PO	W	L	Sv	Op	Hld	H-A	R^L	RA	ERA	FIP
Wolf R *	*98*	214.3	862	34	34	160	58	1	6	178	24	20	.741	7	5	2	11	7	0	0	0	.012	-.095	3.40	3.23	4.00
Kershaw C *	*98*	171.0	701	31	30	185	91	4	1	119	7	14	.727	6	7	7	8	8	0	0	0	-.023	-.050	2.89	2.79	3.06
Billingsley	*76*	196.3	823	33	32	179	86	7	7	173	17	24	.697	7	9	1	12	11	0	0	0	.010	-.006	4.31	4.03	3.77
Broxton J	*47*	76.0	300	73	0	114	29	1	1	44	4	1	.730	7	1	0	7	2	36	42	1	-.170	.038	2.84	2.61	1.98
Belisario R	*41*	70.7	299	69	0	64	29	7	6	52	4	6	.724	6	1	0	4	3	0	7	12	-.029	-.088	2.67	2.04	3.26
Kuroda H	*41*	117.3	485	21	20	87	24	1	1	110	12	8	.712	10	0	1	8	7	0	0	0	.009	-.022	4.53	3.76	3.61
Sherrill G *	*41*	27.7	111	30	0	22	11	2	0	19	1	1	.766	2	0	0	1	0	1	3	11	-.056	-.109	0.65	0.65	3.01
Troncoso R	*38*	82.7	357	73	0	55	34	9	3	83	3	11	.683	5	2	0	5	4	6	7	14	.050	-.042	3.27	2.72	3.31
Weaver J	*33*	79.0	355	28	7	64	33	9	5	87	7	6	.671	9	2	0	6	4	0	0	0	-.089	-.046	3.87	3.65	3.78
Mota G	*28*	65.3	273	61	0	39	24	8	5	53	6	5	.764	6	1	0	3	4	0	2	2	-.074	.013	3.44	3.44	4.12
McDonald J	*21*	63.0	280	45	4	54	34	5	5	60	6	7	.680	4	2	0	5	5	0	0	5	-.022	.060	4.86	4.00	4.29
Padilla V	*19*	39.3	159	8	7	38	12	0	0	36	4	6	.676	1	3	0	4	0	0	0	0	.021	-.033	3.43	3.20	3.46
Kuo H *	*17*	30.0	124	35	0	32	13	2	2	21	2	1	.747	2	0	0	2	0	0	1	14	-.011	-.032	3.00	3.00	3.18
Stults E *	*16*	50.0	223	10	10	33	26	2	4	51	3	5	.694	3	3	1	4	3	0	0	0	-.112	.009	4.86	4.86	4.29
Garland J	*14*	36.3	154	6	6	26	9	2	0	37	4	4	.696	0	0	0	3	2	0	0	0	-.078	-.035	3.96	2.72	3.73
Vargas C	*9*	11.0	43	8	0	10	4	0	1	7	1	2	.778	0	0	0	0	0	0	0	0	-.025	-.199	1.64	1.64	3.88
Haeger C	*9*	19.0	79	6	3	15	7	0	2	13	4	1	.804	3	0	0	1	1	0	0	0	-.181	.055	3.32	3.32	5.73
Milton E *	*8*	23.7	108	5	5	20	6	0	2	30	2	1	.628	0	1	1	2	1	0	0	0	.052	-.006	4.56	3.80	3.57
Wade C	*8*	27.7	121	27	0	18	10	3	1	28	3	2	.719	1	0	0	2	3	0	6	7	-.043	-.000	5.53	5.53	4.13
Elbert S *	*7*	19.7	83	19	0	21	7	0	0	19	4	3	.706	1	1	0	2	0	0	0	3	.069	-.054	5.03	5.03	4.73
Leach B *	*6*	20.3	88	38	0	19	12	3	1	16	3	2	.736	0	1	1	2	0	0	0	4	-.037	.052	5.75	5.75	4.68
Schmidt J	*4*	17.7	83	4	4	8	12	1	3	16	1	1	.729	6	0	0	2	2	0	0	0	.210	.056	6.11	5.60	5.36
Ohman W *	*3*	12.3	54	21	0	7	8	1	0	12	4	3	.771	3	0	0	1	0	1	2	4	.081	.209	5.84	5.84	7.93
Schlichting	*1*	2.7	15	2	0	2	5	0	0	1	1	0	.857	0	0	0	0	0	0	0	0	.217	-.068	6.75	3.38	12.15

Italicized stats have been adjusted for home park.

Batted Ball Pitching Stats

	% of PA		% of Batted Balls					Out %		Runs Per Event				Total Runs vs. Avg.				
Player	K%	BB%	GB%	LD%	FB%	IF/F	HR/OF	GB	OF	NIP	GB	LD	OF	NIP	GB	LD	FB	Tot
Kershaw C	26	13	39	19	42	.14	.05	77	84	.04	.03	.37	.08	1	-6	-10	-22	-37
Wolf R	19	7	40	18	42	.11	.10	80	85	.02	.01	.36	.16	-8	-11	-7	-5	-32
Broxton J	38	10	56	16	28	.05	.10	72	86	-.02	.06	.21	.15	-7	1	-12	-9	-27
Kuroda H	18	5	49	17	33	.12	.11	80	80	-.01	.01	.41	.23	-8	-5	-1	1	-14
Belisario R	21	12	56	16	28	.04	.08	74	89	.05	.04	.33	.10	1	0	-6	-8	-13
Billingsley C	22	11	45	18	36	.05	.09	74	83	.04	.04	.35	.17	1	-0	-8	-5	-13
Mota G	14	11	36	17	47	.17	.08	82	83	.08	-.01	.34	.15	2	-5	-3	-2	-9
Sherrill G	20	10	43	23	35	.08	.04	88	87	.04	-.03	.32	.06	-0	-3	-1	-4	-8
Troncoso R	15	10	55	19	26	.07	.05	73	83	.07	.04	.36	.09	2	1	-1	-10	-8
Kuo H	26	12	46	15	39	.11	.08	79	83	.03	.02	.38	.15	-0	-2	-3	-2	-7
Padilla V	24	8	47	20	33	.17	.14	73	84	-.00	.05	.38	.21	-2	1	-1	-2	-3
Garland J	17	6	46	21	33	.13	.09	74	77	.00	.04	.36	.19	-2	-0	0	-1	-3
Wade C	15	9	36	16	48	.09	.08	69	86	.06	.07	.34	.13	0	1	-2	-1	-1
McDonald J	19	14	44	17	39	.11	.10	63	89	.08	.11	.33	.12	4	6	-4	-5	1
Stults E	15	13	35	17	48	.10	.05	77	81	.11	.02	.50	.14	4	-2	1	-1	3
Milton E	19	7	30	23	47	.22	.07	61	81	.02	.16	.46	.13	-1	3	3	-2	3
Weaver J	18	11	41	23	36	.08	.09	77	85	.06	.04	.45	.16	1	-1	8	-3	5
MLB Average	***18***	***10***	***43***	***19***	***38***	***.10***	***.11***	***75***	***83***	***.05***	***.04***	***.39***	***.19***	--	--	--	--	--

Fielding Stats

Name	INN	SBA/G	CS%	ERA	WP+PB/G	PO	A	TE	FE
Catchers									
Martin R	1201.0	0.74	25%	3.37	0.517	1039	87	7	0
Ausmus B	244.7	0.66	22%	3.64	0.405	203	11	0	0
Ellis A	27.7	0.33	0%	3.25	0.325	36	2	0	0

Name	Inn	PO	A	TE	FE	FPct	DPS	DPT	ZRDif	OOZ	Dif
First Base											
Loney J	1341.0	1269	85	3	4	.995	14	3	.030	28	-13
Loretta M	119.0	122	9	0	0	1.000	0	0	.113	3	-9
Mientkiewicz	12.0	9	0	0	0	1.000	0	0	--	0	--
Blake C	1.3	2	0	0	0	1.000	0	0	--	--	--
Second Base											
Hudson O	1272.0	325	359	2	6	.988	31	42	-.017	40	4
Castro J	94.7	29	24	0	2	.964	4	3	--	3	--
Belliard R	87.0	11	19	1	0	.968	2	4	--	0	--
Abreu T	9.0	4	3	0	0	1.000	0	1	--	1	--
Loretta M	6.3	2	2	0	0	1.000	0	1	--	0	--
DeWitt B	4.0	2	1	0	0	1.000	0	0	--	0	--
Shortstop											
Furcal R	1282.0	187	419	10	10	.968	37	32	.005	65	12
Castro J	170.0	20	39	0	1	.983	1	5	-.071	6	-3
Hu C	13.0	1	1	0	0	1.000	0	0	--	0	--
DeWitt B	8.0	1	2	0	0	1.000	0	0	--	0	--
Third Base											
Blake C	1161.0	99	263	5	4	.973	28	2	.055	41	-6
Loretta M	131.7	11	31	0	2	.955	2	1	.128	7	12
Belliard R	79.7	8	13	0	0	1.000	0	1	--	1	--
DeWitt B	68.0	5	13	1	0	.947	1	0	--	3	--
Castro J	22.7	2	5	0	0	1.000	0	0	--	1	--
Abreu T	10.0	1	3	0	0	1.000	0	0	--	1	--
Martin R	0.3	0	0	0	0	.000	0	0	--	--	--

Name	Inn	PO	A	TE	FE	FPct	DPS	DPT	ZRDif	OOZ	Dif
Left Field											
Ramirez M	812.0	139	3	0	4	.973	0	0	-.007	29	-15
Pierre J	653.3	128	1	0	0	1.000	0	0	.016	27	-9
Castro J	4.0	0	0	0	0	.000	0	0	--	--	--
Blake C	2.0	0	0	0	0	.000	0	0	--	--	--
Repko J	2.0	1	0	0	0	1.000	0	0	--	0	--
Center Field											
Kemp M	1355.0	367	14	0	2	.995	4	0	-.032	82	-7
Pierre J	102.0	28	0	0	1	.966	0	0	-.036	11	40
Repko J	9.0	1	0	0	0	1.000	0	0	--	0	--
Paul X	7.0	1	0	0	0	1.000	0	0	--	0	--
Right Field											
Ethier A	1365.0	279	6	1	6	.976	0	0	.014	53	-13
Kemp M	50.0	10	0	0	0	1.000	0	0	--	2	--
Hoffmann J	32.0	10	1	0	0	1.000	1	0	--	2	--
Paul X	12.0	1	0	0	0	1.000	0	0	--	0	--
Repko J	7.0	1	0	0	0	1.000	0	0	--	0	--
Jones M	7.0	2	0	0	0	1.000	0	0	--	1	--

Milwaukee Brewers

Stat Facts:

- Craig Counsell's 17 line drive runs tied for the major league lead
- In 114 IP, David Bush surrendered the most HBP (15) in the majors
- Braden Looper allowed the most HR (39) and ER (113) in the majors
- Looper's FIP (5.70) was highest of any ML pitcher with at least 162 IP
- Jeff Suppan's FIP (5.60) was 2nd-highest
- Suppan had the fewest PRC (39) among ML pitchers with at least 162 IP
- The Brewers were the only NL team with 2 full-season regulars with GPAs over .300
- The DER behind Manny Parra (.631) was lowest of any ML pitcher with at least 100 IP
- Yovani Gallardo allowed 19 SBs in 21 attempts
- Todd Coffey induced 13 DPs in 83 IP
- Prince Fielder played the most innings (1431) of any player at any position

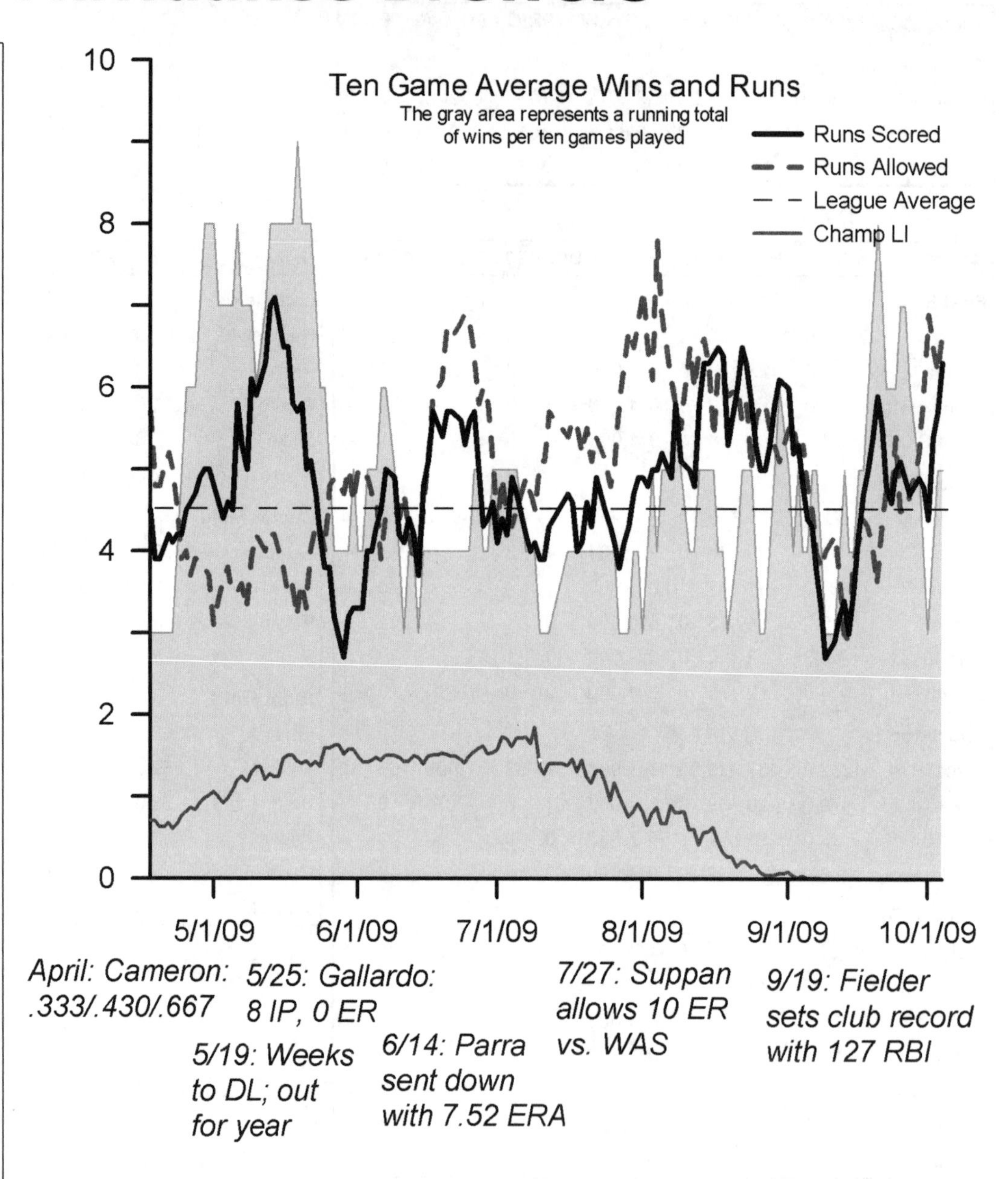

Team Batting and Pitching/Fielding Stats by Month

	April	May	June	July	Aug	Sept/Oct
Wins	12	18	12	9	13	16
Losses	10	10	15	17	14	16
RS/G	4.5	4.9	4.9	4.4	5.6	4.8
RA/G	4.4	4.1	5.4	5.8	5.5	5.0
OBP	.346	.332	.341	.336	.354	.338
SLG	.432	.405	.438	.429	.451	.407
FIP	4.60	4.78	4.70	5.69	4.93	4.30
DER	.717	.733	.671	.681	.676	.677

Batting Stats

Player	*BR*	Runs	RBI	PA	Outs	H	2B	3B	HR	TB	K	BB	IBB	HBP	SH	SF	SB	CS	GDP	H-A	L^R	BA	OBP	SLG	*GPA*
Fielder P *	*135*	103	141	719	431	177	35	3	46	356	138	110	21	9	0	9	2	3	14	-.026	.039	.299	.412	.602	*.336*
Braun R	*128*	113	114	708	445	203	39	6	32	350	121	57	1	13	0	3	20	6	7	-.024	.103	.320	.386	.551	*.311*
Cameron M	*85*	78	70	628	423	136	32	3	24	246	156	75	3	4	0	5	7	3	12	-.001	.072	.250	.342	.452	*.267*
Hart C	*58*	64	48	472	325	109	24	3	12	175	92	43	0	6	1	3	11	6	9	.052	-.021	.260	.335	.418	*.255*
McGehee C	*58*	58	66	394	263	107	20	1	16	177	67	34	2	1	0	4	0	2	13	-.046	.014	.301	.360	.499	*.287*
Counsell C *	*56*	61	39	459	305	115	22	8	4	165	54	42	0	6	3	4	3	4	12	-.008	.019	.285	.357	.408	*.263*
Kendall J	*47*	48	43	526	356	109	19	2	2	138	58	46	6	17	6	5	7	2	11	.022	.002	.241	.331	.305	*.225*
Lopez F +	*45*	44	32	297	182	83	20	2	3	116	41	37	1	1	0	0	0	3	3	.013	.020	.320	.407	.448	*.295*
Hardy J	*43*	53	47	465	334	95	16	2	11	148	85	43	0	2	1	5	0	1	14	.025	-.035	.229	.302	.357	*.225*
Weeks R	*25*	28	24	162	110	40	5	2	9	76	39	12	0	3	0	0	2	2	1	.093	-.032	.272	.340	.517	*.282*
Gamel M *	*19*	11	20	148	98	31	6	1	5	54	54	18	2	1	0	1	1	0	1	-.027	-.028	.242	.338	.422	*.257*
Catalanotto	*19*	18	9	162	106	40	6	3	1	55	23	14	5	2	0	2	2	0	2	.025	.202	.278	.346	.382	*.251*
Hall B	*17*	22	24	234	181	43	12	0	6	73	72	19	0	0	0	1	1	0	10	.093	.038	.201	.265	.341	*.205*
Gerut J *	*17*	23	21	177	131	38	7	0	5	60	21	14	0	1	0	1	4	2	6	.036	.112	.236	.299	.373	*.228*
Escobar A	*15*	20	11	134	89	38	3	1	1	46	18	4	0	2	2	1	4	2	0	-.085	.141	.304	.333	.368	*.242*
Rivera M	*12*	10	14	132	94	26	7	0	2	39	32	15	3	2	0	1	1	0	6	.066	.025	.228	.326	.342	*.232*
Gallardo Y	*3*	6	8	66	49	10	2	0	2	18	23	2	0	0	5	1	0	0	1	-.003	.045	.172	.197	.310	*.166*
Bourgeois J	*2*	6	3	40	32	7	0	0	1	10	7	3	0	0	0	0	3	0	2	.031	.133	.189	.250	.270	*.180*
Looper B	*2*	3	8	73	48	12	0	0	0	12	18	2	0	0	11	0	0	0	0	-.058	.046	.200	.226	.200	*.152*
Iribarren H	*1*	1	1	14	10	3	2	0	0	5	5	1	0	0	0	0	0	0	0	.352	.264	.231	.286	.385	*.225*
Suppan J	*1*	4	5	56	37	6	1	0	0	7	12	4	0	0	10	0	0	0	1	.001	.044	.143	.217	.167	*.139*
Duffy C *	*1*	3	3	37	29	4	1	0	0	5	12	4	0	0	1	0	0	0	1	.181	.152	.125	.222	.156	*.139*

Only includes batters with at least one Base Run. Italicized stats have been adjusted for home park.

Batted Ball Batting Stats

	% of PA		% of Batted Balls					Out %		Runs Per Event				Total Runs vs. Avg.				
Player	K%	BB%	GB%	LD%	FB%	IF/F	HR/OF	GB	OF	NIP	GB	LD	OF	NIP	GB	LD	FB	Tot
Fielder P	19	17	41	16	43	.06	.23	74	81	.10	.04	.50	.37	17	-1	5	42	63
Braun R	17	10	47	19	34	.17	.21	67	78	.06	.09	.42	.37	2	14	9	23	48
Lopez F	14	13	50	22	27	.03	.05	72	78	.11	.07	.45	.17	5	4	8	-2	15
McGehee C	17	9	38	22	40	.11	.15	69	84	.04	.06	.35	.24	-1	2	3	8	13
Cameron M	25	13	35	17	48	.10	.14	69	86	.04	.07	.42	.22	1	2	-4	9	9
Weeks R	24	9	38	19	44	.13	.22	61	88	.01	.12	.39	.31	-1	3	-0	5	6
Hart C	19	10	41	17	42	.07	.09	68	81	.05	.08	.33	.19	0	5	-5	3	3
Counsell C	12	10	44	21	35	.11	.04	76	90	.10	.03	.53	.03	5	-1	17	-18	3
Gamel M	36	13	23	27	51	.05	.14	71	81	.01	.06	.40	.26	-1	-1	0	3	1
Catalanotto F	14	10	52	15	33	.18	.03	70	81	.08	.07	.43	.12	1	3	-0	-4	-0
Escobar A	13	4	52	17	31	.06	.03	61	83	.00	.13	.29	.07	-2	5	-2	-4	-2
Rivera M	24	13	33	18	49	.22	.06	70	87	.05	.05	.43	.09	0	-0	-0	-4	-4
Gerut J	12	8	50	19	31	.16	.14	79	94	.08	.01	.33	.16	0	-2	-1	-3	-5
Kendall J	11	12	44	20	36	.12	.02	74	90	.13	.05	.35	.00	8	2	1	-24	-13
Hall B	31	8	39	18	43	.13	.11	86	83	-.02	-.05	.42	.20	-5	-6	-2	-1	-15
Hardy J	18	10	46	14	40	.09	.09	74	90	.05	.04	.39	.12	-1	0	-7	-8	-15
MLB Average	***18***	***10***	***43***	***19***	***38***	***.10***	***.11***	***75***	***83***	***.05***	***.04***	***.39***	***.19***	--	--	--	--	--

Pitching Stats

Player	PRC	IP	BFP	G	GS	K	BB	IBB	HBP	H	HR	DP	DER	SB	CS	PO	W	L	Sv	Op	Hld	H-A	R^L	RA	ERA	FIP
Gallardo Y	*86*	185.7	793	30	30	204	94	5	5	150	21	15	.719	19	2	0	13	12	0	0	0	-.024	.024	3.78	3.73	3.94
Looper B	*50*	194.7	866	34	34	100	64	6	5	226	39	19	.696	5	3	3	14	7	0	0	0	-.023	-.037	5.69	5.22	5.70
Coffey T	*44*	83.7	336	78	0	65	21	3	3	76	8	13	.711	3	1	0	4	4	2	6	27	.029	-.077	3.01	2.90	3.59
Hoffman T	*42*	54.0	210	55	0	48	14	2	1	35	2	3	.759	1	0	0	3	2	37	41	0	-.010	-.059	1.83	1.83	2.58
Suppan J	*39*	161.7	748	30	30	80	74	8	11	200	25	22	.676	6	3	2	7	12	0	0	0	.036	-.007	5.90	5.29	5.60
Parra M *	*31*	140.0	671	27	27	116	77	5	1	179	19	15	.631	8	2	0	11	11	0	0	0	-.030	-.030	6.94	6.36	4.82
Villanueva C	*29*	96.0	422	64	6	83	35	8	2	102	13	10	.671	5	1	0	4	10	3	8	9	.037	.012	5.44	5.34	4.09
Bush D	*27*	114.3	508	22	21	89	37	2	15	131	19	14	.675	12	4	0	5	9	0	0	0	-.011	-.009	6.61	6.38	5.07
DiFelice M	*24*	51.7	219	59	0	48	15	6	1	49	6	1	.705	2	0	0	4	1	0	1	9	.002	-.083	3.66	3.66	3.38
Vargas C	*23*	30.3	116	28	0	20	11	1	1	18	2	2	.793	3	2	2	1	0	0	2	11	-.005	.020	1.78	1.78	3.78
Stetter M *	*20*	45.0	203	71	0	44	27	6	5	37	4	3	.715	1	1	1	4	1	1	2	20	-.050	-.065	3.80	3.60	4.08
McClung S	*20*	62.0	278	41	2	40	39	1	1	62	11	8	.727	6	1	0	3	3	0	1	5	-.036	-.010	4.94	4.94	6.05
Narveson C *	*19*	47.0	205	21	4	46	16	1	2	45	7	2	.687	5	1	0	2	0	0	0	0	-.023	.050	4.21	3.83	4.21
Smith C	*18*	46.0	200	35	0	35	19	0	3	41	11	4	.758	0	0	0	0	0	0	1	0	-.093	-.029	4.11	4.11	6.17
Burns M	*13*	51.7	227	15	8	39	17	2	1	60	10	8	.663	0	0	0	3	5	0	0	0	-.088	-.036	6.27	5.75	5.09
Weathers D	*6*	24.0	107	25	0	10	11	1	2	26	3	5	.691	1	0	0	1	3	0	1	8	-.100	.009	5.63	4.88	5.44
Axford J	*4*	7.7	34	7	0	9	6	1	0	5	0	0	.737	1	0	0	0	0	1	1	0	-.205	.248	3.52	3.52	2.76
Julio J	*3*	17.3	88	15	0	13	15	0	4	15	2	0	.722	3	0	0	1	1	0	1	0	-.057	-.111	8.83	7.79	6.44
Colome J	*2*	6.3	28	5	0	3	0	0	0	11	1	2	.542	1	0	0	0	0	0	0	0	-.139	.075	5.68	5.68	4.26
Butler J	*1*	4.0	27	3	0	3	6	0	1	7	0	0	.588	0	0	0	0	0	0	0	0	--	-.088	9.00	9.00	6.90

Italicized stats have been adjusted for home park.

Batted Ball Pitching Stats

	% of PA		% of Batted Balls					Out %		Runs Per Event				Total Runs vs. Avg.				
Player	K%	BB%	GB%	LD%	FB%	IF/F	HR/OF	GB	OF	NIP	GB	LD	OF	NIP	GB	LD	FB	Tot
Hoffman T	23	7	39	14	46	.17	.04	67	92	-.00	.09	.24	.02	-3	2	-8	-10	-19
Gallardo Y	26	12	45	19	36	.06	.13	77	83	.04	.04	.34	.22	0	-3	-10	-0	-13
Coffey J	19	7	52	17	31	.05	.11	77	85	.01	.02	.36	.18	-4	-2	-4	-3	-12
Vargas C	17	10	40	14	45	.11	.06	85	88	.06	-.03	.29	.08	0	-3	-3	-3	-8
DiFelice M	22	7	26	20	54	.17	.09	74	81	.00	.06	.37	.18	-3	-1	-1	1	-4
Stetter M	22	16	37	13	50	.08	.07	78	80	.08	.03	.46	.14	3	-1	-3	-1	-1
Narveson C	22	9	31	21	47	.09	.12	63	87	.02	.12	.34	.18	-2	3	-1	1	1
Smith C	18	11	32	17	51	.10	.17	73	91	.06	.04	.32	.21	1	-1	-3	5	2
Weathers D	9	12	46	18	35	.10	.12	76	78	.15	.01	.41	.23	2	-1	1	1	3
Villanueva C	20	9	40	22	38	.08	.11	75	82	.03	.03	.45	.19	-2	-1	7	1	5
McClung S	14	14	37	19	45	.06	.13	80	86	.12	-.01	.38	.19	6	-4	0	4	6
Burns M	17	8	33	24	44	.11	.15	76	80	.03	.01	.41	.28	-1	-3	5	8	10
Bush D	18	10	34	21	45	.07	.13	75	82	.06	.04	.44	.23	1	-1	7	12	19
Looper B	12	8	46	17	36	.09	.17	75	83	.07	.04	.39	.28	1	2	1	24	29
Parra M	17	12	48	18	34	.11	.14	67	85	.07	.09	.50	.21	6	13	11	2	31
Suppan J	11	11	49	18	33	.10	.15	75	79	.12	.04	.42	.28	11	2	7	15	36
MLB Average	***18***	***10***	***43***	***19***	***38***	***.10***	***.11***	***75***	***83***	***.05***	***.04***	***.39***	***.19***	--	--	--	--	--

Fielding Stats

Name	INN	SBA/G	CS%	ERA	WP+PB/G	PO	A	TE	FE
Catchers									
Kendall J	1162.0	0.60	17%	4.96	0.441	882	61	8	0
Rivera M	271.0	0.76	22%	4.38	0.332	234	14	0	0
Corporan C	2.0	0.00	0%	0.00	0.000	2	1	0	0

Name	Inn	PO	A	TE	FE	FPct	DPS	DPT	ZRDif	OOZ	Dif
First Base											
Fielder P	1431.0	1387	66	1	6	.995	7	1	-.039	28	-15
McGehee C	4.0	3	0	0	0	1.000	0	0	--	--	--
Second Base											
Lopez F	542.3	105	176	3	5	.972	21	26	.007	12	-5
Counsell C	396.3	92	131	0	0	1.000	15	19	.070	13	5
Weeks R	303.7	66	95	3	3	.964	7	13	.040	17	28
McGehee C	179.7	37	61	0	2	.980	4	9	.036	7	11
Catalanotto F	7.0	1	0	0	0	1.000	0	0	--	--	--
Iribarren H	6.0	3	4	0	0	1.000	2	0	--	0	--
Shortstop											
Hardy J	949.3	146	318	4	4	.983	31	29	.043	30	-7
Escobar A	300.0	59	94	3	3	.962	10	9	-.001	11	-2
Counsell C	185.7	35	70	0	1	.991	8	12	-.036	8	5
Third Base											
McGehee C	530.3	31	111	4	9	.916	12	0	-.064	21	-2
Hall B	457.0	33	123	4	0	.975	13	0	.038	24	11
Counsell C	255.7	27	58	2	2	.955	5	0	.019	9	-6
Gamel M	191.0	19	35	2	5	.885	4	0	.013	5	-15
Iribarren H	1.0	0	0	0	0	0.000	0	0	--	--	--

Name	Inn	PO	A	TE	FE	FPct	DPS	DPT	ZRDif	OOZ	Dif
Left Field											
Braun R	1364.0	304	8	2	0	.994	2	0	.025	57	-9
Catalanotto F	35.0	4	0	0	0	1.000	0	0	--	0	--
Duffy C	18.0	4	0	0	0	1.000	0	0	--	2	--
Gerut J	7.0	1	0	0	0	1.000	0	0	--	0	--
Nelson B	6.0	3	0	0	0	1.000	0	0	--	0	--
Bourgeois J	3.0	0	0	0	0	0.000	0	0	--	--	--
Hall B	1.0	2	0	0	0	1.000	0	0	--	1	--
Iribarren H	1.0	0	0	0	0	0.000	0	0	--	--	--
Center Field											
Cameron M	1267.0	404	4	0	4	.990	1	0	.029	67	-15
Gerut J	113.3	25	1	0	1	.963	0	0	-.084	3	-41
Duffy C	32.0	11	0	0	0	1.000	0	0	--	2	--
Patterson C	21.0	6	0	0	0	1.000	0	0	--	2	--
Hall B	1.0	1	0	0	0	1.000	0	0	--	0	--
Right Field											
Hart C	930.3	187	3	1	4	.974	0	0	.008	37	-12
Catalanotto F	230.7	60	2	1	0	.984	0	0	.035	10	-9
Gerut J	172.7	43	0	0	0	1.000	0	0	.041	6	-17
Bourgeois J	45.0	14	0	0	0	1.000	0	0	--	2	--
Hall B	36.0	13	0	0	0	1.000	0	0	--	1	--
Duffy C	11.3	6	1	0	0	1.000	0	0	--	1	--
Nelson B	8.0	1	0	0	0	1.000	0	0	--	0	--
McGehee C	1.0	0	0	0	0	0.000	0	0	--	--	--

Minnesota Twins

Stat Facts:

- Joe Mauer led the majors in BA and OBP
- Mauer led the AL in SLG and GPA
- Mauer hit just 1 infield pop-up
- Nick Blackburn allowed the most hits (240) in the majors
- Carl Pavano allowed 13 SBs in 13 attempts
- Scott Baker's's R^L (.055) was highest of any ML pitcher with at least 162 IP
- The Twins' defensive runs (-35) ranked 28th in the majors
- The Twins' -59 middle infield plus/minus ranked last in the majors
- The Twins' outfield throwing ranked 29th in the majors
- Francisco Liriano had 6 pickoffs and 9 caught stealing
- Mike Redmond had 8 GIDPs in 147 PAs
- Alexi Casilla stole 11 bases in 11 attempts

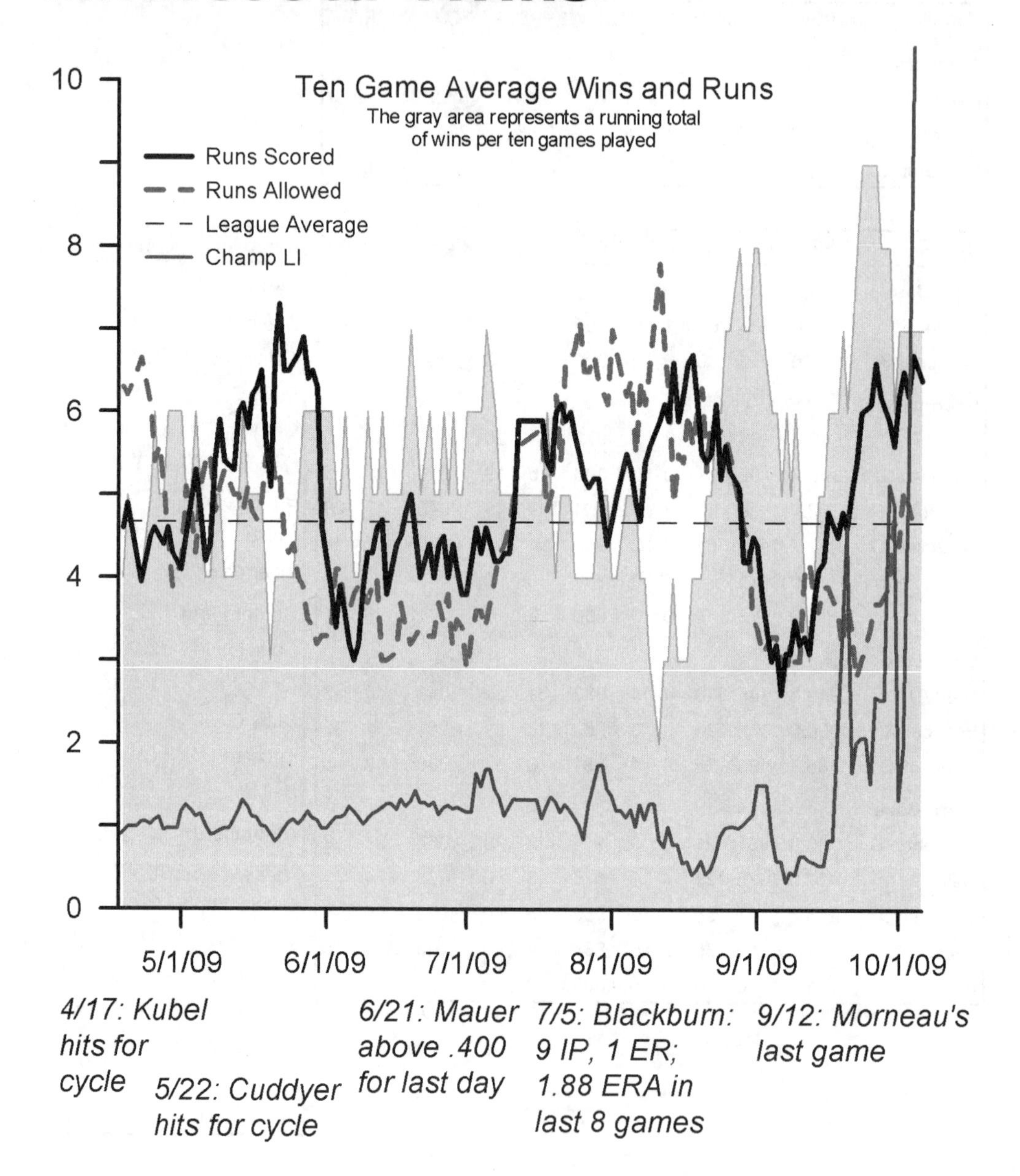

Team Batting and Pitching/Fielding Stats by Month

	April	May	June	July	Aug	Sept/Oct
Wins	11	14	15	12	14	21
Losses	11	16	12	12	14	11
RS/G	4.2	5.6	4.1	5.3	5.3	5.3
RA/G	5.3	4.6	3.4	5.8	5.4	4.0
OBP	.328	.360	.331	.334	.350	.355
SLG	.386	.461	.406	.417	.448	.440
FIP	4.58	4.97	3.87	4.56	4.18	4.50
DER	.692	.709	.715	.678	.663	.700

Batting Stats

Player	*BR*	Runs	RBI	PA	Outs	H	2B	3B	HR	TB	K	BB	IBB	HBP	SH	SF	SB	CS	GDP	H-A	L^R	BA	OBP	SLG	*GPA*
Mauer J *	*118*	94	96	606	346	191	30	1	28	307	63	76	14	2	0	5	4	1	13	.048	.058	.365	.444	.587	*.347*
Cuddyer M	*97*	93	94	650	449	162	34	7	32	306	118	54	3	6	0	2	6	1	22	.029	.059	.276	.342	.520	*.284*
Span D *	*95*	97	68	676	415	180	16	10	8	240	89	70	3	10	12	6	23	10	7	.025	-.030	.311	.392	.415	*.280*
Kubel J *	*94*	73	103	578	374	154	35	2	28	277	106	56	9	3	0	5	1	1	13	.024	.112	.300	.369	.539	*.301*
Morneau J *	*91*	85	100	590	381	139	31	1	30	262	86	72	12	3	0	7	0	0	12	.027	.026	.274	.363	.516	*.292*
Young D	*44*	50	60	416	305	112	16	2	12	168	92	12	1	4	0	5	2	5	17	-.017	.041	.284	.308	.425	*.245*
Harris B	*42*	44	37	453	324	108	22	1	6	150	78	29	0	3	1	6	0	2	16	.091	.042	.261	.310	.362	*.230*
Punto N +	*41*	56	38	440	287	82	15	1	1	102	70	61	1	1	13	6	16	3	7	-.011	.005	.228	.337	.284	*.223*
Crede J	*40*	42	48	367	264	75	16	1	15	138	56	29	1	2	0	3	0	0	6	.012	-.072	.225	.289	.414	*.234*
Gomez C	*32*	51	28	349	251	72	15	5	3	106	72	22	0	4	7	1	14	7	1	-.057	-.009	.229	.287	.337	*.213*
Cabrera O	*30*	42	36	260	181	70	13	3	5	104	32	11	0	0	1	6	2	0	9	-.062	.046	.289	.313	.430	*.248*
Tolbert M +	*20*	28	19	231	155	46	7	1	2	61	37	21	1	0	10	2	6	2	1	-.002	.111	.232	.303	.308	*.213*
Casilla A +	*18*	25	17	256	188	46	7	3	0	59	36	22	0	3	2	1	11	0	6	-.012	-.023	.202	.280	.259	*.190*
Buscher B *	*17*	14	12	164	107	32	3	1	2	43	35	24	0	3	0	1	0	0	3	-.026	.009	.235	.360	.316	*.241*
Morales J +	*16*	14	7	134	86	37	6	0	0	43	22	14	1	0	0	1	0	0	4	-.026	.115	.311	.381	.361	*.262*
Redmond M	*10*	9	7	147	111	32	5	1	0	39	19	11	0	1	0	0	0	0	8	-.005	.095	.237	.299	.289	*.207*

Only includes batters with at least one Base Run. Italicized stats have been adjusted for home park.

Batted Ball Batting Stats

	% of PA		% of Batted Balls					Out %		Runs Per Event				Total Runs vs. Avg.				
Player	**K%**	**BB%**	**GB%**	**LD%**	**FB%**	**IF/F**	**HR/OF**	**GB**	**OF**	**NIP**	**GB**	**LD**	**OF**	**NIP**	**GB**	**LD**	**FB**	**Tot**
Mauer J	10	13	48	23	30	.01	.21	71	82	.14	.06	.40	.33	13	8	16	22	59
Kubel J	18	10	39	20	42	.06	.17	81	77	.05	-.00	.46	.31	1	-7	9	26	29
Morneau J	15	13	41	16	43	.13	.17	75	84	.10	.04	.41	.27	9	-0	-1	17	24
Cuddyer M	18	9	44	16	40	.16	.19	75	79	.04	.03	.44	.34	-1	-2	1	23	21
Span D	13	12	53	19	28	.05	.06	68	82	.10	.09	.37	.13	9	18	1	-10	18
Morales J	16	10	49	24	27	.00	.00	74	77	.07	.03	.40	.07	1	0	3	-4	0
Buscher B	21	16	33	26	40	.12	.06	76	88	.09	.02	.34	.08	3	-1	1	-5	-2
Cabrera O	12	4	44	17	39	.06	.06	71	86	.00	.06	.45	.11	-3	2	2	-3	-2
Crede J	15	8	30	16	53	.15	.12	78	88	.05	.02	.39	.17	-1	-3	-2	2	-4
Young D	22	4	50	16	34	.04	.12	71	76	-.04	.05	.36	.24	-11	2	-4	5	-7
Redmond M	13	8	55	21	24	.00	.00	80	82	.06	-.00	.35	.02	-0	-2	1	-6	-8
Harris B	17	7	51	15	34	.10	.06	65	85	.02	.09	.38	.11	-4	9	-4	-9	-8
Tolbert C	16	9	50	16	34	.19	.05	77	79	.05	.03	.33	.11	-0	-0	-4	-7	-11
Gomez C	21	7	45	19	35	.20	.05	77	81	.01	.05	.36	.14	-4	1	-3	-9	-16
Casilla A	14	10	52	12	36	.16	.00	78	80	.08	.03	.26	.04	1	1	-8	-10	-17
Punto N	16	14	48	19	33	.09	.01	79	89	.10	.02	.38	-.00	8	-2	-2	-20	-17
MLB Average	***18***	***10***	***43***	***19***	***38***	***.10***	***.11***	***75***	***83***	***.05***	***.04***	***.39***	***.19***	--	--	--	--	--

Pitching Stats

Player	PRC	IP	BFP	G	GS	K	BB	IBB	HBP	H	HR	DP	DER	SB	CS	PO	W	L	Sv	Op	Hld	H-A	R^L	RA	ERA	FIP
Baker S	*85*	200.0	828	33	33	162	48	1	4	190	28	11	.722	10	3	1	15	9	0	0	0	-.036	.055	4.46	4.37	4.16
Blackburn N	*77*	205.7	882	33	33	98	41	1	3	240	25	19	.691	12	2	3	11	11	0	0	0	-.003	-.033	4.51	4.03	4.45
Nathan J	*60*	68.7	271	70	0	89	22	1	2	42	7	3	.762	5	0	0	2	2	47	52	0	-.042	.004	2.10	2.10	2.93
Guerrier M	*47*	76.3	304	79	0	47	16	2	4	58	10	7	.771	4	2	0	5	1	1	4	33	.041	.031	2.71	2.36	4.37
Mijares J *	*44*	61.7	253	71	0	55	23	1	2	50	7	6	.729	5	0	1	2	2	0	1	27	.019	-.104	2.48	2.34	4.05
Liriano F *	*42*	136.7	609	29	24	122	65	0	6	147	21	11	.676	15	9	6	5	13	0	0	0	-.038	-.077	6.12	5.80	4.96
Duensing B *	*38*	84.0	359	24	9	53	31	1	3	84	7	11	.706	1	3	2	5	2	0	0	1	-.058	-.046	3.96	3.64	4.19
Slowey K	*35*	90.7	394	16	16	75	15	1	5	113	15	7	.651	10	3	0	10	3	0	0	0	-.015	-.073	4.96	4.86	4.32
Pavano C	*29*	73.7	320	12	12	59	16	1	3	85	7	5	.664	13	0	0	5	4	0	0	0	.003	.020	4.76	4.64	3.56
Perkins G *	*27*	96.3	423	18	17	45	23	0	1	120	13	11	.683	7	0	0	6	7	0	0	0	-.054	.039	5.98	5.89	4.76
Dickey R	*24*	64.3	293	35	1	42	30	1	4	74	8	6	.675	5	1	1	1	1	0	0	1	.010	.046	4.76	4.62	5.04
Crain J	*20*	51.7	230	56	0	43	27	3	5	48	3	6	.697	4	1	1	7	4	0	0	4	.007	-.126	4.88	4.70	3.97
Keppel B	*19*	54.0	242	37	0	32	21	2	5	63	4	7	.661	2	1	1	1	1	0	1	4	.047	-.018	5.00	4.83	4.30
Swarzak A	*15*	59.0	268	12	12	34	20	0	2	76	12	8	.670	1	2	0	3	7	0	0	0	.045	-.049	6.56	6.25	5.80
Rauch J	*14*	15.7	64	17	0	14	6	1	1	13	1	3	.714	0	0	0	5	1	0	2	5	-.115	.069	1.72	1.72	3.38
Ayala L	*12*	32.3	138	28	0	21	8	0	3	38	4	7	.667	4	1	1	1	2	0	3	1	.131	-.158	5.01	4.18	4.52
Manship J	*9*	31.7	146	11	5	21	15	0	1	39	4	3	.667	6	0	0	1	1	0	0	0	-.109	.029	5.97	5.68	5.02
Mahay R *	*6*	9.0	39	16	0	8	3	1	2	7	1	0	.720	0	1	0	1	0	0	0	2	.235	-.008	3.00	2.00	4.19
Breslow C *	*4*	14.3	64	17	0	11	11	0	1	11	3	1	.763	1	2	2	1	2	0	0	2	.050	.020	6.91	6.28	6.89
Henn S *	*3*	11.3	50	14	0	9	8	1	1	9	2	1	.767	1	1	0	0	3	0	1	2	.111	.271	7.15	7.15	6.01
Humber P	*2*	9.0	50	8	0	9	9	2	0	17	1	2	.484	1	0	0	0	0	0	0	0	-.043	-.039	8.00	8.00	4.97

Italicized stats have been adjusted for home park.

Batted Ball Pitching Stats

	% of PA		% of Batted Balls					Out %		Runs Per Event				Total Runs vs. Avg.				
Player	**K%**	**BB%**	**GB%**	**LD%**	**FB%**	**IF/F**	**HR/OF**	**GB**	**OF**	**NIP**	**GB**	**LD**	**OF**	**NIP**	**GB**	**LD**	**FB**	**Tot**
Nathan J	33	9	41	12	47	.18	.12	79	77	-.02	.01	.24	.25	-6	-3	-11	0	-20
Baker T	20	6	33	19	47	.15	.11	76	85	-.00	.04	.37	.17	-12	-3	-2	-1	-18
Guerrier M	15	7	42	18	40	.09	.12	83	91	.02	-.01	.31	.14	-3	-5	-4	-3	-16
Mijares J	22	10	38	12	51	.15	.10	69	88	.03	.08	.42	.12	-1	1	-6	-4	-10
Duensing B	15	9	45	15	40	.07	.07	71	86	.07	.06	.34	.11	1	3	-5	-5	-7
Crain J	19	14	43	16	41	.05	.05	75	87	.08	.03	.48	.09	3	-0	-0	-5	-2
Pavano C	18	6	41	21	39	.13	.09	76	73	-.00	.05	.38	.22	-4	1	2	3	0
Ayala L	15	8	38	20	42	.07	.10	82	72	.05	-.03	.39	.25	-0	-3	1	4	2
Blackburn N	11	5	46	18	37	.10	.10	76	79	.03	.04	.40	.19	-8	1	5	5	4
Manship J	14	11	44	19	36	.13	.12	77	83	.09	.03	.52	.18	1	-1	4	-0	4
Perkins G	11	6	47	14	39	.07	.10	66	84	.05	.09	.29	.18	-2	11	-7	3	5
Keppel R	13	11	50	21	28	.06	.06	73	72	.09	.06	.33	.23	2	2	1	1	7
Dickey R	14	12	47	18	35	.03	.11	77	77	.09	.02	.38	.24	3	-1	1	5	8
Slowey K	19	5	32	20	48	.14	.12	66	83	-.02	.10	.43	.21	-7	4	5	6	9
Swarzak A	13	8	36	19	45	.05	.13	71	87	.07	.06	.42	.19	0	1	4	6	11
Liriano F	20	12	40	19	41	.08	.14	70	87	.06	.08	.45	.19	3	5	4	3	15
MLB Average	***18***	***10***	***43***	***19***	***38***	***.10***	***.11***	***75***	***83***	***.05***	***.04***	***.39***	***.19***	--	--	--	--	--

Fielding Stats

Name	INN	SBA/G	CS%	ERA	WP+PB/G	PO	A	TE	FE
Catchers									
Mauer J	939.0	0.68	24%	4.29	0.307	724	31	3	0
Redmond M	330.7	1.01	5%	5.31	0.354	228	8	0	0
Morales J	183.3	0.93	5%	4.07	0.687	135	9	1	0

Name	Inn	PO	A	TE	FE	FPct	DPS	DPT	ZRDif	OOZ	Dif
First Base											
Morneau J	1071.0	952	90	1	2	.997	8	1	.025	37	0
Cuddyer M	296.0	278	14	3	1	.986	1	1	-.013	10	-1
Buscher B	72.3	69	6	0	0	1.000	1	0	--	4	--
Harris B	9.0	11	0	0	0	1.000	0	0	--	--	--
Huber J	3.0	0	0	0	0	0.000	0	0	--	0	--
Tolbert M	1.0	1	0	0	0	1.000	0	0	--	--	--
Second Base											
Casilla A	571.3	141	170	0	5	.984	9	25	-.054	10	-10
Punto N	510.3	119	150	0	0	1.000	12	23	-.012	9	-10
Tolbert M	285.0	74	110	1	1	.989	10	19	.012	4	-13
Harris B	85.3	19	24	0	0	1.000	0	2	--	2	--
Cuddyer M	1.0	1	1	0	0	1.000	0	1	--	--	--
Shortstop											
Cabrera O	501.0	102	155	5	6	.959	21	12	-.030	11	-16
Punto N	491.0	100	153	5	1	.973	16	13	.000	20	2
Harris B	451.0	64	150	3	3	.973	14	9	.008	14	-7
Tolbert M	8.0	2	4	0	0	1.000	1	1	--	0	--
Casilla A	2.0	0	1	0	0	1.000	1	0	--	0	--
Third Base											
Crede J	728.0	60	171	0	4	.983	18	0	.081	39	12
Harris B	312.0	20	57	1	5	.928	0	0	-.010	5	-26
Buscher B	195.7	19	31	1	0	.980	3	0	.038	6	-11
Tolbert M	190.3	11	43	0	1	.964	5	0	-.074	17	48
Punto N	27.0	3	6	0	0	1.000	1	0	--	2	--

Name	Inn	PO	A	TE	FE	FPct	DPS	DPT	ZRDif	OOZ	Dif
Left Field											
Young D	806.7	175	4	1	4	.973	1	0	-.032	38	-3
Span D	438.0	115	3	0	2	.983	0	0	.033	27	11
Kubel J	208.3	51	1	0	0	1.000	0	0	-.013	14	17
Center Field											
Gomez C	848.7	297	3	0	1	.997	0	0	.035	74	19
Span D	587.3	179	1	0	1	.994	1	0	.021	40	0
Cuddyer M	17.0	10	0	0	0	1.000	0	0	--	1	--
Right Field											
Cuddyer M	991.7	199	5	1	1	.990	0	0	-.032	29	-23
Span D	242.0	56	2	0	2	.967	1	0	-.001	17	18
Kubel J	219.3	52	0	0	0	1.000	0	0	-.057	12	3

New York Mets

Stat Facts:

- Luis Castillo had the most sacrifice hits (19) of any non-pitcher in the majors
- Castillo turned the fewest DPs (38) of any second baseman with at least 1,000 innings
- David Wright's LD% of 26% tied for highest in the majors
- Only 8% of Wright's outfield flies were home runs
- Ryan Church hit zero infield pop-ups
- For the second straight year, Pedro Feliciano led the majors in appearances
- Sean Green's GB% (66%) was highest in the majors
- Johan Santana's IF/F rate (.16) was highest of any ML pitcher with at least 162 IP
- Santana allowed just 1 SB in 3 attempts
- 98% of the outfield flies allowed by Fernando Nieve were outs
- The Mets' GDP defense ranked last in the majors
- Cory Sullivan had more triples (5) than doubles and home runs combined (4)

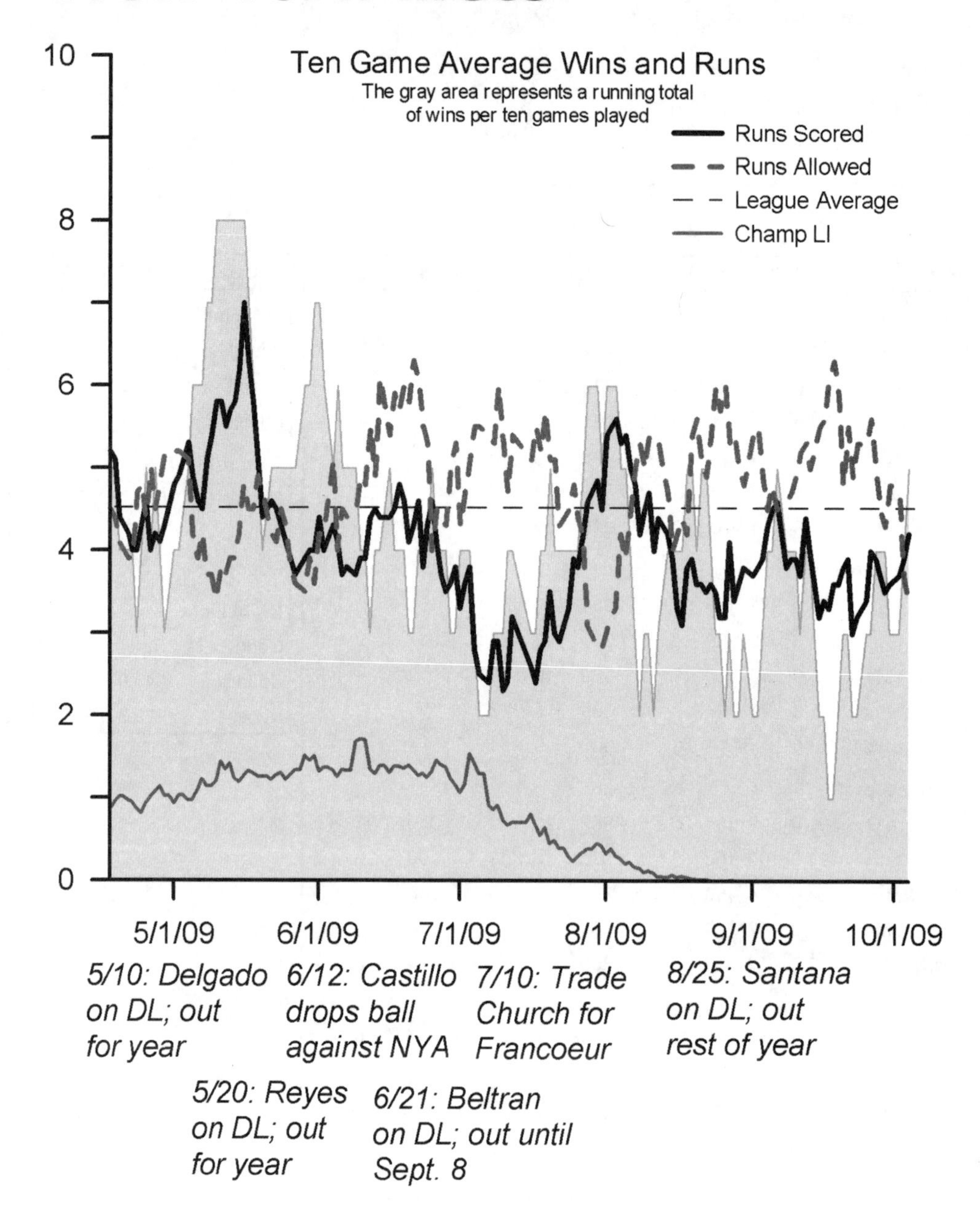

Team Batting and Pitching/Fielding Stats by Month

	April	May	June	July	Aug	Sept/Oct
Wins	9	19	9	12	10	11
Losses	12	9	18	14	19	20
RS/G	4.6	4.9	4.0	3.6	4.0	3.8
RA/G	4.6	4.0	5.4	4.2	5.2	4.6
OBP	.362	.363	.324	.310	.328	.326
SLG	.411	.413	.378	.359	.402	.401
FIP	4.19	3.75	5.10	4.59	4.53	4.68
DER	.700	.687	.706	.697	.672	.714

Batting Stats

Player	BR	Runs	RBI	PA	Outs	H	2B	3B	HR	TB	K	BB	IBB	HBP	SH	SF	SB	CS	GDP	H-A	L^R	BA	OBP	SLG	GPA
Wright D	88	88	72	618	396	164	39	3	10	239	140	74	8	3	0	6	27	9	16	-.016	.124	.307	.390	.447	.295
Castillo L +	64	77	40	580	360	147	12	3	1	168	58	69	3	1	19	5	20	6	15	.069	-.036	.302	.387	.346	.268
Murphy D *	63	60	63	556	388	135	38	4	12	217	69	38	4	0	4	6	4	2	13	.044	.029	.266	.313	.427	.255
Beltran C +	58	50	48	357	218	100	22	1	10	154	43	47	10	1	0	1	11	1	9	-.078	.026	.325	.415	.500	.320
Pagan A +	54	54	32	376	248	105	22	11	6	167	56	25	2	0	5	3	14	7	3	.062	-.018	.306	.350	.487	.287
Tatis F	45	42	48	379	258	96	21	4	8	149	54	22	3	9	4	4	4	1	13	.012	.027	.282	.339	.438	.269
Francoeur J	44	40	41	308	205	90	20	2	10	144	46	11	3	3	0	5	1	3	3	-.004	.091	.311	.338	.498	.284
Sheffield G	42	44	43	312	205	74	13	2	10	121	46	40	3	2	0	2	2	1	10	-.005	.005	.276	.372	.451	.288
Santos O	29	28	40	306	217	73	14	1	7	110	44	15	1	2	2	6	0	0	9	.016	-.042	.260	.296	.391	.238
Cora A *	27	31	18	308	208	68	11	1	1	84	28	25	1	3	8	1	8	3	2	-.022	-.038	.251	.320	.310	.228
Church R *	26	26	22	255	176	65	16	0	2	87	36	17	4	2	2	2	6	2	7	-.069	.119	.280	.332	.375	.250
Reyes J +	21	18	15	166	110	41	7	2	2	58	19	18	1	0	0	1	11	2	2	.099	.139	.279	.355	.395	.266
Delgado C *	18	15	23	112	69	28	7	1	4	49	20	12	0	4	0	2	0	0	3	.043	-.020	.298	.393	.521	.316
Sullivan C *	18	17	15	157	108	34	2	5	2	52	22	19	1	0	0	2	7	1	5	.116	.107	.250	.338	.382	.254
Schneider B	16	11	24	194	138	37	11	0	3	57	21	18	1	1	2	3	0	0	5	.002	.179	.218	.292	.335	.221
Hernandez A	14	14	14	149	107	34	6	2	2	50	22	13	1	0	0	1	2	2	4	-.162	-.013	.252	.315	.370	.241
Reed J *	12	9	9	178	129	39	6	2	0	49	36	14	1	0	1	1	0	3	4	-.001	-.099	.242	.301	.304	.217
Castro R	10	5	13	87	62	20	5	0	3	34	16	8	1	0	0	0	0	0	3	.101	-.050	.253	.322	.430	.259
Valdez W	7	11	7	95	71	22	3	2	0	29	10	8	0	1	0	0	0	1	6	-.044	-.129	.256	.326	.337	.238
Thole J *	7	2	9	59	37	17	2	1	0	21	5	4	0	0	0	2	1	0	1	.023	.083	.321	.356	.396	.266
Martinez F *	6	11	8	100	75	16	6	0	1	25	14	5	0	3	1	0	2	0	0	-.057	.061	.176	.242	.275	.183
Evans N	6	5	7	69	54	15	5	1	1	25	20	4	0	0	0	0	0	0	4	.083	.111	.231	.275	.385	.226
Santana J *	3	1	4	57	35	7	3	0	0	10	14	5	0	0	10	0	0	0	0	-.177	.009	.167	.255	.238	.179
Perez O *	2	1	0	24	16	6	0	0	0	6	7	1	0	0	1	0	0	0	0	.009	-.176	.273	.304	.273	.211
Nieve F	1	0	1	9	6	3	0	0	0	3	3	0	0	0	0	0	0	0	0	.105	.150	.333	.333	.333	.240
Martinez R	1	1	4	44	36	7	2	0	0	9	9	1	0	0	0	1	1	0	1	.123	.137	.167	.182	.214	.139
Figueroa N	1	1	3	25	19	3	0	1	0	5	8	1	0	0	2	0	0	0	0	-.008	-.074	.136	.174	.227	.139
Green A	1	0	0	5	3	1	0	0	0	1	1	1	0	0	0	0	0	0	0	--	.588	.250	.400	.250	.249

Only includes batters with at least one Base Run. Italicized stats have been adjusted for home park.
Batted ball stats are listed after fielding stats.

Pitching Stats

Player	PRC	IP	BFP	G	GS	K	BB	IBB	HBP	H	HR	DP	DER	SB	CS	PO	W	L	Sv	Op	Hld	H-A	R^L	RA	ERA	FIP
Santana J *	74	166.7	701	25	25	146	46	3	3	156	20	11	.702	1	2	2	13	9	0	0	0	-.028	.046	3.62	3.13	3.79
Pelfrey M	49	184.3	824	31	31	107	66	8	7	213	18	17	.679	16	6	2	10	12	0	0	0	-.051	-.004	5.47	5.03	4.32
Hernandez L	35	135.0	593	23	23	75	51	3	1	164	16	21	.669	8	5	3	7	8	0	0	0	.002	.009	5.53	5.47	4.67
Redding T	33	120.0	525	30	17	76	50	5	2	122	18	12	.718	3	1	0	3	6	0	0	0	-.015	-.048	5.40	5.10	5.01
Figueroa N	27	70.3	320	16	10	59	24	4	9	80	8	3	.668	4	2	0	3	8	0	0	0	-.008	.004	4.22	4.09	4.19
Maine J	27	81.3	349	15	15	55	38	2	4	67	8	3	.750	5	4	0	7	6	0	0	0	-.102	.096	4.65	4.43	4.55
Feliciano P	26	59.3	242	88	0	59	18	4	0	51	7	5	.703	0	0	0	6	4	0	2	24	-.074	-.088	3.79	3.03	3.40
Rodriguez F	26	68.0	295	70	0	73	38	6	1	51	7	5	.722	7	2	0	3	6	35	42	0	-.042	.070	4.50	3.71	3.80
Stokes B	25	70.3	316	69	0	45	38	7	2	72	6	13	.684	2	0	0	2	4	0	2	10	-.035	-.095	4.22	3.97	4.39
Parnell B	24	88.3	413	68	8	74	46	2	4	101	8	8	.658	1	2	0	4	8	1	5	16	-.045	-.003	5.71	5.30	4.28
Green S	23	69.7	316	79	0	54	36	5	9	64	5	7	.693	2	1	0	1	4	1	3	14	.037	-.040	4.78	4.52	4.26
Misch P *	19	59.0	251	22	7	23	19	2	2	62	9	5	.732	1	1	1	3	4	0	1	0	.034	.050	4.12	4.12	5.32
Nieve F	17	36.7	161	8	7	23	19	1	1	36	4	4	.719	2	1	0	3	3	0	0	0	-.056	.118	3.19	2.95	4.87
Perez O *	15	66.0	324	14	14	62	58	2	4	69	12	3	.691	5	3	2	3	4	0	0	0	.029	-.147	6.95	6.82	6.36
Takahashi K	14	27.3	116	28	0	23	14	1	2	23	2	4	.720	0	0	0	0	1	0	0	0	.038	.095	2.96	2.96	4.07
Dessens E	13	32.7	130	28	0	14	10	1	2	24	5	3	.808	0	0	0	0	0	0	0	0	-.109	-.000	3.31	3.31	5.29
Niese J *	9	25.7	110	5	5	18	9	0	0	27	1	3	.659	1	2	1	1	1	0	0	0	.128	.043	4.21	4.21	3.31
Putz J	8	29.3	135	29	0	19	19	4	0	29	1	1	.688	4	1	0	1	4	2	4	10	-.026	-.110	5.52	5.22	3.83
Stoner T	3	9.0	36	4	0	5	3	0	0	9	2	2	.731	1	0	0	0	0	0	0	0	-.251	.123	4.00	4.00	5.93
Broadway L	3	14.7	67	8	0	9	6	0	0	19	0	3	.615	0	1	0	0	0	0	0	0	.081	-.094	6.75	6.75	3.15
Fossum C *	3	4.0	19	3	0	3	4	0	0	4	0	1	.667	2	0	0	0	0	0	0	0	.083	-.181	2.25	2.25	4.65
O'Day D	1	3.0	17	4	0	2	1	0	1	5	0	0	.538	0	0	0	0	0	0	0	0	-.339	.103	6.00	0.00	3.82
Switzer J *	1	3.3	17	4	0	3	2	0	1	4	1	0	.700	0	0	0	0	0	0	1	1	-.279	.263	8.10	8.10	7.95

Italicized stats have been adjusted for home park.

Batted Ball Pitching Stats

	% of PA		% of Batted Balls					Out %		Runs Per Event				Total Runs vs. Avg.				
Player	K%	BB%	GB%	LD%	FB%	IF/F	HR/OF	GB	OF	NIP	GB	LD	OF	NIP	GB	LD	FB	Tot
Santana J	21	7	36	17	48	.16	.10	73	83	.00	.05	.43	.17	-9	1	-2	-2	-13
Maine J	16	12	35	21	44	.12	.09	84	86	.09	-.00	.33	.13	4	-5	-2	-5	-8
Rodriguez F	25	13	35	19	46	.18	.10	74	88	.05	.06	.41	.14	1	-1	-2	-5	-7
Feliciano P	24	7	57	16	28	.07	.17	80	71	-.01	.00	.39	.35	-4	-2	-4	3	-6
Dessens E	11	9	38	14	48	.06	.11	90	90	.10	-.05	.43	.14	1	-4	-1	-0	-5
Takahashi K	20	14	39	16	45	.12	.07	76	82	.08	.03	.48	.14	1	-1	-0	-1	-1
Nieve F	14	12	36	18	46	.06	.08	66	98	.10	.09	.42	.04	2	1	1	-5	-1
Niese J	16	8	48	19	33	.07	.04	72	67	.04	.06	.31	.21	-0	1	-1	0	-0
Misch P	9	8	41	20	39	.08	.13	80	81	.11	.02	.28	.21	1	-3	-2	4	1
Putz J	14	14	47	19	34	.16	.04	75	69	.12	.04	.31	.22	3	-0	-1	-0	2
Green S	17	14	66	14	20	.02	.12	77	75	.10	.03	.46	.28	5	0	-2	-2	2
Stokes B	14	13	44	22	35	.16	.09	80	77	.10	-.01	.39	.22	5	-5	3	1	4
Figueroa N	18	10	37	24	39	.14	.11	76	85	.05	.05	.40	.17	1	-0	6	-2	4
Redding T	14	10	36	16	48	.11	.10	72	85	.07	.06	.43	.16	2	2	-0	2	5
Parnell R	18	12	47	16	37	.11	.09	65	81	.07	.11	.37	.16	4	9	-4	-3	6
Pelfrey M	13	9	51	19	30	.07	.10	73	80	.07	.05	.37	.19	2	8	2	-3	9
Hernandez L	13	9	40	22	38	.07	.09	74	77	.07	.04	.36	.21	2	-1	6	9	16
Perez O	19	19	28	20	52	.08	.13	65	87	.12	.11	.41	.19	11	2	0	4	17
MLB Average	***18***	***10***	***43***	***19***	***38***	***.10***	***.11***	***75***	***83***	***.05***	***.04***	***.39***	***.19***	--	--	--	--	--

Fielding Stats

Name	INN	SBA/G	CS%	ERA	WP+PB/G	PO	A	TE	FE
Catchers									
Santos O	680.3	0.58	20%	4.46	0.265	502	26	1	1
Schneider B	437.3	0.58	32%	4.63	0.309	329	25	0	0
Castro R	181.0	0.70	43%	4.23	0.298	159	9	0	1
Thole J	127.3	0.35	20%	4.24	0.495	72	3	1	0

Name	Inn	PO	A	TE	FE	FPct	DPS	DPT	ZRDif	OOZ	Dif
First Base											
Murphy D	849.3	790	74	4	6	.989	12	0	.043	44	17
Tatis F	296.7	274	28	0	1	.997	2	1	.034	12	6
Delgado C	217.7	192	9	0	2	.990	0	0	-.032	3	-21
Evans N	38.0	36	2	0	1	.974	0	0	--	1	--
Reed J	23.3	26	1	1	0	.964	0	0	--	0	--
Cora A	1.0	0	0	0	0	.000	0	0	--	--	--
Second Base											
Castillo L	1146.0	266	344	5	5	.982	28	38	-.025	26	-5
Cora A	131.3	38	40	0	2	.975	2	5	-.083	6	18
Hernandez A	53.7	11	14	0	0	1.000	0	4	--	1	--
Tatis F	51.3	8	13	0	0	1.000	0	0	--	0	--
Reyes A	20.0	4	3	0	0	1.000	0	0	--	0	--
Martinez R	17.0	3	6	0	0	1.000	2	1	--	0	--
Valdez W	3.0	0	0	0	0	.000	0	0	--	--	--
Green A	3.0	0	1	0	0	1.000	0	0	--	1	--
Shortstop											
Cora A	466.3	106	140	3	3	.976	13	21	-.066	18	0
Reyes J	305.3	50	90	1	4	.966	5	5	.017	12	1
Hernandez A	289.7	40	88	4	2	.955	8	8	-.043	11	-0
Valdez W	210.7	41	69	0	1	.991	6	10	.029	8	-0
Martinez R	81.3	12	26	2	2	.905	2	4	--	3	--
Berroa A	57.7	7	22	0	2	.935	3	1	--	2	--
Reyes A	8.0	2	3	0	0	1.000	1	1	--	0	--
Tatis F	7.0	4	2	0	0	1.000	0	1	--	0	--
Third Base											
Wright D	1232.0	119	224	9	9	.950	18	0	-.015	50	-1
Tatis F	192.0	22	45	1	1	.971	3	0	.092	12	21
Valdez W	1.0	0	0	0	0	.000	0	0	--	--	--
Green A	1.0	0	0	0	1	.000	0	0	--	0	--

Name	Inn	PO	A	TE	FE	FPct	DPS	DPT	ZRDif	OOZ	Dif
Left Field											
Sheffield G	358.3	78	3	0	2	.976	0	0	-.044	10	-22
Sullivan C	227.0	50	2	0	0	1.000	0	0	-.005	10	-6
Murphy D	213.7	56	1	1	2	.950	1	0	-.033	19	39
Tatis F	178.7	56	0	0	0	1.000	0	0	.086	7	-11
Pagan A	146.7	40	0	0	0	1.000	0	0	.106	12	31
Reed J	141.3	39	1	0	0	1.000	0	0	.077	6	-8
Martinez F	82.0	17	1	0	0	1.000	0	0	--	3	--
Evans N	74.3	16	1	0	0	1.000	0	0	--	4	--
Valdez W	4.0	2	0	0	0	1.000	0	0	--	0	--
Center Field											
Beltran C	676.0	208	3	1	1	.991	1	0	.003	40	-9
Pagan A	506.3	132	4	2	0	.986	0	0	.042	25	-19
Reed J	86.7	29	0	0	0	1.000	0	0	--	5	--
Martinez F	64.0	21	0	0	0	1.000	0	0	--	6	--
Church R	49.0	15	0	0	0	1.000	0	0	--	3	--
Sullivan C	44.0	14	1	0	0	1.000	0	0	--	2	--
Right Field											
Francoeur J	637.3	137	5	0	1	.993	0	0	-.023	31	-4
Church R	469.0	105	3	0	1	.991	3	0	.053	30	12
Sheffield G	143.7	18	1	0	0	1.000	0	0	.029	3	-31
Martinez F	56.0	11	0	0	0	1.000	0	0	--	1	--
Reed J	49.0	11	0	0	0	1.000	0	0	--	1	--
Pagan A	44.0	11	1	0	0	1.000	0	0	--	3	--
Sullivan C	17.0	4	0	0	0	1.000	0	0	--	1	--
Brown E	8.0	1	0	0	0	1.000	0	0	--	--	--
Tatis F	2.0	0	0	0	0	0.000	0	0	--	--	--

Batted Ball Batting Stats

	% of PA		% of Batted Balls					Out %		Runs Per Event				Total Runs vs. Avg.				
Player	**K%**	**BB%**	**GB%**	**LD%**	**FB%**	**IF/F**	**HR/OF**	**GB**	**OF**	**NIP**	**GB**	**LD**	**OF**	**NIP**	**GB**	**LD**	**FB**	**Tot**
Beltran C	12	13	45	20	35	.13	.12	66	82	.13	.09	.45	.21	8	7	8	3	25
Wright D	23	12	38	26	36	.08	.08	69	73	.05	.06	.39	.22	3	3	12	4	22
Pagan A	15	7	41	21	38	.07	.06	72	74	.03	.07	.44	.19	-3	5	7	3	13
Francoeur J	15	5	34	24	42	.11	.11	74	83	-.01	.04	.43	.19	-4	-0	9	3	8
Sheffield G	15	13	47	15	38	.23	.15	64	87	.11	.10	.32	.23	5	6	-4	0	8
Delgado C	18	14	39	20	41	.03	.13	83	73	.09	-.02	.51	.28	2	-2	2	4	6
Reyes J	11	11	41	19	40	.18	.05	62	77	.11	.12	.27	.15	2	4	-2	-2	3
Tatis F	14	8	47	19	34	.09	.09	76	79	.06	.03	.39	.19	-0	-2	2	-0	0
Castillo L	10	12	59	23	19	.03	.01	73	80	.14	.05	.30	.08	10	6	0	-18	-1
Sullivan C	14	12	47	20	34	.03	.05	87	81	.10	-.04	.42	.15	2	-4	2	-1	-1
Hernandez A	15	9	55	21	25	.04	.08	80	79	.06	.01	.40	.14	-0	-2	1	-3	-3
Church R	14	7	48	22	31	.00	.03	82	76	.05	-.01	.40	.14	-1	-3	4	-3	-4
Murphy D	12	7	40	19	41	.09	.07	77	82	.05	.03	.37	.14	-2	-1	1	-3	-5
Martinez J	14	8	52	10	38	.07	.04	85	81	.05	-.01	.42	.11	-0	-1	-2	-2	-6
Santos O	14	6	40	22	38	.09	.08	79	79	.01	.00	.33	.16	-3	-4	1	-1	-7
Schneider B	11	10	57	13	30	.18	.08	80	82	.10	.01	.39	.15	1	-2	-3	-4	-7
Reed J	20	8	57	19	24	.17	.00	77	83	.02	.02	.43	.06	-2	-1	0	-7	-9
Cora A	9	9	47	20	33	.14	.01	81	84	.12	.01	.35	.05	2	-3	1	-11	-11
MLB Average	***18***	***10***	***43***	***19***	***38***	***.10***	***.11***	***75***	***83***	***.05***	***.04***	***.39***	***.19***	--	--	--	--	--

New York Yankees

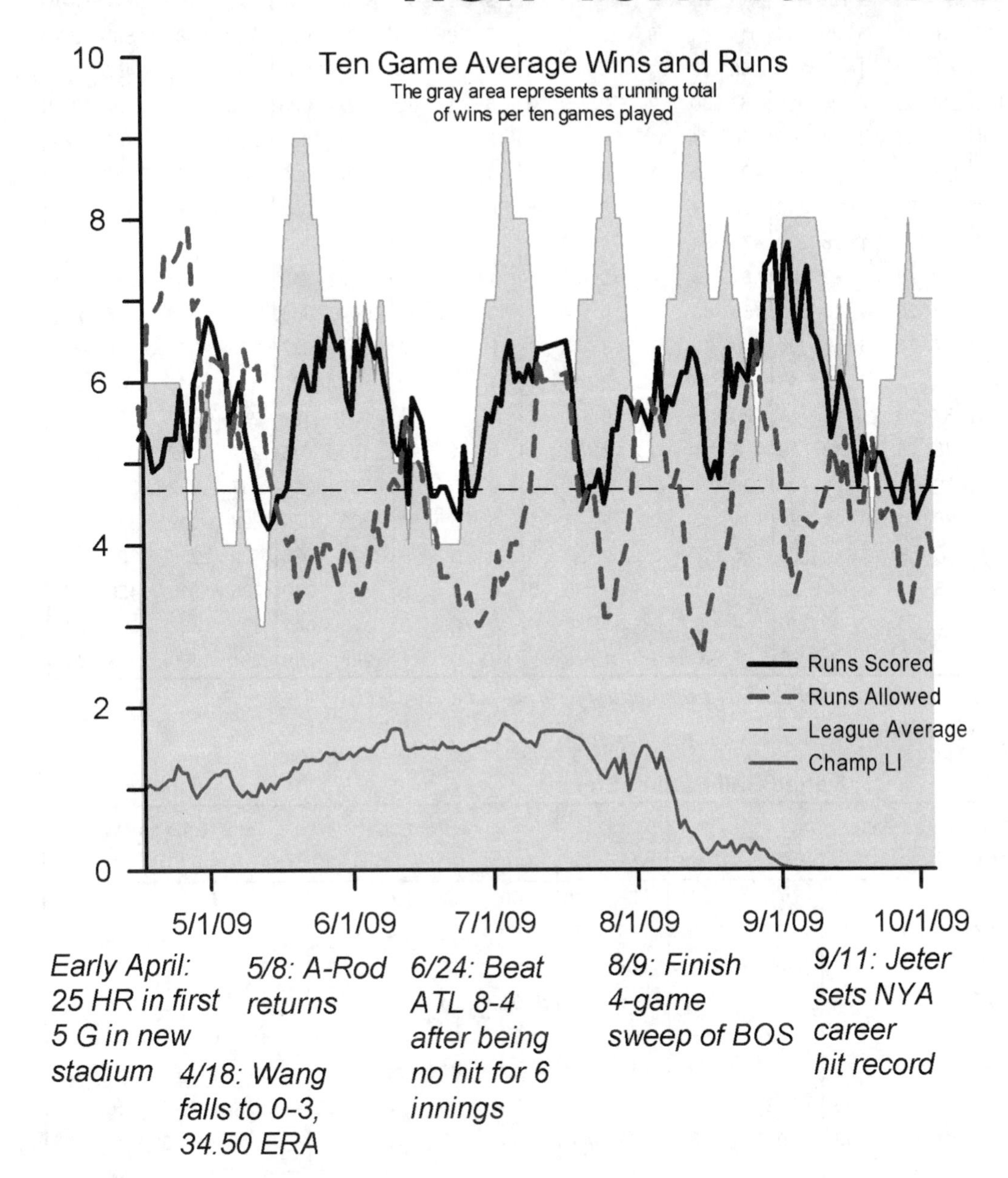

Stat Facts:

- Derek Jeter stole 30 bases in 35 attempts
- Jeter hit just 1 infield pop-up
- Jeter made the fewest OOZ plays (25) of any shortstop with at least 900 innings
- Johnny Damon stole 12 bases in 12 attempts
- Joba Chamberlain led the AL with 12 hit batsmen
- Chamberlain's 26 stolen bases allowed was 2nd-highest
- Andy Pettite's R^L was just .001
- Alex Rodriguez's L^R was just .002
- 91% of the groundballs allowed by Mariano Rivera were outs, highest rate in the majors
- 57% of the outfield flies allowed by Chien-Ming Wang were outs, lowest rate in the majors
- Wang allowed 10 SBs in 42 innings
- The team ERA with Jorge Posada catching (5.04) was over 1.5 runs higher than their other catchers

Team Batting and Pitching/Fielding Stats by Month

	April	May	June	July	Aug	Sept/Oct
Wins	12	17	15	18	21	20
Losses	10	11	11	9	7	11
RS/G	5.8	5.5	5.4	5.4	6.3	5.5
RA/G	6.2	4.5	3.9	4.7	4.4	4.5
OBP	.362	.349	.354	.370	.361	.372
SLG	.473	.497	.433	.483	.507	.467
FIP	4.94	5.14	4.01	4.10	3.95	4.13
DER	.686	.709	.716	.700	.692	.691

Batting Stats

Player	BR	Runs	RBI	PA	Outs	H	2B	3B	HR	TB	K	BB	IBB	HBP	SH	SF	SB	CS	GDP	H-A	L^R	BA	OBP	SLG	GPA
Teixeira M +	121	103	122	707	444	178	43	3	39	344	114	81	9	12	0	5	2	0	13	.034	-.008	.292	.383	.565	.314
Jeter D	111	107	66	716	445	212	27	1	18	295	90	72	4	5	4	1	30	5	18	.021	.066	.334	.406	.465	.299
Cano R *	98	103	85	674	462	204	48	2	25	331	63	30	2	3	0	4	5	7	22	.027	.003	.320	.352	.520	.288
Damon J *	95	107	82	626	404	155	36	3	24	269	98	71	1	2	2	1	12	0	9	.037	.038	.282	.365	.489	.287
Rodriguez A	90	78	100	535	332	127	17	1	30	236	97	80	7	8	0	3	14	2	13	-.007	.002	.286	.402	.532	.314
Swisher N +	90	84	82	607	387	124	35	1	29	248	126	97	2	3	3	6	0	0	13	-.038	.007	.249	.371	.498	.291
Matsui H *	82	62	90	528	336	125	21	1	28	232	75	64	1	4	0	2	0	1	4	-.039	-.033	.274	.367	.509	.292
Posada J +	66	55	81	438	287	109	25	0	22	200	101	48	4	2	0	5	1	0	13	.078	-.019	.285	.363	.522	.294
Cabrera M +	62	66	68	540	369	133	28	1	13	202	59	43	4	4	4	4	10	2	15	.004	.006	.274	.336	.416	.255
Gardner B *	35	48	23	284	189	67	6	6	3	94	40	26	0	3	6	1	26	5	3	-.022	-.027	.270	.345	.379	.250
Hinske E *	14	13	14	98	67	19	3	0	7	43	25	10	1	2	0	2	1	0	2	-.078	.023	.226	.316	.512	.270
Pena R +	13	17	10	121	85	33	6	1	1	44	20	5	0	0	1	0	4	1	2	-.051	-.177	.287	.317	.383	.238
Hairston J	10	15	12	93	60	18	5	0	2	29	8	11	0	3	2	1	0	1	1	.105	.015	.237	.352	.382	.254
Molina J	9	15	11	155	114	30	4	0	1	37	28	14	0	1	1	1	0	0	6	-.007	.000	.217	.292	.268	.199
Cervelli F	9	13	11	101	70	28	4	0	1	35	11	2	0	0	4	1	0	3	1	-.006	.025	.298	.309	.372	.232
Ransom C	6	11	10	86	67	15	9	1	0	26	25	7	0	0	0	0	2	0	3	.072	-.076	.190	.256	.329	.197
Nady X	3	4	2	29	22	8	4	0	0	12	6	1	0	0	0	0	0	0	2	--	.036	.286	.310	.429	.247
Miranda J *	2	2	3	9	6	3	0	0	1	6	4	0	0	0	0	0	0	0	0	-.398	-.043	.333	.333	.667	.317
Cash K	1	1	3	28	21	6	2	0	0	8	5	0	0	1	0	1	0	0	1	-.267	.218	.231	.250	.308	.189

Only includes batters with at least one Base Run. Italicized stats have been adjusted for home park.

Batted Ball Batting Stats

	% of PA		% of Batted Balls					Out %		Runs Per Event				Total Runs vs. Avg.				
Player	K%	BB%	GB%	LD%	FB%	IF/F	HR/OF	GB	OF	NIP	GB	LD	OF	NIP	GB	LD	FB	Tot
Teixeira M	16	13	36	20	44	.10	.20	79	80	.09	.02	.40	.33	11	-5	6	36	47
Jeter D	13	11	57	20	23	.01	.15	75	74	.10	.04	.42	.29	8	5	14	8	34
Rodriguez A	18	16	42	20	38	.07	.24	77	85	.11	.02	.40	.34	13	-3	3	21	34
Cano R	9	5	47	20	33	.07	.13	74	78	.04	.04	.40	.25	-4	2	12	16	27
Damon J	16	12	41	16	42	.13	.15	69	82	.08	.09	.38	.24	6	10	-3	12	25
Matsui H	14	13	38	20	42	.13	.19	80	83	.11	.02	.38	.29	8	-4	3	17	25
Swisher N	21	16	38	16	46	.12	.19	80	84	.09	.00	.44	.30	13	-7	-3	18	22
Posada J	23	11	36	21	43	.07	.18	75	80	.04	.02	.40	.31	0	-3	3	17	17
Cabrera M	11	9	50	21	30	.10	.12	77	87	.09	.02	.36	.17	2	-2	5	-5	1
Pena R	17	4	37	24	39	.11	.03	71	87	-.02	.06	.46	.04	-2	1	4	-4	-1
Gardner B	14	10	49	18	33	.15	.05	73	83	.08	.05	.42	.12	2	1	1	-6	-3
Cervelli F	11	2	46	20	34	.11	.04	71	88	-.04	.06	.40	.05	-2	1	1	-3	-3
Molina J	18	10	39	19	42	.11	.02	72	88	.05	.04	.28	.02	-0	-0	-3	-7	-10
MLB Average	***18***	***10***	***43***	***19***	***38***	***.10***	***.11***	***75***	***83***	***.05***	***.04***	***.39***	***.19***	--	--	--	--	--

Pitching Stats

Player	PRC	IP	BFP	G	GS	K	BB	IBB	HBP	H	HR	DP	DER	SB	CS	PO	W	L	Sv	Op	Hld	H-A	R^L	RA	ERA	FIP
Sabathia C *	*116*	230.0	938	34	34	197	67	7	9	197	18	23	.711	13	7	3	19	8	0	0	0	-.021	-.041	3.76	3.37	3.40
Burnett A	*94*	207.0	896	33	33	195	97	0	10	193	25	19	.696	23	12	4	13	9	0	0	0	-.017	.051	4.30	4.04	4.43
Pettitte A *	*78*	194.7	834	32	32	148	76	1	4	193	20	21	.689	14	8	6	14	8	0	0	0	.040	.001	4.67	4.16	4.22
Rivera M	*60*	66.3	257	66	0	72	12	1	1	48	7	4	.745	2	1	0	3	3	44	46	0	.005	.018	1.90	1.76	2.93
Chamberlain	*56*	157.3	709	32	31	133	76	2	12	167	21	16	.675	26	8	1	9	6	0	0	0	.015	-.002	5.38	4.75	4.88
Hughes P	*52*	86.0	351	51	7	96	28	1	5	68	8	7	.715	5	2	0	8	3	3	6	18	.042	-.071	3.24	3.03	3.28
Aceves A	*41*	84.0	337	43	1	69	16	2	5	69	10	5	.734	10	2	1	10	1	1	2	5	-.087	.039	3.86	3.54	3.77
Robertson D	*24*	43.7	191	45	0	63	23	1	1	36	4	0	.680	2	2	1	2	1	1	1	5	-.082	.051	3.92	3.30	3.08
Gaudin C	*23*	42.0	188	11	6	34	20	1	3	41	7	3	.718	0	1	1	2	0	0	0	0	-.013	-.054	3.43	3.43	5.31
Coke P *	*22*	60.0	238	72	0	49	20	4	1	44	10	8	.772	2	2	0	4	3	2	7	21	-.048	-.074	5.10	4.50	4.57
Bruney B	*19*	39.0	175	44	0	36	23	3	1	36	6	3	.716	2	0	0	5	0	0	1	14	.004	.045	3.92	3.92	4.96
Mitre S	*11*	51.7	241	12	9	32	13	0	3	71	10	6	.645	3	1	0	3	3	0	0	0	-.019	-.154	7.84	6.79	5.40
Albaladejo J	*10*	34.3	158	32	0	21	16	2	3	41	6	4	.679	3	2	1	5	1	0	1	1	-.084	.080	6.03	5.24	5.72
Veras J	*8*	25.7	118	25	0	18	14	0	4	23	5	0	.766	1	0	0	3	1	0	0	3	-.108	-.055	5.96	5.96	6.42
Ramirez E	*7*	22.0	110	20	0	22	18	0	0	25	6	0	.688	3	1	0	0	0	0	0	1	.015	-.006	6.14	5.73	7.19
Tomko B	*7*	20.7	85	15	0	11	7	0	0	19	5	3	.774	3	0	0	1	2	0	0	0	-.035	.171	5.23	5.23	6.29
Melancon M	*7*	16.3	74	13	0	10	10	0	4	13	0	3	.720	2	0	0	0	1	0	1	0	.116	-.086	4.41	3.86	4.54
Wang C	*6*	42.0	206	12	9	29	19	1	2	66	7	5	.597	10	3	1	1	6	0	0	0	.026	-.085	9.86	9.64	5.41
Marte D *	*2*	13.3	62	21	0	13	6	1	1	15	3	1	.692	1	0	0	1	3	0	1	5	.197	-.224	9.45	9.45	5.52
Towers J	*2*	5.3	25	2	0	2	1	1	1	6	0	0	.667	0	0	0	0	0	0	0	0	.096	.269	5.06	3.38	3.00
Dunn M *	*1*	4.0	20	4	0	5	5	0	0	3	1	0	.778	0	0	0	0	0	0	0	0	-.005	-.061	6.75	6.75	7.69

Italicized stats have been adjusted for home park.

Batted Ball Pitching Stats

	% of PA		% of Batted Balls					Out %		Runs Per Event				Total Runs vs. Avg.				
Player	K%	BB%	GB%	LD%	FB%	IF/F	HR/OF	GB	OF	NIP	GB	LD	OF	NIP	GB	LD	FB	Tot
Sabathia C	21	8	43	20	37	.09	.08	77	84	.01	.02	.36	.15	-9	-6	-5	-13	-33
Rivera M	28	5	51	22	27	.15	.15	91	79	-.04	-.05	.39	.26	-8	-8	-1	-3	-20
Hughes P	27	9	34	22	44	.14	.10	76	89	.00	.03	.39	.13	-4	-3	-1	-7	-15
Aceves A	20	7	35	17	48	.13	.10	80	85	-.00	.00	.40	.15	-5	-5	-2	-2	-13
Coke P	21	9	35	20	45	.12	.15	90	91	.02	-.05	.33	.19	-2	-5	-3	1	-8
Pettitte A	18	9	43	19	38	.09	.10	72	83	.05	.06	.32	.18	-1	5	-6	-2	-4
Robertson D	33	13	36	23	41	.12	.11	78	82	.01	.04	.42	.21	-1	-1	-0	-1	-4
Burnett A	22	12	43	18	39	.06	.11	76	82	.05	.03	.36	.20	3	-3	-8	4	-3
Bruney B	21	14	32	16	52	.12	.10	69	80	.07	.07	.39	.18	2	-0	-2	1	1
Veras E	15	15	33	20	48	.13	.15	85	93	.12	-.01	.46	.18	3	-2	1	0	2
Gaudin C	18	12	42	21	37	.08	.14	76	89	.07	.04	.39	.20	2	-0	1	0	3
Ramirez E	20	16	36	16	48	.12	.21	68	83	.09	.11	.35	.30	2	2	-1	4	7
Albaladejo J	13	12	53	19	28	.15	.21	77	73	.11	.03	.37	.40	2	1	1	4	8
Mitre S	13	7	58	18	24	.02	.22	75	80	.04	.05	.41	.36	-1	3	3	7	11
Chamberlain J	19	12	43	21	36	.11	.14	70	88	.07	.07	.38	.20	7	7	3	-1	15
Wang C	14	10	53	20	27	.10	.19	70	57	.08	.06	.41	.50	2	3	3	10	18
MLB Average	***18***	***10***	***43***	***19***	***38***	***.10***	***.11***	***75***	***83***	***.05***	***.04***	***.39***	***.19***	--	--	--	--	--

Fielding Stats

Name	INN	SBA/G	CS%	ERA	WP+PB/G	PO	A	TE	FE
Catchers									
Posada J	785.0	1.18	22%	5.04	0.562	648	48	5	2
Molina J	356.7	0.71	18%	3.31	0.454	366	21	1	0
Cervelli F	241.3	0.78	38%	3.43	0.261	207	14	1	0
Cash K	67.0	1.48	18%	3.49	0.403	57	10	0	0

Name	Inn	PO	A	TE	FE	FPct	DPS	DPT	ZRDif	OOZ	Dif
First Base											
Teixeira M	1303.0	1222	49	1	3	.997	7	0	.016	37	-6
Swisher N	104.0	89	5	0	1	.989	0	0	.018	2	-15
Miranda J	23.0	19	1	0	0	1.000	0	0	--	1	--
Ransom C	8.0	5	2	0	0	1.000	1	0	--	1	--
Molina J	6.3	4	2	0	0	1.000	0	0	--	0	--
Posada J	5.0	3	2	0	0	1.000	0	0	--	0	--
Second Base											
Cano R	1399.0	308	424	4	8	.984	36	55	.015	44	4
Pena R	32.3	7	10	0	0	1.000	1	1	--	1	--
Hairston J	9.0	3	2	0	0	1.000	0	0	--	0	--
Ransom C	9.0	4	2	0	0	1.000	1	0	--	0	--
Shortstop											
Jeter D	1260.0	206	340	5	3	.986	36	34	.045	25	-18
Pena R	145.0	21	40	1	2	.953	4	5	.052	4	-11
Hairston J	28.3	6	10	0	0	1.000	0	2	--	2	--
Ransom C	16.0	2	5	0	0	1.000	0	0	--	0	--
Third Base											
Rodriguez	974.3	66	200	3	6	.967	16	0	.012	37	-4
Ransom C	164.0	10	31	3	1	.911	2	0	-.148	8	7
Pena R	135.3	10	30	0	2	.952	5	0	.045	3	-19
Hairston J	76.0	3	20	1	1	.920	2	0	--	6	--
Berroa A	63.0	6	16	2	1	.880	3	0	--	1	--
Hinske E	35.3	3	3	0	0	1.000	0	0	--	0	--
Molina J	2.0	0	0	0	0	0.000	0	0	--	--	--

Name	Inn	PO	A	TE	FE	FPct	DPS	DPT	ZRDif	OOZ	Dif
Left Field											
Damon J	1117.0	220	6	1	4	.978	2	0	.013	46	-9
Cabrera M	204.3	38	0	1	0	.974	0	0	-.008	7	-16
Hairston J	65.0	17	1	0	0	1.000	0	0	--	6	--
Swisher N	36.0	10	0	0	0	1.000	0	0	--	1	--
Hinske E	17.0	7	0	0	0	1.000	0	0	--	1	--
Guzman F	10.0	3	0	0	0	1.000	0	0	--	1	--
Center Field											
Cabrera M	806.3	226	2	0	0	1.000	1	0	.011	34	-26
Gardner B	628.7	186	3	0	2	.990	2	0	-.011	49	10
Hairston J	15.0	3	0	0	0	1.000	0	0	--	0	--
Right Field											
Swisher N	1052.0	239	2	1	4	.980	1	0	.021	55	0
Cabrera M	177.0	36	1	1	1	.949	0	0	-.012	10	4
Hinske E	129.0	25	0	0	0	1.000	0	0	.092	4	-21
Nady X	46.0	10	0	0	0	1.000	0	0	--	2	--
Duncan S	24.3	5	0	0	0	1.000	0	0	--	2	--
Hairston J	15.0	2	0	0	0	1.000	0	0	--	0	--
Guzman F	6.0	1	0	0	0	1.000	0	0	--	0	--

Oakland Athletics

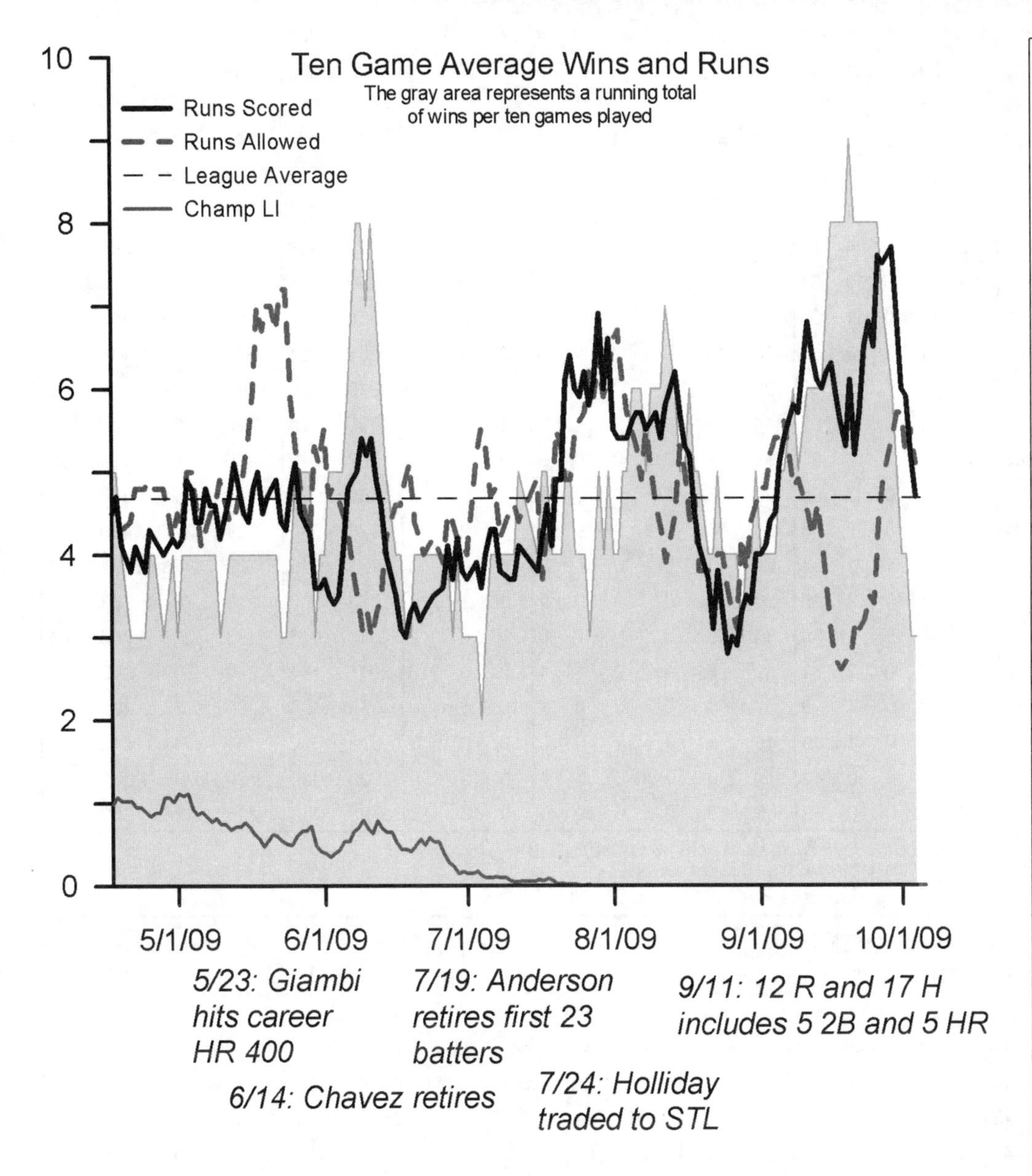

Stat Facts:

- Andrew Bailey had the most PRC (76) of any reliever in the majors
- Jack Cust walked or struck out in 46% of his PAs
- Brad Ziegler induced 17 DPs in 73 IP
- The A's -53 middle infield plus/minus ranked 29th in the majors
- Mark Ellis turned the fewest DPs (31) of any second baseman with at least 900 innings
- Ellis made the fewest OOZ plays (19) of any second baseman with at least 900 innings
- Dallas Braden had the most IP (139) of any pitcher in the majors with zero SB allowed
- Michael Wuertz struck out 34% of the batters he faced, and walked 8%
- Russ Springer's GB% (18%) was lowest in the majors
- Springer's FB% (60%) was highest in the majors
- Among players with more than 400 PAs, the A's highest GPA (.273) was achieved by Rajai Davis

Team Batting and Pitching/Fielding Stats by Month

	April	May	June	July	Aug	Sept/Oct
Wins	8	11	13	12	14	17
Losses	11	18	15	14	15	14
RS/G	4.2	4.3	4.1	5.3	4.3	5.7
RA/G	4.3	5.7	3.9	5.5	4.4	4.3
OBP	.313	.319	.305	.351	.317	.357
SLG	.322	.378	.377	.429	.407	.442
FIP	4.52	4.33	3.67	4.58	4.32	3.64
DER	.707	.671	.695	.678	.684	.684

Batting Stats

Player	BR	Runs	RBI	PA	Outs	H	2B	3B	HR	TB	K	BB	IBB	HBP	SH	SF	SB	CS	GDP	H-A	L^R	BA	OBP	SLG	GPA
Cust J *	86	88	70	612	398	123	16	0	25	214	185	93	5	2	0	4	4	1	7	.044	.062	.240	.356	.417	.270
Kennedy A *	80	65	63	587	390	153	29	1	11	217	86	45	2	4	5	3	20	6	8	.006	.053	.289	.348	.410	.264
Suzuki K	77	74	88	614	430	156	37	1	15	240	59	28	0	8	1	7	8	2	14	-.040	-.005	.274	.313	.421	.251
Sweeney R *	68	68	53	534	361	142	31	3	6	197	67	40	1	3	2	5	6	5	14	-.058	.013	.293	.348	.407	.264
Davis R	64	65	48	432	295	119	27	5	3	165	70	29	0	7	2	4	41	12	12	.035	.001	.305	.360	.423	.273
Holliday M	63	52	54	400	258	99	23	1	11	157	58	46	3	6	0	2	12	3	8	.024	-.017	.286	.378	.454	.289
Cabrera O	48	41	41	448	315	116	23	0	4	151	39	25	1	0	5	4	11	4	13	.028	-.038	.280	.318	.365	.239
Ellis M	48	52	61	410	291	99	23	0	10	152	54	23	1	2	3	5	10	3	10	-.029	-.001	.263	.305	.403	.243
Giambi J *	39	39	40	328	223	52	13	0	11	98	72	50	1	7	0	2	0	0	6	.055	-.042	.193	.332	.364	.246
Pennington C	30	27	21	229	160	58	11	3	4	87	46	19	0	1	1	0	7	5	5	-.034	-.104	.279	.342	.418	.264
Barton D *	27	31	24	192	120	43	12	1	3	66	25	26	0	2	1	3	0	2	1	-.079	-.120	.269	.372	.413	.276
Crosby B	27	35	29	272	193	53	10	2	6	85	44	24	0	2	4	4	2	1	7	.025	.082	.223	.295	.357	.226
Hairston S	25	24	35	248	185	55	13	1	7	91	38	8	0	2	0	5	3	2	5	.002	.012	.236	.262	.391	.220
Garciaparra	19	17	16	169	119	45	8	0	3	62	28	8	1	0	0	1	2	0	4	.069	.023	.281	.314	.388	.243
Powell L +	19	19	30	155	111	32	7	0	7	60	36	14	0	0	0	1	0	0	3	.028	-.112	.229	.297	.429	.246
Patterson E	17	15	11	110	68	27	5	1	1	37	25	14	0	0	0	2	6	1	0	.033	-.049	.287	.373	.394	.272
Buck T *	11	11	10	115	83	23	3	0	3	35	20	10	0	0	0	0	1	1	0	.033	.108	.219	.287	.333	.217
Hannahan J *	11	12	8	134	98	23	6	2	1	36	36	13	0	1	1	0	0	0	2	.115	.015	.193	.278	.303	.205
Everidge T	9	13	7	97	72	19	6	0	2	31	17	8	1	2	1	1	0	0	6	-.015	.134	.224	.302	.365	.232
Carson M	3	1	5	22	15	6	0	0	1	9	7	0	0	0	0	1	0	0	0	.068	.088	.286	.273	.429	.235
Cunningham A	2	6	6	57	48	8	2	0	1	13	16	3	0	1	0	0	0	0	3	.078	.032	.151	.211	.245	.159
Gonzalez E	1	0	0	2	0	2	0	0	0	2	0	0	0	0	0	0	0	0	0	-.700	.000	1.000	1.000	1.000	.714
Petit G	1	2	1	31	26	7	1	0	0	8	6	0	0	0	0	0	0	0	2	-.303	.085	.226	.226	.258	.170

Only includes batters with at least one Base Run. Italicized stats have been adjusted for home park.

Batted Ball Batting Stats

	% of PA		% of Batted Balls					Out %		Runs Per Event				Total Runs vs. Avg.				
Player	K%	BB%	GB%	LD%	FB%	IF/F	HR/OF	GB	OF	NIP	GB	LD	OF	NIP	GB	LD	FB	Tot
Holliday M	15	13	45	16	39	.13	.11	70	83	.10	.07	.43	.20	6	5	0	2	13
Cust J	30	16	37	20	43	.02	.18	76	83	.04	.04	.36	.28	4	-2	-7	13	8
Davis R	16	8	46	20	34	.14	.03	68	76	.04	.07	.44	.14	-1	6	7	-6	5
Sweeney R	13	8	45	24	31	.09	.05	75	77	.07	.04	.35	.15	0	1	8	-5	5
Kennedy A	15	8	41	24	36	.05	.07	80	81	.05	.01	.41	.14	-0	-6	13	-4	3
Barton D	13	15	31	20	48	.05	.05	77	80	.13	.03	.34	.13	4	-1	0	-0	3
Patterson E	23	13	34	20	46	.06	.03	67	76	.05	.10	.49	.12	1	1	2	-1	2
Pennington C	20	9	42	18	39	.11	.07	71	78	.03	.07	.39	.18	-1	3	-0	-1	1
Giambi J	22	17	36	14	50	.04	.11	83	85	.09	-.02	.39	.18	7	-5	-6	3	-2
Powell L	23	9	38	18	44	.11	.17	75	94	.02	.04	.37	.21	-1	-1	-2	1	-3
Suzuki K	10	6	44	19	36	.10	.09	76	86	.06	.04	.36	.14	-3	1	3	-5	-3
Garciaparra N	17	5	33	24	43	.14	.06	70	87	-.01	.05	.39	.09	-3	0	3	-4	-3
Buck T	17	9	30	23	47	.15	.09	80	90	.04	.02	.29	.11	-0	-1	-1	-2	-4
Hannahan J	27	10	37	17	46	.08	.03	77	85	.02	.02	.49	.06	-1	-1	-1	-4	-7
Ellis M	13	6	40	20	39	.12	.06	76	88	.03	.03	.41	.09	-3	-2	5	-10	-10
Hairston S	15	4	35	11	55	.19	.08	70	81	-.02	.07	.32	.16	-4	1	-7	0	-10
Crosby B	16	10	44	15	40	.13	.09	74	89	.06	.05	.29	.12	0	1	-6	-5	-10
Cabrera O	9	6	46	20	34	.12	.04	74	83	.07	.04	.33	.08	-2	2	0	-12	-12
MLB Average	***18***	***10***	***43***	***19***	***38***	***.10***	***.11***	***75***	***83***	***.05***	***.04***	***.39***	***.19***	--	--	--	--	--

Pitching Stats

Player	PRC	IP	BFP	G	GS	K	BB	IBB	HBP	H	HR	DP	DER	SB	CS	PO	W	L	Sv	Op	Hld	H-A	R^L	RA	ERA	FIP
Bailey A	76	83.3	323	68	0	91	24	3	0	49	5	4	.764	1	0	0	6	3	26	30	2	-.022	.005	1.84	1.84	2.54
Anderson B *	68	175.3	735	30	30	150	45	1	3	180	20	24	.673	14	4	4	11	11	0	0	0	-.016	.036	4.83	4.06	3.77
Cahill T	60	178.7	773	32	32	90	72	1	4	185	27	20	.714	17	10	2	10	13	0	0	0	.001	-.067	4.99	4.63	5.41
Braden D *	57	136.7	589	22	22	81	42	2	2	144	9	10	.692	0	2	2	8	9	0	0	0	-.008	-.071	4.15	3.89	3.78
Wuertz M	54	78.7	304	74	0	102	23	1	0	52	6	5	.711	9	3	1	6	1	4	6	23	-.093	-.001	2.86	2.63	2.43
Ziegler B	39	73.3	313	69	0	54	28	4	1	82	2	17	.632	3	1	1	2	4	7	10	14	-.009	-.099	3.31	3.07	3.10
Gonzalez G *	31	98.7	455	20	17	109	56	2	1	113	14	10	.629	4	2	2	6	7	0	0	0	.044	.101	6.20	5.75	4.50
Outman J *	31	67.3	276	14	12	53	25	0	0	53	9	7	.762	1	0	0	4	1	0	0	0	.000	-.113	4.01	3.48	4.47
Breslow C *	30	55.3	217	60	0	44	18	0	2	37	5	6	.764	7	3	1	7	5	0	2	13	-.063	.013	3.25	2.60	3.86
Mazzaro V	26	91.3	423	17	17	59	39	3	4	120	12	10	.644	8	3	1	4	9	0	0	0	.006	-.022	6.01	5.32	4.92
Kilby B *	23	17.0	65	11	1	20	4	0	0	10	1	0	.775	1	0	0	1	0	0	0	1	-.134	.081	1.06	0.53	2.31
Tomko B	21	36.7	142	6	6	22	6	0	1	31	7	6	.764	1	1	0	4	1	0	0	0	.056	-.020	2.95	2.95	5.05
Gonzalez E	20	65.3	299	26	6	39	28	4	6	76	4	6	.671	3	2	0	0	4	0	0	0	-.062	-.113	5.65	5.51	4.17
Springer R	19	41.7	191	48	0	47	14	2	0	52	5	1	.624	4	0	0	0	1	0	1	7	-.120	-.113	4.32	4.10	3.36
Casilla S	13	48.3	233	46	0	35	25	3	3	61	6	4	.652	3	2	1	1	2	0	0	5	-.107	-.072	6.70	5.96	4.91
Gray J	12	26.3	116	24	0	19	4	1	2	30	3	3	.648	0	0	0	0	1	0	0	1	.030	-.024	4.10	3.76	3.80
Meloan J	11	8.3	29	6	0	11	2	0	0	3	0	0	.813	0	1	0	0	0	0	0	0	.115	-.156	1.08	0.00	1.27
Cameron K	10	18.3	74	11	0	15	6	0	0	15	1	3	.712	1	1	0	0	0	1	1	1	-.101	.013	3.44	3.44	3.25
Blevins J *	9	22.3	90	20	0	23	6	1	0	19	2	2	.712	0	0	0	0	0	0	0	0	.126	.029	4.84	4.84	2.97
Eveland D *	8	44.0	221	13	9	22	26	1	0	70	4	10	.604	5	0	0	2	4	0	0	0	-.082	.029	7.98	7.16	5.08
Giese D	7	22.0	94	7	1	11	9	1	0	22	5	3	.754	2	0	0	0	3	0	0	0	.079	-.000	5.32	5.32	6.24
Mortensen C	4	27.7	133	6	6	11	12	0	2	37	5	1	.670	5	2	0	2	4	0	0	0	-.178	-.136	9.11	7.81	6.26
Gallagher S	2	14.3	71	6	2	10	7	0	2	21	1	0	.608	2	1	0	1	2	0	0	0	-.033	-.160	10.05	8.16	4.59
Rodriguez H	2	4.0	20	3	0	4	2	0	1	4	0	0	.615	1	0	0	0	0	0	0	0	.183	-.250	4.50	2.25	3.44
Reineke C	1	5.0	22	1	1	1	0	0	1	7	2	1	.722	0	0	0	0	0	0	0	0	--	-.214	7.20	7.20	8.59

Italicized stats have been adjusted for home park.

Batted Ball Pitching Stats

	% of PA		% of Batted Balls					Out %		Runs Per Event				Total Runs vs. Avg.				
Player	K%	BB%	GB%	LD%	FB%	IF/F	HR/OF	GB	OF	NIP	GB	LD	OF	NIP	GB	LD	FB	Tot
Bailey A	28	8	42	13	45	.10	.06	76	86	-.01	.03	.27	.10	-7	-2	-12	-8	-29
Wuertz M	34	8	45	14	40	.11	.10	71	82	-.03	.08	.37	.18	-8	1	-8	-4	-19
Breslow C	20	9	32	21	47	.15	.08	71	93	.03	.06	.24	.08	-1	-0	-5	-7	-13
Outman J	19	9	38	19	43	.12	.11	80	91	.03	.00	.37	.12	-1	-4	-2	-5	-11
Anderson B	20	6	51	15	34	.11	.13	70	84	-.00	.06	.40	.20	-11	9	-7	-2	-11
Braden D	14	7	36	21	43	.09	.05	72	85	.05	.07	.36	.09	-2	5	3	-11	-5
Tomko B	15	5	36	19	45	.10	.15	78	92	-.00	.02	.31	.18	-2	-1	-2	1	-4
Ziegler B	17	9	62	18	20	.07	.05	69	70	.05	.07	.36	.19	-0	6	-1	-5	-0
Gray J	16	5	56	16	28	.04	.13	68	71	-.00	.08	.32	.28	-2	2	-1	2	1
Springer R	25	7	18	22	60	.13	.08	65	79	-.01	.10	.45	.17	-3	1	3	2	2
Gonzalez E	13	11	41	18	41	.07	.05	76	74	.10	.04	.41	.18	4	-1	2	2	7
Mortensen C	8	11	54	20	26	.00	.18	72	87	.14	.07	.40	.27	2	3	2	2	9
Casilla J	15	12	50	20	30	.10	.11	67	85	.09	.10	.45	.18	3	6	4	-2	10
Eveland D	10	12	56	18	25	.05	.10	68	76	.14	.07	.46	.22	4	5	5	1	14
Gonzalez G	24	13	46	18	36	.10	.13	68	75	.04	.08	.45	.29	2	6	1	7	15
Cahill T	12	10	48	18	34	.07	.14	79	85	.10	.01	.45	.22	6	-7	9	8	16
Mazzaro V	14	10	39	21	40	.08	.10	72	79	.08	.06	.40	.20	3	3	7	6	19
MLB Average	***18***	***10***	***43***	***19***	***38***	***.10***	***.11***	***75***	***83***	***.05***	***.04***	***.39***	***.19***	--	--	--	--	--

Fielding Stats

Name	INN	SBA/G	CS%	ERA	WP+PB/G	PO	A	TE	FE
Catchers									
Suzuki K	1173.3	0.75	17%	4.24	0.291	923	68	3	0
Powell L	274.0	0.66	45%	4.50	0.328	214	13	2	1

Name	Inn	PO	A	TE	FE	FPct	DPS	DPT	ZRDif	OOZ	Dif
First Base											
Giambi J	450.0	441	17	0	3	.993	2	0	-.087	8	-17
Barton D	416.7	418	25	0	1	.998	4	0	.005	24	23
Crosby B	268.0	235	13	0	0	1.000	1	0	.132	3	-23
Everidge T	166.0	138	11	0	1	.993	1	0	.068	3	-16
Garciaparra	101.3	95	5	0	0	1.000	3	0	-.327	6	25
Powell L	40.3	39	4	0	1	.977	0	0	--	2	--
Kennedy A	3.0	1	0	0	0	1.000	0	0	--	--	--
Hannahan J	2.0	1	0	0	0	1.000	0	0	--	--	--
Second Base											
Ellis M	906.7	197	285	1	4	.990	31	31	.017	19	-7
Kennedy A	421.0	87	121	5	2	.967	15	15	-.069	8	-8
Petit G	50.0	14	15	1	0	.967	1	3	--	2	--
Crosby B	37.0	12	8	0	1	.952	1	2	--	1	--
Patterson E	30.7	9	9	1	1	.900	1	0	--	0	--
Hannahan J	2.0	0	0	0	0	.000	0	0	--	--	--
Shortstop											
Cabrera O	887.7	156	273	5	9	.968	27	33	-.043	24	-11
Pennington	533.7	90	181	4	4	.971	18	22	-.008	10	-20
Crosby B	26.0	1	8	0	0	1.000	2	0	--	0	--
Third Base											
Kennedy A	691.7	50	156	6	7	.941	7	0	-.017	26	-4
Hannahan J	335.3	35	89	3	1	.969	9	0	.080	27	39
Crosby B	297.3	23	72	2	5	.931	5	0	-.101	15	9
Chavez E	67.0	5	15	0	0	1.000	2	0	--	1	--
Garciaparra	32.0	1	8	0	0	1.000	0	0	--	0	--
Petit G	24.0	1	4	0	0	1.000	0	0	--	1	--

Name	Inn	PO	A	TE	FE	FPct	DPS	DPT	ZRDif	OOZ	Dif
Left Field											
Holliday M	812.7	189	6	1	3	.980	1	0	.058	52	14
Hairston S	361.3	90	1	0	0	1.000	1	0	.064	23	13
Patterson E	179.3	33	1	0	0	1.000	0	0	-.047	11	11
Sweeney R	44.0	8	2	0	0	1.000	0	0	--	1	--
Buck T	29.0	0	0	0	0	0.000	0	0	--	--	--
Cunningham	17.0	1	0	0	0	1.000	0	0	--	--	--
Denorfia C	2.0	0	0	0	0	.000	0	0	--	--	--
Carson M	2.0	0	0	0	0	.000	0	0	--	--	--
Center Field											
Davis R	856.3	259	8	1	3	.985	1	0	-.001	62	4
Sweeney R	452.7	146	4	0	1	.993	0	0	.032	44	29
Hairston S	106.0	30	0	0	1	.968	0	0	-.074	6	-11
Patterson E	30.0	6	0	0	0	1.000	0	0	--	1	--
Denorfia C	2.3	0	0	0	0	.000	0	0	--	--	--
Right Field											
Sweeney R	600.0	165	5	1	1	.988	2	0	.045	43	19
Cust J	401.7	69	1	0	2	.972	1	0	-.151	16	-12
Buck T	217.7	61	0	0	0	1.000	0	0	.053	12	3
Cunningham	119.0	21	0	0	1	.913	0	0	-.066	5	-10
Carson M	54.0	12	0	0	0	1.000	0	0	--	3	--
Davis R	35.0	6	0	0	0	1.000	0	0	--	2	--
Patterson E	12.0	2	0	0	0	1.000	0	0	--	0	--
Kennedy A	5.0	1	0	0	0	1.000	0	0	--	0	--
Denorfia C	2.0	0	0	0	0	.000	0	0	--	--	--
Crosby B	1.0	0	0	0	0	.000	0	0	--	--	--

Philadelphia Phillies

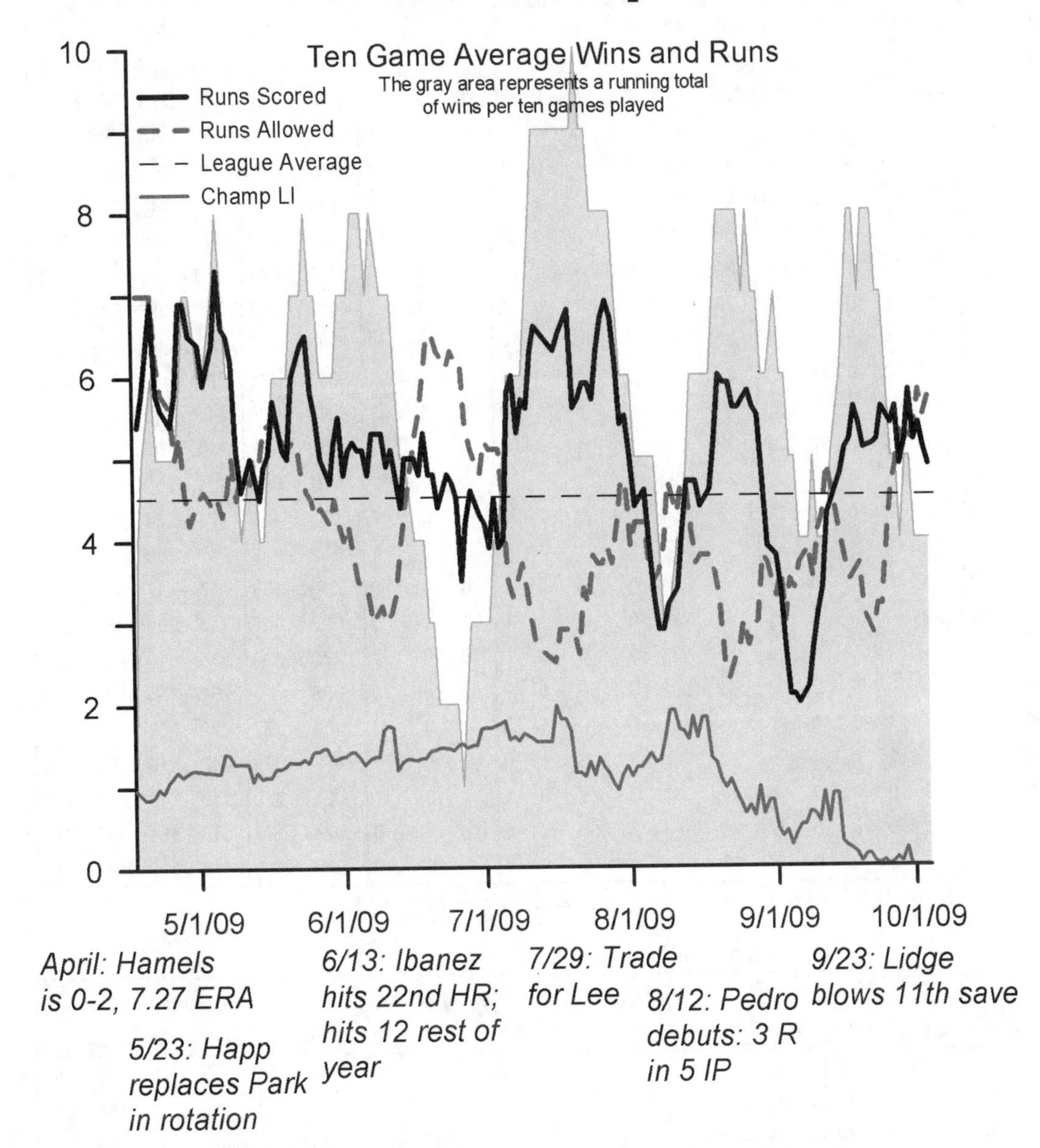

Stat Facts:

- Jimmy Rollins made the most outs (519) of any batter
- Shane Victorino led the majors with 13 triples
- Victorino's 17 line drive runs tied for the major league lead
- Chase Utley led the majors with 24 HBPs
- Utley stole 23 bases in 23 attempts
- Utley had the highest ZR (.846) of any regular second baseman
- Ryan Howard's L^R of .128 was highest of any regular
- Howard hit just 2 infield pop-ups
- 26% of Howard's outfield flies were home runs
- 89% of the outfield flies allowed by Joe Blanton were outs
- Matt Stairs walked in 20% of his PAs
- Brett Myers allowed 18 home runs in 71 IP

Team Batting and Pitching/Fielding Stats by Month

	April	May	June	July	Aug	Sept/Oct
Wins	11	17	11	20	16	18
Losses	9	11	15	7	11	16
RS/G	6.0	5.3	4.8	5.7	4.5	4.6
RA/G	5.6	4.8	4.8	3.6	3.6	4.3
OBP	.349	.344	.320	.353	.319	.325
SLG	.464	.467	.422	.442	.470	.426
FIP	5.66	4.75	4.68	4.00	3.79	3.95
DER	.691	.703	.681	.725	.693	.681

Batting Stats

Player	BR	Runs	RBI	PA	Outs	H	2B	3B	HR	TB	K	BB	IBB	HBP	SH	SF	SB	CS	GDP	H-A	L^R	BA	OBP	SLG	GPA
Howard R *	117	105	141	703	456	172	37	4	45	352	186	75	8	6	0	6	8	1	11	-.008	.128	.279	.360	.571	.299
Utley C *	115	112	93	687	415	161	28	4	31	290	110	88	3	24	0	4	23	0	5	-.023	-.027	.282	.397	.508	.300
Werth J	105	98	99	676	432	153	26	1	36	289	156	91	8	8	0	6	20	3	11	.008	.086	.268	.373	.506	.289
Victorino S	94	102	62	694	452	181	39	13	10	276	71	60	1	6	4	4	25	8	5	.027	.022	.292	.358	.445	.267
Ibanez R *	87	93	93	565	380	136	32	3	34	276	119	56	8	4	0	5	4	0	16	-.016	-.038	.272	.347	.552	.288
Rollins J +	83	100	77	725	519	168	43	5	21	284	70	44	1	2	2	5	31	8	7	.026	-.017	.250	.296	.423	.234
Feliz P	62	62	82	625	439	154	30	2	12	224	68	35	3	3	2	5	0	1	12	.021	-.018	.266	.308	.386	.231
Ruiz C	46	32	43	379	250	82	26	1	9	137	39	47	8	4	4	2	3	2	8	.115	.042	.255	.355	.425	.261
Dobbs G *	17	15	20	169	118	38	6	0	5	59	29	11	1	1	0	3	1	0	2	-.040	-.074	.247	.296	.383	.224
Stairs M *	16	15	17	129	83	20	4	0	5	39	30	23	3	3	0	0	0	0	0	-.043	.147	.194	.357	.379	.250
Francisco B	14	10	13	104	75	27	9	0	5	51	24	5	0	1	0	1	1	4	1	.038	-.135	.278	.317	.526	.269
Coste C	13	12	8	118	79	25	8	0	2	39	27	14	1	1	1	0	0	0	2	.113	.005	.245	.342	.382	.245
Bako P *	11	12	9	130	93	26	4	0	3	39	32	13	2	1	0	0	0	1	2	-.033	.162	.224	.308	.336	.218
Mayberry J	6	8	8	60	47	12	3	0	4	27	23	2	0	1	0	0	0	0	2	-.001	.083	.211	.250	.474	.226
Bruntlett E	5	15	7	118	89	18	7	0	0	25	26	5	0	3	2	3	2	0	2	-.001	.120	.171	.224	.238	.157
Cairo M	5	6	2	47	34	12	2	1	1	19	4	0	0	1	1	0	0	0	1	-.032	-.129	.267	.283	.422	.228
Tracy A *	2	1	1	12	7	5	0	1	0	7	3	0	0	0	0	0	0	0	0	.133	.364	.417	.417	.583	.327
Park C	2	1	1	18	12	2	0	0	1	5	5	3	0	0	1	0	0	0	0	-.090	-.046	.143	.294	.357	.217
Marson L	2	3	0	20	14	4	1	0	0	5	7	3	0	0	0	0	0	0	1	-.232	--	.235	.350	.294	.226
Hoover P	1	0	1	4	1	3	0	0	0	3	1	0	0	0	0	0	0	0	0	.233	--	.750	.750	.750	.515
Myers B	1	2	0	20	14	4	1	0	0	5	4	1	0	0	1	0	0	0	0	.104	-.277	.222	.263	.278	.184
Lee C *	1	2	1	33	27	7	2	0	0	9	13	0	0	0	0	0	0	0	1	-.024	.028	.212	.212	.273	.160
Moyer J *	1	2	2	59	38	5	0	0	0	5	21	6	0	1	9	1	0	0	1	.025	.029	.119	.240	.119	.135
Hamels C *	1	6	5	69	52	9	3	0	0	12	29	1	0	0	7	0	1	0	0	.024	.129	.148	.161	.197	.119
Blanton J	1	4	1	69	48	7	0	0	0	7	21	4	0	1	9	0	0	0	0	-.009	-.089	.127	.200	.127	.119

Only includes batters with at least one Base Run. Italicized stats have been adjusted for home park.

Batted Ball Batting Stats

	% of PA		% of Batted Balls					Out %		Runs Per Event				Total Runs vs. Avg.				
Player	K%	BB%	GB%	LD%	FB%	IF/F	HR/OF	GB	OF	NIP	GB	LD	OF	NIP	GB	LD	FB	Tot
Utley C	16	16	34	18	48	.07	.14	71	84	.12	.07	.39	.23	18	3	1	18	41
Howard R	26	12	36	23	41	.01	.26	78	77	.03	.01	.34	.43	-2	-7	-0	47	38
Werth J	23	15	36	20	44	.09	.21	72	82	.07	.06	.34	.33	8	0	-4	27	31
Ibanez R	21	11	43	15	42	.04	.21	75	81	.04	.03	.39	.37	-0	-2	-5	32	25
Victorino S	10	10	45	22	33	.17	.05	72	83	.11	.07	.43	.13	6	9	17	-13	19
Ruiz C	10	13	42	19	39	.09	.09	76	89	.15	.04	.34	.13	8	1	-1	-4	4
Francisco B	23	6	28	26	46	.12	.17	81	80	-.02	.00	.41	.29	-2	-1	2	4	3
Stairs M	23	20	47	11	42	.10	.18	79	87	.10	.02	.35	.26	4	-1	-4	2	1
Coste C	23	13	37	25	37	.11	.08	93	65	.05	-.07	.41	.25	1	-4	2	1	-0
Bako P	25	11	46	20	34	.07	.12	76	78	.03	.04	.30	.21	-1	-0	-2	-0	-3
Dobbs G	17	7	29	20	51	.06	.08	78	84	.02	.02	.29	.14	-2	-2	-2	0	-4
Rollins J	10	6	40	19	41	.14	.10	77	89	.07	.04	.36	.14	-2	-0	2	-6	-7
Feliz P	11	6	44	21	35	.10	.07	81	81	.05	.00	.34	.15	-3	-7	4	-5	-10
Bruntlett E	22	7	34	22	44	.06	.00	89	85	-.00	-.05	.32	.02	-2	-3	-2	-6	-12
MLB Average	***18***	***10***	***43***	***19***	***38***	***.10***	***.11***	***75***	***83***	***.05***	***.04***	***.39***	***.19***	***--***	***--***	***--***	***--***	***--***

Pitching Stats

Player	PRC	IP	BFP	G	GS	K	BB	IBB	HBP	H	HR	DP	DER	SB	CS	PO	W	L	Sv	Op	Hld	H-A	R^L	RA	ERA	FIP
Happ J *	87	166.0	685	35	23	119	56	2	5	149	20	19	.728	4	4	1	12	4	0	0	0	.046	-.029	2.98	2.93	4.35
Blanton J	80	195.3	837	31	31	163	59	4	8	198	30	15	.698	8	4	0	12	8	0	0	0	-.008	.018	4.10	4.05	4.45
Hamels C *	75	193.7	814	32	32	168	43	4	5	206	24	16	.674	18	11	5	10	11	0	0	0	-.047	-.019	4.41	4.32	3.71
Moyer J *	50	162.0	699	30	25	94	43	1	10	177	27	13	.707	14	5	4	12	10	0	0	1	.019	-.040	5.06	4.94	5.12
Madson R	40	77.3	320	79	0	78	22	3	3	73	7	10	.681	5	1	1	5	5	10	16	26	.046	-.030	3.38	3.26	3.16
Lee C *	35	79.7	328	12	12	74	10	0	2	80	7	5	.672	0	1	1	7	4	0	0	0	-.038	.045	3.95	3.39	2.89
Park C	31	83.3	362	45	7	73	33	3	5	84	5	9	.667	2	2	0	3	3	0	1	13	.003	-.023	4.64	4.43	3.44
Durbin C	24	69.7	314	59	0	62	47	2	7	56	8	3	.747	5	1	0	2	2	2	3	8	-.008	-.001	4.91	4.39	5.10
Myers B	24	70.7	304	18	10	50	23	1	4	74	18	6	.722	3	3	2	4	3	0	0	3	.036	.121	4.84	4.84	6.15
Eyre S *	23	30.0	128	42	0	22	16	0	1	22	3	3	.779	1	0	0	2	1	0	0	13	.101	-.034	1.80	1.50	4.68
Martinez P	21	44.7	191	9	9	37	8	0	4	48	7	1	.696	4	0	0	5	1	0	0	0	-.062	-.006	3.63	3.63	4.34
Walker T	18	35.3	150	32	0	27	9	1	3	31	4	1	.729	3	0	0	2	1	0	0	1	-.041	.023	3.06	3.06	4.03
Condrey C	18	42.0	174	45	0	25	14	3	1	37	4	6	.731	2	0	0	6	2	1	2	7	-.000	.054	3.64	3.00	4.06
Lidge B	12	58.7	283	67	0	61	34	3	5	72	11	4	.622	11	1	1	0	8	31	42	1	-.052	-.031	7.82	7.21	5.35
Kendrick K	11	26.3	112	9	2	15	9	0	1	27	1	6	.686	0	0	0	3	1	0	0	0	.004	-.046	3.76	3.42	3.64
Taschner J *	8	29.3	143	24	0	19	20	2	2	38	3	3	.636	4	2	0	1	1	0	1	0	-.066	.012	5.52	4.91	5.23
Romero J *	8	16.7	73	21	0	12	13	0	2	13	2	4	.750	2	0	1	0	0	0	1	6	.092	.139	3.24	2.70	5.97
Lopez R	6	30.0	137	7	5	19	11	1	0	42	3	5	.625	3	1	0	3	1	0	0	0	-.084	-.018	7.20	5.70	4.18
Bastardo A *	5	23.7	106	6	5	19	9	0	2	26	4	1	.694	2	1	1	2	3	0	0	0	-.039	.008	6.85	6.46	5.14
Escalona S *	5	13.7	60	14	0	10	5	1	3	12	0	1	.714	1	0	0	1	0	0	0	2	.124	.016	4.61	4.61	3.22
Register S	1	2.0	11	1	0	1	1	0	1	3	0	0	.625	2	0	0	0	0	0	0	0	--	-.070	4.50	4.50	5.15
Carpenter D	1	5.7	32	3	1	5	4	0	1	11	1	1	.524	1	0	0	1	0	0	0	0	.095	.139	11.12	11.12	6.33

Italicized stats have been adjusted for home park.

Batted Ball Pitching Stats

	% of PA		% of Batted Balls					Out %		Runs Per Event				Total Runs vs. Avg.				
Player	K%	BB%	GB%	LD%	FB%	IF/F	HR/OF	GB	OF	NIP	GB	LD	OF	NIP	GB	LD	FB	Tot
Happ J	17	9	38	19	43	.10	.10	78	82	.04	.02	.33	.18	-2	-5	-7	1	-13
Madson R	24	8	46	22	32	.06	.11	76	88	-.00	.03	.41	.14	-5	-2	2	-6	-10
Lee C	23	4	38	24	38	.11	.08	76	85	-.05	.04	.44	.13	-9	-1	7	-6	-8
Condrey C	14	9	55	20	24	.06	.13	82	81	.06	-.01	.29	.23	-0	-3	-1	-1	-6
Eyre S	17	13	33	21	46	.10	.08	79	88	.09	-.00	.23	.13	2	-2	-3	-2	-5
Kendrick K	13	9	56	22	22	.05	.06	79	88	.07	-.00	.36	.05	0	-2	1	-4	-4
Walker T	18	8	38	15	48	.13	.09	68	88	.03	.09	.32	.14	-1	1	-3	-1	-4
Hamels C	21	6	40	21	39	.13	.12	74	82	-.01	.05	.41	.21	-14	2	6	3	-3
Park C	20	10	44	24	33	.13	.07	73	82	.04	.04	.38	.14	0	0	3	-7	-3
Durbin C	20	17	39	18	42	.16	.12	82	84	.10	.00	.34	.19	8	-4	-4	-1	-1
Blanton J	19	8	41	20	39	.12	.15	71	89	.02	.07	.38	.20	-7	4	0	1	-0
Martinez P	19	6	29	27	44	.05	.12	90	78	-.00	-.04	.33	.26	-3	-4	2	6	1
Bastardo A	18	10	23	25	52	.15	.06	82	87	.06	-.01	.60	.09	0	-2	6	-2	3
Lopez R	14	8	35	26	39	.12	.08	76	61	.05	.03	.29	.32	-0	-0	1	5	6
Moyer J	13	8	41	19	40	.13	.14	77	83	.05	.03	.37	.24	-2	-3	1	11	8
Taschner J	13	15	40	24	37	.14	.09	68	86	.13	.08	.41	.16	4	2	4	-1	8
Myers B	16	9	47	18	35	.12	.25	81	88	.05	.01	.45	.36	-0	-3	3	11	10
Lidge B	22	14	39	19	42	.09	.16	67	84	.07	.08	.53	.26	3	3	5	6	17
MLB Average	***18***	***10***	***43***	***19***	***38***	***.10***	***.11***	***75***	***83***	***.05***	***.04***	***.39***	***.19***	--	--	--	--	--

Fielding Stats

Name	INN	SBA/G	CS%	ERA	WP+PB/G	PO	A	TE	FE
Catchers									
Ruiz C	882.3	0.78	20%	4.00	0.184	707	49	3	0
Bako P	299.3	0.54	17%	3.91	0.421	254	9	2	3
Coste C	211.0	0.73	12%	4.69	0.171	164	6	0	0
Marson L	52.0	0.69	50%	5.71	0.173	48	6	0	0
Hoover P	11.0	1.64	0%	6.55	0.818	9	1	0	0

Name	Inn	PO	A	TE	FE	FPct	DPS	DPT	ZRDif	OOZ	Dif
First Base											
Howard R	1388.0	1300	95	6	8	.990	6	0	.034	31	-12
Dobbs G	41.0	24	1	0	1	.962	0	0	--	0	--
Tracy A	10.0	8	1	0	0	1.000	0	0	--	0	--
Coste C	9.0	9	0	0	0	1.000	0	0	--	--	--
Bruntlett E	7.3	6	0	0	0	1.000	0	0	--	--	--
Second Base											
Utley C	1357.0	354	408	4	8	.984	34	58	.033	35	-2
Bruntlett E	65.3	20	20	0	2	.952	2	5	--	2	--
Cairo M	33.3	10	9	0	0	1.000	1	2	--	1	--
Shortstop											
Rollins J	1364.0	212	389	3	3	.990	37	31	.001	44	-6
Bruntlett E	75.0	13	18	1	0	.969	1	0	--	3	--
Cairo M	13.0	1	4	0	0	1.000	0	0	--	0	--
Feliz P	3.0	0	0	0	0	0.000	0	0	--	0	--
Third Base											
Feliz P	1342.0	110	312	4	11	.966	33	0	.028	32	-18
Dobbs G	88.7	3	25	0	0	1.000	1	0	--	2	--
Bruntlett E	15.7	0	1	0	0	1.000	0	0	--	0	--
Cairo M	9.0	1	1	0	0	1.000	0	0	--	0	--

Name	Inn	PO	A	TE	FE	FPct	DPS	DPT	ZRDif	OOZ	Dif
Left Field											
Ibanez R	1123.0	213	9	1	1	.991	0	0	-.030	41	-14
Mayberry J	96.3	25	0	0	0	1.000	0	0	--	6	--
Dobbs G	83.0	17	0	0	0	1.000	0	0	--	3	--
Francisco	71.3	19	0	0	0	1.000	0	0	--	4	--
Stairs M	43.0	14	1	0	0	1.000	1	0	--	1	--
Werth J	28.3	3	1	0	0	1.000	0	0	--	0	--
Bruntlett E	10.0	5	0	0	1	.833	0	0	--	2	--
Center Field											
Victorino S	1330.0	336	8	0	1	.997	1	0	.011	63	-21
Werth J	62.3	23	0	1	1	.920	0	0	--	5	--
Francisco	62.0	21	1	0	0	1.000	0	0	--	2	--
Bruntlett E	1.0	0	0	0	0	.000	0	0	--	--	--
Right Field											
Werth J	1288.0	327	10	0	4	.988	4	0	.018	77	8
Stairs M	51.0	9	1	0	0	1.000	1	0	--	2	--
Francisco	48.0	11	1	0	0	1.000	0	0	--	4	--
Mayberry J	30.7	6	1	0	0	1.000	1	0	--	3	--
Bruntlett E	22.3	4	1	0	0	1.000	0	0	--	1	--
Dobbs G	15.0	6	0	0	0	1.000	0	0	--	4	--

Pittsburgh Pirates

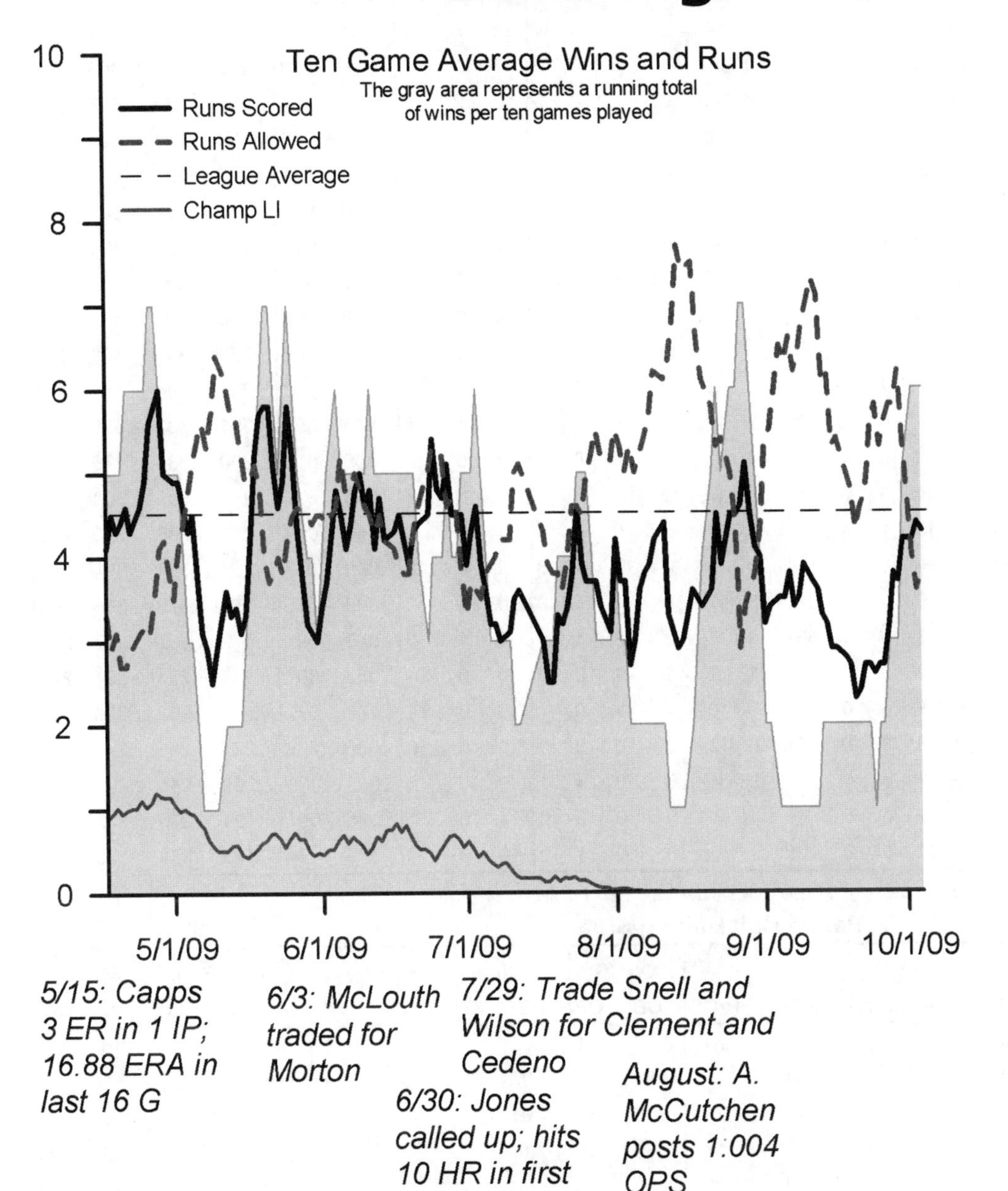

Stat Notes:

- The DER behind Kevin Hart (.609) was lowest of any ML pitcher with at least 50 IP
- Pat Maholm induced 33 DPs, tied for most in the NL
- Maholm's R^L (-.106) was lowest of any ML pitcher with at least 162 IP
- Zach Duke's R^L was just .001
- Duke allowed just 7 SBs in 15 attempts
- 20% of Garrett Jones's outfield flies were home runs
- 23% of Jack Wilson's fly balls were infield pop-ups
- Ross Ohlendorf tied for the ML lead with 8 pickoffs
- Brandon Moss made 56 OOZ plays in 665 innings in right field
- Brian Bixler struck out 26 times in 46 PAs
- Andrew McCutchen had more sacrifice flies (4) than GIDPs (3)
- Charlie Morton induced 18 DPs in 97 IP

Team Batting and Pitching/Fielding Stats by Month

	April	May	June	July	Aug	Sept/Oct
Wins	11	11	14	8	9	9
Losses	10	18	13	17	19	22
RS/G	4.8	3.9	4.6	3.3	3.9	3.5
RA/G	3.6	4.9	4.2	4.6	5.5	5.4
OBP	.335	.327	.338	.282	.313	.315
SLG	.415	.378	.407	.372	.406	.353
FIP	4.77	4.42	4.47	4.20	4.76	4.47
DER	.740	.686	.712	.677	.665	.686

Batting Stats

Player	*BR*	Runs	RBI	PA	Outs	H	2B	3B	HR	TB	K	BB	IBB	HBP	SH	SF	SB	CS	GDP	H-A	L^R	BA	OBP	SLG	*GPA*
McCutchen A	*74*	74	54	493	317	124	26	9	12	204	83	54	2	2	0	4	22	5	3	.054	.035	.286	.365	.471	*.288*
LaRoche A	*66*	64	64	590	406	135	29	5	12	210	84	50	1	8	6	2	3	1	16	.029	.050	.258	.330	.401	*.254*
Jones G *	*62*	45	44	358	230	92	21	1	21	178	76	40	8	1	0	3	10	2	6	.047	.124	.293	.372	.567	*.315*
Sanchez F	*47*	45	34	382	260	105	28	3	6	157	60	20	4	2	2	3	5	1	9	.011	.016	.296	.334	.442	*.266*
LaRoche A *	*45*	46	40	368	255	80	25	1	12	143	81	41	6	0	0	3	2	2	9	.135	.071	.247	.329	.441	*.264*
Young D +	*40*	40	43	388	273	94	16	2	7	135	90	29	0	3	1	1	2	0	13	-.010	-.041	.266	.326	.381	*.247*
Moss B *	*40*	47	41	424	306	91	20	4	7	140	84	34	3	4	0	1	1	5	7	.045	.006	.236	.304	.364	*.232*
Morgan N *	*34*	39	27	321	217	77	6	5	2	99	49	29	2	5	5	4	18	10	6	.012	.116	.277	.351	.356	*.252*
Doumit R +	*32*	31	38	304	222	70	16	0	10	116	49	20	6	1	0	3	4	0	12	.009	-.008	.250	.299	.414	*.243*
McLouth N *	*29*	27	34	195	127	43	7	1	9	79	29	21	0	4	0	2	7	0	2	.060	-.032	.256	.349	.470	*.280*
Wilson J	*29*	26	31	286	200	71	18	1	4	103	31	15	2	0	3	2	2	1	4	.012	-.003	.267	.304	.387	*.238*
Milledge L	*27*	20	20	239	164	64	11	0	4	87	37	12	0	3	2	2	6	4	4	.013	.050	.291	.333	.395	*.254*
Vazquez R *	*20*	17	16	239	159	47	7	0	1	57	47	31	4	2	0	2	1	0	2	.065	-.058	.230	.335	.279	*.225*
Jaramillo J	*20*	20	26	224	165	52	14	0	3	75	33	17	2	0	1	0	1	0	11	.046	-.076	.252	.309	.364	*.235*
Pearce S	*19*	19	16	186	133	34	13	1	4	61	43	21	0	0	0	0	1	0	2	.046	.092	.206	.296	.370	*.230*
Cedeno R	*18*	17	21	170	118	40	4	1	5	61	29	9	2	2	4	0	2	0	3	.009	-.017	.258	.307	.394	*.241*
Hinske E *	*16*	18	11	126	79	27	9	0	1	39	27	17	0	3	0	0	0	0	0	.040	-.016	.255	.373	.368	*.265*
Diaz R	*12*	9	19	138	99	36	7	0	1	46	9	3	0	3	1	2	0	1	5	-.049	-.091	.279	.307	.357	*.232*
Monroe C	*7*	8	16	87	66	17	2	0	3	28	21	7	1	1	0	0	0	0	4	.053	.097	.215	.287	.354	*.222*
Cruz L	*4*	5	2	78	56	15	1	0	0	16	7	6	1	1	0	1	0	0	1	.063	-.017	.214	.282	.229	*.188*
Bixler B	*4*	5	3	46	34	10	5	0	0	15	26	2	0	0	0	0	1	0	0	-.036	.252	.227	.261	.341	*.207*
Duke Z *	*3*	1	5	79	48	12	2	0	0	14	18	4	0	0	14	1	0	0	0	.003	-.038	.200	.246	.233	*.173*
Walker N +	*2*	5	0	40	30	7	1	0	0	8	11	4	0	0	0	0	1	0	1	.095	-.097	.194	.275	.222	*.183*
Hart K	*1*	1	1	20	14	2	0	0	0	2	4	3	0	0	1	0	0	0	0	.029	--	.125	.263	.125	*.153*

Only includes batters with at least one Base Run. Italicized stats have been adjusted for home park.

Batted Ball Batting Stats

	% of PA		% of Batted Balls					Out %		Runs Per Event				Total Runs vs. Avg.				
Player	K%	BB%	GB%	LD%	FB%	IF/F	HR/OF	GB	OF	NIP	GB	LD	OF	NIP	GB	LD	FB	Tot
Jones G	21	11	40	18	41	.05	.20	73	81	.05	.05	.49	.33	1	1	4	16	22
McCutchen A	17	11	42	19	39	.08	.10	64	85	.07	.12	.40	.18	4	12	2	1	18
Sanchez F	16	6	43	23	34	.04	.06	70	83	.01	.07	.44	.12	-4	4	10	-5	5
McLouth N	15	13	41	14	45	.10	.14	78	88	.10	.02	.46	.20	3	-1	-1	3	4
Hinske E	21	16	45	15	40	.19	.04	69	83	.08	.10	.47	.11	2	3	-1	-3	1
LaRoche A	22	11	38	21	41	.10	.13	87	80	.04	-.04	.46	.24	0	-9	4	5	1
Morgan N	15	11	52	19	29	.05	.03	73	71	.08	.05	.32	.16	2	3	-2	-4	-1
Milledge L	15	6	41	21	39	.11	.05	69	85	.02	.08	.42	.08	-2	3	4	-6	-1
Diaz R	7	4	56	18	26	.06	.03	77	79	.07	.02	.35	.13	-1	1	0	-2	-2
Cedeno R	17	6	52	13	35	.14	.14	69	78	.01	.07	.23	.27	-2	2	-5	2	-3
Doumit R	16	7	42	18	40	.09	.12	77	81	.02	.01	.34	.21	-3	-3	-2	3	-5
Wilson J	11	5	41	16	43	.23	.05	73	82	.04	.07	.44	.11	-2	3	1	-7	-5
Pearce S	23	11	38	19	43	.06	.08	80	80	.04	.03	.27	.17	-0	-1	-4	-1	-6
Vazquez R	20	14	47	19	34	.09	.02	77	83	.08	.03	.37	.04	3	-1	-1	-9	-7
LaRoche A	14	10	49	17	34	.14	.09	77	81	.07	.03	.34	.19	3	-2	-5	-3	-8
Young D	23	8	46	22	33	.17	.10	76	81	.01	.02	.45	.18	-4	-3	5	-5	-8
Jaramillo J	15	8	49	20	32	.18	.07	83	79	.04	-.03	.42	.16	-1	-6	2	-4	-8
Moss B	20	9	45	20	36	.05	.07	81	81	.03	.00	.35	.16	-2	-6	-2	-3	-13
MLB Average	***18***	***10***	***43***	***19***	***38***	***.10***	***.11***	***75***	***83***	***.05***	***.04***	***.39***	***.19***	**--**	**--**	**--**	**--**	**--**

Pitching Stats

Player	*PRC*	IP	BFP	G	GS	K	BB	IBB	HBP	H	HR	DP	DER	SB	CS	PO	W	L	Sv	Op	Hld	H-A	R^L	RA	ERA	FIP
Duke Z *	*72*	213.0	891	32	32	106	49	0	3	231	23	23	.699	7	8	4	11	16	0	0	0	-.039	.001	4.27	4.06	4.29
Ohlendorf R	*66*	176.7	725	29	29	109	53	1	7	165	25	18	.729	12	8	8	11	10	0	0	0	-.055	-.039	4.08	3.92	4.76
Maholm P *	*62*	194.7	836	31	31	119	60	4	6	221	14	33	.661	15	6	4	8	9	0	0	0	-.035	-.106	4.72	4.44	3.82
Morton C	*33*	97.0	416	18	18	62	40	0	5	102	7	18	.685	9	4	1	5	9	0	0	0	-.058	-.094	4.55	4.55	4.20
Karstens J	*28*	108.0	471	39	13	52	45	5	2	115	12	11	.711	9	2	1	4	6	0	0	1	-.023	-.007	5.50	5.42	4.80
Chavez J	*24*	67.3	286	73	0	47	22	3	1	69	11	3	.717	3	0	0	1	4	0	4	15	-.040	.063	4.41	4.01	4.77
Meek E	*22*	47.0	195	41	0	42	29	2	0	34	2	7	.730	4	2	0	1	1	0	1	4	-.070	-.032	3.45	3.45	3.64
Snell I	*22*	80.7	360	15	15	52	44	3	1	87	7	11	.680	8	4	1	2	8	0	0	0	-.009	-.018	5.58	5.36	4.55
Grabow J *	*21*	47.3	209	45	0	41	28	2	2	43	4	6	.701	3	1	1	3	0	0	2	16	-.049	.006	3.61	3.42	4.29
Hanrahan J	*16*	31.3	134	33	0	37	20	1	1	23	0	2	.697	4	2	0	0	1	0	0	7	.049	-.024	3.45	1.72	2.70
Burnett S *	*15*	32.3	133	38	0	23	15	4	3	22	3	5	.764	4	0	0	1	2	1	2	6	-.065	-.022	3.34	3.06	4.23
Jackson S	*15*	43.0	186	40	0	21	22	3	0	38	2	4	.738	5	0	0	2	3	0	1	4	.081	-.006	4.19	3.14	4.10
Capps M	*14*	54.3	251	57	0	46	17	3	3	73	10	7	.629	6	0	0	4	8	27	32	1	-.094	-.056	5.96	5.80	4.79
McCutchen D	*13*	36.3	155	6	6	19	11	2	1	38	6	1	.729	3	0	1	1	2	0	0	0	.017	.035	4.21	4.21	5.08
Vasquez V	*11*	44.7	206	14	7	29	18	1	3	58	6	6	.653	0	0	0	2	5	0	0	0	-.084	-.031	6.04	5.84	4.94
Hart K	*9*	53.3	254	10	10	39	26	2	2	74	8	9	.609	10	2	1	1	8	0	0	0	.049	.027	7.93	6.92	5.10
Bautista D	*4*	13.7	61	14	0	15	7	0	1	15	1	2	.622	0	1	0	1	1	0	1	1	-.096	.038	5.27	5.27	3.66
Veal D *	*4*	16.3	87	19	0	16	20	0	2	18	2	1	.660	1	1	1	1	0	0	0	1	-.142	-.082	7.16	7.16	6.82
Gorzelanny T	*3*	8.7	36	9	0	7	4	0	0	6	0	0	.760	0	0	0	3	1	0	1	1	.085	.117	5.19	5.19	2.92
Dumatrait P	*2*	13.0	64	15	0	7	11	0	0	13	4	1	.738	0	1	0	0	2	0	1	1	-.003	.025	7.62	6.92	8.61
Hansen C	*2*	6.3	30	5	0	5	4	0	1	6	1	0	.737	1	0	0	0	0	0	0	0	.022	.187	5.68	5.68	5.99
Yates T	*2*	12.0	56	15	0	9	7	1	1	14	2	2	.649	0	1	0	0	2	0	0	3	-.087	-.326	9.00	7.50	5.57
Bootcheck C	*2*	14.7	70	13	0	13	9	0	1	16	1	0	.674	2	0	0	0	0	0	0	1	-.031	-.019	11.05	11.05	4.31
Hacker E	*1*	3.0	14	3	0	1	2	0	0	4	0	1	.636	0	0	0	0	0	0	0	0	.181	.025	6.00	6.00	4.48
Ascanio J	*1*	2.7	13	2	0	2	0	0	1	4	0	0	.600	1	0	0	0	1	0	0	0	.050	-.579	6.75	6.75	2.78

Italicized stats have been adjusted for home park.

Batted Ball Pitching Stats

	% of PA		% of Batted Balls					Out %		Runs Per Event				Total Runs vs. Avg.				
Player	K%	BB%	GB%	LD%	FB%	IF/F	HR/OF	GB	OF	NIP	GB	LD	OF	NIP	GB	LD	FB	Tot
Hanrahan J	28	16	27	25	48	.11	.00	90	84	.05	-.06	.41	.03	1	-3	1	-5	-6
Meek E	22	15	52	19	29	.06	.06	79	87	.07	.01	.46	.10	3	-2	0	-5	-5
Jackson S	11	12	44	19	38	.11	.04	75	96	.12	.04	.45	-.00	3	-0	2	-9	-4
Burnett S	17	14	43	23	34	.13	.12	81	91	.09	.02	.25	.16	2	-1	-2	-2	-4
Ohlendorf R	15	8	41	17	42	.09	.11	75	89	.05	.04	.41	.16	-2	-0	-0	-1	-3
Duke Z	12	6	48	19	33	.06	.11	77	83	.04	.03	.38	.18	-6	-1	5	-0	-3
Grabow J	20	14	41	16	43	.05	.07	65	84	.08	.09	.29	.12	3	2	-4	-2	-2
McCutchen D	12	8	40	20	40	.08	.14	80	89	.06	.02	.39	.18	-0	-1	1	1	0
Morton C	15	11	49	18	33	.13	.08	71	85	.08	.05	.39	.15	3	3	-0	-6	0
Chavez J	16	8	39	20	41	.13	.14	75	88	.04	.05	.35	.22	-1	0	0	3	2
Maholm P	14	8	52	18	30	.09	.08	72	75	.05	.05	.36	.22	-2	8	-1	1	7
Karstens J	11	10	39	16	46	.12	.08	77	80	.10	.03	.42	.19	4	-0	-0	5	9
Vasquez V	14	10	38	21	41	.13	.11	74	80	.08	.05	.46	.24	1	1	5	4	11
Capps M	18	8	41	19	41	.12	.15	68	78	.03	.07	.45	.29	-1	2	3	8	12
Snell I	14	13	39	22	38	.06	.08	77	84	.10	.04	.46	.15	5	-0	9	-1	13
Hart K	15	11	44	23	33	.05	.12	68	80	.08	.08	.48	.22	2	3	9	3	18
MLB Average	*18*	*10*	*43*	*19*	*38*	*.10*	*.11*	*75*	*83*	*.05*	*.04*	*.39*	*.19*	--	--	--	--	--

Fielding Stats

Name	INN	SBA/G	CS%	ERA	WP+PB/G	PO	A	TE	FE
Catchers									
Doumit R	615.3	0.80	20%	4.48	0.366	418	53	4	2
Jaramillo J	520.0	0.81	23%	5.04	0.381	322	28	4	0
Diaz R	283.0	1.05	18%	4.04	0.572	188	23	2	0

Name	Inn	PO	A	TE	FE	FPct	DPS	DPT	ZRDif	OOZ	Dif
First Base											
LaRoche A	756.7	776	59	0	1	.999	9	0	-.037	37	15
Pearce S	362.0	360	30	2	0	.995	2	0	.096	22	26
Jones G	255.7	246	37	0	1	.996	2	0	.002	10	5
Hinske E	44.0	39	3	0	0	1.000	1	0	--	1	--
Second Base											
Sanchez F	739.7	184	224	0	2	.995	16	46	-.017	18	-3
Young D	448.3	102	131	2	2	.983	10	21	-.003	6	-14
Vazquez R	161.0	33	50	0	0	1.000	5	7	.031	3	-9
Cruz L	39.3	6	11	0	0	1.000	0	1	--	0	--
Bixler B	30.0	4	12	0	1	.941	1	0	--	1	--
Shortstop											
Wilson J	650.7	105	242	5	2	.980	35	24	.052	33	12
Cedeno R	367.0	66	133	0	4	.980	14	12	-.057	23	24
Vazquez R	189.7	37	54	0	1	.989	6	4	.003	8	4
Cruz L	134.0	37	48	1	1	.977	3	4	.108	4	-8
Bixler B	77.0	15	24	1	1	.951	0	3	--	6	--
Third Base											
LaRoche A	1246.0	97	321	6	8	.968	31	3	.023	48	-3
Vazquez R	83.7	7	20	0	0	.964	3	0	--	0	--
Walker N	69.7	6	15	0	1	.955	0	1	--	1	--
Hinske E	19.0	0	3	0	0	1.000	0	0	--	1	--

Name	Inn	PO	A	TE	FE	FPct	DPS	DPT	ZRDif	OOZ	Dif
Left Field											
Morgan N	530.7	141	5	0	1	.993	1	0	-.028	51	46
Milledge L	500.0	111	6	0	0	1.000	0	0	-.013	37	24
Moss B	170.7	46	1	0	1	.979	0	0	.051	12	20
Jones G	127.0	24	0	0	0	1.000	0	0	-.024	4	-19
Monroe C	62.0	17	0	0	0	1.000	0	0	--	3	--
Young D	26.0	6	1	0	1	.875	0	0	--	4	--
Salazar J	2.0	0	0	0	0	.000	0	0	--	--	--
Center Field											
McCutchen	952.7	263	10	1	1	.993	1	0	-.046	72	8
McLouth N	380.0	117	5	0	0	1.000	2	0	.017	27	3
Morgan N	71.7	22	1	0	0	1.000	0	0	--	6	--
Salazar J	13.0	7	1	0	0	1.000	0	0	--	0	--
Bixler B	1.0	0	0	0	0	.000	0	0	--	--	--
Right Field											
Moss B	665.0	171	8	1	0	.994	4	0	-.024	56	32
Jones G	343.3	76	4	0	0	1.000	0	0	-.010	23	15
Young D	218.0	60	0	0	1	.984	0	0	.092	12	3
Hinske E	111.7	30	3	0	0	1.000	0	0	.012	7	11
Monroe C	59.0	14	0	0	0	1.000	0	0	--	5	--
Doumit R	9.0	2	0	0	0	1.000	0	0	--	0	--
Pearce S	9.0	1	0	0	0	1.000	0	0	--	0	--
Salazar J	3.3	0	0	0	0	.000	0	0	--	--	--

San Diego Padres

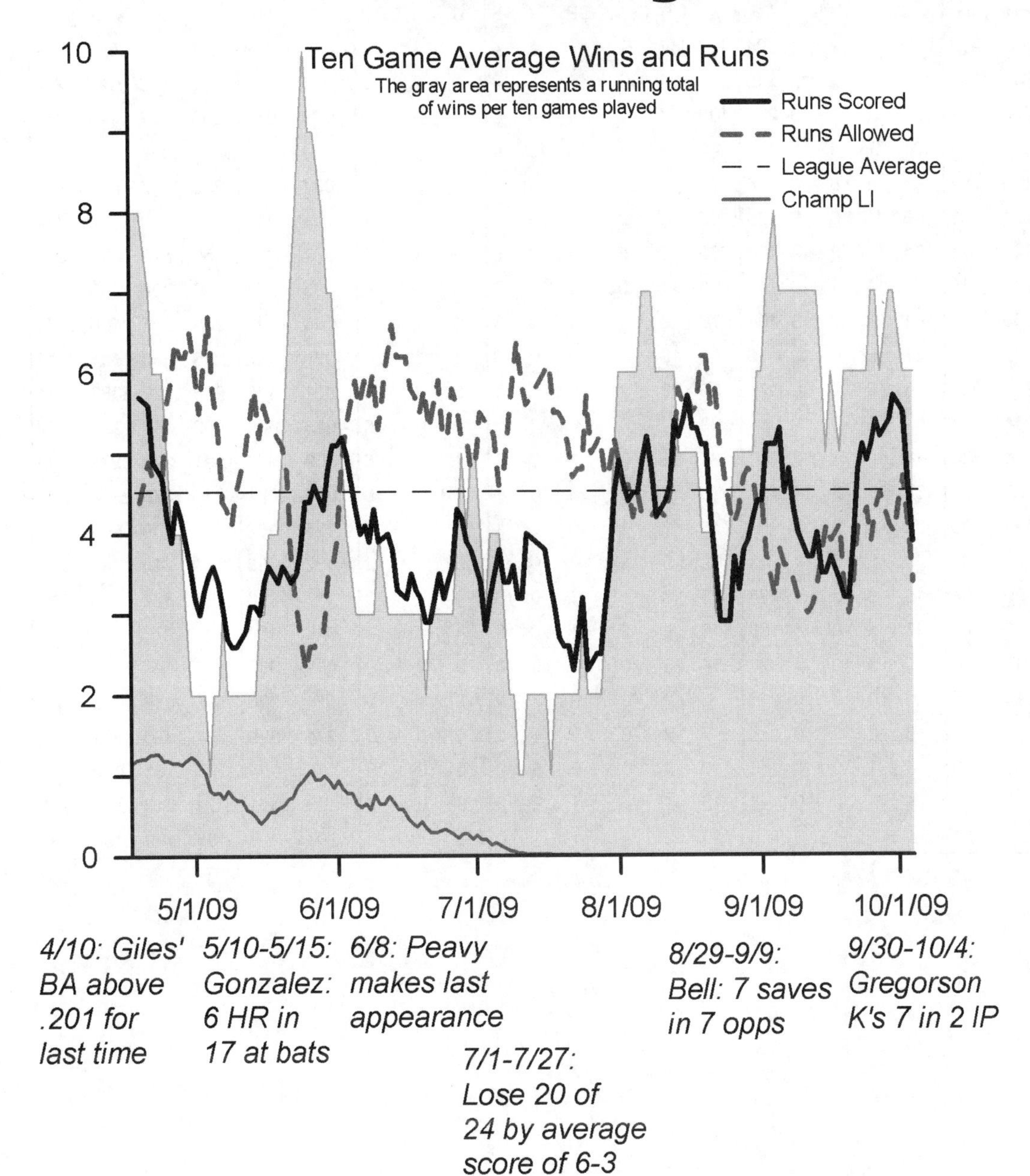

Stat Facts:

- Adrian Gonzalez walked in 18% of his PAs
- Gonzalez tied for the ML lead with 18 DPs started at first base
- Luis Rodriguez walked 15% of the time, and struck out just 9%
- Josh Geer allowed 27 home runs in 103 IP
- Kouzmanoff committed zero throwing errors, and only 3 fielding errors
- David Eckstein made just 2 errors
- Everth Cabrera made 23 errors, most by any player
- Cla Meredith induced 9 DPs in 37 IP
- Chris Young allowed 20 SBs in 20 attempts
- Kevin Correia allowed just 7 SBs in 14 attempts
- Eliezer Alfonzo was over 11 times more likely to strike out than to walk
- Nearly a quarter of Kyle Blanks's outfield flies were home runs

Team Batting and Pitching/Fielding Stats by Month

	April	May	June	July	Aug	Sept/Oct
Wins	11	14	9	8	15	18
Losses	11	14	17	20	14	11
RS/G	4.4	3.7	3.5	3.6	4.3	4.2
RA/G	5.2	4.1	5.5	5.4	4.9	3.6
OBP	.332	.308	.307	.302	.343	.332
SLG	.421	.375	.350	.363	.417	.363
FIP	4.40	3.89	4.96	4.35	4.48	3.69
DER	.680	.721	.700	.686	.681	.706

Batting Stats

Player	BR	Runs	RBI	PA	Outs	H	2B	3B	HR	TB	K	BB	IBB	HBP	SH	SF	SB	CS	GDP	H-A	L^R	BA	OBP	SLG	GPA
Gonzalez A *	113	90	99	681	423	153	27	2	40	304	109	119	22	5	1	4	1	1	23	-.044	.099	.277	.407	.551	.349
Headley C +	70	62	64	612	422	142	31	2	12	213	133	62	3	5	0	2	10	2	19	-.053	-.031	.262	.342	.392	.274
Kouzmanoff K	61	50	88	573	419	135	31	1	18	222	106	27	3	11	0	6	1	0	25	-.038	.050	.255	.302	.420	.262
Eckstein D	52	64	50	568	381	131	27	2	2	168	46	39	1	9	13	4	3	1	8	-.026	-.007	.260	.323	.334	.249
Cabrera E +	49	59	31	438	292	96	18	8	2	136	88	46	5	5	8	2	25	8	3	-.037	-.031	.255	.342	.361	.265
Gwynn T *	48	59	21	451	296	106	11	6	2	135	65	48	2	2	5	3	11	7	2	.011	.088	.270	.350	.344	.264
Venable W *	41	38	38	324	225	75	14	2	12	129	89	25	2	4	2	0	6	1	6	-.062	.083	.256	.323	.440	.278
Hairston S	36	26	29	216	143	59	14	1	10	105	45	17	0	1	1	0	8	1	4	-.005	.111	.299	.358	.533	.320
Hundley N	34	23	30	289	198	61	15	2	8	104	76	28	1	1	1	3	5	1	2	.006	-.049	.238	.313	.406	.263
Blanks K	26	24	22	172	116	37	9	0	10	76	55	18	1	6	0	0	1	1	4	-.027	-.082	.250	.355	.514	.313
Blanco H	25	21	16	232	161	48	12	0	6	78	50	26	2	0	1	1	0	0	5	.031	.150	.235	.320	.382	.261
Rodriguez L	18	18	16	251	171	42	6	0	2	54	23	37	4	0	3	3	1	0	5	-.056	.069	.202	.319	.260	.226
Giles B *	16	18	23	254	188	43	10	1	2	61	31	26	2	1	0	1	1	0	6	.009	.087	.191	.277	.271	.209
Gonzalez E	15	16	18	169	127	33	8	2	4	57	36	11	0	3	0	2	1	2	5	.056	-.029	.216	.278	.373	.237
Salazar O	15	12	19	121	85	29	8	2	3	50	16	12	1	0	0	1	0	0	6	-.125	.062	.269	.339	.463	.292
Gerut J *	11	17	14	121	90	25	6	0	4	43	22	5	1	0	0	3	2	0	2	-.182	-.055	.221	.248	.381	.225
Macias D *	8	8	7	90	64	15	6	0	1	24	15	13	1	1	0	0	0	1	2	.117	-.030	.197	.322	.316	.243
Burke C	7	8	5	89	67	17	5	0	1	25	16	6	0	1	0	0	4	1	1	.016	-.101	.207	.270	.305	.215
Alfonzo E	5	6	8	117	94	20	3	0	2	29	34	3	0	0	0	0	0	0	0	.019	.032	.175	.197	.254	.165
Durango L +	3	3	0	14	6	6	0	0	0	6	2	2	0	0	1	0	2	1	0	-.074	-.025	.545	.615	.545	.449
Young C	2	2	2	26	17	6	0	0	0	6	7	2	0	0	1	0	0	0	0	.214	.099	.261	.320	.261	.227
Geer J	1	2	1	31	20	4	1	0	0	5	10	2	0	0	5	0	0	0	0	-.174	.004	.167	.231	.208	.169
Stauffer T	1	1	0	27	19	4	0	0	0	4	13	1	0	1	2	0	0	0	0	-.120	-.151	.174	.240	.174	.165
Wilson J	1	2	1	43	34	4	2	0	0	6	9	3	1	1	1	0	0	0	0	-.207	.092	.105	.190	.158	.136

Only includes batters with at least one Base Run. Italicized stats have been adjusted for home park.
Batted ball stats are listed after fielding stats.

Pitching Stats

Player	PRC	IP	BFP	G	GS	K	BB	IBB	HBP	H	HR	DP	DER	SB	CS	PO	W	L	Sv	Op	Hld	H-A	R^L	RA	ERA	FIP
Correia K	*70*	198.0	830	33	33	142	64	6	4	194	17	19	.703	7	7	1	12	11	0	0	0	-.026	-.009	4.18	3.91	3.77
Bell H	*40*	69.7	278	68	0	79	24	1	0	54	3	9	.703	5	1	1	6	4	42	48	0	.005	-.119	2.71	2.71	2.43
Gregerson L	*36*	75.0	318	72	0	93	31	9	3	62	3	5	.681	1	1	0	2	4	1	7	27	-.130	-.109	3.48	3.24	2.19
Peavy J	*32*	81.7	335	13	13	92	28	0	1	69	7	5	.696	9	2	0	6	6	0	0	0	-.027	-.107	4.19	3.97	3.08
Mujica E	*31*	93.7	393	67	4	76	19	4	0	101	14	9	.683	3	3	0	3	5	2	3	11	-.049	-.045	4.52	3.94	3.95
Stauffer T	*28*	73.0	316	14	14	53	34	1	5	71	8	11	.704	1	2	0	4	7	0	0	0	-.030	.050	3.82	3.58	4.69
Gaudin C	*27*	105.3	476	20	19	105	56	3	5	105	7	10	.653	4	4	0	4	10	0	0	0	.071	-.064	5.90	5.13	3.67
Thatcher J *	*26*	45.0	188	52	0	55	18	7	4	37	2	5	.679	5	1	1	1	0	0	1	9	-.043	-.078	2.80	2.80	2.28
Adams M	*26*	37.0	136	37	0	45	8	1	0	14	1	0	.817	2	1	0	0	0	0	1	15	-.049	-.015	2.19	0.73	1.64
Richard C *	*22*	64.0	276	12	12	48	34	0	0	60	7	9	.690	5	5	3	5	2	0	0	0	-.140	-.028	4.36	4.08	4.67
Geer J	*21*	102.7	438	19	17	54	23	0	4	116	27	10	.715	2	1	3	1	7	0	0	0	-.059	.029	6.40	5.96	6.31
Young C	*19*	76.0	336	14	14	50	40	3	2	70	12	3	.746	20	0	1	4	6	0	0	0	-.118	.080	5.57	5.21	5.43
LeBlanc W *	*18*	46.3	194	9	9	30	19	1	4	35	6	3	.785	1	1	1	3	1	0	0	0	-.119	.078	3.69	3.69	4.96
Perdomo L	*17*	60.0	268	35	0	55	34	3	0	57	11	4	.708	5	1	0	1	0	0	1	0	-.069	-.090	5.40	4.80	5.25
Burke G	*15*	45.7	204	48	0	33	23	5	1	48	4	4	.685	1	2	0	3	3	0	2	10	-.084	-.129	4.53	4.14	4.09
Latos M	*14*	50.7	212	10	10	39	23	1	0	43	7	6	.741	4	3	0	4	5	0	0	0	.043	-.076	5.15	4.62	4.71
Meredith C	*11*	36.7	165	35	0	20	13	4	2	47	1	9	.628	7	1	0	4	2	0	3	1	-.036	-.016	4.66	4.17	3.31
Webb R	*8*	25.7	117	28	0	19	11	1	1	27	3	2	.687	0	0	0	2	1	0	0	6	-.089	-.068	4.91	3.86	4.48
Ramos C *	*7*	14.7	62	5	2	10	4	0	0	19	0	4	.583	3	1	1	0	1	0	0	0	.118	-.250	3.07	3.07	2.61
Moreno E	*6*	22.3	108	19	0	15	15	3	2	28	3	3	.644	3	2	0	1	3	0	1	4	-.097	-.075	5.24	4.84	5.43
Russell A	*5*	12.3	61	15	0	14	11	0	0	13	0	0	.611	2	1	0	3	1	0	0	4	-.044	-.028	4.38	3.65	3.56
Ekstrom M	*4*	18.3	83	12	0	19	8	0	1	21	3	3	.654	4	0	0	0	0	0	0	0	.115	.018	6.87	6.38	4.68
Banks J	*4*	22.7	100	6	3	9	4	1	1	30	6	1	.700	4	2	0	1	1	0	0	0	-.066	-.053	7.15	7.15	6.33
Hill S	*3*	12.0	56	3	3	7	3	0	1	15	1	1	.636	1	0	0	1	1	0	0	0	.139	-.011	5.25	5.25	4.07
Silva W	*2*	24.7	121	6	6	11	15	0	0	34	4	4	.637	0	0	0	0	2	0	0	0	-.172	.071	10.22	8.76	6.19
Sanchez D	*1*	11.0	57	12	0	2	8	1	1	18	3	2	.651	0	0	0	1	1	0	1	5	-.099	.186	9.00	9.00	8.51
de la Cruz E	*1*	3.3	17	3	0	2	6	0	0	2	0	1	.778	1	0	0	0	0	0	0	0	.281	-.272	5.40	5.40	7.35
Carrillo C	*1*	10.3	60	3	3	4	12	2	2	16	4	1	.684	0	0	0	1	2	0	0	0	-.217	.153	13.06	13.06	10.89

Italicized stats have been adjusted for home park.
Batted ball stats are listed after fielding stats.

Fielding Stats

Name	INN	SBA/G	CS%	ERA	WP+PB/G	PO	A	TE	FE
Catchers									
Hundley N	643.3	0.92	15%	4.00	0.490	515	35	5	1
Blanco H	508.0	0.73	34%	4.69	0.319	444	28	0	0
Alfonzo E	255.3	0.85	38%	4.51	0.352	203	23	0	1
Lobaton J	44.0	0.61	33%	5.32	0.205	52	2	1	0

Name	Inn	PO	A	TE	FE	FPct	DPS	DPT	ZRDif	OOZ	Dif
First Base											
Gonzalez A	1359.0	1224	136	2	4	.995	18	1	-.003	50	2
Blanks K	45.0	36	3	0	0	1.000	0	0	--	3	--
Salazar O	36.0	30	4	0	0	1.000	0	0	--	3	--
Gonzalez E	9.0	6	0	0	0	1.000	0	0	--	--	--
Headley C	1.0	1	0	0	0	1.000	0	0	--	--	--
Second Base											
Eckstein D	1093.0	228	326	1	1	.996	20	53	-.038	33	3
Rodriguez L	226.0	51	69	1	2	.976	6	8	-.085	1	-23
Gonzalez E	110.0	20	20	1	2	.930	2	2	-.003	1	-18
Salazar O	16.3	4	6	1	1	.833	0	1	--	0	--
Burke C	4.0	0	0	0	0	0.000	0	0	--	--	--
Lobaton J	1.0	0	0	0	0	0.000	0	0	--	--	--
Shortstop											
Cabrera E	896.7	140	304	9	14	.951	36	24	-.055	42	9
Rodriguez L	263.7	45	74	3	0	.975	14	7	-.038	8	-8
Burke C	184.3	27	52	4	2	.929	4	4	-.099	7	-0
Wilson J	106.0	13	20	2	0	.943	2	1	-.158	1	-29
Third Base											
Kouzmanoff	1186.0	94	214	0	3	.990	19	0	.041	34	-13
Headley C	225.7	10	39	2	3	.907	2	0	-.004	4	-24
Gonzalez E	28.0	2	6	0	1	.889	0	0	--	2	--
Burke C	7.0	1	0	0	0	1.000	0	0	--	--	--
Wilson J	1.3	0	0	0	0	0.000	0	0	--	--	--
Blanco H	1.0	0	0	0	0	0.000	0	0	--	--	--
Rodriguez L	1.0	0	0	0	0	0.000	0	0	--	--	--

Name	Inn	PO	A	TE	FE	FPct	DPS	DPT	ZRDif	OOZ	Dif
Left Field											
Headley C	982.3	215	5	1	2	.987	2	0	.003	50	1
Hairston S	131.0	36	1	0	0	1.000	0	0	.040	8	11
Blanks K	110.0	26	1	0	0	1.000	0	0	.065	3	-23
Salazar O	102.7	19	0	0	0	1.000	0	0	.040	5	-2
Macias D	80.7	14	0	0	0	1.000	0	0	--	3	--
Venable W	32.3	5	0	0	1	.833	0	0	--	0	--
Durango L	10.0	2	0	0	0	1.000	0	0	--	1	--
Hundley N	1.0	1	0	0	0	1.000	0	0	--	0	--
Gonzalez E	0.7	0	0	0	0	0.000	0	0	--	--	--
Center Field											
Gwynn T	812.0	269	4	2	5	.975	0	0	.009	65	12
Hairston S	290.7	70	1	0	1	.986	0	0	-.025	22	8
Gerut J	191.7	56	2	0	0	1.000	0	0	-.006	19	31
Venable W	117.0	30	1	0	0	1.000	0	0	.028	7	-8
Macias D	32.3	5	0	0	0	1.000	0	0	--	0	--
Durango L	7.0	1	1	0	0	1.000	0	0	--	--	--
Right Field											
Giles B	502.7	113	6	0	0	1.000	3	0	-.032	21	-10
Venable W	493.7	123	2	0	1	.992	0	0	-.033	39	27
Blanks K	174.0	29	0	0	0	1.000	0	0	-.019	5	-23
Gonzalez E	98.3	24	0	0	0	1.000	0	0	--	5	--
Gwynn T	81.3	28	1	0	1	.967	1	0	--	9	--
Macias D	43.7	5	0	0	1	.833	0	0	--	0	--
Gerut J	29.0	7	0	0	0	1.000	0	0	--	4	--
Salazar O	28.0	6	0	0	0	1.000	0	0	--	1	--

Batted Ball Batting Stats

	% of PA		% of Batted Balls					Out %		Runs Per Event				Total Runs vs. Avg.				
Player	**K%**	**BB%**	**GB%**	**LD%**	**FB%**	**IF/F**	**HR/OF**	**GB**	**OF**	**NIP**	**GB**	**LD**	**OF**	**NIP**	**GB**	**LD**	**FB**	**Tot**
Gonzalez A	16	18	39	21	40	.05	.23	81	84	.13	-.01	.35	.35	22	-10	2	33	47
Hairston S	21	8	33	21	46	.22	.19	61	84	.02	.12	.43	.28	-2	3	3	5	10
Blanks K	32	14	37	13	51	.19	.24	68	76	.03	.08	.49	.42	-0	1	-3	8	6
Salazar O	13	10	43	15	42	.21	.10	80	75	.08	-.02	.53	.24	1	-2	1	2	1
Cabrera E	20	12	63	15	23	.08	.04	71	74	.06	.08	.40	.18	2	13	-6	-9	1
Headley C	22	11	45	17	38	.09	.08	71	74	.04	.05	.36	.22	0	2	-7	4	-1
Venable W	27	9	44	16	40	.07	.16	75	81	-.00	.03	.45	.28	-4	-1	-3	7	-1
Gwynn A	14	11	46	24	30	.06	.02	77	80	.09	.04	.36	.09	4	-1	5	-12	-3
Hundley N	26	10	31	22	47	.14	.11	72	88	.01	.06	.47	.15	-3	-1	3	-3	-3
Blanco H	22	11	41	16	43	.10	.08	73	89	.04	.06	.50	.10	0	0	0	-5	-4
Gonzalez E	21	8	39	18	43	.06	.06	78	89	.02	.02	.47	.09	-2	-2	1	-4	-6
Gerut J	18	4	43	19	38	.08	.12	83	93	-.03	.00	.36	.13	-3	-2	-1	-2	-7
Rodriguez L	9	15	41	18	40	.08	.03	84	96	.17	-.02	.40	-.02	7	-5	0	-13	-11
Kouzmanoff K	18	7	44	20	36	.07	.12	83	76	.01	-.02	.35	.25	-7	-12	-2	9	-11
Alfonzo E	29	3	43	18	40	.19	.08	85	92	-.08	-.00	.38	.08	-5	-2	-2	-5	-13
Eckstein D	8	8	46	19	34	.15	.02	76	85	.12	.05	.34	.04	4	2	0	-23	-16
Giles B	12	11	44	19	37	.11	.03	87	89	.10	-.03	.33	.03	2	-6	-3	-11	-17
MLB Average	***18***	***10***	***43***	***19***	***38***	***.10***	***.11***	***75***	***83***	***.05***	***.04***	***.39***	***.19***	--	--	--	--	--

Batted Ball Pitching Stats

	% of PA		% of Batted Balls					Out %		Runs Per Event				Total Runs vs. Avg.				
Player	**K%**	**BB%**	**GB%**	**LD%**	**FB%**	**IF/F**	**HR/OF**	**GB**	**OF**	**NIP**	**GB**	**LD**	**OF**	**NIP**	**GB**	**LD**	**FB**	**Tot**
Adams M	33	6	51	7	42	.21	.04	83	88	-.04	.00	.49	.02	-5	-2	-6	-7	-20
Bell H	28	9	48	18	35	.10	.06	72	82	-.01	.05	.29	.13	-5	-0	-7	-7	-19
Correia K	17	8	45	19	36	.09	.09	78	84	.04	.02	.40	.15	-4	-5	2	-9	-16
Gregerson L	29	10	46	21	33	.16	.06	76	78	.01	.03	.38	.16	-4	-2	-2	-7	-15
Peavy J	27	9	41	19	40	.11	.10	71	86	-.00	.07	.41	.15	-5	1	-3	-6	-12
Thatcher J	29	12	44	18	38	.12	.06	71	91	.02	.07	.46	.05	-1	1	-1	-7	-8
LeBlanc W	15	12	36	17	47	.11	.10	84	90	.09	-.01	.37	.12	2	-4	-2	-3	-6
Latos M	18	11	36	19	45	.08	.12	77	89	.06	.02	.27	.16	1	-1	-4	-0	-5
Mujica E	19	5	39	17	44	.08	.11	68	88	-.02	.09	.39	.15	-7	7	-1	-1	-2
Stauffer T	17	12	44	20	36	.06	.09	79	84	.08	.01	.40	.17	3	-3	2	-2	0
Meredith C	12	10	62	19	19	.04	.04	63	86	.09	.10	.32	.06	1	5	-0	-5	1
Richard C	17	12	49	17	34	.05	.12	67	85	.08	.08	.27	.19	3	4	-5	-0	1
Webb R	16	10	57	18	25	.10	.16	79	75	.06	.01	.47	.31	0	-1	1	1	1
Gaudin C	22	13	45	20	36	.07	.07	70	77	.06	.06	.40	.17	3	2	-0	-3	1
Burke G	16	12	48	17	35	.02	.08	73	76	.08	.05	.33	.19	2	1	-2	1	2
Young C	15	13	30	18	52	.17	.12	66	95	.10	.12	.36	.12	4	4	-2	-5	2
Banks J	9	5	34	21	45	.08	.18	79	86	.05	.04	.42	.27	-1	0	2	4	6
Perdomo L	21	13	52	18	30	.04	.20	75	83	.06	.04	.38	.34	2	0	-1	6	6
Moreno E	14	16	36	14	50	.24	.11	63	72	.13	.11	.49	.26	3	2	0	2	7
Silva W	9	12	46	22	32	.17	.16	70	90	.15	.06	.46	.20	3	2	4	0	9
Geer J	12	6	42	18	40	.05	.20	78	76	.04	.02	.28	.37	-3	-2	-5	29	19
MLB Average	***18***	***10***	***43***	***19***	***38***	***.10***	***.11***	***75***	***83***	***.05***	***.04***	***.39***	***.19***	--	--	--	--	--

San Francisco Giants

Stat Facts:

- Tim Lincecum led the NL with 139 PRC and 261 strikeouts
- Lincecum's FIP (2.37) was lowest of ML pitchers with at least 162 IP
- Lincecum's K% (29%) was highest of ML pitchers with at least 162 IP
- Edgar Renteria's LDR of .29 was lowest among ML regulars
- Andres Torres put the ball in play 108 times, and had 20 extra-base hits, including 8 triples
- Bengie Molina led the majors with 11 sacrifice flies
- Molina tied for the lowest BB% (3%) among major league regulars
- Jeremy Affeldt induced 18 DPs in 62 IP
- Affeldt's FB% (18%) was lowest among ML pitchers with at least 60 IP
- Randy Winn's L^R of -.126 was lowest of any regular in the majors
- Jonathan Sanchez allowed 24 SBs, most in the NL
- Sanchez's BB% (13%) was highest of ML pitchers with at least 162 IP

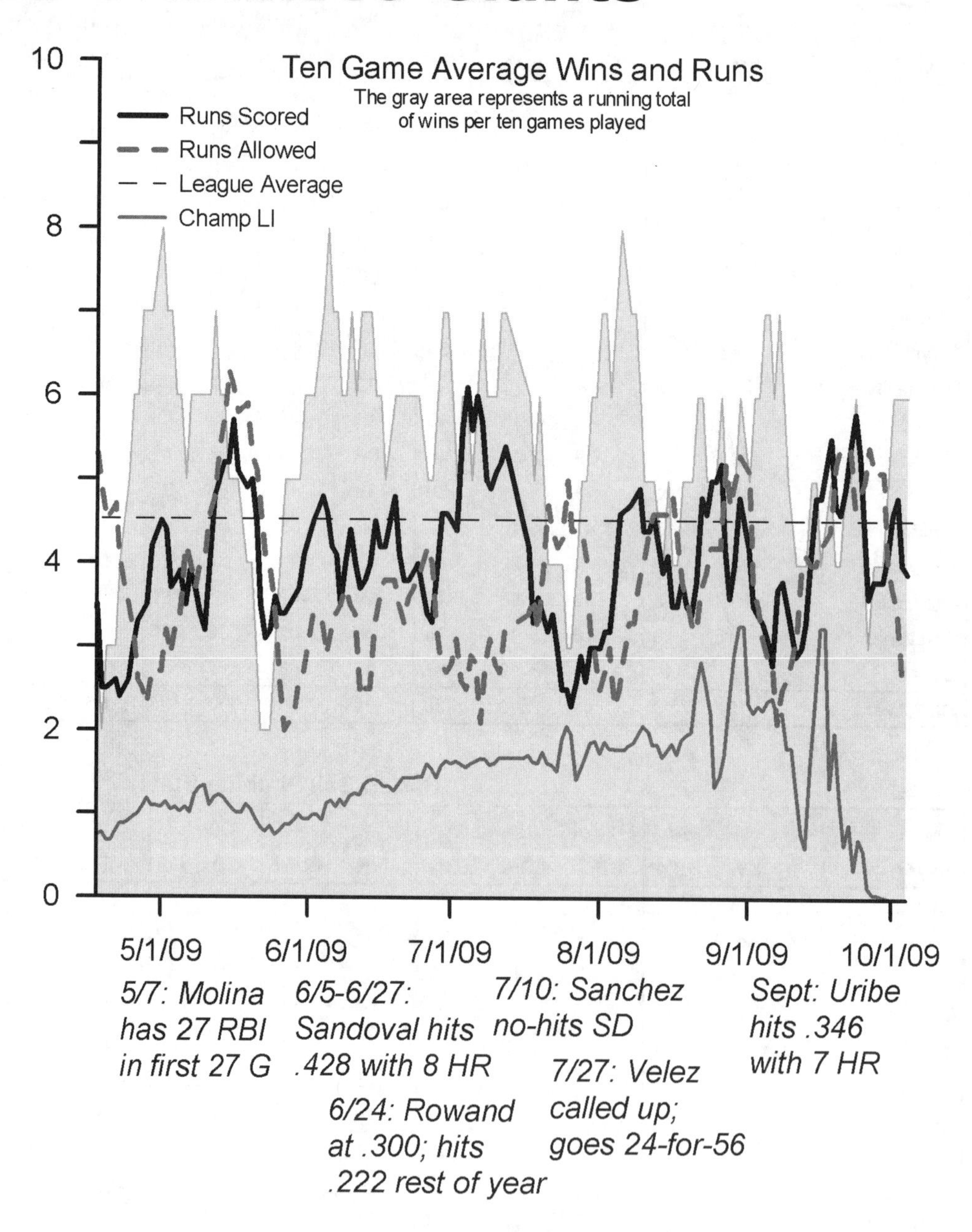

Team Batting and Pitching/Fielding Stats by Month

	April	May	June	July	Aug	Sept/Oct
Wins	10	15	17	14	16	16
Losses	10	14	10	13	12	15
RS/G	3.9	4.0	4.4	3.6	4.4	4.1
RA/G	4.0	4.0	3.3	3.5	4.2	3.7
OBP	.318	.314	.308	.287	.326	.303
SLG	.383	.360	.424	.358	.427	.381
FIP	3.98	3.88	3.88	3.50	3.76	4.11
DER	.692	.692	.718	.723	.705	.723

Batting Stats

Player	*BR*	Runs	RBI	PA	Outs	H	2B	3B	HR	TB	K	BB	IBB	HBP	SH	SF	SB	CS	GDP	H-A	L^R	BA	OBP	SLG	*GPA*
Sandoval P +	*112*	79	90	633	398	189	44	5	25	318	83	52	13	4	0	5	5	5	10	.044	.039	.330	.387	.556	*.310*
Rowand A	*67*	61	64	546	382	130	30	2	15	209		30	2	14	0	3	4	1	12	-.009	-.047	.261	.319	.419	*.246*
Winn R +	*65*	65	51	597	405	141	33	5	2	190	93	47	2	1	3	8	16	2	6	-.052	-.126	.262	.318	.353	*.229*
Uribe J	*64*	50	55	432	291	115	26	4	16	197	82	25	2	1	3	5	3	1	7	.088	-.022	.289	.329	.495	*.269*
Molina B	*60*	52	80	520	375	130	25	1	20	217	68	13	3	5	0	11	0	0	14	.076	.058	.265	.285	.442	*.236*
Renteria E	*46*	50	48	510	364	115	19	1	5	151	69	39	5	1	5	5	7	2	17	-.010	-.008	.250	.307	.328	*.218*
Lewis F *	*42*	49	20	336	227	76	21	3	4	115	84	36	3	5	0	0	8	4	4	.047	.090	.258	.348	.390	*.252*
Ishikawa T *	*42*	49	39	363	250	85	10	2	9	126	89	30	3	4	1	2	2	2	7	.146	.037	.261	.329	.387	*.242*
Velez E +	*35*	40	31	307	220	76	13	5	5	114	55	16	1	2	2	2	11	5	6	.008	-.080	.267	.308	.400	*.236*
Schierholtz	*34*	33	29	308	215	76	19	2	5	114	58	16	3	1	0	6	3	1	5	-.012	-.123	.267	.302	.400	*.234*
Torres A +	*29*	30	23	170	112	41	6	8	6	81	45	16	0	1	1	0	6	1	0	.035	.132	.270	.343	.533	*.285*
Burriss E +	*17*	18	13	220	161	48	6	0	0	54	34	14	1	2	1	1	11	4	3	-.047	.067	.238	.292	.267	*.196*
Garko R	*12*	10	12	127	90	27	3	1	2	38	10	9	0	3	0	0	0	0	2	-.135	.075	.235	.307	.330	*.219*
Whiteside E	*11*	15	13	134	102	29	6	1	2	43	30	4	1	3	0	0	0	0	4	.107	-.161	.228	.269	.339	*.204*
Sanchez F	*9*	11	7	107	76	29	1	0	1	33	16	2	0	0	2	1	0	0	3	-.033	.079	.284	.295	.324	*.212*
Aurilia R	*8*	10	16	133	101	26	2	0	2	34	24	8	1	0	0	3	0	0	5	.064	.023	.213	.256	.279	*.183*
Bowker J *	*7*	7	7	73	54	13	2	2	2	25	18	4	0	1	0	1	1	0	0	.095	.222	.194	.247	.373	*.202*
Downs M	*4*	6	2	60	46	9	2	0	1	14	13	6	1	0	0	1	1	0	2	.141	-.088	.170	.250	.264	*.177*
Cain M	*2*	2	3	73	51	9	2	1	0	13	31	4	0	0	9	0	0	0	0	.021	.070	.150	.203	.217	*.144*
Lincecum T *	*2*	8	3	86	57	10	1	0	0	11	36	6	0	0	13	1	0	0	1	.106	.087	.152	.219	.167	*.139*
Holm S	*1*	1	0	9	5	2	0	0	0	2	0	2	0	0	0	0	0	0	0	-.107	-.271	.286	.444	.286	*.269*
Frandsen K	*1*	3	1	54	45	7	2	0	0	9	4	3	0	1	0	0	0	0	2	-.037	.030	.140	.204	.180	*.135*
Martinez J *	*1*	2	0	9	6	2	1	0	0	3	1	0	0	0	1	0	0	0	0	-.275	-.825	.250	.250	.375	*.204*
Guzman J	*1*	0	0	20	17	5	0	0	0	5	3	0	0	0	0	0	0	0	2	.000	-.038	.250	.250	.250	*.173*

Only includes batters with at least one Base Run. Italicized stats have been adjusted for home park.

Batted Ball Batting Stats

	% of PA		% of Batted Balls					Out %		Runs Per Event				Total Runs vs. Avg.				
Player	**K%**	**BB%**	**GB%**	**LD%**	**FB%**	**IF/F**	**HR/OF**	**GB**	**OF**	**NIP**	**GB**	**LD**	**OF**	**NIP**	**GB**	**LD**	**FB**	**Tot**
Sandoval P	13	9	45	19	36	.08	.15	68	83	.07	.09	.48	.25	2	13	13	15	43
Uribe J	19	6	39	21	40	.12	.14	75	78	-.00	.04	.40	.28	-6	-0	4	12	10
Torres A	26	10	34	16	49	.08	.14	82	63	.01	.01	.44	.41	-1	-1	-2	10	7
Lewis F	25	12	52	21	27	.11	.08	65	83	.04	.11	.40	.17	0	8	1	-6	3
Velez E	18	6	54	17	29	.06	.06	72	80	.00	.06	.41	.17	-4	3	0	-3	-3
Rowand A	23	8	45	16	39	.13	.12	73	78	.01	.05	.42	.23	-6	3	-4	4	-4
Ishikawa T	25	9	45	18	37	.05	.11	69	84	.01	.07	.32	.19	-3	3	-5	1	-4
Garko R	8	9	43	18	39	.20	.06	80	87	.14	.02	.30	.08	1	-1	-1	-4	-5
Sanchez F	15	2	52	26	22	.05	.06	78	100	-.06	.02	.40	-.01	-3	-1	3	-5	-6
Schierholtz N	19	6	45	21	35	.06	.07	73	86	-.01	.05	.39	.12	-5	1	2	-5	-6
Whiteside D	22	5	41	17	42	.18	.06	77	81	-.03	.01	.42	.14	-3	-2	-1	-3	-8
Aurilia R	18	6	48	13	40	.20	.06	81	87	.00	-.01	.39	.09	-2	-3	-3	-4	-11
Molina B	13	3	31	17	53	.11	.10	84	81	-.02	-.03	.36	.18	-9	-11	-3	10	-12
Winn R	16	8	46	22	32	.06	.01	74	84	.04	.05	.36	.07	-2	1	5	-17	-13
Burriss E	15	7	56	17	27	.12	.00	78	89	.03	.03	.39	-.02	-1	-0	-1	-11	-14
Renteria E	14	8	48	21	31	.10	.05	77	85	.06	.02	.29	.08	-1	-2	-4	-15	-22
MLB Average	***18***	***10***	***43***	***19***	***38***	***.10***	***.11***	***75***	***83***	***.05***	***.04***	***.39***	***.19***	--	--	--	--	--

Pitching Stats

Player	PRC	IP	BFP	G	GS	K	BB	IBB	HBP	H	HR	DP	DER	SB	CS	PO	W	L	Sv	Op	Hld	H-A	R^L	RA	ERA	FIP
Lincecum T	*139*	225.3	905	32	32	261	68	2	6	168	10	14	.709	20	5	0	15	7	0	0	0	-.031	-.014	2.76	2.48	2.37
Cain M	*115*	217.7	886	33	33	171	73	6	3	184	22	19	.731	11	9	0	14	8	0	0	0	-.012	.016	3.02	2.89	3.86
Zito B *	*76*	192.0	818	33	33	154	81	8	8	179	21	24	.704	11	9	0	10	13	0	0	0	.003	-.036	4.17	4.03	4.23
Sanchez J *	*64*	163.3	710	32	29	177	88	5	6	135	19	10	.707	24	5	2	8	12	0	0	1	-.029	-.026	4.52	4.24	4.13
Affeldt J *	*46*	62.3	248	74	0	55	31	3	3	42	3	18	.737	4	1	1	2	2	0	0	33	.076	.063	2.02	1.73	3.50
Wilson B	*38*	72.3	303	68	0	83	27	4	1	60	3	6	.677	5	1	0	5	6	38	45	1	-.027	.036	3.36	2.74	2.39
Medders B	*33*	68.7	300	61	0	58	32	5	3	63	6	5	.711	2	1	0	5	1	1	4	8	.025	-.049	3.41	3.01	3.91
Johnson R *	*32*	96.0	412	22	17	86	31	2	2	97	19	9	.701	7	3	2	8	6	0	1	0	-.063	-.026	5.16	4.88	4.90
Howry B	*28*	63.7	268	63	0	46	23	6	2	50	5	2	.745	4	0	0	2	6	0	3	10	-.027	-.064	3.68	3.39	3.62
Miller J	*27*	56.7	236	44	0	36	27	2	1	47	7	7	.758	2	1	0	3	3	0	0	1	-.029	-.074	3.18	3.18	4.86
Penny B	*21*	41.7	161	6	6	20	9	0	0	31	5	6	.780	1	1	1	4	1	0	0	0	-.089	.030	2.81	2.59	4.40
Romo S	*16*	34.0	143	45	0	41	11	0	1	30	1	2	.674	2	0	0	5	2	2	2	10	-.001	.051	3.97	3.97	2.18
Valdez M	*13*	49.3	225	48	0	38	28	2	0	57	5	7	.643	4	4	0	2	1	0	3	4	-.045	.059	6.02	5.66	4.51
Runzler D *	*11*	8.7	38	11	0	11	5	0	1	6	1	0	.750	1	0	0	0	0	0	0	2	-.122	-.229	1.04	1.04	4.19
Sadowski R	*9*	28.3	128	6	6	17	17	1	1	28	2	4	.692	1	0	0	2	4	0	0	0	-.121	-.046	4.76	4.45	4.67
Bumgarner M	*8*	10.0	40	4	1	10	3	1	0	8	2	1	.760	0	0	0	0	0	0	0	0	.058	-.281	1.80	1.80	4.35
Martinez J	*5*	30.0	148	9	5	19	12	2	1	46	4	3	.616	5	0	0	3	2	0	0	0	.057	-.125	8.10	7.50	4.72
Joaquin W	*5*	10.7	51	10	0	12	7	0	2	10	1	0	.690	2	0	0	0	0	0	0	0	.053	.072	4.22	4.22	4.65
Matos O	*1*	6.0	31	5	0	5	1	0	0	11	2	0	.565	1	0	0	0	0	0	0	0	-.088	.088	10.50	9.00	6.32

Italicized stats have been adjusted for home park.

Batted Ball Pitching Stats

	% of PA		% of Batted Balls					Out %		Runs Per Event				Total Runs vs. Avg.				
Player	K%	BB%	GB%	LD%	FB%	IF/F	HR/OF	GB	OF	NIP	GB	LD	OF	NIP	GB	LD	FB	Tot
Lincecum T	29	8	48	19	33	.07	.06	75	87	-.01	.05	.37	.09	-17	-1	-13	-29	-60
Cain M	19	9	39	19	42	.11	.09	82	84	.03	-.00	.38	.16	-6	-11	-4	-7	-28
Wilson B	27	9	46	18	36	.09	.03	74	81	.00	.05	.47	.08	-4	-0	-1	-10	-15
Affeldt J	22	13	65	17	18	.07	.11	80	83	.06	-.02	.32	.20	2	-6	-5	-6	-15
Howry B	17	9	33	16	51	.13	.06	70	90	.05	.09	.39	.07	-0	1	-3	-8	-9
Penny B	12	6	54	13	33	.14	.14	80	91	.03	.00	.30	.19	-2	-2	-4	-1	-9
Zito B	19	11	38	22	40	.12	.11	78	87	.06	.01	.39	.16	2	-7	4	-7	-8
Romo S	29	8	32	15	53	.15	.03	68	77	-.01	.08	.42	.12	-3	0	-2	-2	-7
Sanchez J	25	13	41	16	43	.11	.11	75	83	.05	.05	.43	.20	3	-0	-8	-1	-6
Medders B	19	12	34	27	39	.14	.09	84	90	.06	-.02	.40	.10	2	-5	6	-7	-5
Miller J	15	12	41	16	43	.07	.11	78	88	.09	.02	.33	.16	2	-2	-4	-1	-4
Sadowski R	13	14	51	20	29	.15	.09	72	86	.12	.05	.34	.12	3	1	-0	-3	1
Valdez M	17	12	45	24	31	.04	.11	73	88	.08	.04	.43	.14	3	-0	6	-2	6
Johnson R	21	8	45	19	35	.12	.20	72	83	.01	.06	.42	.32	-4	1	1	9	7
Martinez J	13	9	54	21	25	.11	.16	73	71	.07	.05	.48	.37	1	1	5	3	10
MLB Average	***18***	***10***	***43***	***19***	***38***	***.10***	***.11***	***75***	***83***	***.05***	***.04***	***.39***	***.19***	--	--	--	--	--

Fielding Stats

Name	INN	SBA/G	CS%	ERA	WP+PB/G	PO	A	TE	FE
Catchers									
Molina B	1042.0	0.93	21%	3.75	0.466	942	77	3	1
Whiteside E	314.0	0.80	29%	3.01	0.602	286	25	3	2
Posey B	40.0	0.45	50%	3.60	0.450	32	4	0	0
Sandoval P	27.0	0.67	50%	1.67	0.333	21	2	0	0
Holm S	23.0	0.39	0%	4.30	0.783	14	1	0	0

Name	Inn	PO	A	TE	FE	FPct	DPS	DPT	ZRDif	OOZ	Dif
First Base											
Ishikawa T	817.3	745	55	1	2	.996	9	0	.058	26	-3
Garko R	230.7	219	14	0	1	.996	0	0	-.051	5	-13
Sandoval P	207.0	181	10	1	2	.985	0	0	.004	10	14
Aurilia R	158.3	125	14	0	0	1.000	2	0	.018	5	-3
Bowker J	18.7	15	0	0	0	1.000	0	0	--	0	--
Guzman J	14.0	10	0	0	0	1.000	0	0	--	1	--
Second Base											
Burriss E	494.0	115	131	2	5	.972	11	19	-.021	12	-3
Uribe J	299.7	59	82	0	1	.993	11	5	.033	10	6
Velez E	215.7	55	68	3	3	.953	3	5	-.005	3	-14
Sanchez F	210.0	44	65	2	1	.973	4	7	.023	7	6
Downs M	143.0	31	42	0	0	1.000	5	7	-.033	2	-14
Frandsen K	73.7	21	22	1	0	.977	3	6	--	1	--
Rohlinger R	10.0	5	3	0	0	1.000	0	1	--	0	--
Shortstop											
Renteria E	1071.0	161	299	7	7	.970	31	25	.036	28	-12
Uribe J	318.7	61	94	1	3	.975	9	11	-.012	9	-10
Frandsen K	42.7	4	12	0	1	.941	1	0	--	0	--
Rohlinger R	13.0	4	5	0	0	1.000	1	1	--	1	--
Third Base											
Sandoval P	1028.0	70	195	7	3	.960	13	0	-.032	32	-10
Uribe J	323.3	28	67	0	4	.960	8	0	.033	18	14
Aurilia R	65.7	3	11	0	0	1.000	2	0	--	1	--
Rohlinger R	29.0	2	7	0	0	1.000	0	0	--	2	--

Name	Inn	PO	A	TE	FE	FPct	DPS	DPT	ZRDif	OOZ	Dif
Left Field											
Lewis F	589.7	127	3	1	2	.977	1	0	-.007	33	6
Winn R	319.7	72	1	0	0	1.000	0	0	.074	12	-13
Velez E	288.7	49	2	0	2	.962	0	0	.033	11	-12
Torres A	163.3	33	1	0	0	1.000	1	0	.032	8	-1
Bowker J	84.7	20	1	0	0	1.000	0	0	--	7	--
Center Field											
Rowand A	1127.0	299	5	0	3	.990	2	0	.002	78	1
Torres A	152.3	53	1	0	0	1.000	1	0	.046	12	11
Winn R	101.3	23	1	0	0	1.000	1	0	.019	4	-28
Velez E	65.3	13	0	0	1	.929	0	0	--	4	--
Right Field											
Winn R	770.0	187	3	0	0	1.000	1	0	.051	48	10
Schierholtz	597.7	135	10	1	1	.986	2	0	.013	43	20
Torres A	35.3	7	0	0	0	1.000	0	0	--	5	--
Bowker J	29.0	6	0	0	0	1.000	0	0	--	2	--
Velez E	14.0	3	0	0	0	1.000	0	0	--	0	--

Seattle Mariners

Stat Facts:

- The Mariners earned the most team defensive runs (109) in the majors, by a landslide
- Ichiro Suzuki led the AL with 15 intentional walks
- Suzuki's GB% (56%) was highest among AL regulars
- Suzuki grounded into just 1 double play
- 63% of Suzuki's ground balls were outs, lowest rate among AL regulars
- Suzuki's 33 ground ball runs led the majors by a landslide
- Felix Hernandez was third in the majors with 141 PRC
- Jose Lopez had the lowest H-A (-.079) of any regular in the majors
- Ronny Cedeño had the lowest OBP (.213) of anyone in the majors with at least 200 PAs

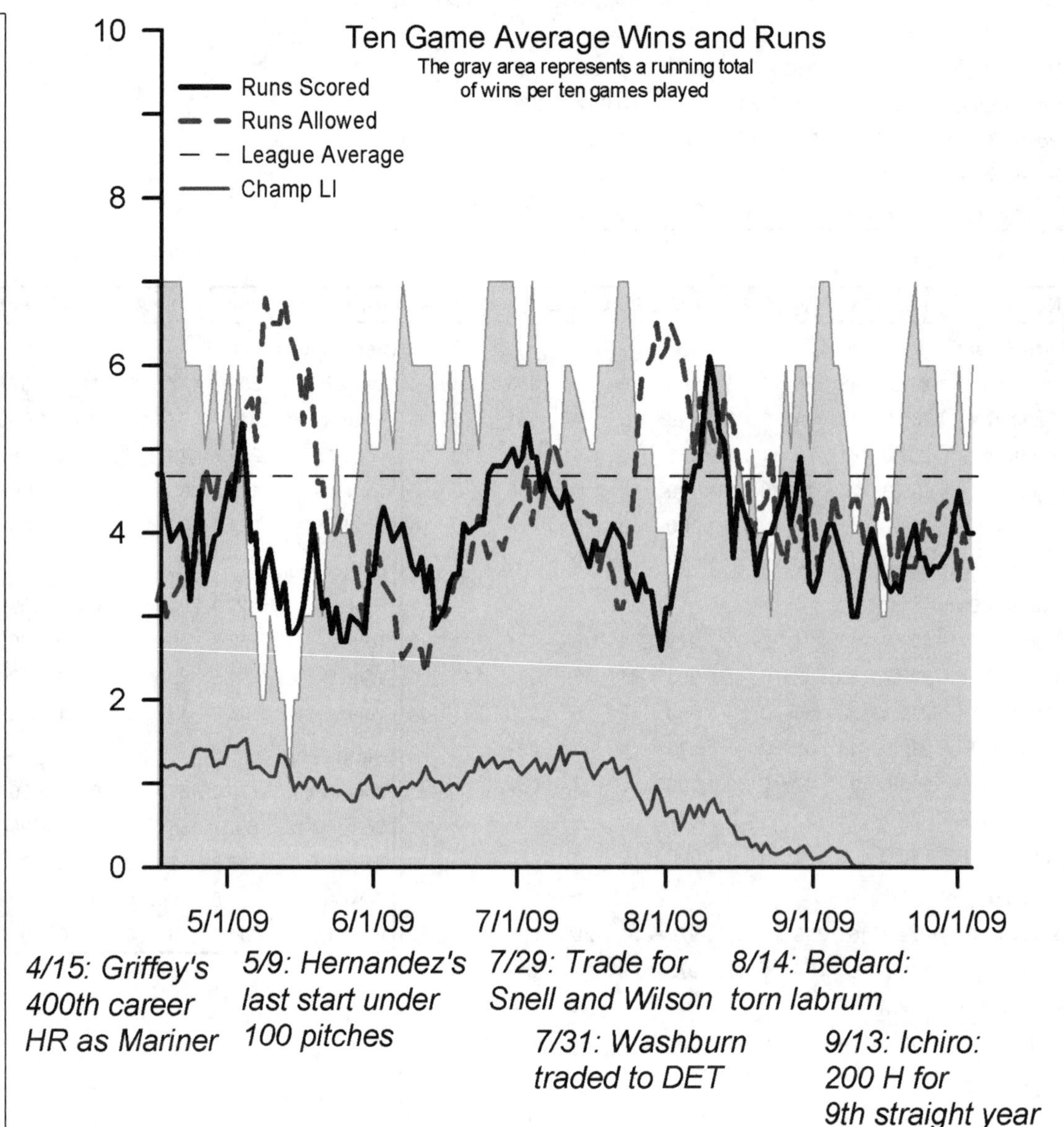

Team Batting and Pitching/Fielding Stats by Month

	April	May	June	July	Aug	Sept/Oct
Wins	13	11	15	14	15	17
Losses	9	18	10	13	14	13
RS/G	4.2	3.6	4.0	3.7	4.4	3.8
RA/G	3.8	5.0	3.4	4.9	4.7	3.7
OBP	.311	.311	.327	.307	.314	.314
SLG	.372	.398	.430	.381	.412	.412
FIP	3.70	4.89	4.02	5.20	4.89	3.90
DER	.703	.689	.723	.731	.728	.716

Batting Stats

Player	*BR*	Runs	RBI	PA	Outs	H	2B	3B	HR	TB	K	BB	IBB	HBP	SH	SF	SB	CS	GDP	H-A	L^R	BA	OBP	SLG	*GPA*
Suzuki I *	*99*	88	46	678	424	225	31	4	11	297	71	32	15	4	2	1	26	9	1	.038	.012	.352	.386	.465	*.299*
Branyan R *	*77*	64	76	505	329	108	21	1	31	224	149	58	6	9	1	6	2	0	6	.034	.034	.251	.347	.520	*.295*
Lopez J	*76*	69	96	653	474	167	42	0	25	284	69	24	5	6	3	7	3	3	25	-.079	.004	.272	.303	.463	*.260*
Gutierrez F	*76*	85	70	629	424	160	24	1	18	240	122	46	3	3	13	2	16	5	14	.051	.091	.283	.339	.425	*.267*
Griffey Jr.	*54*	44	57	454	310	83	19	0	19	159	80	63	2	1	0	3	0	0	6	.107	-.018	.214	.324	.411	*.256*
Beltre A	*46*	54	44	477	351	119	27	0	8	170	74	19	1	7	0	2	13	2	19	-.026	.082	.265	.304	.379	*.239*
Sweeney M	*33*	25	34	266	178	68	15	0	8	107	31	17	2	4	0	3	0	0	4	-.024	-.030	.281	.335	.442	*.269*
Johjima K	*27*	24	22	258	186	59	11	0	9	97	28	12	0	5	1	1	2	2	4	-.052	-.027	.247	.296	.406	*.242*
Johnson R	*22*	21	27	290	215	55	19	2	2	84	60	26	1	2	3	1	1	1	11	-.036	-.053	.213	.289	.326	*.218*
Chavez E *	*18*	17	13	182	122	44	3	1	2	55	22	14	1	0	5	2	9	1	4	-.011	.051	.273	.328	.342	*.240*
Betancourt Y	*17*	15	22	245	178	56	10	1	2	74	18	10	0	0	8	3	3	1	9	.038	.053	.250	.278	.330	*.214*
Hannahan J *	*16*	15	11	167	117	34	8	0	3	51	35	17	0	1	0	1	1	1	2	-.052	.067	.230	.311	.345	*.233*
Balentien W	*15*	18	13	170	124	33	10	0	4	55	43	13	1	0	0	2	1	0	2	.010	-.035	.213	.271	.355	*.217*
Wilson J	*14*	16	10	138	100	32	8	1	3	51	32	6	0	2	2	0	1	2	2	-.087	.017	.250	.294	.398	*.239*
Langerhans R	*13*	12	10	122	80	22	6	1	3	39	28	14	1	1	3	3	0	1	0	-.050	.027	.218	.311	.386	*.244*
Carp M *	*10*	7	5	65	38	17	3	1	1	25	10	8	0	2	0	1	0	0	1	.072	.036	.315	.415	.463	*.312*
Cedeno R	*10*	15	17	206	163	31	4	2	5	54	50	10	1	1	9	0	3	2	6	.008	.005	.167	.213	.290	*.174*
Hall B	*9*	10	12	131	99	24	8	1	2	40	48	8	0	0	0	3	1	2	1	-.093	-.059	.200	.244	.333	*.199*
Saunders M *	*8*	13	4	129	97	27	1	3	0	34	40	6	0	0	1	0	4	1	1	-.066	.065	.221	.258	.279	*.191*
Wilson J	*8*	11	8	116	85	24	5	0	1	32	17	6	0	0	2	1	1	0	2	-.070	.003	.224	.263	.299	*.199*
Woodward C	*5*	7	5	74	52	16	1	0	0	17	15	5	0	0	1	1	1	0	1	.058	-.152	.239	.288	.254	*.199*
Tuiasosopo M	*3*	2	2	25	17	5	1	0	1	9	5	2	0	0	0	1	0	0	0	-.085	.170	.227	.280	.409	*.235*
Moore A	*2*	4	2	24	19	5	1	0	1	9	7	0	0	1	0	0	1	0	1	-.308	.042	.217	.250	.391	*.217*
Shelton C	*2*	1	4	28	20	6	2	0	0	8	11	2	0	0	0	0	0	0	0	.174	.214	.231	.286	.308	*.212*
Quiroz G	*1*	0	2	15	10	4	0	0	0	4	3	0	0	0	1	0	0	0	0	.042	.538	.286	.286	.286	*.206*

Italicized stats have been adjusted for home park.

Batted Ball Batting Stats

	% of PA		% of Batted Balls					Out %		Runs Per Event				Total Runs vs. Avg.				
Player	**K%**	**BB%**	**GB%**	**LD%**	**FB%**	**IF/F**	**HR/OF**	**GB**	**OF**	**NIP**	**GB**	**LD**	**OF**	**NIP**	**GB**	**LD**	**FB**	**Tot**
Suzuki I	10	5	56	18	26	.09	.08	63	85	.04	.12	.41	.14	-4	33	10	-10	30
Branyan R	30	13	33	17	50	.03	.22	78	84	.03	.03	.45	.32	-0	-4	-3	23	15
Sweeney M	12	8	38	18	44	.09	.09	73	83	.07	.06	.37	.15	0	1	1	1	3
Griffey Jr. K	18	14	37	16	47	.11	.14	84	83	.09	-.01	.37	.22	7	-8	-6	8	1
Gutierrez F	19	8	45	19	36	.08	.12	70	82	.02	.06	.37	.21	-5	5	-1	2	1
Wilson J	23	6	41	24	35	.18	.11	74	80	-.02	.04	.40	.20	-3	-1	2	-1	-3
Lopez J	11	5	41	19	41	.07	.12	80	83	.03	.00	.36	.20	-7	-9	1	11	-3
Langerhans R	23	12	37	16	47	.14	.10	71	89	.05	.08	.39	.14	0	0	-2	-2	-3
Hannahan J	21	11	42	19	39	.09	.08	79	84	.04	.02	.39	.13	-0	-1	-0	-2	-4
Johjima K	11	7	50	13	36	.13	.14	75	89	.06	.05	.28	.19	-1	2	-6	-1	-6
Chavez E	12	8	53	19	28	.11	.06	75	94	.07	.04	.35	.05	-0	2	-1	-7	-7
Balentien W	25	8	43	13	44	.12	.09	78	83	-.01	.04	.45	.16	-3	-1	-3	-2	-8
Hall B	37	6	40	17	43	.09	.07	80	81	-.05	.01	.56	.16	-5	-2	-0	-2	-9
Wilson J	15	5	44	17	39	.11	.03	83	87	.01	-.01	.39	.05	-2	-2	-1	-5	-9
Saunders M	31	5	47	15	39	.10	.00	77	81	-.05	.03	.46	.06	-4	2	-2	-5	-10
Beltre A	16	5	46	16	38	.10	.06	70	85	.01	.05	.42	.11	-6	3	1	-9	-11
Betancourt Y	7	4	40	18	41	.20	.03	78	83	.05	.01	.34	.08	-2	-3	-1	-8	-14
Johnson R	21	10	46	21	33	.20	.04	80	88	.03	-.00	.46	.05	-1	-5	3	-12	-15
Cedeno R	24	5	49	9	41	.13	.11	81	88	-.03	-.01	.22	.18	-5	-2	-10	-3	-21
MLB Average	***18***	***10***	***43***	***19***	***38***	***.10***	***.11***	***75***	***83***	***.05***	***.04***	***.39***	***.19***	--	--	--	--	--

Pitching Stats

Player	PRC	IP	BFP	G	GS	K	BB	IBB	HBP	H	HR	DP	DER	SB	CS	PO	W	L	Sv	Op	Hld	H-A	R^L	RA	ERA	FIP
Hernandez F	141	238.7	977	34	34	217	71	0	8	200	15	24	.706	20	8	1	19	5	0	0	0	.019	-.014	3.05	2.49	3.18
Washburn J *	76	133.0	531	20	20	79	33	1	3	109	11	13	.743	3	3	0	8	6	0	0	0	-.046	-.064	2.84	2.64	3.87
Bedard E *	50	83.0	348	15	15	90	34	0	4	65	8	3	.717	5	3	1	5	3	0	0	0	-.007	.016	3.14	2.82	3.65
Aardsma D	46	71.3	296	73	0	80	34	3	0	49	4	3	.742	2	2	0	3	6	38	42	6	.028	-.012	2.90	2.52	2.98
Rowland-Smit	40	96.3	401	15	15	52	27	0	4	87	9	8	.735	0	1	0	5	4	0	0	0	-.048	-.041	4.02	3.74	4.29
Lowe M	34	80.0	339	75	0	69	29	1	0	71	7	6	.705	2	2	0	2	7	3	13	26	-.012	-.081	4.39	3.26	3.65
White S	31	64.3	261	52	0	28	20	1	2	50	3	5	.745	5	3	3	3	2	1	3	15	-.044	.032	3.22	2.80	3.91
Vargas J *	30	91.7	385	23	14	54	24	1	3	98	16	13	.701	2	6	2	3	6	0	0	0	-.056	.016	5.20	4.91	5.13
Batista M	27	71.3	326	56	0	52	39	1	2	79	7	10	.668	7	2	0	7	4	1	5	14	-.012	-.084	4.67	4.04	4.69
Morrow B	27	69.7	313	26	10	63	44	1	0	66	10	6	.694	5	1	0	2	4	6	8	1	-.058	-.073	4.91	4.39	5.10
Jakubauskas	26	93.0	390	35	8	47	27	3	2	91	15	8	.732	2	2	2	6	7	0	1	3	.031	-.046	5.81	5.32	5.12
Snell I	24	64.3	289	12	12	37	39	0	1	61	7	6	.737	2	1	0	5	2	0	0	0	.011	.004	4.48	4.20	5.32
Fister D	24	61.0	256	11	10	36	15	0	2	63	11	9	.719	0	1	0	3	4	0	0	0	-.035	.008	4.28	4.13	5.19
Olson G *	23	80.3	347	31	11	47	34	0	4	79	19	11	.741	5	3	0	3	5	0	0	5	-.053	-.001	5.83	5.60	6.51
Kelley S	19	46.0	191	41	0	41	9	1	3	45	9	5	.721	2	0	0	5	4	0	4	9	.024	.110	4.50	4.50	4.67
French L *	8	38.0	179	8	7	23	17	0	1	54	9	6	.643	1	1	1	3	3	0	0	0	-.033	.005	7.58	6.63	6.48
Silva C	5	30.3	142	8	6	10	11	0	3	41	5	4	.681	1	1	0	1	3	0	0	0	-.086	-.123	8.60	8.60	6.06
Corcoran R	4	19.0	91	16	0	6	17	0	1	25	2	8	.646	1	1	0	2	0	0	1	2	.056	-.069	6.16	6.16	6.77
Messenger R	4	10.3	43	12	0	5	0	0	0	13	3	1	.714	0	0	0	0	1	0	0	1	.079	-.116	4.35	4.35	6.00
Stark D	2	11.0	54	9	0	7	10	0	0	13	2	1	.657	2	3	0	0	1	0	0	0	.174	-.168	7.36	6.55	7.01

Italicized stats have been adjusted for home park.

Batted Ball Pitching Stats

	% of PA		% of Batted Balls					Out %		Runs Per Event				Total Runs vs. Avg.				
Player	K%	BB%	GB%	LD%	FB%	IF/F	HR/OF	GB	OF	NIP	GB	LD	OF	NIP	GB	LD	FB	Tot
Hernandez F	22	8	53	17	30	.07	.08	76	86	.01	.03	.38	.13	-11	-2	-11	-21	-46
Washburn J	15	7	36	21	43	.08	.07	78	92	.03	.01	.33	.06	-4	-5	-1	-16	-26
Aardsma D	27	11	25	21	54	.08	.05	73	90	.02	.05	.35	.04	-2	-2	-4	-11	-18
Bedard E	26	11	42	17	40	.09	.09	79	80	.02	.02	.38	.17	-2	-3	-5	-3	-12
White S	11	9	48	16	36	.11	.05	82	84	.09	-.00	.37	.09	1	-4	-2	-7	-11
Rowland-Smith R	13	8	39	18	43	.13	.08	77	87	.06	.03	.32	.12	-1	-0	-3	-6	-11
Lowe M	20	9	39	21	40	.04	.08	74	88	.02	.05	.37	.12	-3	-1	0	-5	-8
Kelley S	21	6	31	17	51	.12	.13	57	94	-.01	.15	.32	.13	-3	4	-3	-1	-3
Snell I	13	14	37	21	41	.08	.06	77	88	.13	.04	.35	.09	6	-1	1	-6	0
Fister D	14	7	41	20	39	.04	.15	76	89	.03	.03	.36	.20	-2	-0	1	3	2
Jakubauskas C	12	7	45	14	41	.11	.13	77	81	.06	.03	.33	.25	-1	0	-6	9	2
Morrow B	20	14	37	20	43	.10	.13	68	90	.08	.08	.35	.17	4	2	-1	-1	4
Batista M	16	12	47	18	35	.10	.10	71	78	.09	.06	.34	.20	4	2	-2	1	5
Vargas J	14	7	37	21	42	.10	.13	79	88	.04	.01	.44	.18	-2	-4	7	4	5
Olson G	14	11	34	19	47	.13	.18	76	93	.09	.02	.38	.22	3	-3	1	7	9
Silva C	7	10	45	22	33	.11	.15	71	83	.16	.08	.36	.27	2	2	2	3	10
French L	13	10	30	24	46	.06	.13	63	90	.09	.11	.46	.17	1	2	7	3	14
MLB Average	***18***	***10***	***43***	***19***	***38***	***.10***	***.11***	***75***	***83***	***.05***	***.04***	***.39***	***.19***	--	--	--	--	--

Fielding Stats

Name	INN	SBA/G	CS%	ERA	WP+PB/G	PO	A	TE	FE
Catchers									
Johnson R	684.3	0.76	29%	3.22	0.552	511	42	2	2
Johjima K	580.0	0.59	50%	4.84	0.341	413	35	1	0
Burke J	96.7	0.74	38%	2.98	0.652	68	6	0	1
Moore A	57.0	0.16	0%	2.53	0.474	40	2	0	0
Quiroz G	34.7	0.26	0%	5.19	0.779	25	2	0	0

Name	Inn	PO	A	TE	FE	FPct	DPS	DPT	ZRDif	OOZ	Dif
First Base											
Branyan R	1034.0	947	74	2	8	.990	7	1	.000	44	8
Carp M	127.3	115	15	0	0	1.000	3	0	.113	9	36
Lopez J	122.0	115	8	0	0	.992	1	0	.085	7	23
Hannahan	90.0	92	8	0	0	1.000	2	1	--	4	--
Sweeney M	35.0	29	0	1	1	.935	0	0	--	0	--
Shelton C	35.0	31	2	0	0	1.000	1	0	--	1	--
Burke J	9.0	7	1	0	1	.889	0	0	--	1	--
Second Base											
Lopez J	1234.0	235	351	4	11	.975	34	50	-.020	36	2
Cedeno R	82.7	22	21	0	1	.977	3	6	--	2	--
Tuiasosopo	56.0	12	20	0	0	1.000	2	2	--	0	--
Woodward	35.0	8	3	0	0	1.000	1	0	--	1	--
Wilson J	26.0	6	13	0	0	1.000	1	3	--	2	--
Hall B	19.0	3	3	0	0	1.000	0	0	--	0	--
Shortstop											
Betancourt	548.0	101	159	3	6	.967	14	22	-.076	15	-11
Cedeno R	344.7	44	114	2	3	.969	10	7	.063	4	-27
Wilson J	273.3	42	74	0	2	.983	8	8	-.029	5	-20
Wilson J	266.7	47	75	2	3	.961	7	7	-.070	15	18
Hannahan	11.0	0	4	0	0	1.000	0	0	--	0	--
Woodward	9.0	2	0	0	0	1.000	0	0	--	--	--
Third Base											
Beltre A	988.3	103	224	7	7	.959	19	0	.016	61	20
Hannahan	277.7	18	60	2	1	.963	10	0	.067	13	5
Woodward	123.0	9	38	1	3	.922	6	1	.057	7	15
Wilson J	29.0	2	6	0	0	1.000	0	0	--	1	--
Hall B	17.7	1	4	0	0	1.000	1	0	--	1	--
Cedeno R	17.0	0	3	0	0	1.000	0	0	--	0	--

Name	Inn	PO	A	TE	FE	FPct	DPS	DPT	ZRDif	OOZ	Dif
Left Field											
Balentien	338.7	83	5	0	1	.989	0	0	-.010	15	-6
Saunders	312.3	89	0	0	1	.989	0	0	-.008	19	10
Chavez E	293.3	81	1	1	0	.988	1	0	.041	24	31
Langerhans	230.7	68	1	0	0	1.000	0	0	.056	11	-3
Hall B	176.7	43	1	0	1	.978	0	0	.077	10	6
Griffey Jr. K	60.0	9	0	0	0	1.000	0	0	--	1	--
Cedeno R	41.0	11	0	0	0	1.000	0	0	--	4	--
Center Field											
Gutierrez F	1353.0	445	6	4	3	.985	2	0	.035	113	16
Chavez E	67.0	17	1	0	0	1.000	0	0	--	5	--
Langerhans	32.3	16	0	0	0	1.000	0	0	--	3	--
Right Field											
Suzuki I	1291.0	317	5	1	2	.988	2	0	.043	83	12
Hall B	72.0	22	2	0	0	1.000	0	0	--	5	--
Balentien	25.7	5	0	0	0	1.000	0	0	--	1	--
Griffey Jr. K	23.0	4	0	0	0	1.000	0	0	--	1	--
Chavez E	23.0	6	0	0	0	1.000	0	0	--	2	--
Langerhans	18.0	1	0	0	0	1.000	0	0	--	--	--

St. Louis Cardinals

Stat Facts:

- Albert Pujols led the majors (again) in Base Runs, GPA, and IBB
- Pujols had 93 extra-base hits and 64 strikeouts
- Skip Schumaker's GB% of 61% was highest among major league regulars
- Schumaker's FB% (17%) was lowest in the majors
- Adam Wainwright led the NL with 970 BFP
- Joel Pineiro induced 33 DPs, tied for most in the NL
- Pineiro allowed just 1 SB in 5 attempts in 214 IP
- Pineiro's GB% (60%) was highest of any ML pitcher with at least 162 IP
- Pineiro's FB% (24%) was lowest of any ML pitcher with at least 162 IP
- Pineiro's BB% (4%) was lowest in the majors
- Chris Carpenter allowed 7 home runs in 193 IP
- P.J. Walters allowed 6 home runs in 16 IP

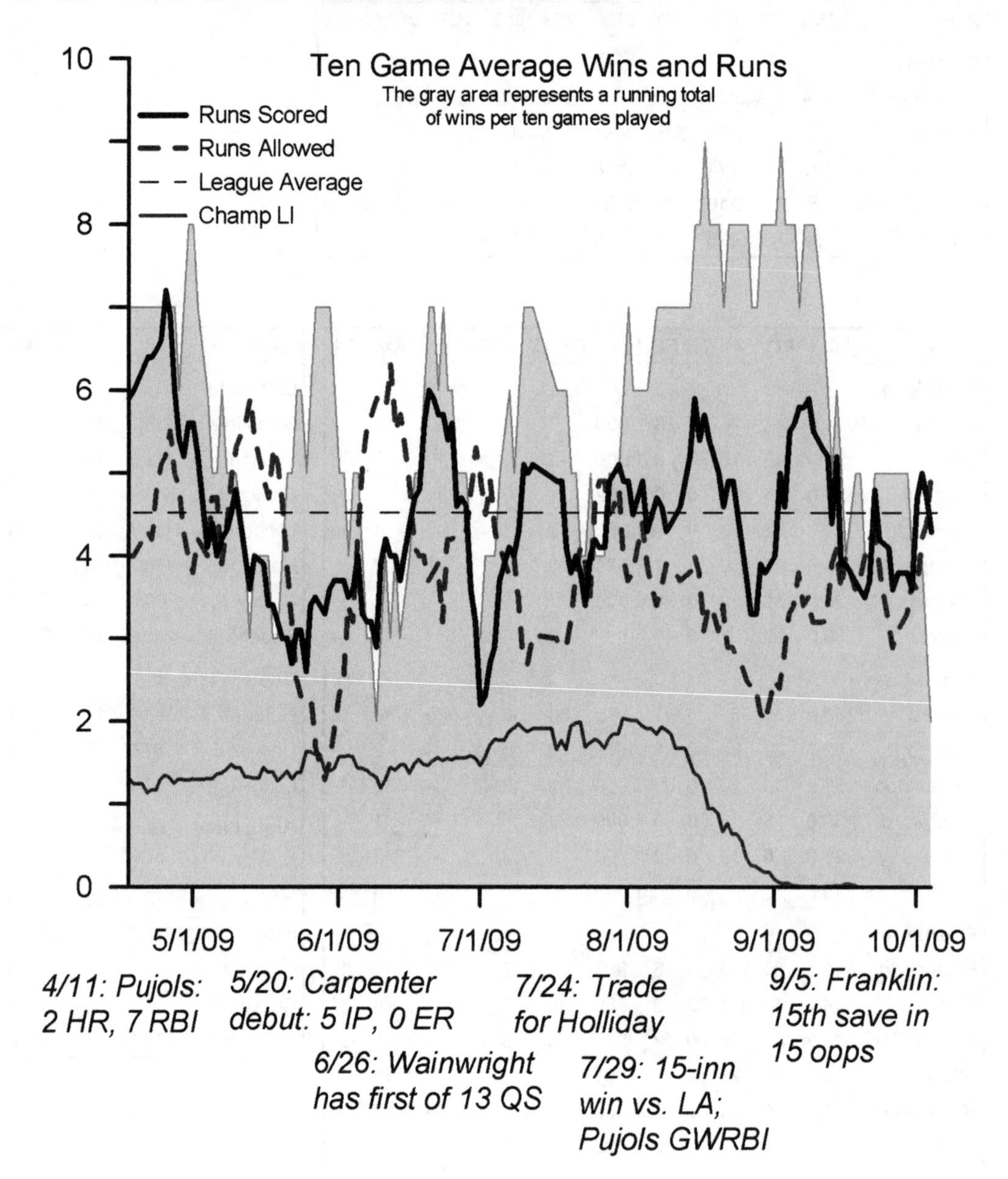

Team Batting and Pitching/Fielding Stats by Month

	April	May	June	July	Aug	Sept/Oct
Wins	16	13	12	16	20	14
Losses	7	14	17	11	6	16
RS/G	5.8	3.5	4.1	4.6	4.5	4.8
RA/G	4.2	3.7	5.0	3.6	3.0	4.2
OBP	.369	.299	.310	.336	.338	.344
SLG	.450	.389	.405	.418	.416	.417
FIP	3.84	3.94	4.62	3.77	3.52	3.54
DER	.683	.714	.705	.680	.709	.683

Batting Stats

Player	BR	Runs	RBI	PA	Outs	H	2B	3B	HR	TB	K	BB	IBB	HBP	SH	SF	SB	CS	GDP	H-A	L^R	BA	OBP	SLG	GPA
Pujols A	145	124	135	700	409	186	45	1	47	374	64	115	44	9	0	8	16	4	23	.008	.026	.327	.443	.658	.372
Schumaker S	75	85	35	586	377	161	34	1	4	209	69	52	2	0	1	1	2	2	4	-.005	.095	.303	.364	.393	.268
Ludwick R	72	63	97	542	365	129	20	1	22	217	106	41	3	7	1	4	4	2	6	-.066	-.008	.265	.329	.447	.265
Molina Y	63	45	54	544	370	141	23	1	6	184	39	50	2	6	6	1	9	3	27	.038	-.011	.293	.366	.383	.266
Rasmus C *	60	72	52	520	361	119	22	2	16	193	95	36	3	3	5	2	3	1	5	.019	.100	.251	.307	.407	.245
Holliday M	52	42	55	270	161	83	16	2	13	142	43	26	5	4	0	5	2	4	5	.064	-.043	.353	.419	.604	.347
Ryan B	51	55	37	429	292	114	19	7	3	156	56	24	3	6	6	3	14	7	9	.024	-.032	.292	.340	.400	.259
Ankiel R *	41	50	38	404	294	86	21	2	11	144	99	26	4	3	0	3	4	3	5	-.008	.041	.231	.285	.387	.230
Duncan C *	32	25	32	304	208	59	15	2	5	93	67	41	1	0	0	3	0	1	6	-.074	.021	.227	.329	.358	.243
DeRosa M	29	31	28	262	189	54	10	1	10	96	58	18	0	4	1	2	2	1	5	-.123	.033	.228	.291	.405	.237
Thurston J *	28	27	25	307	218	60	17	4	1	88	56	33	5	3	3	1	4	2	9	.060	-.012	.225	.316	.330	.229
Lugo J	24	24	13	170	110	41	9	4	2	64	27	17	0	1	2	2	6	0	3	.026	-.048	.277	.351	.432	.272
Greene K	16	21	24	193	142	34	7	0	6	59	35	15	1	3	2	3	2	1	5	-.002	-.018	.200	.272	.347	.214
Barden B	11	13	10	114	82	24	3	0	4	39	21	6	0	2	2	1	0	0	3	-.053	-.055	.233	.286	.379	.228
Greene T	10	9	7	116	86	24	5	0	2	35	32	4	0	3	1	0	3	0	2	.007	-.023	.222	.270	.324	.207
LaRue J	9	10	6	112	82	25	3	0	2	34	22	3	0	4	1	0	1	0	3	-.049	.003	.240	.288	.327	.216
Stavinoha N	8	6	17	91	69	20	7	0	2	33	15	2	0	0	0	2	1	0	2	.028	.066	.230	.242	.379	.208
Wainwright A	5	7	4	96	73	16	5	1	2	29	26	1	0	0	6	0	0	0	0	-.012	-.128	.180	.189	.326	.170
Freese D	5	3	7	34	22	10	2	0	1	15	7	2	0	0	0	1	0	0	1	.026	-.315	.323	.353	.484	.286
Carpenter C	3	3	7	69	53	11	3	0	1	17	13	2	0	1	3	0	0	0	1	.007	-.048	.175	.212	.270	.166
Hoffpauir J	2	1	2	16	10	3	2	0	0	5	2	4	0	0	0	0	0	0	1	--	-.271	.250	.438	.417	.308
Lohse K	2	3	2	45	29	8	0	0	0	8	7	1	0	2	5	0	0	0	0	.079	.260	.216	.275	.216	.182
Glaus T	2	2	2	32	25	5	2	0	0	7	8	3	0	0	0	0	0	0	1	-.040	-.067	.172	.250	.241	.177
Robinson S	1	1	1	26	20	6	1	0	0	7	2	0	0	0	0	1	1	0	1	-.056	-.102	.240	.231	.280	.178
Pineiro J	1	4	4	79	57	9	2	0	0	11	33	4	0	0	9	0	1	0	0	-.013	-.132	.136	.186	.167	.128

Only includes batters with at least one Base Run. Italicized stats have been adjusted for home park.

Batted Ball Batting Stats

	% of PA		% of Batted Balls					Out %		Runs Per Event				Total Runs vs. Avg.				
Player	K%	BB%	GB%	LD%	FB%	IF/F	HR/OF	GB	OF	NIP	GB	LD	OF	NIP	GB	LD	FB	Tot
Pujols A	9	18	39	16	46	.12	.21	69	86	.19	.07	.47	.31	28	6	8	37	79
Holliday M	16	11	43	17	40	.09	.18	60	78	.08	.13	.42	.33	2	8	2	12	25
Schumaker J	12	9	61	22	17	.10	.05	74	74	.08	.06	.37	.18	3	9	9	-11	9
Ludwick R	20	9	33	18	49	.11	.13	71	86	.03	.07	.39	.19	-3	1	-0	6	5
Lugo J	16	11	43	20	38	.09	.05	73	85	.07	.05	.50	.12	1	0	4	-3	2
Ryan B	13	7	51	19	30	.13	.01	71	80	.05	.07	.44	.09	-2	7	6	-12	-0
Molina Y	7	10	51	20	29	.05	.05	78	79	.16	.01	.34	.14	8	-5	3	-6	-1
Barden B	18	7	51	19	31	.04	.17	85	85	.01	-.03	.43	.23	-1	-3	0	0	-3
Duncan C	22	13	51	15	35	.12	.08	72	82	.06	.06	.35	.17	2	2	-6	-4	-5
DeRosa M	22	8	42	16	42	.08	.14	70	85	.01	.08	.25	.23	-3	2	-7	3	-5
LaRue J	20	6	49	15	36	.17	.08	78	77	-.00	.02	.41	.18	-2	-1	-1	-1	-5
Greene T	28	6	44	18	38	.11	.08	72	82	-.03	.06	.31	.15	-3	2	-2	-2	-6
Rasmus C	18	8	35	20	46	.05	.10	72	88	.02	.06	.33	.13	-5	3	-4	-3	-8
Greene K	18	9	31	18	51	.03	.09	88	87	.04	-.05	.30	.13	-1	-5	-4	-1	-9
Thurston J	19	12	45	25	30	.25	.02	79	86	.06	.02	.38	.05	2	-2	3	-13	-10
Ankiel R	24	7	40	15	45	.13	.10	75	82	-.01	.04	.42	.19	-7	-1	-5	0	-12
MLB Average	***18***	***10***	***43***	***19***	***38***	***.10***	***.11***	***75***	***83***	***.05***	***.04***	***.39***	***.19***	--	--	--	--	--

Pitching Stats

Player	PRC	IP	BFP	G	GS	K	BB	IBB	HBP	H	HR	DP	DER	SB	CS	PO	W	L	Sv	Op	Hld	H-A	R^L	RA	ERA	FIP
Wainwright A	128	233.0	970	34	34	212	66	1	3	216	17	22	.685	12	5	1	19	8	0	0	0	-.048	-.072	2.90	2.63	3.92
Carpenter C	121	192.7	750	28	28	144	38	1	7	156	7	26	.729	2	4	1	17	4	0	0	0	.028	-.023	2.29	2.24	4.56
Pineiro J	78	214.0	865	32	32	105	27	1	8	218	11	33	.700	1	4	0	15	12	0	0	0	-.037	-.011	3.95	3.49	4.58
Franklin R	43	61.0	250	62	0	44	24	3	1	49	2	5	.732	1	1	1	4	3	38	43	1	-.072	.010	1.92	1.92	3.82
Lohse K	34	117.7	512	23	22	77	36	2	3	125	16	7	.695	4	1	0	6	10	0	0	0	-.048	.015	5.28	4.74	4.78
Miller T *	30	43.7	173	70	0	46	11	1	2	31	5	4	.734	1	1	1	4	1	0	1	13	-.025	-.153	2.27	2.06	4.66
McClellan K	29	66.7	288	66	0	51	34	2	2	56	4	8	.711	0	0	0	4	4	3	6	15	.038	.043	3.65	3.38	3.58
Wellemeyer T	27	122.3	561	28	21	78	57	2	3	160	19	20	.646	5	1	0	7	10	0	0	0	-.017	-.095	6.47	5.89	3.96
Hawksworth B	23	40.0	160	30	0	20	15	3	1	29	2	5	.779	0	1	0	4	0	0	0	2	-.063	-.067	2.25	2.03	4.40
Thompson B	22	80.0	345	32	8	34	23	2	7	85	8	13	.700	2	1	0	2	6	0	0	0	-.025	-.001	5.06	4.84	4.19
Boggs M	21	58.0	268	16	9	46	33	0	4	71	3	10	.621	3	2	1	2	3	0	0	1	.007	-.140	4.34	4.19	4.46
Motte J	19	56.7	244	69	0	54	23	1	2	57	10	6	.690	0	1	1	4	4	0	3	15	.018	-.100	5.08	4.76	4.94
Reyes D *	18	41.0	180	75	0	33	21	1	3	35	2	1	.694	4	3	3	0	2	1	1	18	.001	-.113	3.73	3.29	1.11
Smoltz J	15	38.0	158	7	7	40	9	1	0	36	3	1	.689	2	1	0	1	3	0	0	0	-.021	.038	4.26	4.26	3.07
Perez C	9	23.7	106	29	0	30	15	0	3	17	3	1	.709	1	2	1	1	1	1	2	3	.066	-.047	4.56	4.18	4.99
Boyer B	4	16.3	70	15	0	9	5	0	1	14	1	1	.759	2	0	0	0	0	0	0	2	.229	.057	5.51	4.41	6.99
Kinney J	2	15.3	81	17	0	8	11	1	2	23	2	1	.638	3	0	0	1	0	0	1	2	-.051	.171	8.80	8.80	6.47
Walters P	2	16.0	80	8	1	14	9	1	0	21	6	2	.647	1	0	0	0	0	0	0	0	.044	-.170	10.69	9.56	4.22

Italicized stats have been adjusted for home park.

Batted Ball Pitching Stats

	% of PA		% of Batted Balls					Out %		Runs Per Event				Total Runs vs. Avg.				
Player	K%	BB%	GB%	LD%	FB%	IF/F	HR/OF	GB	OF	NIP	GB	LD	OF	NIP	GB	LD	FB	Tot
Carpenter C	19	6	55	17	28	.09	.05	81	80	-.00	-.00	.39	.12	-12	-13	-7	-20	-52
Wainwright A	22	7	51	19	30	.10	.09	73	83	-.00	.05	.35	.17	-14	4	-8	-15	-32
Pineiro J	12	4	60	16	24	.08	.06	76	82	.00	.03	.43	.14	-12	2	1	-20	-29
Franklin R	18	10	46	20	34	.08	.04	80	85	.05	.00	.33	.07	0	-3	-2	-8	-13
Hawksworth B	13	10	54	14	32	.08	.06	80	85	.09	.01	.27	.12	1	-2	-4	-4	-9
Miller T	27	8	35	20	45	.12	.11	74	87	-.01	.04	.32	.15	-3	-1	-3	-2	-9
McClellan K	18	13	50	19	31	.12	.08	74	92	.08	.04	.40	.06	3	-1	0	-10	-8
Smoltz J	25	6	36	19	46	.08	.07	79	81	-.03	.02	.46	.13	-4	-1	0	-2	-6
Reyes D	18	13	53	16	31	.06	.03	74	79	.08	.06	.44	.09	2	1	-1	-5	-2
Perez C	28	17	36	23	41	.13	.10	80	89	.06	.02	.49	.13	1	-1	1	-2	-1
Motte J	22	10	38	17	45	.12	.16	73	83	.03	.04	.42	.27	-1	-1	-1	6	3
Thompson B	10	9	53	19	28	.10	.10	79	81	.10	.02	.42	.21	2	-2	4	-1	4
Lohse K	15	8	45	19	36	.08	.12	74	83	.04	.05	.36	.21	-2	3	0	4	5
Boggs M	17	14	53	18	29	.13	.07	67	77	.09	.10	.44	.20	4	6	2	-2	11
Wellemeyer T	14	11	37	21	42	.12	.13	65	85	.09	.08	.41	.20	5	7	8	6	26
MLB Average	***18***	***10***	***43***	***19***	***38***	***.10***	***.11***	***75***	***83***	***.05***	***.04***	***.39***	***.19***	--	--	--	--	--

Fielding Stats

Name	INN	SBA/G	CS%	ERA	WP+PB/G	PO	A	TE	FE
Catchers									
Molina Y	1176.7	0.37	33%	3.48	0.306	884	82	4	1
LaRue J	254.0	0.46	23%	4.46	0.283	174	13	1	0
Pagnozzi M	9.0	2.00	50%	3.00	0.000	9	1	0	0
Freese D	1.0	9.00	0%	18.00	0.000	1	0	0	0

Name	Inn	PO	A	TE	FE	FPct	DPS	DPT	ZRDif	OOZ	Dif
First Base											
Pujols A	1376.0	1473	185	2	10	.992	17	2	.025	76	21
Duncan C	27.0	26	3	0	1	.935	0	0	--	2	--
Glaus T	10.0	15	0	0	0	1.000	0	0	--	0	--
Molina Y	10.0	10	1	0	0	1.000	0	0	--	0	--
DeRosa M	8.0	6	0	0	0	1.000	0	0	--	0	--
Freese D	4.0	7	0	0	0	1.000	0	0	--	--	--
LaRue J	3.0	7	0	0	0	1.000	0	0	--	--	--
Greene T	1.0	1	0	0	0	1.000	0	0	--	--	--
Pagnozzi M	1.0	1	0	0	0	1.000	0	0	--	--	--
Second Base											
Schumaker	989.3	188	347	5	4	.983	22	55	-.013	21	-6
Lugo J	168.3	33	59	1	1	.979	2	9	-.101	7	14
Thurston J	138.0	32	48	2	0	.976	3	10	.079	5	9
Ryan B	95.7	21	31	0	1	.981	3	5	--	5	--
Hoffpauir J	22.0	1	10	0	0	1.000	1	1	--	0	--
Greene T	18.3	4	6	0	0	1.000	1	1	--	0	--
Barden B	7.0	4	0	0	0	1.000	0	0	--	--	--
DeRosa M	2.0	0	0	0	0	0.000	0	0	--	--	--
Shortstop											
Ryan B	830.7	145	354	3	5	.984	42	26	.033	54	27
Greene K	240.3	43	80	2	5	.946	7	10	-.098	16	28
Greene T	184.7	28	65	1	2	.969	8	4	-.014	9	10
Lugo J	158.0	35	55	1	1	.978	8	6	-.029	7	6
Barden B	27.0	4	11	0	0	1.000	2	0	--	0	--
Third Base											
DeRosa M	519.0	41	99	0	0	1.000	8	0	-.018	15	-13
Thurston J	463.0	38	109	3	7	.936	9	0	.016	22	6
Barden B	216.7	9	50	1	3	.937	3	0	.088	3	-28
Greene K	96.0	5	27	1	0	.970	5	0	--	3	--
Greene T	61.0	3	8	1	0	.917	1	0	--	1	--
Freese D	41.3	6	5	0	0	1.000	1	0	--	1	--
Glaus T	40.7	1	6	0	1	.875	0	0	--	3	--
Hoffpauir J	3.0	0	1	0	0	1.000	0	0	--	0	--

Name	Inn	PO	A	TE	FE	FPct	DPS	DPT	ZRDif	OOZ	Dif
Left Field											
Holliday M	540.7	86	1	0	1	.989	0	0	.066	14	-24
Duncan C	507.3	79	3	0	3	.965	1	0	-.026	20	-11
Ankiel R	153.3	41	2	0	0	1.000	1	0	.076	9	8
Schumaker	82.3	16	0	0	1	.941	0	0	--	1	--
Stavinoha	77.0	6	0	0	0	1.000	0	0	--	2	--
Rasmus C	43.0	9	0	0	0	1.000	0	0	--	4	--
Thurston J	17.0	3	0	0	0	1.000	0	0	--	0	--
DeRosa M	10.0	5	0	0	0	1.000	0	0	--	2	--
Ludwick R	8.0	1	0	0	0	1.000	0	0	--	0	--
Robinson S	2.0	0	0	0	0	0.000	0	0	--	--	--
Center Field											
Rasmus C	945.7	258	3	0	5	.981	1	0	.019	52	-13
Ankiel R	458.7	134	1	2	2	.971	0	0	.005	32	2
Schumaker	23.7	8	0	0	0	1.000	0	0	--	1	--
Ludwick R	7.0	2	0	0	0	1.000	0	0	--	1	--
Greene T	3.0	1	0	0	0	1.000	0	0	--	0	--
Robinson S	2.7	0	0	0	0	0.000	0	0	--	--	--
Right Field											
Ludwick R	1068.0	210	9	0	1	.995	4	0	-.039	44	-11
Ankiel R	183.7	28	2	1	0	.968	1	0	.015	5	-25
Stavinoha	67.3	6	0	0	0	1.000	0	0	--	2	--
Rasmus C	46.7	9	0	0	1	.900	0	0	--	4	--
Robinson S	41.3	6	0	0	0	1.000	0	0	--	3	--
Schumaker	25.3	5	0	0	0	1.000	0	0	--	1	--
DeRosa M	8.0	2	0	0	0	1.000	0	0	--	2	--

Tampa Bay Rays

Stat Facts:

- Jason Bartlett's LD% of 26% tied for highest in the majors
- B.J. Upton's LDR of .50 was highest among ML regulars
- Dioner Navarro had the fewest Base Runs (27) of any ML player with at least 400 PAs
- Evan Longoria led the AL with 27 GIDPs
- Gabe Kapler's L^R (.181) was highest in the majors among players with 200 PAs
- Carlos Peña walked or struck out in 45% of his PAs
- 26% of Peña's outfield flies were home runs
- 86% of Peña's ground balls were outs, highest rate of any major league regular
- David Price induced just 2 DPs in 128 IP
- The DER behind Dan Wheeler (.799) was highest of any ML pitcher with at least 50 IP
- Wheeler's R^L (-.164) was lowest of any ML pitcher with at least 50 IP

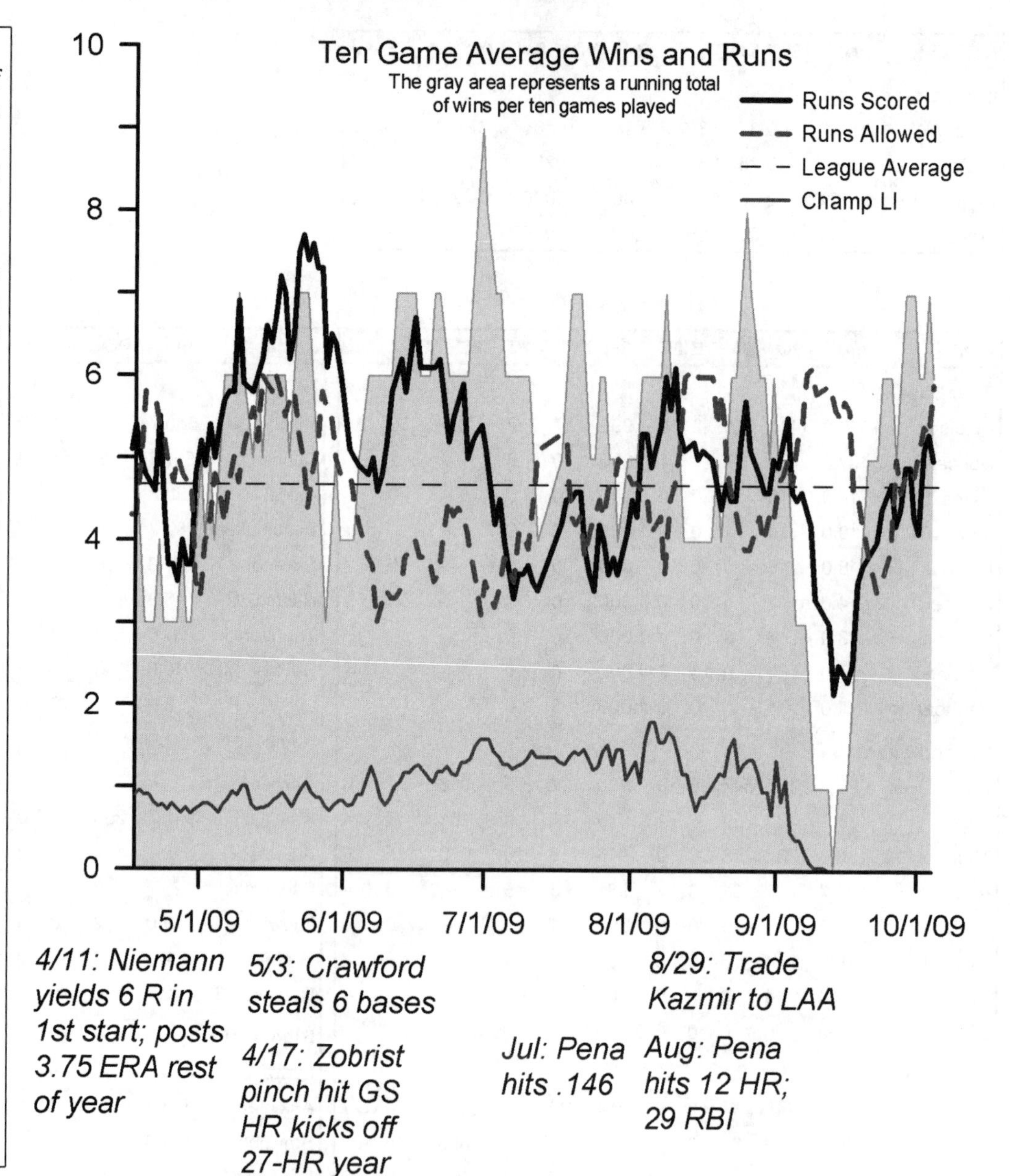

Team Batting and Pitching/Fielding Stats by Month

	April	May	June	July	Aug	Sept/Oct
Wins	9	16	19	12	15	13
Losses	14	14	7	12	12	19
RS/G	4.8	6.1	5.7	3.9	5.1	4.0
RA/G	4.5	5.2	3.4	4.8	4.7	5.1
OBP	.342	.362	.366	.317	.345	.322
SLG	.448	.455	.498	.384	.459	.393
FIP	4.57	4.74	3.98	4.25	4.55	4.40
DER	.708	.674	.737	.682	.720	.683

Batting Stats

Player	*BR*	Runs	RBI	PA	Outs	H	2B	3B	HR	TB	K	BB	IBB	HBP	SH	SF	SB	CS	GDP	H-A	L^R	BA	OBP	SLG	*GPA*
Zobrist B +	*107*	91	91	599	365	149	28	7	27	272	104	91	4	2	1	4	17	6	7	.048	.043	.297	.405	.543	*.321*
Longoria E	*102*	100	113	671	447	164	44	0	33	307	140	72	11	8	0	7	9	0	27	-.026	.007	.281	.364	.526	*.298*
Crawford C *	*101*	96	68	672	444	185	28	8	15	274	99	51	1	8	2	5	60	16	7	.004	.053	.305	.364	.452	*.280*
Bartlett J	*93*	90	66	567	352	160	29	7	14	245	89	54	2	5	4	4	30	7	5	-.046	.030	.320	.389	.490	*.301*
Pena C *	*91*	91	100	570	372	107	25	2	39	253	163	87	11	9	0	3	3	3	5	.063	.038	.227	.356	.537	*.298*
Upton B	*69*	79	55	626	446	135	33	4	11	209	152	57	0	3	3	3	42	14	7	.037	-.044	.241	.313	.373	*.237*
Burrell P	*50*	45	64	476	327	91	16	1	14	151	119	57	2	2	0	5	2	0	6	.052	-.027	.221	.315	.367	*.236*
Aybar W +	*41*	38	41	336	225	75	12	0	12	123	54	34	2	2	1	3	1	0	4	.053	.065	.253	.331	.416	*.256*
Gross G *	*35*	31	36	326	223	64	16	1	6	100	79	42	1	0	1	1	6	3	2	-.008	-.020	.227	.326	.355	*.238*
Iwamura A *	*33*	28	22	260	166	67	16	2	1	90	44	24	0	1	1	3	9	1	1	-.020	-.095	.290	.355	.390	*.260*
Kapler G	*29*	26	32	238	167	49	15	1	8	90	39	29	1	0	1	3	5	2	9	.027	.181	.239	.329	.439	*.261*
Navarro D +	*27*	38	32	410	310	82	15	0	8	121	51	18	1	5	8	3	5	2	14	-.011	.076	.218	.261	.322	*.200*
Zaun G +	*13*	11	14	99	71	27	7	0	4	46	18	4	0	1	0	0	0	2	2	-.005	-.135	.287	.323	.489	*.271*
Brignac R *	*11*	10	6	93	68	25	8	2	1	40	20	3	0	0	0	0	2	2	1	.056	.246	.278	.301	.444	*.249*
Hernandez M	*8*	12	12	107	81	24	3	1	1	32	12	7	0	0	1	0	2	1	5	.105	-.019	.242	.292	.323	*.215*
Joyce M *	*5*	3	7	37	26	6	1	0	3	16	7	3	0	1	0	1	1	0	0	.152	.010	.188	.270	.500	*.249*
Dillon J	*5*	4	2	35	22	9	0	0	1	12	4	3	0	2	0	0	0	0	1	.264	-.183	.300	.400	.400	*.283*
Sonnanstine	*1*	3	1	12	8	3	1	0	0	4	6	1	0	0	0	0	0	0	0	.104	.166	.273	.333	.364	*.243*
Richard C *	*1*	1	0	23	17	2	0	0	0	2	7	4	0	0	0	0	0	0	0	-.166	.175	.105	.261	.105	*.145*

Only includes batters with at least one Base Run. Italicized stats have been adjusted for home park.

Batted Ball Batting Stats

	% of PA		% of Batted Balls					Out %		Runs Per Event				Total Runs vs. Avg.				
Player	K%	BB%	GB%	LD%	FB%	IF/F	HR/OF	GB	OF	NIP	GB	LD	OF	NIP	GB	LD	FB	Tot
Zobrist B	17	16	42	20	39	.05	.18	69	82	.10	.08	.39	.30	13	6	3	20	42
Longoria E	21	12	39	19	42	.03	.17	76	79	.05	.02	.44	.29	3	-5	5	25	28
Bartlett J	16	10	35	26	39	.07	.09	70	79	.07	.07	.37	.20	3	5	13	6	27
Pena C	28	17	29	17	54	.12	.26	86	84	.06	-.03	.44	.40	8	-7	-6	32	27
Crawford C	15	9	52	19	29	.08	.10	68	81	.06	.09	.38	.21	1	14	4	-1	18
Iwamura A	17	10	44	21	36	.03	.02	71	75	.05	.07	.33	.14	0	3	-0	-2	2
Aybar W	16	11	42	22	36	.07	.14	76	87	.07	.04	.31	.19	2	0	-1	0	1
Kapler G	16	12	36	22	41	.19	.14	84	90	.08	-.02	.40	.19	2	-4	3	-1	-0
Hernandez M	11	7	57	17	25	.05	.05	78	85	.06	.01	.37	.06	-0	-1	-0	-4	-5
Gross G	24	13	40	23	36	.08	.09	72	94	.05	.08	.35	.09	1	2	-1	-9	-6
Upton BJ	24	10	44	15	40	.08	.07	69	86	.02	.08	.50	.12	-5	8	-2	-11	-10
Burrell P	25	12	34	18	48	.08	.11	76	87	.04	.03	.38	.15	0	-4	-5	-2	-11
Navarro D	12	6	37	20	43	.18	.07	85	86	.03	-.04	.34	.10	-4	-11	-1	-9	-25
MLB Average	***18***	***10***	***43***	***19***	***38***	***.10***	***.11***	***75***	***83***	***.05***	***.04***	***.39***	***.19***	--	--	--	--	--

Pitching Stats

Player	PRC	IP	BFP	G	GS	K	BB	IBB	HBP	H	HR	DP	DER	SB	CS	PO	W	L	Sv	Op	Hld	H-A	R^L	RA	ERA	FIP
Garza M	95	203.0	861	32	32	189	79	0	11	177	25	18	.715	3	4	0	8	12	0	0	0	-.027	.049	4.12	3.95	4.26
Shields J	88	219.7	930	33	33	167	52	1	1	239	29	24	.681	5	2	1	11	12	0	0	0	-.032	-.005	4.63	4.14	4.10
Niemann J	78	180.7	769	31	30	125	59	1	9	185	17	22	.692	24	6	1	13	6	0	0	0	-.010	-.019	4.18	3.94	4.14
Price D *	47	128.3	557	23	23	102	54	0	4	119	17	2	.724	8	6	3	10	7	0	0	0	-.066	-.025	5.05	4.42	4.68
Howell J *	44	66.7	278	69	0	79	33	3	3	47	7	5	.731	3	2	1	7	5	17	25	4	.033	.073	2.97	2.84	3.67
Cormier L	35	77.3	331	53	0	36	25	2	1	75	6	7	.719	6	1	0	3	3	2	2	6	.001	-.001	3.61	3.26	4.20
Kazmir S *	33	111.0	504	20	20	91	50	0	5	121	15	8	.673	3	1	0	8	7	0	0	0	.008	.029	6.24	5.92	4.79
Wheeler D	30	57.7	219	69	0	45	9	2	0	41	11	4	.799	5	0	0	4	5	2	6	16	.033	-.164	3.43	3.28	4.47
Balfour G	26	67.3	289	73	0	69	33	0	2	59	6	9	.698	6	1	0	5	4	4	9	18	-.039	-.007	5.08	4.81	3.86
Sonnanstine	21	99.7	459	22	18	60	34	3	2	131	19	12	.657	1	2	0	6	9	0	0	0	-.024	.109	7.68	6.77	5.46
Choate R *	18	36.3	142	61	0	28	11	3	0	28	4	6	.758	2	1	0	1	0	5	5	9	.038	-.163	3.72	3.47	3.74
Nelson J	16	40.3	182	42	0	36	27	1	1	32	7	2	.748	6	0	0	3	0	3	4	7	.016	.040	4.91	4.02	5.67
Davis W	15	36.3	150	6	6	36	13	1	0	33	2	2	.687	4	1	0	2	2	0	0	0	-.001	.012	4.71	3.72	2.92
Shouse B *	10	28.0	122	45	0	17	7	3	2	31	5	4	.692	2	0	0	1	1	0	1	10	.007	-.150	4.82	4.50	4.94
Springer R	7	15.3	65	26	0	11	3	1	1	16	4	1	.739	2	0	0	1	3	1	2	7	-.071	-.050	4.11	4.11	5.73
Isringhausen	6	8.0	37	9	0	6	5	0	2	6	0	1	.708	2	0	0	0	1	0	1	0	-.114	.009	2.25	2.25	4.32
Bradford C	4	10.3	55	20	0	6	2	1	0	22	1	1	.522	3	0	0	1	0	0	1	2	.000	-.412	4.35	4.35	3.58
Thayer D	4	13.7	59	11	0	8	1	0	0	18	3	1	.681	1	0	0	0	0	1	1	0	.002	.135	5.93	4.61	5.09
Percival T	3	11.3	52	14	0	7	5	0	1	14	3	1	.694	4	1	0	0	1	6	6	0	-.240	-.345	6.35	6.35	6.99
Abreu W	3	3.7	15	2	0	3	2	0	0	3	0	1	.700	0	0	0	0	0	0	0	0	-.244	-.118	2.45	2.45	3.19
Bennett J	2	12.7	70	11	0	4	11	0	1	24	2	4	.577	0	0	0	0	0	0	0	0	-.129	-.173	9.95	9.95	7.45

Italicized stats have been adjusted for home park.

Batted Ball Pitching Stats

	% of PA		% of Batted Balls					Out %		Runs Per Event				Total Runs vs. Avg.				
Player	K%	BB%	GB%	LD%	FB%	IF/F	HR/OF	GB	OF	NIP	GB	LD	OF	NIP	GB	LD	FB	Tot
Garza M	22	10	40	18	43	.10	.11	76	85	.04	.03	.36	.18	-2	-3	-9	-1	-15
Howell J	28	13	49	16	35	.07	.14	78	91	.03	.02	.43	.18	-0	-3	-4	-4	-11
Wheeler D	21	4	31	13	56	.09	.13	86	90	-.04	-.02	.43	.19	-5	-5	-4	3	-10
Choate R	20	8	65	10	25	.00	.16	79	90	.02	.01	.37	.19	-1	-2	-4	-2	-9
Balfour G	24	12	36	21	43	.10	.07	71	88	.04	.05	.39	.10	0	-0	-0	-6	-7
Cormier L	11	8	52	17	30	.06	.07	81	81	.08	.01	.39	.15	0	-2	0	-4	-6
Niemann J	16	9	41	20	39	.12	.09	75	86	.05	.03	.39	.14	-1	0	4	-9	-6
Davis W	24	9	39	25	36	.14	.06	79	86	.01	.01	.37	.12	-2	-2	1	-4	-6
Price D	18	10	41	19	39	.10	.12	82	81	.05	.01	.32	.23	1	-5	-6	5	-5
Shields J	18	6	42	20	37	.08	.12	70	82	-.00	.07	.34	.22	-13	7	-1	8	1
Nelson J	20	15	32	17	50	.12	.14	70	95	.09	.08	.38	.15	3	1	-2	-0	2
Shouse B	14	7	61	23	16	.00	.33	75	70	.05	.04	.25	.57	-0	0	-1	3	2
Kazmir S	18	11	36	19	45	.09	.10	69	80	.06	.08	.34	.21	2	4	-2	8	11
Sonnanstine A	13	8	43	19	38	.07	.15	70	83	.06	.08	.41	.25	-0	6	5	13	24
MLB Average	***18***	***10***	***43***	***19***	***38***	***.10***	***.11***	***75***	***83***	***.05***	***.04***	***.39***	***.19***	--	--	--	--	--

Fielding Stats

Name	INN	SBA/G	CS%	ERA	WP+PB/G	PO	A	TE	FE
Catchers									
Navarro D	921.3	0.78	24%	4.23	0.401	732	47	4	0
Hernandez M	264.3	0.58	24%	4.43	0.238	217	11	1	1
Zaun G	207.7	0.65	7%	4.94	0.173	168	6	0	1
Riggans S	34.0	0.53	0%	3.71	0.265	29	1	1	0

Name	Inn	PO	A	TE	FE	FPct	DPS	DPT	ZRDif	OOZ	Dif
First Base											
Pena C	1155.0	1055	71	2	8	.991	6	0	-.073	36	-3
Aybar W	204.3	168	18	0	1	.995	2	0	-.055	7	-0
Richard C	55.0	59	2	1	0	.984	0	0	--	1	--
Zobrist B	13.0	6	1	0	1	.875	1	0	--	0	--
Second Base											
Zobrist B	714.7	143	225	2	2	.989	16	25	.047	31	16
Iwamura A	555.3	114	163	2	4	.979	15	22	-.054	28	23
Aybar W	139.3	35	46	0	4	.942	3	10	-.123	4	1
Dillon J	10.0	1	1	0	0	1.000	0	0	--	1	--
Brignac R	8.0	0	4	0	0	1.000	0	0	--	0	--
Shortstop											
Bartlett J	1153.0	170	339	13	7	.962	25	28	-.018	64	17
Brignac R	211.7	26	62	1	1	.978	2	7	-.059	8	-0
Zobrist B	62.0	9	16	1	1	.926	3	2	--	5	--
Third Base											
Longoria	1302.0	112	302	9	4	.970	41	2	.026	64	8
Aybar W	114.0	8	26	0	2	.944	2	0	-.046	4	-6
Zobrist B	5.7	0	0	0	0	.000	0	0	--	--	--
Dillon J	4.0	0	1	0	0	1.000	0	0	--	0	--
Iwamura A	1.0	1	0	0	0	1.000	0	0	--	--	--

Name	Inn	PO	A	TE	FE	FPct	DPS	DPT	ZRDif	OOZ	Dif
Left Field											
Crawford	1282.0	327	6	1	3	.988	1	0	.020	105	32
Kapler G	73.7	8	0	0	0	1.000	0	0	--	0	--
Zobrist B	38.0	8	0	0	0	1.000	0	0	--	4	--
Perez F	31.0	10	0	0	0	1.000	0	0	--	5	--
Burrell P	2.0	0	0	0	0	.000	0	0	--	--	--
Center Field											
Upton B	1228.0	375	6	1	3	.990	1	0	.006	80	-3
Kapler G	68.0	27	1	0	0	1.000	0	0	--	4	--
Perez F	52.0	19	0	0	0	1.000	0	0	--	7	--
Zobrist B	46.7	15	0	0	0	1.000	0	0	--	4	--
Joyce M	32.0	9	0	0	0	1.000	0	0	--	1	--
Right Field											
Gross G	638.7	149	6	3	0	.981	1	0	.034	36	4
Kapler G	414.3	108	4	2	0	.982	0	0	-.007	35	32
Zobrist B	329.3	89	5	0	0	1.000	4	0	.030	28	33
Joyce M	36.0	6	0	0	0	1.000	0	0	--	2	--
Burrell P	7.0	2	0	0	0	1.000	0	0	--	0	--
Perez F	2.0	0	0	0	0	.000	0	0	--	--	--

Texas Rangers

Stat Facts:

- Chris Davis struck out 36% of the time, and walked 6%
- Marlon Byrd tied for the AL lead with 10 sacrifice flies
- The Rangers' +41 middle infield plus/minus ranked second in the majors
- The Rangers' GDP defense ranked second in the majors
- The Rangers' bunt defense ranked 29th in the majors
- Ian Kinsler stole 31 bases in 36 attempts
- Omar Vizquel had the most PAs (195) of anyone in the majors with 0 GIDPs
- Neftali Feliz's LD% (5%) was lowest in the majors
- 81% of the groundballs allowed by Scott Feldman were outs
- Elvis Andrus committed 14 throwing errors, most by any player
- Kevin Millwood's ERA (3.67) was much better than his FIP (4.89)
- Nearly a quarter of Nelson Cruz's outfield flies were home runs

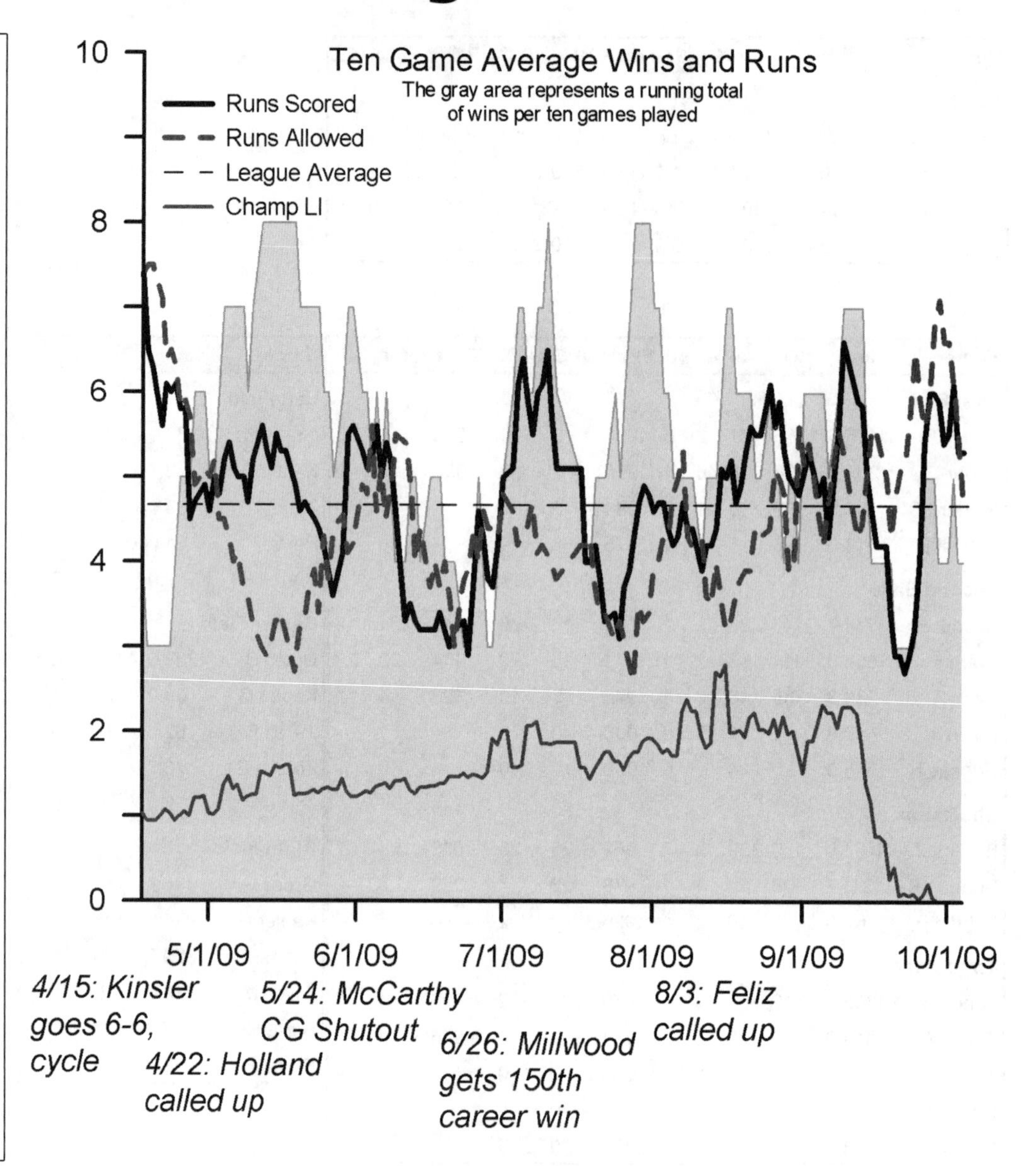

Team Batting and Pitching/Fielding Stats by Month

	April	May	June	July	Aug	Sept/Oct
Wins	10	20	11	17	14	15
Losses	11	9	15	8	15	17
RS/G	5.9	5.1	3.8	4.9	4.8	4.7
RA/G	6.0	3.7	4.5	3.8	4.6	5.1
OBP	.329	.333	.288	.312	.334	.318
SLG	.497	.483	.388	.452	.452	.407
FIP	5.73	4.51	4.73	4.04	4.63	4.03
DER	.687	.726	.698	.718	.691	.683

Batting Stats

Player	*BR*	Runs	RBI	PA	Outs	H	2B	3B	HR	TB	K	BB	IBB	HBP	SH	SF	SB	CS	GDP	H-A	L^R	BA	OBP	SLG	*GPA*
Young M	90	76	68	593	386	174	36	2	22	280	90	47	2	1	0	4	8	3	16	.037	-.010	.322	.374	.518	.289
Kinsler I	90	101	86	640	437	143	32	4	31	276	77	59	0	6	3	6	31	5	9	.085	.079	.253	.327	.488	.261
Byrd M	79	66	89	599	407	155	43	2	20	262	98	32	2	10	0	10	8	4	11	.036	-.033	.283	.329	.479	.260
Cruz N	77	75	76	515	355	120	21	1	33	242	118	49	6	2	0	2	20	4	9	.051	-.040	.260	.332	.524	.272
Murphy D *	63	61	57	494	325	116	24	1	17	193	106	49	3	1	2	9	9	4	5	.001	.068	.269	.338	.447	.256
Andrus E	61	72	40	541	362	128	17	8	6	179	77	40	0	6	12	3	33	6	4	.057	.033	.267	.329	.373	.234
Blalock H *	57	62	66	495	360	108	21	4	25	212	108	26	2	3	0	4	2	0	6	-.044	.039	.234	.277	.459	.232
Davis C *	47	48	59	419	304	93	15	1	21	173	150	24	2	2	0	2	0	0	6	-.009	.080	.238	.284	.442	.231
Hamilton J *	42	43	54	365	254	90	19	2	10	143	79	24	2	1	0	4	8	3	5	-.065	-.072	.268	.315	.426	.241
Jones A	42	43	43	331	229	60	18	0	17	129	72	45	3	2	0	3	5	1	7	.049	.008	.214	.323	.459	.253
Saltalamacch	29	34	34	310	222	66	12	0	9	105	97	22	1	1	3	1	0	2	3	.057	-.004	.233	.290	.371	.217
Borbon J *	25	30	20	179	115	49	4	0	4	65	28	15	0	1	6	0	19	4	3	.096	.205	.312	.376	.414	.265
Vizquel O +	19	17	14	195	130	47	7	2	1	61	27	13	0	0	5	0	4	0	0	.004	.162	.266	.316	.345	.222
Teagarden T	19	26	24	218	161	43	13	0	6	74	76	14	0	1	3	2	0	0	6	.015	.080	.217	.270	.374	.209
Rodriguez I	9	14	13	104	81	24	8	0	2	38	18	5	0	0	0	1	1	0	7	-.001	.016	.245	.279	.388	.216
German E	6	9	4	50	32	14	4	0	0	18	7	4	0	0	0	0	1	0	0	.090	.065	.304	.360	.391	.252
Richardson K	1	2	0	6	3	3	0	0	0	3	2	0	0	0	0	0	0	0	0	.420	-.525	.500	.500	.500	.340
Gentry C	1	4	1	19	15	2	1	0	0	3	5	2	0	0	0	0	0	0	0	.379	.128	.118	.211	.176	.135

Only includes batters with at least one Base Run. Italicized stats have been adjusted for home park.

Batted Ball Batting Stats

	% of PA		% of Batted Balls					Out %		Runs Per Event				Total Runs vs. Avg.				
Player	K%	BB%	GB%	LD%	FB%	IF/F	HR/OF	GB	OF	NIP	GB	LD	OF	NIP	GB	LD	FB	Tot
Young M	15	8	45	22	33	.02	.15	72	81	.05	.05	.39	.26	-1	4	11	14	28
Cruz N	23	10	38	16	46	.11	.24	76	85	.03	.03	.39	.35	-3	-2	-5	25	15
Kinsler I	12	10	30	16	54	.11	.13	79	88	.10	.03	.42	.19	5	-3	-1	13	15
Byrd M	16	7	41	19	41	.07	.11	69	85	.03	.09	.41	.18	-4	8	5	4	12
Murphy D	21	10	38	19	43	.10	.12	70	83	.03	.07	.41	.22	-1	2	1	5	8
Jones A	22	14	34	16	50	.13	.16	71	83	.07	.07	.30	.26	4	1	-7	8	6
Borbon J	16	9	54	19	27	.13	.14	61	88	.05	.13	.31	.18	0	8	-2	-3	3
Hamilton J	22	7	36	22	42	.03	.08	80	84	-.00	.01	.46	.15	-5	-4	7	-1	-3
Blalock H	22	6	37	18	44	.08	.17	78	88	-.02	.03	.36	.25	-9	-3	-3	12	-3
Rodriguez I	17	5	53	17	30	.04	.09	79	86	-.01	-.01	.45	.15	-2	-2	1	-1	-4
Vizquel O	14	7	34	22	43	.13	.02	75	87	.04	.05	.43	.03	-1	-1	4	-8	-6
Davis C	36	6	35	21	44	.03	.20	74	80	-.05	.04	.34	.33	-14	-2	-6	15	-7
Teagarden T	35	7	42	17	41	.06	.11	63	83	-.04	.10	.42	.20	-7	2	-3	-1	-9
Andrus E	14	9	55	22	23	.09	.07	76	86	.06	.04	.36	.12	-0	3	3	-15	-9
Saltalamacchia J	31	7	36	23	41	.07	.13	68	90	-.03	.08	.36	.15	-7	1	-2	-4	-12
MLB Average	***18***	***10***	***43***	***19***	***38***	***.10***	***.11***	***75***	***83***	***.05***	***.04***	***.39***	***.19***	--	--	--	--	--

Pitching Stats

Player	*PRC*	IP	BFP	G	GS	K	BB	IBB	HBP	H	HR	DP	DER	SB	CS	PO	W	L	Sv	Op	Hld	H-A	R^L	RA	ERA	FIP
Millwood K	*91*	198.7	850	31	31	123	71	0	11	195	26	27	.711	13	8	0	13	10	0	0	0	-.012	-.016	3.99	3.67	4.89
Feldman S	*83*	189.7	791	34	31	113	65	0	9	178	18	26	.722	15	7	0	17	8	0	0	0	.009	.025	4.13	4.08	4.40
O'Day D	*49*	55.7	216	64	0	54	17	1	4	36	3	6	.754	7	4	0	2	1	2	2	20	.007	-.058	1.94	1.94	3.03
Hunter T	*46*	112.0	475	19	19	64	33	2	2	113	13	10	.702	9	3	1	9	6	0	0	0	-.033	-.090	4.42	4.10	4.44
Wilson C *	*43*	73.7	323	74	0	84	32	3	6	66	3	7	.657	4	2	0	5	6	14	18	19	-.105	-.038	3.54	2.81	2.87
Holland D *	*41*	138.3	611	33	21	107	47	0	4	160	26	16	.672	8	3	3	8	13	0	1	2	.075	-.010	6.38	6.12	5.19
Padilla V	*38*	108.0	475	18	18	59	42	0	8	120	12	18	.686	3	4	2	8	6	0	0	0	.052	-.068	5.08	4.92	4.93
McCarthy B	*36*	97.3	420	17	17	65	36	0	3	96	13	9	.713	5	2	0	7	4	0	0	0	-.059	-.037	5.09	4.62	4.79
Nippert D	*33*	69.7	300	20	10	54	29	0	4	64	7	6	.714	12	1	2	5	3	0	0	1	.002	-.046	4.00	3.88	4.37
Feliz N	*31*	31.0	117	20	0	39	8	0	3	13	2	1	.815	1	0	0	1	0	2	3	9	.053	-.071	1.74	1.74	2.58
Francisco F	*27*	49.3	203	51	0	57	15	1	1	40	6	2	.702	4	0	0	2	3	25	29	4	-.010	-.000	3.83	3.83	3.37
Jennings J	*25*	61.0	272	44	0	44	28	3	2	67	7	8	.675	7	3	0	2	4	1	2	12	-.045	-.054	4.57	4.13	4.57
Mathis D	*21*	42.7	172	24	2	25	10	0	2	39	4	8	.725	0	0	0	0	1	1	1	1	.033	-.019	3.59	3.16	4.08
Harrison M *	*18*	63.3	283	11	11	34	23	0	2	81	9	9	.660	3	3	1	4	5	0	0	0	-.022	-.133	6.11	6.11	5.15
Guardado E *	*14*	38.3	166	48	0	20	15	1	2	39	8	4	.727	4	2	0	1	2	0	2	5	.057	.056	4.93	4.46	6.11
Grilli J	*11*	26.3	113	30	0	27	14	0	1	21	2	2	.725	2	0	0	2	2	0	0	4	.127	.024	4.78	4.78	3.84
Eyre W	*7*	18.0	72	17	0	8	6	2	0	18	0	5	.690	0	1	0	0	0	0	0	0	-.049	-.052	4.50	4.50	2.97
Moscoso G	*6*	14.0	64	10	0	12	6	0	1	15	1	1	.682	1	0	0	0	0	0	0	0	.158	-.153	4.50	3.21	3.91
Benson K	*4*	22.3	114	8	2	11	12	0	3	33	6	1	.671	0	0	0	1	1	0	0	0	-.003	.176	9.27	8.46	7.71
Strop P	*2*	7.0	30	7	0	9	4	0	0	6	0	1	.647	0	0	0	0	0	0	0	0	.347	.162	7.71	7.71	2.33
Madrigal W	*2*	12.7	67	13	0	5	12	1	1	18	2	1	.660	0	0	0	0	0	0	0	0	.021	-.216	9.95	9.95	7.30

Italicized stats have been adjusted for home park.

Batted Ball Pitching Stats

	% of PA		% of Batted Balls					Out %		Runs Per Event				Total Runs vs. Avg.				
Player	**K%**	**BB%**	**GB%**	**LD%**	**FB%**	**IF/F**	**HR/OF**	**GB**	**OF**	**NIP**	**GB**	**LD**	**OF**	**NIP**	**GB**	**LD**	**FB**	**Tot**
O'Day D	25	10	41	16	42	.12	.04	79	90	.02	.00	.44	.02	-2	-3	-2	-10	-17
Feldman S	14	9	47	21	33	.10	.10	81	83	.07	-.00	.33	.18	2	-12	-1	-6	-16
Feliz N	33	9	38	5	57	.14	.06	76	90	-.01	.06	.29	.06	-2	0	-6	-5	-13
Wilson C	26	12	55	20	25	.13	.07	73	87	.03	.06	.46	.10	-1	3	1	-10	-7
Francisco F	28	8	29	21	50	.14	.11	63	94	-.01	.11	.43	.11	-4	1	0	-4	-6
Mathis D	15	7	50	19	31	.07	.10	82	83	.04	-.02	.37	.17	-1	-4	-0	-1	-6
Nippert D	18	11	41	18	41	.14	.09	72	87	.06	.05	.35	.13	1	1	-3	-4	-5
Grilli J	24	13	38	14	48	.06	.06	81	79	.05	.01	.52	.19	1	-2	-1	1	-1
McCarthy B	15	9	39	19	42	.06	.10	79	83	.06	.02	.33	.18	0	-2	-2	4	-0
Hunter R	13	7	37	20	42	.11	.09	77	85	.05	.03	.41	.14	-2	-1	6	-3	1
Millwood K	14	10	42	19	39	.11	.12	79	83	.07	.02	.37	.19	3	-5	1	4	3
Guardado E	12	10	37	21	42	.08	.14	70	93	.10	.06	.35	.17	1	0	1	1	4
Jennings J	16	11	44	19	38	.11	.11	78	83	.07	.02	.51	.18	2	-2	5	-0	5
Padilla V	12	11	49	20	31	.06	.11	74	85	.10	.04	.36	.18	5	1	2	-2	5
Benson K	10	13	27	20	52	.07	.12	75	84	.15	.05	.51	.20	3	-0	4	4	10
Harrison M	12	9	47	23	31	.10	.15	74	87	.08	.04	.43	.21	1	1	8	1	11
Holland D	18	8	41	19	39	.05	.16	71	84	.04	.06	.37	.26	-2	5	1	17	21
MLB Average	***18***	***10***	***43***	***19***	***38***	***.10***	***.11***	***75***	***83***	***.05***	***.04***	***.39***	***.19***	--	--	--	--	--

Fielding Stats

Name	INN	SBA/G	CS%	ERA	WP+PB/G	PO	A	TE	FE
Catchers									
Saltalamacchia J	714.0	0.98	22%	4.08	0.315	502	28	6	1
Teagarden T	491.7	0.81	34%	4.56	0.329	360	31	5	0
Rodriguez I	214.0	0.50	42%	4.88	0.379	168	11	2	1
Richardson K	15.0	1.20	0%	6.00	1.200	13	0	0	0

Name	Inn	PO	A	TE	FE	FPct	DPS	DPT	ZRDif	OOZ	Dif
First Base											
Davis C	825.3	845	47	1	2	.997	5	3	-.034	21	-9
Blalock H	567.7	535	26	1	5	.989	6	0	-.003	14	-10
Jones A	39.7	32	1	0	0	1.000	0	0	--	0	--
German E	2.0	0	0	0	0	0.000	0	0	--	--	--
Second Base											
Kinsler I	1258.0	249	451	2	9	.985	42	58	.022	47	10
Vizquel O	126.0	23	49	0	0	1.000	7	5	.085	0	-27
German E	34.0	4	13	1	0	.944	1	2	--	1	--
Arias J	16.7	4	4	0	0	1.000	0	2	--	1	--
Shortstop											
Andrus E	1238.0	261	407	14	8	.968	40	50	.045	45	-2
Vizquel O	196.7	32	76	0	0	1.000	11	8	.102	8	2
Third Base											
Young M	1165.0	72	208	3	6	.969	25	0	-.042	41	-6
Vizquel O	101.0	5	22	0	0	1.000	2	0	.288	5	8
Davis C	85.0	9	8	1	1	.895	1	0	--	0	--
German E	72.0	5	12	2	2	.810	1	0	--	1	--
Blalock H	9.0	0	3	0	0	1.000	0	0	--	2	--
Arias J	2.0	0	0	0	0	0.000	0	0	--	--	--

Name	Inn	PO	A	TE	FE	FPct	DPS	DPT	ZRDif	OOZ	Dif
Left Field											
Murphy D	858.3	195	4	0	1	.995	1	0	.014	38	-6
Byrd M	305.7	73	0	0	0	1.000	0	0	-.012	21	18
Borbon J	128.0	31	0	0	3	.912	0	0	.035	5	-11
Jones A	98.7	24	0	0	0	1.000	0	0	--	6	--
Boggs B	26.0	8	0	1	0	.889	0	0	--	2	--
Cruz N	17.0	7	0	0	1	.875	0	0	--	1	--
German E	1.0	0	0	0	0	0.000	0	0	--	--	--
Center Field											
Byrd M	889.0	242	5	0	3	.988	4	0	-.005	55	-6
Hamilton J	472.7	132	2	0	0	1.000	1	0	.031	33	2
Gentry C	33.0	8	1	0	0	1.000	1	0	--	2	--
Borbon J	26.0	7	0	0	0	1.000	0	0	--	3	--
Boggs B	11.0	1	0	0	0	1.000	0	0	--	0	--
Murphy D	2.0	0	0	0	0	0.000	0	0	--	--	--
Golson G	1.0	1	0	0	0	1.000	0	0	--	0	--
Right Field											
Cruz N	1035.0	294	11	1	2	.990	2	0	.012	76	21
Hamilton J	210.0	53	2	0	1	.982	0	0	.012	7	-19
Murphy D	74.0	19	3	0	1	.957	1	0	--	2	--
Byrd M	52.0	17	1	0	0	1.000	0	0	--	8	--
Jones A	50.0	6	0	0	0	1.000	0	0	--	1	--
Gentry C	13.0	3	0	0	0	1.000	0	0	--	0	--

Toronto Blue Jays

Stat Facts:

- Roy Halladay was second in the majors with 145 PRC
- Halladays BB% (4%) was lowest in the AL
- Aaron Hill led the majors with 734 plate appearances
- Hill turned 74 DPs, most in the majors
- Ricky Romero induced 36 DPs, most of any pitcher in the majors
- The Blue Jays' +42 middle infield plus/minus was best in the majors
- The Blue Jays' -51 outfield plus/minus was 29th in the majors
- Vernon Wells's ZR (.892) was lowest of any center fielder with at least 1,000 innings
- The Blue Jays' outfield throwing ranked 2nd in the majors
- The Blue Jays' bunt defense ranked last in the majors
- Scott Richmond had the most IP (139) of any pitcher in the majors with zero HBP
- Marc Rzepczynski induced zero infield pop-ups

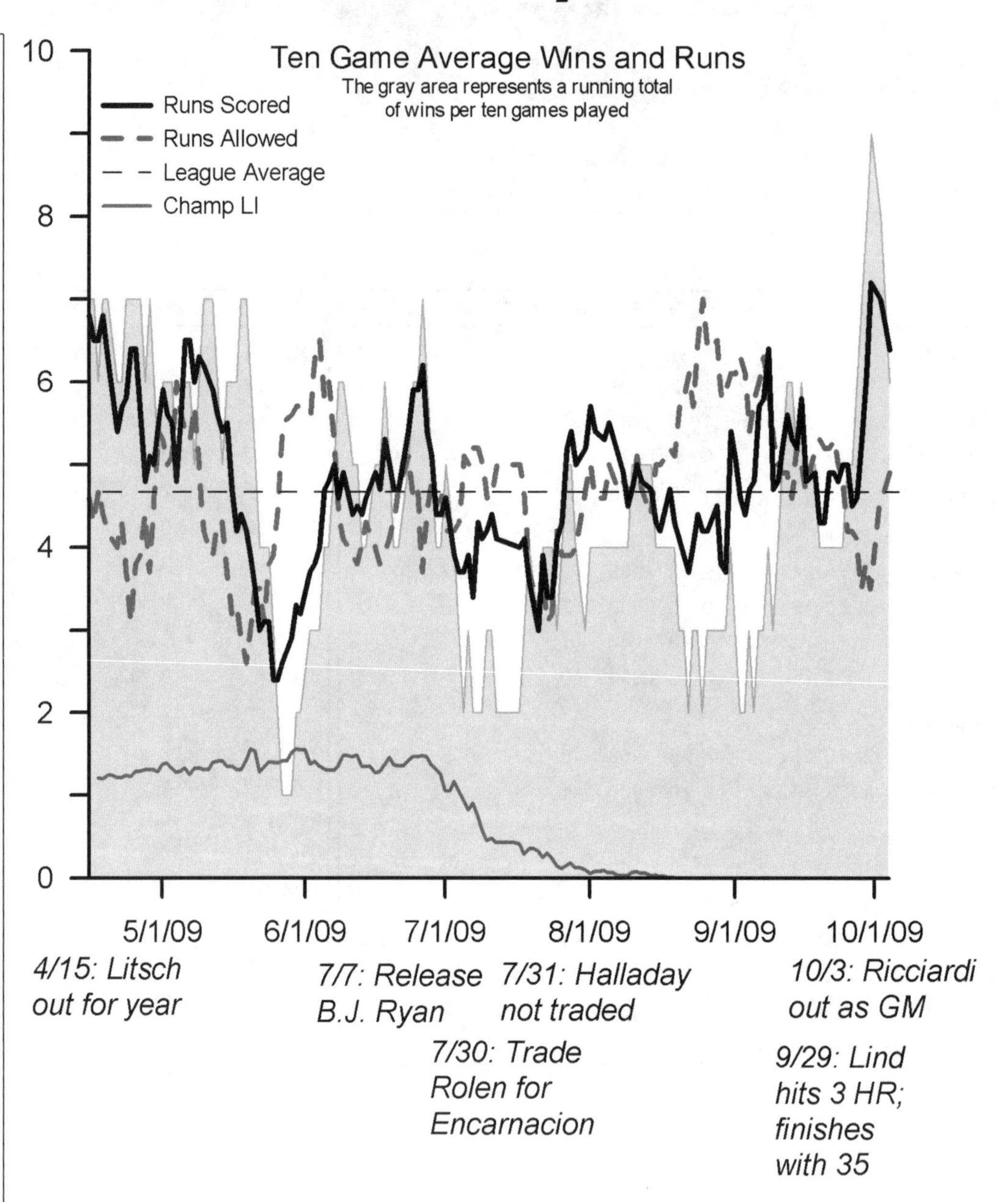

Team Batting and Pitching/Fielding Stats by Month

	April	May	June	July	Aug	Sept/Oct
Wins	15	14	12	8	10	16
Losses	9	15	14	16	16	17
RS/G	5.9	4.4	4.7	4.5	4.7	5.3
RA/G	4.7	4.4	4.4	4.3	5.7	5.0
OBP	.366	.337	.327	.298	.333	.333
SLG	.472	.414	.425	.426	.438	.465
FIP	4.47	4.43	4.17	4.07	4.49	4.68
DER	.711	.704	.687	.682	.654	.667

Batting Stats

Player	*BR*	Runs	RBI	PA	Outs	H	2B	3B	HR	TB	K	BB	IBB	HBP	SH	SF	SB	CS	GDP	H-A	L^R	BA	OBP	SLG	*GPA*
Lind A *	*107*	93	114	654	424	179	46	0	35	330	110	58	7	5	0	4	1	1	15	-.001	.067	.305	.370	.562	*.301*
Hill A	*101*	103	108	734	506	195	37	0	36	340	98	42	1	5	1	4	6	2	17	.006	.024	.286	.330	.499	*.268*
Scutaro M	*88*	100	60	680	429	162	35	1	12	235	75	90	0	4	5	7	14	5	12	-.033	.009	.282	.379	.409	*.268*
Wells V	*73*	84	66	684	488	164	37	3	15	252	86	48	2	1	0	5	17	4	18	-.047	-.045	.260	.311	.400	*.235*
Overbay L *	*70*	57	64	500	319	112	35	1	16	197	95	74	6	0	0	3	0	0	8	.007	.121	.265	.372	.466	*.278*
Rios A	*56*	52	62	479	338	115	25	2	14	186	78	31	1	6	0	6	19	3	14	.081	-.003	.264	.317	.427	*.245*
Rolen S	*54*	52	43	373	234	108	29	0	8	161	42	26	1	4	0	5	4	2	2	.016	.071	.320	.370	.476	*.280*
Bautista J	*48*	54	40	404	266	79	13	3	13	137	85	56	1	4	6	2	4	0	9	.036	.074	.235	.349	.408	*.254*
Barajas R	*43*	43	71	460	336	97	19	0	19	173	76	20	2	1	3	7	1	0	4	-.037	.057	.226	.258	.403	*.213*
Snider T *	*32*	34	29	276	189	58	14	1	9	101	78	29	1	3	2	1	1	1	5	.040	.041	.241	.328	.419	*.248*
Millar K	*26*	29	29	283	205	56	14	0	7	91	49	31	0	1	0	0	0	0	10	-.038	.037	.223	.311	.363	*.226*
Ruiz R	*24*	25	17	130	86	36	7	0	10	73	35	10	0	4	0	1	1	1	6	-.131	-.086	.313	.385	.635	*.325*
Encarnacion	*21*	25	23	173	119	37	5	1	8	68	29	13	0	3	0	3	1	0	2	-.044	-.002	.240	.306	.442	*.243*
McDonald J	*14*	18	13	156	115	39	7	0	4	58	18	1	0	2	1	1	0	2	1	.024	-.020	.258	.271	.384	*.214*
Chavez R	*13*	10	15	168	123	41	8	0	2	55	23	6	0	0	3	0	1	1	4	.019	-.002	.258	.285	.346	*.210*
Inglett J *	*11*	11	6	99	65	25	4	1	0	31	21	8	0	1	1	0	3	1	0	.014	.065	.281	.347	.348	*.238*
Phillips K *	*2*	1	2	18	14	5	3	0	0	8	4	0	0	0	0	0	0	0	1	-.268	.283	.278	.278	.444	*.231*
Barrett M	*1*	3	2	19	15	3	0	0	1	6	5	1	1	0	0	0	0	0	0	-.091	-.144	.167	.211	.333	*.175*
Adams R *	*1*	2	0	21	16	4	0	0	0	4	1	1	0	0	0	0	0	0	0	-.571	.165	.200	.238	.200	*.154*

Only includes batters with at least one Base Run. Italicized stats have been adjusted for home park.

Batted Ball Batting Stats

	% of PA		% of Batted Balls					Out %		Runs Per Event				Total Runs vs. Avg.				
Player	K%	BB%	GB%	LD%	FB%	IF/F	HR/OF	GB	OF	NIP	GB	LD	OF	NIP	GB	LD	FB	Tot
Lind A	17	10	43	20	37	.08	.21	79	80	.05	.01	.45	.35	1	-5	12	29	37
Hill A	13	6	39	20	41	.12	.17	72	86	.04	.05	.35	.25	-5	3	2	19	19
Overbay L	19	15	42	20	37	.04	.13	81	81	.09	.00	.45	.25	9	-6	6	9	17
Scutaro M	11	14	37	19	44	.06	.05	71	88	.14	.06	.44	.07	16	3	10	-14	15
Rolen S	11	8	33	25	42	.05	.06	68	88	.08	.10	.43	.07	1	5	15	-7	14
Ruiz R	27	11	49	11	40	.00	.31	70	68	.02	.04	.39	.56	-1	0	-3	13	10
Bautista J	21	15	41	17	42	.10	.13	76	87	.08	.02	.48	.18	6	-3	-0	-1	2
Snider T	28	12	44	15	41	.08	.15	73	79	.02	.04	.48	.28	-1	0	-3	4	0
Encarnacion E	17	9	34	20	46	.08	.15	86	91	.05	-.03	.39	.19	-0	-3	1	2	-1
Rios A	16	8	41	18	41	.11	.11	73	86	.03	.05	.39	.17	-2	1	1	-1	-2
McDonald J	12	2	32	17	50	.22	.08	70	85	-.05	.07	.37	.12	-3	1	-0	-2	-5
Millar K	17	11	32	17	51	.10	.08	88	83	.07	-.06	.43	.14	2	-8	-1	-0	-7
Chavez R	14	4	46	21	34	.13	.05	79	89	-.02	.01	.40	.06	-3	-1	2	-6	-8
Wells V	13	7	43	15	42	.15	.07	70	88	.05	.07	.49	.09	-2	7	3	-16	-8
Barajas R	17	5	29	14	57	.13	.11	79	83	-.01	.02	.30	.18	-8	-5	-11	7	-18
MLB Average	***18***	***10***	***43***	***19***	***38***	***.10***	***.11***	***75***	***83***	***.05***	***.04***	***.39***	***.19***	--	--	--	--	--

Pitching Stats

Player	*PRC*	IP	BFP	G	GS	K	BB	IBB	HBP	H	HR	DP	DER	SB	CS	PO	W	L	Sv	Op	Hld	H-A	R^L	RA	ERA	FIP
Halladay R	*145*	239.0	963	32	32	208	35	0	5	234	22	24	.684	18	6	0	17	10	0	0	0	-.023	.019	3.09	2.79	3.15
Romero R *	*77*	178.0	771	29	29	141	79	0	10	192	18	36	.663	9	7	4	13	9	0	0	0	.001	.027	4.45	4.30	4.42
Tallet B *	*55*	160.7	717	37	25	120	72	2	6	169	20	12	.697	7	5	2	7	9	0	0	0	-.016	.045	5.55	5.32	4.73
Richmond S	*46*	138.7	610	27	24	117	59	1	0	147	27	10	.700	6	3	1	8	11	0	0	0	-.030	-.080	5.84	5.52	5.29
Frasor J	*40*	57.7	227	61	0	56	16	3	2	43	4	5	.732	6	2	0	7	3	11	14	4	-.043	-.103	2.65	2.50	2.93
Camp S	*37*	79.7	333	59	0	58	29	4	4	73	7	12	.715	0	1	0	2	6	1	1	6	-.034	-.035	4.07	3.50	3.97
League B	*32*	74.7	313	67	0	76	21	2	7	72	8	13	.662	9	1	0	3	6	0	3	9	.047	-.027	4.82	4.58	3.59
Rzepczynski	*31*	61.3	261	11	11	60	30	0	1	51	7	7	.706	7	3	2	2	4	0	0	0	-.056	-.016	3.96	3.67	4.23
Cecil B *	*31*	93.3	422	18	17	69	38	0	5	116	17	11	.655	4	4	0	7	4	0	0	0	.013	-.017	5.69	5.30	5.46
Carlson J *	*26*	67.7	291	73	0	51	21	3	3	67	7	4	.703	3	1	0	1	6	0	3	12	.008	.018	4.92	4.66	3.96
Downs S *	*26*	46.7	200	48	0	43	13	1	2	46	4	4	.681	1	1	0	1	3	9	13	10	-.102	.033	3.47	3.09	3.36
Accardo J	*15*	24.7	107	26	0	18	17	1	2	23	2	5	.691	2	3	0	0	0	1	1	4	-.003	.173	2.92	2.55	4.97
Purcey D *	*14*	48.0	223	9	9	39	30	1	1	54	6	5	.667	6	2	0	1	3	0	0	0	-.101	-.135	6.56	6.19	5.07
Hayhurst D	*14*	22.7	97	15	0	13	9	2	2	23	2	3	.704	0	0	0	0	0	0	0	0	-.044	-.101	2.78	2.78	4.38
Janssen C	*11*	40.0	192	21	5	24	14	1	2	59	5	6	.605	0	1	0	2	4	1	1	2	.083	.014	6.53	5.85	4.74
Ray R	*8*	24.3	101	4	4	13	6	0	2	23	4	2	.737	5	1	0	1	2	0	0	0	-.108	.043	5.55	4.44	5.25
Murphy B *	*6*	11.3	45	8	0	6	8	0	0	4	1	1	.900	0	0	0	0	0	0	0	0	.169	-.018	3.18	3.18	5.40
Ryan B *	*6*	20.7	95	25	0	13	17	2	1	22	5	4	.712	1	3	1	1	1	2	4	2	-.179	-.123	6.53	6.53	7.40
Roenicke J	*4*	17.7	84	13	0	19	12	1	1	19	2	0	.660	4	0	0	0	0	0	0	1	-.077	-.191	7.64	7.13	4.55
Bullington B	*4*	6.0	31	4	0	5	6	1	0	7	0	0	.650	0	0	0	0	0	0	0	0	--	.132	3.00	3.00	4.02
Wolfe B	*3*	15.3	77	14	0	11	7	1	1	25	5	3	.623	0	0	0	2	2	0	1	0	.014	-.051	8.80	8.22	7.36
Litsch J	*2*	9.0	42	2	2	8	1	0	1	14	4	1	.643	1	1	0	0	1	0	0	0	-.117	.239	9.00	9.00	7.86
Mills B *	*1*	7.7	42	2	2	9	6	0	0	14	4	0	.565	0	1	0	0	1	0	0	0	-.020	-.124	14.09	14.09	9.97

Italicized stats have been adjusted for home park.

Batted Ball Pitching Stats

	% of PA		% of Batted Balls					Out %		Runs Per Event				Total Runs vs. Avg.				
Player	K%	BB%	GB%	LD%	FB%	IF/F	HR/OF	GB	OF	NIP	GB	LD	OF	NIP	GB	LD	FB	Tot
Halladay R	22	4	50	20	29	.13	.12	79	77	-.04	.01	.38	.24	-23	-7	2	-4	-33
Frasor J	25	8	38	18	43	.12	.05	76	89	-.00	.03	.38	.06	-3	-2	-2	-8	-16
Camp S	17	10	55	17	28	.06	.11	82	80	.05	-.01	.44	.21	0	-5	-0	-2	-7
Rzepczynski M	23	12	51	20	28	.00	.15	81	90	.04	-.00	.41	.20	0	-3	0	-2	-4
Downs S	22	8	56	21	24	.03	.13	78	75	.01	.03	.34	.27	-2	-0	-1	-0	-4
League B	24	9	56	18	26	.02	.15	77	82	.01	.02	.50	.26	-3	-1	2	-0	-3
Carlson J	17	9	37	20	43	.10	.09	80	83	.04	.02	.42	.15	-1	-3	3	-1	-2
Ray R	13	8	48	12	40	.13	.15	78	87	.06	.04	.45	.23	-0	0	-1	1	0
Accardo J	17	18	46	13	41	.11	.08	71	83	.12	.05	.45	.14	3	0	-1	-1	1
Purcey D	18	14	32	19	49	.10	.09	64	85	.09	.12	.42	.15	3	3	1	0	7
Romero R	18	12	54	19	27	.09	.14	76	78	.06	.03	.40	.26	5	-0	3	0	9
Tallet B	17	11	36	21	43	.06	.09	79	83	.07	.02	.40	.17	4	-4	5	4	9
Janssen R	13	8	50	24	26	.08	.14	73	74	.07	.05	.45	.30	1	2	8	3	14
Richmond S	19	10	34	22	45	.10	.15	80	82	.04	.02	.41	.26	-1	-7	7	16	15
Cecil B	16	10	43	20	38	.08	.15	72	79	.06	.06	.36	.29	2	4	1	13	20
MLB Average	*18*	*10*	*43*	*19*	*38*	*.10*	*.11*	*75*	*83*	*.05*	*.04*	*.39*	*.19*	--	--	--	--	--

Fielding Stats

Name	INN	SBA/G	CS%	ERA	WP+PB/G	PO	A	TE	FE
Catchers									
Barajas R	974.3	0.69	29%	4.26	0.305	806	55	8	0
Chavez R	399.0	1.02	36%	4.85	0.361	327	40	2	0
Barrett M	39.3	0.46	0%	4.35	0.915	34	1	0	0
Phillips K	38.3	1.41	17%	5.87	0.704	28	2	1	0

Name	Inn	PO	A	TE	FE	FPct	DPS	DPT	ZRDif	OOZ	Dif
First Base											
Overbay L	1055.0	1028	102	1	1	.998	12	0	.053	34	-2
Millar K	386.7	376	27	1	3	.990	0	0	-.063	16	7
Ruiz R	9.0	7	1	0	0	1.000	0	0	--	--	--
Second Base											
Hill A	1372.0	307	484	3	4	.991	45	74	.027	51	10
McDonald J	55.0	8	30	0	0	1.000	4	3	--	2	--
Inglett J	20.0	5	6	0	0	1.000	0	1	--	0	--
Scutaro M	4.0	0	2	0	0	1.000	0	0	--	1	--
Shortstop											
Scutaro M	1252.0	190	421	3	7	.984	49	44	-.002	61	10
McDonald J	198.3	38	66	0	1	.990	11	11	-.005	12	22
Third Base											
Rolen S	779.0	62	168	4	1	.979	14	1	.063	45	16
Encarnacion	364.0	27	77	5	2	.937	6	0	.028	15	-0
Bautista J	209.0	18	48	1	2	.957	3	1	.033	7	-8
McDonald J	78.0	3	17	1	1	.909	2	0	--	3	--
Millar K	21.0	4	4	0	0	1.000	1	1	--	0	--

Name	Inn	PO	A	TE	FE	FPct	DPS	DPT	ZRDif	OOZ	Dif
Left Field											
Lind A	475.7	80	1	1	0	.988	0	0	-.060	10	-29
Snider T	435.3	87	3	0	1	.989	0	0	-.008	17	-11
Bautista J	322.3	54	8	1	0	.984	2	0	-.057	8	-26
Inglett J	115.0	25	0	0	0	1.000	0	0	.106	6	2
Dellucci D	49.7	8	0	0	0	1.000	0	0	--	0	--
Adams R	31.0	1	0	0	0	1.000	0	0	--	0	--
McDonald J	22.0	3	0	0	0	1.000	0	0	--	2	--
Center Field											
Wells V	1356.0	352	6	0	1	.997	1	0	-.039	72	-15
Rios A	61.0	19	0	0	0	1.000	0	0	--	4	--
Bautista J	32.3	9	0	0	0	1.000	0	0	--	4	--
Inglett J	1.0	0	0	0	0	.000	0	0	--	--	--
Right Field											
Rios A	914.7	217	4	0	3	.987	0	0	.007	45	-3
Bautista J	286.3	69	3	0	0	1.000	0	0	.016	20	18
Snider T	173.3	36	0	1	2	.923	0	0	.025	8	-6
Inglett J	76.7	10	2	0	2	.857	0	0	--	1	--

Washington Nationals

Stat Facts:

- Elijah Dukes was thrown out in 10 of 13 stolen base attempts
- Josh Bard allowed .599 WP+PB per game
- John Lannan induced 33 DPs, tied for most in the NL
- Lannan's K% (10%) was lowest of any ML pitcher with at least 162 IP
- Cristian Guzman tied for the lowest BB% (3%) among major league regulars
- Guzman committed 15 fielding errors, most by any player
- Mike MacDougal induced 11 DPs in 50 IP
- Colin Balester allowed 10 home runs in 30 IP
- The DER behind Garrett Mock (.625) was lowest of any ML pitcher with at least 60 IP
- Craig Stammen allowed 17 SBs in 19 attempts
- Ryan Zimmerman made the most OOZ plays (101) of any third baseman
- Daniel Cabrera walked 18% of the batters he faced, and struck out 8%

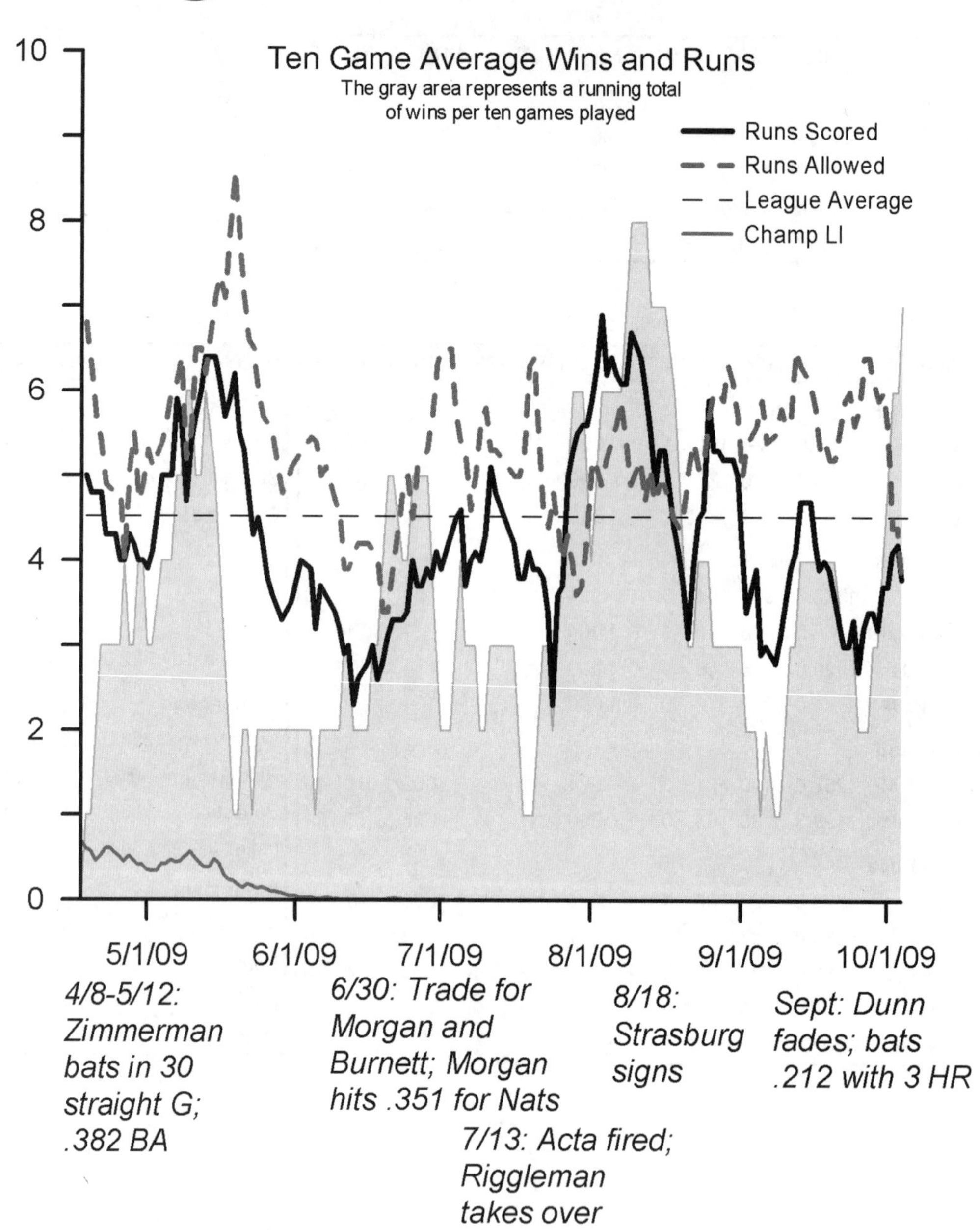

Team Batting and Pitching/Fielding Stats by Month

	April	May	June	July	Aug	Sept/Oct
Wins	5	8	9	10	14	13
Losses	16	20	17	18	15	17
RS/G	4.5	5.0	3.4	4.6	5.0	3.7
RA/G	5.9	6.3	4.7	4.9	5.2	5.3
OBP	.356	.347	.324	.352	.339	.306
SLG	.416	.433	.362	.418	.430	.377
FIP	5.35	4.72	4.26	4.37	5.57	4.62
DER	.683	.664	.699	.681	.702	.695

Batting Stats

Player	*BR*	Runs	RBI	PA	Outs	H	2B	3B	HR	TB	K	BB	IBB	HBP	SH	SF	SB	CS	GDP	H-A	L^R	BA	OBP	SLG	*GPA*
Dunn A *	*109*	81	105	668	409	146	29	0	38	289	177	116	16	4	0	2	0	1	8	-.035	.060	.267	.398	.529	*.308*
Zimmerman R	*104*	110	106	694	454	178	37	3	33	320	119	72	9	2	0	9	2	0	22	.002	-.018	.292	.364	.525	*.292*
Willingham J	*74*	70	61	502	330	111	29	0	24	212	104	61	2	12	0	2	4	3	11	-.059	.072	.260	.367	.496	*.286*
Johnson N *	*55*	47	44	424	262	104	16	2	6	142	66	63	3	6	0	2	2	2	11	.042	-.057	.295	.408	.402	*.281*
Guzman C +	*55*	74	52	555	394	151	24	7	6	207	75	16	0	1	6	1	4	5	9	.035	.022	.284	.306	.390	*.233*
Harris W *	*49*	47	27	393	255	76	18	6	7	127	62	57	1	9	3	1	11	4	4	.078	.055	.235	.364	.393	*.260*
Dukes E	*44*	38	58	416	291	91	20	4	8	143	74	46	2	3	0	3	3	10	8	.003	.002	.250	.337	.393	*.247*
Morgan N *	*31*	35	12	212	134	67	9	2	1	83	25	11	0	4	5	1	24	7	3	.016	.065	.351	.396	.435	*.284*
Bard J +	*27*	20	31	301	217	63	18	0	6	99	50	24	1	1	1	1	0	1	5	.027	.000	.230	.293	.361	*.220*
Gonzalez A	*27*	31	33	316	223	77	16	3	1	102	27	14	1	3	2	6	1	1	8	.014	.155	.265	.299	.351	*.220*
Hernandez A	*20*	25	23	255	182	58	9	2	1	74	41	20	1	0	3	1	5	3	6	-.040	.071	.251	.310	.320	*.217*
Belliard R	*19*	26	22	204	148	46	7	1	5	70	40	14	0	0	1	2	2	0	7	.046	.015	.246	.296	.374	*.224*
Nieves W	*19*	20	26	249	173	58	6	0	1	67	45	17	1	3	0	5	1	0	7	-.069	-.056	.259	.313	.299	*.214*
Kearns A	*17*	20	17	211	153	34	6	2	3	53	51	32	1	5	0	0	1	1	12	.042	-.027	.195	.336	.305	*.225*
Flores J	*16*	13	15	106	66	28	3	2	4	47	26	11	1	0	1	1	0	0	1	-.072	-.051	.301	.371	.505	*.291*
Maxwell J	*14*	13	9	102	69	22	4	1	4	40	32	12	0	1	0	0	6	1	1	-.016	-.071	.247	.343	.449	*.264*
Desmond I	*14*	9	12	89	61	23	7	2	4	46	14	5	0	0	1	1	1	0	2	-.064	-.066	.280	.318	.561	*.281*
Morse M	*7*	4	10	55	40	13	3	0	3	25	16	3	0	0	0	0	0	0	1	.252	-.071	.250	.291	.481	*.249*
Orr P *	*7*	5	10	81	57	19	2	1	1	26	15	3	0	0	0	3	2	1	0	-.064	.120	.253	.272	.347	*.207*
Stammen C	*2*	1	4	37	25	6	3	0	0	9	10	2	0	0	4	0	0	0	0	-.092	.120	.194	.242	.290	*.180*
Bernadina R	*1*	1	0	5	3	1	1	0	0	2	1	1	0	0	0	0	1	0	0	--	-.213	.250	.400	.500	*.302*
Martis S	*1*	4	2	27	19	5	1	0	0	6	6	0	0	0	3	0	0	0	0	-.255	.003	.208	.208	.250	*.155*
Olsen S *	*1*	1	1	22	13	2	0	0	0	2	7	3	0	0	4	0	0	0	0	.194	.168	.133	.278	.133	*.157*
Rivera S +	*1*	2	0	5	2	1	0	0	0	1	0	1	0	0	1	0	0	0	0	.308	-.308	.333	.500	.333	*.305*
Lannan J *	*1*	1	0	65	49	9	1	0	0	10	21	2	0	0	5	0	0	0	0	.037	-.002	.155	.183	.172	*.124*
Milledge L	*1*	1	1	26	21	4	0	0	0	4	10	1	0	1	0	0	1	0	1	-.007	.116	.167	.231	.167	*.144*

Only includes batters with at least one Base Run. Italicized stats have been adjusted for home park.

Batted Ball Batting Stats

	% of PA		% of Batted Balls					Out %		Runs Per Event				Total Runs vs. Avg.				
Player	K%	BB%	GB%	LD%	FB%	IF/F	HR/OF	GB	OF	NIP	GB	LD	OF	NIP	GB	LD	FB	Tot
Dunn A	26	18	31	20	49	.08	.23	76	82	.07	.03	.40	.36	13	-4	-1	32	40
Zimmerman R	17	11	40	19	42	.10	.18	69	87	.06	.07	.41	.26	3	5	4	18	30
Willingham J	21	15	36	22	42	.07	.19	72	84	.08	.06	.32	.29	7	1	-2	16	22
Johnson N	16	16	43	23	34	.09	.06	72	86	.12	.05	.42	.11	11	1	9	-8	13
Morgan N	12	7	58	19	23	.03	.03	74	72	.06	.05	.47	.16	-0	5	3	-3	5
Harris W	16	17	38	15	47	.08	.06	76	85	.13	.05	.41	.13	11	0	-4	-3	4
Flores J	25	10	28	18	54	.16	.13	63	78	.02	.10	.49	.26	-0	1	1	3	4
Maxwell J	31	13	48	14	38	.10	.21	59	93	.02	.15	.38	.27	-0	3	-2	1	1
Dukes E	18	12	44	16	40	.09	.08	69	87	.07	.07	.38	.13	3	5	-4	-5	-1
Belliard R	20	7	43	21	36	.13	.11	78	88	.01	.00	.37	.16	-3	-3	1	-2	-7
Kearns A	24	18	46	19	36	.07	.07	84	87	.08	-.05	.41	.11	4	-6	-1	-5	-8
Guzman C	14	3	54	17	29	.06	.05	71	85	-.03	.07	.46	.09	-10	11	5	-15	-9
Hernandez A	16	8	56	19	25	.13	.03	80	82	.04	.01	.40	.09	-1	-1	0	-8	-10
Bard J	17	8	40	19	41	.16	.08	81	89	.04	.01	.43	.10	-1	-4	1	-8	-11
Gonzalez A	9	5	43	23	34	.09	.01	78	87	.06	.02	.37	.03	-2	-2	6	-13	-11
Nieves W	18	8	62	19	19	.09	.03	75	84	.03	.04	.35	.05	-2	1	-1	-10	-12
MLB Average	***18***	***10***	***43***	***19***	***38***	***.10***	***.11***	***75***	***83***	***.05***	***.04***	***.39***	***.19***	--	--	--	--	--

Pitching Stats

Player	PRC	IP	BFP	G	GS	K	BB	IBB	HBP	H	HR	DP	DER	SB	CS	PO	W	L	Sv	Op	Hld	H-A	R^L	RA	ERA	FIP
Lannan J *	68	206.3	875	33	33	89	68	5	6	210	22	33	.707	10	7	4	9	13	0	0	0	-.038	.049	4.36	3.88	4.68
Clippard T	35	60.3	246	41	0	67	32	1	1	36	9	7	.781	1	1	0	4	2	0	1	3	-.012	.133	2.98	2.69	4.46
Zimmermann J	32	91.3	391	16	16	92	29	0	4	95	10	8	.645	8	5	2	3	5	0	0	0	-.040	-.016	5.03	4.63	3.64
Stammen C	27	105.7	448	19	19	48	24	1	3	112	14	6	.716	17	2	0	4	7	0	0	0	-.009	-.015	5.71	5.11	4.70
Martin J	24	77.0	341	15	15	37	24	4	6	85	14	4	.723	0	1	0	5	4	0	0	0	.049	-.015	4.68	4.44	5.57
Mock G	23	91.3	422	28	15	72	44	3	1	114	9	14	.625	3	3	1	3	10	0	2	4	.024	-.045	6.41	5.62	4.24
Detwiler R *	23	75.7	341	15	14	43	33	3	2	87	3	9	.665	6	3	3	1	6	0	0	0	-.053	-.017	5.11	5.00	3.80
Martis S	22	85.7	377	15	15	34	39	3	4	83	11	7	.740	3	0	0	5	3	0	0	0	-.057	-.116	5.46	5.25	5.43
MacDougal M	17	50.0	221	52	0	31	31	3	3	45	3	11	.706	4	1	0	1	1	20	21	0	-.041	.000	4.50	3.60	4.55
Villone R *	17	48.7	228	63	0	33	29	4	2	54	6	4	.677	0	1	1	5	6	1	4	7	-.011	-.018	4.62	4.25	5.06
Beimel J *	16	39.7	172	45	0	24	15	4	1	38	3	2	.713	0	1	0	1	5	1	5	10	-.145	-.012	3.86	3.40	3.83
Bergmann J	15	48.0	213	56	0	40	25	7	3	50	7	9	.674	4	1	0	2	4	0	1	10	-.061	-.099	5.25	4.50	4.69
Olsen S *	15	62.7	289	11	11	42	25	2	0	83	11	5	.640	5	4	3	2	4	0	0	0	-.053	-.007	6.46	6.03	5.19
Hernandez L	14	48.7	213	8	8	27	16	2	0	56	3	6	.677	3	1	0	2	4	0	0	0	.050	.037	5.36	5.36	3.71
Burnett S *	13	25.3	104	33	0	20	13	4	0	14	3	0	.809	3	1	1	1	1	0	1	5	-.045	.022	3.20	3.20	4.18
Rivera S	8	38.3	176	30	0	21	14	4	3	48	7	5	.664	1	1	1	1	3	0	1	2	.022	.008	6.57	6.10	5.45
Tavarez J	8	35.0	169	42	0	32	27	2	2	34	1	1	.654	5	1	0	3	7	1	2	5	-.006	-.105	6.94	4.89	4.01
Hanrahan J	7	32.7	163	34	0	35	14	0	2	50	3	2	.550	2	1	0	1	3	5	10	2	-.057	.009	7.71	7.71	3.67
Balester C	6	30.3	135	7	7	20	14	0	0	34	10	2	.736	0	2	0	1	4	0	0	0	.095	-.060	7.12	6.82	7.50
Wells K	6	26.3	117	23	0	18	18	1	0	23	1	2	.725	4	1	0	0	2	2	2	5	.011	-.079	6.49	6.49	4.21
Cabrera D	5	40.0	207	9	8	16	35	1	2	48	4	6	.667	3	0	0	0	5	0	0	0	-.018	-.100	8.78	5.85	6.35
Sosa J	5	22.3	103	18	0	17	12	2	0	28	5	3	.667	0	0	0	2	1	2	2	3	-.173	-.147	6.45	6.45	5.88
Kensing L	4	28.0	132	26	0	12	12	1	0	40	7	4	.673	2	0	0	1	1	1	3	1	-.168	.106	8.68	8.68	6.72
Hinckley M *	3	9.7	44	14	0	3	11	0	1	8	1	3	.750	0	0	0	0	0	0	1	4	.136	-.288	4.66	4.66	7.60
Colome J	3	15.0	75	16	0	12	6	1	1	23	1	0	.600	4	0	0	1	1	0	1	0	.108	-.091	8.40	8.40	3.62
Estrada M	2	7.3	33	4	1	9	4	0	0	6	1	0	.684	0	0	0	0	1	0	0	0	-.108	-.178	7.36	6.14	4.11
Shell S	2	5.0	22	4	0	5	2	0	0	5	1	0	.714	0	0	0	0	0	0	0	1	-.030	.329	5.40	5.40	4.95
Segovia Z	1	10.3	47	8	0	4	6	1	0	11	1	2	.694	0	0	0	1	0	0	1	0	-.137	-.151	8.71	7.84	5.09
Ledezma W *	1	5.7	30	5	0	8	4	0	0	8	1	0	.529	1	0	0	0	0	0	0	0	-.010	-.110	11.12	9.53	4.74

Italicized stats have been adjusted for home park.
Batted ball stats are listed after fielding stats.

Fielding Stats

Name	INN	SBA/G	CS%	ERA	WP+PB/G	PO	A	TE	FE
Catchers									
Bard J	630.7	0.71	14%	4.95	0.599	397	27	4	1
Nieves W	553.7	0.76	28%	5.06	0.423	380	41	5	0
Flores J	205.7	0.66	27%	5.16	0.613	139	10	0	1
Burke J	34.3	0.52	50%	4.72	0.262	27	1	0	0

Name	Inn	PO	A	TE	FE	FPct	DPS	DPT	ZRDif	OOZ	Dif
First Base											
Johnson N	806.3	833	67	2	4	.992	9	2	-.006	29	2
Dunn A	540.0	531	37	1	6	.986	6	1	-.131	7	-21
Morse M	46.0	46	6	0	0	1.000	0	0	--	3	--
Belliard R	31.0	31	3	0	1	.971	0	0	--	2	--
Willingham	1.0	0	0	0	0	0.000	0	0	--	--	--
Second Base											
Hernandez	497.0	132	174	2	4	.981	12	20	.046	9	-9
Gonzalez A	363.0	86	121	0	1	.995	17	17	-.038	8	-5
Belliard R	316.7	73	116	2	1	.984	11	15	.058	15	20
Orr P	123.0	31	51	0	2	.976	9	6	.078	3	-3
Harris W	82.0	21	26	0	2	.959	4	2	--	3	--
Desmond I	39.7	12	12	1	1	.923	1	1	--	0	--
Cintron A	3.0	1	0	0	0	1.000	0	0	--	--	--
Shortstop											
Guzman C	993.7	154	353	5	15	.962	34	34	-.016	43	5
Gonzalez A	279.3	39	84	5	4	.932	6	6	-.067	15	15
Desmond I	136.3	37	43	3	1	.952	5	8	-.063	3	-16
Cintron A	15.0	4	2	1	0	.857	0	0	--	1	--
Third Base											
Zimmerman	1337.0	117	325	13	4	.963	25	3	.014	101	34
Harris W	32.0	4	8	1	0	.923	2	0	--	2	--
Orr P	30.0	2	6	2	0	.800	0	0	--	1	--
Belliard R	16.0	0	5	0	1	.833	1	0	--	2	--
Gonzalez A	4.7	0	0	0	0	0.000	0	0	--	0	--
Morse M	4.0	1	2	0	0	1.000	0	0	--	1	--

Name	Inn	PO	A	TE	FE	FPct	DPS	DPT	ZRDif	OOZ	Dif
Left Field											
Willingham	691.7	165	2	1	4	.971	1	1	.032	41	9
Dunn A	505.0	99	2	1	4	.953	0	0	-.062	20	-11
Harris W	175.7	34	0	0	0	1.000	0	0	-.047	12	18
Padilla J	24.7	7	1	0	0	1.000	0	0	--	1	--
Dukes E	11.7	1	0	0	0	1.000	0	0	--	0	--
Morse M	9.7	4	0	0	0	1.000	0	0	--	1	--
Hernandez	2.0	0	0	0	0	0.000	0	0	--	--	--
Bernadina R	2.0	1	0	0	0	1.000	0	0	--	0	--
Maxwell J	2.0	0	0	0	0	0.000	0	0	--	--	--
Center Field											
Harris W	467.3	143	1	0	1	.993	0	0	.004	28	-8
Morgan N	391.0	135	7	2	1	.979	1	0	.029	41	37
Dukes E	272.7	79	6	0	1	.988	0	0	-.032	26	27
Maxwell J	203.3	58	1	0	0	1.000	1	0	.001	17	16
Milledge L	42.3	11	0	0	0	1.000	0	0	--	3	--
Kearns A	19.0	3	0	0	0	1.000	0	0	--	1	--
Patterson C	18.0	3	0	0	0	1.000	0	0	--	0	--
Bernadina R	7.7	3	0	0	0	1.000	0	0	--	0	--
Padilla J	3.0	0	0	0	0	0.000	0	0	--	0	--
Right Field											
Dukes E	548.3	129	6	1	6	.951	1	0	-.015	30	3
Kearns A	363.0	81	5	0	0	1.000	0	0	-.015	15	-11
Willingham	264.3	68	0	0	1	.971	0	0	.057	12	-7
Dunn A	180.0	43	0	0	3	.935	0	0	-.147	8	-8
Morse M	23.0	7	0	0	0	1.000	0	0	--	1	--
Padilla J	13.0	3	0	0	0	1.000	0	0	--	1	--
Patterson C	11.7	3	0	0	0	1.000	0	0	--	1	--
Maxwell J	9.0	2	0	0	0	1.000	0	0	--	0	--
Desmond I	7.0	3	0	0	0	1.000	0	0	--	0	--
Bernadina R	3.0	0	0	0	0	0.000	0	0	--	--	--
Harris W	1.0	0	0	0	0	0.000	0	0	--	--	--
Orr P	1.0	0	0	0	0	0.000	0	0	--	--	--

Batted Ball Pitching Stats

	% of PA		% of Batted Balls					Out %		Runs Per Event				Total Runs vs. Avg.				
Player	K%	BB%	GB%	LD%	FB%	IF/F	HR/OF	GB	OF	NIP	GB	LD	OF	NIP	GB	LD	FB	Tot
Clippard T	27	13	30	13	57	.11	.13	74	86	.04	.04	.28	.19	0	-2	-9	2	-9
Burnett S	19	13	58	18	24	.00	.13	85	93	.07	-.01	.35	.15	1	-2	-2	-3	-6
Beimel J	14	9	39	16	45	.07	.06	66	86	.07	.11	.29	.11	0	3	-3	-2	-2
MacDougal M	14	15	64	16	20	.10	.11	79	88	.13	.01	.43	.16	5	-2	-0	-5	-1
Hernandez L	13	8	43	24	33	.02	.06	75	88	.06	.03	.40	.08	-0	-0	5	-5	-1
Wells K	15	15	50	16	34	.00	.04	83	77	.12	.01	.35	.17	3	-1	-1	-0	-0
Lannan J	10	8	52	18	30	.05	.11	77	85	.10	.03	.40	.17	4	-2	4	-4	3
Zimmermann J	24	8	44	24	32	.16	.13	73	72	.01	.06	.34	.30	-4	2	1	3	3
Stammen C	11	6	47	21	32	.08	.13	82	85	.05	.02	.40	.21	-2	-3	6	2	3
Detwiler R	13	10	43	25	32	.10	.04	72	82	.09	.06	.34	.10	3	2	5	-7	3
Martis S	9	11	40	15	44	.14	.10	74	88	.14	.06	.35	.15	6	2	-4	-1	3
Tavarez J	19	17	50	18	32	.06	.03	74	71	.11	.06	.35	.20	4	1	-1	-0	4
Bergmann J	19	13	36	19	46	.21	.14	69	72	.08	.06	.31	.29	2	0	-2	5	5
Sosa J	17	12	32	20	47	.23	.19	67	86	.08	.09	.47	.27	1	1	2	2	7
Martin J	11	9	37	17	46	.11	.13	72	87	.09	.07	.33	.19	2	4	-2	5	8
Balester C	15	10	37	17	47	.09	.23	78	91	.08	.02	.44	.32	1	-1	1	8	8
Villone R	14	14	39	20	42	.06	.10	72	84	.11	.06	.40	.17	4	1	1	2	9
Rivera S	12	10	56	17	27	.14	.23	72	71	.09	.06	.39	.42	1	2	1	5	9
Kensing L	9	9	39	22	40	.07	.18	83	84	.12	-.02	.53	.27	1	-3	6	5	10
Hanrahan J	21	10	43	24	33	.11	.09	58	80	.03	.16	.52	.19	-0	6	6	-0	12
Cabrera D	8	18	45	22	32	.13	.07	70	79	.21	.06	.39	.16	9	2	4	-1	13
Mock G	17	11	50	17	33	.12	.10	67	75	.06	.09	.44	.24	2	9	2	3	16
Olsen S	15	9	37	22	41	.08	.12	71	79	.06	.07	.45	.25	0	2	8	9	19
MLB Average	***18***	***10***	***43***	***19***	***38***	***.10***	***.11***	***75***	***83***	***.05***	***.04***	***.39***	***.19***	--	--	--	--	--

Appendix: Win Stats

We couldn't fit a major category of stats into our Statistics section: Win Stats. Stats like Win Shares, Wins Above Replacement and Win Probability Added are all the rage in some parts of the baseball world (including ours) but we just didn't have room to include them. So we've created this Appendix. Listed below are our three favorite win stats (Wins Above Replacement, Win Probability Added and Win Shares Above Bench) for all players with at least three expected Win Shares (a measure of playing time).

Actually, we've added a wrinkle: we've calculated WPA and compared it to a replacement level of .300 (that is, a ballclub that plays .300 ball is a "replacement team."). It's called WPAB in the tables (Win Probablity Added vs. Bench, I guess) and it allows you to directly compare WPAB and WAR. You can also directly compare them to WSAB, but you have to divide WSAB by three. Remember that WPA doesn't include the impact of fielding.

These stats are organized by team, in descending WAR order. Many thanks to Fangraphs for the WPA and WAR stats.

Don't forget that you can download a spreadsheet with win stats for every single 2009 major league player from our downloads page. The URL of the Downloads webpage is...

http://www.hardballtimes.com/THT2010Annual/

...the username is "tht10" and the password is "hanley". The spreadsheet contains all of this information and much more.

Team	Name	POS	Age	WSAB	WPAB	WAR
ARI	D Haren	SP	28	17	4.95	6.11
ARI	J Upton	OF	21	9	3.86	4.44
ARI	M Reynolds	3B	25	7	4.83	3.86
ARI	M Montero	C	25	5	2.06	3.30
ARI	M Scherzer	SP	24	5	1.18	3.24
ARI	S Drew	SS	26	4	1.93	2.21
ARI	R Roberts	2B	28	1	0.31	2.07
ARI	F Lopez	2B	29	3	0.78	1.92
ARI	J Garland	SP	29	3	0.49	1.81
ARI	D Davis	SP	33	6	2.16	1.72
ARI	A Ojeda	2B	34	-1	0.63	1.59
ARI	J Gutierrez	RP	25	3	2.92	1.45
ARI	C Qualls	RP	30	3	2.12	1.16
ARI	B Buckner	SP	25	-1	0.30	0.79
ARI	C Snyder	C	28	-1	-0.19	0.57
ARI	E Byrnes	OF	33	-1	-0.74	0.51
ARI	J Rauch	RP	30	1	0.54	0.42
ARI	E Vasquez	RP	25	1	-0.92	0.27
ARI	G Parra	OF	22	0	1.12	0.27
ARI	Y Petit	SP	24	-2	-1.43	0.24
ARI	C Young	OF	25	-1	-1.92	0.19
ARI	A Romero	OF	25	-1	0.11	-0.01
ARI	J Whitesell	1B	27	-0	-0.15	-0.51
ARI	C Tracy	1B	29	-2	-0.33	-0.66
ARI	B Allen	1B	23	-1	-0.10	-0.75
ARI	C Jackson	OF	27	-1	-0.34	-1.07
ATL	J Vazquez	SP	32	12	4.02	6.56
ATL	B McCann	C	25	11	3.04	4.35
ATL	J Jurrjens	SP	23	14	5.07	3.91
ATL	Y Escobar	SS	26	12	3.83	3.91
ATL	M Prado	2B	25	3	2.39	2.89

Team	Name	POS	Age	WSAB	WPAB	WAR
ATL	C Jones	3B	37	8	3.96	2.81
ATL	D Lowe	SP	36	2	-0.23	2.67
ATL	T Hanson	SP	22	7	2.68	2.61
ATL	M Diaz	OF	31	7	4.31	2.37
ATL	R Soriano	RP	29	5	2.67	2.03
ATL	A LaRoche	1B	29	6	1.67	1.94
ATL	N McLouth	OF	27	5	1.01	1.86
ATL	K Kawakami	SP	34	3	0.70	1.73
ATL	D Ross	C	32	3	0.25	1.66
ATL	P Moylan	RP	30	4	1.33	1.46
ATL	O Infante	2B	27	2	0.52	1.12
ATL	M Gonzalez	RP	31	4	1.92	0.91
ATL	C Kotchman	1B	26	2	0.82	0.91
ATL	K Medlen	RP	23	-0	-0.10	0.90
ATL	K Johnson	2B	27	-0	0.50	0.69
ATL	E O'Flaherty	RP	24	2	0.76	0.65
ATL	R Church	OF	30	1	0.30	0.47
ATL	J Schafer	OF	22	-2	-0.99	-0.31
ATL	J Francoeur	OF	25	-3	-0.17	-0.44
ATL	G Anderson	OF	37	-2	0.03	-0.91
BAL	B Roberts	2B	31	8	3.92	3.37
BAL	B Bergesen	SP	23	7	2.31	2.26
BAL	N Markakis	OF	25	5	1.62	1.95
BAL	A Jones	OF	23	5	2.18	1.93
BAL	M Wieters	C	23	1	0.91	1.87
BAL	K Uehara	SP	34	2	0.95	1.63
BAL	L Scott	DH	31	4	1.04	1.51
BAL	F Pie	OF	24	-0	-0.63	1.37
BAL	C Izturis	SS	29	-1	-2.06	1.25
BAL	G Zaun	C	38	3	-0.68	1.12
BAL	J Guthrie	SP	30	3	0.44	1.11

Team	Name	POS	Age	WSAB	WPAB	WAR
BAL	N Reimold	OF	25	3	1.37	1.03
BAL	G Sherrill	RP	32	4	2.39	0.92
BAL	M Mora	3B	37	-2	-1.40	0.85
BAL	M Albers	RP	26	-1	0.69	0.71
BAL	J Berken	SP	25	-3	-0.74	0.65
BAL	J Johnson	RP	26	2	2.28	0.51
BAL	M Hendrickso	RP	35	2	0.75	0.48
BAL	R Hill	SP	29	-3	-0.76	0.38
BAL	D Baez	RP	31	3	0.55	0.28
BAL	D Hernandez	SP	24	1	0.17	0.00
BAL	C Tillman	SP	21	0	0.20	0.00
BAL	C Ray	RP	27	-3	-1.12	0.00
BAL	B Bass	RP	27	1	-0.32	-0.02
BAL	R Andino	SS	25	-3	-0.99	-0.27
BAL	T Wigginton	1B	31	-3	-1.87	-0.30
BAL	A Huff	1B	32	0	1.26	-0.49
BOS	J Lester	SP	25	13	4.47	6.25
BOS	K Youkilis	1B	30	18	3.76	5.53
BOS	J Beckett	SP	29	11	4.32	5.32
BOS	D Pedroia	2B	25	11	1.06	5.22
BOS	J Drew	OF	33	9	1.84	4.61
BOS	J Bay	OF	30	19	5.99	3.40
BOS	J Ellsbury	OF	25	9	1.07	2.07
BOS	V Martinez	C	30	3	1.98	2.06
BOS	B Penny	SP	31	-0	0.20	2.02
BOS	J Papelbon	RP	28	8	6.48	1.95
BOS	T Wakefield	SP	42	5	2.68	1.88
BOS	J Varitek	C	37	1	0.88	1.32
BOS	J Masterson	RP	24	1	1.07	1.26
BOS	A Gonzalez	SS	32	-0	0.24	1.22
BOS	C Buchholz	SP	24	4	1.74	1.22
BOS	M Lowell	3B	35	5	0.20	1.17
BOS	D Bard	RP	24	2	0.50	0.84
BOS	D Ortiz	DH	33	3	2.05	0.70
BOS	H Okajima	RP	33	4	2.69	0.62
BOS	D Matsuzaka	SP	28	0	0.40	0.55
BOS	R Ramirez	RP	27	5	1.72	0.44
BOS	N Green	SS	30	-1	0.15	0.41
BOS	T Saito	RP	39	4	0.23	0.36
BOS	M Delcarmen	RP	27	1	0.56	0.24
BOS	R Baldelli	OF	27	-0	0.47	0.11
BOS	J Lugo	SS	33	1	0.83	-0.26
CHA	G Floyd	SP	26	9	3.78	4.53
CHA	M Buehrle	SP	30	11	3.46	3.37
CHA	J Danks	SP	24	11	3.50	2.88
CHA	P Konerko	1B	33	7	2.84	2.58
CHA	M Thornton	RP	32	7	4.14	2.52

Team	Name	POS	Age	WSAB	WPAB	WAR
CHA	A Pierzynski	C	32	3	1.60	2.49
CHA	A Ramirez	SS	27	3	1.41	2.31
CHA	J Contreras	SP	37	-1	-1.12	2.23
CHA	G Beckham	3B	22	4	1.83	2.13
CHA	S Podsednik	OF	33	5	1.63	1.82
CHA	J Thome	DH	38	6	3.12	1.63
CHA	F Garcia	SP	33	2	0.75	1.59
CHA	D Carrasco	RP	32	4	0.22	1.29
CHA	C Richard	SP	25	3	0.51	1.26
CHA	J Nix	2B	26	1	-0.38	1.06
CHA	O Dotel	RP	35	3	1.50	0.78
CHA	D Wise	OF	31	-1	-0.26	0.56
CHA	B Jenks	RP	28	2	1.52	0.39
CHA	C Getz	2B	25	2	0.32	0.24
CHA	S Linebrink	RP	32	-0	-1.29	0.23
CHA	B Colon	SP	36	1	0.64	0.21
CHA	B Anderson	OF	27	-1	-0.73	0.16
CHA	M Kotsay	1B	33	1	-0.05	0.03
CHA	J Dye	OF	35	5	0.46	-0.14
CHA	C Quentin	OF	26	1	0.53	-0.53
CHA	B Lillibridg	2B	25	-2	-0.61	-0.65
CHA	J Fields	3B	26	-3	-0.25	-0.86
CHA	A Rios	OF	28	-4	-1.22	-1.03
CHN	D Lee	1B	33	14	5.61	5.29
CHN	T Lilly	SP	33	10	2.85	3.68
CHN	R Dempster	SP	32	8	0.64	3.65
CHN	C Zambrano	SP	28	7	2.81	3.60
CHN	R Wells	SP	26	10	2.51	2.99
CHN	R Theriot	SS	29	4	0.09	2.64
CHN	A Ramirez	3B	31	9	3.48	2.56
CHN	K Fukudome	OF	32	7	2.44	2.39
CHN	R Harden	SP	27	4	0.88	1.82
CHN	J Baker	2B	28	3	1.04	1.54
CHN	G Soto	C	26	0	0.26	1.32
CHN	M Bradley	OF	31	2	1.75	1.14
CHN	S Marshall	RP	26	1	1.47	0.92
CHN	C Marmol	RP	26	3	3.45	0.57
CHN	S Fuld	OF	27	2	0.43	0.56
CHN	M Fontenot	2B	29	-1	-1.07	0.47
CHN	R Johnson	OF	32	0	0.39	0.41
CHN	B Scales	OF	31	0	-0.49	0.35
CHN	K Hill	C	30	1	-0.36	0.29
CHN	A Heilman	RP	30	2	-0.15	0.22
CHN	A Guzman	RP	27	4	2.56	0.12
CHN	K Gregg	RP	31	1	0.13	0.00
CHN	A Blanco	2B	25	-1	-0.78	-0.02
CHN	J Fox	3B	26	2	1.17	-0.10

Team	Name	POS	Age	WSAB	WPAB	WAR
CHN	M Hoffpauir	OF	29	-0	0.50	-0.63
CHN	A Soriano	OF	33	1	2.10	-0.80
CHN	A Miles	2B	32	-5	-1.73	-1.28
CIN	J Votto	1B	25	15	7.80	4.43
CIN	B Phillips	2B	28	7	1.83	3.21
CIN	A Harang	SP	31	4	1.11	2.45
CIN	B Arroyo	SP	32	7	2.42	1.79
CIN	C Dickerson	OF	27	2	-0.20	1.68
CIN	J Cueto	SP	23	3	0.81	1.55
CIN	J Bruce	OF	22	3	0.16	1.52
CIN	D Stubbs	OF	24	1	1.12	1.51
CIN	F Cordero	RP	34	6	2.41	1.48
CIN	N Masset	RP	27	6	2.77	1.42
CIN	H Bailey	SP	23	1	0.64	1.37
CIN	P Janish	SS	26	-4	-0.93	1.10
CIN	R Hanigan	C	28	2	-0.26	1.07
CIN	L Nix	OF	28	1	0.75	0.98
CIN	A Rhodes	RP	39	4	2.00	0.98
CIN	S Rolen	3B	34	2	1.26	0.92
CIN	J Gomes	OF	28	5	1.49	0.74
CIN	W Balentien	OF	24	1	-0.09	0.72
CIN	R Hernandez	C	33	5	1.44	0.46
CIN	J Hairston	3B	33	-1	-0.50	0.45
CIN	D Herrera	RP	24	2	0.61	0.43
CIN	J Burton	RP	28	1	0.84	0.34
CIN	C Fisher	RP	26	0	0.55	0.24
CIN	M Owings	SP	26	1	0.65	0.23
CIN	D McDonald	OF	30	-0	0.16	0.07
CIN	A Rosales	3B	26	-2	-0.71	-0.15
CIN	E Encarnacio	3B	26	1	0.29	-0.16
CIN	W Taveras	OF	27	-3	-1.88	-0.28
CIN	J Lehr	SP	31	-0	-0.26	-0.39
CIN	A Gonzalez	SS	32	-0	-0.38	-0.67
CLE	S Choo	OF	26	12	3.78	5.08
CLE	C Lee	SP	30	9	3.59	4.15
CLE	A Cabrera	SS	23	8	3.60	3.08
CLE	V Martinez	C	30	7	3.00	2.79
CLE	G Sizemore	OF	26	5	0.93	2.17
CLE	C Pavano	SP	33	1	1.31	1.90
CLE	K Shoppach	C	29	0	-1.68	1.73
CLE	J Carroll	2B	35	1	0.34	1.51
CLE	A Laffey	SP	24	3	0.70	1.38
CLE	D Huff	SP	24	1	0.49	1.37
CLE	R Garko	1B	28	3	0.51	1.31
CLE	M DeRosa	3B	34	3	2.34	1.28
CLE	J Peralta	3B	27	-2	-0.19	1.22
CLE	T Hafner	DH	32	3	0.99	1.20

Team	Name	POS	Age	WSAB	WPAB	WAR
CLE	J Sowers	SP	26	1	-0.31	1.12
CLE	J Masterson	SP	24	0	0.49	0.80
CLE	F Carmona	SP	25	-3	-1.04	0.45
CLE	K Wood	RP	32	1	1.06	0.42
CLE	M LaPorta	OF	24	-0	-0.43	0.40
CLE	L Valbuena	2B	23	-1	0.47	0.19
CLE	B Francisco	OF	27	1	-0.24	0.10
CLE	T Crowe	OF	25	-2	-0.83	-0.02
CLE	J Lewis	RP	25	-0	0.05	-0.02
CLE	R Perez	RP	27	-3	-1.53	-0.02
CLE	T Ohka	RP	33	-2	-0.70	-0.05
CLE	A Marte	1B	25	-1	0.43	-0.45
CLE	M Brantley	OF	22	1	0.44	-0.56
CLE	C Gimenez	1B	26	-4	-1.16	-0.71
COL	U Jimenez	SP	25	14	4.89	5.68
COL	T Tulowitzki	SS	24	12	2.16	5.47
COL	J Marquis	SP	30	10	4.06	3.79
COL	J Hammel	SP	26	4	0.64	3.75
COL	J de la Rosa	SP	28	7	1.82	3.68
COL	T Helton	1B	35	12	3.94	3.60
COL	S Smith	OF	26	8	1.73	2.77
COL	C Gonzalez	OF	23	4	1.52	2.27
COL	C Iannetta	C	26	4	1.19	2.04
COL	A Cook	SP	30	7	2.37	1.92
COL	C Barmes	2B	30	1	-0.46	1.86
COL	H Street	RP	25	8	4.26	1.55
COL	B Hawpe	OF	30	10	4.12	1.41
COL	I Stewart	3B	24	2	1.86	1.16
COL	Y Torrealba	C	30	4	2.17	0.82
COL	D Fowler	OF	23	6	0.76	0.72
COL	M Daley	RP	27	2	0.56	0.67
COL	R Spilborghs	OF	29	1	0.48	0.25
COL	G Atkins	3B	29	-0	-0.01	-0.46
DET	J Verlander	SP	26	16	6.71	8.24
DET	M Cabrera	1B	26	14	3.34	5.46
DET	E Jackson	SP	25	13	5.15	3.53
DET	C Granderson	OF	28	8	2.16	3.25
DET	P Polanco	2B	33	9	2.79	3.20
DET	B Inge	3B	32	1	2.65	2.43
DET	M Ordonez	OF	35	5	1.76	2.05
DET	R Porcello	SP	20	10	3.05	1.92
DET	R Raburn	OF	28	5	2.64	1.65
DET	C Thomas	OF	25	1	1.46	1.63
DET	A Everett	SS	32	-1	-0.47	0.94
DET	G Laird	C	29	5	-1.22	0.93
DET	B Seay	RP	31	3	0.71	0.77
DET	B Lyon	RP	29	6	1.69	0.74

Team	Name	POS	Age	WSAB	WPAB	WAR
DET	A Galarraga	SP	27	-0	0.30	0.54
DET	N Robertson	RP	31	-1	0.09	0.46
DET	R Santiago	SS	29	2	-0.50	0.44
DET	Z Miner	RP	27	2	0.99	0.35
DET	F Rodney	RP	32	1	4.15	0.32
DET	R Perry	RP	22	1	0.69	0.22
DET	C Guillen	OF	33	1	0.93	0.12
DET	J Anderson	OF	26	-1	-0.23	0.12
DET	M Thames	DH	32	0	-0.60	-0.08
FLA	H Ramirez	SS	25	24	4.76	7.32
FLA	J Johnson	SP	25	16	5.08	5.47
FLA	R Nolasco	SP	26	2	0.10	4.15
FLA	D Uggla	2B	29	6	1.80	2.88
FLA	J Baker	C	28	6	1.36	2.44
FLA	C Coghlan	OF	24	12	2.46	2.39
FLA	C Ross	OF	28	7	2.00	1.92
FLA	R Paulino	C	28	3	0.77	1.63
FLA	J Cantu	1B	27	6	5.04	1.57
FLA	K Calero	RP	34	6	1.83	1.41
FLA	N Johnson	1B	30	3	1.59	1.17
FLA	B Carroll	OF	26	2	0.14	1.16
FLA	B Badenhop	RP	26	3	1.27	0.95
FLA	S West	SP	23	1	0.04	0.94
FLA	A Miller	SP	24	-1	-0.60	0.77
FLA	A Sanchez	SP	25	2	0.88	0.68
FLA	C Maybin	OF	22	-1	0.06	0.64
FLA	W Helms	3B	33	1	0.52	0.58
FLA	D Meyer	RP	27	3	1.68	0.41
FLA	B Sanches	RP	30	4	1.01	0.18
FLA	J Hermida	OF	25	3	1.62	0.17
FLA	C Volstad	SP	22	-1	-0.17	0.08
FLA	R Pinto	RP	26	3	0.83	0.04
FLA	L Nunez	RP	25	2	1.52	0.00
FLA	M Lindstrom	RP	29	-2	1.85	0.00
FLA	R Gload	1B	33	-0	2.68	-0.03
FLA	E Bonifacio	3B	24	-4	-0.68	-0.44
HOU	M Bourn	OF	26	13	2.97	4.16
HOU	W Rodriguez	SP	30	15	3.61	4.03
HOU	H Pence	OF	26	7	2.48	3.38
HOU	R Oswalt	SP	31	6	1.78	3.06
HOU	L Berkman	1B	33	13	3.59	3.03
HOU	M Tejada	SS	35	10	5.05	2.63
HOU	C Lee	OF	33	8	3.36	2.36
HOU	B Moehler	SP	37	-4	-1.30	0.87
HOU	M Hampton	SP	36	2	0.03	0.85
HOU	J Fulchino	RP	29	5	1.12	0.76
HOU	I Rodriguez	C	37	-1	-0.92	0.69

Team	Name	POS	Age	WSAB	WPAB	WAR
HOU	J Valverde	RP	31	7	2.49	0.66
HOU	C Sampson	RP	31	-0	0.44	0.63
HOU	G Blum	3B	36	-1	2.01	0.57
HOU	K Matsui	2B	33	6	-0.01	0.53
HOU	H Quintero	C	29	-1	-0.32	0.50
HOU	J Keppinger	3B	29	-2	0.07	0.39
HOU	R Ortiz	SP	35	-2	-0.06	0.38
HOU	L Hawkins	RP	36	6	1.28	0.34
HOU	F Paulino	SP	25	-6	-1.39	0.01
HOU	T Byrdak	RP	35	3	-0.22	-0.07
HOU	J Michaels	OF	33	0	0.18	-0.26
HOU	C Coste	C	36	-2	0.17	-0.55
HOU	D Erstad	1B	35	-2	-0.77	-0.90
KC	Z Greinke	SP	25	22	8.13	9.42
KC	D DeJesus	OF	29	6	1.57	3.28
KC	B Bannister	SP	28	3	0.43	2.85
KC	A Callaspo	2B	26	7	1.89	2.75
KC	B Butler	1B	23	8	3.80	2.46
KC	M Olivo	C	30	3	0.57	2.18
KC	J Soria	RP	25	6	4.60	1.82
KC	L Hochevar	SP	25	-4	-1.23	1.57
KC	G Meche	SP	30	2	0.29	1.53
KC	R Tejeda	RP	27	4	1.53	1.33
KC	C Crisp	OF	29	1	0.61	1.32
KC	J Buck	C	28	3	0.23	0.94
KC	K Davies	SP	25	2	0.88	0.77
KC	S Ponson	SP	32	-3	-0.48	0.65
KC	B Pena	DH	27	-0	1.05	0.55
KC	A Gordon	3B	25	-1	-0.20	0.41
KC	M Teahen	3B	27	-1	-0.46	0.29
KC	M Maier	OF	27	1	-0.87	0.19
KC	B Chen	SP	32	-0	-0.27	0.13
KC	J Wright	RP	34	0	1.20	0.09
KC	J Cruz	RP	30	-1	-0.09	0.00
KC	R Colon	RP	29	1	-0.11	0.00
KC	W Bloomquist	OF	31	-1	1.17	-0.04
KC	J Anderson	OF	26	-1	-0.54	-0.47
KC	M Jacobs	DH	28	-1	-1.07	-0.73
KC	M Aviles	SS	28	-3	-1.23	-0.99
KC	Y Betancourt	SS	27	-2	-0.91	-1.40
KC	J Guillen	OF	33	-1	0.04	-2.02
LAA	C Figgins	3B	31	13	4.20	5.88
LAA	K Morales	1B	26	14	4.07	4.27
LAA	J Lackey	SP	30	8	3.62	3.92
LAA	J Weaver	SP	26	12	4.28	3.91
LAA	E Aybar	SS	25	8	0.39	3.80
LAA	T Hunter	OF	33	12	3.15	3.77

Team	Name	POS	Age	WSAB	WPAB	WAR
LAA	J Rivera	OF	30	6	2.03	3.45
LAA	M Napoli	C	27	3	1.78	3.19
LAA	M Izturis	2B	28	9	1.21	2.87
LAA	B Abreu	OF	35	12	4.32	2.61
LAA	H Kendrick	2B	25	8	2.09	2.07
LAA	D Oliver	RP	38	6	2.94	1.50
LAA	K Jepsen	RP	24	1	1.77	1.30
LAA	J Saunders	SP	28	7	2.03	1.21
LAA	E Santana	SP	26	2	0.86	1.11
LAA	M Palmer	RP	30	5	1.66	0.90
LAA	V Guerrero	DH	34	2	-0.43	0.76
LAA	J Bulger	RP	30	4	1.78	0.76
LAA	S Loux	RP	29	-2	0.12	0.62
LAA	B Fuentes	RP	33	1	2.17	0.36
LAA	J Arredondo	RP	25	-1	0.73	0.27
LAA	J Mathis	C	26	-0	0.45	0.11
LAA	R Quinlan	1B	32	-1	0.14	-0.87
LAA	G Matthews J	OF	34	4	2.62	-1.15
LAN	M Kemp	OF	24	15	4.77	5.07
LAN	C Blake	3B	35	8	4.58	4.26
LAN	C Kershaw	SP	21	8	3.85	4.19
LAN	R Furcal	SS	31	3	2.14	3.30
LAN	C Billingsle	SP	24	4	0.80	3.15
LAN	R Wolf	SP	32	9	2.38	3.02
LAN	O Hudson	2B	31	7	1.93	2.86
LAN	J Broxton	RP	25	7	4.14	2.86
LAN	A Ethier	OF	27	9	7.22	2.61
LAN	M Ramirez	OF	37	10	3.16	2.58
LAN	H Kuroda	SP	34	2	0.52	2.17
LAN	R Martin	C	26	5	-0.98	2.13
LAN	J Pierre	OF	31	5	0.99	1.82
LAN	J Loney	1B	25	5	2.73	1.39
LAN	R Troncoso	RP	26	3	3.16	0.79
LAN	R Belisario	RP	26	4	-0.47	0.72
LAN	B Ausmus	C	40	1	-0.04	0.60
LAN	J Weaver	RP	32	2	1.47	0.55
LAN	J McDonald	RP	24	-0	-0.04	0.06
LAN	J Castro	SS	37	-0	-0.21	0.05
LAN	G Mota	RP	35	2	-0.42	0.00
LAN	M Loretta	3B	37	-1	-0.46	-0.01
MIL	P Fielder	1B	25	23	9.89	6.71
MIL	R Braun	OF	25	24	6.14	4.68
MIL	M Cameron	OF	36	7	0.68	4.30
MIL	C Counsell	2B	38	6	0.56	2.83
MIL	Y Gallardo	SP	23	8	3.26	2.69
MIL	F Lopez	2B	29	8	0.96	2.63
MIL	C McGehee	3B	26	10	2.72	2.12

Team	Name	POS	Age	WSAB	WPAB	WAR
MIL	R Weeks	2B	26	4	2.04	1.59
MIL	T Hoffman	RP	41	7	2.94	1.50
MIL	J Hardy	SS	26	-3	-0.49	1.42
MIL	J Kendall	C	35	-2	0.22	1.20
MIL	T Coffey	RP	28	4	2.10	0.82
MIL	C Hart	OF	27	1	1.55	0.75
MIL	M Parra	SP	26	-5	-1.22	0.60
MIL	M Gamel	3B	23	2	0.40	0.48
MIL	M DiFelice	RP	32	2	0.61	0.43
MIL	C Villanueva	RP	25	-2	-1.44	0.42
MIL	M Rivera	C	32	1	-0.00	0.42
MIL	D Bush	SP	29	-5	-1.22	0.29
MIL	A Escobar	SS	22	1	1.01	0.28
MIL	B Hall	3B	29	-2	-0.01	0.18
MIL	M Stetter	RP	28	2	1.29	0.00
MIL	F Catalanott	OF	35	1	-0.00	-0.03
MIL	S McClung	RP	28	-1	-0.14	-0.17
MIL	J Gerut	OF	31	-2	-0.35	-0.32
MIL	J Suppan	SP	34	-3	-0.91	-0.47
MIL	B Looper	SP	34	1	0.36	-0.55
MIN	J Mauer	C	26	25	5.09	8.17
MIN	D Span	OF	25	9	1.55	3.85
MIN	S Baker	SP	27	7	2.69	3.52
MIN	J Morneau	1B	28	9	2.26	3.23
MIN	J Kubel	DH	27	12	3.74	2.97
MIN	N Blackburn	SP	27	7	2.87	2.96
MIN	M Cuddyer	OF	30	6	2.24	2.03
MIN	J Nathan	RP	34	8	5.03	1.89
MIN	J Crede	3B	31	-0	1.05	1.84
MIN	C Pavano	SP	33	2	1.00	1.79
MIN	K Slowey	SP	25	2	0.54	1.42
MIN	N Punto	2B	31	2	0.17	1.22
MIN	F Liriano	SP	25	-2	-0.78	1.15
MIN	B Duensing	SP	26	4	1.90	1.12
MIN	G Perkins	SP	26	-1	0.53	1.07
MIN	J Morales	C	26	2	0.17	0.69
MIN	J Mijares	RP	24	4	3.70	0.62
MIN	C Gomez	OF	23	0	-1.23	0.62
MIN	O Cabrera	SS	34	1	0.43	0.46
MIN	M Guerrier	RP	30	6	3.56	0.42
MIN	J Crain	RP	27	1	-0.63	0.39
MIN	B Keppel	RP	27	-0	0.77	0.23
MIN	B Buscher	3B	28	1	0.10	0.20
MIN	M Redmond	C	38	-3	-0.06	0.14
MIN	A Swarzak	SP	23	-1	-0.26	0.02
MIN	R Dickey	RP	34	0	-0.61	0.00
MIN	M Tolbert	2B	27	0	0.83	-0.16

Team	Name	POS	Age	WSAB	WPAB	WAR
MIN	B Harris	SS	28	-1	-0.33	-0.26
MIN	D Young	OF	23	-1	0.86	-1.28
MIN	A Casilla	2B	24	-2	0.03	-1.36
NYA	D Jeter	SS	35	13	3.13	7.41
NYA	C Sabathia	SP	28	14	5.24	5.99
NYA	M Teixeira	1B	29	14	5.47	5.24
NYA	A Rodriguez	3B	33	13	5.15	4.57
NYA	R Cano	2B	26	6	0.22	4.27
NYA	J Posada	C	37	12	2.62	4.00
NYA	N Swisher	OF	28	8	3.26	3.67
NYA	A Pettitte	SP	37	7	3.56	3.34
NYA	A Burnett	SP	32	8	3.02	3.12
NYA	J Damon	OF	35	11	5.51	2.81
NYA	H Matsui	DH	35	12	2.88	2.43
NYA	P Hughes	RP	23	5	3.44	2.25
NYA	B Gardner	OF	25	4	1.36	2.10
NYA	M Rivera	RP	39	8	5.15	1.98
NYA	M Cabrera	OF	24	5	0.55	1.60
NYA	J Chamberlai	SP	23	3	0.30	1.52
NYA	A Aceves	RP	26	4	2.86	1.20
NYA	R Pena	SS	23	1	-0.35	0.54
NYA	P Coke	RP	26	1	1.89	0.10
NYA	J Molina	C	34	1	-1.19	0.07
NYN	D Wright	3B	26	8	5.17	3.34
NYN	C Beltran	OF	32	8	3.48	2.93
NYN	A Pagan	OF	27	6	0.59	2.77
NYN	J Santana	SP	30	11	3.47	2.76
NYN	M Pelfrey	SP	25	-1	-0.37	1.75
NYN	F Tatis	1B	34	1	0.48	1.52
NYN	L Castillo	2B	33	4	1.40	1.52
NYN	O Santos	C	28	2	-0.00	1.03
NYN	L Hernandez	SP	34	-2	-0.05	0.85
NYN	C Delgado	1B	37	3	0.70	0.78
NYN	J Reyes	SS	26	2	0.35	0.74
NYN	P Feliciano	RP	32	4	2.60	0.65
NYN	D Murphy	1B	24	0	0.64	0.61
NYN	N Figueroa	SP	35	2	0.19	0.61
NYN	J Maine	SP	28	2	0.33	0.61
NYN	B Parnell	RP	24	-3	-0.91	0.45
NYN	R Church	OF	30	-1	0.41	0.45
NYN	J Francoeur	OF	25	1	0.05	0.43
NYN	F Rodriguez	RP	27	3	0.87	0.33
NYN	B Schneider	C	32	1	0.28	0.33
NYN	G Sheffield	OF	40	3	2.03	0.15
NYN	C Sullivan	OF	29	1	0.58	0.09
NYN	T Redding	SP	31	-2	0.52	0.07
NYN	A Hernandez	SS	26	1	-0.28	0.00

Team	Name	POS	Age	WSAB	WPAB	WAR
NYN	A Cora	SS	33	-1	-0.07	-0.02
NYN	S Green	RP	30	-0	-0.28	-0.02
NYN	B Stokes	RP	29	1	0.73	-0.02
NYN	O Perez	SP	27	-2	-1.10	-0.04
NYN	P Misch	RP	27	1	-0.08	-0.23
NYN	J Reed	OF	28	-2	-0.16	-0.65
OAK	R Sweeney	OF	24	2	0.54	3.91
OAK	B Anderson	SP	21	4	1.77	3.79
OAK	R Davis	OF	28	6	3.92	3.72
OAK	D Braden	SP	25	5	1.79	2.89
OAK	M Holliday	OF	29	6	1.00	2.88
OAK	K Suzuki	C	25	8	0.50	2.83
OAK	M Wuertz	RP	30	5	3.91	2.42
OAK	A Bailey	RP	25	9	3.76	2.41
OAK	A Kennedy	3B	33	8	2.11	1.79
OAK	B Ziegler	RP	29	2	1.45	1.29
OAK	M Ellis	2B	32	4	0.74	1.19
OAK	G Gonzalez	SP	23	-1	0.27	1.17
OAK	J Cust	DH	30	6	1.60	1.10
OAK	J Outman	SP	24	3	1.09	0.93
OAK	C Pennington	SS	25	3	-0.21	0.88
OAK	V Mazzaro	SP	22	-1	-0.68	0.71
OAK	D Barton	1B	23	2	0.78	0.69
OAK	T Cahill	SP	21	3	1.33	0.65
OAK	C Breslow	RP	28	4	1.20	0.65
OAK	L Powell	C	27	3	0.55	0.61
OAK	J Hannahan	3B	29	-2	-0.78	0.53
OAK	E Gonzalez	RP	26	-2	-0.17	0.52
OAK	O Cabrera	SS	34	1	0.19	0.22
OAK	E Patterson	OF	26	1	0.43	0.20
OAK	S Casilla	RP	28	-2	-0.39	0.00
OAK	T Buck	OF	25	-1	-0.03	-0.20
OAK	N Garciaparr	DH	35	-1	-1.02	-0.37
OAK	S Hairston	OF	29	-1	-0.12	-0.44
OAK	J Giambi	1B	38	0	1.63	-0.49
OAK	B Crosby	3B	29	-3	0.11	-0.67
PHI	C Utley	2B	30	18	5.99	7.67
PHI	R Howard	1B	29	14	8.09	4.89
PHI	J Werth	OF	30	14	3.02	4.73
PHI	R Ibanez	OF	37	8	4.93	4.13
PHI	C Hamels	SP	25	6	2.62	3.76
PHI	S Victorino	OF	28	10	3.77	3.38
PHI	J Rollins	SS	30	6	0.62	2.44
PHI	C Lee	SP	30	5	0.55	2.42
PHI	C Ruiz	C	30	6	1.22	2.23
PHI	J Blanton	SP	28	7	1.57	2.16
PHI	J Happ	SP	26	12	2.55	1.78

Team	Name	POS	Age	WSAB	WPAB	WAR
PHI	C Park	RP	36	1	1.56	1.55
PHI	R Madson	RP	28	5	2.27	1.38
PHI	P Feliz	3B	34	6	1.77	1.19
PHI	J Moyer	SP	46	2	0.36	0.55
PHI	C Coste	C	36	1	-0.12	0.54
PHI	P Bako	C	37	-1	0.10	0.22
PHI	B Lidge	RP	32	-10	-3.06	0.00
PHI	M Stairs	OF	41	1	-0.25	-0.00
PHI	G Dobbs	3B	30	-1	-0.38	-0.03
PHI	B Myers	SP	28	1	0.93	-0.08
PHI	C Durbin	RP	31	0	0.62	-0.10
PHI	E Bruntlett	SS	31	-3	-0.97	-1.09
PIT	A McCutchen	OF	22	10	3.25	3.40
PIT	P Maholm	SP	27	3	1.42	3.20
PIT	G Jones	OF	28	4	2.11	2.57
PIT	A LaRoche	3B	25	2	1.01	2.55
PIT	Z Duke	SP	26	9	0.54	2.48
PIT	F Sanchez	2B	31	4	1.28	1.99
PIT	N Morgan	OF	28	1	0.78	1.88
PIT	J Wilson	SS	31	1	0.56	1.83
PIT	N McLouth	OF	27	5	1.01	1.57
PIT	C Morton	SP	25	2	0.64	1.23
PIT	R Ohlendorf	SP	26	6	1.27	1.11
PIT	R Doumit	C	28	-1	-0.27	0.99
PIT	L Milledge	OF	24	-1	0.56	0.91
PIT	J Jaramillo	C	26	-2	0.19	0.67
PIT	I Snell	SP	27	-1	-0.64	0.60
PIT	A LaRoche	1B	29	-0	0.42	0.41
PIT	E Hinske	OF	31	1	-0.02	0.36
PIT	R Diaz	C	25	-0	0.47	0.34
PIT	R Cedeno	SS	26	2	0.72	0.13
PIT	B Moss	OF	25	-3	0.62	0.10
PIT	D Young	2B	27	1	0.09	0.09
PIT	J Karstens	RP	26	-2	-0.59	0.08
PIT	R Vazquez	SS	32	-2	-0.39	0.03
PIT	J Grabow	RP	30	3	1.63	0.01
PIT	M Capps	RP	25	-5	-1.74	0.00
PIT	J Chavez	RP	25	1	-0.20	-0.02
PIT	S Pearce	1B	26	-1	-0.06	-0.41
SD	A Gonzalez	1B	27	23	5.97	6.35
SD	T Gwynn	OF	26	5	1.63	2.93
SD	K Kouzmanoff	3B	27	6	1.65	2.74
SD	K Correia	SP	28	3	0.46	2.43
SD	S Hairston	OF	29	8	2.19	2.22
SD	H Bell	RP	31	7	2.88	1.95
SD	W Venable	OF	26	3	0.26	1.85
SD	J Peavy	SP	28	1	0.49	1.84

Team	Name	POS	Age	WSAB	WPAB	WAR
SD	L Gregerson	RP	25	3	2.20	1.75
SD	N Hundley	C	25	5	1.34	1.57
SD	C Gaudin	SP	26	-4	-0.44	1.45
SD	C Headley	OF	25	6	2.96	1.19
SD	H Blanco	C	37	2	-0.43	1.17
SD	K Blanks	OF	22	3	1.22	0.94
SD	E Cabrera	SS	22	6	1.97	0.83
SD	D Eckstein	2B	34	6	2.93	0.64
SD	J Gerut	OF	31	-1	-0.13	0.44
SD	O Salazar	OF	31	3	0.50	0.29
SD	C Richard	SP	25	1	0.54	0.17
SD	T Stauffer	SP	27	2	0.45	0.14
SD	E Mujica	RP	25	0	0.20	0.13
SD	C Young	SP	30	-1	-0.37	-0.01
SD	L Perdomo	RP	25	-2	-0.47	-0.14
SD	J Geer	SP	26	-5	-1.08	-0.18
SD	E Gonzalez	2B	31	-1	-0.06	-0.45
SD	E Alfonzo	C	30	-2	-0.56	-0.45
SD	L Rodriguez	SS	29	-1	0.28	-0.49
SD	B Giles	OF	38	-4	-0.31	-1.57
SEA	F Hernandez	SP	23	21	5.72	6.94
SEA	F Gutierrez	OF	26	10	5.45	5.81
SEA	I Suzuki	OF	35	17	6.13	5.08
SEA	R Branyan	1B	33	7	2.52	2.78
SEA	J Washburn	SP	34	11	3.78	2.69
SEA	J Lopez	2B	25	2	1.88	2.63
SEA	A Beltre	3B	30	2	-0.55	2.33
SEA	E Bedard	SP	30	6	2.22	1.91
SEA	D Aardsma	RP	27	8	4.01	1.91
SEA	R Rowland-Sm	SP	26	5	1.01	1.50
SEA	M Lowe	RP	26	3	0.77	1.29
SEA	K Johjima	C	33	2	0.09	0.99
SEA	E Chavez	OF	31	-1	0.07	0.86
SEA	S White	RP	28	4	2.15	0.69
SEA	J Hannahan	3B	29	-1	-0.24	0.65
SEA	R Langerhans	OF	29	0	1.01	0.54
SEA	J Wilson	SS	28	-1	0.28	0.52
SEA	J Vargas	SP	26	1	0.63	0.42
SEA	R Johnson	C	26	4	-0.02	0.38
SEA	D Fister	SP	25	2	0.91	0.34
SEA	I Snell	SP	27	3	0.78	0.29
SEA	M Sweeney	DH	35	3	1.03	0.24
SEA	B Morrow	SP	24	1	-0.85	0.22
SEA	K Griffey Jr	DH	39	2	1.09	0.15
SEA	J Wilson	SS	31	-1	-0.62	0.09
SEA	W Balentien	OF	24	-2	-1.03	0.07
SEA	M Batista	RP	38	2	-0.44	0.05

Team	Name	POS	Age	WSAB	WPAB	WAR
SEA	S Kelley	RP	25	1	1.00	0.04
SEA	C Jakubauska	RP	30	-1	0.17	-0.04
SEA	M Saunders	OF	22	-2	-0.01	-0.09
SEA	G Olson	SP	25	-1	0.71	-0.09
SEA	B Hall	OF	29	-2	0.33	-0.39
SEA	R Cedeno	SS	26	-5	-0.96	-0.71
SEA	Y Betancourt	SS	27	-1	-0.01	-0.77
SF	T Lincecum	SP	25	18	5.71	8.21
SF	P Sandoval	3B	22	18	6.36	5.12
SF	M Cain	SP	24	15	4.60	3.56
SF	J Uribe	3B	30	6	1.69	2.90
SF	B Wilson	RP	27	6	2.68	2.42
SF	B Zito	SP	31	5	1.22	2.22
SF	J Sanchez	SP	26	3	-0.19	2.07
SF	A Torres	OF	31	7	0.75	1.92
SF	A Rowand	OF	31	6	1.43	1.89
SF	R Winn	OF	35	7	2.47	1.81
SF	B Molina	C	34	4	1.31	1.80
SF	F Lewis	OF	28	2	1.02	0.86
SF	T Ishikawa	1B	25	2	-0.02	0.84
SF	J Affeldt	RP	30	6	3.77	0.78
SF	B Howry	RP	35	2	-0.27	0.44
SF	R Johnson	SP	45	0	0.27	0.43
SF	N Schierholt	OF	25	3	0.05	0.31
SF	B Medders	RP	29	4	1.74	0.31
SF	E Renteria	SS	33	0	0.64	0.26
SF	F Sanchez	2B	31	-0	-0.05	0.26
SF	E Velez	OF	27	1	0.82	0.24
SF	E Whiteside	C	29	-0	-0.46	0.12
SF	M Valdez	RP	27	-2	-0.97	0.00
SF	J Miller	RP	31	3	0.33	-0.07
SF	R Garko	1B	28	0	0.22	-0.48
SF	R Aurilia	1B	37	-4	0.46	-0.53
SF	E Burriss	2B	24	-2	-0.10	-0.84
STL	A Pujols	1B	29	28	10.16	8.43
STL	A Wainwright	SP	27	18	5.40	5.69
STL	C Carpenter	SP	34	18	6.74	5.59
STL	J Pineiro	SP	30	9	2.05	4.78
STL	Y Molina	C	26	9	1.01	3.41
STL	B Ryan	SS	27	5	1.83	3.17
STL	M Holliday	OF	29	8	4.43	2.78
STL	C Rasmus	OF	22	4	1.48	2.31
STL	R Ludwick	OF	30	10	2.54	1.70
STL	S Schumaker	2B	29	6	2.20	1.20
STL	R Franklin	RP	36	7	2.96	0.91
STL	K Lohse	SP	30	0	-0.72	0.82
STL	B Barden	3B	28	-1	0.01	0.38

Team	Name	POS	Age	WSAB	WPAB	WAR
STL	M DeRosa	3B	34	-1	0.80	0.37
STL	J LaRue	C	35	-1	-0.35	0.31
STL	K McClellan	RP	25	3	1.07	0.27
STL	J Lugo	2B	33	2	1.03	0.27
STL	J Thurston	3B	29	-1	-0.31	0.19
STL	R Ankiel	OF	29	-2	-0.79	0.07
STL	B Thompson	RP	27	-2	-0.88	0.04
STL	J Motte	RP	27	-1	0.28	-0.02
STL	T Greene	SS	25	-2	-0.75	-0.25
STL	T Wellemeyer	SP	30	-5	-3.40	-0.26
STL	C Duncan	OF	28	0	0.44	-0.36
STL	K Greene	SS	29	-0	-0.56	-0.84
TB	B Zobrist	2B	28	17	5.78	8.50
TB	E Longoria	3B	23	14	3.66	7.27
TB	C Crawford	OF	27	7	1.94	5.43
TB	J Bartlett	SS	29	13	3.53	4.82
TB	J Shields	SP	27	6	2.46	4.07
TB	M Garza	SP	25	7	3.76	3.41
TB	J Niemann	SP	26	8	3.48	3.19
TB	C Pena	1B	31	8	3.36	2.72
TB	B Upton	OF	24	3	1.20	2.70
TB	D Price	SP	23	3	1.61	1.56
TB	A Iwamura	2B	30	1	-0.01	1.23
TB	S Kazmir	SP	25	-1	0.45	1.22
TB	G Kapler	OF	33	1	0.70	1.16
TB	J Howell	RP	26	5	1.69	1.11
TB	G Balfour	RP	31	0	1.27	0.92
TB	G Gross	OF	29	2	-0.87	0.68
TB	L Cormier	RP	28	3	0.57	0.48
TB	A Sonnanstin	SP	26	-4	-1.63	0.26
TB	D Wheeler	RP	31	3	1.97	0.22
TB	M Hernandez	C	30	-1	-0.55	0.17
TB	W Aybar	1B	26	1	1.03	0.10
TB	J Nelson	RP	34	1	0.08	0.00
TB	D Navarro	C	25	-5	-2.45	-0.09
TB	P Burrell	DH	32	0	-0.25	-0.59
TEX	I Kinsler	2B	27	13	2.77	4.64
TEX	M Young	3B	32	7	3.20	3.91
TEX	N Cruz	OF	28	8	2.14	3.65
TEX	S Feldman	SP	26	10	4.05	3.31
TEX	E Andrus	SS	20	6	0.45	3.01
TEX	M Byrd	OF	31	10	2.49	2.42
TEX	K Millwood	SP	34	11	2.82	2.42
TEX	C Wilson	RP	28	5	1.47	1.95
TEX	T Hunter	SP	22	5	1.79	1.83
TEX	J Hamilton	OF	28	4	1.07	1.59
TEX	D O'Day	RP	26	5	2.69	1.36

Team	Name	POS	Age	WSAB	WPAB	WAR
TEX	B McCarthy	SP	25	3	0.70	1.28
TEX	V Padilla	SP	31	3	1.14	1.27
TEX	D Murphy	OF	27	3	0.92	1.18
TEX	O Vizquel	SS	42	2	0.45	1.09
TEX	F Francisco	RP	29	3	2.39	1.08
TEX	D Holland	SP	22	-2	-0.15	1.06
TEX	D Nippert	SP	28	4	1.40	1.00
TEX	A Jones	DH	32	2	0.50	0.80
TEX	M Harrison	SP	23	-0	-0.28	0.60
TEX	J Borbon	DH	23	2	0.10	0.60
TEX	J Saltalamac	C	24	0	-0.61	0.49
TEX	T Teagarden	C	25	-1	-0.49	0.25
TEX	J Jennings	RP	30	1	0.13	0.24
TEX	H Blalock	1B	28	-1	1.70	0.01
TEX	C Davis	1B	23	-0	0.94	-0.62
TOR	R Halladay	SP	32	16	5.67	7.33
TOR	M Scutaro	SS	33	9	2.49	4.43
TOR	A Hill	2B	27	12	4.28	4.26
TOR	A Lind	DH	25	13	4.63	3.69
TOR	S Rolen	3B	34	6	2.25	2.91
TOR	R Romero	SP	24	5	2.15	2.74
TOR	L Overbay	1B	32	3	1.52	1.93
TOR	J Bautista	OF	28	-1	0.51	1.71
TOR	B Tallet	SP	31	0	0.15	1.66
TOR	J Frasor	RP	31	5	3.33	1.40
TOR	M Rzepczynsk	SP	23	2	0.74	1.07
TOR	A Rios	OF	28	1	1.64	1.05
TOR	B League	RP	26	0	-0.19	0.98
TOR	S Downs	RP	33	2	0.50	0.97
TOR	R Barajas	C	33	4	0.44	0.76
TOR	S Richmond	SP	29	-1	-0.53	0.76
TOR	S Camp	RP	33	2	1.81	0.70

Team	Name	POS	Age	WSAB	WPAB	WAR
TOR	J Carlson	RP	28	-0	0.14	0.62
TOR	B Cecil	SP	22	1	1.13	0.40
TOR	T Snider	OF	21	-1	-0.25	0.28
TOR	R Chavez	C	36	0	-0.32	0.24
TOR	E Encarnacio	3B	26	-1	-0.11	0.14
TOR	J McDonald	SS	34	0	-0.77	0.04
TOR	V Wells	OF	30	-4	-0.77	-0.05
TOR	K Millar	1B	37	-2	-0.38	-0.56
WAS	R Zimmerman	3B	24	8	4.45	7.07
WAS	N Morgan	OF	28	4	0.75	2.96
WAS	J Willingham	OF	30	3	0.81	2.30
WAS	J Zimmermann	SP	23	1	-0.04	1.82
WAS	J Lannan	SP	24	5	1.62	1.52
WAS	N Johnson	1B	30	4	3.26	1.27
WAS	R Detwiler	SP	23	-1	0.24	1.26
WAS	A Dunn	1B	29	13	4.09	1.15
WAS	W Harris	OF	31	3	1.20	1.02
WAS	G Mock	SP	26	-3	-1.45	0.97
WAS	C Guzman	SS	31	-2	0.99	0.90
WAS	C Stammen	SP	25	1	-0.74	0.80
WAS	J Bard	C	31	-1	-0.44	0.65
WAS	R Belliard	2B	34	-1	-0.19	0.33
WAS	W Nieves	C	31	-1	-0.58	0.31
WAS	A Hernandez	2B	26	-2	-0.98	0.15
WAS	M MacDougal	RP	32	1	1.88	0.00
WAS	R Villone	RP	39	1	-0.41	0.00
WAS	T Clippard	RP	24	3	1.31	-0.00
WAS	A Kearns	OF	29	-2	-1.17	-0.02
WAS	S Martis	SP	22	1	-0.26	-0.07
WAS	J Martin	SP	26	2	0.07	-0.22
WAS	E Dukes	OF	25	-0	0.44	-0.39
WAS	A Gonzalez	2B	26	-2	0.49	-0.54

The Hardball Times Glossary

A: Assists. The number of times a fielder makes a throw that results in an out.

AB: At-Bats

AB/RSP: At-Bats with Runners in Scoring Position (second and/or third base)

BA: Batting Average; Hits divided by At-Bats

BA/RSP: Batting Average with Runners in Scoring Position (second and/or third base)

BABIP: Batting Average on Balls in Play. This is a measure of the number of batted balls that safely fall in for hits (not including home runs). The exact formula we use is (H-HR)/(AB-K-HR+SF). This is similar to DER, but from the batter's perspective.

BR: Base Runs, a run contribution formula created by David Smyth, which quantifies the number of runs contributed by a batter. The fundamental formula for Base Runs is (baserunners * scoring rate) + home runs. Note that our Base Runs are adjusted for park effects.

BB: Bases on Balls, otherwise known as walks

BFP: Batters Faced by Pitcher; the pitching equivalent of Plate Appearances for batters

CS: Caught Stealing

CWS: Career Win Shares

DER: Defense Efficiency Ratio. The percent of times a batted ball is turned into an out by the team's fielders, not including home runs. The exact formula we use is (BFP-H-K-BB-HBP-0.6*E)/(BFP-HR-K-BB-HBP). This is similar to BABIP, but from the defensive team's perspective.

Dif stands for Difference, and in the fielding stats it represents the difference between the plays made out of zone by a specific player and the major league average number of plays made at that position, per 1,000 innings.

DP: Double Plays

DPS: Double Plays Started, in which the fielder typically gets only an assist

DPT: Double Plays Turned, in which the fielder records both an assist and a putout

ERA: Earned Run Average. Number of earned runs allowed divided by innings pitched multiplied by nine.

ERA+: ERA measured against the league average and adjusted for ballpark factors. An ERA+ over 100 is better than average, less than 100 is below average.

ExpWS: Expected Win Shares. The number of Win Shares an average major leaguer would accrue, given a specific player's playing time.

FB: Fly ball, as categorized by BIS's scorekeepers. Includes both infield and outfield fly balls.

FE: Fielding Errors, as opposed to Throwing Errors (TE)

FIP: Fielding Independent Pitching, a measure of all those things for which a pitcher is specifically responsible. The formula is (HR*13+(BB+HBP)*3-K*2)/IP, plus a league-specific factor (usually around 3.2) to round out the number to an equivalent ERA number. FIP helps you understand how well a pitcher pitched, regardless of how well his fielders fielded. FIP was invented by Tom M. Tango.

FPct: Fielding Percentage, or the number of fielding chances handled without an error. The formula is (A+PO)/(A+PO+E).

G: Games played

GB%: The percent of batted balls that are grounders. GB% is a better way to measure ground ball tendencies than the more common Ground ball/Fly ball ratio (G/F), because ratios don't follow normal scales (a G/F ratio of 2 doesn't equal twice as many ground balls than 1) and definitions of fly balls can be inconsistent.

GIDP (or GDP): The number of times a batter Grounded Into Double Plays

GPA: Gross Production Average, a variation of OPS, but more accurate and easier to interpret. The exact formula is (OBP*1.8+SLG)/4, adjusted for ballpark. The scale of GPA is similar to BA: .200 is lousy, .265 is around average and .300 is a star.

GS: Games Started, a pitching stat.

H-A: Home minus Away, a stat for expressing the "home field advantage" enjoyed by each player. The exact formula is each player's GPA at home minus his GPA on the road. This is calculated for both batters and pitchers; since both tend to perform better at home, H-A is generally positive for batters and negative for pitchers.

Holds: A bullpen stat. According to MLB.com, *A relief pitcher is credited with a hold any time he enters a game in a save situation, records at least one out and leaves the game never having relinquished the lead. A pitcher cannot finish the game and receive credit for a hold, nor can he earn a hold and a save in the same game.*

HRA: Home Runs Allowed, also a pitching stat

HR/Fly or HR/F: Home Runs as a percent of outfield fly balls. Typically, about 11% of outfield flies are hit for home runs.

IBB: Intentional Base on Balls.

IF/Fly or IF/F: The percent of fly balls that are infield flies. Infield flies are those fly balls caught within the infield baselines.

ISO: Isolated Power, which measures the "true power" of a batter. The formula is SLG-BA.

K: Strikeouts

K/G: Strikeouts per Game, the number of strikeouts divided by total number of batters faced, times the average number of batters per game in that specific league (generally around 38 batters a game).

L: Losses

L^R: See R^L.

LD%: Line Drive Percentage. Baseball Info Solutions tracks the trajectory of each batted ball and categorizes it as a ground ball, fly ball or line drive. LD% is the percent of batted balls that are line drives. Line drives are not necessarily the hardest hit balls, but they do fall for a hit around 75% of the time.

LI: Leverage Index. Invented by Tom M. Tango, LI measures the criticality of a play. It is based on the range of potential WPA outcomes of a play, compared to all other plays. 1.0 is an average Index.

NIP: Not In Play; represents plays in which the batter didn't put the ball in play: strikeouts, walks and hits by pitch.

OBP: On Base Percentage, the proportion of plate appearances in which a batter reached base successfully, including hits, walks and hit by pitches.

OF: Outfield Flies. BIS categorizes each fly ball as an infield fly or outfield fly, using the infield baselines as the boundary, depending on where the ball would have landed if not caught.

OOZ: Plays made out of zone. A zone is defined as all areas of the field in which that fielding position successfully converts 50% of chances into outs, on average.

Op: Save Opportunities

OPS: On Base plus Slugging Percentage, a crude but quick measure of a batter's true contribution to his team's offense. See GPA for a better approach.

OPS+: OPS measured against the league average, and adjusted for ballpark factors. An OPS+ over 100 is better than average, less than 100 is below average.

Outs: Outs. Not just outs at bat, by the way, but also outs when caught stealing. Two outs are included when hitting into a double play.

P/PA: Pitches per Plate Appearance.

PA: Plate Appearances, or AB+BB+HBP+SF+SH.

Plus/Minus is a fielding system very similar to Ultimate Zone Rating. It was invented by John Dewan and is tracked by Baseball Info Solutions.

PO: Putouts, the number of times a fielder recorded an out in the field. First basemen and catchers get lots of these. From a pitching perspective, PO stands for pickoffs—the number of times a pitcher picks a base runner off a base.

POS: Position played in the field

PRC: Pitching Runs Created, a stat developed by THT's David Gassko. PRC measures the impact of a pitcher by putting his production on the same scale as a batter's Runs Created. PRC is calculated by inserting the number of runs allowed by a pitcher into a league-average context, and then using the Pythagorean Formula to estimate how many wins that pitcher/team would achieve. That win total is then converted into the number of offensive runs it would take to achieve the same number of wins. The impact of fielders is separated in the process.

Pythagorean Formula: A formula for converting a team's Run Differential into a projected win-loss record. The formula is RS^2/(RS^2+RA^2). Teams' actual win-loss records tend to mirror their Pythagorean records, and variances can usually be attributed to luck.

You can improve the accuracy of the Pythagorean formula by using a different exponent (the 2 in the formula). In particular, a sabermetrician named US Patriot discovered that the best exponent can be calculated this way: (RS/G+RA/G)^.285, where RS/G is Runs Scored per Game and RA/G is Runs Allowed per Game. This is called the PythagoPat formula.

PWins: Pythagorean Wins. See the previous entry.

R: Runs Scored and/or Allowed.

R/G: Runs Scored Per Game. Literally, R divided by games played.

R^L (or L^R): The difference in GPA between a player's performance against left-handed and right-handed pitchers or batters. The order of subtraction depends on the player's natural platoon split—for right-handed batters, for instance, it's L-R. You can read more about R^L in the Stats Introduction of this *Annual.* Note that, for team stats, the formula is the more common L-R for batters and R-L for pitchers.

RBI: Runs Batted In

RISP: Runners In Scoring Position

RS: Runs Scored

Run Differential: Runs Scored minus Runs Allowed

RZR: Revised Zone Rating. RZR measures how often a fielder successfully fields a ball that is hit into his zone. A zone is defined as all areas of the field in which that fielding position successfully converts 50% of chances into outs, on average. RZR differs from the original Zone Rating by removing plays made out of zone and listing them separately.

SB: Stolen Bases

SB%: The percent of time a runner stole a base successfully. The formula is SB/SBA.

SBA: Stolen Bases Attempted.

SBA/G: Stolen Base Attempts per nine innings played.

ShO: Shutouts

SLG and SLGA: Slugging Percentage. Total Bases divided by At-Bats. SLGA stands for Slugging Percentage Against. It represents SLG from the pitcher's perspective.

SO: Strikeouts

Sv: Saves. According to MLB.com, *A pitcher is credited with a save when he finishes a game won by his club, is not the winning pitcher, and either (a) enters the game with a lead of no more than three runs and pitches for at least one inning, (b) enters the game with the potential tying run either on base, or at bat, or on deck, or (c) pitches effectively for at least three innings.*

Sv%: Saves divided by Save Opportunities

TB: Total Bases, calculated as 1B+2B*2+ 3B*3+HR*4

TBA: Total Bases Allowed. A pitching stat.

TE: Throwing Errors, as opposed to Fielding Errors (FE)

UER: Unearned Runs

UERA: Unearned Run Average, or the number of unearned runs allowed for each nine innings pitched.

UZR: A fielding system invented by Mitchel Lichtman, it is similar to John Dewan's plus/minus system. Both systems calculate a fielder's range by comparing his plays made in various "vectors" across the baseball diamond to the major league average rate of plays made in those vectors. Both systems also look at other factors such as the effectiveness of outfield throwing, handling bunts and turning double plays.

W: Wins

WAR: Wins Above Replacement. A relatively new "win stat" that calculates the number of wins a player contributed to his team above a certain replacement level. WAR is calculated at Fangraphs for current seasons and BaseballProjection.com for historical seasons. Though the two implementations vary a bit, they share a common methodology that includes a "linear weights" approach to runs created, advanced fielding metrics, leverage for relievers and replacement levels that vary by position. The methodology was established over time at the *Book Blog* (www.insidethebook.com).

WHIP: Walks and Hits Per Inning Pitched, a variant of OBP for pitchers. This is a popular stat in rotisserie baseball circles.

wOBA: Introduced in *The Book*, this rate stat is similar to OPS and GPA, except that it is set to the scale of OBP.

WPA: Win Probability Added. A system in which each player is given credit toward helping his team win, based on play-by-play data and the impact each specific play has on the team's probability of winning.

WPA/LI: Literally, the WPA of a play divided by its criticality (measured by LI). This stat takes WPA and effectively neutralizes the impact of the game situation. It's another approach for judging player impact on a game—removing the game context but leaving the player's impact on scoring.

WP+PB/G: Wild Pitches and Passed Balls per Nine Innings played. A fielding stat for catchers.

WS: Win Shares. Invented by Bill James. Win Shares is a very complicated statistic that takes all the contributions a player made toward his team's wins and distills them into a single number that represents the number of wins he contributed to the team, times three.

There are three subcategories of Win Shares: batting, pitching and fielding.

We have tweaked James' original formula a bit. Details are available on our website.

WSAge: The average age of a team, weighted by each player's total Win Shares contribution.

WSAB: Win Shares Above Bench. WSAB is a refined approach to Win Shares, in which each player's total Win Shares are compared to the Win Shares an average bench player would have received.

Our research indicates that this is an important adjustment to Win Shares, because it gives greater context to the Win Shares totals. The impact is similar to adding "Loss Shares" for each player.

The bench player is defined as 70% of Expected Win Shares for all players except starting pitchers, for whom it is 50% of Expected Win Shares.

WSP: Win Shares Percentage is a rate stat, calculated as WS/(2*ExpWS). WSP is similar to winning percentage in that .500 is average, but WSP ranges above 1.000 and below .000.

xFIP: Expected Fielding Independent Pitching. This is an experimental stat that adjusts FIP and "normalizes" the home run component. Research has shown that home runs allowed are pretty much a function of flyballs allowed and home park, so xFIP is based on the average number of home runs allowed per outfield fly. Theoretically, this should be a better predictor of a pitcher's future ERA.

ZRDif is used in our fielding tables to show the difference between a player's Revised Zone Rating and the major league average Revised Zone Rating at that position.

Trivia Answers

Dodecatrivia Answers (page 50)

1. The first to 12 losses and wins, respectively, in 2009. The Nationals won this title for the third straight year (they tied with the Royals in 2007), while the Red Sox won after a three-way tie between the Angels, A's and Cardinals in 2008.
2. It was the first 50 home-run season in 12 years (Willie Mays in 1965); it was the only 50-home run season in a 12-team league; and his two best months for homers were July and August. He hit exactly 12 in each month.
3. Career home runs by a player born in North Carolina, the 12th state of the union.
4. Harvey Haddix is the guy, with his famous 12 being the consecutive perfect innings he threw on May 26, 1959. Opposing Lew Burdette won despite giving up 12 hits.
5. The 1984 Red Sox sent Oil Can Boyd, Bruce Hurst and Bob Ojeda to 12-12 records.
6. None other than Wade Boggs who, given his superstitions, would be interested in all those 12s while at the same time being glad it's not 13.
7. Mike Morgan and later Ron Villone became the only two players to take the field for 12 different franchises.
8. By game score, O'Toole's and Deshaies' outings are the two best starts since 1954 to come on 12 days of rest. Woody Fryman's Aug. 1, 1974 shutout was also on that much rest and had the same score as Deshaies', but there was no additional 12 to link him to.
9. Kurowski's hit, done as it was in the 12th-ever All-Star Game (he just happened to drive in his regular-season teammate, which was conveniently misleading), was the 12th and final hit of the game. The only other time an All-Star team's final hit total matched the number of the game was July 11, 1939, when the NL had seven hits. Given that it would take about 80 hits to match the feat today, I don't see it happening soon.
10. It's the all-time leaderboard for starts at DH for NL teams.
11. Every one of these guys was named for a Presidential candidate who never won. The full names:

    C: Winfield Scott Hastings

    1B: William Jennings Kenworthy

    2B: William Jennings Bryan Herman (take that, the Kenworthys!)

    SS: Henry Clay Baldwin

    3B: William Jennings Bryan Patterson

    LF: George Brinton McClellan Rooks

    CF: Stephen Arnold Douglas Behel

    RF: Samuel James Tilden Sheckard

    SP: William Jennings Bryan Harriss (that's as many guys on the team with his full name as times he lost the presidency)

    P: James Blaine Baskette

    P: Winfield Scott Camp

    RP: William Jennings Buckner

Makes you wonder if Mr. Bryan handed out free silver to those who would name their child after him.

12. The 12 most frequent last names in the United States as of 1990 are listed in alphabetical order. The active streaks in which the majors have fielded at least one player with that last name are listed in reverse order of length. Match the names to the active streak. I've listed their longest historical streak after the semicolon unless the active one is longest, in which case there's something else to identify them.

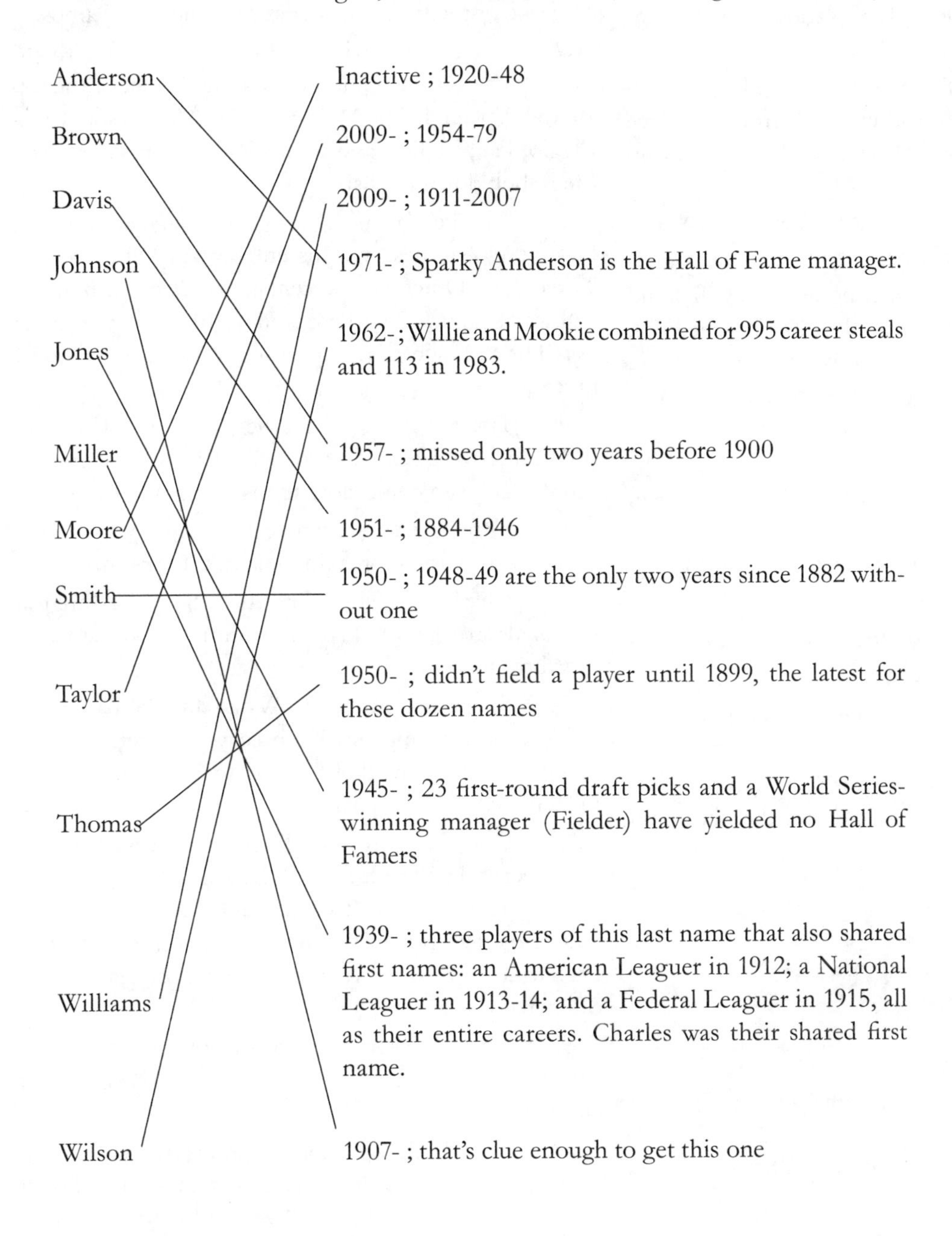

Time Machine: Emit Enihcam Answers (page 103)

1. The Reds, with their first title in 1990 and their back-to-backs in 1976-75.

2. The 1896 Orioles. The National League, of course, didn't expand until 1899.

3. The 2000-1999 Rangers went from last place to the division title; the 1999-98 Cubs went from last place to the wild card; and the "Miracle Marlins" would do the same in 1998-97.

4. Charlie Manuel, in the very first World Series ever played. Okay, it's a cheapie.

5. Larry Walker's .379 batting average will stand the test of time, now that teams play shorter schedules. It was so much harder to sustain a batting average then, with so many more games. New players these days will never appreciate how hard it was back in the day.

6. Mike Matheny's 64 OPS+ was surpassed by Bob Swift (61) who in turn was surpassed by Bill Bergen (21).

7. Greg Maddux on July 15, 1996 and Andy Pettitte on Aug. 19 of the same year.

8. Barry Bonds on May 30, Sammy Sosa on June 30, and Alex Rodriguez before that.

9. Cal Ripken played his 1,153rd consecutive game, surpassing Miguel Tejada.

10. Rickey Henderson stole his 623rd base, breaking Kenny Lofton's record (who in turn had broken Juan Pierre's record in 1994).

Time Machine: The Advanced Class Answers (page 130)

1. Billy O'Brien of the 1887 Washington Nationals who, given the 1884 Chicago madness, could be considered one of the first nonasterisked home run champs.

2. Rabbit Maranville's 7,887 outs are now 17th all-time. Since Winfield bumped Maranville out of the top 10, Cal Ripken, Eddie Murray, Rickey Henderson, Craig Biggio, Paul Molitor and Rafael Palmeiro have shuffled the Rabbit down the list.

3. Charlie Bennett, longtime slugger for the Detroit Wolverines, was his era's Adam Dunn, with a Three True Outcomes percentage of 25.6 (55 homers, 478 walks, and 572 strikeouts in 4,310 plate appearances). The low side of the qualifiers was Joe Start, at 7.4 percent.

4. Isolated Power. Brouthers' was .177, Cravath's .191. Since Babe Ruth exceeded 3,000 plate appearances, no one has even come close to matching him in ISO.

5. Offensive winning percentage. Joe Mauer came ridiculously close to breaking Piazza's record this year.

6. Charlie Geggus for the 1884 Washington Nationals struck out 7.92 per nine innings and was never heard from again.

7. Single-season HBP. White hit 35 batters in 1884, Gus Weyhing hit 37 three years later, and Joe McGinnity hit 41 in 1900. Wood in 2003 and Murphy in 1969 each checked in at 21.

8. Fred Corey finished 17 games as a pitcher over his career and finished seven of those in 1882. His career OPS+ was 93 over 432 games, and his career ERA+ was 91 over 93 games. By those measures, he was Mike Pagliarulo and Bobby Witt in the same package. Make of it what you will.

9. John Clarkson gave up 161 home runs over his career, but many were from the White Stockings' era of cheap home runs.

10. Award yourself double points if you arrived at Shane Reynolds and his K/BB ratio as the correct answer. He was over 4.00 in 1998 and 1999, putting him second all-time to Tommy Bond's absurd 4.83. Reynolds ended his career at 3.35, good for 17th in the modern era and 22nd all-time. Award yourself stalker points if you found that I went to Faulkner University for my undergraduate studies, that it used to be called Alabama Christian College, and that Shane pitched there before moving on to the University of Texas at Austin.

The Virtual Who's Who

Dave Allen is a graduate student studying ecology at the University of Michigan. He writes about baseball for baseballanalysts.com and fangraphs.com. Recently, with a group of the best baseball analysts, he started Complete Game Consulting. They look to answer baseball questions using the data provided by new tracking technologies.

Sky Andrecheck is a statistician for a research company in Washington, DC. Sky writes about baseball and sabermetrics regularly on the web at Baseball Analysts. He is a life-long Cubs fan.

Ben Badler writes for *Baseball America* about scouting and player development, with an emphasis on evaluating minor league prospects and Latin American amateur players. He graduated with a degree in sport management from the Isenberg School of Management at UMass-Amherst.

Richard Barbieri has written for The Hardball Times since 2007. He grew up and lives in New York City, and enjoys putting his degree in history to use when he writes his column.

Carolina Bolado lives in New Jersey and works by day making restaurant menus available online to the masses and by night fixing punctuation on The Hardball Times' website. In the precious few hours that she is not glued to her computer, she can be found riding her bicycle, experimenting with new recipes in the kitchen, or rooting for her hometown Marlins.

A graduate of Michigan State University, **Brian Borawski** is a CPA who owns his own small business consulting practice as well as other business ventures. A lifelong Tigers fan, Brian writes about his favorite team at Tigerblog (www.tigerblog.net) and he's a member of SABR's Business of Baseball committee.

Craig Brown is a soft-tossing left hander with a minus breaking ball. He lives in Kansas City with his wife and two daughters where he writes for Royals Authority and hosts a weekly radio show in between soccer games and dance recitals. He doesn't trust The Process.

Evan Brunell is a recent graduate of Northeastern University and has owned a sports blog network, MVN.com, since December 2003. In addition to writing for the Hardball Times, Brunell has an ESPN-affiliated Red Sox blog at firebrandal.com and contributes to HEATER Magazine as well as Rotoworld.com. His free time is spent playing baseball games, meaning baseball truly is a 24/7 vocation for him.

Craig Calcaterra writes the ShysterBall blog at The Hardball Times, contributes to the Circling the Bases blog at NBC Sports.com and, when he can find the time, practices law for a mid-sized Midwestern government. He is married with two children (Mookie, 5 and Tyrus Raymond, 4). He makes his home in New Albany, Ohio, but hears there might be an opening for a minor league manager in Salem next spring.

Matthew Carruth works as a software engineer by day and writes for The Hardball Times among others by night. A graduate of the University of Pennsylvania, he also runs StatCorner.com and specializes in rooting for losing teams.

Warren Corbett was batting champion of the Bearden, Tennessee, Little League before the vast right-wing conspiracy ended his playing career: right-handed pitchers began throwing curveballs. He has written for SABR's Baseball Biography Project and is the author of "The Wizard of Waxahachie: Paul Richards and the End of Baseball as We Knew It." He is editor of a trade publication in Washington, D.C.

Corey Dawkins is a Certified Athletic Trainer who has been an avid fantasy baseball player for the last 15 years. After working with major Division I football and baseball teams, he's begun to focus on tracking injuries and seeing how much they influence both fantasy baseball and real baseball. Corey would like to thank his wife as he prepares for the launch of Injurytool.com for the upcoming season.

For the past twenty-five years, Baseball Info Solutions owner **John Dewan** has collected, published and analyzed in-depth baseball statistics. He is the author of the award-winning *The Fielding Bible* and the *The Fielding Bible—Volume II* (published this year). He announces his annual Fielding Bible Awards on November 1 in The Bill James Handbook and at www.fieldingbible.com.

Joe Distelheim is a retired newspaper editor who has seen Super Bowls, national political conventions, Pete Rose flattening Ray Fosse in Cincinnati, several presidents, the Delaware State Fair and more grammatical errors than Barack Obama had votes. But has never seen his Cubs in a World Series.

Mike Fast enjoys learning about the physics of baseball, the intricacies of pitching, and anything baseball related. He has fond memories of competitive Kansas City Royals baseball from the last millennium. He lives in Austin, Texas, where he enjoys his growing family and works as an engineer. He is part of an exciting new venture with Complete Game Consulting, a team of top baseball analysts applying PITCHf/x and HITf/x data and other advanced techniques to tackle previously unanswerable questions about the game.

David Gassko is a current student and former major league consultant. It usually works the other way.

Jonathan Halket is an economist by day and night. He received his PhD from New York University and a BA from Amherst College. He is currently a fellow at University College London, where he might catch a cricket match if he has a free week or two.

Brandon Isleib grew up reading Bill James books, inheriting a love of semicolons, numbered two-item lists, and sabermetrics—in some order. He is a geek in lawyer's clothing in the middle of Alabama.

Ben Jacobs is a copy editor for the Rochester (N.Y.) Democrat and Chronicle. He is a diehard Red Sox fan and would like to thank his wife, Stacy, for putting up with his baseball mania.

Chris Jaffe is the author of *Evaluating Baseball's Managers, 1876-2008* which comes out this off-season from McFarland Publishers. In his normal life, he is a history instructor.

Like Shakespeare and Charles Dickens, **Bill James** is a writer and has a beard. He is the proprietor of Bill James Online.com, which is the kind of web site that Charles Dickens would have if he were alive today.

Max Marchi lives in Italy. He graduated from the University of Bologna more than nine centuries after it was founded. When he gets home from work he tries to catch up with the games played the night before—thanks to MLB.TV. He met Ramona in November, so she didn't become aware of his addiction until four months later.

Jack Marshall is an ethicist, lawyer, speaker and stage director who cares more about baseball than any of those things. He is the president of ProEthics, an ethics training and consulting firm in Alexandria, Virginia, and writes about right and wrong in sports, politics and popular culture on his website,The Ethics Scoreboard, and his blog, Ethics Alarms. With Pulitzer Prize-winning historian Ed Larson, he is the co-author/editor of *The Essential Words and Writings of Clarence Darrow*, published by the Modern Library.

Jeremiah Oshan is a former editor and writer of things that used to be called "newspapers." The apex of his prestigious writing career was covering the Single-A High Desert Mavericks where he once interviewed such legends as pitcher Javier Lopez and slugger Bill Hall. A graduate of The San Jose State University, he's now plying his trade in Seattle.

Greg Rybarczyk is a reliability engineer and baseball consultant who has tracked every one of the 20,000-plus MLB home runs since 2006. Home run details and much more can be found at his website, www.hittrackeronline.com. From November through March Greg hibernates in a pleasant suburb of Portland, OR with his very understanding wife and two children.

Jeff Sackmann is the creator of MinorLeagueSplits.com. With Kent Bonham, he founded CollegeSplits.com, which provides data on amateur baseball to half of the 30 Major League teams. Jeff is also the author of several test-preparation guides, including Total GMAT Math, Total GMAT Verbal, and Total GRE Math.

Sean Smith has been a fan of baseball and the Angels since 1982. He lives in Maryland with his wife, two cats, and a daughter who in the last year has learned to clap for Mike Napoli and shout "Aybar!" during Angel games.

Dave Studenmund (who is the General Manager of the Hardball Times, created the Baseball Graphs Website (mentioned in both *Fantasyland* and Joseph Adler's *Baseball Hacks*), has been quoted in the *New York Times*, *Wall Street Journal* and *Sports Illustrated* and was called a "national treasure" by Rob Neyer) doesn't like to brag.

By day, **Tom Tango** works in the development of computer systems. By night, he is co-author of *The Book: Playing the Percentages In Baseball*, runs the Tangotiger.net website, blogs at InsideTheBook.com, and consults with pro teams in MLB and the NHL. By weekend, he is a stay-at-home dad. He prefers his weekends.

Steve Treder has been a writer for The Hardball Times since its founding in 2004. He's also been a frequent presenter/contributor to other forums, such as the SABR national convention, the NINE Spring Training Conference, and the Cooperstown Symposium. He roots for the Giants from his home in Santa Clara, California.

By night, **Bryan Tsao** is the editor of the Hardball Times website. By day, he is a user experience designer for Watercooler, a startup that develops social games and communities on the Facebook platform. He is a proud alum of UC San Diego and UC Berkeley, and roots for the A's in his spare time.

TUCK!'s award-winning cartoons, illustrations, and comics have appeared in a diverse assortment of avenues. Notable placements and contributions include Pulitzer and Gannett Newspapers, Marvel and Image Comics, and, for the last three seasons, www.hardballtimes.com.

John Walsh is a research physicist by day, baseball researcher by night. Despite living four thousand miles from Fenway Park, he remains an avid Red Sox fan.

Craig Wright worked 21 years in major league baseball pioneering a career that integrated science and baseball. He is the primary author of the book *The Diamond Appraised* and currently writes a baseball column under the same name. Subscription information can be found at diamondappraised.com. Craig also researches and writes *A Page from Baseball's*

Past, one of the longest running pre-game radio shows in baseball history. A delightful text version of these stories, delivered to your email inbox, can be subscribed to at pagefrombaseballspast.com.

Geoff Young is the founder of Ducksnorts, one of the world's first baseball blogs. Since 1997, he has written countless articles and published three books under that name. He is a regular contributor to The Hardball Times, and his work also appears at Baseball Daily Digest and Baseball Prospectus. He is a proud alum of the University of San Diego and still lives in that fine city with his wife, Sandra, who waits patiently for him to grow up and do something useful.

Also Available from ACTA Sports

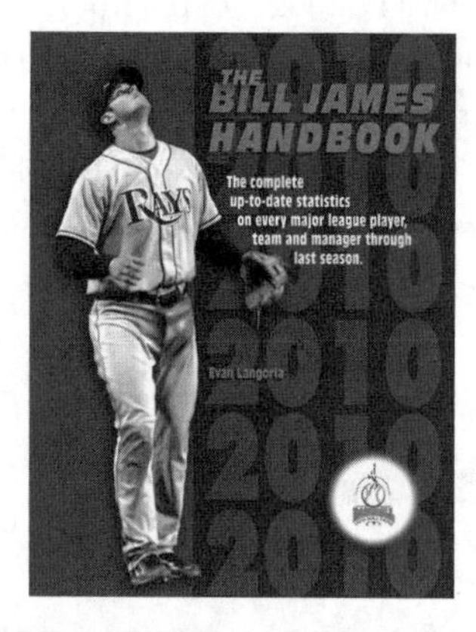

THE BILL JAMES HANDBOOK 2010

BILL JAMES
and BASEBALL INFO SOLUTIONS

Every year, thousands of avid baseball fans eagerly await ***The Bill James Handbook***—the best and most complete annual baseball guide available. Full of exclusive stats, this book is the most comprehensive resource of every hit, pitch and catch in Major League Baseball's 2009 season. Key features include the Fielding Bible Awards, Hitter and Pitcher Projections, and Career Data with more statistical categories than any other book.

$23.95, paperback
$28.95, spiral-bound
Available Now

THE BILL JAMES GOLD MINE 2010

BILL JAMES

Starting in the 1970s, a night watchman from Kansas forever changed the way that many people view baseball analysis and ultimately the game itself. In his latest work, Bill James continues that tradition with ***The Bill James Gold Mine 2010***—a groundbreaking collection of original essays, statistical profiles, and hidden "nuggets" of information worth their weight in gold.

$23.95, 320 pages, paperback
Available February 2010

THE FIELDING BIBLE—VOLUME II

JOHN DEWAN
and BASEBALL INFO SOLUTIONS

First published in 2006, *The Fielding Bible* completely changed the entire perception of fielding statistics in Major League Baseball. Using the revolutionary Plus/Minus approach to fielding analysis previously available exclusively to Major League Baseball teams, John Dewan and Baseball Info Solutions have moved the conversation forward on this important and often overlooked part of the game.

$23.95, 240 pages, paperback
Available Now

GRAPHICAL PLAYER 2010

JOHN BURNSON and WRITERS FROM *HEATER* MAGAZINE

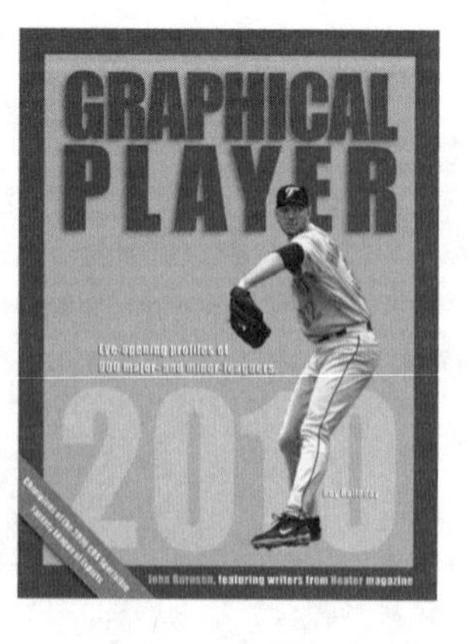

In ***Graphical Player***, John Burnson offers a new approach to ballplayer analysis: visually analyzing charts and graphs to uncover trends and tendencies among players. With full profiles of 900 major and minor league players, key features include daily game logs (now for three years), support for point leagues (including yearly and weekly trends), auction dollar values, and the Graphical Minors—profiles of baseball's top prospects.

$21.95, paperback
Available December 1, 2009

TRADED: INSIDE THE MOST LOPSIDED TRADES IN BASEBALL HISTORY

DOUG DECATUR

This book uses Bill James' Win Shares to evaluate the most lopsided trades in baseball history while also going beyond the numbers to look at the real people involved in the greatest deals of all time. What was the most lopsided trade in history? Here's a hint: It included Curt Schilling.

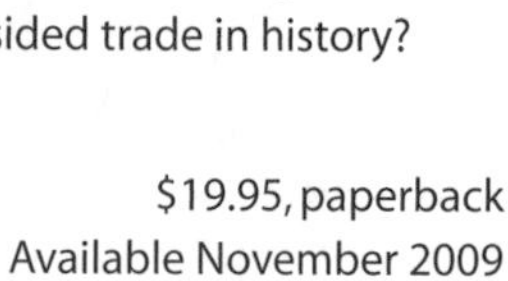

$19.95, paperback
Available November 2009